Washington's
Circle

By David S. Heidler and Jeanne T. Heidler

Washington's Circle: The Creation of the President

Henry Clay: The Essential American

Daily Life in the Early American Republic, 1790–1820

Indian Removal

Manifest Destiny

The Mexican War

*Old Hickory's War: Andrew Jackson
and the Quest for Empire*

*Pulling the Temple Down: The Fire-Eaters
and the Destruction of the Union*

The War of 1812

WASHINGTON'S
CIRCLE

The Creation of the President

DAVID S. HEIDLER

and

JEANNE T. HEIDLER

Random House | New York

ISBN 978-1-4000-6927-9
eBook ISBN 978-0-679-60383-2

Printed in the United States of America on acid-free paper

www.atrandom.com

2 4 6 8 9 7 5 3 1

First Edition

Book design by Virginia Norey

To
Leslie Fruecht Bentley
and
the memory of
J. Stephen Bentley II

The character of sages,
the conscience of Samaritans

Contents

Introduction

Before George Washington became his country's first president he had already achieved something impossible. He had defeated the most powerful empire in the world. Possibly there were other men who could have beaten Britain and secured American independence, but nobody else in the world could have completed the task so gracefully. It was at the close of the Revolution that His Excellency General Washington, commander in chief of the Continental Army, achieved true greatness. In a simple ceremony at the Maryland State House in Annapolis, he surrendered his authority to the republic, turned over the army to the Congress, and went home. Few outside the United States believed he would do this. History, after all, is littered with the debris of ambition. Told about Washington's plans, King George III reportedly exclaimed, "He will be the greatest man in the world!"[1] Americans certainly thought it was time somebody noticed.

A smattering of American biographers already had, and their successors soon grew to legions. The fanciful creations of Parson Mason Weems gave us the cherry tree story and Washington's solemn childhood declaration "I cannot tell a lie," while modern, more reliable writers have skillfully placed the man in his time and charted his impact on it. A great and good man will always merit yet another biographer because of his complexity and importance, but this is not a biography of this great and good man. Rather it is the story of the people who helped to shape his presidency, people who were indispensable in his final and most demanding job. Having retired to his farm, Washington was called back into service to guide the establishment of a republic that could distinguish liberty from license and make government a servant rather than a master. Washington's circle helped him summon the finest instincts of a proud and self-reliant people. Without this circle the mystery of his unique role in doing so remains too opaque and enigmatic. To view the first president in isolation, his achievement in starting everything from scratch seems miraculous, and his gifted counselors become merely men with oversized egos whose personal clashes squandered their genius. It then becomes difficult to understand why they drifted away to be replaced in the end by less talented strangers, men George Washington should not have trusted and the reason, as a result, his second term was less than triumphal.

George Washington's wide range of acquaintances makes for an enormous group, and by necessity many will appear in these pages very sparingly or not at all. For example, people from Washington's youth, his neighbors in Fairfax County and across the Potomac in Maryland, and the builders, managers, and overseers of Mount Vernon do not have a part to play. The frontiersman Christopher Gist guided young George Washington through the Ohio Country in 1753 and pulled him from the freezing Allegheny during their return journey, a deed that likely saved Washington's life, but his relations with Washington were limited to the 1750s. The same is true for Washington's mentors, whether the powerful Fairfax family or Virginia's colonial governor Robert Dinwiddie. British general Edward Braddock taught Washington what not to do with an army, and Braddock's successor John Forbes showed him how to manage one effectively, but their lessons helped him win his country's Revolutionary War rather than set up its government. His cousin Lund Washington was essential in overseeing the extensive renovations of Mount Vernon's mansion house during the Revolution while George Washington was absent, yet it was a personal service that came to an end several years before Washington became president, and by then Lund was going blind on the little piece of land that Washington had deeded him. Dr. James Craik's attachment to Washington was lengthy and durable, making Craik the oldest and possibly the dearest friend the squire of Mount Vernon ever had, but he did not touch on his presidency. All these and others are intriguing in their own ways, and each had a part in making George Washington into the man who became president, but they are not part of the story of his eight years in the office and the making of the presidency beyond the man.

As a consequence, the criteria for the circle should be obvious: These are the people who had close involvement in the country's major events and who were intimately involved with Washington as a private and public figure during the opening years of the constitutional republic. They include the heads of executive departments, the secretaries who by 1793 were being collectively called the cabinet. Alexander Hamilton at Treasury and Thomas Jefferson at the State Department figure prominently by this measure alone, but they made other contributions worth exploring as well—some superb, others much less so. Henry Knox would never be as celebrated as his colleagues and for good reason, but he nevertheless cooked up the plan to pacify the Indians on the country's frontiers. Washington measured it as among his presidency's most significant initiatives, and it was the one he most closely superintended. Knox also had difficulties just as challenging as those of his associates. As the secretary of war, Knox had to run a military department that lacked a military and cope with war scares that loomed and receded in a dangerous world. Edmund Randolph as attorney general and then Jefferson's successor at State was a relative youth whose admiration of George Washington reflected Randolph's belief that his fellow Virginian was the greatest man he had ever known. Yet Randolph was no callow hero worshipper. He alone continued to understand the primary purpose and best methods of the executive branch as both colleagues and chief began to lose sight of one and falter in the other. Randolph reminded Washington of someone, at least before he reminded him of someone else, and the consequences of that transformation have the shadows of a Shakespearean tragedy.

In addition to Washington's official family, there was his real one. The plain little widow he married was an unlikely match for the dashing militia colonel, but Washington saw something in Martha Custis from the start, and anyone with a trace of discernment would eventually see it as well. In Washington's home, Harvard man Tobias Lear was a rarity, the fixture not related by blood or marriage. Lear was, rather, the general's right-hand man who became the first presidential secretary. His responsibilities were so extensive that they would beggar the most grinding workhorse's imagination, and he routinely rose to their challenges. Lear would also prove that, given the right temptations and the wrong circumstances, every man can disappoint.

Outside of cabinet and household, advisers and extensions of Washington's executive authority were part of this indispensable circle. Even before the beginning of Washington's first term, James Madison was a trusted counselor who became Washington's unofficial prime minister, helping to set proper precedents and appropriate relations between executive and legislative branches. Their partnership was most remarkable, however, for how it slowly, painfully collapsed. Gouverneur Morris and John Jay were friends who Washington so trusted that he assigned them to delicate diplomatic missions crucial to the success of his presidency and the nation, yet they became victims of domestic divisions caused by worsening relations with France and Great Britain, forcing the president to desert one man and sustain the other. The political costs were significant.

Martha Washington's grandchildren did not shape her husband's presidency, but they show us important things about the man, as do certain members of his family, such as Washington's mother and the nephew he entrusted with Mount Vernon's care when he left to become president. Members of the government who would seem to merit inclusion in the inner circle—men such as John Adams and the second cabinet—are certainly important in their own right, but Washington's own preferences and quirks rendered them curiously ancillary rather than central to his story during this time. Two figures were of seismic importance during the Revolution—the Marquis de Lafayette as the son Washington never had, and Benedict Arnold as the American Judas—and cast long shadows over Washington's life as president in unexpected ways.

None of these people would have been as famous or as influential had it not been for George Washington. Some would have achieved distinction but at most only as talented provincials, lesser lights in the British imperial galaxy. If they had staged the Revolution, Washington's absence would have diminished its chances of success, making it likely that those now judged by history as patriots would have been punished then as traitors. If their bid for independence had succeeded, the lack of a unifying character could have frustrated their efforts to form a more perfect union, and fears that a strong-arm character could become a king would likely have thwarted the formation of a strong constitutional government.

Because of these likelihoods, the story of George Washington tends to become a sprawling epic regardless of efforts to limit its span or scope. It is a hallmark of his life. Never was anyone more unprepared for fame. Never was anyone so obviously suited to it once it came, beginning with the fact of his appearance. He was an enormous man for his time, standing six feet three inches with enviable posture and a muscular physique. His arms and legs were long, his hands and feet large. He had broad shoulders, but broad hips as well, making him pear-shaped with a relatively small chest and thin torso. His neck was strong, and his face was pleasantly proportioned with blue eyes set somewhat far apart. He had a heavy brow, a strong chin, and a prominent nose whose wide bridge gave him the appearance of an inscrutable lion. Fair and prone to sunburns, he was usually flushed, the complexion of a drinker, but in Washington's case of an outdoorsman. For years he wore his long auburn hair tied in a queue and continued the style during his presidency as the reddish strands were going white and thinning. His dental troubles began in his twenties, and he usually kept his mouth set to hide them, but he could forget himself when excited and reveal the flaw. By the late 1780s, he was all but toothless and had to wear dentures that were a mélange of animal and human teeth (the myth of wooden ones is just that). Kept taut by springs, the hinged contraption was embarrassing in the way it made his lips bulge while causing him considerable pain as the day passed.[2]

Even as his face and physique succumbed to age, Washington still conjured admiration. The painter Gilbert Stuart at first thought him unimpressive—his shoulders too narrow, hips too wide, hands too large—but Stuart admitted that something about the man struck him as "singularly fine." When Stuart's wife glimpsed Washington entering her husband's studio, she plainly stated that he was simply "the most superb looking person" she had ever seen.[3] In 1798, a visitor from Poland saw a man altogether different from what he had expected. "The portraits we have of him in Europe do not resemble him much," he said. "We spoke with Mrs. Washington," he continued, "of the little likeness there is between the General and his portraits."[4] It was the rare instance of a man being larger than life both as an image and a person.

Filling a room, however, is hardly the same as filling an entire country. Washington's impressive physical presence would hardly have been enough if not matched by a distinctive nature. Even when excited, he rarely revealed his emotions, and in his youth he resolved to control his fierce temper. Sometimes that temper slipped its leash, but normally George Washington seemed placid to the point of reticence. He spoke slowly, walked deliberately, and gazed intently into a companion's eyes during conversation. He did not gesticulate broadly. He was courtly and impressive, even when young, adopting the manner while avoiding affectation. He was also distant and remote, preserving from preference rather than design the sense of mystery that can make a man into a monument while he still breathes. "His reserve is always extreme and sometimes icy," said a French diplomat, speaking for the multitude that found Washington a man easy to revere but difficult to know.[5]

His sense of dignity was highly developed and his manner cordial but detached. Except in extremely rare instances, Washington had acolytes rather than friends, and adversaries usually became enemies. Like most people, he liked pleasant relations more than contentious ones, but he took offense easily and had a long memory for slights. He was interested in most people, but he seldom empathized with them. His manner toward peers was courtly, but his treatment of inferiors could be harsh and even forbidding. He liked children and was usually avuncular with them, but he could just as easily be demanding and disapproving. His attitude toward animals was equally uneven. He saw them as livestock to be shorn or slaughtered, and he once directed his manager at Mount Vernon to hang dogs he suspected of killing sheep. Yet he could display tenderness toward animals that was odd for his time. His love of horses was natural for a man in his place, but his fondness for the nearly tame deer of Mount Vernon exasperated his gardener and bewildered neighbors accustomed to treating destructive ruminants as prey rather than pets.

The contrasting elements of his temperament marked a special quality in George Washington, one that made his seemingly incongruous parts into a harmonious whole. He was obsessed with exerting control but careful to avoid abusing the power that came with it. He wanted the farms at Mount Vernon to run with clockwork efficiency but allowed the deer to run rampant. He wanted the new government to provide stability and security but was committed to limiting its authority and constraining its reach. He was reluctant to serve but was willing to sacrifice. It all made him particularly suited for accomplishing something even more incredible than winning the Revolutionary War and retiring to his farms. The tall squire from a rural Virginia county was destined to convince his country that it could sustain a republic protective of its liberty, committed to orderly governance, and scornful of autocrats. The rest of the world doubted it could be done. More than a few Americans did, too.

In fact, the stakes of the experiment he would superintend were exceedingly high, and failure would have been calamitous, which made the long odds against success all the more daunting. Americans struck many European observers as too individualistic to be governable, and their country seemed too vast and variegated for coherency. The skeptics had a point since even astute observers could not comprehend America's enormity. The country had boundaries, but the distance between them gave the impression of boundlessness. The Atlantic lapped an eastern coast that stretched from near the tropics of Georgia's sandy beaches to the rocky shores of Massachusetts. A thousand miles to the west the Mississippi started as a modest rivulet in the far northern wilderness but grew grand, broad, and muddy as it pulled water from dozens of tributaries to empty the middle of the continent into the Gulf of Mexico. Spain was there in the South, but its territory was already a fragile marker of a waning empire.

From this southern border north to the Great Lakes, another thousand miles, were the United States—the citizens at the time were careful about the plural. The space dwarfed Old Europe, inspiring awe in visitors who saw journeys through dense forests consume days passing into weeks and then months and with travelers never encountering another person or finding anything resembling a road. During the Revolution, the Earl of Carlisle had been fascinated by America's colorful autumn and overwhelmed by the country's size. "The rivers are immense," Ambrose Serle, the secretary to the British commander, marveled, "the climate violent in heat and cold; the prospects magnificent; the thunder and lightning tremendous." The countryside just outside Philadelphia caused a traveler to exclaim, "Everything here is new; everything appears as if made yesterday."[6]

A letter from rural Massachusetts took three weeks to reach Georgia.[7] Stagecoaches could use up nearly two weeks rattling down from

Boston to Baltimore along the best developed and most traveled roads. Heading west meant high adventure and usually great peril. Starting from New York City at a smart pace one could trek upstate in about a week, but Canandaigua was the end of the actual as well as the proverbial road. The same for a journey beginning in Philadelphia, which would pull up in Wheeling some fourteen days later, a distance just under four hundred miles but at least speeded by a road; after Wheeling rose mountains and trees, and after the mountains, more trees, until a dogged traveler slogged into the swamps of the Maumee River or a broad prairie with seas of grass, their blades like razors and taller than a horse's head.

Most headed southwest through the lush Shenandoah Valley along the aptly named Wilderness Road, which featured much wilderness and occasionally a road. They climbed through the Cumberland Gap and descended into Kentucky or Tennessee. A fellow traveling from Philadelphia not burdened with too much baggage and kinfolk could cover the six hundred miles to Knoxville in about a month. Families took three times as long. Once arrived they fanned out to unsettled tracts to fell trees and scratch the earth. If they were lucky, blockhouses might protect them from frequently hostile Indians who objected to the settlers' rude fences, obstructions that included pasturage and meager crops. The nearest neighbor was likely a half-day's ride away.

The epic opportunities offered by the vast land were countless, but so were the equally epic obstacles. Aside from confronting the grinding hardships and ceaseless dangers of the frontier, the American people as a whole, including those who lived in the civilized East, faced significant difficulties in conceiving of themselves as one nation, let alone as indivisible. In fact, many believed that resisting that very concept best preserved liberty and justice. They argued that central authority could never govern such a diverse place and its varied people without imposing standards that would be at best arbitrary and ultimately despotic. In colonial times—just the day before yesterday for Americans of the 1780s—Boston was closer to London in spirit than to its neighbor Charleston geographically. The Revolution had not changed that, and the Revolutionary War's unifying purpose of Britain as a common enemy was now absent.

Regional differences were stark. New England neighbors met as equals to confront challenges and solve problems, often in raucous town meetings but nevertheless in a spirit of cooperation. New Englanders believed piety and moral improvement were crucial to order and stability. Government was integral to promoting Good Causes. Civic virtue was a corporate exercise involving church elders, town aldermen, even congressional delegations, all working in concert to advance the common interest. The nation was an organic creature, the body entire, and preserving its health was simply another obligation, the appropriate province of government.

Southerners didn't see it that way. Plantation agriculture kept the region rural; town meetings did not occur because there were precious few towns. Instead, southerners relied on hierarchical relationships with planters at the top of a social structure too vertically linear to be described as even pyramidal. A mass of poor whites was at its base, and slaves were completely under it. County courts with lifetime judges reflected the will of the upper class, and slavery made white unity and consensus imperative. To cope with slavery's social onus and economic burdens, white southerners prized harmony and frowned on variety. Slavery also made most southern whites of all classes intensely libertarian. Suspicion greeted anything that threatened the status quo. Resistance to outside meddling already framed southern attitudes toward other parts of the country. The politics of deference defined this world, one that discordantly embraced the ethics of personal liberty while protecting the pathologies of chattel bondage.

The incompatible visions of the sprawling land worried doubters. The practical problems of erecting a functioning government to reconcile those visions alarmed them. Americans knew that despotism is most dangerous when rooted in a Good Cause. If given the means, those who embrace the Good Cause will eventually find a way to coerce less enlightened neighbors. It only seemed a matter of time before New England's desire to improve the world would clash with the South's insistence that it remain just the way it was.

And that was one of the murkier problems, one vividly perceived but for the time placed in the shadow of more apparent perils such as a hostile frontier, aggressive neighbors, and predatory rivals in an opportunistic world. America was the kind of place that always before and everywhere else had required a crown and council for governance and prosperity, the people knowing their place as subjects, the imperium bound together by the blood of royals, justified by a state-sanctioned church, and sustained by the sword. The rest of the world thought it was only a matter of time before that was America's fate. The rest of the world could not conceive that Americans did not need a king, could not know that Americans had something better: an improbable Virginia farmer and his unlikely companions.

This is their story.

Washington's
Circle

1

"A Citizen of So Much Consequence"

The presidency had "no enticing charms, and no fascinating allure-
ments" for George Washington.[1] By 1789 and in his fifty-seventh
year, he had become proof of the Talmudic story of how a man comes
into the world with his fists clenched wanting everything but leaves it
with his hands open desiring nothing. For years ambition had been
Washington's master, driving him as a youth to seek glory for the fame
and approval that came with it. Age hammered most of that out of him,
but even on the eve of the Revolution, a residue of the deep-rooted impulse remained. He had worn his old Virginia militia uniform to the
Continental Congress in 1775 just in case anyone needed a reminder of
his military experience. During the Revolution he won the world's applause and his countrymen's admiration, and he enjoyed both without
acting as if either mattered. He was a proud man taught by observation
and experience the wages of arrogance and the perils of heedless certainty.

Washington's country wanted him for its chief magistrate and
thereby confronted him with another kind but equally troubling test of
reputation. There is every reason to believe Washington did not want
the post. He was tired. Nobody could know the toll levied by eight years
fighting the British for American independence. Nobody could know
how much the four years following the end of the Revolutionary War
had made him happy. He grew things on the ground above the majestic
river he loved, living in the house he loved with the woman he loved

and surrounded by little ones and their friends, grandchildren, and gig-gling nieces and nephews growing up and making their way, often with his help, which made him happier still. He complained about the place called Mount Vernon becoming "a well-resorted tavern," but the people who filled it as guests kept out of his way during the day and filled his evenings with bright conversation and quiet admiration. Leaving Mount Vernon was like being cast out of Eden and instantly led to Gol-gotha, the place of skulls. He had wanted everything when young with clenched fists. Now an old man, his hands were open, and he wanted nothing.

Out of Eden, this famous and admired man had reluctantly attended the convention in Philadelphia to frame a new government. That enter-prise alone risked his reputation, and only entreaties from friends ap-pealing to his sense of duty had persuaded him to go. He presided over the gathering during its four months of heated debates with the impas-sive detachment that had made him famous and admired, the Ameri-can Cincinnatus who had set aside his sword to return to his plow. The delegates had been angry, stubborn in their opinions, suspicious of one another, and resolutely opposed to this and then that measure, but in the end they were collectively superb. Washington watched, pleased to see something grow, like a healthy stand of wheat or a blooded colt finding its legs. He almost never spoke at the convention but quietly voiced opinions at evening dinners with small groups of fellow delegates. He had been the first to sign the document called the Constitution, confi-dent that it did what was best for the country. He pushed for its ratifica-tion with a fierce resolve of his own, a feeling that ran so deep that he could not brook opposition to it. One of his oldest friends could not agree. He was a friend no more.

Yet despite his confidence in having done right, a strange sense of inadequacy leavened his dread as the new government took shape in New York City. He had worried that merely by attending the conven-tion he was violating his pledge that after the Revolution he would leave public life forever, but that had been the vanity of a man eager to pre-serve his repute for keeping promises. Now it wasn't vanity that robbed him of sleep and clouded his days. For the first time in his life, George Washington was afraid that a challenge was beyond him. What his country wanted was too large, too demanding, too complex for a Virginia farmer who stumbled over his words in public and might just simply stumble under the weight of these new incalculable burdens. He was too old, too feeble, too ignorant. His eyes were failing, his memory sometimes was fogged, and people everyone else clearly heard seemed to be mumbling to him. He had nothing to prove. He had everything to lose. People already called him the "father of his country," a pleasant tribute, a bauble of public acclaim, but it was a bauble, like a fading epaulet on a tunic stored in a forgotten trunk.

That September of 1788 George Washington had received a letter from Alexander Hamilton, his former military aide and a fellow delegate to the convention. Hamilton urged him to accept the presidency. The advice was familiar enough to be dreary. "The new government in its commencement may materially depend" on your acceptance. By "serving in the Constitutional Convention" and supporting its product, you in essence agreed to "filling the station in question." Hamilton echoed other correspondents but with more presumption: Your country needs you, the new government needs you, only your reputation can give this experiment the chance it needs. And there was an admonition wrapped in adulation: "A citizen of so much consequence as yourself . . . has no option but to lend his services if called for." With as much a command as a compliment, Hamilton went to the heart of the issue. If the new government failed, Washington's place in history would be in jeopardy. Everyone who framed the new government would be blamed, including George Washington. Especially George Washington.[2]

Alexander Hamilton sent hard words despite their flattery. Could it be possible that Washington's every sacrifice during the war would count for nothing if he did not drink from this last bitter cup? Would every indignity borne, every conspiracy thwarted, every battle lost and won become as nothing if he did not do this last thing? "A citizen of so much consequence as yourself . . . has no option but to lend his services if called for," Hamilton intoned.[3] The message had a presumptuous air, which was Hamilton's habit, but the words "has no option but to lend his services" were like a hammer on Washington's conscience.

This and other letters from Hamilton were part of a growing plea from a growing chorus that staggered George Washington. As the convention designed the office described in Article II of the Constitution, every power given it and even the vague reach of its responsibilities had been crafted with him in mind. What had he been thinking when he left for Philadelphia in May 1787 and in the months that followed? Was his expectation of his certain selection so high that the choice of someone else would have left him feeling discarded and downcast? George Washington acted the part of a leader so convincingly during the war that his headquarters became a stage, his movements a pageant, and the quiet humility of his resignation at Annapolis at the end of the war a grand finale. The suggestion that he was now being coy, that he wanted to be coaxed and appear as if answering a call rather than grabbing a prize, derives mainly from the seeming inevitability of his presidency. The truth of the matter was the actor was now old, the play not only untried but unwritten, and the supporting cast uncertain. He was not being coy. At the moment of inevitability, he could not quite believe it. His response to these many entreaties were tortured motifs of fatalism and quiet desperation over the bitter cup he would gladly pass to another, but no one else was there.

Hamilton's words were like a hammer, but other friends, James Madison and Gouverneur Morris chief among them, coaxed more softly. Madison first met George Washington in 1781 when the general visited Philadelphia shortly after his victory at Yorktown, but they didn't form a friendship until the mid-1780s. It was an in-between time for Madison. He had quit the Congress to become a member of Virginia's House of Delegates, where he fought for religious freedom. The two shared an interest in western commerce, and from that blossomed the kind of relationship Madison had formed with Thomas Jefferson. Jefferson's departure for France as the new American minister had left a void in Madison's life.

It became apparent that Madison and Washington also shared a vision about the potential for America to be a great nation. Their mutual acquaintances formed a circle of influence that included young Virginia governor Edmund Randolph, but their shared concerns over crippled commerce spurred action more than political theorizing. Virginia's quarrels with Maryland over navigation of the Potomac prompted citizens of the two states to meet in the spring of 1785. Washington opened Mount Vernon to them for the occasion. The meeting was limited to discussing navigation and usage of shared waterways such as the Potomac River and Chesapeake Bay, but it was successful in producing a compact that both states ratified. Its most important contribution was showing that interstate cooperation was possible between suspicious rivals. From it, Madison ran with the idea of a larger gathering with a broader purpose. All the states should meet to "remedy defects" of the present government. He persuaded the Virginia state legislature to issue the general invitation to the states in January 1786, and Maryland agreed to host at its state capital.

The Annapolis Convention met for three days in September, but the result was disappointing. Nine states planned to attend, but only five delegates made it in time. The rest were either late, or absent because their states didn't bother to appoint anyone. Maryland did not even send someone across the street to look in on the proceedings. Hamilton was there, as were Madison and Edmund Randolph, and they managed at the end to salvage the event from complete futility. Hamilton insisted that the convention invoke the authority of the Congress to call yet another meeting, this one to gather in Philadelphia with the stated purpose of addressing deficiencies in the Articles of Confederation. That was the meeting that became the Constitutional Convention, the convocation that George Washington had fretted about, presided over, and now could blame for all his trouble, the thing that could save the country from ruin and damn him to purgatory with the same stroke.

As he headed back to the Congress in the summer of 1788, Madison stopped at Mount Vernon. It was his and Washington's custom never to divulge their conversations, but the subject of the presidency had to figure prominently during this visit. After arriving in New York City, Madison kept up the pressure, but Washington still demurred, and Madison became mildly relentless. He returned in December to spend Christmas at Mount Vernon. By then eleven states had ratified the Constitution, two more than necessary to put it into effect. The old Congress was now a relic as the new government was scheduled to convene. Elections had already begun filling the new legislature. The Electoral College was slated to choose the president.

A letter came from Gouverneur Morris in New York. Morris had met Washington during the Revolution and had been among the few members of the Continental Congress to visit the encampment at Valley

Forge in the horrid winter of 1777–78. The sight had shaken Gouverneur Morris like nothing in his experience. The instant he returned to the Congress, he began talking himself hoarse and working tirelessly to get those forlorn soldiers clothes, shoes, food, money, weapons, encouragement. Washington liked him immensely.[4]

Morris's resolute behavior during the Revolution, his commitment to nationalism, his impressive learning, and his sober pragmatism for all his sophisticated charm were among the traits that miffed some as much as they impressed Washington. As a youth, Morris had learned not to take himself or the world too seriously. He looked askance at politics as a process in which "the madness of so many is made the gain of so few."[5] In 1780, Morris had lost a leg in what he called a carriage accident but rumor said was caused by a fall from a lady's balcony when her husband unexpectedly showed up. As a consequence, he had the look of a peg-legged pirate to match a devil-may-care attitude mixed with flawless manners and a ready wit. It all made him the target of tittering gossip. His lost leg was legendary and still a subject of hushed conversation in New York drawing rooms even years later. Nobody believed the carriage accident story, and Morris didn't care. Leaping from a bedroom window with an irate husband on his heels was better theater. It made prim John Jay assess the missing limb by muttering that he wished Morris "had lost something else."[6]

As he was writing to Washington in the fall of 1788, Morris was preparing for an extended trip to Europe. Its purpose was mostly business, but Morris was never far from pleasure and was looking forward to the change. Like Hamilton, he paused to remind George Washington of his obligations but took a different tack, characteristically sugaring his wisdom with wit. He explained that he had not sent any of his Chinese pigs Washington admired because the boar had developed a wandering eye for "meer common sows." Worse, his well-bred "consort" had exacted revenge by becoming the "Paramour of a Vulgar Race." The results were an estranged couple and depressingly unexceptional piglets. Washington would have chuckled. The farmer appreciated barnyard humor.

But Morris's next sentences raised the gloomy refrain: All would be well, presumably even in pig land, when Washington became the president.[7] The farmer put the letter away, but a few weeks later another arrived without the sugar. In fact, it was decidedly tart. "You must be President," Morris announced in exasperation. "No other Man can fill that Office." No other man could "awe the Insolence of opposing Factions." Morris then swung his own version of Hamilton's hammer: the tarnished reputation. "On the other Hand you will, I firmly expect," he cheerfully said, "enjoy the inexpressible Felicity of contributing to the Happiness of all your Countrymen; even of those who hate because they envy, and envy because they cannot, dare not, imitate you."[8] Here were blows of a different sort, the artistry of Gouverneur Morris appealing to duty and playing to vanity with the reference to reputation. The delegates in Philadelphia had made Morris the stylist for the Constitution. Washington held in his hands the reason why.

He trusted these men. The dozens who dared write obviously were the voices of scores more in timid silence and legions who kept quiet in the certainty that no persuasion was necessary, that Washington would do his duty as always. He could not ignore this. He had no choice, except possibly to be president briefly to have things settled. He then could slip away. Two years at most would be his sentence, he thought. He did not formally announce anything, but reports told of him quietly putting his Virginia affairs in order, an unmistakable signal that he was preparing a journey to New York City, the temporary capital. When he arranged a loan, everyone was certain. In addition to setting up a new household, he intended to bear his travel costs, another sign of his long-range intentions, for he would owe only a few for a formal loan rather than many for small kindnesses that in the end would prove more costly to repay. Friends besieging him for places in the government were bad enough, but the swarms of strangers had begun filling the letter pouches from Alexandria, and so far he had no obligations to any of them for anything. He would keep it that way. He would stay in no private homes en route to New York. He would not accept private hospitality when he arrived there. He intended to pay from his own pocket for food and drink as he went and arrange rent at going rates for his residence in the city.[9]

The presidency, after all, was not a prize. The country was obligated to him for nothing more than the office's constitutionally stipulated salary as set by Congress, and Washington would try to refuse that. Private citizens owed him only the chance to make things work. He waited for the official notification "with feelings not unlike those of a culprit who is going to the place of his execution." He knew he had no sly tricks up his sleeve to pull this last trick off with aplomb. Instead of tricks, possibly "integrity & firmness," even if lacking in "political skill," would be enough.[10]

It was April. He heard a man arrive at Mount Vernon's front door. Everything, everything and all, distilled to this moment. He went to greet the rider.

On the morning of April 6, 1789, the United States Senate conducted its first official business by counting the electoral ballots in the first presidential election. Any drama stemming from this event derived from its solemnity, and when President Pro Tempore John Langdon finished the tally, there were no surprises. Washington was unopposed, which meant all 69 electors had voted for him, but they spread their second vote among 10 other candidates. John Adams topped that list with 34 votes, which made him vice president. The Senate immediately named messengers to inform Washington and Adams of their election. Charles Thomson, the former Congress's secretary, was selected for the errand to Washington's estate in Virginia.

Thomson left New York City on April 7, 1789, on a long journey of some 250 miles. On the eighth day he reached the Potomac, the last of the "many large rivers" he would later complain about crossing.[11] The Potomac was indeed large, a sweeping watercourse that sluiced through Virginia's western piedmont and tumbled in a series of rapids and falls to the Tidewater, the region near enough Chesapeake Bay to mirror its ebb and flow and admit Atlantic commerce. The river had been a timeless constant in George Washington's life, a liquid tether around his heart.

Thomson took a ferry across the Potomac, passed through Alexandria, and was soon riding on roads through old-growth forests that opened on cultivated fields. As the sun reached high meridian, he came upon an unpretentious whitewashed gate, the entrance to the grounds of Mount Vernon's main house, which sat about a mile to the east. The path before him led downward on a slight grade into a thick copse of

oak trees. The effect was tranquil and reassuring, a different world
from the rough-hewn one outside the estate's fences. Everything within
gave testimony to the owner's passion for system and order. But the
magnificent setting more than rivaled the serenity of the place. Thomson's eyes were drawn toward what appeared to be a white stone house
sitting above a large meadow of long grass that rippled in the breeze.
One visitor had aptly described it as "altogether the most charming Seat
I have seen in America."[12]

Up close everything seemed intimate, even the house, which sat in-
vitingly behind a bowling green. Thomson followed the neatly edged
drive that arced toward the house, trees placed at perfect intervals. On
either side what seemed uncleared forests were actually planned "Wil-
dernesses" planted symmetrically to hide the estate's vegetable gardens
and slave quarters. The trees presented a delightful variety and were
trimmed to display their most appealing features.

Attention to the house's architecture revealed its asymmetrical plan,
something counter to popular fashion. Its exterior accommodated its
interior rather than the other way around. Windows were placed at
imperfect intervals, and the house's cupola sat slightly off its center. The
exterior stone facings were another visual trick, for they were actually
wooden panels beveled and painted with a sand-laced concoction.
Thomson might have pondered how the place suited George Washington as much as it reflected his personality. The house's imperfections
balanced form and utility. Grand from a distance, the aesthetic flour-
ishes were revealed to be prudent and frugal at close inspection. Its
owner was like that.

It was noon when Thomson arrived at the mansion. Usually Washington would have been riding his circuit of farms, and a visitor would
have been seated in the house's central passage that bisected the mansion and opened on the rear piazza with its sweeping view of the Potomac below and Maryland beyond. An important guest like Thomson,
though, was allowed to wait in the formal parlor, an airy room of wood
panels painted Prussian blue. Thomson did not have to wait. George
Washington knew that Thomson was coming from New York with
news of the election. A letter from Henry Knox had told him so.[13]
Washington apparently had calculated the time of Thomson's arrival

and abandoned his daily program accordingly. Their meeting at the front door of Mount Vernon was cordial but formal, and Charles Thomson would have known that to be Washington's way.

They walked through the formal parlor into the New Room, the house's most formal setting, started during the Revolution and finished after it. With its high ceiling and ornately painted panels, it was appropriate for the event about to unfold. Despite its historic significance and the impressive backdrop, the ceremony was simple. Thomson read the paragraph he had prepared.

> *Sir, the President of the Senate, chosen for the special purpose, having opened and counted the votes of the electors in the presence of the Senate and House of Representatives, I was honored with the commands of the Senate to wait upon your Excellency with the information of your being elected to the office of President of the United States of America. This commission was entrusted to me on account of my having been long in the confidence of the late Congress, and charged with the duties of one of the principal civil departments of the Government. I have now, sir, to inform you that the proofs you have given of your patriotism and your readiness to sacrifice domestic ease and private enjoyments to preserve the happiness of your country did not permit the two Houses to harbor a doubt of your undertaking this great and important office, to which you were called, not only by the unanimous vote of the electors, by the voice of America.*
>
> *I have it, therefore, in command to accompany you to New York, where the Senate and House of Representatives are convened for the dispatch of public business.*[14]

Thomson ended by stating that they would begin their journey at Washington's convenience. He then read the official communication from John Langdon announcing the unanimous election. Days earlier, Washington had prepared a response, and now he slowly read a carefully fashioned declaration of his willingness to serve that was framed in humble reluctance. "I wish," Washington read from the paper, "that there may not be reason for regretting the choice, for, indeed, all I can promise is to accomplish that which can be done by honest zeal."[15] He said he would be ready to travel as soon as possible, no later than the day after the next.

This brief ceremony in Mount Vernon's New Room marked the beginning of the American presidency with its nebulous and potentially fearsome power. The certainty that republican restraint would guide George Washington's every move had made the office possible for a country cautious about kings. The simplicity of the exchange between Charles Thomson and George Washington was more than appropriate then. It was reassuring.

Luckily, Washington's sure-footed sense of the apt carried over to other matters as well. Before Thomson's arrival, Washington's former military aide and occasional secretary, David Humphreys, had drafted an inaugural address at Washington's request, partly because of his literary experience (he was a part-time poet and playwright) and partly because he was at hand. Yet Humphreys responded with such a will that the bulk of the draft alone gave Washington pause. At seventy-four pages, it would have taxed him beyond his endurance and his audience beyond its patience. What Humphreys found to go on about at such length can only be dimly imagined. In the nineteenth century, historian Jared Sparks was editing an edition of Washington's papers when he inexplicably seized upon the idea of cutting up the only surviving draft of the entire address because it was in Washington's handwriting, the result of his editorial practice of making changes to drafts he carefully copied verbatim. The small fragments made grand souvenirs, which Sparks gave away to countless friends and acquaintances. Reassembling this draft in a coherent form has proved impossible, but bits reclaimed suggest how Washington viewed his coming responsibilities and the way the government would work, which was born out in what he did say and how he behaved once in the presidency.

James Madison visited Mount Vernon that February, and Washington had him review the Humphreys draft. Madison was likely tactful, but he made plain to Washington that it would not do. They conferred to write a much shorter address, and that was the one Washington packed.[16] Humphreys didn't mind. His good humor was unshakable, and for that reason Madison was the trusted adviser, but Humphreys remained a treasured friend, and more. After the war, Washington had urged the Confederation government to make him its minister of foreign affairs, a post that went to John Jay, so Humphreys went abroad to help Benjamin Franklin and John Adams negotiate trade treaties. Adams was so impressed by Humphreys that he hoped David would interest his daughter Nabby. She didn't take to him, possibly because he was the fellow who talked a bit too loud, laughed a little too long, recited verse when prose would do, and spoke when silence was better.[17]

Washington usually did not like this sort of man, but something about David Humphreys charmed him from the start and never wore thin. When Humphreys returned to the United States in 1786, he found his parents ill, and when they both died the following year, he was worse than at loose ends. The unshakably cheerful man was nearly heartbroken. He proposed to spend the winter of 1787–88 at Mount Vernon, and Washington was eager to have him. "The only stipulations I shall contend for are, that in all things you shall do as you please," Washington told him. "I will do the same; and that no ceremony may be used or any restraint imposed on any one."[18] There were few people who enjoyed such latitude with George Washington, and Humphreys became a fixture at the mansion, part of a plan that originally had him organizing Washington's papers and outlining a biography. Organization was not Humphreys's strong suit, and though he could write a splendid letter when pressed into service, both the catalog and the biography proved too much of a challenge.

While Humphreys lived at Mount Vernon, he worked under the vague title of secretary. Someone else, however, was doing the real labor that went with that designation. Washington quickly realized that he needed a secretary when he returned from the war in 1783. By then Martha's son from her first marriage had died, leaving a young widow and four small children. Washington and Martha took the two youngest, Nelly and Wash (pet names for the more impressive Eleanor Parke Custis and George Washington Parke Custis) into their home to ease the burdens on their mother, Eleanor.

Because Wash and Nelly's tutor left about this time, Washington needed a replacement teacher as well as a secretary, and he asked his friend General Benjamin Lincoln in Massachusetts to help him find a man. Lincoln recommended young Tobias Lear. The lad was from New Hampshire, a Harvard graduate who had traveled abroad, was fluent in French, had fine handwriting, and could turn a phrase. He was at the time teaching school, which rounded out his qualifications perfectly. In February 1786, Washington offered the twenty-three-year-old the position as his private secretary, bookkeeper, and tutor to the children. Lear was to earn an annual salary of $200 as well as have room, board, and laundry. As was the custom with such employees, he would live as a member of the family.[19]

Teaching Nelly and Wash was unexpectedly rewarding, and they grew fond of him, bestowing upon him a child's highest tribute, a diminutive as a nickname. For the rest of his life, much of it spent in the company of these children growing up, Lear would be Uncle Toby to them. Everybody began calling him Toby. Martha's kindness was immediate and motherly. He was soon helping her with spelling and suggesting better phrasing when she had to write a letter, bringing Harvard gently to the Potomac and making her laugh.

Still, the arrangement almost went awry at the start. His place in the family seemed highly provisional in the eyes of its patriarch, who never called him Toby—who never called him much anything at all. Washington's cold formality made Lear uncomfortable. In the first days of his employment, he made the cardinal mistake of tardiness, showing up late for work twice, which was twice too many times. Lear faulted his watch, and Washington told him to purchase a more reliable timepiece or he would hire a more reliable secretary. He was not speaking in jest. And thus it was for months, until Lear had a chance to see his employer dealing with strangers and casual acquaintances. The young man had a revelation: Washington treated everyone he did not know well the same way he treated Lear. The secretary relaxed, and in due course the general warmed. In a few months, Lear considered himself "rather as [a] son of the family than in any other light."[20]

Lear brought order to the chaotic ledgers of Mount Vernon's farms, taught the children, and became fast friends with Washington's nephew and farm manager George Augustine Washington as well as his bride, who happened to be Martha's niece. He handled General Washington's massive correspondence as though born for the job. Yet even on the eve of Washington's presidency, Lear remained unsettled about his future.

He was never quite able to let go of the idea that something more meaningful awaited him than the post of factotum, no matter that it was for the most important man in America. He never treated his work with Washington as a temporary arrangement, but he never embraced it as permanent either, pointing to an admirable ambition in one sense, but also exposing a small fault line in an otherwise sterling character that one day would lead him astray.

Lear liked Mount Vernon, though he was never reconciled to slavery. He conceded that Washington treated his slaves well, "but," he sighed, "they still are slaves."[21] Even so, Toby Lear never had any doubts about his boss. "George Washington is, I believe," he concluded, "almost the only man of an exalted character who does not lose some part of his respectability by an intimate acquaintance."[22] In a few years, Lear would leave his secretary's post and strike out on his own to pursue business ventures. He did not yet know that he had already found his destiny in the routines of a bustling household filled with laughing children, a kind woman, and a graceful if aloof giant. The knowledge would come in time, just as Washington's affection had been slow but sure to appear. When the time came, Tobias Lear would be at George Washington's deathbed, holding the giant's hand, weeping.

Before Thomson's summons, Washington had visited his mother in Fredericksburg that March. Their relationship was complicated. Mary Ball Washington was the second wife and produced the second and larger family of Augustine ("Gus") Washington. George was the oldest of this brood and had four surviving siblings. Washington's grandfather had died when Gus was only four, and Gus died at forty-nine when George was eleven. His father's death and his family history impressed the boy with the brevity of life and the usual fate of Washington men. There would hardly be a time in George's life that he did not contemplate his own death as a potentially imminent event, no matter his age. Possibly it made him fearless, but it also made him more mature than most boys his age. The two lessons this otherwise shadowy paternal presence provided could be simply stated but were keenly important. Life is short. Stay busy.

His father's death also meant that unlike his older half brothers,

George would not be sent to England for his schooling. Instead, he remained with his mother, a woman contemporaries described as imperious, if they were kind. Less charitable people found her unpleasant and said so, perhaps too quickly. When Gus died, Mary Ball Washington stood at the head of a young family with the delicate task of balancing her obligations to her children against commitments to the adult boys from her husband's first marriage. On the Rappahannock River at Ferry Farm she held the roof over their heads in trust for George, who was supposed to take title in 1748. It could not have been easy.

On the other hand, she made it no easier from the start almost to the finish. Washington loved his mother from filial duty, which is to say he loved her because he was supposed to. As an adult and the head of the family, he wrote her regularly, but the letters usually contained advice and sometimes included reprimands. He visited, but out of obligation rather than affection, and the impression emerges that he simply did not like her. He had reason not to. Her ways were demanding and her words sharp. She was difficult by habit and often groused about her lack of money and the shortcomings of her children. She never visited Mount Vernon during Washington's marriage, and Martha Washington seems to have met her only once when the Washingtons as newlyweds stopped briefly at Fredericksburg on the way to Mount Vernon.

Washington's sister Betty became a saint in this awkward family association. Washington allowed his mother to remain at the Rappahannock River farm far beyond the five years allotted her in Augustine's will, but she finally turned it over to him in 1771. Washington bought her a home in Fredericksburg the following year so she could be close to Betty, whose husband Fielding Lewis was then building a large house on his plantation just outside of town.[23] Betty was attentive, but Mary Ball Washington regularly appealed to the children for money, and during the Revolution she finally crossed a line. Citing Washington's service—about which she was customarily dismissive—she petitioned the Virginia General Assembly for a pension. Bleating about finances to the family was one thing; humiliating the family with public pronouncements about neglect and penury was quite another. He wrote to the Speaker of the Virginia Assembly that he and his siblings "would feel much hurt, at having our mother a pensioner." That put a mild stamp on his feelings. Washington was never angrier with her.[24]

He got past it, but their arm's-length relationship never changed. When Washington's younger brother John ("Jack") died in early 1787, Mary renewed her complaints about poverty and neglect, and in February he sent her a stern note with £15, money he said he could barely spare. He then launched into a recitation of why she should live with one of her children, but not with him. "My house is at your service," he said tersely, and the narrowly disguised insincerity of that opening was unmasked by his adding in the same breath, "I am sure, and candor requires me to say, it will never answer your purposes in any shape whatsoever."[25]

As always, duty more than affection compelled his farewell visit in 1789. In addition to her complaints about poverty, Mary Ball Washington constantly bemoaned her poor health, but his mother's illness was clearly serious this time, and he likely suspected that this would be their last meeting. In the months that he contemplated the presidency, she had shown the signs of the cancer that was killing her, and the ordeal strangely revived a dormant affection for her son, particularly when he came down with rheumatism. She began saying things more tenderly than she had in years, asking after him, and worrying about him. He rode away from the little frame house in Fredericksburg certain only in the knowledge that life was fragile, especially for Washingtons. As his mother withered away that spring and summer, she would not rest until she received a regular report of his hale health. Betty told him so. It must have made him sad.

The young nephew Washington planned to leave in charge of Mount Vernon was a reminder of grim reality, too. George Augustine Washington had his instructions and was committed to doing well, but Washington worried. George Augustine was engaging, earnest, and capable, but he was also seriously ill. He had served during the war on the Marquis de Lafayette's staff and after the war was often referred to as "the major" from the colonial habit of transforming military ranks into durable titles. It was an honorable marker of experiences that certainly had prepared him for the demands of running Mount Vernon.[26] Yet by 1789 he occasionally coughed up blood and increasingly wore the wan complexion of a consumptive. Because the march of the illness was slow, everyone hoped that he could beat it.

He had come to Mount Vernon four years earlier to become a partner with his uncle in its management. He was also set to marry the fetching girl who lived there. She was Martha's niece from her sister who had died in 1777. Frances Bassett, always known as Fanny, had become like a daughter to Mrs. Washington, and her courtship with the major was as pleasant for her aunt as it was exciting for the youngsters. Fanny was a delicate beauty of eighteen with soft eyes and flowing hair, and though Washington accepted the romance between Fanny and his nephew more than he approved of it, he had to concede they were in love. "Neither directly nor indirectly have I ever said a syllable to Fanny or George upon the subject of their intended connexion," he told Fanny's father, "but as their attachment to each other seems to have been early formed, warm and lasting, it bids fair to be happy."[27]

And so it was, as long as it lasted. Fanny and George Augustine married on October 15, 1785, the first wedding at Mount Vernon. After losing a baby boy, the couple soon had a growing family with a daughter and two sons.[28] Meanwhile, Washington treated this nephew as a son and wanted him to build a house near the estate. He persuaded George Augustine to plant crops on part of Mount Vernon's farms and confided that if he outlived Martha there would be no heir because he did not intend to "marry a girl." Instead he planned to break up Mount Vernon and bequeath George Augustine property on Dogue Neck that spanned more than two thousand acres.[29]

The promise was certainly an incentive for George Augustine to prove himself worthy of it. Washington showered the major with instructions after he became president, drafting voluminous letters on Sunday afternoons to assign chores and tasks, contemplate projects, and comment on the detailed reports he expected his manager to draft for a Thursday dispatch out of Alexandria.[30] This item needed tending to, he would write, or that article required attention, he would remind. Page after page followed page after page, all filled with strong, clear handwriting that flowed with almost no interlined corrections or incomplete thoughts. Washington was never regarded as highly articulate or facile with words, but when it came to Mount Vernon, he was a freshet of them.[31]

In the end, Washington's generous plans for his nephew were unnecessary. Within a year of Washington's departure for New York the major was slowly surrendering to tuberculosis. The following year his decline gained momentum, and some days he could not get out of bed. Eventually Washington had to hurry back to Virginia.[32] George Augustine lingered for months after this scare, and there was some hope that he was on the mend as Washington sheltered him from workaday concerns by dealing directly with overseers. Then in early 1793 the major took another turn for the worse. Martha wrote to Fanny on February 10, 1793, to say that she was "sincearly sorry to hear that the pore majors complaints continue," but by then the complaints were at an end. George Augustine Washington had been dead five days.[33] Life was fragile, especially for Washingtons.

2

"The Most Insignificant Office"

In the new constitutional government's first days, the Senate argued at length about appropriate titles for officials, particularly for George Washington. Makeshift titles for the president had popped up in print in various places, some of them—such as "his Most Serene Highness"—distasteful for a republic at its outset.[1] John Adams regarded this matter as something he could sink his teeth into, and he ultimately made a fool of himself by insisting that lofty titles were necessary for the president, vice president, and senators. At this early stage, the men in the Senate were prepared to be charitable, even to the point of reckoning Adams's idea as a mark of his concern for the new government's prestige. A majority agreed on "His Highness, the President of the United States of America, and Protector of the Rights of the Same." Some senators, however, thought the episode confirmed what they already knew about Adams. The plump little man became a comic figure whose concern for titles was lampooned with one reserved especially for him in cloakroom conversations: "His Rotundity."[2]

Worse, the issue did not end with the Senate's overblown title for the president but became overblown itself as a cause for extended debate. It spilled into the House where the open forum showed the public how foolish Congress could be when it put its collective mind to it: The members of the brand-new national legislature had a mountainous debt with an empty treasury but were squabbling over the trivial question of what to call one another. In any case, the House of Representatives quickly formed a consensus that the Senate's proposed title for the executive of a republic was not only unseemly but silly. The Senate responded by requesting that the House appoint members to a joint committee to confer about a better title. The House, to its credit, refused. Members flatly declared that there should not be a title at all. Congressman James Madison's leadership in framing this blunt response made the sagacious conclude that he was doing Washington's bidding. Possibly they were correct. Madison related the fiasco to Jefferson in Paris, who replied that it was "the most superlatively ridiculous thing" he had ever heard. He also reminded Madison that Benjamin Franklin had said John Adams was "always an honest man often a great one but sometimes absolutely mad."[3] And Jefferson liked Adams.

Madison and the House prevailed in this superlatively ridiculous thing. By never designating a title, the legislature allowed republican simplicity, like nature, to take its course. Washington would be "President of the United States." Adams unfortunately remained His Rotundity because he was temperamentally unsuited for his job. He was opinionated and knowledgeable, a storehouse of political history spanning the centuries and able to summon obscure facts as well as salient details from an encyclopedic memory. But Adams never understood that in politics being too smart could be incredibly stupid. He never understood why people did not heed his advice or reward him with the recognition he deserved. He resented the legislative purists who frowned on presiding officers participating in debates, and sometimes he could not keep silent, launching into lectures that spewed precedents, minutiae, and facts that were sometimes pertinent to the discussion, sometimes bewilderingly irrelevant. Soon, very few senators could abide him, and most resorted to cold civility.

John Adams had known George Washington since the early days of the Revolution, but they were never friends. Adams nominated Washington in May 1775 to command the Continental Army, but that was merely part of New England's ploy to court Virginia's friendship and dispel the impression of revolutionary regionalism. They were a study in contrasts in almost every respect. Washington was tall with a physique that recalled athleticism and agility; Adams was short with the squat figure of a scrivener. Washington's blue eyes had a steady gaze; Adams had protruding eyes that were usually blinking and animated, some would say darting. Adams was a Harvard man who read voraciously and talked back to books by scribbling furiously in their margins. Washington was an outdoorsman who soldiered, then farmed, and had to copy portions of what he read to have it stick in his memory. Adams was a New Englander from a modest family who had become a modestly situated lawyer. Washington hailed from the middling ranks of a planter elite but by young adulthood had climbed to its upper echelons. Adams argued freely and expressed his opinion with peppery phrases on any subject with equal surety, a habit that irked Benjamin Franklin no end. Washington had early cultivated an aloof manner to hide his bashful nature that caused him to speak only when necessary and always after carefully considering his words.

Even men who did not like Washington admired him, but Adams often irritated people without any offsetting advantages. He could be petty in his jealousies and say acid things about people that he later had cause to regret, and he had done as much with George Washington and would continue to do so after Washington's death, as when he bitterly remarked that Washington would never have commanded the army or become president if he had not married a "rich widow."[4]

Just how much Washington had heard of Adams's occasional disparagement of him is difficult to judge, but they were never friends, and Adams's resentment over Washington's popularity and acclaim could have been part of the reason. Adams believed himself Washington's superior in intellect and qualifications but had the good sense, for a change, not to say so, at least not right away.

John and Abigail Adams were abroad during the drafting and ratification of the Constitution because he was the country's minister to Great Britain, but he enthusiastically supported it and wanted a significant role in the new government. That he had become a contender for the vice presidency only through the elimination of more appealing candidates was hurtful. Many wanted Henry Knox or Nathaniel Gorham or John Hancock, but they had not attracted much support, and the field had dwindled to New York governor George Clinton and

Adams, at which point Hamilton had acted on his animus against Clinton rather than his preference for Adams. In fact, the disappointing vote totals that stung Adams with a plurality of only 34 out of 69 were partly because Alexander Hamilton worked behind the scenes to prevent Adams from tying Washington in the Electoral College. With each elector casting two votes, a majority chose the president while the runner-up became vice president. Hamilton and others worried that those electors casting votes for both Washington and Adams would prevent Washington from winning outright. Adams knew nothing about this, but if he had known, it would have been doubly painful. Hamilton's intrigue proved unnecessary—some electors did not like Adams—but Hamilton's ability to persuade electors in the Northeast to throw away their second vote by casting it on nonstarters was chicanery tinged with spite. Adams had puffed himself up during the process to say he would deign to accept the vice presidency and certainly nothing lower, but between his reputation and Hamilton's antics, he was lucky to get anything at all.

Adams swallowed his pride, but the little man had begun his job in simmering humiliation and promptly made things worse for himself. Many of his contemporaries and even some friends came to believe that his time at European courts had washed much of the republicanism out of him, and for most of the first term, even Washington took little notice of him. Yet, he and his family were an important part of the administration, partly for the observations they would make on the political and social events of the presidency, but also for the loyalty Adams exhibited toward the president and his policies, a loyalty that never wavered over the entire eight years. Late in his presidency, George Washington would realize John Adams's true worth, and for the little man from Massachusetts, that was better than never.

Pennsylvania's William Maclay was one senator who dismissed aristocratic pretensions and elaborate ceremony with the disdain of a rugged man with broad experience. Just five years Washington's junior, Maclay lived a life that was a striking mirror of the president-elect's. Like Washington, he had started out as a surveyor and had fought in the French and Indian War and the Revolution. Not many people impressed Maclay, including George Washington and especially John

Adams. He was wary of the very concept of executive authority, and though the debate on titles had amused him as much as anyone, he also was alert to the sinister side of the new government. He is most famous for the biting observations he made about everybody in his diary, and the opening days of the government gave him an ample supply of targets to skewer. Adams was chief among them, so it is probably wise to consider Maclay's prejudices when weighing his remarks about the vice president, whom he called "Bonny Johnny Adams" and described as "mantling his visage with the most unmeaning simper that ever dimpled the face of folly."[5]

It does not strain credulity, however, to see Adams, per Maclay, exploding during discussions about the upcoming inaugural ceremonies. Adams was troubled about his own status when Washington was to return to the Senate chamber after being sworn in. He finally exclaimed, "I am Vice-President. In this I am nothing, but I may be everything." Even his friends must have looked down, but Adams continued. "But I am president also of the Senate," he rambled. "When the President comes into the Senate, what shall I be? I can not be [president] then. No, gentlemen, I can not. I wish gentlemen to think what I shall be." He fell into his chair exhausted by the conundrum. It was the title controversy all over again, with Adams, an intellectual titan, straining at another gnat. Too many senators already had an idea of what John Adams was and always would be.[6]

Throughout his presidency, Washington was kind to John Adams, and Adams was grateful for being included in social events. Yet Adams never became Washington's confidant. He was never consulted on important matters of state until late in Washington's presidency, and that was because by then Washington felt so isolated within a less congenial circle that he was finding friends wherever he could. Over the years, Adams eventually settled into a routine, learned to hold his tongue in the Senate, and became resigned to his dull existence. He told Abigail that "my Country has in its Wisdom contrived for me, the most insignificant Office that ever the Invention of Man contrived or his Imagination conceived: and as I can do neither good nor Evil, I must be born away by Others and meet the common Fate."[7] She loved him more than life, making him a lucky man, which he knew. They addressed each other in letters as "Dear Friend," and reading those words from the man who was not only her dear friend but her hero would have hurt her heart.

On April 16, 1789, Washington, Humphreys, and Thomson left Mount Vernon for New York City, retracing Thomson's steps in about the same amount of time it had taken him to ride south. The travelers stopped in Alexandria for a dinner in honor of the newly elected president, a preview of things to come. Every town on the way to New York held receptions for General Washington. It was gratifying to see any vestigial rancor over ratification fade away as thousands of Americans paid tribute to the man unanimously chosen as their first president, but it played havoc with the traveling schedule, and Washington felt the hurry of a man who is late. He resigned himself to the growing throngs, the endless toasts, and the troubling adulation that threatened dashed expectations if things didn't go well.

Philadelphia's dignitaries met Washington outside of town with horses for him, Humphreys, and Thomson to enhance the spectacle of their progress into the town. Washington had an especially large white stallion to make him fully visible for crowds of craning necks. Philadelphians had decorated the bridge over the Schuylkill River, and as Washington and his companions crossed it, the roar that rose in the city had the power of a physical blow, startling the animals into a stuttering canter and rattling windows. A lavish dinner at City Tavern awaited them with plates piled with food and delicacies, and wine and endless toasts made their beds refuges when all was done.

Crossing the Delaware River into New Jersey the next morning, they met mounted troops and infantry who escorted them to Trenton. A little more than a dozen years earlier, Washington had staged the daring Christmas raid on the Hessian outpost in Trenton, the Delaware then clogged with ice and the smell of failure as thick as gunpowder; but he hadn't failed, and victory at Trenton had saved his army, his generalcy, and his country, at least for that year. Trenton was special, and Trenton acted like it. As at Philadelphia, Washington was to enter the town on an impressive mount provided for the occasion, but as he approached Trenton there stood a large array of people, all female and apart from everyone else. Little girls dressed in white stared up at him in awe, young women in bright spring garb smiled, and Trenton's matrons stood with chins slightly lifted and faces appropriately solemn— the "Virgins fair, and Matrons grave"—a perfectly conceived frame for the flower-covered arch behind them. At its top were the words "The Defender of the Mothers will also Defend the Daughters." They were singing as the children tossed flowers in the road in front of Washington's horse. The song had been written just for that day.[8]

New York City also planned an epic spectacle for Washington's arrival. He crossed Newark Bay on April 23, 1789, in an elaborately decorated barge sporting a red canopy; boats large and small followed behind. Musicians and singers aboard the barge kept up a serenade as they passed Staten Island's batteries firing a thirteen-gun salute. Only eleven states had ratified the Constitution by then, but optimism about the other two was buoyant. Another barge from lower Manhattan carried an official escort of dignitaries that included Henry Knox and John Jay. Careful timing synchronized the movement of the two crafts. Thousands waited at the tip of the island, and a Manhattan battery fired its own thirteen-gun salute as Washington's barge approached. Every church bell in New York City began tolling. Governor George Clinton extended the official welcome over the din of cheers and bells. Clinton ended with the offer of an honor guard to escort Washington to his lodgings. "You will give yourself no further trouble," Washington replied, "as the affection of my fellow-citizens is all the guard I want."[9] That day, it was all the guard he needed.

Clinton accompanied Washington to the house that Lear had rented and prepared for the president at 3 Cherry Street, not far from the East River. The site is now under the Brooklyn Bridge and marked only by a plaque, the house having been demolished in 1856, but in 1789 Cherry was one of Manhattan's fashionable streets. Lear had done the best he could on short notice to make the house comfortable, and its owner Samuel Osgood (soon to be Washington's first postmaster general) had taken trouble to acquire new furnishings.

Despite all efforts, the house was clearly too small. Washington's family would have to be accommodated, but so would Lear, Humphreys, and another secretary. Washington's office was on the first floor along with the formal dining room and a smaller casual one toward the rear of the house. The second floor consisted of a drawing room and family bedrooms, while Washington's secretaries were consigned to cramped quarters on the third floor where servants and slaves were lodged, as well as in the attic. It was much too cozy, especially when David Humphreys could not sleep and paced the room reciting verses and trying out dialogue for a play he was writing. The public areas made formal events feel crowded, and soon Washington began searching for a larger place. He eventually would find it in the spacious Alexander Macomb residence on Broadway.[10]

That first day, however, it was good to have anywhere to light after the long, tiring journey. Seeing George Clinton also helped to relax Washington, for theirs was a happy reunion between old friends. Clinton had been part of the opposition to New York's ratification of the Constitution, and a political feud with Alexander Hamilton had lately become vicious and personal, but Washington and Clinton had developed an immediate friendship during the earliest days of the Second Continental Congress that time, distance, and disagreement could never lessen. Clinton showed his esteem by naming his only son George Washington Clinton, one of his daughters Martha Washington Clinton, and steadfastly praising their eponyms without stint or hesitation. On the night the British evacuated New York City, he and Washington had celebrated with raised glasses and a hearty meal. After Washington resigned his commission that December, he had written a note to Clinton expressing thanks for his support and ending with a heartfelt declaration: "Permit me still to consider you in the Number of my friends, and to wish you every felicity." Clinton's political divergence from Washington's ideas would never result in Washington diverging from Clinton.[11]

That sort of loyalty became difficult when the governor and Alexander Hamilton became sworn enemies and created a remarkably toxic political environment in New York. Elites such as the Schuyler and Livingston families despised Clinton because he appealed to middle- and lower-class interests. Armed with considerable popular support, Clinton was a formidable and fearless enemy. Gouverneur Morris said that Clinton "had an aversion to councils, because (to use his own words) the duty of looking out for danger makes men cowards."[12] With Hamilton, he proved the point with a vengeance, and Hamilton returned the favor in spades. They were caught up in the shifting factions of New York state politics as Clinton continued to build new coalitions to oppose Philip Schuyler's Federalists, and the most prominent Federalist in Schuyler's camp was his son-in-law, young Hamilton.

Some had thought George Clinton would be a perfect vice president, and Clinton quietly encouraged the idea. His supporters had a point. He would have brought into the government a voice for the large number of Antifederalists troubled by the Constitution but not adamantly opposed to it. In doing so, Clinton could have provided philosophical as well as geographical balance, a compelling combination at the government's outset. Yet Hamilton and Schuyler used every ounce of their influence to portray Clinton as a dangerous radical who would serve only to thwart the new government at every turn. They were able to block his candidacy.[13]

Washington felt himself badly served by these feuds. He was certainly used to being caught in the middle of them. During ratification he had learned that Clinton's people were accusing Hamilton of merely using Washington for his own advancement, which was little more than a standard debating point of the Antifederalists but one Washington found distasteful. When Hamilton wrote to Washington asking him to refute the charge, he obliged with a complimentary letter to his former aide.[14]

The bad blood between the Clinton and Schuyler factions was only warming, however, and there would be little Washington could do about it. As Washington was preparing to travel to New York, Hamilton had plunged into a newspaper war with Clinton supporters over the governor's bid for reelection. An angry political disagreement brought out the best of Hamilton's fighting trim, but it also could rouse his worst instincts. Aside from his many admirable qualities, Hamilton had a vicious streak that almost always was uncovered in these episodes, making him a good man to have on one's side, but always at some cost. His way of waging political combat could ruin friendships and create implacable enemies. This was his way in the Clinton fight. From February 20 through April 9, 1789, Hamilton published sixteen attacks in the form of letters signed "HG," a pseudonym that did not in the least disguise their author. He questioned Clinton's military performance during the Revolution, a criticism that had never occurred to Hamilton before politics estranged them. He accused Clinton of being something worse than an ordinary Antifederalist; he was, said Hamilton, "an enemy of the American Union."[15]

Yet if Hamilton thought he could estrange Washington from Clinton, he was brought up short when Washington arrived in New York that April. Much to Hamilton and Schuyler's dismay, Washington not only made a conspicuous show of his affection for Clinton; he spent his first night at a dinner hosted by the governor, a legendary host whose beverage board alone could warm the iciest guest. At one particularly heroic entertainment, Clinton had "135 bottles of Madeira, 36 bottles of port, 60 bottles of English beer, and 30 large cups of rum punch" on hand for 120 people.[16] Washington continued to show warm cordiality for the governor, helping him to win reelection and always including him and his wife, Sarah, on guest lists. Clinton took an oath to support the Constitution, and Washington's early federal appointments in New York were generally made with an eye to pleasing him.[17]

That first night, an elaborate fireworks display and a huge backlit transparency depicting Washington capped off celebrations for a rousing end to the day. The celebratory mood would continue throughout the week before Washington's inauguration and hide some of the less attractive aspects of the place. The words "New York City" or "Manhattan" now summon images of a bustling metropolis with enormous buildings and street canyons that span like a spiderweb from shore to shore, east and west and north and south. Yet New York City in 1789 was a provincial village by modern standards. Most of its activity was confined to the southern part of Manhattan with farms, dense woods, and the occasional dirt road covering the rest of the island. The city contained about thirty thousand people, including some two thousand slaves. Commercially it had the advantages of an accessible harbor connected to the interior by the Hudson River. Culturally it had access to the grandest traditions that Europe could export, including a diverse population of immigrants, but it lagged behind Philadelphia in the arts and in architecture. Politically it was such a Federalist stronghold that opponents of the Constitution, such as Clinton, had succeeded in placing the ratification convention in a more neutral site at Poughkeepsie.

New York City threatened to riot if Poughkeepsie made the wrong decision.

The riot, in fact, was a venerable New York City tradition for expressing displeasure about almost anything. During the ratification debates in 1788, a turbulent protest left several buildings wrecked. It started after boys playing near a hospital caught sight of dismembered body parts and alerted the community, which rapidly ginned up a rumor about medical students robbing graves for anatomy lessons. Authorities locked up a few students to protect them, but a series of riots broke out for several days and finally focused on the jail. Clinton called out the militia and joined prominent citizens in leading the troops to protect the prisoners. The mob was singularly unimpressed. Rioters greeted the august assemblage by hurling rocks, brickbats, and curses. John Jay and Baron Friedrich von Steuben suffered nasty head wounds, and a rock grazed Clinton's arm. Although under orders not to fire, the militia leveled muskets and sent two volleys into the crowd, leaving three dead and finally persuading the mob the fun was over. It dispersed. Jay, knocked cold, was taken back to his house where he was bedridden for days with his face bruised black and blue and his eyes swollen shut. Meeting in the shadow of this infamous "Doctors' Riot," delegates in Poughkeepsie had every incentive to make the right decision about the Constitution.[18]

As Washington arrived in the city a mere year later, representatives and senators had every reason to feel a bit uneasy given this unruly past. New York's chronic shabbiness could be hidden by the dark of night and festive fireworks, but it was made quite evident in the cold light of day. The city was a patchwork of overlapping communities that had grown haphazardly out of the Dutch village founded in the previous century.[19] Fires during the war had devastated lower Manhattan, but rebuilding had not resulted in renovation. The streets were "badly paved, very dirty & narrow as well as crooked, & filled up with a strange variety of wooden & Stone & brick Houses full of Hogs and mud."[20] One can presume that it was the streets, not the houses, filled with hogs and mud, but residents did complain about the incessant noise of the place, such as that made by squealing hogs chased by howling dogs.

New York City was also a medley of bad odors. Many streets were too narrow for sidewalks, and in defiance of city ordinances poorer inhabitants threw garbage into them. The sewage system was primitive, with much waste disposed of by "slaves, a long line of whom might be seen late at night winding their way to the river, each with a tub on his head." That was in the more fastidious parts of town. Elsewhere people emptied slop jars of their "night soil" onto unpaved streets where an abundance of horse manure and urine was churned into a mixture that reeked of ammonia and excrement. Street lamps had been put up here and there, but they were seldom lit. It was perhaps nicer, if not always safer, to have the dark.[21]

While settling into the Cherry Street house the week before his inauguration, Washington tried to make calls on members of Congress and city officials, but office seekers overwhelmed him. He left all of the details of the inaugural ceremony to others and finally resigned himself to running through visits with an almost comical routine. A senator described how Washington would arrive on horseback, dismount, bow, remount, bow again from the saddle, and ride away.[22]

Inauguration Day mercifully arrived. On the morning of April 30 the church bells again commenced tolling as a committee of congressmen and senators arrived at Cherry Street with South Carolina senator Ralph Izard at its head. This group would escort Washington to the ceremony at New York's City Hall, newly dubbed Federal Hall after extensive remodeling supervised by Pierre L'Enfant, a young French engineer from the war. Washington knew him, his primitive pronunciation of his name coming out as "Monsieur Lanfang."[23] When Washington arrived in New York, L'Enfant's Federal Hall project was not quite finished, which caused the week's delay. It was a small warning about L'Enfant's methods, which missed deadlines while busting budgets.

The building's new interior had the House of Representatives and galleries in an octagonal room on the ground floor. The Senate chamber on the second floor needed no gallery because the Senate had decided to conduct closed sessions. Washington walked briskly into that chamber in the early afternoon of April 30, 1789. He was dressed in a brown suit Tobias Lear had purchased for the occasion, ensuring that it was of American broadcloth to promote the idea of national self-sufficiency.

Silver buttons set off the coat, and a ceremonial sword at Washington's side added a formal touch. Everyone stood, but after Washington bowed in acknowledgment, everyone sat down. The English Parliament remained standing for the king; American legislators would show respect but not deference.

Vice President Adams greeted Washington before escorting him to the presiding officer's chair, which was normally reserved for Adams, constitutionally designated as president of the Senate. Other than breaking tie votes and standing by in case George Washington died, it was his only specific duty in the new government. Adams forgot to deliver the short speech he had prepared for the occasion. The slip was emblematic of the disappointments that dogged his career. Like most of the others, this one was his fault.

Washington made his way toward L'Enfant's new balcony overlooking the intersection of Wall and Broad streets. A multitude filled the streets and roofs around Federal Hall. Adams motioned Washington through the doors, and he appeared before a hushed crowd and slowly bowed. The gesture had the seeming effect of slowly summoning a vast noise, a growing roar of cheers intermingled with stamping and whistling. Chancellor Robert R. Livingston, the highest-ranking judicial figure in New York, stood ready to administer the oath. He, too, knew Washington from the Revolution and was a representative of the complexly interlinked families that enjoyed status and privilege in New York State. Washington had fond memories of Livingston's mother befriending Martha when she visited the army's New York encampments.

A momentary panic had seized Livingston as Washington was set to appear. It turned out that no one had brought a Bible for the ceremony. Invoking his authority as the grand master of the St. John's Masonic Lodge, Livingston had its Bible rushed to Federal Hall. Secretary of the Senate Samuel Otis was to hold the Bible, but he was a diminutive man dwarfed by the tall figures of Livingston and Washington. When he placed the Bible on a satin red cushion, he seemed unsure about the best way to present it for Washington's comfort.

Washington placed his hand on the Bible with Otis slightly bowing and clutching the cushion. The crowd became eerily silent. Livingston spoke the oath, pausing for Washington to repeat its phrases, now familiar but entirely new in their first use on April 30, 1789. When Washington completed his pledge to faithfully execute his office and uphold the Constitution, some heard him proclaim, "So help me God," though that remembrance surfaced some years later. Everyone, however, saw Otis awkwardly raise the cushion toward Washington's face. It seemed to surprise Washington. He motioned for Otis to lower it and then bowed to kiss it. Livingston was already turning toward the crowd, and his shouting voice broke the silence: "Long Live George Washington, President of the United States!"[24] Livingston's proclamation was not yet finished before the cheering people sent a wall of noise across Wall Street that assumed the same physical force as the cheers that had charted Washington's journey from Mount Vernon. A flag went up atop Federal Hall, the signal for an artillery salute. Washington bowed to the crowd, turned slowly, and walked back to the Senate chamber to deliver his inaugural address.[25]

Washington began another tradition with this speech, one that most presidents have emulated as a show of humility before the majesty of the people. He expressed concern that he was not worthy of the responsibility entrusted to him but that he would not ignore the call of a country whose "every step . . . seems to have been distinguished by some token of providential agency." That agency had brought them all together at this moment with Washington's halting delivery of an address that offered little in specifics, for it reflected his agreement with Madison that Congress represented the will of the people, and he was only their steward. At most he asked Congress to honor the pledge to consider amendments to the Constitution as a good faith gesture to erase the divisions from ratification. He offered to serve without salary to continue the tradition he had established at the head of the Continental Army, when his only compensation had been reimbursement for expenses. He closed with an appeal to the "Parent of the Human Race" for "His divine blessing."[26]

The address was fewer than five hundred words long and took less than fifteen minutes to deliver. Its brevity was matched by a lack of urbanity in its delivery, which was becoming. A young Massachusetts congressman named Fisher Ames described the feelings of many. He was more deeply moved by the man than his words. "Time has made havoc upon his face," Ames noted. Something about Washington touched him, "his aspect grave, almost to sadness."[27] The deep voice had sometimes paused incongruously, as was Washington's way, but it had also quavered. It was odd for a large man obviously accustomed to being in command. Everyone's eyes had trailed down from the time-scarred face to the papers in his hands, finally fixing on the hands themselves. Throughout the quarter hour of this first inaugural address, George Washington's hands had been trembling.[28]

Washington's first presidential deed after the inauguration ceremony was to go to church. In the company of Congress and prominent citizens, he crossed the street from Federal Hall and entered St. Paul's Chapel to attend a two-hour service. The gesture was more than symbolic. Each of the six paragraphs in the inaugural address he had just delivered contained a reference to God as a higher power and the ultimate authority. Washington spoke of "fervent supplications to that Almighty Being who rules over the universe," expressed the hope that "His benediction may consecrate," paid "homage to the Great Author of every public and private good," invoked God as a "providential agency," noted "the propitious smiles of Heaven," and prayed for "the preservation of sacred fire of liberty and the destiny of the republican model of government."

This was not Deism, a creation of the Enlightenment that appealed to the rationalism of intellectuals uncomfortable with the supernatural aspects of religion. The God of Deism was detached, a master mechanic who had created a perfect machine that once thumped into motion ran perpetually without the need for superintendence and certainly without random instances of divine intervention. Deism is often touted as the faith of the American Founders, which makes the mistake of lumping all Deists together by ignoring that Deism was no more monolithic than denominational Christianity. Jefferson and Franklin are always cited as the most obvious Deists, and Washington is frequently added to the list as a passive participant—a reluctant Anglican at best, a secular realist at heart. Yet, his inaugural address contained the same sentiments he expressed throughout his life. His reference to the "sacred fire of liberty" echoed his self-admonition meticulously copied from a seventeenth-century text, *Rules of Civility & Decent Behaviour in Company and Conversation,* when Washington was only a teenager: "Keep alive in Your Breast that Little Spark of Celestial fire Called Conscience."[29]

Nevertheless, few agree about Washington's religious beliefs. It is true that after the Revolution, he ceased taking communion. Historian Mary Thompson, whose knowledge is unsurpassed on the subject, has posed the possibility that the Episcopal Church's selection of Samuel Seabury as its first bishop may have deeply troubled Washington. Seabury headed the High Church Anglican wing of the Episcopal Church that insisted on apostolic succession and refused non-Anglicans communion. In addition, Seabury had been an outspoken Loyalist during the war. In any case, Washington identified more closely with the Low Church Anglicans who embraced broader views about inclusion.[30] Thompson believes that Washington in his later years became uncomfortable with the Episcopalian teachings of his youth. In short, his concept of Christian charity became both broader and simpler.[31] He proclaimed days of thanksgiving and prayer (the first, near the end of 1789) and expressed his gratitude for the prayers of others and the beneficence of God. Like so much about Washington, his actions rather than his words disclosed his convictions.[32]

Even though Washington never explicitly explained his own beliefs in a concise manifesto, he obviously believed in God as a participant, "an agency," in the lives of men and women and nations.[33] His recurring references to a supreme being coincided with his habit of often quoting the Bible in his letters, demonstrating a clear and thorough knowledge of the Old and New Testaments. Possibly Washington set aside time in the early morning for private prayer. He plainly directed that grace precede meals at his table. He attended church regularly, served on his Episcopal vestry, and supported the church financially. He made no secret of his belief that active church membership was an important seam in a community's fabric that tied society together.

Moreover, to take Washington at his word in scores of writings that mirror his inaugural address, he believed that religion in general and Christianity in particular were essential to the success of republican government. Religion encouraged civic virtue and responsibility. During the Revolution, he ordered soldiers to attend religious services. While president, he rarely missed Sunday services, and his only activity on the Sabbath was the appropriately restful one of writing his lengthy letters to Mount Vernon's managers.[34]

Yet he also believed in absolute freedom of conscience. It remained a constant principle. In the summer of 1790, he wrote to the Hebrew Congregation of Newport, Rhode Island, an illustrative expression of it. Americans through their republican government gave "to bigotry no sanction, to persecution no assistance."[35] It was the statement of a man sufficiently confident in his faith and in his country that neither he nor it saw cause to trespass on the faith of others.

That night, Washington attended a reception at Robert R. Livingston's home and another at Henry Knox's where he watched rockets light the sky. Wealthy New Yorkers competed to display the most elaborate transparency, that popular though pricey method for festively illuminating pictures. Many depicted scenes from the country's brief past and featured giant images of Washington. French minister Elénor-François-Elie, Comte de Moustier, scored a triumph with a huge display that illustrated not only the history of the United States but also showed scenes prophesying the future greatness of the nation. The country was broke, enemies prowled its borders, and the world was inclined to believe that Moustier's optimistic vision of American prospects was more wishful than prophetic.

Yet standing at the center of a swirling pool of hope and anxiety was the tall figure with impeccable posture, his head tilted back, his face impassive as his eyes tracked the sparkling arcs of rockets. The odds were long, but that April night in America, anything was possible, even a solvent treasury and peaceful border, even friendly commerce with a world that was spinning its way toward an American dawn. The transparencies told a story, but the rockets rushing upward were more than an ornament. They were an emblem. George Washington and his friends watched them.

3

"Not the Tincture of Ha'ture About Her"

Martha Washington stayed at Mount Vernon when her husband left for New York City, but their separation was always meant to be temporary and brief. She was even less happy than he about this latest call to duty and would have liked nothing better than to remain in Virginia. She loved the house, the grounds, the vista, the life. She could set her own routines and, at worst, had to cope with her husband's celebrity, which meant an endless parade of visitors, but even that bother after a time became tolerable because everyone was awed by him and nice to her. But for all her fondness for that life in that place, she loved him more. She could not bear to be without him, and only a few weeks after his departure her yearning to see him tempered the anxiety of moving as she heard the family coach arriving back from New York. He had sent it as soon as he could.

He had brought her to Mount Vernon thirty years before, almost to the day that she was leaving it that spring in 1789. In 1759 they were newlyweds as they made their way toward the house on the Potomac, approaching it from the west, the vantage that always made a lasting impression on new visitors. Spring meant the grounds were at their best, and orchards filled the air with sweet scents. The new husband was vexed that incomplete renovations filled the house with the odor of wet paint and drying plaster. The bride had not minded in the least.[1]

In those first months, soft days passed into pleasant nights cooled by

Potomac breezes. The house high atop its impressive little mountain smelled of linseed oil and trembled during the day from hammering workmen, but she didn't care, and even a case of the measles had not dampened her spirits. Things had worked out pretty well after all for the little Dandridge girl who had known so much heartbreak so early. Her children played, her husband was attentive even when busy, and she was mistress of a fine farm. Though they were of that class of colonial Virginia who often arranged matrimony with money in mind, there was always the chance that hearts would follow. In fact, hers already had.[2]

Martha Dandridge was born on the Pamunkey River at Chestnut Grove on June 2, 1731, the eldest of eight children who had to take on considerable responsibility helping a mother who was frequently pregnant or nursing the latest addition to the family. The Dandridge children had an adequate education, but important social skills such as dancing were more valuable in Martha's world than spelling. She became a practiced dancer. She never mastered spelling.[3]

Her parents introduced her to Williamsburg society in 1746 when she was just fifteen. The custom was suited to the time. In those days, a woman was considered middle-aged in her midtwenties, and Martha's entrance into the capital's social whirl was the normal course for a girl nearing marriageable age. Shorter than five feet and a bit squat in figure, she was as physically attractive as she would ever be in her life, and that was not much. But there was something else about her. She had a beguiling charm that made her popular, not because she was pretty but because she was nice. She laughed easily and often, and always at other people's jokes, never at other people. She doubtless realized that she was not much to look at, nor the sort of girl who made clever remarks or came up with sharp repartee, so she cultivated a natural talent for making everyone else feel smart and witty.

Even so, young Martha was hardly besieged by suitors, which is probably why she wound up with an unlikely one. Daniel Parke Custis had never married, an oddity for a man his age, which at thirty-seven made him twice as old as Martha and almost as old as her mother. The

Dandridges might have frowned, but Daniel's family was wealthy. Daniel's father, however, opposed his son's plan to marry a lowly Dandridge and even threatened to disown him. The couple persisted, and their commitment outlived the old man. With the passing of his father, Daniel Parke Custis became wealthy with an inheritance impressive by any standard. He owned almost eighteen thousand acres of land in King William, Northampton, and Hanover counties. Little Martha Dandridge had most definitely married up, yet her life was not luxurious. The couple settled where Daniel had been living for years while managing the farms, a place prosaically named White House. It was also on the Pamunkey not far from Chestnut Grove and much like the house where Martha had grown up.

Included in Daniel Custis's inheritance were some three hundred slaves, an enormous number that made him one of the largest slaveholders in North America. Martha's feelings about slavery were typical of the benign but unquestioning white person in British North America. Slavery was part of the way things were, part of the system of rank and caste that, for all she knew, affected the lives of all people everywhere. Quaker abolitionism was a nascent force at best in the mid-eighteenth century, often despised and even persecuted, and unlikely in any case to have intruded upon the thoughts of a young plantation mistress on the Pamunkey River. In her cloistered world, the clear distinction was for whites to be free and blacks to be slaves. Martha Custis would not have thought about it much beyond that. In fact, her acceptance of the world as she found it was part of a larger piety that required respect for God's plan, mysterious as it might be. The philosophical underpinning of slavery did not have to be plainer than that for a twenty-year-old woman who had never known any other way. Slavery simply was.

In her view of that world, the obligation of whites within the system of slavery was to make it as tolerable as possible with kindness and forbearance. Cruelty was a sin. Martha Custis could not be cruel. But at the same time, she was limited in her understanding of the world as it moved around her. This was the case throughout her life, beginning at Chestnut Grove, continuing at White House, and then over the years at Mount Vernon. She believed that the people living in slavery also accepted it as the natural way of things. Because acting as if this were true was a sensible way to make their lives easier, most slaves reinforced this impression, and Martha was not alone in thinking that the occasional slave who rebelled by shirking work or feigning illness or—at the extreme—by running away was an aberration. Something was wrong with the person, who happened to be a slave, rather than slavery, which simply was the way of the world.

As the years wore on, she would not change this view, but events would first rattle and then shatter it. Her experiences as the wife of General Washington and then President Washington took her, as they did him, to new places far from the Pamunkey and the Potomac, places where new ideas were seeking to reconcile the unsightly disparity between a land proclaiming liberty while much of it was forging shackles. Stubbornness and provincialism could bolster her certainties about the rectitude of slavery for a time, but not forever.

Daniel and Martha's firstborn died at three years old, and though her grief receded in time, the death of her second child in April 1757 made her obsessively protective of the two who survived, John Parke ("Jacky") and Martha Parke ("Patsy"). Martha could be strict about some things, and usually more so with girls. But Martha's ordinary way of dealing with children was affection tending to outright indulgence.

In July 1757, she lost Daniel. He was only forty-five, and his illness's unexpected appearance and rapid march made his passing seem like a bad dream. Everybody was stunned.[4] In fact, it all happened so quickly that Daniel died without a will, which placed the sizable Custis estate under terms of English common law and required someone to tie up loose ends and resolve questions. According to the latest biographies, Martha astonished everyone in what proved to be her finest hour. Over the autumn, winter, and spring after Daniel's death, she remained steady and resolute, dealing with attorneys, colonial authorities, London agents, and her grieving children, always with the same sure hand and even temper.

The clear intent of the common law made matters seem simple enough on paper: Martha received a third of the estate, and Jacky and

Patsy would have the rest with Martha holding their portions in trust until they came of age. Yet details complicated everything. The vast acreage would all go to Jacky because the intestate condition of the Custis fortune required that land be bequeathed to the male heir. On reaching his majority Jacky would inherit the nearly eighteen thousand acres with slaves to one-third of the estate's assessed value. Patsy's share was money and stocks to a third, and Martha's the same with slaves included. Keeping track of the slaves would become a confusing tangle because Martha's share—designated as "dower" slaves—never belonged to her but were merely at her service until she died. They then would revert to the estate to be distributed among heirs or descendants of heirs. Even after the Revolution when Virginia relaxed its proscriptive laws limiting emancipation, freeing these slaves would have been quite expensive. Their assessed value would have to be paid to the estate for distribution to the heirs.

That was Martha's situation in the spring of 1758. In March she was visiting her neighbors the Chamberlaynes at Poplar Grove. Two riders approached the yard and dismounted. While one held the horses, the taller one strode to the door. It was there in a neighbor's parlor that Colonel Washington just happened to run into the Widow Custis. They were married the following January.

The best anyone can do is guess why Washington showed up at the Chamberlaynes that day. The meeting has the look of being arranged. Martha may not have known he was coming, but he most likely knew she was there.[5] In any case, their subsequent meetings were few, probably not more than three, making the courtship quite brief. The brevity and background of their association suggests it was a business arrangement rather than a love match. Certainly it was an unlikely match from several perspectives, and an unwise one for Martha. George had no real assets, had accumulated a fair amount of debt, had a demanding mother ensconced in the only house he owned, and was at the time leasing the one he lived in from his former sister-in-law.[6] Yet none of that mattered to Martha. She may have been swept off her feet—Washington was tall, athletic, and gracious. There was also a steadiness about George Washington that a young widow with two small children and numerous responsibilities would have found reassuring. At some point in June 1758, eleven months after Daniel's death, Martha and George came to an understanding, possibly even a formal engagement. He had by then received a ring purchased through the mail from Philadelphia. On January 6, 1759, they were married at White House.

We know little about the women in George Washington's life before he married Martha Custis, with one notable exception. After Sally Cary Fairfax died in England in 1811, her possessions eventually made their way back to America. In a bundle of papers were two letters George Washington had written her in September 1758, but it was not until 1871, a half century after Sally's death, that the first of them became public. It was a love letter.

It was also quite troubling. Sally was the wife of Washington's close friend, his mentor from youth and longtime neighbor, George William Fairfax. We will never know if George Washington and Sally Fairfax ever acted on his feelings.[7] What we do know is that in the late summer of 1758, Washington as a colonel in the Virginia militia was about to begin a dangerous campaign on the western frontier. He wrote Sally two extraordinary letters. In the first, he appears to answer her joshing remark about his impatience to have the campaign completed so he could marry the widow Custis. "'Tis true, I profess myself a votary of love," Washington responded. "I acknowledge that a lady is in the case, and further I confess that this lady is known to you." This was so far, so good. But in the next two sentences Washington veered into strange romantic territory. "Yes, Madame," he explained, "as well as she is to one who is too sensible of her charms to deny the Power whose influence he feels and must ever submit to. I feel the force of her amiable beauties in the recollection of a thousand tender passages that I could wish to obliterate, till I am bid to revive them."[8]

The flowery phrase in Washington's opening has tagged the note as "the votary of love" letter, and its convoluted declarations have caused some to explain that actually he was professing himself a "votary of love" to Martha Custis. Yet, the interpretation is doubtful. Washington's reference to "a thousand tender passages" could not have been referring to Martha. From their first meeting in May until mid-September, the two could not have had a fraction of a thousand passages, tender or otherwise. The gist of what Washington was saying was, "I love you," and asking, in equally stammering fashion, "Do you love me?"

That Martha appears at all in the exchange between Washington and Sally Fairfax gives the tale a sad and troubling twist. To be sure, Washington had already come to some understanding that summer with Martha, an arrangement serious enough to merit a ring. As a consequence, Washington was not only declaring his love to his friend's wife; he was also being disloyal to the woman he had pledged to marry. Sally's response was as prompt as a courier could deliver it, and it was apparently either cool in tone or tried to treat Washington's letter as a joke. Incredibly, he tried again: "Dear Madam: Do we still misunderstand the true meaning of each other's Letters? I think it must appear so, tho' I would feign hope the contrary as I cannot speak plainer without, But I'll say no more, and leave you to guess the rest."

But he did say more, returning to the subject near the end of his letter: "I should think my time more agreable spent believe me, in playing a part in Cato, with the Company you mention, and myself doubly happy in being the Juba to such a Marcia, as you must make."[9] For modern readers, it's likely an obscure reference, but Sally would have understood it completely. *Cato* was a popular play of the time whose characters Juba and Marcia are star-crossed lovers.

Sally possibly never answered this letter, and Washington never wrote her again in the same way. It was a rare instance of uninhibited emotion. Pleading Washington's youth as an excuse for his behavior is difficult. At twenty-six, he was hardly callow. In the end, he was lucky to have found two sober young women—one aware of her station and the obligations it imposed, and the other a cheerful intended who knew something of the world and had known great sadness, greeting almost every disappointment with resolve spiced by laughter. As it turned out, the result was not a tragedy, but neither was it a fairy tale, except for the fact that the people who deserved to end up living happily ever after more or less did. In less than four months after writing the letters to Sally Fairfax, George Washington married Martha Custis.

They were neighbors until 1773 when the Fairfaxes visited England on what should have been a temporary trip, but the American Revolution dissuaded them from returning, and Sally's husband died in 1787.

Forty years after George Washington had told her that he loved her, she received a letter from him that was tinged with whimsy and colored by nostalgia. He made reference to a note he was enclosing from Martha, one he actually had written for Martha to copy. In it, he had Martha invite Sally to come back to Virginia to live out her life down the road from Mount Vernon as they all spun out their final years. Sally would not.[10] She had settled in Bath, and there she grew old as gout swelled and gnarled her fingers.

"It has been the maxim of my life," she once wrote about something else, "to go without what I wanted ever so much if I could not pay instantly."[11] It would seem that she was true to her word in applying the maxim broadly. Sally Cary Fairfax's good sense ensured all their futures, the best for George Washington's country, and the best for him, as it happened.[12] Sally was always to be the girl he once secretly adored, but she remained a sensible woman with her own sentimental secret. Washington apparently destroyed her letters to him from the fall of 1758, but she saved his. She carried them to England, stowed them safely away, and they were thus finally found. They are bittersweet reminders of going without, when the cost of having is too high.

The sixteen years that followed Martha Washington's first spring at Mount Vernon would have their times of heartbreak, but the estate's world and the people in it became as natural for her as drawing breath. There were few frills at Mount Vernon. Life was simple and ordered by strict routines.

The Washingtons rose early. She ran the household while he toured the plantation's farms. The tradition of social events from Washington's active bachelor days continued with Martha easily folded in. Neighbors for plantation people were hardly handy, the extent of one's property usually making "next door" a day away, and the overnight guest was a usual fixture on any given evening.

They never had children of their own, but more precisely, Martha never bore Washington a child. Children, however, became a permanent feature at Mount Vernon. The marriage brought the Custis children to the estate, and there were nieces and nephews and small friends, then grandchildren to start the cycle anew. It was a happy setting with lots of places to play, run with abandon, swim, ride, and have parties. An elderly lady fondly remembered a time at Mount Vernon when a traveling dance instructor arrived to hold lessons for children who gathered there from neighboring farms. She saw Washington peeking in one of the doors. She never forgot his smile.[13]

Martha was an indulgent mother, especially with Jacky, and the predictable consequences drove George Washington to distraction. He learned to hold his tongue about the children, but he quietly fretted over Jacky refusing to study and filling his days with mindless amusements. Patsy was better, but sadly ill health rather than firm guidance was the reason. As she entered puberty she began having the tonic-clonic seizures of a confirmed epileptic. Doctors employed a variety of futile treatments, many of them little more than medieval superstitions. Late one summer afternoon in 1773 the horrible spasms came, but this time they ended once and for all. After a two-minute episode, Martha's "Little Patt" would be seventeen forever. Washington wrote: "It is an easier matter to conceive than to describe the distress of this Family."[14]

Shortly after his sister's death, Jacky married Eleanor Calvert from Maryland across the Potomac at Mount Airy in February 1774; the groom was nineteen and his bride freshly sixteen. In a couple of years they started a family, giving Martha a new batch of children to fuss over, worry about, and spoil. Her Jacky was now John Parke Custis and in possession of his inheritance. He became a burgess, just as his stepfather had.

The war with Britain took Jack Custis in a strange way. He never served in the army, and there was no shame in that, but in the fall of 1781 as the siege of Yorktown was ending with the British planning to surrender, he resolved to see something of the American Revolution since it was happening in his own backyard. Visiting the lines, he fell ill with a complaint vaguely described as "camp fever," which was likely typhus and thus much more serious than anyone realized. He was taken to Eltham, the home of Burwell Bassett and his wife, Martha's sister, but his condition steadily worsened until he died just two weeks later. His mother and Eleanor were at his bedside. Jack was twenty-six.[15]

Martha was beyond consolation, and Eleanor was a widow at twenty-three, an oddly piercing repeat of Martha's fate twenty-five years earlier, with double the orphans. The two oldest girls stayed with their mother while Martha took in the very young other daughter and the baby son to lighten Eleanor's load. The arrangement was sensible enough, but it also had the effect over time of making the siblings virtual strangers. That was inevitable given their ages: Wash was a mere babe in arms, and his sister Nelly was two. Over time they came to regard the Washingtons more as their parents than grandparents, and the attachment to their mother, Eleanor, became increasingly tenuous until it almost did not exist at all. When Nelly was sixteen, Martha planned for her to spend the winter with her mother. Nelly dreaded the prospect.[16]

These children grew up as George and Martha grew old. In considering Wash, Washington might have taken some comfort in remembering how the boy's father had been shown little direction when he was young but had turned out all right as age and the right girl settled him. But Washington systematically lectured the boy to the point of hectoring him. Wash didn't seem to mind, and his high spirits sometimes tickled even Washington. Wash could not stay in a school to save his life. During an educational career that was doggedly optimistic on Washington's part, but casual and unenthusiastic on Wash's, he attended the Academy and College of Philadelphia, the College of New Jersey, and St. John's College at Annapolis, distinguishing himself at each place by either being expelled or simply being withdrawn to save everyone the embarrassment of another failed experiment.[17]

Nelly, on the other hand, could do no wrong. In part this was because she was truly sweet natured. But it was also because with Nelly the Calvert and Custis lines had achieved something visually miraculous. The pretty child became a stunning girl during Washington's presidency in New York City and Philadelphia. She was ten at the beginning and eighteen at the end, schooled and groomed and admired as she attended girls' academies and received private instruction.[18] Long hours of practice developed her into an accomplished musician. Washington appreciated her talent so much he bought her no less than two expensive imported harpsichords. He could never carry a tune himself, but when Nelly played it was magic, and he noticed how everyone listened. He also noticed how men in deep conversation with one another lost their train of thought and stopped in midsentence when Miss Custis entered a room. People as diverse as the architect Benjamin Latrobe ("more perfection of form, of expression, of color, of softness, and of firmness of mind than I have ever seen before or conceived consistent with mortality"), the Polish expatriate Julian Niemcewicz ("the divine Miss Custis with her hair blown by a storm"), and Henrietta Liston, the wife of the British minister ("most beautiful girl"), sang Nelly's praises. A large part of her charm was that Nelly Custis could not see what all the fuss was about.[19]

In the spring of 1789, George Washington looked forward to his family's arrival in New York because Wash needed supervision and Nelly needed attention. The brief separation was trying on both him and Martha, and both looked forward to putting their household together again. During all their years together, Martha wore a locket that contained his miniature portrait and a lock of his hair. She called him "Pappa" when they were with close friends and family; during the Revolutionary War, she began calling him "the General."[20] It was a pet name.

The travelers bound for New York from Mount Vernon that spring included six slaves, two of them Martha's maids Oney Judge and Molly. Christopher Sheels and Oney's half brother Austin were to become waiters in the president's house, and Giles and Paris would be coachmen. Washington had arranged to have his sister's twenty-year-old son Robert Lewis escort the family to New York and become a junior secretary on the presidential staff.

On May 16, 1789, they began a journey that reprised Martha's role during the Revolutionary War. When their sixteen years of peaceful retirement had ended with her husband taking up arms against Great Britain, she had not merely kept the home fires burning. Whenever possible, she took them to him, rarely missing any chance or shying from any peril to do so. Bad roads, uncertain accommodations, poor food, and inclement weather were bad enough, but she risked British capture while traveling miles upon miles. Like young Lewis in 1789, her escorts then had been more for company than protection.

She had never flinched from her duty. The example of "Lady Washington" inspired officers and regular soldiers alike. While her behavior fixed her in the popular imagination as an icon of the patriot cause, the experiences also broadened Martha's world. She saw regions of the country she could have only imagined before and met people she would not have otherwise known. Some of the people she met were famous and some would become famous, but most would remain obscure. Her world expanded, but her good character was constant. She treated everyone just the same, just as she always had.

At headquarters she had been a leavening presence, which was part of her personality. Young ladies giggled over handsome Alexander Hamilton, and he never passed up a romantic opportunity, so she named her randy tomcat "Hamilton."[21] She also became an active witness to the war. For want of clothes soldiers froze in desolate winter encampments, for want of shoes they left footprints streaked with blood in the snow, and she saw. Congress and commissary failed to supply soldiers with basic needs, so she joined patriotic ladies to collect private donations from women throughout the country. Pennies and shillings were the normal sums from a hard-pressed population, but every bit helped. Martha quietly chipped in money to match her time and effort. In one season she donated £6000.[22]

George Washington saw her devotion to him, to the country's cause, and to the ragtag army fighting for it. He had to love her for this. The war took a lifetime to end but they endured its hardships together, and its triumphant conclusion was a miracle they shared. The Washingtons had returned to their home above the Potomac the same people but greatly changed. They were confident that life would grant them the wish expressed by Eloisa to Abelard: "the world forgetting, by the world forgot."[23] Neither of them had ever wanted to leave Mount Vernon again.

Martha's caravan stopped first at Abingdon, the home of Nelly and Wash's mother, Eleanor Stuart, and their stepfather, Dr. David Stuart, one of Washington's closest personal friends. Outside of Baltimore they stayed with Mrs. Charles Carroll, whose husband was in the U.S. Senate. After Baltimore, Martha's procession began to resemble her husband's of weeks before, except the pace was much more leisurely. When Lady Washington stopped in Philadelphia at the home of Mary and Robert Morris, she lingered for several days.

New York City gave Martha her own grand celebration. Washington boarded the presidential barge for the trip to New Jersey to meet Martha and escort her to the city. Just as before, Governor Clinton was waiting on the wharf, and crowds hurrahed her and the children all the way to the Cherry Street house.

As she sorted out the details of arranging schooling for the children and settling in at 3 Cherry Street, Martha quickly had confirmed what she already knew: Life in New York would little resemble life at Mount Vernon. Her role was now more visible and more important than running a household on a large rural plantation. She became the official hostess of the government and the feminine face of her husband's administration. Washington had hired a steward who shouldered many of the chores Martha had seen to in Virginia. He was Samuel Fraunces, the former owner of Fraunces Tavern at the corner of Dock and Broad streets, famous for being the place where Washington had said farewell to his officers at war's end.[24] Fraunces supervised some two dozen servants and saw to meal preparation in consultation with Mrs. Washington.

She had to dive right in. Shortly after her arrival, she held a large dinner at the presidential residence. Martha knew the art of feeding a multitude since every meal at Mount Vernon included friends, family, and even curiosity seekers, many showing up with little if any notice. Dinners in New York, however, were formal affairs that required elaborate planning and elegant execution. It should have overwhelmed this ordinary woman unused to ceremony and equipped by custom and temperament only for the task of taking care of children and a husband. She excelled. In fact, she attended official functions, hosted dinners, staged social events, and acted the part of the most important woman in New York without seeming to act any part at all. From the start she refused to put on airs or pretend to social knowledge that she did not have. Rather, she charmed everyone with her tried and true habit of being more interested than interesting. Soon enough, the round little lady with the mop cap and ready smile bewitched men and women alike. The day after Abigail Adams arrived in New York she called on Martha, and the two instantly became friends and were frequent companions. Abigail found Martha "modest and unassuming, dignified and femenine," with "not the Tincture of ha'ture about her."[25]

While New York was effusive in its adoration of Martha Washington, the depth of her husband's affection for her remains a mystery. She kept her counsel about her marriage in ways that frustrate an understanding of it. Destroying correspondence was the best way to preserve privacy because it obliterated the documentary record, something Martha Washington elected to do before she died. As a result, only four letters to her from George Washington survived her, two written from Philadelphia in 1775 when he was departing for Boston to take command of the Continental Army. They are loving letters, if not love letters per se, but intimate in tone. His salutations are tender. "My dearest," he opens, and soon tells his "Patsy," Washington's nickname for her, that "I should enjoy more real happiness and felicity in one month with you, at home, than I have the most distant prospect of reaping abroad, if my stay was to be Seven times Seven years." And in the second letter, written just minutes before he began his journey, he plainly states, "I retain an unalterable affection for you, which neither time or distance can change."[26]

Martha Washington obviously wanted to keep these letters, and the other two she seems to have overlooked, possibly because they concerned commonplace matters. Students of George and Martha Washington have had to make do with this meager documentary record to speculate by extrapolation, and the resulting conclusions have been mixed. In fact, the assessments of George Washington's wife and their feelings for each other have always told more about their authors and the times they lived in than about George or Martha or their lives together. For lack of evidence, observers either have been quite unkind to Martha Washington or extravagantly praiseful of her, with many falling along a range between these two extremes.

It was obvious to some, for instance, that Washington married her only for her money, as some people said at the time. How could it be otherwise since she was nothing but an ill-educated frump, unable to write a literate sentence or grace a parlor with flair and elegance? Others insist Washington was smitten from the moment he saw her, a bereaved widow who was captivating in her composure and self-reliance, her hazel eyes bewitching and her trim figure or busty plumpness (the description changes according to the feminine ideal of the writer's time) spurring him to ardent pursuit. For some, the courtship was brief because marriage was nothing more than a business arrangement, while others think it was abbreviated because the lovers could not put brakes on their passion. It was a loveless union because it was childless, proof of their distance and disregard. Or they were completely devoted to each other, brimming with so much love that they were able to shower it on Martha's children and grandchildren. To some it is obvious that Washington loved another woman, and they submit that Martha was a shrew who destroyed his letters to hide the deceit of their marriage from the world. Others clearly see Martha as his soul mate, his confidante in things major and minor. She burned the letters because she had been forced to share so much of their lives with the public that she would be damned if she would do it in death.

In short, George and Martha Washington were everything or nothing to each other. She was a bank account and he a glorified business manager; she a passionate lover, he a gallant Galahad. As a consequence, when Martha burned the letters she did more than pull a shade on the window of their marriage. She opened the door to everyone to imagine its contours, its purpose, and its meaning. Possibly everyone is wrong.

What is clear is that she proved to be the perfect wife for a taciturn man. She was modest in dress and manner, stolid, reliable, unpretentious, kind, and practical. In sharing his public duties, she was a stoic partner, and as a social arbiter the best complement to his tendency to sit silent at meals, sometimes bored enough to drum his utensils between courses. After the Revolution and the fame that came with it, she always had guests at her table and could have probably counted on one hand the number of times she and Washington dined alone. On the eve of his presidency, an event that she dreaded, she continued to entertain, charming any and all, whether bon vivants and worldly Europeans or dour Quakers and prim maidens.

She did not battle her weight the way modern women do nor try to disguise her age with gaudy dresses and glittering jewelry. Instead she let nature take its course and her appetite have its way. The result was the grandmotherly image that Americans have exclusively as George Washington's wife, in all times and at all ages. By the late 1780s she had become "rather fleshy" with "a large portly double chin." She dressed plainly in long-sleeved black satin gowns with linen handkerchiefs and aprons for trim rather than use. Her only adornment might be black bows on her French-style mop cap. But it was her "open & engageing Countenance," always adorned with a smile, that people most remembered and never went out of style.[27]

She remained kind and trusting despite her discomfort with the constraints the presidency imposed. She responded to criticism of him like a lioness, but she never exhibited a shred of envy toward the wealthy women in their circle in New York and Philadelphia or a particle of jealousy toward those always deemed more fashionable, more intelligent, and more attractive. She embraced women who were close friends of her husband, including Eliza Powel and even Robert Morris's wife, Mary, who was sometimes openly unkind to Martha.[28] She worried about making social mistakes that might embarrass her family and often consulted the ruling mavens with an endearing innocence. She could never spell and sometimes used awkward, inelegant phrases, so for important correspondence, she had her husband draft the letter that she then laboriously copied. The facts present us with Martha as a plain, plump woman, neither clever nor quick.[29]

And yet she really was someone else, too. Young Martha Dandridge had learned early that even a plain girl is made attractive by being interested rather than interesting. Martha Washington never forgot it. She brimmed with love, freely gave it away with both hands, laughed often, embraced her family, and easily made friends and kept them. Once at a dinner party later in Washington's presidency, Mary Morris was seated on George Washington's right and whispered to him that the cream in the dessert that Martha was spooning into her mouth had curdled. Martha was on her husband's left and heard the remark but said nothing. She continued eating the dessert. Mary told and retold this story to her friends, a spiteful show of discourtesy to illustrate Martha's provincialism. Martha never said a word about this, one way or another.[30]

George Washington had to love this woman. She was his kind of girl.

4

"His Person Is Little and Ordinary"

It's easy to forget how young they all were when they fought Britain for independence and then set up a government like nothing the world had seen. Because they managed to achieve these feats, they became "Founding Fathers," and their image for history would be of men always old and often stern. Yet at the beginning of the drama in 1774, Thomas Jefferson was thirty-one, John Jay twenty-eight, Henry Knox twenty-four, James Madison twenty-three, and Alexander Hamilton only nineteen. George Washington was the relatively "old man" of the group at forty-two, but Washington was one of those people born "old." The rest were youngsters, and none more so than James Madison. Even the teenager Hamilton looked older.

His friends called him Jimmy and always spelled it "Jemmy," the kind of diminutive that stubbornly attaches to the physically unimpressive. He was shy and retiring in large groups, and his dour black suits that were meant to hide his youth and frail frame actually had the effect of almost hiding him altogether. He was small (some say five feet four inches, others five six) and never weighed more than a hundred pounds at his stoutest. His handshake was soft, his bow uncertain, his gaze usually cast downward, his tongue often at a loss for words. Most people saw a funny little man. Women ignored him.

The oldest son of a large family, Madison grew up in the tobacco culture of plantation Virginia but never took much interest in it. He buried himself in books, and they became his constant companions. He began his daily reading before dawn with folio pages flying like the hours until he lit candles into the night, absorbing anything and everything of the mind rapidly, thoroughly, relentlessly. His private tutors and accomplished teachers were astonished by his facility for mastering scores of learned disciplines, especially ancient languages, philosophy, history, and political theory. They suspected they were seeing a large genius despite the small packaging.

It took him only two years to complete an ambitious program of study at the College of New Jersey in Princeton. He chose the school instead of William and Mary to avoid what he regarded as Williamsburg's unhealthy climate, but unyielding intellectual effort took a heavier toll than the York River's marsh fevers. Madison had always been high strung and had always complained of being sickly, but finishing college scared him almost to death. Serious chronic illness dogged him for the rest of his life, and possibly it was all in his mind. He never called it epilepsy—there was a stigma attached even to the milder forms of the malady that came as mental fogs—but whatever ailed him resembled it to the extent that it cast him into spells of mental and physical torpor. The fear of aggravating his condition made him physically nervous. He avoided taxing activities ranging from sea voyages to military service, but anxiety over getting sick could make him sick. He fought these panic attacks until the day he died—at eighty-five.[1]

Madison returned to Virginia in 1772, studied law, and sat in the House of Burgesses from 1776 to 1779. Thomas Jefferson saw something remarkable in him right away, possibly because the two shared a passion for religious liberty that made them obvious collaborators in legislating it for Virginia. Yet Madison would display an uncanny habit of making older, more experienced men into admirers as well as mentors. They formed a lasting friendship that later would have more consequential results on a larger stage.

When Madison went to the Congress in 1780 he found everything about it an ordeal. The futility that enervated the proceedings was bad enough, but the place full of strangers was terrifying for a shy, little man who was twenty-nine but looked fifteen. Often nobody bothered to hear his hushed voice. Still, beneath the retiring manner and diffident bearing, he was ambitious. For a time the words flowed only in letters to his friend Jefferson, but in a few months he found a niche as an industrious lieutenant for congressional leaders. They were amazed that the little Virginian could put together unlikely coalitions out of thin air. Legislative inertia tutored him in the political art of the possible. After a while, his hushed voice could silence every murmur in a room. At parties people were suddenly delighted by his unexpectedly wicked sense of humor. In the right company, he could be ribald, causing men to chuckle and look at one another with surprise. (Years later as secretary of state, he paid for a Tunisian diplomat's visit to a prostitute with what he described as "appropriations to foreign intercourse.")[2] In Congress, colleagues who had talked over him now listened, even if they had to cup their ears. Those who still took Jemmy Madison lightly found themselves on the receiving end of a calmly delivered, steadily cadenced bolt of lightning. Some never regained consciousness, so to speak, in the pursuit of their public careers. Many didn't know what had hit them.

In November 1782, Colonel Alexander Hamilton, recently of the Continental Army, took his seat in New York's congressional delegation. Madison watched the twenty-five-year-old tornado operate at parties, talk for hours without the slightest hesitation, whirl when answering a question, bounce on the balls of his feet in debate, all bright brass and crackling intelligence. The two men agreed on many things and often worked together, and they would become the driving force behind the Constitutional Convention, but Madison wasn't sure about Hamilton's brash manner and evident disdain for people he thought stupid. As for Hamilton, he snapped to a rapid and decisive judgment the moment he saw Madison in action. For some, Jemmy Madison would always be a peculiar little man, but Alexander Hamilton knew lightning when he saw it.

Madison was among the first to realize that the American Revolution's legacy rested on the survival of the American union. Setting up a new government during the war had been only part of the problem. Armed with Enlightenment teachings lauding natural rights, Americans were trying to set up a new species of government—something the likes of which the world had never seen. America's colonial experience had encouraged suspicions of government as grasping. Distrust of government was the father of security, went the reasoning. As Thomas Jefferson would later say, "Free government is founded in jealousy, and not in confidence."[3]

Under that formulation, America's first constitution, the Articles of Confederation, created the freest government on earth, for it was definitely founded in jealousy and gradually inspired only dwindling confidence. Almost a club sealed by handshake, it was hardly even a confederation. There were positives in this first government, though. It embraced the principle that limited government best protected freedom and that the proximity of government to governed increased its efficiency and responsiveness. It also gave the country time to win the war, to settle into the peace, and to think. Time might have been the Confederation's greatest gift of all, except affairs began taking troubling turns in 1786, and many feared time might be running out.

By then Madison had concluded that the Articles of Confederation had been a creature of the moment, and that the moment had passed. The central government it established was meant to deal with issues that states had in common—especially foreign relations—and little else. The trouble was that by making clear what the Confederation could not do, the Articles made it virtually impossible for it to do anything at all. The Congress was clumsy by design, and Americans had accepted this unlikely arrangement because they were in no mood to create an American parliament with intrusive powers like the one they were casting off. Debt mounted, and inflated currency became worthless.

But there was hope. A common political heritage from English common law and the philosophical foundation of the Enlightenment united the thirteen jealous rivals in spite of themselves. There was also the influence of exceptional young people, men willing to experiment and innovate, men such as James Madison. When the economy went into free fall in 1786 as British manufacturers began dumping surplus goods in their former colonial markets, Madison enlisted Alexander Hamilton to action. Just as Washington had encouraged Madison to push for the reform of a more stable union, Madison was key in summoning George Washington from his retirement as essential to the effort's success.

If possible, Madison had intensified his reading schedule to prepare for the convention in Philadelphia. Friend Thomas Jefferson sent him

crates of books covering political philosophy, and Madison not only devoured them over the summer of 1786. He formulated the nationalist
Virginia Plan that would be the convention's starting point for debate
the following spring in Philadelphia. Like Madison, most delegates
wanted reliable finances administered by a stronger central government. None of them wanted anything resembling hereditary monarchy, but anarchy appalled them, and mobs frightened them. As a
consequence, Madison's idea was to bring about an essential change in
the relationship of the central government to the states.

The Virginia Plan is often called the "large-state plan," which ob-
scures Madison's real purpose in drafting it. His idea was not to promote the interests of the large states but to create an all-powerful
national government. In fact, he wanted to create a national government so powerful that it would essentially shrivel the role of the states
to administrative entities. In his original vision, Madison's bicameral
legislature with both houses based on population would have favored
the large states, but more important for him was the fact that it would
have eliminated the power of *any* state, large or small, to frustrate the
national government.[4] The small states objected, and what developed
was not just an argument over form but a disagreement about the
amount of power the national government was to have by way of its
structure.

The "Great Compromise" that resolved this dispute over the extent
of central governmental power marked a defeat for Madison's doctrine
of supreme nationalism. Small states surrendered the House of Representatives, which would be apportioned according to population, but
their victory in securing equal representation in the Senate guaranteed
the preservation of state sovereignty within a federal rather than a nationalist system. Preserving that distinction was key to easing the acceptance of the Constitution, because federalism allowed the states to
remain independent of central (national) authority in the exercise of
their individual affairs. As it happened, states were so protective of their
sovereignty that they would want additional guarantees regarding it.

Madison's disappointments in Philadelphia continued as the weeks
wore on, including the elevation of state legislatures as appointive bod-
ies for senators and the defeat of a national veto on state legislation. The
significant dilution of his vision for a national government would have

discouraged a lesser man, but Madison took his half loaf and pressed on. Washington was not just grateful for this show of maturity; he was impressed by it. Washington's scrupulous adherence to formality made his letters begin with the salutation "Sir" for acquaintances and "Dear Sir" for friends. Intimate friends and close relatives merited "My Dear Sir" and the especially rare close of "Affectionately." Washington's letters to Jemmy Madison began starting and ending that way.[5]

Madison helped to secure Virginia's ratification of the Constitution in the summer of 1788, but the consent of the states had been only the first difficult step in forming the new government. Washington believed that a friendly U.S. Senate was crucial to success, and he pressed Madison to seek a seat in it. Yet the Virginia General Assembly was estimated to be two-thirds opposed to the Constitution and possibly would be active in undermining the government it created. Madison's chances for acquiring a Senate seat were accordingly slight, and though he showed strongly, he still came in third behind Richard Henry Lee and William Grayson, both opponents of ratification.[6]

The result likely relieved Madison because he preferred a place in the House of Representatives, though his chances in that election were slim as well. The Virginia General Assembly drew House districts to marginalize Federalists and create artificial Antifederalist majorities. This method of disenfranchising opponents became a standard trick. Years later, it would be called "gerrymandering" after Elbridge Gerry, whose 1812 redistricting initiative in Massachusetts produced an ungainly grouping of counties that on a map resembled a salamander. Long before that, Madison became one of the first targets of the technique. He had to work to overcome the disadvantage.

It was bad enough having to campaign. Although the political class sanctimoniously sniffed at the prospect of grubbing for office, the tradition of persuading voters with entertainments was an old practice that even George Washington had resorted to during his days as a member of colonial Virginia's House of Burgesses. The tactic was described as "swilling the planters with bumbo," a reference to the rum punch served at the events. Yet Madison truly had disdain for "an electioneering appearance, which I have always despised and wish to shun."[7] For

Madison in 1789, however, he had the added burden of bad health and abysmal weather to cope with. During the five weeks he campaigned across his district, he suffered from an onset of his chronic problem of the piles (hemorrhoids) that made travel excruciating. Icy January winds made outdoor events an ordeal, and one appearance left his ears badly frostbitten. His efforts were mainly directed at stopping rumors about his nefarious intentions to discard all pledges about amendments to the Constitution, which were designed to make more attractive his opponent, the young Antifederalist James Monroe.

Madison and Monroe were friends, which made the contest awkward in addition to uncomfortable. Friends warned Madison away from possibly thinking Monroe callow in youth or tender in friendship. "Let me apprise you," Edward Carrington said, "that you are upon no occasion of a public nature to expect favors from this Gentleman."[8] Monroe was an aberration among the Antifederalists because at thirty he was a youngster among old men. The Federalists in the main had been the youthful characters during the fight over the Constitution— men such as the authors of that series of newspaper articles arguing for ratification collectively known as *The Federalist*. Those authors were Madison, Alexander Hamilton, and John Jay, and they were the purveyors of innovation against old heads.

Yet there was Monroe, the seeming antithesis of the Antifederalist movement and the obvious opposite of little Jemmy Madison. Monroe had dark good looks, an easy manner, and an impressive record for one so young. He had given up his education at William and Mary to fight in the Revolution but made up for it afterward by reading law under Thomas Jefferson. In addition to serving in the Virginia General Assembly, he had represented the state in the Confederation Congress. He suspected that nationalist actions would always be at the expense of Virginia, and he thought that most Virginians on sober reflection would have rejected the Constitution for that reason alone, had not Washington's reputation "carried the government."[9]

Madison ran a vigorous campaign despite his ailments. He dutifully made public appearances to speak and answer questions, though the weather kept the crowds sparse. He wisely resorted to writing letters to key people that plainly declared his determination to amend the new Constitution as promised.[10] His speeches and letters "smelt of the lamp," as a saying of the time described burning the midnight oil, meaning the compositions kept him up nights.[11] As Madison's announcements circulated, as they were meant to, some scoffed that Madison's pose was merely a play for votes.[12] Yet Madison meant it, and the people believed him. Bearing up under his blistered ears and more embarrassing maladies, Madison won the election on February 2, 1789, but it was close enough to convince him that any less of an effort would have elected Monroe. Out of 2,380 votes, Madison's margin was a mere 326. Both of the state's senators were Antifederalists, and the close calls in House elections proved the new national government still remained a source of concern for many Virginians.

Washington knew this as he contemplated the presidency, and Madison's advice carried the greatest weight with him. In fact, the small man became his closest counselor. It was a natural arrangement as everyone sorted out what the Constitution was meant to do as to form and authority. Madison knew that the people's patience would soon wear thin if the government did not quickly establish sensible procedures and consequently delayed real achievements. His sense of urgency made Madison invaluable in hurrying the resolution of important issues. Where everything was new and untried, they sought precedents from elsewhere, and that made Madison into something that nobody could have foreseen. He became President Washington's "prime minister" in the American House of Commons. Not everyone was happy about it.

Nevertheless, Madison was an indispensable bridge between budding executive wishes and developing congressional policy. He visited George Washington almost every evening after the House adjourned. They often huddled for hours despite grumbling from those who had thought in Philadelphia that the Senate should be the president's chief counselor. Others were grateful that Madison, "a great friend to a strong" government, had the president's ear.[13] Nobody could have guessed that Madison also had the president's pen. Washington had worked from Madison's draft for his inaugural address. Congress then selected Madison to write the House of Representatives' response to the inaugural address, meaning that Madison was answering an address he had largely written. There was more. Washington asked Madison to write a response to the House's response and, while he was at it, to write the response to the Senate's response as well. None of these tasks was especially taxing since they repeated platitudes about how pleased everyone was with everyone else, but Washington's reliance on Madison to handle even the ceremonial aspects of government was telling.

Madison spoke more than twice as much as any other congressman during the first session. His quiet demeanor continued to disarm the unschooled. Harvard-educated Fisher Ames was among those at first taken in. He noted how Madison always spoke "low" and how "his person is little and ordinary." He conceded that Madison was "very pure, perspicuous, and to the point," and could be "cool" with "an air of reflection," but he also found "little Jemmy . . . very timid" and lacking "manly firmness and energy of character."[14] So said the rod to the lightning.

Finances were the government's biggest problem as trickling revenue allowed an already mountainous public debt to grow while accumulating interest, all in arrears. The amounts were terrifying. The states owed a total of $21 million. Some owed far less than others, which was another complication. The country owed almost $12 million on foreign loans. The central government owed its own citizens a whopping $42.5 million. In sum, the total of $75 million could be calculated in modern worth at about $2 trillion in purchasing power but as much as $30 trillion in labor value. The numbers obscure their enormity. The classic method of equating spending velocity to available volume puts them into perspective. At the rate of spending $1 million a day, it would take more than five thousand years to exhaust $2 trillion.

The Confederation Congress had not been able to levy taxes, and that power under the Constitution, even with some important restrictions, was seen as a great strength. Beyond that, however, nobody was certain how to use it. At first Congress resorted to customary methods of raising revenue, such as taxes on transactions—specifically, a tariff on imports. Madison spoke strongly in favor of the measure, and apparently with Washington's blessing urged the House to place higher duties on those countries that did not have commercial treaties with the United States. Madison was aiming specifically at Great Britain, still America's leading trading partner. He hoped that discrimination, as he called it, would pressure Britain to settle differences that had survived the peace negotiations of 1783. Such sanctions are always the first diplomatic resort of the militarily weak.

They are always controversial, however, because they impose hardships on those who employ them. This first tariff law wound up imposing a relatively low duty of about 8 percent on the value of certain imports, and, despite Madison's wishes, revenue was its main goal; it provided only a low protective wall around infant American manufacturing. Farmers did not want to buy goods priced artificially higher by import duties, and merchant shippers did not want to irritate Britain, the country's main source of trade. Economic policy as a diplomatic weapon would cause endless arguments in the years to come.

Washington's only firm recommendation to Congress in his inaugural address was that it was "expedient at the present juncture" to calm Antifederalist apprehensions about the new government by fulfilling promises from the ratification debates. That meant the consideration of constitutional amendments to address concerns about fundamental liberties. Washington must have insisted on the point, because Madison was more than hesitant about it. He had been reluctant to encourage the consideration of amendments when they were broached in Philadelphia, and he winced when they later became a subject in the ratification conventions. Madison had even argued with Thomas Jefferson about the matter, exchanging letters in which he pointed out how the act of specifying certain liberties for protection could be interpreted as allowing the government to restrict others. Jefferson disagreed because he thought that without any specification the courts would later have to step in to define them. The result would increase judicial power. Courts armed with such power for a good cause could later promote bad ones.

Possibly these arguments persuaded Madison. Perhaps Washington convincingly argued that even if Antifederalists' alarm was imaginary, caviling over it was irrelevant. Perceptions that the Constitution failed to guarantee individual rights would hobble confidence in the government. Many states had ratified the document with the understanding that the specific assurance of these protections would be among the new government's first order of business. Madison resolved to carry the matter before Congress, but he was at first hardly happy about it. What happened to him in the course of the process was consequently telling.

Getting it done proved surprisingly difficult. On May 4, 1789, Madison told the House of Representatives that he would be proposing amendments, but many supporters as well as opponents remained skeptical. More than a few members knew about Madison's lack of enthusiasm for the idea and suspected that he was merely going through the motions to make good on a promise from his campaign for Congress. It did seem as if Madison was merely setting aside his resistance rather than ardently pursuing a goal.

Under the Constitution, amendments could be proposed in either of two ways: A new constitutional convention requested by two-thirds of the states could convene, or a two-thirds vote of both houses of Congress could hash out particulars in committee and general debate. Madison assayed a new convention as dangerous because it could follow the lead of the Philadelphia convention to throw out the Constitution and start from scratch. Better to draft the amendments himself and guide them through the relatively controlled environment of Congress.

Madison soon discovered a troubling reality about Congress. It rarely could be more than partially controlled, and he struggled against opponents ready to wreck everything with unreasonable and even frivolous suggestions.[15] By July, the House had to resort to a committee to draft recommendations, but opponents continued their obstruction. The reasons for opposition varied. Some feared that amending the Constitution would weaken the new government before it could get up and running. They wanted to discover if amendments were necessary and first gain the experience to determine their substance. Others, mirroring Madison's original objections, worried that naming specific rights would have the unintended consequence of limiting principles better preserved and more broadly defined by inference than by enumeration.

Only after Madison in exasperation produced a letter from Washington that approved of the proposed amendments did critics desist. Even this seemingly decisive gesture did not shorten debate, however. After considerable talk the House finally adopted seventeen proposals. The Senate talked some more and combined the seventeen to produce twelve, mainly altering their language to limit federal rather than state power. In this form they sought to safeguard the most cherished American principles: freedom of religion, speech, and the press; the right to bear arms and to be tried by a jury; and the right to assemble and petition the government for redress of grievances. Cruel and unusual punishments were forbidden, and private property was guaranteed against arbitrary seizure by the government.

Yet Madison's original objection about enumerating certain rights while omitting others led him to insist on what became the Ninth Amendment, the declaration that naming certain rights "shall not be construed to deny or disparage others retained by the people." To soothe worries that had emerged in state ratification conventions, the language of what became the Tenth Amendment reserved all powers not explicitly delegated to or prohibited by the federal Constitution "to the States respectively, or to the people." Only ten of the twelve proposed amendments were approved by the states. The two dealing with congressional compensation and House apportionment failed, leaving the rest as the first changes to the Constitution, known eventually as the Bill of Rights, though not until almost a century after their passage. The achievement struck some as mixed. Richard Henry Lee believed the new amendments were not comprehensive and specific enough and was "grieved to see too many look at the rights of the people as a miser examines a security, to find a flaw in it."[16]

Nonetheless, the strong central government was on record as committed to the protection of minority rights and individual liberties. For James Madison, the process seemed to push him through a remarkable transformation. Where he stood at its conclusion was noticeably different from where he had began. The unabashed nationalist's preferred amendments pointed to a shift away from his stand at Philadelphia in 1787 and afterward in *The Federalist*. Possibly the reservations of people he greatly respected, such as Jefferson, had given him pause. The potential of the central government to gather unto itself immense power seems to have suddenly begun to trouble him. Fisher Ames noticed that Madison was "not a little of a Virginian" and was "afraid of their State politics, and of his popularity there, more than I think he should be."[17] For whatever reason, the president's unofficial prime minister was possibly having second thoughts about what they had created.

James Madison could do little about presidential relations with the Senate, which could be unexpectedly fractious in the opening months of Washington's presidency. Early that summer Washington learned that

Thomas Jefferson wanted to come home but only temporarily. He had grown fond of Paris and had made many friends in the French intelligentsia. Paris had also become the center of seemingly world-changing events, the first impact of the wind from America as the spirit of *liberté* and *égalité* from the American Revolution finally made its way across the Atlantic. Jefferson wanted to bring his two daughters home, though, especially the older girl, Patsy. Her attendance at a convent school had almost persuaded her to convert to Catholicism and become a nun. Jefferson did not mind the faith—one Christian denomination was pretty much the same as another for him—but Patsy was too young for a world-changing decision of her own. He thought she needed to breathe some American air.

To make the trip Jefferson required an official leave of absence from his post as U.S. minister to France, and this small procedural matter caused the first instance in which the executive was at odds with the legislature, specifically the Senate. Washington told John Jay, who had agreed to remain temporarily in charge of foreign affairs as he had in the Confederation, to grant Jefferson the request and was surprised when several senators objected. The president, they said, had "transgressed his Powers . . . without consulting the Senate." Nobody lodged an official protest this time, but several mused that Washington's stature was causing Congress to allow a troubling growth of presidential power. "There is danger," said one senator, ". . . that some points may be conceded to him from a sense of his virtue & a confidence that he will never make an improper use of his power."[18]

Here, then, was an unanticipated issue, but it was also a healthy sign that the system was working as planned. The Senate's sense of its prerogative in the scheme of governmental things was precisely the sort of check that was supposed to balance the president's powers. Washington understood that, but imperfectly as it turned out. He had never objected to the idea of the Senate acting as an advisory board. He thought its role as a small, select assembly (composed of only twenty-two men in 1789, before North Carolina and Rhode Island ratified the Constitution) was partly to consult with the president. He even supported setting aside a special chamber in a new capitol as neutral ground where the president and Senate could confer regularly. Yet as Congress began creating executive departments in late July, plans on paper sometimes clashed with actual procedures. Congress built the government from the ground up in all of six weeks that summer, but there were bumps: some memorable, instructive, and precedent setting.

One of the first bumps occurred when Congress created hundreds of new government positions. It was Washington's job to fill these positions. Usually Washington followed the guiding principles for appointments that he had set down before he arrived in New York. All appointees were to be well qualified. They did not have to agree with Washington politically, but neither could they be opposed to the Constitution. Jobs would fall evenly so that all parts of the nation were represented. Whenever possible and if not contrary to the public good, veterans would be given preference. When the nature of a post was advisory, Washington wanted people he knew; in all other cases he had to rely on recommendations from people he trusted. Washington was determined never to appoint his relatives. To avoid the appearance of nepotism, he refused to appoint nephew Bushrod Washington as a U.S. attorney despite the young man's clear qualifications. "No slip will pass unnoticed," he rightly worried, as ". . . a supposed partiality for friends and relations."[19]

As a matter of policy Washington's appointments sailed through the confirmation process with such ease that when one did not, it shocked him. In early August, the president appointed Benjamin Fishbourne (sometimes spelled Fishbourn) as the naval officer of the port of Savannah, but the Senate rejected the appointment without explanation. Washington learned that Georgia senator James Gunn opposed Fishbourne, though he did not know why (Gunn had a political ally in mind for the job) and his efforts to discover Gunn's objection flared into another controversy. Washington sent a curt letter detailing Fishbourne's qualifications and lauding his character, but the president's request for an explanation for Fishbourne's rejection raised senatorial hackles. The language of Washington's letter was heated, but the Senate coldly made clear that nothing required it to explain its reasons to the chief executive for doing anything, including the rejection of his appointments. Washington likely fumed, but if so, he held his tongue and on reflection was sorry he had made the fuss, if not the request. In fact, when he promptly sent the Senate another nomination for the post, he repeated his desire that the Senate explain its reasons for rejecting any future appointments.[20] The incident possibly established the tradition of senatorial courtesy—the practice of asking senators for prior approval of appointments made in their home states—but Washington never formally consented to such vetting. His informal consultation with members from both houses of Congress about possible appointees was always informational at most, and he did not always approve their choices or bow to their objections.[21]

Following the tiff over Fishbourne, however, Washington at least wanted to set up formal procedures for consulting with the Senate. A committee met with him and proved so deferential that everyone considered the exercise a waste of time. At most, it became clear that the Senate preferred oral communications, while Washington wanted them in writing. He asked Madison to assist, and cobbling together everybody's imperfect understanding of the situation resulted in a sort of ad hoc procedure that had the advantage of flexibility. Washington would continue making appointments in writing but would confer in person on treaties. Everybody soon had reason to regret the latter part of that arrangement.

Under it, Washington tried to consult with the Senate regarding a treaty with Indians, the first and, as it happened, the last effort to obey the Constitution's instruction to seek the upper chamber's "advice" as well as its "consent" for such initiatives. When Washington arrived in the Senate chamber, John Adams relinquished the vice president's chair and read the proposed treaty aloud twice before calling for a vote to record the sense of the Senate. The episode then took its unfortunate turn. Several senators began asking what had happened to the "advice" part of the formula, and Washington became first impatient and then visibly agitated. When he audibly muttered, "This defeats every purpose for my coming here," everything stopped. Senators were gazing at him, some puzzled, some worried, a few angry.

Washington instantly realized that he had said something highly charged and resolved to say nothing more. His emotionless expression and relaxed manner disguised the fact he was boiling, and after only a few minutes of additional senatorial deliberations, he left the chamber. A few days later, he tried again, hoping for a more productive result, but it seemed to him that the Senate was incapable of doing anything, whether it was to decide weighty matters of state or have its quill pens trimmed, without interminable discussions. Senators finally agreed to the treaty as originally proposed, which made the prelude all the more exasperating. Washington would never repeat this ordeal.[22] The executive would conclude future diplomatic initiatives before anything was submitted to the Senate. As a nod to the "too many cooks" maxim, there was wisdom in removing the Senate from the negotiating chores of international diplomacy, but it happened by accident, the result of Washington's impatience and the Senate's love of hearing itself talk.

It was after submitting the twelve amendments to the states that Congress set about creating executive departments. Madison led the discussions and the drafting of legislation that created the State Department (July 27, 1789), War Department (August 7), and Treasury Department (September 2).[23] In creating the executive, Congress found its real strong suit, the one that would exceed all others for all of its history. Congress could debate endlessly, dither over the important, and fixate on the trivial, but it was matchless in its ability to grow government.

The initial session of the First Congress warmed up the body to this institutional motif not by establishing the executive departments per se, for State, War, and Treasury were obviously necessary for a working government. But Congress left open the number of government positions in the actual offices. They could be paltry or sizable, depending on the personality of the boss. The Treasury, for example, would eventually top out with thirty-five clerks and assistants, and not just because it was supervising the large customs apparatus that Congress authorized on July 31, 1789. Alexander Hamilton believed in government. The State Department, on the other hand, would be headed by a man careless with his own money but extremely mindful about spending that of others. State would make do with five clerks.[24]

Early in the debate, several congressmen insisted that even having executive departments would resemble a king and his cabinet unless their heads answered directly to the legislature, as they had under the Articles of Confederation. It was a touchy subject, and Washington was mindful of it. He did not even use the term "cabinet" until 1793. Yet, the larger question was whether departments would be placed directly under the president and answer exclusively to him. In addition, the removal of federal appointees, particularly those confirmed by the Senate, became an issue. The Constitutional Convention had left the question unanswered, and now more than a few senators concluded that provision for Senate confirmation of appointees meant the need for Senate approval of dismissals as well.

Downstairs in Federal Hall, Madison headed off what he knew George Washington would not abide. The president had made clear to his friend that extending the Senate process to dismissals would be an unacceptable intrusion in the presidential bailiwick. Departments were the only sensible administrative arrangement for a coherent executive branch, and the executive would have to be the master in his own house if they were to function properly. Washington insisted that he have his way, and Madison argued the common sense of the position. A confirmed appointee should serve only at the president's pleasure. No executive should be expected to live with a subordinate in whom he had lost confidence. When Madison's opponents insisted that a president with such arbitrary power of removal could encourage a "tendency to establish a monarchical" government, Madison deflected such emotionally charged language, and the House rejected it.[25]

The Senate reared up on hind legs again when the House suggested that the president could make low-level appointments without Senate confirmation. There were stern reminders that Washington's honor and decency were as mortal as he and could be no basis on which to shape precedents and adopt traditions. Senator William Maclay distilled the sentiment: "The virtues of the present Chief Magistrate are brought forward as a reason for vesting him with extraordinary powers." He trembled at the prospect. "No nation ever trod more dangerous ground," since Washington's "virtues will depart with him, but the powers which you give him will remain."[26]

As a technical question of procedure, the issue assumed a maddening longevity that would have been less likely if anyone but George Washington had been president. Raising the specter of kings was more than a debating device. It was the heart of the issue, which was the likelihood of power amassing in one branch of government, whether for good or for ill. It was always for good at first, always for ill at the end. The staunch nationalists in Philadelphia had nodded over that reality. Madison could work his persuasive magic to make State, War, and Treasury primarily accountable to the president, but constitutional stipulations required that the Treasury also be accountable to Congress. As with the requirement of explicit congressional declarations to wage war, Americans had removed from the presidency the absolute and kingly power of the sword. They were determined to deprive the executive of the absolute power of the purse as well.

And yet, the removal issue remained, and the final stages of its debate became so divisive that when the Senate finally voted, it was evenly divided. John Adams cast the deciding vote, breaking the tie in the first instance of his wielding one of the few clearly designated constitutional duties given the vice president. It was a profoundly important vote, perhaps the most important of his tenure as president of the Senate, for Adams cast it in favor of presidential prerogative. The deed caused a kind of stunned incredulity, as though the men fearful of what the government could become were seeing their worst fears coming to pass. For them, the veil was lifted on the future to reveal teeming hordes of parasitical beseechers and favor seekers, ensconced, unaccountable, and irremovable. A vast federal dinner bell clanged amid the shout *Come and get it!* as the slumbering leviathan stirred.

Many alarmed Virginians saw it this way. Jemmy Madison was still arguing the case for preserved executive prerogatives, but as more people would gradually realize, he was "not a little of a Virginian."

5

"Republican Court"

Horseback riding was Washington's favorite exercise, and after arriving in New York he worked off nervous energy by overdoing it. It almost killed him. In mid-June, a small irritation on his left buttock changed from a minor saddle sore to a painful boil. Mindful of presidential dignity, public reports described the wound's location as Washington's upper thigh, but nothing in the days that followed could disguise the fact that it was turning into a serious infection. As it grew outward and inward, "a very large tumor" hardened beneath the skin, and a "disorder commenced in a fever which . . . greatly reduced him."[1] The illness was doing much more than greatly reducing him. By the time doctors hurried to Cherry Street, Washington was lucky to be alive. The physicians instantly recognized the malady. Cutaneous anthrax is usually transmitted by an open wound's contact with an infected animal, which is likely what had turned Washington's carbuncle into the telltale sore of flaming red skin with a black circle in the center, the site of the infection.

The doctors measured the mass as the size of two fists and judged his fever high enough to be "threatening."[2] Washington recognized a euphemism better than most and wanted the hard truth instead, even if it was the worst news possible. "Whether tonight, or twenty years hence, it makes no difference," he said. "I know that I am in the hands of a good providence."[3] The doctors were not ready to hand him off just yet, but the need for immediate surgery to save his life invited equally dangerous infections. They had no choice. Washington consented to the operation.

Two physicians, a father and son, came to the bedroom at Cherry Street on June 17, 1789, to conduct a procedure more resembling a butcher's job than a doctor's. After a brief preparation, the son's scalpel commenced cutting away the infected mass, but there seemed no end to it, and the initial cut turned into a wholesale excavation. Washington had no anesthesia but neither flinched nor made a sound. The father knew that leaving in place any trace of infection would make the operation pointless, so he finally blurted out as his son paused, "Cut away— deeper, deeper still!" The son continued slicing. "Don't be afraid," the father exclaimed, not to Washington but to his son; he glanced at the president, certainly in amazement, and said, "You see how well he bears it!"[4]

Washington bore it well enough to let them finish the grisly task and close the wound. A silent crowd had assembled on Cherry Street. They were a reflection of a government that had to contemplate losing its best hope of survival. Efforts at secrecy were no more effective then than now, and citizens knew the illness was dire by the frequent visits of doctors with worried frowns.

By late June, Washington's fever had broken and his appetite returned. The doctors knew he would live, but he was badly mangled and could not sit normally for weeks. He resumed work and eased back into a partial social schedule at the end of July, but he found it difficult to stand, impossible to sit, and embarrassing to recline. Sleep was fitful because his left side was so tender, and his right side soon became numb. Lear blocked off Cherry Street with rope barriers to divert passing carriages and had the sidewalks covered with straw to deaden pedestrians' footsteps.

Washington gradually and painfully returned to a public routine, reassuring the worried public by appearing in a carriage fitted out with a mattress so he could lie on his side. He began receiving visitors for no other reason than to show people he was not a complete invalid. It worked, and public concern waned. James Madison continued to fret, but that was his way. The personal blow of losing George Washington would have been sobering, but the blow to the country would have been horrible. "His death at this present moment," Madison flatly observed, "would have brought on another crisis in our affairs."[5]

The tumor did not kill him, but office seekers threatened to by sapping his energy. Before Washington got sick, he was being swamped with perpetual visitors wanting government jobs and favors. He asked Madison, Hamilton, Jay, and Livingston to suggest protocols for managing visitors and events. The pressure had made him mildly desperate. He even consulted John Adams.

How a president should handle social events seemed frivolous on its face, but it wasn't frivolous in the least. Accommodating anyone who appeared at his office door meant constant interruptions that left him little time for real work. Washington worried that cutting off visits would make him seem aloof, but indiscriminately attending social functions did more than consume enormous blocks of time. It ran the risk of unseemly familiarity. Washington was determined not to demean the presidency, no matter the political costs.

Everyone agreed that the dignity of the office required formal protocols to govern the president's availability and social schedule. The degree of formality, however, gave rise to differing opinions. Hamilton said Washington should keep as great a distance as possible between himself and the people. He should visit no one and invite only important government officials and distinguished citizens to dine. Hamilton recommended that Washington hold a weekly levee under formal rules of etiquette for dress and behavior and open only to consequential people. As it happened, Washington would adopt this suggestion, even though it early showed how tin-eared Hamilton could be about governing a republic. Even the word "levee" brought to mind the trappings of royalty, and bringing to mind such things would gradually become a political problem for Washington as he listened more exclusively to Hamilton's advice.

Livingston was concerned about the appearance of favoritism and thought the president should not return visits or accept invitations to private homes. But he saw the problem of isolation if Washington limited his contact with ordinary people. Anticipating a modern concern for diversity for diversity's sake, Livingston suggested that Washington appoint people from varied backgrounds to executive branch posts for no other reason than to have their different perspectives. Young men from good families could attend social events to collect gossip, he mused. Some of Livingston's ideas gave the impression that he was simply thinking out loud.

For his part, Adams provided sound and sensible advice. He told Washington to invite whomever he pleased to his house but never to return visits. The exception would be a visit from a fellow head of state, which was highly unlikely. Otherwise, Adams saw no reason for Washington to become a prisoner of his office. He could, for example, attend informal tea parties at people's homes without degrading the presidency.

Washington pieced together the advice and formed his own social strategy. His secretaries published the official policy in the newspapers to forewarn New York's social mavens and avoid any confusion.

Under the new rules, it worked like this. On Tuesday afternoons, the president held an official levee for gentlemen. After the men assembled, one of Washington's secretaries announced him as he entered the room. He would be in formal dress, which was invariably a black velvet suit, a hat he never donned but tucked under his arm, and a ceremonial sword rattling at his side. As each man was announced to him—usually by David Humphreys, whose voice was loud enough to vanquish Washington's deafness—and after an exchange of bows (Washington did not shake hands) the guest joined the other men, eventually forming a semicircle around the president, who positioned himself next to the fireplace. Doors closed at 3:15 P.M., sharp. Following introductions Washington worked the semicircle to talk briefly to each man about such things as the weather. At the end, guests individually bowed and said good-bye to Washington at the fireplace. No matter the topic of discussion or the (unlikely) liveliness of the gathering, these events always ended at 4:00.[6] Formality was carried to an extreme. Introductions continued as part of the event long after Washington knew every face and every name.

Friday evenings from seven to ten o'clock were set aside for Martha's levee, an event called a "drawing room" for mixed company. Light refreshments included coffee, tea, and desserts, with ice cream a favorite.

Mingling was more informal. Arriving guests were presented by one of Washington's secretaries to Martha at her place on an elevated settee. As with her husband's more formal gathering, the introductions at Martha's soirees continued for even her closest friends.

The exception was Abigail Adams. When she attended, she was always installed on the settee to Mrs. Washington's right. Washington was careful to preserve this place of honor for her, politely intervening with anyone who presumed to take it by offering his arm for a turn around the room and then making certain that Abigail was seated properly. She appreciated the attention; her husband treasured it for her.

Often the entire three hours raced by at these pleasant functions, but it was understood that the evening was over when Martha rose and announced she was retiring. Everyone, including Washington, enjoyed Martha's event more than the deadly dull Tuesday afternoon levee. Washington found them "of a more familiar and sociable kind."[7] He dressed less formally, forgoing the hat and sword, and mingled rather than received guests. Martha's Friday evenings gave him the chance to banter with the leading ladies of New York society, one of the few times he could play the gallant charmer. The company of women achieved the impossible for George Washington. It made him easygoing.

Even though Martha's social activities were not as constrained as her husband's, she followed a strict routine of her own. She received ladies at her home and returned calls without fail within three days. With a regimen far more inflexible than at Mount Vernon, she described herself as little more than a state prisoner, forbidden to appear unaccompanied in public and having to have her hair "set and dressed every day." Her wry aside to Fanny, who was back in Virginia enjoying the slow rhythms of Mount Vernon, was more plaintive than amusing: "You would I fear think me a good deal in the fashion if you could but see me."[8]

Martha also attended Washington's Thursday afternoon dinners, which were for mixed company except when the entire Senate attended. Even on those occasions, Martha was the hostess. Government people, influential citizens, and diplomats were the usual guests, and despite the occasional presence of ladies, they were tedious affairs. Because invitations went out in rotation to achieve geographic balance, lively conversation was unfortunately not the goal. Trusted advisers and close friends attended according to the calendar just like everyone else. James Madison was not invited more often than anyone else. Washington's close friend Senator Robert Morris of Pennsylvania did not appear except when his name came round in the order of things. Thursdays were work. It felt like it. Adding to the impression, Washington would not tolerate tardiness, and an invited guest who appeared a few seconds after 4:00 would find the doors of the residence closed. Except for the possibility of slighting the president, a late arrival was lucky.

Washington avoided preprandial socializing, making for a somber pantomime as diners approached the table with little conversation to leaven proceedings. When ladies were included, the Washingtons sat across from each other at the middle of the table with everyone else arranged according to rank and importance. When ladies did not attend, Martha sat at the head of the table.

After sitting down, everyone could at least look forward to a culinary treat. Samuel Fraunces took pride in these dinners. But he also ran up bills that dismayed Washington. During the first three months of Washington's presidency, Fraunces purchased "butcher's meat, bacon, tongue, geese, ducks, turkeys, chickens, birds, scale fish, lobsters, crabs, oysters, cured fish, eggs, cheese, bread, biscuit, cake, vegetables, butter, ice cream, preserves, fruit, melons, nuts, citrons, and honey," not to mention, "Madeira, Claret, Champagne, Sherry, Arrack, Spirits, Brandy, Cordials, Porter, Beer, and Cider."[9] As expenses mounted, Washington sternly instructed Fraunces to economize, but the steward was uncompromising: "He may discharge me, he may kill me if he will, but while he is President of the United States, and I have the honor to be his Steward, his establishment will be supplied with the very best of everything that the whole country can afford."[10]

Several courses made up a dinner. They began with soup followed by a variety of meats and different types of fish, assorted fowls, and vegetables. Desserts could be delectations prepared by local bakers. Fruits, an abundance of nuts, and cheeses finished the meal. Dinner was eaten in silence, and chat did not enliven things afterward. A Massachusetts congressman remembered his Thursday dinner party being "as grave as at a funeral."[11]

In the place of chitchat were the toasts, which could be many and varied to match the company. At meal's end, Washington would start off by drinking to the health of each guest. With glasses filled and refilled, everyone responded. Maclay thought the custom absurd: "Such a buzz of 'health sir,' and 'health, madam,' and 'thank you, sir,' and 'thank you, madam,' never had I heard before."[12] Foreigners found it simply peculiar. Enough people drinking to one another's health left everyone tipsy.[13] Finally, the ladies withdrew as a prelude to the final act of the evening, which might feature Washington telling a story, or an especially intrepid guest trying out one of his own.

As somber as they were, these were expensive affairs to stage, and they severely strained Washington's budget. As he had done during the Revolution, he had wanted only his expenses covered in lieu of a salary, but Congress insisted that the Constitution be followed to the letter. He relented. With an annual salary of $25,000, Washington had to cover everything connected to living in New York City as would any private citizen, including his house and entertainment, but with the extra burden that everything had to be fitting for the presidency.

Despite the pinch of finances, he refused to become a penurious hermit at Cherry Street. Since he could not by choice visit private homes, he regularly went to plays and often treated friends to tickets to accompany him and Martha. He had seen his first play when traveling with his brother Lawrence in Barbados, and the magical quality of a night spent in the company of an audience never waned for him.

Washington enjoyed homegrown playwrights such as young William Dunlap, whose farce *Darby's Return* featured a character who encounters leaders of the new American government. Dunlap played on raucous theater customs of the day that had plays rarely staged as written. Tragedies could conform to an audience's mood to end happily, and everything was often abbreviated to allow for wide variety on the playbill. A night at the theater resembled the modern "review" wherein a medley of sketches bounced between farce and tragedy. Audience commentary invigorated proceedings, and the lampoons of familiar people in *Darby's Return* along with the irreverent catcalls from the galleries could make the president laugh aloud, a reaction that often startled companions who did not know him well. Theater owners loved for Washington to attend. They advertised his plans in newspapers to boost the box office.[14]

Measures to establish the dignity of the presidency were bound to create the impression that rules for formal behavior and appropriate dress were pretentious. Yet it would be incorrect to think that people caviled at protocol because it seemed snobbish. Class division obviously existed in America, and people did not reject social rank if it had resulted from merit achieved through hard work. Rules, protocols, clothes, and customs became problems, rather, because they were suddenly being associated with government, and that reminded people of royalty. Natural aristocrats were already American icons. Kings were objects of scorn because monarchy was not an earned honor, and its unmerited power was also something to be feared.

Washington's natural dignity was itself destined to become a source of problems in light of these attitudes. He believed that formal dress and an elaborate retinue were the most obvious ways to create respect for the new government. He traveled the town in a large coach with six matching cream-colored horses, four servants, and two gentlemen on horseback. While admirers believed "he ought to have still more state, & time will convince the Country of the necessity, of it," the jury in 1789 was very much out on the matter.[15] As it happened, it was not out for long, and ultimately the verdict would not be favorable.

George Washington could do nothing about the public's adulation, though it worried some people early. Philadelphia physician Benjamin Rush was disappointed by Washington's unanimous election because it demonstrated an "idolatrous and exclusive attachment" to a man. "Monarchy," he darkly concluded, "is natural to Americans."[16] When Washington's journey from Mount Vernon to New York resembled a royal progress, Rush developed a new fear. After watching the frenzied reaction to Washington's arrival in Philadelphia, he worried that "we ascribe all the attributes of the Deity to the name of General Washington." That was bad enough for the political future of the republic, but Rush trembled over the country's worshipping a graven image. God would punish the United States for that.[17] The intense anticipation in the days leading up to Washington's inauguration caused John Trumbull, hardly a critic, to sniff at "the odour of incense" as the people went "through all the Popish grades of worship."[18]

To his credit, Washington found it troubling, too. As he arrived in New York City, the reception all but unnerved him, especially the multitude of watercraft in the harbor with snapping flags and banners as the barge brought him nearer and nearer to the roaring crowd on Manhattan. He had a premonition. The adoration was "pleasing" because it was so obviously sincere, but it created "sensations so painful" because he knew it could vanish overnight. As Washington rode that ornately decorated barge, he might have recalled the murmured warning to the Roman hero: *All glory is fleeting.*[19]

Washington's formality and ostentation caused muted criticism expressed, at first, only in diaries and private letters. Senator Maclay understood why the president could not be available to just anyone, but the practice of limiting his appearances to public venues at strictly controlled times made him resemble "an Eastern Lama," an impression offensive to a republican people.[20] The first public grumbling wasn't Washington's fault but was provoked by an otherwise harmless bit of fluff in a newspaper. To generate support for the government, avid Federalists had moved a thirty-eight-year-old Boston newspaper editor named John Fenno to New York to publish the *Gazette of the United States.* With its first issue on April 1, 1789, the one-sheet newspaper became an unofficial organ of the administration.[21] Fenno's gushing admiration of Washington could be embarrassing, but his reports on social and political events were sometimes cringe worthy. Describing a Friday night drawing room, he mentioned the daughters of the late William Alexander and set off a controversy.[22]

Alexander had lived for many years at Basking Ridge, a small village in New Jersey where he dabbled in astronomy and lived off rents from his lands, but mostly he was known as an eccentric who claimed to be an English peer. An English jury had settled the title of Lord Stirling on him in 1759, but the House of Lords never recognized it as valid. Nevertheless, for the rest of his life (he died in 1783) William Alexander called himself Lord Stirling, and Americans thought the moniker a harmless conceit. Washington had known him before the war and always held him in regard, even though Major General Stirling's performance in some crucial battles was, at best, only adequate. Stirling married into the Livingston family of New York and had three children, the two oldest girls named Catharine ("Kitty") and Mary. They married well, Kitty to William Duer in 1779, and some have suggested Washington gave away the bride, though that is not likely.[23]

What was certain, however, was Kitty Duer's place in New York society. Her husband was a successful speculator, and they lived in luxury while setting fashions. Kitty had helped prepare the house at 3 Cherry Street for Washington's residence, and both she and her sister Mary Alexander Watts (Mary had married the wealthy financier Stephen Watts) were at Martha's first drawing room on May 29, 1789.

These two were routinely referred to as Lady Kitty and Lady Mary because of their father's assumed title, but the practice was highly colloquial, and the sobriquets were more pet names than expressions of deference. Fenno's use of the titles in his newspaper, however, struck people as unctuous. It did not help that Martha Washington also was often referred to as Lady Washington, a mark of respect by soldiers during the Revolution that later suggested a troubling pattern. Critics pointed to the government's "Republican Court" of self-titled aristocrats as a sign that European elitism was alive and well in America. They found it odd that the country that had expended so much "energy to get rid of Monarchy" was now "making every effort to fix another."[24]

The men who were busy setting up the executive branch hardly noticed this little controversy, but they should have. Calling a couple of women from New Jersey "Ladies" was trivial in itself, but public sensitivity over it was not. The hypercritical response to privilege deriving from birth spelled trouble, and the implications for legitimate government could not be ignored forever. The Senate's presuming itself to be a sort of American House of Lords by conducting debates behind closed doors was a terrible way to start its existence. Washington questioned friends, such as David Stuart in Virginia, about the people's mood. Stuart was observant and discerning, and he was also family of a sort because he had married Jack Custis's widow, so he could be more candid about how questions of etiquette and titles had the potential to transform from trite concerns to real controversies.

In fact, Stuart was among the few men who gave Washington unvarnished advice by talking to the president as an equal, an invaluable quality in a counselor to a powerful man. Senate secrecy, said Stuart, incensed Virginians, and Washington sadly had to agree that the upper house was making a grave mistake, one that had dogged the Continental and Confederation congresses when they closed their sessions to the public. The House of Representatives stood in marked contrast by opening its doors, making the Senate's practice even more suspicious. Public pressure would eventually force a change, but not until 1795, and by then cries over monarchism, privilege, aristocracy, and the incipient tyranny that went with them were in full voice. The Senate opening its doors was a tardy concession that did little more than assure the people that Senate proceedings were as tedious as they were pretentious. By then, other, more concrete, concerns had emerged.

Unflattering perceptions worried Washington because he wanted to make the new government a popular as well as a legitimate institution. He tried to counter the impression of his isolation by taking walks before his three o'clock dinner. The results were disappointing. Washington usually overawed, and citizens could manage only the smallest of small talk when they tried at all. Washington was never comfortable with the ritual, either, and he would pretend to have other purposes for it, such as an errand or the laughable deceit of checking his watch against a clock tower.[25] He could never abandon his excessive formality. When important callers interrupted his family dinner, Washington changed into formal attire, completed the interview, and changed back into his everyday clothes before returning to the table.[26] It was simply who he was, a creature of habit and routine.

When the capital moved to Philadelphia at the end of 1790 the Washingtons had a more impressive house but did not change their fixed program except in two respects. Because they had spent time in Philadelphia during the war, he and Martha had more friends there, and they periodically invited them to informal "family" dinners or for an evening of quiet conversation. Alas, the other change was not politically adroit. The presidential residence in Philadelphia was more commodious and allowed for more grandly conceived entertainments. Some critics called the affairs regal.

They always liked Philadelphia better than New York because it offered a more intimate social life, but the public knew little about this, which was too bad. Robert and Mary Morris lived next door, and Samuel and Eliza Powel were regular companions. The Washingtons especially enjoyed the Powels because Eliza never stood on ceremony with either of them, something that was rare for Washington and refreshing to Martha. The Powels never stood on ceremony with anyone—including each other, in fact—and were the kind of people who did not let their money bend their manners, which were easy and unaffected. They were a seemingly mismatched couple who bewildered superficial observers. Eliza was all sparkles. Samuel was quiet and bookish. His family's wealth could have been credited for his successful courtship of her, except Eliza was a Willing and just as rich, her family rivaling the Powels and Binghams as Philadelphia's most moneyed clan. She could have married anyone in Philadelphia, but she chose him, and he her.

Washington liked them both, as did Philadelphia, its citizens making Samuel their mayor whenever he chose to serve. Washington had always enjoyed the company of women, but Eliza Powel was one of the few people he knew, male or female, who could be familiar without being forward. Abigail Adams described her as "a friendly, affable, good woman, sprightly, full of conversation." She was also well versed in politics and saw the success of the new government as something of a personal project, even though she thought women were unsuited for politics because "their Imagination runs Riot."[27] Her drawing room featured effervescent parties where conversations sorted out the affairs of the day. Eliza never hesitated to weigh in.

Levees and formal dinners continued for the Washingtons as they had in New York, though critics calling them antirepublican began to increase and gradually became less reluctant to speak out. Senator Maclay groused about such trappings suborning virtue. Good republicans, he said, attended presidential affairs because they were "borne down by fashion and a fear of being charged with a want of respect to General Washington." He pondered that "if there is treason in the wish I retract it, but would to God this same General Washington were in heaven! We would not then have him brought forward as the constant cover to every unconstitutional and irrepublican act."[28] Abigail Adams represented the other pole in this heretofore silent but obvious divide. She found the events enchanting and argued that there was no other way for a president and his wife to entertain "consistent with the Rank they hold."[29]

It wasn't happening yet, but those afraid of kings and princes would eventually imagine ermine and opulence as well as power and purpose. They would have been surprised to see the patterns of the existence established at the Cherry Street house in New York and continued at High Street in Philadelphia. As he did in Virginia, Washington kept to the same schedule each day. He rose early, usually before the servants, and ambled through the house. He inspected the stables, pulled up horses' hooves to see about shoes, rubbed their noses, maybe pulled a carrot from his pocket for a treat, and watched with emotionless blue eyes as it was crunched down. Back inside, he read newspapers and answered mail. He had been up for hours by the time he had breakfast with the family at seven o'clock. Then he worked with the secretaries and met appointments, one after another and seemingly without end. His exercise was either on horseback or a brisk walk in the neighborhood before the midafternoon dinner with the families, the official one of secretaries ("the gentlemen of the household") and the other of his kin.[30] Afterward, he returned to work until eight P.M., had a light supper, and gathered again with the family. When conversation lagged, someone read aloud, often Toby Lear. The household was in bed by ten o'clock at the latest. The next morning was the same, as was the next. The levees, dinners, and impressive entourage were the public face of the president's existence, but George Washington's evenings were altogether different. Nelly played the harpsichord. Toby read aloud. Martha sewed.

That was George Washington's glamorous and regal life as the president of the United States. The public knew nothing of this, which was too bad.

6

"A Stranger in This Country"

When Washington became ill that summer in 1789, his sister Betty wrote him that their mother was obsessed with his health. She would not believe he was recovering until she heard from him directly. In only a few more weeks, Mary Ball Washington was dead from the breast cancer that had been withering her away for months.[1] The presidential residence observed a period of mourning, making the house even more private for the family but not necessarily somber for the president. Washington's fatalism over death was unusual even for a time when it was easy to die. Beginning with a baby sister, then his father, his many brothers, and the stepchildren, he had been losing loved ones since he was ten years old. But his acceptance of death was only part of what those endless seasons of constant loss had done to him. He expected death and was seldom shocked when it came. He kept sadness to himself and could seem cold.

His condolences had all the warmth of so many bills of lading.[2] When Martha's daughter Patsy died at Mount Vernon in 1773, Washington spoke of the family's distress as a collective lament, but did not mark his own as particularly notable. It can only be guessed what he said to Martha in that long night after the girl's hideous spasms had twisted the life out of her. When his mother died, Washington wrote his sister Betty a letter that typified his reaction to death as nature's toll and the obligation of dignified people to meet it with reserve. "Awful, and affecting as the death of a Parent is," he said, "there is consolation in knowing that Heaven has spared ours to an age, beyond which few attain and favored her with the full enjoyment of her mental faculties, and as much bodily strength as usually falls to the lot of four score." He barely paused before giving his sister instructions about Mary Ball Washington's estate.[3]

He had begun his presidency with an illness so dire that many, including himself, had despaired of his life. His troubled relationship with his mother could not account for all of his seeming detachment when he heard the news that August afternoon in New York City, but we shall never know how much of it was from his temperament, and how much was from possible indifference. He did not like to talk about it, and if he said anything to Martha, she kept it in confidence, as she did everything about him and her without exception.

Meanwhile, he kept to his regular routine, signed the bills sent to his desk, and met his appointments. When Congress adjourned on September 29, 1789, he looked forward to the company of the compact bundle of energy who tapped on the door at Cherry Street each day. That was Alexander Hamilton, who asked no questions, ventured no speculation, and knew his business and went about it with brusque efficiency. The refuge of immutable and unchanging facts likely comforted Washington. Hamilton talked of numbers and ledgers—things that could not sicken, things that would not die.

Today the most famous member of Washington's war staff is Alexander Hamilton, who is often thought to have been his most important aide. The description would have surprised both of them, as well as their colleagues. Hamilton's distinction came later, which made his service as Washington's subordinate during the war an interlude rather than a milestone. In fact, their relationship would falter near war's end and have to await its revival years later, an association with profound consequences for them and for the country.

None of that was apparent, however, when Hamilton came to Washington's headquarters in the spring of 1777. Born in the British West Indies in either 1755 or 1757 (the dates are muddled), Hamilton was the illegitimate child of a Scottish father and French Huguenot mother. He grew up on the island of St. Croix, where he learned a clerk's trade but also devoured everything in print that came his way. He developed an agile mind that impressed his elders even while he was still in his teens.

Yet Hamilton's confused parentage was embarrassing, and the implications of his illegitimacy shaped a personality that would obsessively seek success, acclaim, and even simple approval. At the same time, he inclined toward somber dissatisfaction, a habit of tarnishing any achievement, large or small, with impulsive bursts of unhealthy introspection. Later these traits were mistaken for arrogance because Hamilton eventually wore condescension more openly than was wise, but it was also another manifestation of his unquenchable thirst for the admiration of strangers as well as the devotion of friends. As he grew up his flair for words flourished and his sense of self made at least the appearance of confidence a second nature. His driving ambition, though, was immediate, and it made the boy feel smothered in St. Croix, a beautiful place blighted by slavery in its cruelest form and a metaphor for the larger world as Hamilton would always see it: All metals were alloyed, all people were flawed, and all things lovely merited suspicion because they were likely incubating disease.

His desires made him cavil over his clerk's duties, which he described as a "grov'ling condition," and he longed for a way "to exalt my Station."[4] The chance to do just that came when Hamilton attracted sponsors and patrons who arranged for his education in the mainland colonies, first in New Jersey and then at King's College in New York City. The war cut his formal education short when Hamilton joined an independent New York artillery company. By then he was as fairly well formed as he ever would be, which is to say he was brash, daring, and had cultivated a stunning presence to match his intellect. His frame was diminutive and his face had an almost feminine delicacy, but men fell silent in his presence if he wanted them to, and women tried to catch their breath, if he wanted them to.

When he joined Washington's staff, Hamilton was still quite young but prodigiously gifted. What distinguished Hamilton most, aside from a facile pen and a quick grasp of the complicated, was his insatiable quest for self-improvement. He made up for his abbreviated schooling with compulsive reading in broad subjects but always with a specific purpose. He discovered an aptitude for political economy, and even his demanding duties at headquarters could not distract him from such abstruse works as Malachy Postlethwaite's *Universal Dictionary of Trade and Commerce.* These studies bolstered his reading of David Hume and others to convince him that mercantilism could be adjusted to promote fiscal policy and government credit. Hamilton concluded that government intervention in markets otherwise unregulated could make them thrive. He thought about such things when he was twenty-five years old.

Yet Hamilton's coiled mental spring was not the stuff of the diffident accountant. He was notorious among his colleagues for romantic escapades and a hair-trigger temper. Both were attributable to youth, and Washington overlooked them, up to a point, possibly because he saw something beyond the diligence and drive in the young man, something sad and yearning. "I am a stranger in this country," Hamilton confided to his closest friend, another of Washington's aides named John Laurens.[5]

Hamilton's marriage to Elizabeth Schuyler of a top-tier New York family in December 1780 presumably would end the romances as well as the alienation, but it did not, and Hamilton's temper visibly remained in any case. One day he recoiled over a perceived slight from Washington, spoke sharply to him, and angrily resigned. Hamilton rebuffed Washington's effort to reconcile, and the contact the men had afterward was slight—consisting only of letters about minor matters until the writing of the Constitution came up. Yet the young man's admiration for Washington seemed to endure as would a plant in dormancy, evidently withered but awaiting rejuvenation. Beneath his impetuous anger, Hamilton never relinquished the muted praise he had spoken of his chief two years after their first meeting. "Whoever knows his character," Hamilton said, "will be satisfied."[6] It was a rare observation for a man who saw all metals as alloyed.

Washington was always willing to put up with Hamilton more than Hamilton was Washington. He wasn't disloyal to Washington the general, and he would not be disloyal to Washington the president, either, but Hamilton's loyalty was a quirky creature. His critics would have called it opportunism, but it possibly had something to do with his and Washington's opposing views of human nature. Washington believed that virtue bolstered by religious instruction was the republic's best guarantor. Hamilton doubted that virtue existed outside of fable and fancy. In an older man, that opinion could be described as cynicism stemming from experience, but a younger man's jaded perspective likely results from the shock of discovering that a world seemingly full of promise is keenly flawed. Disappointment and loss can do that, and Hamilton certainly experienced his share of disappointment, beginning with an embarrassing mother and a shadowy father. Yet the severest blow seems to have fallen on him during the Revolutionary War, when he met and lost the closest friend he would ever have.

John Laurens was a courageous South Carolinian with a rash streak to match young Hamilton's. Despite their almost immediate and deep friendship, they made a strange pair. They were roughly the same age, but their paths to Washington's headquarters had been starkly different. Laurens was everything Hamilton was not. He was the scion of wealthy planters who was schooled by tutors and educated abroad. Rather than a shadowy father, John had a famous and accomplished one in Henry Laurens, a president of the Continental Congress, whose Carolina empire rested on rice and slavery. Yet the inexplicable fact that opposite personalities often are drawn to each other was never more apparent than in Alexander Hamilton and John Laurens, and it was after they became friends, not because of it, that they discovered a common purpose in their feelings about slavery. Possibly Hamilton developed his opposition to slavery from seeing it in the West Indies, but if so he never mentioned it. Laurens, on the other hand, was more open and direct about his feelings regarding the chief mainstay of his family's wealth. John and his father could no longer accommodate the unsettling contradiction of talking about human liberty while owning human beings.

When Laurens proposed enlisting slaves in the army with emancipation an incentive to serve, Hamilton had to be impressed that his friend irreverently carried the idea to South Carolina and fought as tirelessly for it as he did against the British. The proposal appalled Carolinians, but Laurens continued his advocacy until the day he was killed in a skirmish on the Combahee River outside Charleston in August 1782, just months after the climactic battle at Yorktown; it would be only a few more months before the final peace ended the war. It seemed a horrible waste, and hearing the news challenged Alexander Hamilton's icy control. "The world will feel the loss of a man who has left few like him behind," Hamilton wrote. For the remainder of his days, he would never meet anyone like John Laurens, "a friend I truly and most tenderly loved."[7]

What might have remained of young Hamilton's idealism does not seem to have survived this loss. His causes became more practical, if no less ambitious, and his manner more self-serving while less engaging. The optimistic patriot gave way to the cynical politician as Hamilton mastered the law, entered Congress, and quickly joined the faction desiring a stronger central government. How far he was willing to go to realize that goal has raised questions about his possible involvement in a troubling episode at the close of the Revolution.

Practically on the eve of peace in the spring of 1783, the Continental Army appeared ready to stage a mutiny directed by its senior officers. The grievance was the thwarting by the states of the Congress's effort to pay soldiers and fund veterans' pensions. Tense meetings between the army and congressional leaders produced no solution but did persuade, it was said, important officers that a military coup was the only solution. The army encampment at Newburgh, New York, became the center of this plot, and a meeting on March 15, 1783, was to be its decisive moment. General Washington sympathized with the discontent, but the rumors about military insurrection infuriated him.

He appeared at the March 15 meeting to plead for patience, lest brute force ruin everything they had spent eight years fighting to secure. The result was one of the most famous exploits of George Washington's career. Unable to talk the gathering down, he began to read an encouraging letter from a congressman. But he faltered over the first sentences. He could not make out the words. His grumbling audience fell silent as he pulled a pair of spectacles from his pocket. They were a recent capitulation to presbyopia and something most of them had never seen Washington wear. Suddenly, it struck them all how very old he looked, how worn down he was from the strapping forty-three-year-old he had been at the start of the war, now a year past midcentury and wearing the weight of the world, poignantly, on the wide bridge of his nose. "Gentlemen," he said quietly, with just a trace of embarrassment, "you will permit me to put on my spectacles, for I have not only grown gray but almost blind in the service of my country." He read the letter, but they did not hear it. They did not need to. Their heads were lowered. Many were weeping.[8]

The collapse of the Newburgh Conspiracy through the irresistible influence of Washington at this crucial moment makes a grand story, but some historians doubt that it's true. At least, there is doubt that it happened just this way. Did nationalists in Congress engineer this crisis and exaggerate its dangers to convince their reluctant colleagues that the country needed a stronger central government? Robert Morris, James Madison, and Alexander Hamilton led the nationalist faction. The officers who petitioned Congress and held the tense meetings with Morris and others were Washington's closest friends and most trusted confidants in the army's officer corps. Was there collusion between the army and the nationalists to force the question of taxation and make a compelling case for enhanced national authority? Did it include Washington as a knowing participant? If so, the way things ended at the March 15 meeting could have been staged in cooperation with trusted lieutenants, including even the dramatic scene with Washington's spectacles as an especially effective touch.[9]

Historians have not settled the question and never will, for we likely know everything we shall ever know about the events at Newburgh in the spring of 1783. The evidence for calculated manipulation is more circumstantial than documentary and requires a fair amount of inference, which makes it thin enough to discount, at least in the estimation of some scholars.[10] The interpretation of the conspiracy as high theater also seems to exaggerate the influence Washington's associates could exert on him to break character and engage in dramatic playacting during a potentially combustible situation. Army discontent was real and on the edge of ugly. That same year a mutiny by Pennsylvania militia became serious enough to frighten Congress out of Philadelphia, the beginning of its wanderings that would finally end with it setting up in New York City. Did Alexander Hamilton represent a type of nationalist whose desires to change the nature of the government made him willing to risk its very existence?

★ ★ ★

As the Confederation government faltered, Hamilton with Madison continued to promote a nationalist agenda. Their partnership helped bring about the Annapolis Convention and from that the Constitutional Convention in Philadelphia, where Hamilton spoke only once but at length to explain his plan for an ideal American government. It would have closely followed the British model. The states would have been all but eliminated, and the national legislature's upper chamber would have become an American House of Lords with members serving for life. The American executive—Hamilton called him a "governor"—would have become a sort of American king by serving for life and possessing an absolute veto. In retrospect, it was a peculiar vision, but at the time Hamilton's ideas were not greeted with derision or dismissed out of hand. He pitched his idea in mid-June 1787, early enough in the convention for delegates to consider anything and everything for a new government. But it was simply an unlikely formula, and in a few weeks the convention's progress made his ideas a footnote. Yet, the delegates had heard Alexander Hamilton say these things, and they would remember them differently as the years passed and politics became vexed and vicious. Suspicions about Hamilton's fidelity to republicanism had dogged him for years. In addition to his possible involvement with the Newburgh Conspiracy, rumors alleged that he wanted Congress overthrown and Washington made a dictator.[11] His remarks in Philadelphia were not at all seditious, but they were curious, and James Madison never forgot that Hamilton had made them. Thomas Jefferson would come to know that Hamilton had said them.

During the ratification debates Hamilton dissembled and equivocated to erase residual suspicions caused by his strange speech in Philadelphia, and his entries for *The Federalist* also disguised his real feelings about the Constitution and what it would allow the government to do. After the Constitution was put in place, he intended to put in motion elaborate plans to consolidate more power in a national government than anyone could have imagined. As early as the spring of 1789, people were touting Hamilton for the post of "financier-general," and long before the creation of the Treasury Department, he was talking about funding the public debt and raising money by selling public lands. Beneath it all, though, was his goal to "triumph altogether over the state governments."[12]

After Congress created executive departments in 1789, Washington wanted his old friend Robert Morris to head up the Treasury Department, a reprise of his role as chief financial officer during the latter part of the Revolution and the early years of the Confederation. Morris was not interested, but along with Madison and others he recommended Hamilton. It was an intriguing suggestion.

It was soon clear to the new president that his former aide was poised to save his country with an imaginative financial program that few would understand and some would abhor. But Hamilton brought problems with his genius. Whether his pessimism derived from his illegitimacy, impoverished youth, or disillusionment over losing a friend is hard to say, for there was so much wrong with the fellow who always appeared to be so right. Having to struggle for social advancement and economic security against the prejudices of people put off by a bastard who often acted like one was enough burden for any man. Progress against personal and public challenges might have been proof that anyone could succeed in America regardless of his past, but that offered little comfort for a driven man with great talent and a large ego.

His marriage into the Schuyler family had elevated him into the American aristocracy, and though he obviously loved Betsey Schuyler, the old problem of inconstant loyalty sooner or later cropped up with his wife as it did with everybody else. Eventually his marriage would be a bit unfulfilling, and there would be at least one other woman, possibly more. Something other than sexual desire drove him to affairs. Private happiness and professional success were never enough for a man who could not shake dark thoughts nor turn away from dire predictions. Hamilton never thought of American citizens as intuitively astute about money, liberty, or order. As far as he could see, they spent too much, confused freedom with license, and tended to fly into rages over trivial irritations. Kids saw a disembodied arm through a hospital window, and New Yorkers were suddenly burning down buildings and stoning their betters. People like that could not even be shepherded. Their instincts were seldom sound, and their passions were seldom restrained. People like that had to be herded. They had to be controlled.

He almost never talked about this so explicitly, and describing it so bluntly simplifies the complexity of a character that mystified even his friends, devastated his wife when she found out about his most notorious dalliance, and should have given George Washington pause. He almost would, once or twice, but never with as much resolve as he would have with other men. Not just the complexity of Hamilton's character but the intricacies of his relationship with Washington would come to puzzle men such as Thomas Jefferson and James Madison. At a loss for an easy explanation, they eventually would gravitate to the worst one, whether it had merit or not. For George Washington that was the cost of trusting a brilliant man with a peculiar sense of loyalty.

Because Hamilton would have a more direct relationship with the legislature than the rest of the administration, he gradually assumed increasing authority in framing as well as influencing economic policy. In responding to the House's requests for information, he was overwhelmingly comprehensive, and few in the legislature could comprehend his reports entirely. It became easier just to allow Hamilton to draft legislation that answered the country's fiscal needs. His regular meetings with congressmen to hash out economic questions marked a less-than-subtle shift in the relationship between the executive and legislative branches of the government.

The economic crisis of mounting debt and wrecked credit threatened to topple the constitutional experiment before it could begin. The very size of the problem established the rising importance of the man dealing with it. Multiplying responsibilities to cope with a multifaceted problem made Hamilton's department the largest in the executive branch. The administration and collection of the main sources of revenue through import duties and sumptuary taxes necessitated the large staff of clerks at the capital and hundreds of customs officials, lighthouse keepers, and revenue men all over the country. Hamilton's reach stretched from his office to the Congress and beyond to the woods of Maine District and the pine barrens of the Georgia frontier. The instant the Senate confirmed Alexander Hamilton on Friday, September 11, 1789, his broad, encompassing influence was assured, and James Madison's days as Washington's "prime minister" were numbered. The consequences would be politically and personally profound.

Hamilton was at his desk the Monday after his confirmation and immediately began displaying a superhuman capacity for work. Congress wanted a report on possible ways to address the debt crisis but did not expect it until the second session in early 1790. Even so, that gave Hamilton not much more than a hundred days to gather data and draft some proposals. At the same time, he would have to assemble his department, establish workaday routines, install the Customs Service, and staff it with reliable employees. Nobody expected much more than some sketched-out ideas in draft form as a starting point for discussion.

Nobody yet had any idea that Alexander Hamilton never slept, always worked, and had a mind so acutely honed to the digestion, manipulation, and calculation of numbers that his skills resembled those of an idiot savant—except that Hamilton was all savant and nothing idiotic. He could summon astonishing powers for everything from a sparkling conversation to a sexual liaison. Brimming with purpose, he was also a selfless patriot who could have made millions in the pursuit of his own interests had he not chosen to pauper himself in the public's service. He was scrupulously honest, despite doubts that would later arise. "You remember the saying with regard to Caesar's Wife," he told someone who had proposed an innocent financial undertaking. "I think the spirit of it applicable to every man concerned in the administration of the finances of a country." Hamilton was not just mouthing a platitude. "With respect to the conduct of such men," he insisted, "*Suspicion* is ever eagle eyed, And the most innocent things are apt to be misinterpreted."[13]

Such honesty and the knowledge that public confidence required the appearance of it in all things was something he shared with Washington as a facet of his character, and with Thomas Jefferson as well. It was a defining trait of the "genius" of the Founders, which meant for these people something other than incredible mental acuity. It embraced a man in his entirety, what George Washington in his youth described as the celestial spark of conscience. While some doubted Alexander Hamilton's celestial spark, none would ever question his genius. In time, some would fear it.

★ ★ ★

Washington's trip to New England in the fall of 1789 provides an indication of how similar his vision of the new federal union was to Alexander Hamilton's. Washington did not usually meditate on political philosophy, but stature and pride of place were issues he thoroughly understood—practical manifestations of ego that were exasperating but inescapable. With the Constitution, the federal government was supposed to transcend local interests, but only if it could find ways to exercise authority over the states without riling them up at the beginning. Here was a practical rather than a philosophical question. New Englanders would be a test of how effective Washington's reputation could be in the balance between localism and loyalty to the federal experiment.[14]

On the morning of October 15, 1789, he and a small entourage headed for Boston for a week's stay. The journey was heartening as crowds in towns along the way cheered themselves hoarse. Vice President Adams ventured ahead to make sure everything was prepared for the president's arrival, and the people of the city were near bursting with excitement by the time he arrived. Throngs shoved and necks craned to catch a glimpse of him. The celebrations planned for every day of his week promised to be tiring but propitious, and the visit was being scored a success before it had even begun—until an incident ruined everyone's good mood.

Governor John Hancock wanted the presidential party to attend a celebratory dinner at his home as a welcome to the city, and Washington had gladly accepted. However, when Washington arrived on the Boston Neck, the governor was not there. The day was cold and drizzly, and Washington curtly asked if there was another way into Boston. Told there was not, he very nearly canceled his visit but relented when he was told that the city fathers as well as a large gathering were waiting for him. His entrance was triumphal as always, but at the statehouse the set of his jaw showed he was still upset. He expected Hancock to visit his rooms, but the governor did not come, and the omission became impossible to overlook.

President Washington meant to outrank Governor Hancock, a protocol that required Hancock's symbolic submission by coming first to the chief executive. When a note arrived from Hancock explaining that his health would not permit him to come to Washington's lodgings in advance of the planned dinner, the president perceived a ploy to establish a state governor as the equal of the president of the United States. He responded with a chilly note: If the governor was too ill to come to Washington's lodging, he was obviously too ill to entertain. Washington remained at the inn and had a quiet supper with John Adams.

Alexander Hamilton would have exulted over this insistence of subordinating a state to federal authority, and Washington's stand is usually lauded as appropriate. Yet John Hancock was likely acting on republican principle. The president of the United States was not a king, not an emperor, not a tsar, but a fellow citizen clothed in temporary (and limited) powers by the republic to administer the laws. In 1789 the office itself was less than a year old, lacked the trappings of tradition, and commanded respect solely through the stature of its current occupant. George Washington's popularity in the country, and especially in Boston, where citizens recalled the frantic evacuation of the British in the spring of 1776, was simply unassailable. The truth of the matter was that John Hancock's gesture, whatever its motive, was unpopular because it embarrassed the city by making George Washington—not the president, but George Washington—dine alone at his inn on his first night in town. Or, more accurately, dine with John Adams, which many people thought even worse. This distinction between the popularity of the man and reverence for the office makes the matter dubious.

Even worse, Hancock could have been telling the truth that poor health prevented his standing on ceremony. Severe gout had plagued him for years and would kill him in only a few more. Dinner guests pitied his appearance and looked away from the wheelchair that forced him to eat at a small separate table. On the day Washington arrived, the weather was abysmal, the wet and cold causing Hancock to suffer more than usual. In fact, the entire city became sick from the raw weather, and people referred to it as "the Washington cold" or "Washington's influenza."[15] Hancock very possibly did not appear at Boston Neck because he could not. He might not have thought anything about staying in and waiting for Washington to come to dinner, where the president would sit at the main table with all the important guests while a servant pushed Hancock to the makeshift one, apart.

Washington's note sent a spear of pain through Hancock worse than the gout. On the next day, he asked if he could call on the president. Washington coldly informed the governor that he had about an hour in the early afternoon free, but after that he would be engaged. Hancock was at Washington's door in thirty minutes. According to some accounts, when servants carried Hancock inside, Washington was stunned by his wretched appearance. They had not seen each other since the Revolution, but the square-jawed patriot had become a gnarled shell with bloated limbs wrapped in red flannel. George Washington immediately dropped his curt manner. Hancock was sick, after all.

The two had set a precedent, which was important but not necessarily laudable. Those around Washington saw his popularity as good for the country, something that "answered a good political purpose."[16] If opposition to the government was seen as opposition to Washington, the government seemed unassailable. Yet it also carried risks to have so much depend "on the life of one man."[17]

The other risks were not so readily apparent. This first presidential tour solidified the concept of Washington as defining a national identity. Hamilton was among those who believed European veneration of monarchs was a wholesome expression of both political and spiritual unity, something that could be adapted to the American setting for an executive with limited power. Celebrations that hailed royal births, coronations, and kings' birthdays were soon associated with George Washington. His birthday would resemble a national holiday, with balls and concerts in his honor. But devotees of republican government were not sure about the wholesomeness of these practices. They privately worried that Washington's closest associates could be moving the nation toward monarchy with such trappings, veneration that held dangers despite constitutional limitations on presidential power. They squinted but kept silent. For the time being, it was wiser to keep their misgivings to themselves. John Hancock would have understood why.[18]

New Year's festivities could not distract Washington from drafting his annual message, that day's version of the State of the Union address. The Constitution requires that the president will, from "time to time," inform the Congress accordingly but says nothing about the time or manner of doing so. Washington did not relish having to deliver the speech, but he wanted to communicate his views to Congress in person. He did so every year of his presidency, and his successor John Adams continued the practice. The third president, Thomas Jefferson, preferred to send his message in written form to Congress, but only partly because he loathed public speaking. By the time Jefferson was president, the annual message had fallen into disfavor for resembling the king's address from the throne to Parliament, and every president after Jefferson followed his precedent until Woodrow Wilson revived the personal appearance. Wilson saw nothing untoward in addressing Parliament from the throne.

Washington did, but he was working from a different set of circumstances, one of which was the need to establish his office as a coequal branch of government. At 11 A.M. on January 8, 1790, with considerable ceremony, the president of the United States left his residence in his cream-colored carriage. At its front rode two secretaries atop Washington's matching white stallions. Tobias Lear sat in the carriage with Washington, and the president's nephew Robert Lewis rode his horse behind it. Chief Justice Jay, Alexander Hamilton, and Henry Knox followed, each in a separate carriage.[19] When Washington arrived at Federal Hall, the doorkeepers of the House and Senate escorted him into the Senate chamber. Members of the House and Senate stood when he entered and remained standing until he sat down in John Adams's ornate chair. Washington's retinue filed in to stand at the rear of the chamber throughout the address. Washington stood to give his speech. Congressmen and senators stood as well. In a departure from their behavior at the inaugural address, they remained standing throughout the address. The government was changing before their very eyes.

Washington opened by congratulating Congress on the favorable reputation of the government and urged the continuation of the good work started in the last session, including measures to ensure the common defense, provide for diplomatic representatives to foreign countries, create procedures for naturalizing immigrants, and establish a uniform currency. One of the longest sections of his address called for "the promotion of science and literature" through either the creation of a national university or aid to institutions of higher learning already in existence. These were important matters, but they were only a preamble to the part of the message everyone had been anticipating. In the closing portion of his message, Washington recommended the adoption of measures to "support the public credit" for the sake of "the national honor and prosperity."[20]

Six days later Alexander Hamilton delivered to Congress the *Report on Public Credit,* and all other government business came to a standstill. It was an astonishing piece of work. Beyond lengthy, it was epic in the reach of its data and spectacular in the scope of its solutions. Hamilton proposed to fund the debt with interest-bearing government securities issued to the government's creditors. These were to be redeemed at some future date, which would perpetuate the debt but provide assurance that the nation would meet its financial obligations. Hamilton said the United States owed in principal and interest almost $12 million to foreigners and about $40 million domestically. This much was known and had always been assumed as the obligations outstanding, but Hamilton went further. He pegged collective state debt at $25 million and proposed to assume it as a federal obligation as well. The mechanics of this were as ambitious as the scope. Hamilton planned to pay the accrued interest in specie (hard money) and gradually retire the principal as money became available. A benefit of his approach was a gradual schedule that would not require drastic increases in government revenue.[21] Instead, he planned to pay off the debt with a sinking fund tied to post office revenues, customs duties, and excise taxes. The Treasury would buy government securities on the open market to place those securities in government hands.[22]

Congress in the main thought the plan generally sensible and its recommendations sound, but that was at first blush. It would be fair to say that a goodly number of them did not understand its particulars as well as they should have, nor would some ever understand what the *Report on Public Credit* intended, which was more than funding the debt. Possibly George Washington was among this number. His lack of interest in the minutiae of the debt and how to resolve it allowed Hamilton to work on his plan outside presidential supervision. Hamilton consulted the plans framed by Robert Morris during the Confederation, asked James Madison about the best ways to raise revenue, and pored over reports written by Thomas Jefferson about reducing the country's foreign debt. He read widely in diverse authorities including Blackstone, Montesquieu, Hobbes, and Hume. He digested the modern thinking of men such as Jacques Necker, Louis XVI's beleaguered finance minister who was struggling with a massive debt problem in France, one ironically caused in part by funding the American Revolution.

Hamilton was convinced of the general rule that a nation's standing in the world and with its citizens depended less on its real financial solvency than the perception of its financial solvency. The essential and inescapable reality was clear: Any economic transaction involving credit results in debt, and someone will eventually want the money. The ability to pay that debt carried advantages beyond a tidy ledger with neatly balanced columns of assets and liabilities. It determined the ability to borrow money in the future. Paying off the debt was clearly important, but colliding with that goal was the certainty that raising taxes could cripple an economy, making it impossible to function after paying a portion of the bills. The trick was to create the confidence that the debt would indeed be paid down, and eventually off, no matter what otherwise happened.

The trick was to be achieved through an incredibly complex web of funding over a span of decades rather than years. Central to accepting this protracted schedule was the acceptance of debt as a useful economic tool rather than a burden, the idea that it wasn't the debt that was the problem, but the kind of creditor who held it. Debt in the right hands— say, America's wealthiest class—would give the right people a material stake in the country's survival. They would be compelled to act in the country's interest out of their self-interest to be repaid. Hamilton's policy did not expect good people to do the right thing but made it worthwhile for anybody, good or bad, to do the right thing. Yet the translation of that concept into policy was one of the things that troubled people more from instinct than reason. Opposition arose to the federal assumption of state debts because adding to the national debt seemed contrary to the goal of retiring it. And even at this early stage of what would become a great national struggle, some sensed that Hamilton's seemingly nonsensical purpose was the madness of the fox. Was he using this carrot of assumption to place states under the stick of federal authority?

Many cried foul because they were from fiscally responsible states that had taken pains to pay off their debt from the Revolution. Austerity measures and higher taxes had been the hefty price for those policies, and the men who had endured them bristled over bailing out spendthrift neighbors. As one group pointed out an objection, another parsed the plan to discover additional ones, and soon small pockets of opposition were forming over this, that, and the other—enough to drive Mr. Hamilton mad for real, a fox in a swarm of bees. Fears that the government would use the cry of necessity to renege on constitutional guarantees against direct taxes found voice. Still others proposed outright repudiation for at least part of the debt, such as the mountains of interest that had grown since the war, suggestions that horrified Hamilton. Even the hint of repudiation would destroy the abstraction of responsibility needed to establish confidence in American credit.

Other opponents were just as baffling in refusing to shake the idea that all debt was equally bad, whether through profligate loans or new government securities. They suspected what seemed to be a sly avoidance of taxes, the quickest and surest way to pay off the entire debt, as a trick to avoid paying off the debt (which, in fact, it was). Debt was never beneficial, they muttered, and claiming it was encouraged the government in "wanton expeditions, wars & useless expences."[23]

But it was James Madison who stunned everybody. In the midst of the House debate, Madison objected to current holders of government securities being the only ones to benefit from them. He proposed an alternative, what became known as "discrimination," a convoluted scheme to divide the proceeds of securities between original purchasers and current owners, hence to discriminate somehow between the two. Although his proposal did not seem more than a repair for a particular part of Hamilton's plan, Madison's initiative actually became the main assault on Hamilton's entire program. The insistence that original holders be compensated to some extent conveyed the impression that not doing this would be a callous dismissal of their original sacrifice. They had invested in the uncertain quest for American independence when it really mattered and had fallen prey to speculators using the Confederation's financial problems. Confidence men had played on ignorance and distress to purchase those securities for a pittance. The implication was that the original investors had been cheated in those transactions and now were going to be cheated again by Hamilton's plan.

It was true that speculation had run rampant in the 1780s, and the activity was easy to portray as sinister because a few men with disposable capital and the audacity to risk it had done it. Speculators, for example, had focused on acquiring the final settlement certificates issued to soldiers, which was easy because soldiers were eager for ready cash and sold the certificates at considerable discounts almost as soon as they received them. Speculators had gambled large sums on discounted purchases of all sorts of government securities, with the result that by 1787 virtually all the public debt had already fallen into the hands of secondary purchasers. It made for a powerful political argument to point to these people as vultures, but Madison's embrace of discrimination amounted to a brazen reversal of the position he had taken in 1783, when he opposed fellow Virginians on the very same issue. He had said nothing about such an idea as discrimination in Philadelphia in 1787, and as late as 1789 he had not posed it as an alternative to any funding plan. Then suddenly in the spring of 1790, Madison developed a profound sympathy for original holders of securities, despite the fact that the transfer of securities had been a long process of fits and starts over the 1780s that could not have anticipated Hamilton's plans.

Nobody had been cheated. Speculators had taken risks. Sellers had been paid. Madison knew this. Instead of compassion, his motive was likely to rebuke the move toward nationalism that had begun to worry him, the glimmers of that worry appearing as early as late 1789. He tried to cloak this maneuver by seeming to protect the interests of widows, orphans, bilked veterans, and small storekeepers who had invested in America's future, only to be cheated out of the proceeds by moneyed interests.[24]

Whatever Madison's motive, his proposal shocked Alexander Hamilton even more than the suggestions for partial repudiation, not only for what it envisioned but because of who had envisioned it: James Madison. Hamilton's partner for the better part of a decade in the titanic struggle to create a central government capable of disciplining the states and promoting a national program was suddenly opposing a key element of the plan to realize their old dream. It baffled others, too. For almost a year, Madison had been the voice of the administration in the House, behaving much like a prime minister in the constitutional system. Now, as he spoke out against something that George Washington obviously supported, people listened in amazement. Madison's size and shyness still caused some to misjudge the quiet, pale, and gifted man's power and misgauge his determination, but Hamilton wasn't one of them. Jemmy might be "no bigger than half a piece of soap" in the estimation of the unschooled, but Hamilton knew lightning when he saw it.[25] He was terrified that this opponent would stop everything.

Alexander Hamilton was powerful, too, in his ability to report directly to the House of Representatives. It is impossible to overstate how much influence that gave him in determining not just the course of legislation but its substance. Hamilton's reports and lesser communications kept his hands on the legislative levers of power. Madison now began to see that as a remarkably bad idea, something more than a bridge to the executive. When Hamilton wanted something, as he did with this funding and assumption scheme, he flirted with the unconstitutional practice of drawing up a bill that he expected Congress to approve. Too intimate a tie between the legislature and executive threatened the separation of powers and tended to monarchy and ministerial control, casting the Treasury head in the role of prime minister, which was sobering. James Madison in that role had really been more of a liaison between executive and legislature. The distinction was important. Madison was not a member of the administration.

Hamilton thought his friend had become a turncoat willing to stab him in the back. Madison thought his friend had been revealed. Years later in 1834, after most of the participants in the battles of the Washington administration were long in their graves, Madison heard that a new biography of Alexander Hamilton would discuss Madison's desertion of the Treasury secretary. Madison had spent as much time thinking about it at age eighty-three as he had at thirty-nine on the afternoon he proposed discrimination. No, he insisted, Hamilton had deserted him by blurring the lines separating government power between coequal branches, a consolidation of authority that was completely at odds with the Constitution's aim of limiting as well as enabling government.[26]

During ratification, Madison had observed, "If men were angels, no government would be necessary." It is a phrase often remembered. What is often not remembered is that Madison had immediately followed it by saying, "If angels were to govern men, neither external nor internal controls on government would be necessary."[27] In 1790, he watched Alexander Hamilton pull aside this and that legislator, speaking quickly while glancing around for another to collar and persuade, smiling and flattering with a hand on the shoulder and a pat on the back. It gave James Madison pause.

"If angels were to govern men?" Was he looking at a fallen one?

7

"A Certain Species of Property"

Bad feelings in the funding and assumption debates ran high, but arguments over controversial petitions dealing with slavery in early 1790 made them seem mild.[1] In February, Quaker antislavery organizations in Philadelphia filed three of these calling for the immediate end to the international slave trade and the gradual abolition of slavery. The subject made the House more than uncomfortable because many southern members all but frothed at the mouth when the subject of gradual abolition came up in any setting. The last of these petitions, however, caused particular dismay. The president of the Pennsylvania Society for Promoting the Abolition of Slavery had signed it. His name was Benjamin Franklin.

Franklin had owned slaves at one time, but it was when he was much younger, and his thinking about the matter had ripened with age. He was lighthearted by nature, but there was nothing lighthearted about slavery in Franklin's world. He saw the coffles of people with large frightened eyes, wrists and ankles chafed to bleeding by their fetters, children torn from mothers, people inspected like horses with lips pushed roughly back over their teeth to display their gums, the awful ringing of chains, the awful music of money—there was nothing but a nasty ugliness about it all. Benjamin Franklin wanted it ended. He wanted its victims educated and trained to make their way in freedom.[2]

These petitions outraged men from the Deep South, who protested "in the strongest terms" their submission to a committee to produce a report.[3] A report was the last thing southerners wanted to see about this issue, but James Madison argued that deviating from regular procedures would only give the petitions more publicity. He shared the fears of the Upper South and mid-Atlantic states that the Quaker petitions were harbingers of something wider, larger, and ultimately irresistible. Northern and southern differences over this fundamental point of human freedom could pose a dangerous threat to the Union. Slavery was too important to those who owned slaves. If it became all-important to those who wanted to do something about it, the nation would not survive.

George Washington had privately expressed mild disgust over Quakers ever since 1777 when they sold food at markets in the Valley Forge region while the army starved. He thought their ideas about slavery were half-baked, and he was certain they would harden proslavery attitudes, which he believed congressional anger proved. It would have been best not to have the issue broached at all, but once raised, the House should dispense with it as quickly as possible.

That slavery had already become something people did not want to talk about was a problem in itself. Southerners did not want to talk about it because it embarrassed or angered them. They felt the stain of hypocrisy with their high talk of liberty, and they feared the prospect of abolition because it was economically disastrous and socially terrifying.

The "reasonable" position held that the debates raised unnecessarily provocative issues best left alone, which made the problem insoluble. Trying to calm southerners by telling them that they should simply let debate run its course and that nothing would come of it was unconvincing because it was obviously not true. Madison was aware of this and greatly disturbed by it.

Moreover, slavery troubled James Madison. It simultaneously repelled him because he shared the sensibilities of Benjamin Franklin, and constrained him because of the economic needs of the planter class. Presumptions about race that were endemic to educated white people of the eighteenth century did not always resemble the bigotry of later times, for they emerged from an Enlightenment aesthetic informed by rationalism. Madison was, in that regard, not a racist but a racialist whose empirical observations of black people could not imagine them beyond the degraded state of slavery. This ran quite deep in him. Because of it, he saw no viable solution to slavery in the short term and doubted that gradual abolition could succeed. He was not alone or unique, and his attitude was not a sectional one. "I wish myself that Congress would prefer the white people of the country to the blacks," muttered Connecticut lieutenant governor Oliver Wolcott, Sr. "After they have taken care of the former, they may amuse themselves with other people. The African trade is a scandalous one; but let us take care of ourselves first."[4]

Lurking behind these widespread attitudes, of course, were the two questions essential to any moral wrong awaiting redress: If not us, who? If not now, when? Could James Madison have asked himself those questions? He was most peculiar in that this apostle of empiricism would never allow contrary experiences to change his mind about slavery. Madison grew up with a slave named Billey Gardiner given to him by his grandmother. Billey Gardiner tended to Madison as a valet and filled the role of a companion. He accompanied Madison when he traveled to Congress during the Revolution, and those lengthy stays in the North set Madison to thinking.

He arranged for Billey's eventual freedom by selling him to a Philadelphia Quaker with the stipulation that Billey learn a trade. Knowing that Pennsylvania law treated such sales as indentures to end after seven years, Madison on the face of it was repaying a loyal servant with an affectionate gesture. Yet Madison made the arrangement from utilitarian rather than altruistic motives. Billey's time in the North had introduced him to countless examples of blacks living in freedom that made him unsuited for life among slaves at Montpelier. And Madison's long and intimate acquaintance with Billey Gardiner had created a sense of the man's worth that inspired trust. In the early 1790s, Gardiner still lived in Philadelphia, and Madison often hired him to purchase implements and tools for Montpelier, important tasks that required skillful bargaining and the honest handling of money. The example of Billey Gardiner, however, was singularly uninformative for James Madison, who must have seen other Billey Gardiners in his long experience with slavery. Yet Madison made no arrangements in his will to free a single slave. This brilliant child of the Enlightenment with an all-encompassing mind and boundless vision could never see beyond the coffles, shackles, and skin.[5]

Unlike Madison, Thomas Jefferson seems to have thought about slavery a lot. Jefferson never reconciled his devotion to liberty with his ownership of slaves, which left him open to charges of hypocrisy for his entire public career. Also like Madison, his belief in the inherent intellectual and physical inferiority of people of African descent kept him from publicly denouncing slavery. Though Washington harbored these same reservations, he at least had the financial wherewithal to arrange a measure of emancipation in his will. Jefferson's spending and debts made a similar arrangement financially impossible for him. Jefferson also believed that slaves made free would threaten the progress gained from the Revolution. As historian Bernard Bailyn has pointed out, Jefferson even came to believe that the expansion of slavery was necessary to maintain southern power as a counterweight to growing corruption in the North.[6] Many scholars doubt that Jefferson, despite his soaring words and admirable aims, ever seriously opposed slavery other than as a mere philosophical exercise.[7] The spring was never wound tighter in Thomas Jefferson than on this issue, a jumble of conflicts and hypocrisies that Madison had all but resolved not to think about, while Jefferson apparently thought about it more or less all the time. "I tremble for my country," he said as he surveyed slavery, "when I reflect that God is just; that his justice cannot sleep forever."[8]

The report on the 1790 Quaker petitions took several weeks to appear, but when it did another firestorm immediately flared up. Possibly the debates over Hamilton's funding and assumption plans had everyone on edge by then, because the report on antislavery was a milk-and-water creation hardly worthy of the violent response. As expected, the committee agreed that Congress had no constitutional right to interfere with the slave trade before 1808. Yet it tendered a mild recommendation that Congress and the states strive to find ways to look into the possibility of eliminating slavery's worst abuses while also looking into ways to investigate possible plans to eliminate slavery. That was enough to set off southern members. They shook fists and shouted insults at Quakers in the gallery. The most pointed remarks foreshadowed southern proslavery arguments that others would take decades to develop. Their appearance in 1790 was the very thing that alarmed Madison more than ever. He participated in the successful effort to remove everything southerners found objectionable from the report, and the palliating gesture won the measure a thin majority.[9] Washington wrote David Stuart that the petitions had "at length been put to sleep," but not much else. Washington suspected the issue would awaken and cause trouble before 1808.[10]

During the debates, Benjamin Franklin went to bed to die and then heard about the evisceration of the antislavery petitions. The news made him decide that he was not ready to die just yet, and he dictated to his grandson a satire skewering the southern position on slavery, his last bit of satire and his last public effort. Benjamin Franklin's death on April 17, 1790, silenced a voice that could exert more influence than almost any other American's on matters of public concern. Yet in the challenge of slavery, Franklin's stature had made no difference. His name on those petitions had neither persuaded his opponents nor comforted his friends. Though Franklin died, slavery yet lived, a sobering testament to the durability of ringing chains and the ability of otherwise good men to abide the ugliness of it all.

John Trumbull's portrait of George Washington during the Revolution features a black man. A 1780 French engraving of Washington presenting the Declaration of Independence does so, too. In both pictures the men are tending to Washington's horse, clearly indicating they are servants. But it is certain that they were more than that, or less than that, in point of fact. These men were slaves.

George Washington had owned slaves for as long as he could remember, beginning with his inheritance of ten people from his father. As with Martha, for much of his adult life the immorality of slavery did not trouble him because it did not occur to him. His was a world built by, powered by, and framed by slavery—and not just in Virginia, nor just in the southern colonies. This was the world as these people found it. Yet, by the end of the eighteenth century, slavery in the United States was dying everywhere except in the South. There it thrived and was populated by individual people with names and faces, people who exhibited the same range of emotions as people anywhere, people who reacted to the world and to their treatment with entirely predictable responses. The question for southerners was not just what slavery did to blacks as a race but what it did to them as human beings. Answers to that question could range from brutish racism (since blacks were degenerate and intellectually inferior, they were slaves) to moderate enlightenment (blacks were as they were because of slavery, not slaves because they were blacks). It was possible to hold both of these views in some measure at the same time. It could be most disconcerting.

Untroubled by slavery when growing up, Washington as an adult bought slaves because they were necessary to grow tobacco, which is what he intended to do with Mount Vernon when he began leasing it in 1754. He was also not averse to selling slaves, and did so throughout his life, sometimes for the simple purpose of raising cash.[11] He pursued fugitives and enlisted the aid of neighbors and authorities in reclaiming them. If slaves were difficult, broke the rules, or stole, they were punished, severely if the offense was serious. Washington did not like managers and overseers to resort to the whip, but he did not subscribe to soft altruism. He was a steely realist in all but a handful of his human relations, and his attitude toward the slave class was seldom branded by benevolence outside the accepted protocols of the institution. Slaves were meant to work, and Washington believed that the very nature of slavery discouraged them from doing so with any enthusiasm. They could not improve their good names, and they could not add luster to their reputations. He would not work slaves who were ill, but he also would not be taken advantage of. Doctors were consulted if necessary, not only to treat the ill but also to determine if sicknesses were feigned.[12]

By the year of Washington's death, 1799, more than three hundred slaves lived at Mount Vernon, far more than were needed to run the place efficiently. As the years had passed, Washington's distaste for breaking up families made for fewer sales, and the numbers grew accordingly. He had seen this state of affairs coming soon after his decision to transform Mount Vernon from a tobacco plantation into a collection of grain and produce farms. There were far more black people than white on his plantation—about 90 percent of the people there were slaves—and the interaction made for a curious mix of control and congeniality, of patriarchy and accommodation. Weddings and other family celebrations sometimes included slaves as fellow celebrants rather than servants, pointing to emotional bonds between slaves and the Washington family that are impossible to dismiss as merely slaves pretending to have affection to curry favor, or whites patronizing their inferiors to salve troubled consciences.

And yet there was the other, less appealing, side of the coin. A visitor from Poland who had seen the inside of a Russian prison found what he saw as he traveled through Virginia equally unsettling. He had a queasy feeling of disgust over slavery. Its victims were wretched; its drivers wicked. When he tried to get a closer look at a slave working in a field, a menacing white man brandishing a musket ran toward him. Though never as coarse or cruel, life at Mount Vernon could have its grim moments, too. After he had retired from the presidency, Washington was escorting a visitor from Britain around the farms when the man was suddenly struck by his host's altered behavior. Washington's affable cordiality and courtliness vanished, and his voice became hard with a sharp edge. He was talking to his slaves. He seemed, for no particular reason, to be angry. But he had a reason. He was talking to slavery.[13]

In Thomas Jefferson's first draft of the Declaration of Independence, he blamed slavery in the English colonies on King George III. Jefferson insisted that the Crown had not only pressed slavery upon the colonists but had also blocked all efforts to eradicate it. The Continental Congress struck this passage from the declaration, not because it was in large part inaccurate, but because it made southerners uncomfortable. While Americans who owned slaves disagreed with the British government over the meaning of liberty, they also wrestled with a profound paradox. The acerbic lexicographer and social commentator Samuel Johnson dryly noted in 1775, "How is it that we hear the loudest yelps for liberty among the drivers of Negros?"[14]

During the Revolutionary War, Washington did a fair amount of thinking about slavery. His war experiences changed him in many ways, including his ideas about labor in the plantation South. In part it was a practical matter, as when he saw the efficiency of northern agriculture, but there was also a philosophical element. Vermont, New Hampshire, and Massachusetts eliminated slavery during the war, and Pennsylvania adopted a plan of gradual emancipation. In the years to come, New York, New Jersey, Connecticut, and Rhode Island would do so as well. As these states embraced the morality of matching rhetoric about liberty with real action, they also showed that emancipation was achievable without undue social or economic disruption. Even Virginia relaxed its law that had made freeing slaves legally impossible without permission from the governor and council. Yet all meaningful initiatives occurred in the North, which meant that the South was already confronting the reality of slavery becoming its "peculiar" institution. Even worse, evidence pointed to the fact that the situation would never change.[15]

As Washington saw parts of the country where slavery was either waning or moribund, the contrast to Virginia rattled him. Other, more personal, forces worked on him as well during the long years away from home. One of them might have been the remarkable black poet Phillis Wheatley.[16] In the early 1760s, she was brought from Africa to Boston aboard the slave ship *Phillis* when less than ten years of age. Her first name came from the ship, but her surname was from the family who purchased the child solely to save her from slavery.[17] Efforts to provide Phillis with a rudimentary education were limited to Susannah Wheatley's homeschooling, but they lifted a veil. The child was a prodigy. She studied history, languages, and religion, and began to write poetry. At twenty she visited London and began publishing verse that resembled Alexander Pope's. She returned to Massachusetts as the colonies were mounting their rebellion against Britain, and she expressed her admiration of George Washington with a poetic tribute.[18] Wheatley sent him a copy, and we know that he read it because he sent her a note of thanks. This had to impress him in regard to the intellectual capabilities of a specific black person, if not the intellectual potential of black people generally. There is no denying, however, that Washington regarded Phillis Wheatley to be someone "favoured by the Muses, and to whom Nature has been so liberal and beneficent in her dispensations."[19]

Another black person who impressed him was a companion he brought from home. William Lee first came to Mount Vernon in the fall of 1767 when Washington purchased him from the estate of John Lee. He was quite young, probably about sixteen. Washington called him "Billy." As was his custom, Washington was not interested in a slave's surname. When he thanked Phillis Wheatley for her poem, his salutation was to "Mrs. Phillis."[20] Listed in Washington's account ledger as "Mulatto Will," the young man came at the high price of more than £61 because he was light-skinned and suitable for work in the mansion.[21]

Billy soon became Washington's manservant and from that post became something of a factotum. William Lee was an effective one too, for he was industrious as well as resourceful. He rose in the morning when Washington did, no matter the hour and possibly earlier. He accompanied him on trips to Williamsburg for meetings of the burgesses, trekked with him in the wilderness, and became the master of the hunt for the more or less constant rounds of chasing foxes that Washington so loved. He was evidently a skilled horseman and good with animals.

When Congress appointed Washington to command the Continental Army outside Boston, Billy went with him, and would remain with him throughout the Revolutionary War, riding just behind him into battle as well as on inspections. He was entrusted with Washington's prized telescope, kept his kit, and tended instantly to any of his requests. His constancy through the same hardships that Washington endured both impressed and endeared him to his owner in ways not previously apparent. Along with his deeper understanding of the peculiar status of slavery outside the South came a subtle change in Washington's sense of who Billy Lee was. Though he would never regard him as "Lee," he did begin to call him "William," and occasionally "Will." It was a sign of respect more than the fact that Billy had aged. To Washington he became a man not just through accumulated years but through his behavior as Washington observed it. Fidelity and constancy went far with George Washington.

In the years after the war and before the drafting of the Constitution, emancipation as a moral cause was no longer a quandary for Washington, but it remained a practical problem beset by many difficulties. Washington could claim he was interested in emancipation, but he always stalled on a commitment. Eventually his reluctance revealed that he never intended to make one.

Yet this is not to say that the problem of slavery did not deeply trouble him; it just deeply troubled him in private. On the eve of his presidency, he made plans that seemed to mean he intended to prepare his slaves for freedom with education and training, and then liberate them. The question was always when. Some have speculated that he meant to free his slaves before he became president but reconsidered because of the act's political ramifications. That would mean the decision he seemingly reached years later and expressed in his will had actually been made much earlier.[22] Yet evidence points the other way. When Washington was quite ill, he did not make any arrangements to free his slaves as he faced the possibility of his own death.[23]

Instead, in tandem with his (privately) expressed noble sentiments, he could act in self-interested ways. While he was president and the capital was in Philadelphia, a Pennsylvania law that automatically freed slaves after a six-month residence prompted him to send the few he had brought to staff his residence out of the state, if only briefly. Not only did this flout the letter of Pennsylvania's law that prohibited such dodges; it amounted to a callous calculation ill matched to Washington's lofty personal pronouncements. To be sure, it all made him uncomfortable, but he freely admitted that everything about slavery made him uncomfortable. He did not like to talk about it.

That reticence certainly was the result of a deep conflict that left Washington nonplussed by slavery. Billy Lee might have become William, but William was still a slave—George Washington's property—and that placed permanent limits on him and who he could become, outside the rather superficial tribute of upgrading his given name from a diminutive. During the war, Lee married a free black woman named Margaret Thomas. Several months after his return to Mount Vernon at war's end, Washington tried to have Margaret Lee brought to Mount Vernon. Both William and Margaret wanted this, but Washington's efforts to make it happen were hardly strenuous. "The mulatto fellow William," was the way Washington described Lee to his Philadelphia agent Clement Biddle, and he would only say that William and Margaret Thomas were "attached" with a parenthetical aside "(married he says) to one of his own color a free woman." Washington admitted that Margaret's ill health had led him to believe that "the connection between them had ceased." The idea of a marriage involving a slave was dismissed as a mere attachment or a connection that was only for better and not likely for worse, something that would abide in health but hardly in sickness.[24]

Nothing indicates that Margaret ever came to Mount Vernon. Only a few months later, Lee suffered the first of two serious accidents that at first diminished and finally ended his service to Washington. It happened on a crisp morning in late April 1785. Washington was surveying a parcel of his land near Alexandria when "My Servant William (one of the Chain Carriers) fell, and broke the pan of his knee wch put a stop to my Surveying."[25] Lee was forever afterward a cripple.

Obviously Lee's diminished mobility reduced his usefulness as Washington's factotum. He could no longer ride with ease, which lessened his worth as a companion, as well. All the same he tried to be of value. In November 1786, many of Washington's dogs were locked up because they had contracted rabies, but on a cold day a "Hound bitch" got loose. Will was bitten when he tried to capture her. The dog tore his coat and shirtsleeve, but he insisted his arm was only bruised.[26] He was lucky that the skin was not broken, for rabies would have killed him. As it was, his insistence was remarkable in that he refused to take advantage of an injury that almost anyone, slave or free, would have used to avoid work. William Lee never broke rules, but in this instance he broke the hard and fast one that slaves would not work enthusiastically since they could not add luster to their reputations or their good names. He was a slave, but he did not think of himself as one.

He accompanied Washington to Philadelphia in 1787 for the Constitutional Convention, performing the same duties he had for years as a valet, but more haltingly. Then in 1788 he injured his other leg just as severely as the first when he fell near the post office in Alexandria. Although he was only in his late thirties, the injuries incapacitated him. He could no longer perform his duties, and it was only a matter of time before William Lee would more or less disappear from George Washington's life. He did try to keep Lee near him. Bowing to Lee's desire to be included in his presidential residence in New York City, Washington sent him ahead with Tobias Lear, but by the time Lee reached Philadelphia he could not walk. A physician fashioned braces for him, and with crutches he was just mobile enough to reach New York, but his time there was brief. He could not do anything but get in the way, and Washington soon sent him back to Mount Vernon. On that level, the business was simply business, the normal reaction of an employer ending the employment of someone who is no longer able to do his job. But slavery did not work that way.

William Lee's fondness for drink in his later years is usually attributed to his injuries and his anxiety over what seemed a demotion from the lofty perch of being General Washington's right-hand man. Instead of riding with the general and running important errands, he became an ordinary laborer, doing what he could, helping to milk cows and weed pea patches.[27] In another few years he could not even perform those menial chores. He became a cobbler working in the cabin where he slept, spending his days in the slave quarters mending shoes.

The falls that shattered William Lee's knees were costly accidents for him, for they caused an epic fall in his status. But it actually was one of slavery's more banal cruelties. That was especially true for someone like Lee, who did not have his freedom but did not think of himself as a slave. Another slave would not be so resigned to his fate when he faced even a temporary reduction in rank.

The slave Hercules either was purchased or was born at Mount Vernon in the mid-1750s. He appears in the 1786 slave census as a cook, which meant that he was a relatively young man when he became the chef for the presidential residence in Philadelphia. Washington brought him from Mount Vernon when the government moved the capital from New York City. By then Hercules and his wife, Alice, had three children, the oldest a boy named Richmond, whom Washington abided but did not like. Though Richmond was occasionally dishonest, Washington brought him from Mount Vernon as well to staff the residence, a sign of the favor Richmond's talented and proud father had earned in the household. Hercules, in fact, became a radiant fixture for the family. He ruled over the kitchen with an iron hand, insisting that everything be spotless and orderly. The children gave him a nickname of endearment, calling him "Uncle Harkless," and recalled that he had fastidious manners, flamboyant attire, and great dignity.[28]

He enjoyed a large measure of independence in Philadelphia. Martha gave him tickets to the theater and to the circus, and as long as he fulfilled his duties in preparing meals, he was allowed to pass time in the city as he pleased. Washington even allowed Hercules to sell left-overs from the kitchen, a level of remarkable trust from a man always vigilant for petty theft. Given that, it should not have been surprising that Hercules developed ideas about his station and the nature of his relationship with the Washingtons that were at variance with theirs. In the spring of 1791, that relationship was gravely injured and evidently never healed.

The cause was Washington's attempt to avoid Pennsylvania's Act for the Gradual Abolition of Slavery that had been passed in 1780. Pennsylvania exempted members of Congress (to keep Philadelphia competitive as the site for the nation's capital), but other slaveholding visitors could not keep their slaves in the state beyond six months without setting them free. At first, Washington insisted that everyone in federal service fell under the congressional exemption, but he finally conceded that it was safer to search for ways to evade the law rather than ignore it. He concluded that it required emancipation after six months of *continuous* residence. A slave removed from the state for only a day would reset his six-month clock.[29] Although the Pennsylvania legislature had closed this loophole with a 1788 amendment, Washington still seized upon it in a willful violation of both the spirit and letter of the Pennsylvania law. Beginning in March 1791, he contrived ways to remove his slaves from the state for a short time and then bring them back.

The Washingtons tried to keep secret the reasons for their plans, but Washington's slaves had friends among Philadelphia's free blacks and knew what was happening. The unseemly stratagems employed by Washington, his family, and his staff set Hercules on edge.[30] When he was told in late spring 1791 that he was to go to Mount Vernon to help prepare the house, Hercules suspected that it was merely a scheme to prevent him from taking advantage of the six-month residency limit. It is difficult to judge how much of a turning point this was for his feelings toward the Washingtons, but both Martha and Tobias Lear noticed that the usually cheerful and self-assured chef became withdrawn and gloomy. They tried to reassure him that he was mistaken about the reason for his trip to Mount Vernon, but his sudden realization that George Washington did not trust him deeply wounded Hercules. The family could not shake him from his despond and finally relented. Martha allowed Hercules to stay beyond his six months, and he then went to Mount Vernon.[31]

Martha's gesture seemed to set things right, and Hercules might have given the impression that all was the same as it had been, but it was not. Uncle Harkless continued as the president's chef in Philadelphia, but in 1796 when Washington returned to the capital from a visit to Mount Vernon he left both Hercules and Richmond behind. By the following February, Hercules had vanished. What began several years earlier with the Pennsylvania slave law incident finally came full circle when Hercules was given work at Mount Vernon that he thought humiliating. When an empty house temporarily ended the need for a cook, an overseer had proud Hercules hoeing and weeding in one of the mansion's gardens. For a different reason, William Lee had suffered the same fate, but it was still a harsh reminder that in slavery, pride in specialized work was never a protection from indignity.[32]

When Hercules ran away in 1797, nobody who could return him to slavery ever saw him again. Meanwhile, William Lee remained in Mount Vernon's slave quarters with his awls and needles and leathers. He was often drunk and gained the reputation for being angry. But that was certainly understandable. Hercules was able to run away from the nightmare. William Lee's legs wouldn't work.

Washington loathed slavery because it was immoral to hold men in bondage and hypocritical to talk about liberty while doing so. But he also found slavery offensive because he gradually realized it was bankrupting him. His apprehension that he had too many slaves at Mount Vernon might have prompted him to take a 1786 census. It was in that year that he made one of his most famous pronouncements: "I never mean (unless some particular circumstances should compel me to it) to possess another slave by purchase." He added that he wanted "to see some plan adopted, by which slavery in this country may be abolished," but he also wanted that to happen "by slow, sure, and imperceptible degrees."[33]

When he wrote these words he already had too many slaves to run Mount Vernon profitably, and the situation promised only to get worse.

He was more explicit two years later about having "already as many slaves as I wish." At the same time, he would not break up families or separate them from a place familiar or congenial to them, which limited his ability to address the problem by simply selling excess laborers.[34]

In the fall of 1793 Washington told the British agricultural reformer Arthur Young about an extraordinary plan to which he had given considerable thought.[35] He wanted to rent Mount Vernon's four outlying farms to knowledgeable husbandmen, preferably Englishmen, to help bring about his desire "to liberate a certain species of property which I possess very repugnantly to my own feelings," but which necessity had required him to retain until he could find an alternative.[36]

He conceded that his novel idea could not take form while he was president. This was the political consideration that stayed his hand on emancipation: to alter the status of slavery so radically on his plantation would without question be politically disruptive; it could also be socially disastrous. His example would please some but anger many. It would rob him of the influence necessary to hold the government together, which was the entire reason he had taken on what he considered a thankless job. If he did anything to diminish his influence at this critical time in this particular place, he endangered the success of the experiment in American liberty.[37]

But there was another reason for George Washington to pause over emancipating his slaves. During the years he seriously pondered emancipation, he had to face the reality that he did not own more than half of the slaves who worked at Mount Vernon. They were legally designated as "dower slaves" and had come to him through his marriage to Martha. They had helped to make him a wealthy planter, but they were not his, nor were they actually Martha's. As noted earlier, she held them in trust for the estate of her late husband, which meant that upon her death they were to be distributed among Custis heirs. Because they were in trust, they were neither George nor Martha Washington's to free. That situation was both complicated and made worse by intermarriage between the slaves whom George Washington owned outright and the dower slaves: Children from female dower slaves in these unions were considered dower slaves as well. By emancipating the slaves he legally could, he was likely to shatter those families that included dower slaves—people he could never legally emancipate. The 1786 slave census showed the problem. The second census he compiled thirteen years later showed, of course, that it had gotten worse.[38]

Nor was this all. Dower slaves who ran away were Washington's responsibility. He had to retrieve them or supply their value in cash. The slaves who had made him affluent were bleeding away his wealth, but a fugitive dower slave amounted to a hemorrhage. Taking into account the problem of the dower slaves makes Washington's behavior in attempting to retrieve Oney Judge more understandable if no less troubling.

Oney had many reasons not to think of herself as a slave, and from that collision of perception between her and Martha Washington a great deal of trouble ultimately ensued. Oney was born at Mount Vernon around 1773 to the seamstress Betty, a dower slave, which made Oney a dower slave, too. Betty insisted that Oney's father was the white indentured servant Andrew Judge, though Judge denied it and the Washingtons never acknowledged the claim. Nevertheless, the girl took his name and was so light-skinned and freckled that she could have "passed" for white, as the saying at the time had it.[39]

She was brought into the mansion house when quite young to learn sewing and become a playmate for Nelly Custis. Oney, a slender and delicately formed girl with dark black eyes and hair, was talented with a needle and thread. She was also a convivial companion for Nelly and her friends, something that she would later have cause to regret. Oney became Martha's favorite maidservant and was consequently one of the few slaves whom Washington brought to New York City to serve in the presidential residence. Up to a point, all of this was fine with Oney. Martha was kind to her, as she was to all of the slaves under her roof. Oney, like Hercules, was treated to the theater and the circus, and made to feel like a pet as much as a servant. When Nelly left to attend finishing school in Maryland, Oney had a room all to herself.[40]

But her life in Philadelphia was markedly different in important ways. She was one of two slaves who Martha took out of state in May 1791 to reset their six-month clock under Pennsylvania law. The trip was disguised as a social visit to friends in Trenton, New Jersey, but the slaves knew better.[41]

If Oney's attitude was difficult to judge at the time, it was quite clear later. In the end, all the kindness in the world could not substitute for freedom. And, judging her treatment as more than kindness, Oney evidently thought she was to be free when the Washingtons died, if not before. In 1796, she was shocked that Martha meant to make her a wedding present to her oldest granddaughter Eliza Custis. Eliza had a reputation for being difficult, and as Oney recalled years later, "she was determined never to be her slave."[42]

Oney carefully planned her escape. She used the family's preparation for a trip to Mount Vernon as the reason to pack her things without arousing suspicion. In late May 1796 as the Washingtons sat down to dinner, Oney slipped out of the house and disappeared. For months the Washingtons did not know where she was. Martha vacillated between the conviction that Oney had been lured away by someone, possibly a Frenchman (it was currently fashionable to blame the French for everything), and feelings of betrayal. Either way, what she interpreted as Oney's treachery baffled her. George Washington does not seem to have had any doubts about what had happened. The household steward placed a notice in the *Philadelphia Gazette* that offered a reward for information that could effect Oney's return. The item bluntly said Oney had "absconded."[43]

The free black community in Philadelphia hid Oney until she could find a way north to freedom. In a few weeks, she glided away from Philadelphia aboard the *Nancy,* captained by John Bolles, a name Oney kept secret until Bolles's death "lest they should punish him for bringing me away." The moment Oney left the Washington residence, she became a fugitive from justice according to a federal law enacted three years earlier.[44] Washington could have invoked the Fugitive Slave Act to deploy federal officers to search for and retrieve Oney, but that would have involved the courts, making the incident politically messy.

Oney landed in Portsmouth, New Hampshire, which was bad luck for her, as it turned out. A few weeks later Nelly's friend Elizabeth Langdon recognized Oney as she was strolling on a street in Portsmouth. There was no chance for mistaken identity. Elizabeth, the daughter of Senator John Langdon, had been a frequent visitor to the presidential residence. Whether Elizabeth told Nelly or her father told Washington is not known, but by the summer of 1796, the president knew where the elusive Oney Judge was, and he was determined to get her back.

That Washington was responsible for paying the Custis estate her value does not dilute what followed. He quietly enlisted the Customs Service to make discreet inquiries. Collector of Customs Joseph Whipple suddenly found himself in an exceedingly awkward situation with an exceedingly unpleasant task. Yet, he did as he was told and found Oney. Like the situation, the report he sent to the president was unpleasant. Oney had not been grabbed by anyone but had grabbed freedom the only way she knew how. Whipple predicted that any effort to return her to slavery would cause the good citizens of Portsmouth to riot.[45]

Oney was frightened by the resolve of her owners and the power of the people who would do their bidding. She tried to rebuild the bridge she had burned with flight, but her proposal only made matters worse. She said she would return if Washington pledged to free her in his and Martha's wills. Washington angrily said no: She was faithless in his mind, and he would not reward treachery nor invite the resentment of her "fellow-servants who by their steady attachments are far more deserving than herself of favor."[46]

Whipple's report was disconcerting, though, and it put the matter to rest long enough to suggest that Oney's bid for freedom had been successful. Two years passed as Oney settled in Portsmouth, married a sailor named Jack Staines, and had a child. Then, in 1798, a stranger appeared in Portsmouth and began to ask questions about Oney, which was alarming enough, but the man was from Virginia, which was terrifying. He was, in fact, one of George Washington's nephews, Burwell Bassett, Jr., and he had been sent by his uncle to retrieve Oney.

Possibly this renewed and now relentless pursuit of the young woman was at Martha's request. It seems more likely, however, that Washington had become obsessed with Mount Vernon's deteriorating financial situation and the burden of replacing Oney's value to the Custis estate. He had not pursued Hercules, who he owned outright, with anything like the obsessive attention he devoted to Oney. Yet Bassett was clearly intent on carrying out his mission, with a kidnapping if necessary. Had that happened, the end of this story for Washington would have been much less appealing. As it was, it was bad enough.

John Langdon saved Oney from a return to slavery, and in doing so, consequently if unwittingly saved George Washington from heedlessly staining his reputation. Bassett dined with the Langdon family shortly after arriving in Portsmouth and confidently revealed to them his plans for a forcible abduction. Langdon listened with inscrutable indifference, but he was actually deeply disturbed. He went to Oney's lodgings as soon as he could and told her to hide herself and her family. They fled right away to a nearby village. Bassett never found her.

And thus ended the shabby attempt to retrieve Oney Judge Staines. She lived the rest of her days as a fugitive from justice, always worried that someday another stranger would come and she would not be so lucky. Because Oney was a dower slave, she and her children remained someone's property for the rest of their lives.[47]

Edward Savage's painting *The Washington Family* included a black "servant" standing behind Martha in shadows, and this was likely William Lee. Savage dressed him in something other than livery with a vibrantly colored vest, an arresting contrast to the dark background where he stands. His face if not his clothes is almost swallowed by the shadows. Savage, like other artists who included Lee in their portraits of Washington, took pains to make clear he was wholly African, which he was not. In some reproductions of the Savage painting over the years, Lee becomes nothing at all. He simply vanishes. As some have suggested, placing him in the shadows was perhaps an apt metaphor for slavery in the early republic. Making him go away altogether could seem an appropriate allegory for what happened to him at Mount Vernon after he shattered his legs.[48]

In that, William Lee's life seems to stand as evidence for Washington's coldness as well as his habit of avoiding the inconvenient hypocrisies of slavery. To his credit, in the end he addressed this. He drew up a will that gave his slaves their freedom after Martha's death. (He could do nothing for the dower slaves.) Washington made William Lee the only slave to receive freedom immediately without waiting for Martha's death. Lee could at his choice leave Mount Vernon or remain. In either case, he was to receive $30 every year, a sum with a modern value of about $600.[49] After all the years of pondering, he finally reasoned out how to deal with slavery: For the part of it in his power, he would end it.

William Lee remained at the estate and would die there eleven years after Washington's death. Possibly leaving everything he had ever known was too overwhelming to undertake, especially for a man with his legs. If so, he was a casualty of a system that crushed men's spirit as much as their dignity, making too many of them people who did not know how to be free. He often drank more whiskey than was good for him and had a comfortable annuity to keep it flowing, but in the end he had more than that. It was at least some measure of proof that his companion of old had not cast him off. It wasn't the money or the roof. George Washington bestowed on this good man a unique mark of respect. In his will, the first person Washington mentioned by name was Martha. The second was William Lee.

8

"This May End Disagreeably"

James Madison and Thomas Jefferson had kept in touch during Jefferson's time in Europe by trading letters crammed with politics and philosophy. Jefferson sent Madison crates of books to help him prepare for the Constitutional Convention and afterward criticized the Constitution, but Madison effectively parried the critiques, which was the kind of talent that endeared Madison to Jefferson. For Madison's part, he admired Jefferson immensely for an elegance of style in speech (always soft) and prose (always evocative and often lyrical). He could be pardoned for thinking that there was nobody else in the whole world like Thomas Jefferson, because there wasn't. Philosopher and farmer, wordsmith and scientist, a possessor of such an all-encompassing curiosity that nothing escaped his notice, and the wielder of such a marvelous intellect that nothing confounded his understanding, Jefferson had no peers. He had only friends who admired and enemies who hated.

Clocks were a passion because they were tools for the orderly mind, machines that marked days to sort chores that started before sunrise and lasted into the night, the weapon to tame time and conquer ignorance. Nothing escaped Jefferson's scrutiny: astronomy, physics, medicine, politics, mathematics, whale oil, moose droppings, tobacco leafs, ornithology, the timbre of certain bird trills, the lilt of certain Indian dialects, the day that spring's aroma signaled the time to plant peas, the exact breadth and width of the beam to bear the load of the heaviest roof, the rise of man, the fall of kings, the glory of the Enlightenment, the passion of revolution, the tranquillity of a hearth with laughing children and a dozen books to be read, all at once, annotated, outlined, digested, owned in the mind as well as on a shelf, always going, a brilliant machine oiled to a quiet thrum that occasionally popped like a sparkling firecracker—there was nobody in the world like Thomas Jefferson. "It is wonderful how much may be done," he once told his daughter, "if we are always doing."[1]

In the fall of 1789 he was coming home, temporarily he thought. George Washington would have him stay, and who would not? Abigail Adams thrilled at the prospect of Tom Jefferson coming into the government.[2] Her husband John did, too. While they were abroad Jefferson, John, and Abigail had helped with each other's children, and when Jefferson came to England he and John walked together on tours of English gardens (neither cared for them), a tall shambling redhead nodding and smiling at the peppery bursts that Adams fired off about everything he knew and some things he did not. Jefferson liked this round little companion. Adams liked him right back. Adams never liked anybody right back.

Washington could not count the numerous blessings that would result from having him on board. Brilliant but unassuming, respectful but not awestruck, Jefferson was a fellow Virginian who would provide truthful counsel rather than flattery. His extensive diplomatic experience included an intimate knowledge of France and the enormous changes looming there. Because the French Revolution would have an enormous impact on U.S. foreign policy, Jefferson was simply the ideal man to lead the State Department.

He was also just then aboard a ship. Washington prepared to offer him the position upon his arrival, but he was careful. He suspected— and Madison confirmed—that Tom could be peculiar about things. He would say he could not depart the pleasures of private life and the certainties of routine for the risks of public failure. He would want to go back to Paris and his paintings, books, and salons. So Washington made clear that if Jefferson preferred to return to France, everyone would understand. And yet, the president would have him stay. Washington sent his letter. He knew Madison would help do the persuading.

The quiet Virginian arrived in Virginia and learned from the news-papers that he had received the appointment. He was not pleased.

In Jefferson's bedroom at Monticello a bureau drawer was always locked. He kept the key on his person and must have opened the drawer only when alone, likely late at night with a candle lighting his desk. There he would open the small package. It is impossible to know how often he did this. Possibly it was not often, but certainly occasionally. The contents were odds and ends, a scrap of paper with a verse, some-thing handwritten, other assorted mementos. The most prized posses-sion was in an envelope. He would study these things for a while, and then gently place them back in the drawer, lock it, and slide into bed. The clocks ticked. He would not allow the sun to beat him to his work. He never had.

The locked drawer was one of the reasons it was hard for Thomas Jefferson to come home to his house atop the little mountain within sight of the Blue Ridge, for there were ghosts at Monticello that he could not lock away and had to deal with daily. He mainly did this by keeping busy, which was easy for him because he kept busy by tempera-ment and habit. "Monticello" meant little mountain, and the house nestled in trees on its summit remained very much a work in progress. He would never really finish it, in fact. His years in France had already filled his head with ideas about a dome, colonnades, new styles of win-dows, almost everything. Among his many talents was architecture, and building was a passion. Tearing down in preparation for building was almost as much a passion—a metaphor for his contributions to American independence.

He fully intended his renovations to come years down the road, be-cause he remained committed to returning to France. Jefferson viewed this trip to the United States as a visit to manage affairs that needed his personal attention. Most pressing was his older daughter Martha, named after her mother and called Patsy. She was of age to enter Vir-ginia society, which meant that she was on the matrimonial market. Jefferson hoped she would snag a wealthy son of the state's first families. He could hardly believe it, though. Just months earlier he had been snatching her and her sister Polly from the clutches of proselytizing

Catholics in France. Whether or not Patsy ever seriously contemplated taking the veil, her father was not taking any chances, either with her or her impressionable sister, the girl who looked like her mother and was named Maria (pronounced Mariah) but always called Polly.[3] Patsy was likely to be married to a Virginia planter before too long, and Polly was young but not far behind. It was the way of things, and though Jefferson admired Europe, especially France, his girls were Americans and would marry Americans. He settled them with relatives and planned his trip back to France. He was quite serious about this. He had brought none of his books, artwork, or furniture he had acquired in France. He could not live long without these things.

Peter Jefferson's son had always been bookish, but like his father, Tom developed a passion for the outdoors, sunshine, and riding fast horses perilously at their limit. Like his father, he grew tall and athletic with a shock of red hair, a freckled complexion, blue eyes, and an open expression that matched his open mind. But Tom was different from his father, his mother, and his siblings. He spoke softly. His temper was mellow, and his tendency to withdraw and spend time by himself made him introspective and bashful. Peter Jefferson died in 1757 when Tom was only fourteen, and for a time he was in the care and company almost exclusively of women. However, his father had arranged for friends to see to his education and help him make a start in life.

Tom's early education was in the tradition of planters' children, with private tutors and local schools supplying the basics of learning, but he was luckier than most in meeting accomplished intellectuals who recognized his talents and refined them. Tom mastered classical languages quickly, and for two years after his father's death, he lived with the Reverend James Maury's family to absorb history, grasp science, and develop superhuman reading habits that were both eclectic and disciplined. Nothing in print escaped his notice. He entered William and Mary at age sixteen and became intimate with intellectually formidable men such as William Small and George Wythe, both of whom taught him to think like a scholar and did not discourage his proclivity to write like a poet. He became a tireless investigator of the natural world, watching caterpillars and looking for fossils. Books, however, became and would remain the center of his life. He had accumulated a respectable library at his home Shadwell when the place burned to the ground while he was away. He anxiously inquired about how many books had been saved. None, was the dispiriting answer, but the slaves had risked much to save his fiddle. The logic was clear: There were plenty of books, but only one fiddle. Jefferson began purchasing replacement volumes and new books right away.

The young philosopher also became a lawyer by trade. As with all young men starting out in the lawyering trade, he rode a circuit with fellow attorneys and the judges who presided over the county courts. The experience was good, but he never cared for it, and the law's charms mainly rested in its struggle to establish precision amid ambiguity. Jefferson could understand and sympathize with the goal, because life was often too ambiguous for a young man who craved exactitude in word and deed. That attitude complicated, even stymied, his relations with girls, for the normally cheerful fellow could be hopelessly somber in the company of a pretty girl. He proposed to at least one prospect—his confiding letters to a friend show him to have been miserably in love—but his terms of a delayed marriage while he traveled Europe to increase his fund of knowledge struck Rebecca Burwell as singularly unromantic if not downright peculiar. She said no.

A bit wiser at twenty-three, Jefferson eventually set his cap for Martha Skelton. She was a widow, originally a Wayles, whose first husband Bathurst Skelton had died only two years into their marriage. The suggestion of convenience and arrangement that surrounded George Washington's marriage to Martha Custis never occurred to anyone who knew Tom Jefferson and Patty Skelton. She was a delicate young woman with limpid eyes and ashen hair who combined an extremely appealing appearance with an extremely lively mind. She had other suitors, but Tom was determined, and the little musicales the two staged during evenings—with him bowing his fiddle and her nimbly accompanying him on the fortepiano—discouraged rivals and won Jefferson the day.

They were married on January 1, 1772, and commenced a life that seemed like a fairy tale, beginning with the adventurous wedding trip back to Monticello: The two were snuggled in a sleigh that Jefferson expertly guided through a blizzard in the dark, finally arriving so late at Monticello that everyone was in bed. The only habitable part of the partially finished house was a one-room "pavilion" destined to become a dependency, but he built a large fire in its small hearth and found a bottle of wine behind some books. The firelight danced and threw shadows as they sipped the wine. The snow on the sills made for the new lovers a natural curtain. Happily ever after might have crossed their minds.

The precisely right girl and the imposition of the young man's indomitable routine could not diminish life's ambiguities, though. Jefferson built his house, and continued to build his house, but his place as a burgess thrust him into the intercolonial resistance against Britain, and the Second Continental Congress placed him on the committee with John Adams and Benjamin Franklin that chose him to draft the Declaration of Independence. At home, only two of their seven children survived childhood, and each loss seemed to drain a bit of Patty's vitality away. Her fragile health kept Jefferson close to home during the Revolution. After his work on the declaration, he all but retired from public life, and when he was finally persuaded to serve as governor of Virginia, he immediately and forever afterward regretted it.

Washington never blamed Jefferson for the state's lack of military preparation that the British easily exploited in 1781, but others did. Many Virginians excoriated him for evacuating (they called it "abandoning") Richmond during the British invasion and leaving much of the region defenseless against roving bands of Tory vandals and British redcoats. The Virginia legislature later cleared Jefferson of dereliction when his enemies lodged charges against him as a cynical exercise, but he never forgave the implication of cowardice. It did not have official sanction but would be whispered gossip for years.

Worse was what the war did to Patty. Hurried from Monticello under threat of British capture, she never fully recovered. When she became pregnant again, the difficult term and birth left her dangerously weak, and as the weeks passed, she simply faded away, flickering out on September 6, 1782. "Happily" had been decidedly mixed; "ever after" did not last beyond her thirty-three years.

Nobody has been able to gauge with any adequate measure what Patty's death did to Thomas Jefferson in the long run. In the immediate sense, it drove him close to stark madness. Discipline was damned. He lay abed staring, seldom speaking, sometimes to bolt out of the house and throw himself into the saddle of his fastest horse to pound away at remote paths canopied by colorful leaves, also dying. Everything was dying. His oldest daughter Martha talked to him, stroked his forehead, and brimmed with worry that her papa was dying, too. He wished he could. Placid to the point of entranced, he would burst into tears, refuse food, and then eat only crumbs.

This went on for weeks, and reports seeping out, incomplete as they were, deeply worried his friends. John Adams thought Jefferson might kill himself. The man needed something to do, and in the certainty that work and purpose would be restorative, persistent efforts to draw Jefferson back into public life were unrelenting and eventually persuasive. A month and a half's wallow in grief seems to have allowed Jefferson to find the bottom of his despair, and his clawing climb back to the land of the living began with small gestures, such as personal grooming, regular hours, letters read and answered, and rides with young Patsy, who accompanied him now on quieter paths and whose quiet smile when he slipped toward melancholy seemed like sunshine. He reentered the Congress and threw himself into its work, though like everyone else at this point, he was discouraged by congressional lethargy and national drift.

Jefferson eventually wound up in Paris to help Adams and Franklin negotiate trade treaties and ultimately to follow the retiring Franklin as the U.S. minister to Louis XVI. Convinced that the change would do him good, he had consented to the Confederation's appointment and sailed for France in 1784. At first he took only Patsy, leaving behind Polly and the infant Lucy as too young, but when Lucy died, he brought Polly to France as well. His life mended in the heady atmosphere of Paris's intellectual salons where the talk ranged from natural history to natural rights, and especially focused on the need to curtail the king's authority and establish equitable government that diminished noble privilege and clerical immunities. He also met a charming young artist named Maria Cosway, an exotic intellectual whose English was lilted by a slight Italian accent and whose face and figure bore a remarkable resemblance to his beloved wife's. Cosway was married to a British artist who specialized in miniatures, but Richard Cosway has always been harshly assessed as a bad match for his pretty wife, a man who resembled a monkey and painted like one. The artist John Trumbull introduced Jefferson to Maria Cosway, and for six weeks afterward they were almost inseparable.

He never seemed happier, and certainly their long carriage rides and visits to remote gardens gave them the opportunity to become lovers, but there is no evidence they were anything other than hopeless romantics, an aging man basking in the glow of a pretty woman's company and an intellectually astute woman rather swept off her feet by someone like nobody she had ever met. One afternoon, he tried to show off by leaping over a low wall, a maneuver he had managed a thousand times on the split rail fences of Monticello, but that was before middle age had made the legs heavier and the pivoting hand less sure. He fell hard, broke his right wrist, bruised his hand badly, not to mention his pride, and knocked some sense into himself. What was he doing? He had promised Patty on her deathbed he would never remarry. This young woman causing him to caper like a schoolboy was married as well. What was he doing?

He answered that question with one of the most amazing literary creations of any of the Founders. In a lengthy letter to Maria Cosway, Jefferson set up a dialogue between his heart and his head that parsed the choices between desire and duty—the assertion of reality over romantic fantasy—and concluded that the heart was compelling but the head was correct. Jefferson wrote this remarkable letter with his left hand—he taught himself the art of ambidexterity because of his injured right hand—but its penmanship was as clear as its message. He was saying good-bye to Maria Cosway. They would remain friends for the rest of their lives, but when she returned from England after the "Heart versus Head" letter, he was different, and she had the good sense not to press it. Just like writing clearly with his left hand, Jefferson believed one could do anything if there was will and determination.

Maria Cosway then became an interlude rather than an incident of his Paris days. More lasting and eliciting almost as much enthusiasm were the rumblings of revolution. In 1789, when idle talk in the salons turned unexpectedly to action in the streets, Jefferson viewed these opening acts as heralding great changes not only for France but for all of Europe. He met frequently during the summer of 1789 with prominent figures in the vanguard of France's revolutionary movement, even to the point of committing diplomatic indiscretions. He gave advice about drafting state papers. The Marquis de Lafayette intently listened as Jefferson counseled him and his friends about securing their initial gains against the monarchy. Jefferson does not seem to have been an eyewitness to any of the bloodshed and tended in any case to dismiss lurid reports as exaggerations, which became a bad habit he continued for years, even when trusted friends told him horrifying truths. Jefferson was prepared to accept as necessary some measure of violence to bring about republican government in France, but could he have seen the butchery of the Terror and still remained sanguine?

We shall never know, because he came home with his two daughters in 1789 and had hardly made landfall before learning of his appointment to the State Department. After reading the newspaper story, he received the official proffer, which came with Washington's tepidly offered option that would have allowed Jefferson to return to his post in France. Jefferson's first impulse was to say no and go back to his books and watch the revolution. There the matter remained as 1789 ended.

The congressional recess in the winter of 1789–90 gave Madison the chance to visit Monticello and make a personal appeal for Jefferson to enter the administration. His entreaties worked to the extent that after the visit Jefferson wrote Washington to repeat his reluctance while agreeing to take the post, a classic example of kicking over the freshly drawn pail.[4] Jefferson gave his reasoning to a friend. He was not pleased about becoming secretary of state, but "these things not being created for our convenience, we have no right to decline the post."[5]

Washington's reaction was mixed, for he found Jefferson's sense of duty admirable but his persistent reluctance self-indulgent. He told Jefferson that he did not want him to do anything against his wishes, but the success of the government was crucial for the survival of the nation. To Madison, Washington was more candid: He was "glad [Jefferson] has resolved to accept the appointment of Secretary of State, but sorry it is so repugnant to his own inclinations."[6]

In trying to refuse, Jefferson had been as blunt as he dared, but his reservations unintentionally provided one of the most glaring understatements in American history. By taking the job at the State Department, he said that he could not "but foresee the possibility that this may end disagreeably."[7] He braced to leave his little mountain, pausing first for family, which was always first in Tom Jefferson's world, beginning and ending with the small package of treasures in the bedroom bureau that held her handwriting, her mementos, and, in the envelope most prized, delicate strands of ashen curls that once upon a time had meant happily ever after.

The addition of Jefferson meant that George Washington's official family was finally falling into place. In addition to wanting men he knew and trusted, he carefully chose them to prevent the impression of favoring any particular state. This was one of the reasons he was relieved when the New Yorker John Jay refused to head the State Department and thus allowed him to name the New Yorker Hamilton to Treasury. Even though selecting Jefferson for State seemed to violate the rule because he wanted another Virginian to serve as attorney general, nobody regarded the attorney general as a ministerial post. Rather, he was to advise the president on legal matters and represent the government in cases before the Supreme Court. The position was considered part-time, which had the advantage of allowing its occupant to continue a legal practice to supplement a meager government salary. The attorney general would nonetheless have to reside in the nation's capital much of the year to be at hand when the president needed him.

The meager salary and the need to reside in New York City was a problem when Washington had Madison inquire if their mutual friend Edmund Randolph would be willing to come into the administration. Randolph was more than reluctant. He referred to his wife's poor health, but he also hinted that financial problems would make serving a hardship. Madison would have known about this. Edmund Randolph was always short of funds. Possibly he was a spendthrift, or he could not afford the expectations of a socially prominent wife and the needs of children living among the Virginia elite. Whatever the case, Randolph spent a considerable amount of time worrying about money while fending off a long line of long-suffering creditors.

He did not refuse Washington outright. After Congress passed the Judiciary Act, Washington wrote Randolph conveying his personal regard and emphasizing his need for Randolph's counsel. Madison evidently told Washington about Randolph's money worries, and the president stressed the part-time nature of the job. The attention touched Randolph, and the importance Washington attached to his advice gratified him. He not only relented but also promised that he would be at Washington's side as long as needed. He only wanted to delay his coming to New York until the worst of the winter had passed. Washington quickly agreed. Randolph wanted Madison to find him a house large enough for his family while "cheap in point of rent."[8] He could not bear New York without his Betsy and the children. He firmly resolved to manage his money better.

Jefferson still had doubts about the new government. When the Constitution's ratification process began, he had quietly shared his worries with Madison about the absence of a bill of rights, and though somewhat mollified by the amendments to correct this, he found the strong executive a source of concern. After becoming secretary of state, Jefferson wrote to fellow Virginian George Mason that he would have liked amendments "further than those which have been proposed, and fixing it [the government] more surely on a republican base."[9] Yet Jefferson also trusted Washington completely, and that confidence likely eased his way to the State Department.

Jefferson brought a brimming confidence to the post because of his extensive experience abroad and his thorough understanding of the proper diplomatic functions of the new government.[10] Indeed, as Jefferson understood those functions, they included the country's commercial relations in international markets. He was convinced that American agriculture free from petty European trade barriers could dominate world trade in foodstuffs and staples. With the right government, American farmers would achieve commercial dominance while forming the bedrock of the country's civic virtue, the kind of citizens worthy of a republic and capable of sustaining it. The perception and expectation were characteristic of Thomas Jefferson, a philosopher who reasoned from the utility of a thing to find its abstract advantages.

For example, Jefferson's early crusade against primogeniture and entail in Virginia (the inheritance of estates completely intact by the eldest son) removed a vestige of feudalism that impoverished society. Historian Bernard Bailyn noted that Jefferson believed "poverty . . . was thus a political as well as a social curse; it was the foundation of an unjust concentration of political power, and led inevitably to the destruction of freedom."[11] Work for wages diminished a person's freedom because it tied his tongue to keep from offending an employer and constrained his behavior in a thousand less obvious ways. Jefferson was convinced that the passive, compliant, and controlled cypher that resulted would lead to the republic's ruin. He feared that development far more than he feared civil unrest. Public passivity that derived from an uninformed citizenry would confuse security with tyranny and think the certainties of overreaching authority a good substitute for sovereignty.[12]

All abstractions and theories aside, for Jefferson family came first. He initially planned to depart for New York in February 1790, but he soon told Madison that Patsy would be married that month. It had been a whirlwind courtship between the seventeen-year-old and her cousin Thomas Mann Randolph, Jr. Jefferson had grown up with Randolph's father, was pleased with the match, and would not miss the ceremony. "You see," he told Madison, "that the happiness of a child, for life, would be hazarded were I to go away before." He wrote to Washington the same day, explaining only that he had family matters to attend to and that he would be later than planned.[13] The president must have marveled over dilatory Virginians.

Neither Washington nor Jefferson adequately weighed the awkward consequences of not having anyone in charge of the State Department for the first six months of its existence. The vacancy encouraged Alexander Hamilton to dabble in foreign affairs, and he did so furtively, because he knew that what he was doing would have infuriated the president. To be fair, however, he had some cause for alarm, and his actions from that perspective are understandable, if not admirable.

Hamilton was alarmed because the British were extremely uneasy. Redcoats still occupied the Northwest posts in violation of the Treaty of Paris, but they insisted that Americans had not lived up to their part of the agreement, either. The situation led to belligerent talk about forcibly evicting the British. Meanwhile, Congress pondered punitive duties on British imports. These troubling developments prompted Canada's governor-general Lord Dorchester to send someone to New York to gauge American intentions. Lieutenant Colonel George Beckwith was a logical choice for the job. He knew Americans from the war, but he had also conducted a fact-finding tour for Dorchester in 1787, a trip that had the unfortunate result of making Beckwith look like a spy. Perhaps he was. Beckwith knew influential people and had a talent for disarming them. Once in New York he was soon in touch with Senator Philip Schuyler, Alexander Hamilton's father-in-law. Schuyler soon introduced Beckwith to the new secretary of the Treasury.

Hamilton doubtless thought he was promoting America's best interests by holding private talks with Beckwith, but he was entirely too candid with the British agent, who, after all, could have been a spy. Beckwith was clearly there to advance his government's interests, and he regularly reported to Dorchester, referring to Hamilton with the code name "7" in his dispatches, a device more sinister in appearance than reality. But appearances, as the secretary well knew, counted for a great deal. Because he believed that a prosperous Britain benefited the United States, Hamilton revealed more than his private wishes about improving relations. Dorchester passed along Beckwith's reports to London, and they were of high interest there.

This was quite serious. When Hamilton blithely told Beckwith about his desire to protect British interests, he made a staggering admission in what should have been an adversarial relationship, despite Beckwith's ability to disarm and Hamilton's eagerness to please. Having done this, Hamilton at first kept George Washington in the dark and then deliberately misled him about the substance of these conversations. Washington knew that Hamilton and Beckwith talked, and Washington himself chatted with Beckwith at Tuesday levees, but he would never know that beginning in the fall of 1789 and for several years afterward Alexander Hamilton was disclosing to George Beckwith the administration's private deliberations.

Again, it must be stressed that Hamilton thought he was selling the concept of America as a valuable friend, and never once conceived of selling out America. Yet his government's diplomacy was badly hobbled by the British government occasionally having highly privileged information that he had provided. Jefferson was not the only Virginian who was going to have to cope with that, and without even knowing why.[14]

Before Jefferson arrived in New York, Washington turned to others for advice about foreign affairs, and from conversations and correspondence he formed opinions regarding British attitudes and the French Revolution—opinions that would prove difficult to change. Of considerable influence was his friend Gouverneur Morris, who had been in Paris for almost a year spearheading a scheme to purchase the large American debt to France. Robert Morris and a group of associates had put together the initiative, and that alone made the venture suspect to Thomas Jefferson, at that time still in residence as the U.S. minister. Morris was competing against an international pool that was using Dutch, Swiss, and French bankers to buy up the most vulnerable portions of the debt, and that, too, made Jefferson extremely nervous. Morris's competition had a head start, having begun its scheme in anticipation of the Constitution and the funding plans that were expected to make the American debt crisis a potential bonanza.[15]

Gouverneur Morris did not know Thomas Jefferson well, and Washington had given his friend a letter of introduction to smooth his way to Jefferson's embassy. If Gouverneur Morris had not been associated with Robert Morris in a financial venture Jefferson found questionable, it would have made no difference, because Jefferson almost immediately did not care for the man. As Gouverneur Morris came to know Jefferson, he reciprocated the sentiment. Soon they were barely tolerating each other with a kind of icy civility. Their starkly contrasting views of the French Revolution had something to do with this, but it became more than a personal difference when Morris's unofficial reports in letters to Washington held a bit more sway than Jefferson's official dispatches.

Gouverneur Morris had already seen horrible things happening in Paris. One evening in July 1789, he finished a pleasant dinner with friends and went for a stroll "under the arcade of the Palais Royal" while waiting for his carriage. It was nearing the fabled "blue hour" in Paris, the time when fading light plays tricks with color and hides the squalor normal to cities by casting long shadows and creating a warming coziness. As he strolled, paused, and ruminated, he likely was looking forward to some relaxation, if his latest mistress was free. She was shared with the cunning French diplomat Charles Maurice de Talleyrand, a tribute to the eclectic charms of Adélaïde Marie Emilie, Comtesse de Flahaut. Talleyrand had pride of place since he was actually the father of one of the lady's children, but Morris coped. She lived in the

Louvre in an apartment with a narrow staircase, and the two swains sometimes crossed paths as one was heading out for a dinner and the other in for an assignation. It was all very civilized.

Suddenly, though, Morris was listening to a noisy—and not at all civilized—mob nearing. He stood back, on guard. Then he saw it. "The head and body of M. Foulon are introduced in triumph," he recalled, "the head on a pike, the body dragged naked on the earth."[16] The scene was becoming emblematic of a sickness taking hold and replacing the buoyancy of just months earlier. Those early stages were peaceful and optimistic as intellectuals of the French middle class imposed constitutional limits on Louis XVI's absolutist regime. America was more than pleased. Americans, in fact, were flattered to think that France was becoming the inspired child of the American Revolution. Patrick Henry proclaimed "that America lighted the candle to all the world."[17] Washington received positive reports from Thomas Jefferson and Lafayette, the latter now in exuberant possession of a grand cause that prompted him to gush praise and send mementos such as the key to the main gate of the Bastille, which immediately received and still has a place of honor at Mount Vernon. A few high Federalists warned that rapid change could unhinge a society and that too much democracy was the mother of the mob, but most Americans shared Thomas Jefferson's giddy approval.

Because of what he was seeing on the streets, Gouverneur Morris was not one of them. "This mutilated form of an old man of seventy is shown to Berthier, his son-in-law, the intendant of Paris," he continued in his recollection of the violence near the arcade, "and afterwards *he* is also put to death, and cut to pieces, the populace carrying about the mangled fragments with a savage joy." Nobody could see such scenes and approve of their cause, no matter its purported higher aims. "Gracious God!" Morris despaired, "What a people!"[18]

Morris's reports to Washington gradually altered the president's perception of what was happening in France. Morris was already predicting an ugly turn of events for Louis XVI. Rumors that the king would flee to Spain alarmed him. Louis was "a well meaning Man, but extremely Weak." Even so, if the king left France, Morris was certain of anarchy far worse and more virulent than the mob scenes that he was beginning to witness.[19]

It was in this confusing setting of diametrically opposed reports on events in France that George Washington personally handled his first significant foreign policy initiative, though it had nothing to do with France particularly. It was an attempt to mend relations with Great Britain, which remained as strained as they had been at the end of the Revolution. Americans were convinced that the British in Northwest posts were agitating Indians, an injury to the insult of continued British occupation of forts on American soil. Trade between the two nations remained an issue. Great Britain discriminated against American shipping with high tariffs on imports to England and the outright barring of American ships from trade with the British West Indies, a mainstay of American commerce before the Revolution. The British showed no interest in sending a minister to the United States or having the Washington administration send one to London.

After he had appointed Jefferson to State but before Jefferson had accepted the post, Washington consulted with Hamilton, Jay, and Madison about sending an unofficial emissary to the British government to explore the formal establishment of mutual diplomatic relations. Despite his request for advice, Washington already had someone in mind for the task, and not everyone was pleased that it was Gouverneur Morris. Hamilton, for his part, was delighted by the prospect of improved relations with Great Britain, and he counted Morris a close friend who was in fundamental agreement with Hamilton's view of the European situation. Madison, however, was troubled. He urged the president to wait until Thomas Jefferson arrived to discuss the matter with him. After all, Morris and Jefferson had met in Paris, and Jefferson was more attuned to the situation in Europe than they could be in New York. Most important was Madison's sensible observation that if Jefferson accepted the State Department, he would rightly expect to have some say about such an important appointment, and Madison doubtless knew exactly what Thomas Jefferson would say about it.

At this point, though, John Jay's opinion likely had the most influence. Jay and Gouverneur Morris were the closest of friends, and he enthusiastically endorsed the choice. Coming from the person who had almost singlehandedly managed America's foreign relations for the last few years, the advice sealed Washington's mind.

Morris reluctantly agreed to become the unofficial representative of his government, but he never knew that he was operating at a disadvantage from the start, and not because of anything Thomas Jefferson would do. Using his conversations with Hamilton, George Beckwith alerted London about Gouverneur Morris's mission before even Morris knew about it. The chilly reception he received from the British government wasn't that peculiar, for the British specialized in the diplomatic snub when it came to Americans. Yet Hamilton had appeared too eager with Beckwith, and from that the British understandably assumed that they enjoyed the upper hand in all negotiations. Morris could not raise the slightest interest in opening discussions.

At least he wasn't sorry to put Paris behind him, despite the charms of the Comtesse de Flahaut. When Washington tapped Morris for the London assignment, the savage festival known as the Reign of Terror was still in the future, but the stirring monster could already be seen in the roving mobs, and pikes ready for any aristo's head—ready for any head that was handy eventually. The monster would slip its leash under the press of war, first on the continent and then with much of the world, whipped to frenzy by the paranoid belief among the French that enemies were in their midst. The comtesse would grab up her son and flee the country when it began, but her husband would die on the guillotine, one of the "vermin" expunged by the national razor. The forces of the French Revolution would eventually make the mob the government, and everyone would lose count of the long queue of souls shuffling up the steps of the scaffolds under dozens of national razors.

On March 21, 1790, Jefferson finally arrived in New York. He immediately went to Washington's house on Broadway to pay his respects. He found the president in John Trumbull's painter's chair sitting for one of "his Historical pieces."[20] Jefferson arranged to return the following day to commence a series of wide-ranging discussions on matters that included American captives in the Mediterranean held by Barbary pirates, diplomatic ranks for Americans sent to various nations, consular appointments, and the potential for better commercial relations with Spain. Jefferson filled the time between meetings with Washington by arranging for the shipment of his French household goods and finding a place to live in New York.

The men working under George Washington had to adapt to his administrative methods, which tested their egos and equanimity, including Jefferson's. Washington saw no reason to limit a secretary's influence only to his own department. His experience with his military staff during the war encouraged broad consultation, and his success in turning to a variety of advisers during the early months of his presidency confirmed its advantages. Conferring with many people before making a final decision simply had become Washington's routine for years, but it was bound to cause some measure of confusion, not to mention trouble. When it came to pondering proper ranks for America's diplomats or the level of participation the Senate should have in diplomatic appointments, Washington obviously wanted Jefferson's thoughts. But he also asked other department heads and even people outside the executive branch for their views. It had the appearance of diluting the value of Jefferson's opinion, which could bruise the most easygoing ego, but, worse, it gave the impression of allowing others to meddle in a department that was Jefferson's responsibility. If he was to bear the blame for something going wrong, he at least wanted to have been the sole author of the failure.

Given this practice of seeking advice from many sources, it is strange that Washington did not meet with his cabinet as a group for much of his first term. Instead he placed problems or issues before secretaries and then discussed the matter with each individually, often at breakfast. He could also raise an issue in writing and ask for written responses. He then considered each piece of advice to form policy. For complicated issues, he would have one of his department heads draft a document for review by colleagues. Letters requiring a reply were handed off to the pertinent department head, who would draft a response for Washington's review. Jefferson later lauded the process of consultation and correspondence as keeping the president fully informed about major and minor events and the government's responses, but the method proved less satisfactory as time wore on.[21]

In part, that was because issues became more controversial, and the cabinet became more contentious. As a consequence, late in his first term Washington resorted to meetings of the entire cabinet. He also became more mindful of administrative fences and the touchiness of some in having them breached. It baffled him, because Washington had high hopes for his official family. All were highly capable, and two of his ministers were extraordinarily gifted. Yet Washington wanted something more. "By having Mr Jefferson at the Head of the Department of State, Mr Jay of the Judiciary, Hamilton of the Treasury and Knox of that of War," he said confidently, "I feel myself supported by able Co-adjutors, who harmonise extremely well together."[22] Washington did not expect his subordinates to become bosom friends, but he did want them to get along beyond mere civil courtesies. At first that seemed possible. Jefferson did not know Hamilton and Knox very well, and he had no reason to anticipate serious conflicts with them. Randolph he knew quite well. They were cousins, had been friends for years, and shared an abiding sense of trust and personal loyalty. Years before when Jefferson stopped practicing law, he had turned his clients over to Randolph.

As with any group of intelligent, confident men embarking on an important task, their efforts at first were inclined toward accommodation, the search for common ground, and the commitment to overlook grating crotchets. Washington was not merely being wishful when he saw these men in harmony.

Jefferson was the last of the secretaries to fill his post, but he was no newcomer as far as Congress was concerned. He knew many of the men in the legislature as well as the judiciary from his service in the Confederation before departing for France. Both the passing of years and changes in circumstance, though, meant some old friendships would become fragile while others would deepen. Jefferson's association with John Adams was an example of the former. They had been abroad together during the trying final days of the hapless Confederation and had shared the burdens of official business and family concerns. Yet their ideas on government never really meshed and would continue to diverge under the Constitution.

Jefferson and Madison, however, had formed their friendship on philosophical agreements so essential and unshakable that their renewed relationship evolved into one of profound sympathy and appreciation. They did not always agree or even approach problems in the same way, but they did not have to. Over the years they had developed a mode of discussion that was as compelling on paper as it was in person—a system of argument through mutual respect that always concluded with mutual understanding if not total agreement. Because these two remarkable people after 1790 found themselves together in New York and then in Philadelphia, they conversed rather than wrote about such subjects, depriving posterity of the process of thought that buffeted and shaped opposing views into rough agreements. As the two men's friendship deepened over the years, some in the Washington administration saw a political partnership rather than mutual attachment, a partnership inclined to oppose the direction of the central government. The notion of a loyal opposition was alien to that time—those who opposed the government were presumed to be in conspiracy to overthrow it—so Jefferson and Madison's relationship would become troubling, even threatening, to some, but difficult to classify and gauge as the country confronted serious challenges.[23]

In 1790, however, few knew the official Thomas Jefferson beyond his capacity for thorough work in the Confederation Congress and laudable service abroad. His authorship of the Declaration of Independence would not become common knowledge until years later, and he otherwise seemed a competent, calm man of wide acquaintance and quiet ways. Senator William Maclay took Jefferson's measure during a Senate committee meeting and was unimpressed rather than troubled. He "had a rambling, vacant look, and nothing of the firm, collected deportment which I expected would dignify the presence of a secretary or minister." But Maclay did note that during Jefferson's remarks that were "loose and rambling, . . . some even brilliant sentiments sparkled from him." A month later, Maclay was still making up his mind. Hamilton had "a very boyish, giddy manner," but "Jefferson transgresses on the extreme of stiff gentility or lofty gravity."[24] Hamilton could be difficult to fathom, but Jefferson was a hard man to know.

When Maclay thought Jefferson distant and "vacant," he did not know that the new secretary of state was sick. For more than a month from late April into early June 1790, Jefferson was suffering from one of "his periodical" headaches.[25] They almost always assailed him during times of extreme stress or after he had suffered a great loss. One of his most severe bouts had occurred after Patty's death, and almost every documented incident of this crippling malady happened during or immediately after a stressful situation. Possibly they were migraines, but whatever their cause or nomenclature, they were all but disabling. The pain was sharp and stabbing, depriving him of sleep, distracting him from work, and consigning him to darkened rooms where the light could not seep in and sear his eyes. Possibly the new job and adjusting to Washington's routine caused this event. Jefferson was bedridden for days. He wrote to his daughter in early June that the headache was at last beginning to ease, passing away as it had come. He even joked that an upcoming boat trip would possibly cause enough seasickness to distract him from his throbbing head.[26]

The headaches suggest the charming, timid man was on the inside wound quite tightly, a coiled spring of emotions that drove him to be always doing but sometimes simply drove him. To know Jefferson required breaking through his innate reserve. A young Dutchman described him as having "the shyness that accompanies true worth, which is at first disturbing and which put off those who seek to know him. Those who persist in knowing him soon discern the man of letters, the lover of natural history, Law, Statecraft, Philosophy, and the friend of mankind."[27] Others found him a bit too agreeable. Jefferson adopted Benjamin Franklin's rule "Never contradict anybody" because Jefferson had a physical revulsion over confrontation. He avoided controversy at almost all costs, which made him seem devious to his enemies and duplicitous to those who thought him in agreement only to find him later an opponent.

Jefferson's gradual acquaintance in New York City with prevalent attitudes about governance troubled him. The pomp surrounding the republican court of George Washington too closely resembled the regal ones of European monarchies. Madison had warned Jefferson about this. "The satellites & sycophants which surrounded him [Washington]," Madison muttered, "had wound up the ceremonials of government to a pitch of stateliness which nothing but his personal character could have supported, & which no character after him could ever maintain."[28]

And yet, when it came to his own living conditions, this republican purist would exhibit one of those inconvenient inconsistencies that gave his opponents cause to doubt his sincerity. He wanted the executive to conduct itself in a more republican fashion, but he was hardly austere about his own domicile. Jefferson had purchased beautiful furniture and artwork in Europe, and he found and remodeled a house to display his treasures with little heed to the cost. Jefferson occasionally admitted that he spent more money than he should, but he was one of those people for whom the getting is as exciting as the having, and it made him a compulsive spendthrift.[29]

The State Department had an $8,000 annual budget, $3,500 of which was Jefferson's salary. The balance was to pay his staff of four clerks and a half-time translator. For that amount of money and staffed with that meager manpower, Jefferson was to supervise U.S. foreign relations through remote ministers and scattered consulates, issue copyrights and patents, supervise the coinage of U.S. money (oddly not a function of the secretary of the Treasury), conduct the census, and standardize weights and measures.

For a less industrious man, Jefferson's duties at the State Department would have been overwhelming. The issue of weights and measures provided an example of the seemingly shambling and languid Virginian's attention to detail. Because other nations were already adopting standards of weight and measure to regularize their internal commerce, Congress had seized upon the idea with the feeling of already being behind the rest of the world. Congressional expectations that Jefferson would prepare a report on the matter might not have held out much hope for haste, but, in fact, the task landed squarely in Jefferson's intellectual sweet spot. He found the methodical and scientific task invigorating, and Jefferson had a thorough report ready for Washington more quickly than anyone thought possible.

The achievement, as laudable as it was, pointed to potential problems brewing in Washington's official family, where there was already one genius hard at work. Alexander Hamilton was always pressed, creased, combed, and crisp, creating the impression that intricate work of amazing detail would naturally flow from an office kept shipshape and Bristol fashion in the image of its boss; Jefferson was always rumpled, preoccupied, mumbling, and deliberate, creating the impression of a man constantly searching for a paper he had mislaid. Part of Jefferson's image was a cultivated affectation, but much of it was the actual expression of his temperament. It disguised a mind of tremendous discipline and immense power. He and Hamilton were very different, but they

might have been the perfect complement with an aggregate of intellectual force that would have made the impossible look easy. After twists
of policy and the turns of philosophy had their way, however, and the
natural egotism of supremely talented men came into play, Alexander
Hamilton and Thomas Jefferson would achieve something even more
remarkable. They would make the easy seem impossible.

9

"A Spirit of Accommodation"

In 1790 during the second spring of George Washington's presidency, influenza spread throughout the Northeast and soon laid much of New York City low. Scores of congressmen and senators fell ill, James Madison among them. Theodorick Bland, a promising Virginia congressman who had served as one of Washington's aides during the war, cousin of Thomas Jefferson and Edmund Randolph, was healthy until his bout with the flu. It killed him.

And thus the most serious illness George Washington experienced in his presidency began on Sunday, May 9. He was writing his weekly instructions to Mount Vernon and answering some stray correspondence, his usual routine on Sundays, but he had not gone to church because he did not feel well. He thought it was a bad cold. Three days later, Martha told Abigail Adams that Washington was "a little better" than the day before.[1] Martha's optimism, however, was the last cheerful report from the presidential residence.

By the time Martha was wishing her husband back to health, he was in bed laboring to breathe. The sickness could not have come at a more inconvenient time for the household. The sure-handed Tobias Lear had married his childhood sweetheart Polly Long just weeks earlier and was on his wedding trip. That left secretary William Jackson in charge, and to his credit he did not wait a second longer than alarm would allow to take control of the situation. Jackson summoned doctors, but faced with this illness rather than a removable abscess, there was little they could do. They watched helplessly as the flu became pneumonia.

Washington's decline was rapid and terrifying. Jackson summoned more doctors. Dr. Charles McKnight had served under Washington during the war and was noted for having invented the innovative "flying hospitals," whose mobility allowed for more rapid responses to wounded soldiers. McKnight did not scare easily. What he saw in the bedroom of the Broadway house that May afternoon scared him.[2] The other doctor was John Charlton. He was short, stout, and gruff, carrying the imposing manner of a man who had been a favored physician in the court of King George III before coming to America during the Revolution and remaining in New York City afterward.[3] He examined George Washington and wasted no words: The president's chances of recovery were slim to none.

William Jackson would not hear of it. That night, he sent an express rider to Philadelphia for the eminent physician John Jones, who had been Benjamin Franklin's doctor. Jackson's message to Jones urged secrecy to prevent alarm, but word soon leaked that he had been called. New York had confirmation that Washington was dying. His doctors would have agreed, and by May 15, 1790, everyone in the residence was bracing for the worst. Congressmen, senators, and cabinet members came to the house and found "every eye full of tears."[4] Early that afternoon Washington's struggle for breath had become worse than wheezing. It had the unmistakable sound of a death rattle. Dr. McKnight declared that it would soon end.

About four o'clock, Washington shivered and was suddenly drenched in his own perspiration. The doctors leaped to his bedside, all noting the time and feeling his forehead and wrists. The fever had spiked and was at last broken. Within the hour he began coughing from deep in his chest instead of the shallow rasp of before, and his cough brought up the phlegm and mucus that had been drowning him for days. His breathing evened and slowly lost its labored struggle as the sun set and the night passed. By morning he was conscious. The doctors had been helpless but were now cautiously optimistic in public and privately ecstatic over another miracle settling in on this man. Within a few days they declared him out of danger.

They all had the same prescription as Washington's appetite returned. He sat up blinking at them and mulled their instructions. He would have to follow a less vigorous work schedule and get more exercise. Washington "seemed less concerned himself as to the event, than perhaps almost any other person," as he recovered his strength, but he was realistic enough to know that each rebound from these dire episodes was less thorough than for a resilient young man.[5] Washington knew that another close call would kill him, but like McKnight he did not scare easily.

Everyone else had been terrified. Friends and family felt as if they were in a bad dream, but the political establishment had contemplated something even more profoundly troubling. A congressman wrote that "it is important to us to keep him alive as long as he can live."[6] Senator Pierce Butler observed that "too much hangs on the life of this good man," an observation echoed by Abigail Adams, who plainly stated that the government's survival depended on Washington not just alive but well.[7] David Stuart told fellow Virginian Richard Bland Lee that "his death at the present moment, would in my opinion be more fatal to the government than at any former period."[8] Congressman William Loughton Smith sighed in relief: "Our alarm has been great, equal to the danger to be apprehended from such a calamity."[9]

The new government had weathered its first year, and all its components seemed at last to be falling into place. The cabinet was functioning, Congress bickered but was establishing its procedures and passing legislation, and the Supreme Court and lesser panels had been in session. Yet the competence of excellent ministers and a functioning legislature did not make the government any less an object of suspicion for many. It inspired little affection even among its friends, who were few. George Washington, on the other hand, was the face of rectitude, calm, and steady honesty, the father of his country. Every American was his friend, and they were terrified over losing him.

Funding and assumption continued to vex Congress as James Madison led the opposition with the backing of influential Virginians. Madison's neighbors were incensed over something that had made little sense to

them before Hamilton's plans were published but seemed sinister afterward. Speculators swooping into the state to buy up seemingly worthless securities had baffled Virginians, but they soon concluded it was a
nefarious conspiracy. Those speculators were going to make a fortune
off of investments they had purchased for a song from uninformed regular citizens. Rumor and anxiety could have exaggerated perceptions of
the speculative frenzy, but even if it was widespread, there was nothing
necessarily nefarious about it. There was certainly nothing illegal about
it, and most who hoped to profit from Hamilton's proposals were honest businessmen. Yet just enough of the wrong people were involved to
make the process smell.

Madison heard the rumors of wild speculations not only in Virginia
but throughout the country, which he found distasteful, but more
alarming were warnings from Patrick Henry and others that the
federal government was using Hamilton's methods to consolidate
its power. The states, Henry and his friends said, would cease to exist
except as administrative units. These men were not sounding empty
alarms. Hamilton had privately spoken of wanting to subsume the
states, as had ultranationalists like Oliver Wolcott, Sr., who wrote his
son Oliver, Jr., serving under Hamilton as an auditor in the Treasury
Department, that "the states must be considered as corporations only,
and their laws strictly municipal." Wolcott said that "to effectuate this,
an absorption of the state debts into the national mass might be of much
advantage."[10] It was precisely what Hamilton was trying to do.

Washington remained completely aloof during these initial debates,
but most took his silence as tacit support for Hamilton's plan. At the
same time, he did not denounce Madison's motives for proposing discrimination. Rather he said he was certain that his friend was guided by
principle rather than politics. Other Virginians shared the opinion.[11]

Washington could afford to be detached because it was apparent
from the start that Madison's effort to stop part of Hamilton's plan that
funded the national debt was doomed. Madison lost the vote on it by a
wide margin, and those who did vote with him were mostly fellow Virginians, which meant that Madison had been preaching to the choir.
The assumption of state debts, however, was another matter. It was true
that some thought it seemed reasonable for the federal government to
assume the states' debts as long as direct federal taxation did not pay for

the added burden.[12] But James Madison was not so much worried about the numbers as he was about the consequences to state sovereignty.

Washington still remained silent. Hamilton had proposed the plan from that shadowy area of authority that made the Treasury the part of the executive with direct ties to the legislature, but Washington was not willing to take the executive any farther into the legislative province. He believed that domestic policy was a congressional prerogative, placing funding and assumption beyond his personal influence, if not that of the executive branch. Hamilton could have cursed his chief's concerns for constitutional punctilio. There was every chance that the entire financial plan would collapse in the face of Madison's opposition to assumption.

The House stripped assumption out of the bill, but as Madison feared, funding was passed. The bill's appearance in the Senate placed it in a friendlier venue, where Hamilton had more influence and could use it to restore assumption. Maclay noticed that when the bill was under discussion "all the President's family was there—Humphreys, Jackson, Nelson, etc." Washington's secretaries stood just outside the Senate chamber with Representative John Vining of Delaware, one of Hamilton's strongest supporters, "a standing committee," Maclay punned, "to catch members as they went in or came out."[13] The persuasive tactics worked. The Senate put assumption back in the bill and returned it to the House. Madison was waiting.

Before his illness that spring, President Washington heard plenty of complaints from outside the government about Hamilton's plans. His regular correspondents were mainly in Virginia, and among those his primary source for information remained Dr. David Stuart, the second husband to Eleanor Calvert Custis and stepfather to Martha's grandchildren. He and Eleanor had a happy marriage that produced thirteen children of their own in addition to the two Custis girls he helped raise. "Mr. Stuart goes on in the usual way," Tobias Lear chuckled, "producing a new inhabitant to the U.S. every year."[14]

Stuart was born and educated in Scotland and throughout his life was stereotypically dour and somber. He picked up the nickname "Old Melancholy," and one of the Custis girls described him as a "gloomy mortal." It was not a complaint but an observation, for Stuart was a

kind and unobtrusive stepfather. Martha was grateful that he and Eleanor had found each other, and Washington counted Stuart as more than
a close friend. He was one of the few people who never hesitated to give
Washington bad news, and whether born of his personality or his candid assessment of local opinion, Stuart usually had plenty of bad news
to convey. He once told Washington about complaints that the president's "bows were more distant and stiff" than when he had been simply George Washington of Mount Vernon. Washington bristled at that:
If his bows were stiff it was due to age rather than attitude, he sniffed.[15]
Old Melancholy might have smiled over the explanation.

The doings of Congress that spring of 1790 disturbed Stuart more
than any talk of monarchical levees and stiff bows. Virginians were
angry, and Stuart wanted Washington to know why. In March he wrote
about Virginia senator William Grayson's death with the news that
plans were afoot to replace him with Patrick Henry. Stuart did not
think Henry would accept, but that did not change the fact of Virginia's
growing hostility toward the central government. Even those "who
were warm Supporters of the government, are changing their sentiments," Stuart reported. Recent discussions in the House about abolish-
ing the slave trade were an understandable provocation. Hamilton's
financial program, in addition, was eroding support.[16]

Washington's attention was most likely arrested by Stuart's report
that Virginians were almost universally opposed to assumption and that
James Madison's opposition to it had made him popular beyond measure.[17]

Stuart's letters finally goaded Washington to reveal how he felt about
Hamilton's plans. He had thought about assumption in his customary
way of weighing all sides, but lengthy conversations with Hamilton had
likely convinced him of the idea's wisdom. Washington told Stuart that
Congress understandably thrashed and pondered over an issue with
so many possible ramifications, but the war against Britain had been
a common cause and everyone should help pay for it. Washington
declared that in the long run "under proper restrictions, & scrutiny
into accounts [it] will be found, I conceive, to be just."[18] Beyond that
statement—and it was privately uttered—he would not go. It was Congress's decision to make, and he would abide by it.

Hamilton, however, could not abide by it. While Washington was on the mend, Hamilton had already done some housecleaning and restaffing. Hamilton elevated Tench Coxe from his current post as an assistant secretary, to the second man in the Treasury. Coxe had been a member of the Confederation Congress with Madison and had many acquaintances in the current Congress, whom Hamilton hoped to persuade.[19] Even so, Coxe was a strange choice and one that Hamilton would later regret.[20]

Every trick was for naught, though. Fixed in his belief that restoring American credit required the entire program, not just funding, Hamilton ignored advice to get what he could and secure assumption later. Stymied and frustrated beyond reason, he abandoned all pretense of calm deliberation and told his friends to make any deal they could to secure passage of assumption in the House. Washington did not know about this, though he likely heard the rumors that Pennsylvania would cast deciding votes in return for the permanent capital being located in Philadelphia. If so, the casual use of the residency question as a bargaining chip would have troubled him. He might have shared the view of disgusted congressmen made cynical by "negotiations, cabals, meetings, plots & counterplots" that seemed to be controlling the government. "Such transactions," lamented one, "have more influence on the public business than fair argument & an attention to the general good."[21]

In spite of misgivings, the permanent capital's location appeared to be the only bargaining lever that could secure passage of assumption. Hamilton met with Robert Morris for a dawn stroll along the battery. The Treasury secretary privately promised to support Pennsylvania as quid pro quo for assumption, but he apparently could not line up enough support in the House, and he switched his support to the Potomac to secure votes from Virginia and Maryland.[22] With wheels turning within wheels, bargains half-promised here and half-realized there, and complications growing more complex by the day, Hamilton struggled in a web of pacts and pledges largely of his own making. It was mid-June, and Jemmy Madison still had the votes to stop him.

On June 19, 1790, Thomas Jefferson arrived at Washington's residence on Broadway for an appointment but found Hamilton waiting outside. Hamilton was a miserable sight, "sombre, haggard, & dejected beyond description, even his dress uncouth & neglected." Whether Hamilton was waiting for Jefferson or the meeting was by chance is difficult to say. If Hamilton appeared as Jefferson later described, it may have been affected.

Jefferson recalled that there on the street Hamilton had talked about the significance of assumption for the health of the nation. Without assumption, Hamilton predicted, New England states might leave the Union. Failing to secure assumption, Hamilton said, would force him to resign. In short, the initiative's importance was beyond measure, holding the fate of the cohesive federal compact as well as Washington's official family in the balance. It begged for a compromise to see it through, and since southerners formed the most resolute opposition, Jefferson was crucial to showing them the light.[23] Jefferson listened but apparently did not divulge his thoughts, which were more developed and insightful than many people would have known. At most he declared that his first impression of assumption was not favorable. The stance was consistent with Jefferson's concern that extensive government debt burdened future generations unfairly, binding heirs to the tabs run up by their fathers.[24]

The truth was that he well understood the complicated recommendations Hamilton had made in his *Report on Public Credit*. In fact, he had previously written so cogently about the debt that Hamilton had used some of Jefferson's ideas in his report. If anything, Jefferson's worries were more practical than abstract that June morning, and far more political than economic. The dangerous divisions in Congress hinted at the very disunion of Hamilton's warning. Just a week before this sidewalk meeting with Hamilton, Jefferson had written to friend George Mason about assumption. "It [is] necessary," he concluded, "to give as well as take in a government like ours."[25]

Jefferson suggested that Hamilton and Madison work out a solution by meeting privately, possibly over a private dinner at his rented quarters on Maiden Lane the following day, June 20, 1790. Hamilton agreed, and Jefferson seems to have been certain that Madison would as well. The instant agreement about a dinner party strains credibility, though, and upon close examination everything about the meeting outside the presidential residence compounds too much coincidence. Jefferson and Madison had already been in contact with Tench Coxe, Hamilton's number two man at Treasury, two weeks before the dinner party meeting was presumably arranged that morning on Broadway as a spontaneous event.[26] In short, Jefferson and Madison seem to have been working for a compromise much earlier than the one purportedly fashioned at the dinner party.

According to his account, Jefferson acted as mediator at the dinner with Hamilton, and the results were most promising. Madison did not agree to abandon his objections to assumption, but he would curtail his efforts to stop it. Jefferson suggested that establishing the permanent capital on the Potomac could soothe southern members. That observation further suggested that Richard Bland Lee and Alexander White from Potomac districts in Virginia, and Daniel Carroll and George Gale from Maryland districts across the river could be persuaded to abstain when the Senate again sent assumption back to the House as an amendment to the funding bill. The three realized Pennsylvania's support on residency for the Potomac was necessary, and Hamilton was given the task of working through Robert Morris to secure those votes.[27]

By this account, the dinner on June 20, 1790, at Maiden Lane was a historic event and marks the first significant compromise in the history of the federal government. Whether it happened just the way Jefferson recalled or was a less ad hoc series of negotiations does not detract from the obvious fact that some sort of bargain took place that salvaged Hamilton's plan and placed the permanent capital on the Potomac. It was a first in the American government, but it would be the last for the men who made the arrangement.

Washington's involvement is hard to gauge in the concluding stages of the drama that linked residency to assumption. His secretary William Jackson did quietly continue to line up votes,[28] and many believed Washington was the prime mover in efforts to place the capital on the Potomac, a plan that was not widely popular. William Maclay was certain that "the President of the United States has (in my opinion) had a great influence in this business. The game was played by him and his adherents of Virginia and Maryland, between New York and Philadelphia."[29] The freezing out of Pennsylvania could have caused these sour assessments from a sour personality, but Maclay and other Pennsylvanians had a point. The Potomac Navigation Company, with its ambitious canal project, would benefit from the proposal, and Washington himself had investments in lands that would thrive in the shadow of a new capital.[30]

Everything about residency at first went according to plan. The Senate passed a bill on July 1, 1790, establishing the temporary capital in Philadelphia for ten years and after that moving it permanently to a place of George Washington's choosing on the Potomac. The vote was close, however, at 14–12, which gave opponents in the lower chamber hope. When the bill arrived in the House, New Englanders joined New York efforts to cut out Philadelphia as the temporary capital and keep it in New York. The city was keenly unhappy about losing the capital. Citizens had spent a fortune on plans for a new presidential mansion overlooking the Battery, convinced that such a project would anchor the government in New York. Newspaper editorials extolled the virtues of the city and denigrated the rural primitivism of the Potomac.

The masterstroke of linking residency and assumption proved decisive, however, for even New England was finally willing to abide the government's move south if it meant the end of state debt. Outmaneuvered and then outnumbered, New York forlornly watched Congress pass the residency bill on July 9, 1790, and Washington signed it on July 16. The law gave him almost complete authority over the selection of the site and the planning for the nation's capital. He immediately began putting things in motion.

In the meantime, the House received the funding bill sent from the Senate with the amendment authorizing assumption of state debts. Madison voted against it with the private observation that "the crisis demands a spirit of accommodation to a certain extent."[31] The fated four did their part by not voting at all, which meant that funding passed with assumption intact on July 26, 1790. About $500,000 more than the original plan's sum was slated for Virginia, and an additional $800,000 was promised to heretofore recalcitrant North Carolina. The spirit of accommodation did not come cheap, but Hamilton had his financial program.

And George Washington had his Potomac capital, at least if he could ensure that it was built in ten years. Beginning that fall, he consulted with Madison and Jefferson to choose the site and plan construction.

The Virginia connection between them was important, making them eager to remove any uncertainty about residency, and for a while questions surrounding the new federal district brought Jemmy Madison back to prominence in Washington's circle.

They were vigilant to widely expressed hopes in Pennsylvania that the decade in Philadelphia would make it impossible to move the government elsewhere. As the three conferred in New York City, the blank pages of plans yet to be made and the daunting tasks of building a brand-new city in the middle of nowhere were enough to make the most confident man cringe. Rather than turning to Congress for minor—as well as major—decisions, Washington planned to use every particle of power given him by the Residence Act. He and his advisers knew that asking Congress about the time of day could open the residency question all over again, and doing that was sure to invite steps to block the move to the Potomac. Jefferson and Madison recommended to Washington the appointment of commissioners to handle particulars.[32]

Of several sites vying to become the new federal district, Washington preferred the area around Georgetown, Maryland. That October he rode there to meet with town leaders. His visit was touted as a tour of the broad expanse mentioned in the Residence Act, a relatively large span that stretched from Hagerstown, Maryland, down to Alexandria, Virginia. As Washington traveled the area, locals entertained him, hoping that lavish hospitality would sway his decision, but they were wasting their time. He had already settled on a tract east of Georgetown. His pretending that the matter was still undecided was not unscrupulous but instead stemmed from Washington's thrift. He wanted the government to scoop up the land cheaply before an announcement drove prices up. He enlisted a couple of locals to serve as secret purchasing agents who would acquire land before landowners could guess his decision. Finally on January 21, 1791, President Washington announced the location of the district.

Washington named three men, whom he knew and trusted, to act as essentially unpaid commissioners—they would receive a six-dollar per diem when working on district business—who would oversee the remaining land purchases, the surveying and laying out of lots, and the construction of the public buildings. He called on Thomas Johnson, a well-known Maryland jurist who had been in the Continental Congress, had served as Maryland's first governor after independence, and had worked with Washington for years to improve navigation on the Potomac. Washington also appointed Daniel Carroll of Maryland, who, like Johnson, was a close friend and had been a fellow delegate to the Constitutional Convention. Carroll belonged to one of Maryland's founding families that was quite thick on the ground in Maryland, and especially in the proposed district. One of Carroll's nephews lived there and was trouble waiting to happen.

Finally, Washington named in-law Dr. David Stuart as the third member of the commission. Stuart's candid messages about political events would now be augmented by assessments of the federal project on the Potomac. Indeed, this sole Virginian on the commission became Washington's eyes and ears as the new capital took shape. The three men made their first decision at their initial meeting. The name for the capital was to be "Washington."

For the task of planning the city, Washington inexplicably appointed French engineer and Revolutionary veteran Major Pierre L'Enfant. Almost any of the other candidates would have been better choices—not necessarily for ability but for temperament. The fact that L'Enfant was available seems to have been a paramount reason for his selection, but he also had powerful advocates, including Hamilton, Knox, and Robert Morris. L'Enfant had been wounded in the Revolution as well, which would have raised him in the estimation of Washington. L'Enfant did not, however, have any experience in city planning. More than anything, his appointment marked haste as the order of the day.

Washington, Jefferson, Madison, and the commissioners knew that speed was essential to getting the project started. Everybody, in fact, knew this, except for the man on the ground who was responsible for getting the project started. Early on, Pierre L'Enfant showed a deliberative bent that proved to be the first sign of trouble. Not only did he move slowly; sometimes he did not move at all. Mercurial and almost immediately over his budget, he refused to take advice, much less direction, from the commissioners. Jefferson, like Washington, was an experienced surveyor, and he provided L'Enfant with maps and charts of European cities and drew up a plan of his own. Jefferson hoped to speed the process in this way, but his plan also reflected his desire for republican simplicity.[33]

Washington, however, loved the plan L'Enfant finally produced in August 1791, one that mildly astonished Jefferson and the commissioners. The grandeur of the project exceeded anything they had imagined, and distances were more immense than they thought wise. The symbolism of physically separating Congress from the "Presidential Palace" was not lost on anyone, but the span of that separation laid out by L'Enfant was staggering. After studying the proposed executive residence, David Stuart noted that its grounds were "too extensive" and more appropriate for "a Despotic government." Washington bristled. He defended the scope of the grounds by saying an impressive image was imperative. As for the grand vistas and large distances between buildings, they served the practical purpose of allowing expansion while also projecting power.[34] For Jefferson this was precisely the objection. That Washington did not see it that way was another hint of their diverging attitudes about the federal presence in both symbol and form. That, too, would eventually cause concern.

L'Enfant, however, was the immediate problem. He increasingly resisted direction and defied authority. His artist's temperament could only be indulged for so long. He refused to meet with the commissioners and delayed crucial chores such as laying out streets and selecting sites for public buildings. He had, in short, already made himself unpopular. Then he did the unthinkable.

A partially built house within the district belonged to Daniel Carroll of Duddington, nephew of the commissioner of the same name. Shortly before the land for the district was chosen, Carroll started the house on a lot south of Jenkins Hill, the place designated for the Capitol. L'Enfant informed Carroll that the house protruded into the planned New Jersey Avenue and would have to be torn down. Carroll refused, and L'Enfant threatened to have his workmen raze the property. When Carroll rushed to Annapolis to get an injunction against L'Enfant, the Frenchman abruptly begin demolishing the house. Carroll was incensed, but he showed remarkable forbearance in appealing to the commissioners rather than taking matters into his own hands. Having coped with L'Enfant's dismissive manner for months, the commissioners were equally angry, but before they could act, L'Enfant personally supervised the final demolition of Carroll's house.

Washington received this news "with real mortification."[35] Jefferson told Washington that every explanation L'Enfant had offered was unacceptable. Yet when Washington interceded, he did so gently. He explained to L'Enfant that he simply could not go about tearing down houses and that he must submit to the authority of the commissioners. Washington also placated young Carroll to prevent him from suing in Maryland civil courts. L'Enfant soon replied to Washington with a petulant defense. Most troubling was L'Enfant's gloating explanation that he had quickly destroyed the house to preempt any legal remedy Carroll secured. It made clear that L'Enfant knew American courts had the power to protect property, but he did not feel they could restrain him any more than the commissioners had. When L'Enfant threatened to tear down another house, this one belonging to Commissioner Daniel Carroll's brother-in-law, the commissioners finally stepped in to stop him.

Washington urged Jefferson to meet with L'Enfant. The secretary of state plainly stated that L'Enfant must submit himself to the commissioners' authority. L'Enfant plainly refused. In the shadow of that impasse Washington consulted with Jefferson, Madison, Hamilton, and Randolph in a desperate search for a solution to a bizarre situation. Meanwhile, L'Enfant was not in the least abashed, and he continued to complain about the interference of the commissioners despite repeated instructions to follow their orders. "The conduct of Majr L'Enfant and those employed under him, astonishes me beyond measure!" Washington finally exclaimed in frustration.[36] He sent Tobias Lear to L'Enfant's Philadelphia quarters for a private chat, but the meeting was worse than chilly. L'Enfant was dismissive with Lear, an insult that, by extension, touched George Washington.[37] The following day the president told Jefferson to fire Pierre L'Enfant.

In the aftermath, Washington worried that the touchy Frenchman and his assistants would publish their version of events to cast the president and the commissioners in a negative light, but L'Enfant behaved with laudable restraint and loyalty. He never disclosed any bitterness over his treatment, and only after Washington's death did he mention his experience by insisting that others had misled the president. "I suffered and submitted to all," he wrote two years after Washington died, "out of respect for him."[38]

In the years that followed, L'Enfant was never able to tame his volatile temperament, and all of his subsequent employers sooner or later had to give up by letting him go. He ended up impoverished and reliant on a dwindling number of friends in his last years. In 1825, when he was dying, some of them took him in, a family whose mistress had been a child when he had destroyed Daniel Carroll of Duddington's house on New Jersey Avenue so many years before. She was, in fact, Daniel Carroll's daughter, an unlikely friend, but she made him comfortable as he died in the district, the place George Washington and his associates had only imagined. It would become the place Pierre L'Enfant had seen.

10

"The Sensation of a Philosophic Mind"

Henry Knox was the unlucky man in Washington's cabinet fated to live in the shadow of Alexander Hamilton and Thomas Jefferson. He was neither dim nor dull and had read widely as a youth, embracing Enlightenment idealism as avidly as any Founder. In ordinary company, all these facets of a man would have made him seem capable, even talented, possibly an intellectual with a good head for philosophy—someone who knew how to get things done in a practical world. But Jefferson and Hamilton were far from ordinary, and Knox could never match them in their originality of thought or their boundless energy. So the man who was neither dim nor dull seemed to be precisely those things at the time. Worse, he has seemed to be those things ever since, when he is noticed at all.

Washington did not see it that way. Of all of the men in his official family, he knew Henry Knox best. Washington relied on the stellar lights of his administration for expert advice, but he planned to rely on good old reliable Henry Knox for something else. Washington could confide in Knox about anything with greater ease than with any other man because of what they had done together in the most titanic event of George Washington's life, which was the American Revolution.

Knox was with him at the beginning, suffered with him through the darkest days, was quick-witted when everybody needed laughter, and was silent when quietude was at a premium. He was at Valley Forge when all the world was ice and at Morristown when smallpox threatened to destroy the army the Redcoats could not. He was at West Point when Benedict Arnold's treachery was discovered and at Yorktown when Lord Cornwallis called it quits and lost the war. He was at Fraunces Tavern in lower Manhattan when General Washington had said good-bye as a prelude to laying down his sword, a gathering where men who had stared down death simply stared, their throats tight and their voices husky and halting. The brilliant Mr. Jefferson had never donned a uniform, and the sparkling Colonel Hamilton had by then replaced his with lawyerly broadcloth. But General Henry Knox was there from beginning to end, and General George Washington did not see a man dim and dull. He saw an American hero.

Washington first met Henry Knox in Boston when assuming command of the Continental Army. The young man's earnestness had immediately impressed him. Before the Revolution, Knox was a bookseller by trade if not by choice. His father's untimely death had required him to leave the Boston Latin School and apprentice in a bookshop when he was little more than a child. But Knox had immersed himself in the store's stock, and his studies stoked a native intelligence. He became especially interested in military history, and specifically the use of artillery. Reading became a form of escape for him—a way to stop thinking about his family's straitened financial situation, if only temporarily. At all other times his jovial nature disguised a pathological dread of poverty, something that never left him. No matter how affluent Knox became, he would always fear losing everything. Sometimes it was almost a self-fulfilling prophecy.

The prospect of penury was the only thing that scared Knox, though, and he early earned a reputation for physical recklessness. His Boston was not Beacon Hill gentility but boisterous streets with roving gangs: places where a boy's nimble wit and quicker fists were the weapons of choice—the latter much preferred. He had a way of turning up at public disorders. He was a witness to the Boston Massacre, and some accounts place him at the Boston Tea Party, but his level of participation is shadowy. With the limited prospects of a bookseller, it is little wonder that when he took an interest in plump Lucy Flucker, her family looked askance at him. Worse, as the troubles with Britain intensified in Boston to make it the center of colonial agitation, Knox was an eager revolutionary. That was the final straw for Lucy's Loyalist family. They did not approve. She did not care.

Henry Knox became a newlywed on the eve of the Revolution. He was tall and sandy-haired with a way about him that charmed Lucy, who always called him "Harry" and was selflessly devoted to him for the rest of their lives. She did not mind that he was in the thick of things. There was an air of daring about her Harry, as when he accidentally blew two fingers off his left hand with a hunting rifle the year before their marriage. He nonchalantly tied up the mangled digits with a handkerchief until he could visit a doctor to be sewed up.

He and a friend, the silversmith Paul Revere, worked out a ruse to deceive British soldiers vigilant for sedition. When Redcoats loitered in Knox's bookshop to eavesdrop, Revere would drop by to quarrel with him about loyalty to the Crown. Revere was always the loyal subject and Knox the disgruntled colonial. The British trusted Paul Revere, who was highly active in the Sons of Liberty, while distracting themselves over the bookseller, a decoy.[1] By the time of Lexington and Concord, this type of playacting had put Knox among those at the top of an arrest list, and he was in danger the moment the British recovered from the shock of the skirmish. He and Lucy fled Boston in disguise. There was something about her Harry.

Knox's knowledge of artillery was bolstered by his pre-war membership in gun clubs that gave him practical experience. It came in handy at Bunker (Breed's) Hill before Washington arrived, and by the time the grave Virginian pulled into Cambridge, Knox was highly valued by General Artemas Ward, the man who turned over the ragged army to Washington. The twenty-five-year-old New Englander was as tall as Washington and had a welcoming manner. In those first tense days, it was an endearing quality noticed by the stranger from the South who had also noticed the general chill of other, resentful New Englanders. "General Washington," Knox told Lucy, "fills his place with vast ease and dignity."[2]

The friendliness Washington felt toward Knox became soaring affection after the bookseller pulled off one of the most daring stunts of the war. He took a party of men to captured Fort Ticonderoga on Lake Champlain and brought its cannons to Boston. The simplicity of that sentence disguises the audacity of the deed. Nobody else in the world but George Washington and Henry Knox thought it possible to haul heavy artillery over three hundred miles of terrible terrain with ice-skimmed rivers adding an awful variety to the trip.

Washington had his doubts, but he figured nothing would be lost in the trying, and Knox had developed a first-class case of hero worship that would have goaded him to drive artillery through the gates of hell for His Excellency General Washington. The route from Champlain to Boston was a near facsimile of the gates of hell, and news of Knox's approach with his batteries was so delightfully shocking that it marked one of just two or three times during the eight years of war that Washington almost wept. Installed on Dorchester Heights overlooking the British positions, the cannons threw British general William Howe into a panicked evacuation that lifted the occupation of Boston, boosted American morale, and bought the Continental Army time. George Washington would always remember the moment he galloped out on the road from Cambridge and found Henry Knox shouting orders, directing traffic, and beaming over those great big beautiful guns.

The two men remained close when Washington resigned his commission and returned to Virginia. For about six months after Washington left the service, Knox succeeded to his imminent post as the senior American officer, but that was only because the army was all he knew aside from selling books, and he would not return to his shop. The tug of nostalgia for the finest hours of his life was strong on Henry Knox, which was why he founded the Society of the Cincinnati for former Revolutionary War officers, and he seems to have realized that nothing else he would ever do could match the excitement and achievement of those eight years when he and Washington had taken on the most powerful thing in the world with their nimble wit and quicker fists—the latter much preferred.

In 1785, when Knox became the Confederation's secretary of war, it foreshadowed the narrowing corridors of his public service. He was at the head of a War Department that had plenty of potential wars but no way to fight them. He had to worry about feisty Britons still on the ground in the Northwest, cope with Indians angry over American encroachment, and attempt reforms of state militias, the first (and only) line of defense for a sprawling country with a thousand enemies and only squinting creditors for friends. He grew to despise the Congress for its parsimony and to loathe the state governments for their stubborn refusal to make their militias a viable, unified fighting force. He became a thorough nationalist, a strong supporter of the Constitution, and—for some, including Madison—the preferred candidate to be Washington's vice president. That would have suited Washington just fine, and when it did not happen, he hoped at least to keep Knox in the government. President Washington needed a friend for this new thankless task the way General Washington had needed one for the thankless task in Cambridge almost fifteen years earlier.

The years had made Knox and his wife heavy, Lucy to the point of obesity (Nabby Adams whispered, "Her size is enormous; I am frightened when I look at her"), but George Washington could remember when Lucy was pleasingly plump and Knox strong and athletic. Washington would always see beneath the jowls and under the girth a blond, athletic young man on the road to Cambridge, Lucy's undaunted Harry with his stumpy left hand waving the way for those cannons, ready to war down the lion.[3]

Both Knox and Washington knew that good old reliable Harry could never say no to his hero. Henry and Lucy had named their latest child (of thirteen) George Washington Knox, the most recent tribute of a never-ending admiration. But nobody could have guessed that it was a mistake for him to say yes. As the head of a large family, Knox's old worries about money dogged him as he struggled to get by on a government salary that barely met expenses. Financial opportunities would distract him from his work at the War Department at crucial times, diminishing his primary worth to Washington as a dependable counselor always at hand.

The work held few of the charms and none of the excitement of that earlier time. Heading the War Department in the Washington administration would be taxing and unrewarding, colleagues in the cabinet would be carping and contentious, and the man who once had feared only losing his money would become fearful of almost everything else, too, especially of being dim and dull.

★ ★ ★

The one exception to the tedium for Knox was the quest for peaceful frontiers. During his service to the Confederation, he was forced by the government's empty coffers to find economical ways to deal with unhappy Indians, and he had stretched his thinking for a solution that was not only cheap but humane. His plan was to embrace the central Enlightenment idea that all humans were not only capable of improvement but worthy of it. "How different would be the sensation of a philosophic mind," Knox rhapsodized, "to reflect that instead of exterminating a part of the human race by our modes of population that we had persevered through all difficulties and at last had imparted our Knowledge of cultivation, and the arts, to the Aboriginals of the Country by which the source of future life and happiness had been preserved and extended."[4] In such a world, by Knox's reckoning, Indians would be neighbors instead of aliens—farmers just like the white Americans across the way, helping to clear land and raise barns, practicing the arts of peace on an Edenic frontier. Civilization rather than extermination was rational and kind. President Washington liked the sound of it, even if his experience on the frontier was more informed than the Boston bookseller's. As always with a Knox plan, however, there was nothing to lose in trying.

The land from the Great Lakes to Spanish Louisiana and Florida was in turmoil as land speculators encouraged settlers to move deeper into the wilderness. When Indians violently resisted these encroachments, settlers appealed to state and national governments for protection. In addition to the complication posed by the British occupation of forts in the Northwest, British fur traders wanted to keep their trapping grounds free of settlers. This made the northwestern and the Kentucky frontiers especially volatile, and the bulk of the nation's meager military forces were stationed there. When Washington took office, however, the South became a pressing problem. Spanish trade provided Indians with guns and ammunition, making the two powerful Indian confederations of Creeks and Cherokees armed as well as angry.

White settlement alarmed southern Indians, but Georgia's practice of selling Indian land to speculators enraged them. The Creeks were readying to make war.[5] Faced with belligerent events outpacing his benign plans, Knox considered a preemptive military strike against the Creeks, but Washington correctly gauged a war as the last thing the cash-strapped Treasury needed. Nevertheless, there was no denying that Knox was quite correct that the government's most immediate concern was the possibility of a full-scale Indian war in the South. If the new constitutional Union could not protect its citizens, citizens would have little use for either the Constitution or the Union it created.

Washington wanted to send commissioners to the Creeks, including his secretary David Humphreys to emphasize the initiative's importance. They were told to negotiate peace and regularize relations with a formal treaty rather than merely engage in the traditional presentation of gifts and exchange of vague pledges.

The commissioners left for the South to meet with Creek leader Alexander McGillivray, whose father was a Scot and his mother half-Creek and half-white. McGillivray possessed enormous power as part of the influential Wind Clan, and he augmented the influence of lineage with achievements that made him something of an emperor over his people. Canny at weighing chances and judging odds, he balanced ties to West Florida's Spanish government with a brisk trade from Panton, Leslie and Company, a British firm in Pensacola. McGillivray was not yet forty, but Creeks already called him the "Great Beloved Man."[6]

Because he was known to be worldly, McGillivray seemed a reasonable man to Americans who had never met him, such as Henry Knox and George Washington. The very fact of his consolidated authority promised a more coherent settlement of differences than was likely with the fragmented and hopelessly hostile Indians of the Northwest. The American emissaries the government sent in 1789, however, were woefully uninformed about the man and his temperament. Their abysmal behavior when they met McGillivray and other Creek representatives in Georgia doomed the talks in short order. Humphreys's arrogance and condescension was most offensive, and the meeting broke up before anything meaningful occurred. McGillivray later referred to Humphreys as "that puppy."[7] It was that bad.

By the end of 1789, tensions on the Georgia-Creek frontier were more volatile than in anyone's memory, and Washington resolved to try diplomacy again, this time by inviting a Creek delegation to New York for direct talks.[8] Knox was rather excited by the prospect of laying out his humane solution that he had shared with George Washington in July 1789.

Knox wanted to assimilate American Indians into European American culture through a "Civilization Plan" that would establish schools to teach Indian children English and the rudiments of white culture. Agents living among Indians would teach horticulture, and the government would supply domesticated livestock to smooth the transition. Assimilation had a dual advantage. Because farming would require less land than hunting and gathering, Indians could sell their excess acreage to the government. Second, as the frontier settled into civilization it would require a much smaller (and less expensive) military to keep the peace. Knox championed the idea with such verve that Washington gradually succumbed to its allure, especially since it paid obeisance to Enlightenment notions of rationalism and human rights.

Washington's own experiences with Indians made him wary, though. He had known Indians all his life, but those of his childhood in Tidewater Virginia were different from their frontier counterparts. During his military service in the Ohio Country he had come to know others, the most important an Oneida/Seneca British ally named Tanacharison, whom the British called the Half King. Because he hated the French for killing his father, the Half King was one of the few friends the British and their colonists had in the wilderness where the French were erecting forts to challenge Britain's title.

The Half King was one of Washington's guides during the ill-fated expedition against the French at Fort Duquesne in 1754 and had urged Washington to ambush a French encampment. The deed was a disaster that touched off the French and Indian War, but it was the Half King's behavior in its immediate aftermath that firmly defined Washington's opinion of American Indians. The Half King had walked toward the fallen French commander while saying, "Thou art not dead yet father," before calmly cleaving the Frenchman's skull with several blows of a hatchet. He scooped up the officer's brains with his hands and squeezed them through his fingers. In the words of one account, he "washed his Hands with them."[9] George Washington was twenty-two years old when he saw this happen. He had no quaint illusions about Indians.

When it came to Indians, then, Knox was a romantic and Washington a realist, but their dream of creating harmony through shared customs was born of good motives, and little blame can be attached to them in wishing for a better world. In 1790, the only alternative to Knox's plan was to remove the Indians from violent encounters by driving them west, away from white settlement. Washington hoped to use the humane approach as a basis for negotiations, and for that reason alone Knox's ideas seemed best. If McGillivray would come to New York City, they were certain that this approach as a basis for negotiations would appeal to the reasonable, cosmopolitan Creek leader.

As it happened, it was a propitious time for progress in American Indian relations, but not because of anything the U.S. government had done. Alexander McGillivray sensed it was time to talk to the Americans because he had heard rumors that Great Britain and Spain were on the verge of war over their competing claims for North America's upper Pacific coast. McGillivray knew that if war did break out, securing trade goods from his Scottish partners in Spanish Pensacola could prove difficult. Other changes could also create major inconveniences. Suddenly the United States seemed attractive as a potential counterweight in European quarrels.

Alexander McGillivray and twenty-six Creek headmen set out for New York. McGillivray traveled in a stylish carriage as other Creeks rode on horseback through Georgia and up the coast. Communities along the way turned out for the exotic sight of important Indians in peaceful procession, and town fathers showered them with platitudes of fealty and friendship. If the novelty of these receptions wore thin by journey's end, the Creek headmen were only at the start of the social whirl. New York City greeted them with parties, dinners, and parades.

Washington had set the stage for a grand agreement, and he wanted nothing to spoil it. More than any other initiative in his first two years of office, he saw the possible pacification of Indians as a personal quest—really his first important policy initiative as president.[10] The government arranged for most Creeks to be lodged at a fashionable tavern, but Knox wanted to keep McGillivray away from foreign influences, especially Spain's José Ignacio de Viar and British agent George Beckwith. Knox took McGillivray in as a houseguest at his residence on Broadway, only a few doors down from the president's home.[11]

Meanwhile, social events seemed to overshadow all official negotiations as the Saint Andrew's Society recognized McGillivray's Scottish ancestry by making him an honorary member. The Tammany Society held a grand event for all the headmen. The Creeks fascinated the ladies of New York, including Abigail Adams. They were staying close to the Adamses' residence at Richmond Hill, and she and the vice president had the Creeks over for dinner and watched their ceremonial dances from the windows of the mansion. A headman conferred on Abigail the name "Mammea," as he took her "by the Hand, bowd his Head, and bent his knee."[12] She had moved in the finest salons of Paris and the most fashionable parlors of London, but she admitted she had never seen anything quite so magnificent as these exotic visitors from the South.

Behind all the pomp and pageantry real negotiations proceeded between Knox and McGillivray as Jefferson helped and Washington kept a close watch on the proposed terms. In the agreement that would become the Treaty of New York, the Creeks ceded lands that Georgia had already claimed but in return were granted an annuity. Secret provisions known only to the negotiators and the Senate made McGillivray a U.S. brigadier general with an annual salary of $1,200. Lesser sums went to other Creek headmen. The treaty included references to Knox's civilization program—mainly clauses about schools and instruction in agriculture and providing livestock—but McGillivray does not seem to have troubled himself over the cultural implications of this section, and Knox apparently did not put too fine a point on it. The belief that all would come in the fullness of time evidently guided American attitudes at this crucial moment. The Creeks hoped that they had tied themselves to another friend to play against their Spanish and British ones, and the expectation constrained their behavior.

The Treaty of New York was an impressive agreement, despite its coarser appeals to vanity with foolish army commissions and outright bribes, for it was an attempt to set a new tone in relations between the extant people of a place who found themselves unwittingly part of a new political order. Everyone at least acted as if they realized this. There was an impressive signing ceremony in the Senate chamber and a celebratory banquet with pipes smoked and gifts exchanged afterward. The Creeks had moved like lions through New York society for three weeks, and when they finally headed home they closed an episode that would never be revisited the same way and in the same spirit by any other Indians in America, because relations would never be this hopeful again. It was Henry Knox's most impressive achievement.

It was also, sadly, emblematic of a career that after the Revolution never managed an achievement without a blemish. The tall man in charge and his stately advisers had spoken kind words and uttered seeming truths, but then they were a thousand miles away. The Creek delegation returned to a place where settlers were still yoking their wagons to dray horses and sharpening their axes to put up fences. Creeks could look at their Great Beloved Man in doubt, if not outright despair. Alexander McGillivray was doubtless great and beloved, but he was also unmistakably a prisoner of hard drink, often tipsy and some-times roaring drunk. In New York City, his hosts had been occasionally embarrassed by McGillivray's drinking. Frail from alcoholism, he was consumed by other illnesses as well, possibly venereal. He died just two years after the grand procession and great ceremony of the treaty that was to protect his people while guaranteeing their integration into the white community. In its aftermath Georgians continued their steady march into Creek lands, and clashes broke out here and there over real injuries and imagined wrongs. The reality matched neither Knox's nor McGillivray's vision of cooperation. Henry Knox continued to wish for a world of peace and harmony, and it would have been lovely if only it could have been, but then he was a thousand miles away.

While the tension between Britain and Spain gave the Washington ad-ministration an opportunity to calm down the Creeks, it also presented the United States with its first significant foreign policy problem. As such, it should have been the primary concern of Secretary of State Jef-ferson and, as a contingency should diplomacy fail, of Secretary of War Knox. That it did not work out that way augured later problems in the cabinet.

News of the confrontation between England and Spain reached the United States and Canada in June 1790. Lord Dorchester immediately sent George Beckwith to New York, presumably to gauge American attitudes about a war between Spain and Great Britain. The absence of formal diplomatic relations made it imperative to establish a method to communicate. Yet Beckwith could have been sent to contact pro-British interests in the United States. High officials in London and more than a few Americans thought reconciliation between Britain and her former colonies would occur when the American government collapsed. Beckwith made five journeys to the United States for Dorchester (and by extension the British cabinet) between 1787 and 1792. Beckwith knew how to be a secret agent from his intelligence activities in the latter part of the Revolutionary War, when the British occupation of New York City allowed him to make Loyalist friends there and beyond.

Nothing of a similar nature occurred on the other side of the Atlantic. Gouverneur Morris endured snub after snub from the British government in London, but he never guessed that his hosts' recalcitrance stemmed from information gleaned by Beckwith from Hamilton. This treatment only sharpened the point that Morris's appointment had been a mistake. Washington's choice of him had seemed an unnecessary insult to Thomas Jefferson at the time, and the people Washington had consulted with about Morris indicated that the president was more interested in hearing from those who would only reinforce a decision already made rather than intrude with countervailing views. Madison deduced this and was troubled by it, one of the first instances of his being troubled by something Washington did as president.

Gouverneur Morris tried to find ways the United States could benefit from the dispute between Britain and Spain. Perhaps Americans could bargain with Britain or Spain for neutrality. He continued efforts to engage high-ranking British officials in talks about trade, but he rightly thought that the war scare warranted immediate attention. In the meantime, Britain's preparations for war became peculiarly obnoxious to Americans. Filling the ranks of the Royal Navy required Britain to step up its policy of impressment. Usually this consisted of roving "press gangs" of burly seamen abducting the able-bodied at British pubs and brothels. The practice was more than a century old and consequently a traditional form of recruitment. Yet when it expanded to include waylaying merchant vessels on the high seas, some of its victims were Americans. In the absence of any official status imparted by the American government, Gouverneur Morris could do little but ask that his countrymen caught in this net be released, and he had to be polite while doing so.

George Beckwith, on the other hand, seemed to have the authority, if not the credentials, to hold meaningful talks with the American government. Beckwith, it turned out, was extremely particular about whom he met from the American government. On July 8, 1790, he had a long conversation with Hamilton in which he hinted that London might be willing to grant commercial concessions in exchange for American assistance against Spain. He also reassured Hamilton that Lord Dorchester was doing what he could to discourage the Indians from committing attacks against Americans in the Ohio Country. Hamilton immediately met with Jefferson after his talk with Beckwith, though it is not clear that he told the secretary of state everything he had learned. The two quickly visited Washington with the news, such as it was.[13]

The report was enough to galvanize Washington into one of his consultative frenzies. The president summoned Chief Justice John Jay from the deathbed of his father-in-law, Governor William Livingston of New Jersey. He even talked with John Adams, the last man to hold the position of minister to Great Britain, as well as Knox. The most pressing concern was theoretical but grave: In the event of war, what should the United States do if Britain tried to take Spanish Florida and Louisiana? A successful British campaign in those regions would place them not just to the north of the United States in Canada but also to its west and south. Jefferson raised an additional specter in a written opinion. The British in Louisiana would have control of the Mississippi River and could likely persuade westerners that their future was with the British Empire rather than the feeble American republic. Yet Jefferson's inclination for weighing complexity persuaded him to avoid any Anglo-Spanish conflict. He wrote to his son-in-law that "peace is our business."[14]

Washington weighed opinions and decided to wait. Despite his cooing and billing with Hamilton, Beckwith had no actual authority to offer the United States anything, whether a commercial agreement or a military alliance. If war resulted between Britain and Spain and if the British were serious about official talks, both of those developments would reveal themselves eventually. Washington told Hamilton to continue talking with Beckwith—Hamilton hardly needed the encouragement—to extract as much information as possible without committing to anything. Whether Hamilton told Washington everything that he discussed with Beckwith seems doubtful. On the contrary, Hamilton likely exaggerated Beckwith's gestures of friendship because of his eagerness to promote good relations with the British. In addition to misleading the administration, Hamilton began criticizing Gouverneur Morris to Washington, suggesting that Morris did not know what he was doing or was misinterpreting British overtures. Morris had counted Hamilton as a friend, but the Treasury secretary saw bigger things in play than mere friendship when he unsheathed the ultimate knife for the envoy's back: He told Washington that Gouverneur Morris was not being completely honest about British attitudes.

Nobody could have established meaningful relations with a government under such circumstances. Morris's position lurched from the frustrating to the pathetic. To string the United States along, the British began feigning an interest in his mission, but it was nothing more than a temporary ruse. Hamilton did not stop at undermining Morris's efforts. He also told Beckwith that Jefferson's anti-British views would make him an obstacle in negotiating an alliance. Thus Jefferson became a dupe, dispatching messages to an envoy whose efforts were all but useless and whom he had not even wanted in the first place. Jefferson told Morris to propose only American neutrality in the event of an Anglo-Spanish war. Hamilton told Beckwith that the British should ignore both Jefferson and Morris.[15] One of Hamilton's biographers sums up the result: "In effect, Hamilton was proposing to aid the representative of a foreign power in counteracting the policies of the Secretary of State."[16]

Above both frustration and pathos, George Washington remained the most important person in this foggy intrigue, and he did not want a British alliance. He wanted the country to remain neutral and in a position where a war between Spain and England would not harm it but would possibly provide it some advantages. Washington wondered what Spain might offer for American neutrality. Was this the chance to open the Mississippi and secure shipping rights out of New Orleans?

The United States had a man in Madrid holding the official post of chargé d'affaires, but he had a tendency to drop off the map for extended spans. Fifty-two-year-old William Carmichael was a native of Maryland, had been educated in Scotland, and was active in the Revolution both as a member of the Continental Congress and in diplomatic settings, the latter because of his remarkable fluency in languages. He acquired a reputation, however, for drinking and carousing as he served as volunteer secretary for Silas Deane and later for Benjamin Franklin before being appointed John Jay's private secretary. Jay and Carmichael never hit it off, and, in fact, quickly came to detest each other. Carmichael resented his subordinate position, and Jay distrusted Carmichael as a libertine and liar. He bluntly described Carmichael as "the most faithless and dangerous [man] I have met with, in all my life."[17]

When Jay came back to the United States to take up the foreign office, Carmichael remained in Spain as a testament to the inertia of the Confederation's diplomatic establishment. Jay discovered that Carmichael was not only haughty in manner but stingy with letters. It was a habit, and Washington's government had not heard from him since May 1789. In 1790, the American government no longer had the luxury of indulging the chargé's dilatory nature. It was essential to communicate directly with the Spanish government. Jefferson suggested that Washington send his secretary David Humphreys on a mission to Europe. Humphreys could first meet with Morris in London and then travel through France to find friends of America, such as Lafayette. He would then go to Spain to tell Carmichael to write home and finally travel to Portugal to broach the idea of opening diplomatic relations with Lisbon. The key part of the journey, of course, was to deal with Spain, especially to goad Carmichael to action while determining the pliability of Spain on the important Mississippi question. Washington liked the idea and, with Jefferson's help, prepared papers for Humphreys to take on his journey. It was to be a secret mission, with Humphreys using his seemingly aimless meander as a cover story that he was touring Europe for his own edification.[18] Jefferson did not know Humphreys as well as Washington did, but both men should have known that the concept of secrecy was but wishful thinking for the voluble playwright.

The plan alarmed Hamilton. If Humphreys could wring concessions from Spain, the British might interpret it as a hostile move and refuse to extend commercial concessions to the United States. Hamilton knew Humphreys, though, and without much trouble he persuaded him to meet with Beckwith, a supposedly innocent social call in which poor Humphreys behaved precisely the way Hamilton expected and revealed all. Beckwith sent a dispatch to London, and David Humphreys departed blissfully ignorant that the British government would know his plans before he even arrived in Europe.

A strange calm ensued for the next several weeks before a new wrinkle developed in the Anglo-Spanish crisis. Beckwith raised the possibility that if war did come his government might ask for permission to send troops through U.S. territory to attack Spanish Louisiana and Florida. Beckwith's little aside was actually a bombshell, and it sent the Washington administration reeling. Granting permission would explode Washington's desire for neutrality while placing the British in Louisiana and Florida. Washington wanted to be ready should a formal request come from London, and he began his customary round of consultations. Everyone submitted written opinions. Jefferson said granting the British permission to traipse around the American West was out of the question. The government should use force to stop it as a last resort. Hamilton had it both ways: The government had the right to deny permission but using force to prevent trespass would be highly risky. Henry Knox echoed Hamilton that the United States had its rights, but the man who oversaw America's meager armed forces understood the reality that the country had little chance of stopping the British if they were resolute.[19]

Fortunately, the British never had occasion to ask the United States for the privilege. Spain apologized to Britain for its overzealous assertion of territorial rights in the Pacific Northwest, and the war scare passed as diplomats settled in to hammer out conventions and agreements. The incident itself, however, provided a perfect illustration of what had become ingrained as Washington's way of dealing with unexpected issues as well as workaday matters. He wanted the opinions of as many people as he could reach, and he preferred to have them in writing so he could think through each methodically, systematically, deliberately, and slowly. Wide-ranging discussions between men posturing at a table vaguely irritated him, possibly because of his growing deafness, but certainly because he disliked the ephemeral nature of talk when confronting thorny problems. A written opinion made his advisers think, and the result was a depth to their ideas that avoided the impromptu thought and foolish musing. Washington never had to act in this crisis, but the process forged the best method for obtaining the best responses and served as a dress rehearsal for managing an emergency. Its resolution, however, left undiscovered the tendency of one actor to play all the parts.

The Treaty of New York solved only one of the country's frontier problems. Issues remained in the Northwest. British traders ranging from the occupied posts on American soil were suspected of agitating and arming Indians to harass American settlers in the Ohio Country. To be sure, as long as the British remained, northwestern Indians had no reason to behave peacefully toward American settlers, let alone surrender more land. Westerners resented eastern neglect, especially in Kentucky, where Indian raids were frequent and lethal.[20] Confronted by the ceaseless belligerence of the Indians and the political discontent it generated, Washington and Knox decided that immediate military intervention was necessary. They accordingly ordered Brigadier General Josiah Harmar to march on the center of Indian hostility, a scattering of enclaves called the Miami villages.[21]

If the issue had only been the Indians of the Northwest, it would have been complicated enough, but other factors were involved. The appearance that the United States would resolve its Indian problem with force alarmed pro-British Americans, such as Alexander Hamilton, and caused disagreements in Washington's cabinet. Establishing a decisive Indian policy would prove difficult as Hamilton tried to fend off threats to his plans for better commercial relations with the British, an initiative clouded by British perceptions that an American military expedition against Northwestern Indians was really an excuse to assault Redcoats in the region's posts. To allay British fears, Hamilton revealed the purpose of Harmar's campaign to George Beckwith.

In this impossible situation, the man on the ground in the Ohio Country was told to pacify the region. Josiah Harmar was America's senior army officer at the time, which wasn't saying much because America didn't have much of an army. Harmar had fewer than 350 regular soldiers to command and had to augment this meager number with untrained and poorly armed militia. Manpower was only one of his problems. He operated under the watchful eye of Arthur St. Clair, the influential governor of the Northwest Territory, who had Knox's ear and became a meddlesome force behind Harmar's doomed expedition. St. Clair was responsible for boosting the regular force with unreliable militia and would convey, per Knox's instructions, reassurances to the British about Harmar's mission just as it was commencing, but Beckwith already knew much of this, thanks to Hamilton, so there was plenty of blame to go around for the events about to unfold. Incredibly, neither Washington nor Harmar knew about these candid conversations with the British. Washington would not approve of Knox's behavior in the aftermath. Harmar, on the other hand, would bear all the condemnation for what happened that bleak autumn in the virtually trackless Ohio Country. Rumors that he had taken to drink did not help matters.

From Fort Washington at the new town of Cincinnati, he launched the Washington administration's desired campaign in the early fall of 1790. From the start, it gave cause for worry. Harmar preferred for everything to be in apple pie order before commencing a march, but his desire for fastidious preparation collided with wilderness realities that required resourcefulness. Harmar was an adequate officer but hardly a resourceful leader, and his march out of Fort Washington with 320 regulars and about 1,100 militia did not appear promising, especially since his government thought he was a drunk and the Indians knew he was coming.

11

"A Particular Measure Proceeding
from a Particular Officer"

Almost a year and a half had passed since they had seen Mount Vernon, but the Washingtons were finally going home before settling in Philadelphia. Their leaving New York was sad for the city. New Yorkers were barely reconciled to losing the capital but never to losing George Washington, for many realized that he would not have reason to visit them again. On August 30, 1790, when the presidential barge pushed away from the dock, a large crowd of citizens and dignitaries gathered, but muffled city noises and water slapping against the bulkhead were the only sounds. In striking contrast to April 1789, there were no cheers. "Not a word was heard," Abigail Adams marveled. Rather, each man "took off his Hat bowd and retired."[1]

Two days later the family arrived in Philadelphia for a short visit before continuing to Mount Vernon. The city cheered as its church bells pealed above the din. Philadelphia was ecstatic that the central government was returning. Though the stay was slated for only ten years, any site on the rural Potomac River seemed a million years from fruition and a million miles from civilization. A lot could happen in the span of ten years.

Tobias Lear, his wife, Polly, and a few servants remained in New York to pack up the Broadway house and ship items to Philadelphia and Mount Vernon. With customary attention to detail, Washington gave Lear precise instructions for packing everything. He might have given the same attention to his War Department.

As the weeks passed with Washington at Mount Vernon and the government completing the move to Philadelphia, Josiah Harmar blundered through the Ohio wilderness courting an inevitable disaster. He destroyed a few deserted Indian villages, but with everyone forewarned of his approach, the inhabitants had melted into the woods. Not for long, though. On October 19, 1790, the charismatic Miami leader Michikinikwa, whom whites called "Little Turtle," fell upon a patrol consisting mainly of militia with a few regulars. The militia fled, and the regulars stood their ground to die. The incident stunned Harmar into inaction, but a repeat of it three days later persuaded him to retreat to Fort Washington and bring the campaign to an inglorious end. Harmar and St. Clair tried to frame the disaster as a success, but the reality was that Harmar's jaunt had made things worse by emboldening Indians and embarrassing the United States in the eyes of the British.

Washington was furious. He leaped to blame Harmar and declared he was prepared to do so "from the moment I heard he was a drunkard."[2] Harmar was at fault, but his was not the sole failing, and he was evidently as sober as a judge throughout the misadventure in the wilderness. Rather than reassessing the nature of the military activities in the region, Washington concluded that the problem was the commander and replaced him.

Washington knew Arthur St. Clair far better than he knew Harmar and in a characteristic failure of judgment, he trusted St. Clair beyond a reasonable doubt on familiarity alone. St. Clair was a Scot by birth who saw combat as a British officer during the French and Indian War, though exclusively against the French. He resigned his commission afterward to stay in the United States, settling in Pennsylvania and becoming wealthy and influential. During the Revolution, he was with Washington at Trenton and Princeton and later at Yorktown. After the war, St. Clair served in Congress and was its presiding officer before becoming the governor of the Northwest Territory. Washington's confidence in St. Clair's political and military abilities convinced him that his former comrade in arms was the man to defeat Little Turtle's warriors and bring peace to the northwestern frontier. Although St. Clair's admirable military service was beyond doubt, he had never fought an Indian in his life. Considering this shortcoming in light of St. Clair's new assignment, Washington was as helpful as he could be. He told St. Clair to be vigilant for surprise attacks, which was good advice as far as it went. For Arthur St. Clair and the men under him, it did not nearly go far enough.

Tobias Lear had an unenviable task in the late summer of 1790. After he arrived in Philadelphia, he was to supervise all the construction Washington wanted for the Morris house at High Street. Mary Morris had a sudden illness that prevented the family from moving out on schedule, and the delay kept Lear anxiously counting the hours before the renovations could begin. Washington was not pleased and wrote frequently, urging Lear to hurry the work. When the Morrises did finally leave, the secretary had to cope with a shortage of skilled workers, because Philadelphia was in the middle of a building boom to accommodate the government's return. As the Washingtons prepared to leave Mount Vernon, construction continued on their new house. Even when the changes were completed, the renovated Morris home received mixed reviews. A European described it as "all but monstrous without any kind of architecture."[3]

The Washingtons arrived on November 27, 1790. Vice President Adams with Abigail had arrived a couple of weeks before to settle in at a beautiful though ramshackle mansion called Bush Hill two miles outside of town. Jefferson leased living quarters near the presidential residence on High Street, but he, too, could not move in because of extensive renovations he wanted. Jefferson did this everywhere he lived, treating rented rooms as though they were his own for a lifetime of habitation. In Paris his ideas about gracious living began and ended with living spaces and how they were adorned, and he thought nothing of tearing out walls and rearranging floor plans to suit his aesthetic sense. He rented a house in New York and at his expense renovated it to match the ideal design he had settled on in Paris. He did the same when the capital moved to Philadelphia, incurring significant expenses for temporary comforts. Jefferson's sense of the temporary, however, was relative. One moment of self-imposed unhappiness was one moment too many. There would always be more money (he thought), but moments were fleeting.

In each of these homes, Jefferson followed the pattern of moving from public areas to private spaces seamlessly. A visitor entered into a public drawing room where guests were received. From there, a door led to a more private sitting room that opened onto a library and then into the most private space of the house, his bedroom. The arrangement sought to move "from social intercourse to utter seclusion" without a discernible interruption. Servants' quarters were situated to become almost invisible, an idea he would employ at Monticello.[4]

Jefferson's spacious house swallowed him up, and he invited Madison to live with him when Congress was in session, but his friend politely declined. In addition to it being more appropriate for a member of Congress to live among fellow legislators rather than with a member of the administration, Madison preferred his usual quarters at the House-Trist Boarding House.

Madison usually lodged there when in Philadelphia, but Jefferson noticed that British agent George Beckwith also had a room at Trist's. He worried about stray words and casual asides making the spy's job easier. Madison assured Jefferson that Beckwith would not distract him from his books, papers, and his "little task," a reference to his compiling his notes on the Constitutional Convention, a task that was hardly little.[5]

Hamilton was far less exacting than Jefferson about his living arrangements. Elizabeth and the children would not join him in Philadelphia for a while. He merely wanted an apartment large enough to entertain small groups. His offices at 93 Chestnut Street, on the other hand, were quite large to accommodate his growing staff of clerks. Knox also set up the War Department's offices on Chestnut, while he and Lucy lived near the Adamses at Bush Hill. Randolph rented a house for his large family on High Street, and with that, all were in place when the president arrived in town.

Washington began working on his second annual message before leaving Mount Vernon and put the finishing touches on the speech after he arrived in Philadelphia. It was delivered to the last session of the

First Congress on December 8, 1790, a standard affair with mostly happy news. The government's increasing fiscal solvency and the economy's health through excellent credit was its centerpiece. Yet Washington also mentioned the unsettled Ohio frontier, the impending request from Kentucky for statehood, and the still-uncertain European peace. Most telling, though, was the president's continued reliance on James Madison in framing this address, a situation that recalled their earlier, happier relations before the strain over Hamilton's policies. As before, Madison crafted the House's obligatory response, and composed the president's response to both the House and Senate responses at Washington's request. It was possibly a good result of their work together on the opening phases of the capital, which, considering all the other troubles with that project, was at least one pleasant outcome.

That first autumn in Philadelphia, Washington settled into the new routines of a new city. Lear had arranged for Wash's schooling, though by spring he recommended a change because the lad's Latin was not improving. Lear also managed the servants, an unexpected and additional burden. Lear would have had little involvement with the servants had steward John Hyde run a tighter household. Hyde was one of the staff brought from New York, and the servants held him in mild contempt. Washington did, too, when Hyde planned even more extravagant meals than his predecessor Samuel Fraunces. Hyde resigned in March 1791, Fraunces returned, and an iron-fisted housekeeper named Mrs. Emerson took up the management of the household staff. Lear could breathe a little easier.

Toby and Polly Lear were happy additions for the Washingtons in their new home. Polly became an affectionate companion for Martha and filled a void, for Martha sorely missed the young women relatives she had left at Mount Vernon. Polly was a bright companion and a helpmate who assisted Martha with social events, especially tiresome ones such as the formal Thursday dinners. When Polly had a baby the following spring, Martha Washington's world was very nearly complete. All of the tribulations of presidential society and bothers of city life fell away as she and Polly fussed over and cosseted the new arrival. Toby and Polly named their boy Benjamin Lincoln Lear after the man who had given Lear entrée to the family. Washington stood as the newest Lear's godfather and was not above doing a bit of cosseting of his own.

Philadelphia was a treat and a bane, a mixture of high culture and advanced hygiene with a cost of living that bordered on the unreasonable. "Boston is the Bristol, New York the Liverpool, and Philadelphia the London of America," noted a British visitor.[6] It was an apt observation, but there was a newness to the place where careful planning set Philadelphia apart from any other city in the world. Laid out by founder William Penn, Philadelphia featured a more logical design than New York City. Its wide guttered streets and spacious sidewalks were always cleaner than New York's. Philadelphia was also safer in more of its sections. Benjamin Franklin's Library Company of Philadelphia and the American Philosophical Society provided refinement that was missing in the hurly-burly world of New York finance and speculation. Philadelphia's social scene was more vibrant and its women fetching with "superb complexion[s], beautiful eyes, beautiful hair, beautiful teeth."[7] They were always fashionably attired, often boasting boldly revealing gowns that scandalized Abigail Adams. The women were also politically aware and anything but timid in expressing opinions. Parties were frequent enough to cause Abigail Adams to lament "a very dissipated winter, if I were to accept half the invitations I receive."[8] Social life could take a toll. "A woman of 26 is already faded," marveled a sharp-eyed traveler, "but on the other hand at 14 she is formed."[9]

Prior to the government's arrival, Philadelphia's cultural attractions had not been limited to its upper classes. The city's numerous taverns and public houses held entertainments to draw in customers, a custom that had offended Europeans who found themselves mixing with the common folk listening to raucous music and watching circus-style acts. Their sniffing disapproval came to a partial end when the presence of the American government raised both the rates and the tone of such popular diversions, ultimately depriving the lower class of a small pleasure, another example of government's unintended consequences. Gray's Gardens at the Lower Ferry of the Schuylkill River became popular for its genteel presentations, and staged minor pageants to bid farewell to the Washingtons when they departed for visits to Mount Vernon.[10] It reminded some critics of monarchical ceremony, but they were silent, at first.

The government's first winter in Philadelphia was unusually cold. The Schuylkill froze over in December, and everybody stayed indoors as much as possible. Congress met in the Philadelphia County Court House, for the time being dubbed Congress Hall, where stoked stoves could barely keep the frigid air at bay.[11] Congressional debates, however, soon became heated.

Alexander Hamilton told Washington that "it is always best for the chief magistrate to be as little implicated as possible in the specific approbation of a particular measure proceeding from a particular officer."[12] The advice pertained to the upcoming debate on Hamilton's proposals for new taxes and a national bank. Jefferson and Knox worked with Congress at Washington's request and often with his direct contribution. Hamilton's work was different. He evidently never discussed details of the 1791 proposals with Washington, though they most certainly would have spoken about the subjects generally. In any case, Congress in the main had no reason to believe that messages from the administration were rogue communications, and members in both houses tempered their opposition to proposals because Washington presumably approved of them. Washington could for a time have it both ways: He followed Hamilton's advice to stay above the fray but reaped the benefits of people presuming he silently took sides.

The reports Hamilton placed before Congress in early 1791 responded to an unusual circumstance. The secretary of the Treasury had made a mistake. Hamilton had overestimated the revenue that tariffs would generate, and he had to make up the shortfall. The only solution was to levy new taxes, and in considering that, Congress was sure to pause. A grudging nod to the arithmetic compelled many in Congress to accept import taxes on spirits and an excise on domestic whiskey as necessary evils, but that did not make the measures popular. Madison was among those who swallowed his objections, consoling himself that the excise would at least encourage "sobriety, and thereby prevent disease and untimely deaths."[13] The College of Physicians of Philadelphia applauded the measure as a wholesome way to curb whiskey guzzling, and that moral imperative combined with the mathematical one quashed opposition. It passed both houses with ease. Lost in the haze of necessity and virtue was the fact that Hamilton had achieved a remarkable precedent: If the government wanted to levy a domestic tax, it could.[14]

The proposed Bank of the United States was another matter, although both houses eventually gave Hamilton comfortable victories on that measure as well. The margins disguised more resolute and eventually vocal opposition to the plan as an idea, and the way the bank became law would contribute to the division between Madison and the president. "We are going headlong into the bitterest opposition to Genl Government," a friend warned Hamilton. "I pity you Most sincerly."[15]

Washington did not realize this until later, but Hamilton needed no warnings to see the snares his proposal faced. He was prepared to meet them, he thought, because of his thorough research and detailed plans. He read extensively on the subject and focused particularly on the Bank of England's role in supporting the British economy. The model was instructive, providing a guide for harnessing the potential greatness of an economy to drive its current functions. Years passed before hard data showed that France in 1789 was actually wealthier than Great Britain. France, however, lacked a mechanism—such as the British had in their national bank—to employ that wealth to pay its debts and ensure its future. The difference was social and political chaos versus industrial progress.

Hamilton did not come to this subject fresh. The principle of credit was intimately and rightly tied to banking in Hamilton's studies, the mysteries of high finance being an avocation of his for years. He and Robert Morris had successfully urged the Confederation to charter the Bank of North America at the end of the Revolution and had in its example proof of a small bank's usefulness to a region's economy. Other banks in New York City and Boston provided additional confirmation. Hamilton had written the charter for the one in New York.[16]

It seemed reasonable then to say that if the idea worked in limited applications it would prove proportionately beneficial in a larger one. In simple terms, Hamilton wanted to monetize the debt, and a central bank was a proven way to do it. Monetization is a process whereby something of value is converted into money, or in Hamilton's plan something that could act as money—that is, currency. His plan called for the conversion of the securities from funding and assumption into stock in the bank. The concept was difficult to grasp, especially the part of the formula in which the central bank issued banknotes (the currency) primarily using as collateral the very securities it was converting. The goal was to create money in sufficiently small denominations to perform as circulating currency. By doing that, the bank could significantly increase the money supply, which was how Hamilton intended to transform the country's debt from a negative drag to a positive engine. The bank, however, could not work with halfhearted support. Rather, it had to be generously funded (capitalized), and Hamilton pegged the figure at no less than $10 million, a sum greater than all the specie then circulating in the country. It also surpassed the value of all extant state and regional banks. The Bank of the United States was to be a private corporation with limited government participation, which was a departure from the Bank of England's charter, which Hamilton had closely studied in framing his version.

In addition to the goals of monetizing the debt and increasing the money supply, Hamilton's bank was designed to tie affluent people to the government by giving them a stake in its financial health and thus encouraging them to support its maintenance. Consequently, converted government securities would comprise three-fifths of the initial capitalization of $10 million with the balance in gold and silver. The government would hold 20 percent of the bank's stock, the money for purchasing it to be provided by the bank at a rate of interest below the stock's projected yield. The government would also appoint five of the bank's twenty-three directors. Though technically a private corporation, the bank's operations would be under the scrutiny if not the control of the secretary of the Treasury.

Thus equipped, the Bank of the United States would promote economic growth by expanding credit for the private sector. It would increase the currency supply by issuing banknotes backed by its generous capitalization, while guarding against inflation by controlling that currency from a central authority. Stable but readily available banknotes would encourage commerce that was national rather than regional in scope. The bank would be the government's vault by receiving its deposits and would be a ready creditor in extraordinary situations, providing access to money in any season and untethering the Treasury from payment schedules on tariffs and taxes. The appointment of five of the bank's twenty-three directors did not seem overly intrusive, nor did the plan to have the government hold 20 percent of the corporation's stock, purchased with loans from the bank itself but at special low interest rates. The bank's twenty-year charter placed its renewal or abolishment on a fixed schedule that would give Congress a chance to review its performance.[17]

Hamilton believed that by establishing a bank in Philadelphia the government could more thoroughly supervise the economy, but that aspect of his plan was diluted with the establishment of branches in other cities. The unexpected decentralization of branches did not mollify critics' fears of consolidated power, however. The prospect of a congressionally chartered bank disturbed Madison, for he saw it as more than an extension of Hamilton's previous financial measures to promote good credit and energetic commerce. For him, the bank was another device, like assumption, to suborn the states and centralize power in the federal government. Madison watched uneasily as the House of Representatives was distracted with debates on the whiskey tax while Hamilton craftily had the bank bill originate in the Senate. Not only did this delay the scrutiny of a potentially hostile House; the maneuver delivered a bank conforming almost completely to Hamilton's wishes when the Senate passed the bill on January 20, 1791.[18]

The bill arrived in the House at the end of the month. Madison spoke strongly against it, even though he knew that Washington almost certainly supported it. In addition to risking Washington's displeasure again, Madison labored under the depressing reality that he did not have the votes to stop a measure that either the people would consent to because they did not understand it or enthusiastically support whether they understood it or not. It was possibly mild desperation that prompted Madison to couch his argument in a way that surprised almost everybody, including Alexander Hamilton.

The debate began in the House of Representatives on January 31, 1791. Hamilton's supporters tried to rush the process by calling for a vote on February 1, but the very novelty of the proposal troubled enough members to prolong debate. The delay did not give Madison much time to marshal his argument, but he was as ready as he could be on the following day. Banks were convenient for merchants and governments, he conceded, but in Madison's opinion this exclusive benefit for special interests was the core problem of the proposal. Though he pointedly mentioned how bank failures always injured the community as a whole, he insisted that debating the particulars of this bill was pointless because Congress had no authority to create a bank in the first place.

Madison explained that by listing particular powers, the Framers had meant to make them exclusive beyond which Congress could not legitimately go. Interpreting the "necessary and proper" clause as giving the government unlimited license was to fly in the face of this restrictive intent. Hamilton's proposal was a convenience for a certain class of people, but hardly a necessity for the country as a whole.

The House pondered, but Hamilton was amazed. He vividly remembered—as would be shown—that James Madison had been a proponent after the Revolution of the very concept of implied powers that he now condemned. Yet in early 1791, James Madison spoke with almost unchallenged authority about the intent of the Framers. Hamilton's supporters brought up the Senate's approval of the bank, pointing out that Framers in the upper house obviously had no doubt of the proposal's constitutionality, but Madison snapped that each house should exercise its own judgment. He also stated that the president had the right to apply his judgment to such questions as well.[19]

Invoking Washington's right to exercise his judgment was a veiled reference to the veto power. Madison had to know that Washington narrowly interpreted the presidential veto, however. Washington did not believe the veto was appropriate for mere policy disagreements. In his view, the executive was required to enforce congressional legislation, whether he personally liked it or not, and could only weigh it on constitutional scales. As a coequal branch of government, the executive's role was to check legislative excess, meaning he reviewed bills to make certain they did not exceed constitutional limits.

Madison's appeal to Washington's judgment—that is, the veto pen— was therefore a risky ploy, but it was also all he had, for he knew he was fighting a losing battle. Too many members supported Hamilton simply because they assumed he was doing Washington's bidding, and the vote of 39 to 20 in favor of the bank surprised nobody. In fact, it caused Fisher Ames to remark that it was "strong proof of the little impression that was made" by Madison's argument.[20] That caustic observation reflected a growing suspicion in the House of Madison's motives, but

Washington took note of it. When the bank bill reached the president's desk on February 14, 1791, he asked Edmund Randolph for an opinion on its constitutionality. Washington wanted the thinking of a fellow Framer—the only one aside from Hamilton in the cabinet—as well as his attorney general; it was the first time Randolph was consulted on a matter of real importance. The young man took the request quite seriously.

Unfortunately for Randolph, his written opinion was not what Washington wanted to see. Randolph cited the absence of constitutional authorization to incorporate any entity as the most obvious hindrance to establishing a bank. He noted that even an implied power to incorporate would logically need to be tied to one or more of "the specified powers," or it would have to be "necessary and proper to carry into execution some of the specified powers." But Randolph saw no such flexibility in the Constitution. He told Washington that the bill was unconstitutional.[21]

The president also turned to Jefferson, possibly out of habit for wide consultation, but his rumination about the bank suggests he wanted validation for an opinion already formed. Though Jefferson had many of Madison's same fears about the influence of special interests on Congress, he, like Randolph, raised the constitutional question as most cogent. Jefferson echoed Madison in noting that something being useful or "convenient" to the government did not make it "necessary," let alone proper.[22] He nevertheless gave Washington an excuse to sign the bill by suggesting that any uncertainty about its constitutionality should cause him to defer to the wisdom of Congress. It was an opinion consistent with Jefferson's attitude about legislative supremacy, but the way he offered it was also typical of his obsessive desire to avoid confrontation. Jefferson had strong opinions sincerely held, but something almost always tugged him away from the personal clash as though it were an unforgivable social faux pas. Friends found in that a humble diffidence. Enemies saw it as rank hypocrisy. Both were wrong.

At the moment, Jefferson's ambiguous response introduced the sort of quandary Washington wished to avoid. He went straight to the sources of the debate. He presented Hamilton with Randolph and Jefferson's opinions, asked for a rebuttal, and requested that Madison prepare a detailed message for Congress. Madison was succinct: Washington should simply say, "I object to the bill because it is an essential principle of the Government that powers not delegated by the Constitution cannot be rightfully exercised; because the power proposed by the Bill to be received is not expressly delegated; and because I cannot satisfy myself that it results from any express power by fair and safe rules of implication." Madison also voiced his opposition to the exclusive benefit of the bill as one of the main reasons it lacked merit. If Washington agreed, he could register the complaint in his veto message that only those who lived close to the bank would profit from its services.[23]

Washington waited for Hamilton's response, which took Hamilton longer than usual to draft because he was determined to answer every argument thoroughly. Hamilton took so long, in fact, that Washington worried that his ten-day window to sign the bill would expire to make it law by constitutional default. Hamilton continued to scribble while assuring his nervous chief that neither the day of receipt nor Sundays counted against his time. Washington by that reckoning had until February 25, 1791, to decide. Hamilton fretted about the matter himself. The bill becoming law without the president's signature would be perceived as passive acceptance and tepid support at best. That would be as bad as a veto in a way, so Hamilton hurried against his deadline. Washington had Hamilton's response on February 23.

The result was a calm, measured approach in one of Hamilton's best state papers. In essence he said that the government had the right to enact necessary measures, which was hardly a new argument for him. He made the same point in *Federalist,* no. 31, during the ratification debates when he wrote that there was "no limitation of a power destined to effect a purpose."[24] Citing the doctrine of "implied powers," he noted that Publius had argued for the same thing in *Federalist,* no. 44. Here was the inconsistent stand of James Madison laid bare, though Hamilton cagily neglected to mention that Madison was the author of that entry. It was a subtle touch, and with such deftness Hamilton's rebuttal was a masterful performance that won the day. Washington signed the bill.

Washington did not show any of the opinions to anyone outside his official family nor did he apparently discuss Hamilton's arguments with Jefferson or Randolph, and certainly not with Madison. His circumspection was likely a mistake. Washington certainly meant well in keeping disagreements private, but the act of choosing one opinion over another could not help but create the perception of winners and losers. The losers in such episodes tend to accept their fate rather than brood over it in rough proportion to the consideration given them by the referee. Washington did not yet realize the unhappiness that was simmering under the surface of the "temper and candor" he cheerfully reported as the prevailing mood of debates "more strongly marked . . . Than could have been wished."[25]

In fact, divisions remained quite strongly marked even after Washington signed the bank into law. The perception persisted that the bank was meant to benefit a privileged few, especially speculators and merchant interests, at the expense of the country's farmers. Other critics were more abstract and theoretical, as in their fear that Hamilton's policies were upsetting the balance between the executive and the legislature, tipping power toward the federal government and away from the states, and favoring the North over the South and West. Senator William Maclay knew whom to blame. Unconstitutional laws were being enacted because the people trusted George Washington.[26] Maclay was an early critic of the circumstance, and even at that confined it to his diary. But he was a harbinger, and the prudence of diaries would eventually give way to public outcry in newspapers.

Regardless of Washington's involvement or responsibility, the pattern of Hamilton's financial plans was troubling to Antifederalists who saw consolidation in the federal apparatus and the suborning of the states as the consequence. Without any prompting from Madison or Jefferson, the Virginia legislature the previous fall had passed resolutions denouncing funding and assumption as unconstitutional. The attitude alarmed Hamilton. He told John Jay that "this is the first symptom of a spirit which must either be killed or it will kill the Constitution of the United States." Benjamin Lincoln was even more pointed. He doubted that the Virginia legislature had the right to pass such resolutions, but if such actions became general practice, Lincoln predicted they would "keep the minds of the people at large in a constant state of ferment and irritation."[27]

Yet Hamilton was equally responsible for ferment and irritation.

The bank seemed in the short term another triumph of an unstoppable political force, but in the long term the way he proposed and obtained the bank pointed to trouble. After his success with funding and assumption, he became so sure of his standing with Washington and his strength in the Senate that he began taking for granted the coalition of Federalists who had ratified the Constitution. The slim majority for assumption should have been a warning, but the bank was rammed through the third session of the First Congress not only because of the large Federalist majority but to marginalize Madison and his supporters. Several consequences of that hubris became immediately apparent.[28]

The debate over the bank set the stage for a fight that increasingly divided as it delineated opposing factions. Some historians see the dispute as seminal in the founding of political parties, something that happened despite a universal denunciation of parties as nests of special interests and corrupt practices. Yet the opponents of funding, assumption, and the bank felt more beleaguered than beaten, and by the spring of 1791 they were clustering around the most obvious leader in their ranks, James Madison. The faction was coalescing into a party—some even called it the Madison Party—and from the political reality that mirrors Newtonian physics, that action inevitably led to an equal and opposite reaction in the emergence of the Federalist Party. As the development evolved it would complete the estrangement of James Madison from George Washington, neither the first nor the last man to part ways from Washington in sadness and sometimes in anger.

The Bank of the United States became a lightning rod as well as a catalyst in this emerging confrontation. When the bank's stock went on sale during the summer, everything its opponents feared came to pass. Madison had been appalled by the rampant speculation in funding the national debt, but the frenzy to buy bank stock was even more shocking. He and Jefferson watched the old British system of patronage and influence that had corrupted Parliament taking hold in the U.S. Congress. In that summer of 1791 Madison had his question answered about fallen angels: Hamilton was well on his way to creating a moneyed aristocracy that would destroy representative government by setting up an impenetrable and unaccountable system of cronyism and privilege. Members of Congress who scrambled to buy stock in Hamilton's bank were dancing before a graven idol while tying their material well-being to his policies. They were corrupted, and they sullied the institutions they touched. Madison believed this from his vantage in the legislature. Thomas Jefferson began to see it from his in the administration.[29]

It did not help that an odd quid pro quo played out after Washington signed the bank bill. Washington had decided that the federal district should be larger than originally authorized. He asked Congress to pass a supplemental bill to the Residence Act extending the district's lines to include Alexandria and the area south of the Anacostia River in Maryland. The request seemed routine, but northern members who had objected to the residence deal in the first place apparently held the supplemental bill hostage until Washington approved the bank, which they very much wanted. Sure enough, as soon as Washington signed, the extension of the district passed easily.[30] Jefferson and Madison were helping with the plans for the capital, but they were unsettled by its growing size. The seeming trade of the bank for the district's enlargement tarred the capital with the bank's brush.

12

"Positively Unable to Articulate a Word"

Thomas Jefferson had been hard at work on a report of his own for congressional consideration, and while Congress debated and approved Hamilton's bank, it also considered Jefferson's ostensible evaluation of North American fisheries. The title of the report, which specified its subject as codfish and whales off the New England coast, did not promise to attract much public attention, for it seemingly concerned a narrow part of the population confined to a small segment of the country. Yet Jefferson's assessment of cod catching and whale chasing was actually an epic production. It embraced much more than the concerns of New England fishermen. In it Jefferson unveiled a coherent plan to protect American access to French markets and to emphasize the damaging consequences of Britain's discriminatory trade practices. Washington approved. He had received word from Gouverneur Morris in London that the British had no desire to resolve their differences with the United States. Jefferson's report accordingly recommended that Congress again consider punitive duties against British imports and install measures to help American fishermen compete with the British.

The report complemented James Madison's efforts in the House of Representatives to pass navigation laws aimed at British policy, and in that regard it alarmed Hamilton and his British contact George Beckwith. In addition, the report's appeal to New Englanders challenged their unquestioning allegiance to Hamilton's policies. As Jefferson told

John Hancock, the report attracted Yankees by using whales and cod-fish as bait.[1]

Hamilton had to operate behind the scenes to counter these senti-ments and block Jefferson's efforts. He made no secret to his friends—a group that included Beckwith, of course—that any effort to curb Brit-ish trade would put his financial plans at risk. Sanctions against British imports would invite British retaliation, confine American goods to fewer markets (Hamilton disdained the French as trading partners), and reduce Treasury receipts from import duties. Beckwith helped Hamilton by quietly hinting that the British would soon send a diplo-matic representative to the United States, which convinced Congress to postpone any action and gave Hamilton a temporary victory over James Madison by blocking anti-British legislation in the House. Everyone meanwhile hoped that the new British minister would bring acceptable terms to address the complaints in Jefferson's report.

Neither Jefferson nor Madison thought that likely, and they gloom-ily took stock of yet another Hamilton success, this one scored against a position that even the president supported. Their prospects for altering the situation seemed bleak. From a political standpoint Hamilton was far better organized. He had begun to exercise increasing influence over Henry Knox in Washington's official family, and the Senate was almost automatically friendly to his policies; Oliver Ellsworth, Robert Morris, and Rufus King were staunch supporters. Hamilton had influence that spanned sectional concerns in the House of Representatives with Theo-dore Sedgwick and Fisher Ames, both from Massachusetts, and Wil-liam Loughton Smith of South Carolina. Hamilton also controlled the large and growing patronage of the Treasury Department, which in-cluded tax collectors throughout the country and customs officials in all ports. He had not forgotten the lessons about publicity from the Revo-lution and especially from the ratification struggle, which prompted him to cultivate the press from the start of his tenure. He could rely on the *Gazette of the United States* to promote anything he wanted without question.

In New York the *Gazette*'s editor John Fenno had occasionally pub-lished favorable news about the French Revolution as a favor for Jef-ferson, but the State Department could never match the printing business given to the paper by the Treasury Department, and Fenno remained from first to last a businessman interested in balancing his ledgers. Subsidized by lucrative printing contracts from the Treasury Department, Fenno became an extension of Alexander Hamilton's political will by the time the government moved to Philadelphia, and Jefferson and Madison regarded his paper as one of Hamilton's most dangerous weapons. Worse, Hamilton's camp boasted a growing number of newspapers that suggested a national juggernaut in the making. The *Pennsylvania Packet, The Charleston Evening Gazette, The Massachusetts Centinel,* the *New York Packet, The Providence Gazette* in Rhode Island, and most obviously Fenno's *Gazette of the United States* regularly churned out or reprinted what amounted to government-approved press releases. In the face of this imposing array, Jefferson gave what government business he could to Benjamin Franklin Bache's *General Advertiser,* a paper that catered almost exclusively to a local Philadelphia audience and did not have nearly the reach of even Fenno's paper, let alone its cousins across the republic.[2] Bache was Benjamin Franklin's grandson, the "Benny" who had scribbled his grandfather's final essays at the old man's bedside, but his day had not yet come.

In the meantime, countering Hamilton's national influence became a pressing concern. Madison heard that a friend from college wanted to start a newspaper in Monmouth, New Jersey, to stave off poverty and provide for his bride, who was expecting a baby. Philip Freneau was known as "the Poet of the Revolution" because his patriotic verse had been popular during the war, and it was true that he could turn a phrase better than most. He also had worked as a journalist in New York and had criticized speculators in government securities. Madison and another former classmate, "Light-Horse Harry" Lee, concluded that Freneau was just the man to establish a rival press in Philadelphia. Jefferson was not sure, or at least he hesitated to become involved in a plan that strict rectitude could have judged inappropriate. Then Washington signed the bank bill and Hamilton quashed the recommendations of the fisheries report. At that point, Jefferson convinced himself that he had no choice.

On February 28, 1791, he wrote to Freneau offering him $250 a year as a translator in the State Department and making it clear that his light duties would allow him to pursue other interests, which was a clear reference to editing a newspaper.[3] Freneau himself was not so taken with the plan at first. He initially turned down Jefferson's offer by saying he was ill-suited for the translator's job because his French was rusty, which suggested he either was being coy or was incredibly dense. Assured that he would only have to translate documents from French to English rather than vice versa was more than a hint that translations were not to be his highest priority, but he still demurred. Madison commenced an unrelenting pressure on his old friend, however, and by late summer when financial backing for the new publication was secured, Freneau finally accepted Jefferson's offer. On October 31, 1791, the first issue of the *National Gazette* came off the press.[4] Jefferson, Madison, and Lee did their part, canvassing people all over the nation to buy subscriptions. Madison had a national paper to fight Hamilton's policies. The worry was that it might be too little, too late.

Reports soon trickled into Philadelphia about disaffection over Hamilton's excise on whiskey, especially on the frontier, where distilling grains made them more portable for transport to distant markets. Whiskey was also used as currency on a frontier devoid of money, a situation that made the excise a doubly onerous sales tax. Backwoods resistance to the excise was sufficiently lively to suggest collecting it would be risky, if not impossible. As troubling as these reports were, however, they could at least be attributed to inchoate discontent giving rise to exaggerated rumors. There was nothing undeveloped about southern anger over Mississippi navigation being blocked by Spain, whose agents were also providing a haven for runaway slaves when not choking off western America's lifeline to the world. The American government's inability to solve either problem emphasized its fragile hold on the more remote parts of the country.

Sectional discontent was only one reason that Washington decided to make a tour of the southern states. He would have done so earlier except for North Carolina's reluctance to ratify the Constitution and his own health problems, but North Carolina had finally joined the Union, and he was feeling better. He had the precedent of Rhode Island's delayed ratification, which had caused him to bypass it during his New England tour in the fall of 1789. Both the recalcitrance of "Rogue Islanders" and Washington's avoidance of their home had chagrined

Rhode Island natives, so when confirmation arrived in New York that the state had finally become the thirteenth to accept the new government, Washington made the trip to Rhode Island. He traveled by water in the company of Jefferson, Governor Clinton, William Loughton Smith, and Supreme Court justice John Blair, a mixed group as to politics and temperament to be sure, but it was early enough in the administration not to make much difference.

Rhode Island was like anywhere else in its welcomes and entertainments. Washington spent two days in mid-August 1790 in Newport, where ringing bells and booming cannons greeted him and a sumptuous dinner gave locals the chance to raise glasses and recite tributes that had in their sameness become tedious. And the trip, like all others, produced an amusing anecdote: As he was preparing to leave Newport, Washington sent secretary Thomas Nelson to buy a pair of gloves, but the shopkeeper refused to wait on him. She would not budge from the window where she was waiting to catch a glimpse of the president. Nelson sputtered, tried to explain his errand, and finally returned to tell Washington that he would have to buy his own gloves. The president went to the shop, filling it with his towering presence and leaving his admirer so flabbergasted that she was barely able to complete the transaction. She watched him leave. She would remember it for the rest of her days. And thus Rhode Island was officially welcomed into the Union by Washington's visit, another instance of his presidential wanderings that would in later years give rise to the partly credible claim that Washington slept here, or there, or everywhere.[5]

But it was clear that the trip, like the one to the other parts of New England, was something more than just a presidential procession. That was why Washington's wanderings were important. Governors and dignitaries all seemed to say the same thing during these events. Communities that adorned themselves with flowers or laurels and clad their children in costumes were touching, but the events seemed staged, rehearsed, and lacking a memorable spontaneity, though certainly they were sincere. On the other hand, the wide-eyed clerk stammering and fumbling over her selection of gloves was something else altogether. She was the random flash of a real person, stubborn about her plans to look out her window, genuinely humbled by someone she admired and still able to sell him something as she would any other customer. There was nothing like her anywhere else in the world. For all her life she had been a citizen of Newport, a resident of Rhode Island, a shopgirl surrounded by dry goods and bolts of cloth. But when the enormous man with the huge hands and powder blue eyes walked into her shop, she became an American. She would be an American for the rest of her days. She was why the trips were important.

In the spring of 1791, Washington felt better than he had in months. His previously precarious health had been the last possible impediment to the southern trip, and he now intended to go. Wishing to avoid the Deep South's legendary summer heat, Washington planned to travel immediately after Congress adjourned. The trip was mapped meticulously, and he prided himself on its grueling itinerary, with mornings starting before dawn and double-digit distances covered each day. He suspected southern roads would prove a trial, his progress slow, and the distance daunting. In fact, it would be like a military campaign. He couldn't wait.

Washington's love of travel was one of the few pleasures he had always carelessly indulged. Terrain, weather, and transport offered varied difficulties from hour to hour, making each day an adventure and providing problems to solve, testing resourcefulness, and making the bed or cot or ground feel wonderful at night. Desk work made his backside hurt, particularly after the carbuncle incident, but saddles and coach seats made his heart sing. James Craik, his neighbor and physician, had traveled with him for part of his last and most extensive western journey in the fall of 1784 when Craik had been his only companion at its outset, something of a tradition, for he had been alone with Washington on a 1770 journey down the Ohio River. Craik was Washington's most enduring friend, vigilant to threats and supportive in times of need, spending a lifetime looking after the health of Washington, his friends, and his family. He didn't need anything from Washington and remained with him through the years for the pleasure of his company, which was a rare tribute.

Washington did not have a carriage designed for bad roads over long hauls. He hired Philadelphia carriage maker David Clark to build one with sturdy springs and wheels to handle rutted southern roads. The companions for this trip would also be important, though less personable than Craik. Washington took with him only one secretary, William Jackson, who proved to be a tremendous asset. Jackson knew many important families in the Deep South from his service at Charleston during the Revolution. Washington also brought several servants. He would ride for long stretches in the coach, but he could not bear to travel without a horse. He took his favorite stallion, a majestic white animal named Prescott, and his pet greyhound, the impishly named Cornwallis. As presidential processions went, it was a small entourage even for the time.

They began the adventure on March 21, 1791, riding out of Philadelphia with Thomas Jefferson and Henry Knox accompanying them as far as the Delaware River. Washington stopped at Mount Vernon to inspect the grounds and prepare for his long trip. He wrote a joint communication to Hamilton, Jefferson, and Knox with his detailed itinerary and instructions for handling important matters in his absence. He told them to meet regularly and use their judgment to decide if an emergency required his return.[6]

Washington plotted ambitious daily distances on detailed maps. He intended to start each day at four in the morning to avoid the worst heat, only stopping for breakfast after traveling at least several hours. The trip began inauspiciously nonetheless, testing everyone's patience and resourcefulness early. On the first day "in attempting to cross the ferry at Colchester with the four Horses hitched to the Chariot by the neglect of the person who stood before them, one of the leaders got overboard." The dangling horse's "struggling frightened the others in such a manner that one after another and in quick succession they all go over board harnessed & fastened as they were and with utmost difficulty they were saved."[7]

The incident set the mood for other difficulties, many of them dealing with food and lodging, which Washington more or less expected because he was familiar with the limits of rural areas. Yet circumstances in the South made his resolve to continue his practice of paying his own way for bed and board in public houses impossible to keep. Few inns and taverns dotted the presidential route, because they could not survive amid a sparse and scattered population that rarely traveled. When Washington was lucky enough to find an inn, his companions likely questioned how much luck was really involved. The food was almost always bad, and the beds were usually dirty and uncomfortable.

The routines for this trip fell into the familiar patterns of its predecessors. City fathers and various dignitaries greeted Washington on the outskirts of their towns, and a troop of militia escorted him into them. Washington mounted Prescott to lead the parade. In the towns, he stayed overnight, attended the obligatory dinner in his honor, and sat through "a grand ball and illumination" afterward.[8]

The route followed the North Carolina coast to South Carolina, the most important leg of the journey. As always, Washington wanted to be a living symbol of the new government and project its solidity, a vital task in the South Carolina up-country (the state's western region) where Washington was eager to judge the reaction to the whiskey tax. The Carolina Low Country—the region near the coast that was analogous to the Virginia Tidewater—was the home of the moneyed elite, who were more supportive of the administration than other southerners, including Washington's own Virginia neighbors. To strengthen existing alliances and forge new ones, Washington hoped to bring more of the Carolina men into the government. As part of that plan, he paused at the plantation called Hampton as he neared Charleston. It was the home of the widow Harriott Horry.

Hampton boasted a palatial mansion that had been owned by Daniel Huger Horry. Daniel's marriage to Harriott Pinckney when he was thirty and she nineteen in 1768 had united two powerful Low Country families. She was the daughter of Charles Pinckney and Eliza Lucas Pinckney, which made her the sister of prominent South Carolinians Charles Cotesworth Pinckney and Thomas Pinckney. The Pinckney brothers were among South Carolina's heroes during the Revolution when the British captured both as they defended the state. After the war, they naturally numbered among the state's premier politicians.

Now a widow, Harriott Pinckney Horry managed Hampton, and in the six years before Washington's visit became formidable in her handling of the place and locally famous for the accomplishment. She and her widowed mother, who had taken refuge at Hampton during the Revolution and never left, had, in fact, become legendary in the region much earlier. While a teenager, Harriott's mother Eliza Lucas Pinckney managed her father's South Carolina estates and enlisted slaves to help her experiment with seeds and growing techniques to prove that indigo could thrive in South Carolina. The British textile industry relied on indigo for the dark dye it produced, and Eliza's work introduced a new cash crop in the Lower South. After marrying Charles Pinckney, she kept her hand in the running of family plantations and took over much of the work at the Pinckney estate of Belmont when her husband died in 1758. Harriott and her brothers had this remarkable woman's temperament, inquisitive nature, and love of learning. As a teenager, Harriott had experimented with silk production and pioneered new agricultural techniques and equipment.[9] George Washington could not wait to meet her.

True enough, the Pinckney brothers were the political object of his visit to Hampton, but mother and daughter charmed and amazed him. He sat at a table on May 1 between the daughters of Harriott and Charles Cotesworth, both wearing sashes with Washington's portrait painted on them. The opulence of Hampton was stunning. Harriott presided over a hearty breakfast for Washington and her neighbors in her ballroom. She could have invited a small army: It was seven hundred square feet in size. After breakfast, guests and family adjourned to the veranda for the breeze and conversation. Harriott pointed to a small live oak on the lawn. She told Washington that she was planning to have it removed because it would eventually interfere with the majestic view. "Mrs. Horry, let it stay," said the president. "It can do no harm where it is and I would not think of cutting it down." Strong and sure of her own will, Harriott Pinckney Horry seldom took advice.

More than two centuries later, the tree still stands at Hampton, an enormous, impressive part of the landscape. It is called the "Washington Oak."[10]

Charleston was special. Twelve merchant ship captains sat at the oars of an elaborate barge that took Washington across the Cooper River. They were dressed in "short jackets of light blue silk, black florentine breeches, white silk stockings with light blue silk bow-knots in their shoes" and topped off with "round black hats, with a light blue wide silk sash round the crowns."[11] Assorted vessels flanked the barge, including two with musicians and singers who serenaded the president all the way to Prioleau's Wharf. Governor Charles Pinckney, sometimes referred to as "Young Charles" to distinguish him from his older cousin Charles Cotesworth, waited there. Pinckneys in South Carolina, like Carrolls in Maryland, were thick on the ground.[12]

Washington's procession snaked up one block from the wharf to East Bay and headed down to the Exchange and Provost to ascend to the portico looking down Broad Street. There were additional speeches and a parade, but Washington finally reached his rooms in a private home rented for the visit by the city, which included servants and a housekeeper hired for the week. She was to present Washington with a bill for all expenses at the end of his stay. He intended to honor his pledge to pay his way.

Charleston was special, but the visit soon fell into the familiar pattern of dinners, balls, and tours of military sites. No drudgery or routine, though, could blunt the dazzling effect of Charleston's women. They were so uniformly lovely that Washington noted they "exceeded any thing of the kind I had ever seen."[13] That bit of spice helped leaven the tedium of the trip's purpose, which was to court the state's elite politicians and solidify their support for his administration's policies. Washington took the long view. The powerful Pinckney brothers would play important roles in the government, and Thomas would eventually produce a diplomatic prize beyond price.

Washington left Charleston escorted by members of the Society of the Cincinnati, Governor Pinckney, and Senators Ralph Izard and Pierce Butler. Across the Savannah River was Georgia, and a delegation of Georgia leaders had him board a boat for a downriver cruise to Savannah, where a grand greeting and a two-day festival passed before he could at last count his steps as taking him toward home rather than away from it. At Augusta, he crossed the Savannah River into South Carolina and rode toward the new capital of Columbia through the upcountry. Here was the place that he hoped would alert him to trouble or calm his worries about the government's policies in general and the whiskey tax in particular. South Carolina's new capital was under construction, an experiment in miniature similar to what Washington was attempting on a grand scale on the Potomac.[14]

Both the mood of the citizens and the progress of South Carolina's city planning pleased him. The backcountry of North Carolina awaited him, completely indistinguishable from South Carolina's to the weary eye. At the border thirteen young militiamen had waited in the sun for hours for the president to appear. Among them a young physician named Charles Caldwell was to greet the president, but confronted by the great man, Caldwell forgot his memorized speech and only saluted with his sword. "Not only did I forget my oft-repeated address," Caldwell later remembered, "but I became positively unable to articulate a word." Washington had seen it a hundred times before. He returned the salute and launched into his stock response. He chose to ride Prescott at Caldwell's side as they headed toward Salisbury.[15] The miles unreeled.

He moved quickly into Virginia and back to Mount Vernon. The journey came to a close with his arrival home ahead of schedule, a military precision that made Washington uncharacteristically boast in a letter to Hamilton that because he had determined his "line of march" in advance he had not "departed in a single instance" from it except for an extra day in Columbia. He tended to some farm business, visited the site of the new capital, and was back in Philadelphia by July 6, 1791. Pealing bells and artillery salutes greeted him.[16]

The tour's expenses were easily $2,000, including the coach and horses he bought for the trip, a sum that put a dent into his $25,000 salary, but Washington had seen new things, met new people, and reacquainted with old friends who smiled when they saw him.[17] There had been young, tongue-tied Caldwell, not unlike the shopgirl in Newport. And in the early part of the journey, a mistake had set a pleasant tone for the trip, providing another one of those random flashes of humanity that always seemed to find George Washington. In North Carolina, they were directed to a well-appointed inn for breakfast. The president had already put his companions through the dawn ride of several hours, and they were all famished. The innkeeper's wife seemed flustered at first but soon threw the house into action, and everyone settled in at a bounteous table of pork, fried chicken, turkey, eggs, ham, sausage, hoecakes, and biscuits. Paying for everything himself, Washington was frugal and ate only a boiled egg and drank coffee, but everyone else dug in to the best meal they had enjoyed in days. Washington asked for the bill, but the "innkeeper" revealed himself to be Colonel John Allen and introduced his wife as the lady of the house. Washington slowly realized that this was no inn at all but a private home. The magnificent breakfast was a show of hospitality rather than a commercial transaction. In that regard, Allen would accept no money. He had his horse saddled to escort Washington to the next town.[18] There would be a mayor and a militia in it, a pealing church bell and a rusticated cannon primed for firing. But behind him were Colonel Allen and his lady, assembling all the treasures of their house on a moment's notice, and refusing anything but gratitude in payment. The food had smelled wonderful. It had smelled like America.

The president was not the only wandering soul that summer. While Washington was away from Philadelphia, rumors swirled about Jefferson and Madison's activities, which consisted of a "botanical" expedition through the mid-Atlantic and New England states. The two men always portrayed their trip as a working vacation in which Jefferson observed flora and fauna while Madison made companionable conversation, but conjecture about the trip's real object persists to this day. Robert Troup, a close friend of Hamilton, believed the journey was to establish an opposition party whose motto would be *Carthago delenda est,* a reference to Rome's single-minded aim to destroy an enemy, root and branch. Yet Troup and others could have been a bit keyed up. Nothing alarms a cautious victor more than a wounded but shrewd foe.

The length of their journey raises doubts about Jefferson and Madison's partisan purposes. The first part was likely political because they were overtly political people, and the "botanical" nature of the trip could have been overstated. It is possible, though, that the two were more in search of recreation and relaxation than political opportunities.[19] At most it can be verified that they were eager to gauge popular sentiment in light of Hamilton's string of legislative victories. Dinner-table talk lauding monarchy, the general direction of the First Congress, and troubling publications could have prompted the journey for no other reason than to find out how widespread the cancers were.

They did not avoid political leaders but neither did they seek them out. They likely did not visit Hamilton's political enemy George Clinton in New York, as some alleged, and no evidence places them in the company of Aaron Burr or Robert Livingston, either. They visited Philip Schuyler, Hamilton's father-in-law, who received them with bounteous and jovial hospitality. Ordinary people interested them more. They listened to tradesmen, laborers, and farmers. Among those folk, Jefferson repeated arguments he had rehearsed in his report on the fisheries to promote commerce with France in a region attracted to Britain by habit and trade.

The traveling Virginians did notice scenery, flora, and fauna, as was at least their stated intent. Jefferson was intensely interested in the problem of the Hessian fly, the bane of wheat growers everywhere, and he hoped to compile evidence that it came from someplace abroad, whether the German provinces or, by indirection, eggs in European cargoes. He was frustrated in that endeavor, but he did pursue his private enthusiasm to record Indian vocabularies during an impromptu visit to an Algonquian remnant called the Unquachog. Wholesome activity and rest, sightseeing, scientific inquiry, and a bit of political pulse taking best described the work of these wanderers. Their conversations with people at crossroads and corner markets encouraged them, but their findings did not necessarily convince them of a tide turning against Hamilton's policies.

She was pretty, in her early twenties, and distressed. Her husband had left her stranded in Philadelphia, she explained through her tears, and she needed just a bit of money to return to New York City and her family. She said she knew of the secretary of the Treasury through her husband's former employment as a commissary agent and his subsequent ties to the government; she knew, she said, that the secretary was a kind man who could spare the money, a loan to be sure, and would doubtless want to help her. She told about her young daughter who waited in their small rented rooms. Alexander Hamilton was moved. He told her that he would come to her lodgings later that day, perhaps in the evening, to see that she had what she needed. She told him her name and provided her address. She was Maria Reynolds.

That evening he went wandering and paused before her door. Hamilton's wife, Betsey, and the children were in New York with her father; they would come to Philadelphia later after he had settled in. Hamilton paused, but he finally tapped on Maria Reynolds's door. It opened, and he stepped inside. He had the money, he told her. She was standing very close. Her eyes told him it wasn't only the money she wanted. Hamilton obliged.[20]

13

"Political Heresies"

On April 16, 1791, Nicholas Eveleigh, the comptroller of the Treasury, died after a long illness. The routine matter of replacing him became an unexpected indication of how contentious cabinet relations had become. On the day Eveleigh died, Tench Coxe asked Jefferson to tell Washington that he would like the job, once "decorum permitted."[1] Alexander Hamilton had begun to distrust Coxe as a prelude to loathing him, but at this stage he was irritated with his assistant for helping Jefferson with the fisheries report by providing vital Treasury figures that Hamilton wanted to withhold. Coxe was competent, but he had acquired the unfortunate reputation of a sycophant, and Jefferson did not much like him, either.

When Coxe approached Hamilton about succeeding Eveleigh, Hamilton candidly told him he already had a candidate in mind, which was true. Auditor of the Treasury Oliver Wolcott, Jr., had shown a flair for finance while working under Eveleigh, who had been ill from the moment he became comptroller, requiring Wolcott to perform many of his duties. Yet Hamilton still encouraged Coxe to apply to Washington for the job, which Coxe did indirectly through Jefferson. Jefferson forwarded Coxe's request to Washington without an endorsement, though with a blank commission form. The secretary of state's office was charged with dispensing commission forms, so his including it wasn't a tacit endorsement. Rather, the absence of a recommendation more than indicated that the secretary of state was not interested in the secretary of the Treasury's staff. For his part, Hamilton wrote to Washington recommending Wolcott. He apparently asked Henry Knox and Robert Morris to endorse Wolcott as well. Hamilton was ensuring that Wolcott would get the position, which meant his suggestion that Coxe apply had another purpose.

Hamilton's letter reached Washington first, and, in fact, it was actually an aide-mémoire because they had discussed Eveleigh's replacement before the president left for his southern tour. There was never any doubt that Wolcott would receive the appointment, but when Hamilton heard that Jefferson had sent Coxe's application, he acted furious, as if Jefferson had been trying to interfere in his department. The implication was that Jefferson was trying to plant a spy in Treasury. Jefferson, for his part, did not know the Coxe application had become an issue until he started hearing gossip about his interfering in Hamilton's bailiwick. The gossip could have only originated with Hamilton.[2] In short, the entire affair made little sense unless one believed that Jefferson was trying to place a mole at Treasury. Some historians have precisely concluded this to make sense of the incident. Yet if Jefferson had wanted this result, he was certainly lackadaisical in bringing it about.

Possibly the Coxe application was Hamilton's effort to paint Jefferson as meddlesome and diminish him in the eyes of the president, but he needn't have bothered since Jefferson himself was responsible for another incident that greatly angered George Washington. While touring the South, the president heard that Jefferson had insulted John Adams by committing an incredible indiscretion in print as the secretary of state. It all began in the fall of 1789 when Adams began writing a series of anonymous essays he titled the *Discourses on Davila*. They critically examined the French Revolution and appeared in Fenno's *Gazette of the United States*. Though the essays were unsigned, almost everyone knew Adams to be the author. In 1787, Adams had written a three-volume defense of highly centralized government that he titled *Defence of the Constitutions of the United States of America*, which even a descendant later remarked carried the customary Adams flaw of his taking "too little care of the shape in which his thoughts were clothed."[3] *Discourses* had much the same style. Jefferson concluded from *Defence of Constitutions* that John Adams was a monarchist—an unfair conclusion that Jefferson never abandoned, even in old age.

Jefferson was, therefore, primed to dislike the *Discourses*. Adams cast his essays in the form of a commentary on the seventeenth-century historian Arrigo Caterino Davila's *History of the Civil Wars of France*. His treatment was characteristically voluminous as he denounced the violent overthrow of government and argued that a complete break with the past invited chaos. His views were similar to those more cogently presented in Edmund Burke's *Reflections on the Revolution in France,* which was published in the same year and attracted much more notice than the *Discourses.* Burke's influence as a member of Parliament as well as his reputation for astute political observation inspired Thomas Paine to write a pamphlet in refutation titled *The Rights of Man,* which was published in Great Britain with a dedicatory letter to George Washington, in Paine's estimation the most important defender of the rights he described. Paine, the most effective pamphleteer of the American Revolution, proudly sent the president fifty copies of his latest work.

When the pamphlets arrived in the United States, Secretary of the House John Beckley scrutinized one before loaning it to his friend Madison who, in turn, loaned it to Jefferson. Beckley suggested that Jefferson see to its publication in an American edition, and Jefferson accordingly loaned the much-loaned copy to printer Jonathan Bayard Smith with a cover note. In that note Jefferson expressed his pleasure "that something is at length to be publicly said against the political heresies which have sprung up among us."[4] Smith mistakenly took Jefferson's note as a blurb. When he published *The Rights of Man* he used the quotation in a preface, attributing it to the secretary of state.

Thomas Jefferson was mortified, which was clearly revealed by the way he wrote Washington to explain the accident. He opened as if to inform Washington on the latest news in Philadelphia before approaching the reason for the letter: "The indiscretion of a printer," he gingerly remarked, had caused an embarrassing situation. Jefferson candidly admitted that he meant the Adams essays when referring to "heresies," but he quickly affirmed that Adams was "one of the most honest & disinterested men alive" for whom he had "a cordial esteem, increased by long habits of concurrence in opinion in the days of his republicanism: and even since his apostasy to hereditary monarchy & nobility, tho' we differ, we differ as friends should do."[5] Adams would feel differently, as

Jefferson well knew. He described the prickly vice president's likely reaction to Madison with a priceless understatement: "I . . . think he will be displeased."[6] To be sure, John Adams was angry, but he was also wounded by his supposed friend's words. Abigail Adams was just angry. She attributed Jefferson's behavior to envy and ambition. She was not alone.

The same day that Jefferson sent his letter to Washington, Lear sent the president the Smith edition of Paine's pamphlet with a reference to Jefferson's contribution.[7] If Lear's gesture was to soften the blow, it didn't. Washington cringed. Adams spouting off in anonymous essays was an eccentricity. Jefferson's remark was attributed to him by his title, giving the impression that the endorsement of Paine (and criticism of Adams) was an official statement. Yet Washington was not reacting to mere contretemps. The revolution in France was poised to become a major problem for American foreign policy. Americans could recall Paine as a champion of American independence, but extending that acclaim to him as a champion of the increasingly violent French Revolution was highly uncertain. In that regard, the subject of his pamphlet required official prudence in recognizing it or responding to the events it defended. For the U.S. government and the American people it became an argument about the basic conflict between preserving liberty and maintaining order. It was about more than a breach between old friends or the potential estrangement of a president and a cabinet minister. It was about even more than the direction of the American government. It was about the direction of America.

Those seeking calm were right to want the entire affair to recede, but in early June another series of essays signed "Publicola" began appearing in Benjamin Russell's *Columbian Centinel*. Their direct attack on Paine was an oblique one on Jefferson, who was suspected of writing attacks on Adams (he didn't), and Adams was thought to be Publicola, which he wasn't. In fact, Jefferson and Madison learned rather quickly the author was Adams's son, John Quincy Adams. Anonymity was a very thin veil for the sagacious observer.

Several consequences resulted from these events. First, the public perceived John Adams as a monarchist, a charge that was as unfair as it was enduring. Second, Jefferson and John Adams eventually made a show of patching things up, but they never returned to the trust and friendship of earlier times.[8] The bad taste of the affair lingered, and it was only a matter of time before another incident would estrange them completely. Finally, the display of discord in the administration more than irritated Washington, and his letters and notes to Jefferson showed a hint of a chill. When Washington finally received Jefferson's letter of explanation, after the president arrived at Mount Vernon from his southern trip, he simply replied that "this acknowledgement is all the notice I shall take . . . until I have the pleasure of seeing you."[9] Washington did not thank Paine for his numerous copies of *Rights of Man* for a year. It was not like him to leave unacknowledged even an unsolicited gift, but George Washington was out of sorts.

Washington's posterior carbuncle returned shortly after his trip to the South and required another surgery to excise the infection. Luckily this time the doctors caught the condition early, and the surgery was not as radical as it had been two years earlier. Shortly afterward little Wash took ill with a high fever that preoccupied Martha for more than a month. By September, everybody in the High Street house was ready for a change, and Washington made arrangements to visit Mount Vernon briefly, but it would be a working vacation. Washington would prepare his annual message under a tight deadline, since Congress intended to reconvene at the end of October.

As usual he had asked Hamilton, Knox, and Jay for ideas to include in the annual message, and he rushed his departure for the capital to include a stop at Georgetown, Maryland, to attend the first sale of federal district lots. He met with Jefferson and Madison, who were there for the same purpose, and they gave him some additional ideas for his address. The new capital remained a tie between the three men, who were otherwise growing apart. Jefferson had embarrassed the administration with his careless letter. Madison had been inexplicably obtuse about legislation the president tacitly but doubtlessly endorsed. Jefferson and Madison had been meandering around the countryside planning, it was said, political mischief. Washington pulled the reigns of his horse northward toward Philadelphia. Possibly all of them realized that Madison's advice carried waning weight with George Washington.

In fact, Alexander Hamilton was clearly the prevailing influence in Washington's third annual message. There was, for example, a bit of boasting about the brisk sale of bank stock, not something Washington would have included on his own. Madison again headed the House committee that responded, but the result was more congratulatory than Madison wanted. It was true that the government was entering its fourth year under the Constitution in good shape. Washington looked hale despite recent health problems, and sometimes he was almost cheerful. The economy was prospering, and Europe appeared to be taking the United States more seriously.

George Hammond's arrival seemed to indicate a thaw in British relations, although a slow one. The newly appointed British minister was given his opportunity because senior and mid-level diplomats had no interest in the American posting. At twenty-eight he was young and hardly equipped to cope with the tense situation between the United States and Great Britain in October 1791. Oxford had educated Hammond, and his secretarial duties at the Paris peace negotiations had acquainted him with John Jay and John Adams. Later, he came to know Thomas Jefferson in Paris. Hammond had seen just enough of the world to make him heedlessly confident. Minor diplomatic appointments to Vienna, Copenhagen, and Madrid provided a seasoning of a sort, but none of those places was Philadelphia, and none of the people in them was Thomas Jefferson.

The only regular reports the British had received about the operations of the American government had come from unofficial emissary George Beckwith, who had little regard for America's government or president, possibly because of rather than despite Hamilton's near groveling interviews. Beckwith almost sneered that "the talents of General Washington were greatly overrated in the world" and that he had succeeded partly because of "a good choice of men around him."[10] Young Edward Thornton, mightily impressed with himself as Hammond's secretary, agreed. He described Washington to a friend as foolishly enjoying the pomp and ceremony of his office—he preferred Hammond to visit him "in full dress," sniffed Thornton—but conceded that he had "discernment and penetration" as evidenced by "the judicious choice he has generally made of persons to fill public stations."[11]

Aside from setting up an embassy and, as Thornton noted, dressing up, Hammond's purpose in coming to America was a mystery. To begin, he stood on European diplomatic protocol to tell Jefferson that he would not present his credentials until Washington appointed a counterpart to proceed to Great Britain. The demand made Hammond as well as his hosts the prisoner of the calendar, and once he realized that a place as huge as the United States meant slower communications than between London and Cornwall, he bent the rules a bit. He told Jefferson that Washington's simply announcing an appointment would mark an exchange of ministers. Washington already planned to send Thomas Pinckney of South Carolina to London, and after Hammond was notified of that, he deigned to present his credentials to Secretary Jefferson.

On November 11, 1791, Jefferson formally presented Hammond to President Washington. Pinckney accepted, tying up the protocol package rather tidily, but the breakthrough was short-lived. To his disgust, Jefferson gradually discerned that George Hammond didn't have instructions to do anything other than make a nuisance of himself. His government wanted him to address alleged American violations of the 1783 peace treaty, mediate between the United States and Indians, and prevent the passage of trade legislation discriminating against Great Britain. Each of these tasks was a condescending presumption, but added to their insult was the fact that Hammond had nothing to concede in return.

It was also most peculiar that George Beckwith remained in Philadelphia. Hamilton continued plying unauthorized diplomacy with Beckwith and came close to revealing how elaborate his conversations had been when Beckwith's boss Lord Dorchester offered to mediate between the United States and the northwestern Indians. In response to overtures Hamilton had undertaken without Washington's knowledge, the sudden, inexplicable offer from the Canadian governor-general was more than awkward. Hamilton first tried to cast doubt on the authenticity of Dorchester's communication, and when that lie collapsed, Hamilton resorted to another. He said it was all Beckwith's idea.[12]

Hammond also met with Hamilton, finding him more congenial and "his manners better" than the coldly formal Thomas Jefferson, an attitude Hammond found odd since Jefferson had been friendly in

Paris.[13] Hammond was too young to understand the difference between a drawing room companion and a diplomatic adversary. Edward Thornton liked Jefferson no better than he did Washington. He said that Jefferson had "a face in who no sentiment of the softer or more amiable kind ever attempted an expression," which was a skewed perception of the first order. Thornton also described Jefferson as "cunning," which was more accurate than Thornton, or Hammond for that matter, knew.[14]

And yet Jefferson's cunning did not matter in the least. He was willing to talk to Hammond but preferred meaningful matters be handled in writing. The result was a contentious dialogue in documents that couriers sped from the State Department to the British residence and back, often bearing times of day rather than dates. When Jefferson brought up the British-occupied forts, Hammond's back bowed. "It is scarcely necessary for me to remark to you," he hissed, that Britain had suspended execution of that part of the treaty because Americans had violated Articles, 4, 5, and 6 of the treaty. These articles bore on American payment of outstanding British debts and compensation to Loyalists for confiscated property.[15] Hammond's authority to discuss issues but not resolve them was frustrating, and Jefferson did not hide his exasperation. Hamilton's friendliness was a stark contrast. Jefferson did not know that Hamilton was more than hinting to the British minister that the secretary of state did not represent the true views of the Washington administration. Once Hammond became convinced of that, the secretary of state was, in essence, wasting his time.

Jefferson tried to resolve the disputed portion of the Anglo-American border, but Hamilton whispered to Hammond that British boundary claims were likely correct. Hammond worried that the United States' securing navigation rights to the Mississippi from Spain could jeopardize Britain's similar rights, but Hamilton reassured him that he had nothing to worry about. Jefferson brought up the slaves the British had taken during the Revolution, but Hamilton told Hammond that most Americans did not see it as a major issue.[16] Finally, when Jefferson sent Hammond a lengthy report he had labored over for days—a report that had not only Washington's approval but also ostensibly Hamilton's—Hammond heard from the Treasury secretary that it represented only

Jefferson's views. Jefferson marveled at the British minister's stubborn attitude. He fumed over wasting his time. When Thomas Pinckney arrived in London, he would also fume over wasting his time. Only Alexander Hamilton and George Hammond knew the reasons why.

Washington nominated Pinckney to the British post along with ministers to France and The Hague. These nominations were controversial for at least two reasons, and several senators joined to block them. Some disagreed with the concept of sending diplomats abroad, and others who disapproved of Washington's choices were willing to join the isolationists to block them. The appointments also revived arguments about the meaning of "advice and consent." Washington carefully avoided asking for advice about domestic appointments, but senators contended that the importance of representing America abroad required him to consult with the Senate, perhaps even in person, before submitting names to it. Talk of consultation nearly sent Washington into a rage.[17] Senator Benjamin Hawkins kept Jefferson apprised of the debates (still held behind closed doors), and the secretary of state counseled the president to step lightly.[18]

Jefferson exhibited remarkable forbearance and as a compromise asked Washington to allow him to provide justification for appointing ministers and to defend the nominations. He, too, objected to one of Washington's selections, who happened to be the one provoking the most opposition. Against Jefferson's advice, Washington had decided to send Gouverneur Morris to France as U.S. minister. The erudite Morris, with his reputation for illicit romances and disregard for conventional morality, had attracted a surprising amount of opposition. John Adams thought him a rogue, and Roger Sherman of Connecticut was typical in considering the rakish Morris "an irreligious, & profane man."[19] Washington could use the excuse that Morris was near at hand, having been the president's informal envoy to the British. In addition, Washington simply liked and trusted Gouverneur Morris. Like those senators who knew Gouverneur Morris, Jefferson worried that Morris's penchant for acerbic comments would combine with his animus against the French Revolution to make him unwelcome in Paris. The more enthusiastic revolutionaries were sure to find him objectionable. Still, he was Washington's choice, and Jefferson defended him.

Neither Washington nor Morris knew that Hamilton had undermined Morris's mission to Great Britain, and Hamilton covered his tracks by lobbying hard in the Senate for Morris's confirmation. Hamilton made sure that Morris knew about his support, and a grateful Morris promised confidential information as a reward. Morris thought he knew who all his enemies in the administration were and suspected Thomas Jefferson, his actual superior, to be one of them.[20] When Washington informed Morris of his appointment, Morris knew nothing of Jefferson's defense of him in the Senate.[21] Washington, however, was more pointed. He wanted Morris to know about the Senate's rancorous debate and its charges about his "levity, and imprudence of conversation and conduct" and "habit of expression, [that] indicated a hauteaur disgusting to those who happened to differ from you in sentiment." Washington told Morris to be careful. Morris promised his old friend that he would be.[22]

The French had already sent a new minister to the United States who was a more popular choice in America than Morris would be in France. Jean-Baptiste Ternant had friends in the United States, Washington among them, from his service as a French officer during the Revolutionary War. He also came with a strong recommendation from Lafayette.

Ternant arrived in the United States at an interesting time in Franco-American relations. He was technically the minister of King Louis XVI, but the king's fortunes declined sharply after he and his family were caught trying to flee France on the night of June 20, 1791. Taken back to Paris and confined to the Tuileries Palace, the king and queen of France were virtual prisoners for two years until the radicals of the French Revolution executed them in 1793. Before that, the French National Assembly adopted a new constitution, established a limited monarchy, and essentially forced Louis to accept all changes. Ternant informed Washington of the new constitution, and the president immediately forwarded the information to Congress. The House of Representatives congratulated the French on their new government, an encroachment in foreign affairs that offended the president. Ternant was fated to represent an unsettled government to a contentious one.

He was a survivor and remained in America for the next year and a half as his country transitioned to a constitutional monarchy, became a republic, and killed its king. Through it all he faithfully pursued the aims of each manifestation of his government. He hoped that as the French republicans gained ascendancy the U.S. secretary of state would become an overt champion of France's interests, and Jefferson was certainly a sympathetic observer of France's revolution. Yet he was also determined to observe strict formality toward all diplomats. In the absence of a warm relationship with Jefferson, Ternant, like Hammond, turned to Hamilton, whom he found engaging and solicitous. Ternant was careful with this friend of Britain, but Hamilton surprised everyone by broaching the idea of a commercial treaty with Ternant. Washington instructed Jefferson to pursue it. When Jefferson drew up a proposal, however, Hamilton objected to most of its terms. Jefferson all but threw up his hands.

However, more than personal relations, events in the Caribbean preoccupied Franco-American relations for Ternant's tenure and beyond. In August 1791 a slave uprising began in the French colony of Saint-Domingue on the island of Hispaniola. The colony had been closely following the revolution in France with the hope among whites for greater rights and representation. Meanwhile, the island's slaves, who outnumbered free people by more than six to one, had also heard the revolutionary rhetoric of *liberté* and *égalité* and were inspired to begin a rebellion of their own. It would have repercussions throughout the hemisphere for the next century. Saint-Domingue's colonial government appealed to the United States, beseeching the federal and southern state governments for help in suppressing the uprising. French colonial officials assumed that southerners would want to quash a slave rebellion early.

South Carolina governor Charles Pinckney believed that this was a matter best decided on the federal level. The rebellion started during the congressional recess, and Washington was at Mount Vernon when he first learned of it. Even at this earliest stage, the news was sobering. Tobias Lear received reports that four thousand people had already died in the fighting. Ternant had no instructions from home, but he resented the colony's attempt to negotiate directly with the American government. Jefferson was at Monticello, so Ternant approached Hamilton and Knox, the former for money and the latter for arms. They wrote to Washington recommending that the requests be honored, with expenses charged against the French debt. Ternant's overriding fear was that white colonials, instead of suppressing the rebellion, would use the aid to gain independence from France, which caused him to dispense American aid at a trickle.

Former slaves, ultimately under the leadership of the charismatic Toussaint-Louverture, continued to make gains, and the rationing of American money and supplies did little good. Yet the American die was cast. With great ambivalence the United States provided aid to suppress the uprising for two years. After all, as the ragged empires of old Europe began to fray at their edges, this was the first seeming emulation of the American Revolution in the Western Hemisphere, and with it, as with others to come in Latin America, the constraints of traditional diplomacy with Europe would conflict with American Revolutionary idealism.

The slave element in Saint-Domingue also caused political problems in America, but those can be overestimated in hindsight. Washington obviously feared that if unchecked the idea of a slave rebellion could spread to the United States, but the possible aims of Europe were more troubling at the time. Jefferson was concerned that if France lost the colony to its slaves, Spain or Great Britain would take the prize. And a prize it was. Saint-Domingue produced more sugar than any other Caribbean colony and much of the region's coffee.

Atrocities committed by all factions in Saint-Domingue made the uprising a grotesque affair. For Americans in the last decade of the eighteenth century, reports of the ghastly scenes shaped attitudes about race relations for generations.[23] Americans feared slave rebellion as a contagious disease that could lay waste to the American South. The demographic reality in the South Carolina Low Country—where slaves outnumbered whites nine to one—dwarfed Saint-Domingue's racial imbalance. Confronted by the success of Saint-Domingue's former slaves, Jefferson would eventually conclude that only concessions to Toussaint-Louverture could restore peace. Returning his followers to slavery was impossible, and the worsening conditions for whites could only encourage slaves throughout the Caribbean to assert their numerical advantage and take control.[24] It was an attempt to quarantine what Americans regarded as a virulent disease made real by the refugees in their midst. Some of them had brought the few slaves they still held.

14

"Sweets of Office"

Everything Alexander Hamilton had done thus far during Washington's presidency had been to strengthen the United States economy and polish America's image in the world. He believed that funding and assumption had gone a long way toward accomplishing the latter and that the establishment of the Bank of the United States had already provided a boost to American businesses. For the nation to compete internationally and to achieve economic independence, however, Hamilton believed it needed to enlarge its manufacturing capability. It was the final piece of the puzzle.

He led by example in promoting private enterprise, after a fashion. In the late summer of 1791, he collaborated with associates to charter the Society for Establishing Useful Manufactures (SEUM) in New Jersey to build a manufacturing town that could showcase modern machinery and industrial proficiency. Eventually the SEUM settled on a site at the falls of the Passaic River to be named after New Jersey's governor William Paterson, a bit of back scratching for future favors. The society's founders planned to use the falls to power textile mills, and they hired Pierre L'Enfant to design the canals and water traces. They hoped to import foreign labor and mechanics familiar with European textile production. The initial investors would realize little to no profits, but they laid the groundwork for one of the first great industrial towns in the United States.[1]

That was the private part of the enterprise. Hamilton, however, believed that private ventures such as the SEUM needed help from the federal government at their inception because European manufacturers were already so well established. Inspired by that belief, he submitted the *Report on Manufactures* to Congress in early December 1791. Coming a year after his controversial bank proposal, this newest series of recommendations was sure to be disputed. Hamilton hoped to head off opposition by having Madison and Jefferson read the proposal before it was submitted to Congress, but it made no difference.[2] Madison and Jefferson found the *Report on Manufactures* alarming.

The gist of the report was the recommendation that Congress raise tariffs whose revenue would provide bounties to American industry. The plan would give American manufacturers enough protection from established foreign competition to encourage growth. Madison had, at times, supported a protective tariff, but in this case he and Jefferson disagreed with the idea of bounties going to industries selected by the U.S. government under the increasing elasticity of the "necessary and proper" clause. Madison again argued that broad interpretation made the Constitution meaningless. "The parchment," he cried, "had better be thrown in the fire at once."[3] Paying people to make one thing rather than another intruded government into the free market to decide which businesses succeeded and which failed, and they insisted that the policy would lead to corruption. When people had a reason to influence government to gain its support against foreign competition, it would only be a matter of time before they were bidding for government support against domestic competitors.

Jefferson was more than discouraged. It seemed that this latest proposal would also pass Congress and be signed into law by the president despite his objections. He met with Washington on February 29, 1792, ostensibly to discuss moving the Post Office Department from Treasury to State, but the conversation became more than that. It was to be one of the most significant of the missed opportunities in the relationship between these two men.

Jefferson explained that the post office sensibly belonged under State because it fit with the other home office responsibilities of his department. Hamilton controlled an enormous amount of patronage by having both customs and the post office in his wield. Jefferson did not divulge another reason he wanted to wrest the post office from Hamilton—Jefferson hoped to disseminate his faction's message more effectively through the mail. Washington would have seen this. Perhaps Jefferson sensed the delicacy of the post office subject. He assured Washington that he was not merely seeking more power for himself, and confided his intention to resign at the end of Washington's first term.

The statement seemed to sadden the president. "In an affectionate tone," the president expressed concern at Jefferson's decision. He then confided that he, too, wanted to retire. He had accepted the presidency reluctantly, and now, almost three years into his term, he worried that some would say "that having tasted the sweets of office he could not do with out them." More important, Washington explained that he was tired. He admitted he was deaf and that his memory was slipping. Thomas Jefferson must have been sad, like the officers at Newburgh, to see how very old George Washington looked. He listened as Washington gave the main reason he wanted to go home: He could not bear the partisan bickering any longer.

Jefferson saw his opening: All Washington needed to do was look to Hamilton's policies for the cause of partisan rancor. Jefferson explicitly cited the *Report on Manufactures*.[4] Washington was silent, which was too bad. He, too, believed that Hamilton's bounty scheme was unconstitutional, but he did not open his mind to Jefferson. The proposal would have to run its course in Congress before the president could state his opinion. Standing on form was typical for Washington, and possibly it was in this conversation a convenient way to avoid exchanging confidences with a man who had recently irritated him. But it would have been good for Jefferson to know that George Washington agreed with him on a crucial constitutional issue. Like the spectacles at Newburgh years before, it might have made all the difference.

As it was, Jefferson would never have occasion to know. Hamilton's proposals finally overreached congressional acceptance of government growth. The recommendations in the *Report on Manufactures* were not passed, and a bill with bounties never came to Washington's desk. A point of agreement between Washington and his fellow Virginians remained unstated and unexplored. Hamilton had at last lost in the legislature, but nothing indicated he was other than ascendant with the executive. That enduring impression for Thomas Jefferson made all the difference in the world.

In the Ohio wilderness, Arthur St. Clair failed to detect the presence of Little Turtle's warriors until they surprised his force of about 1,400 men on the morning of November 4, 1791, sending them fleeing in all directions. Only about one-third of the men made it back to Fort Washington unscathed. This second disaster sent Washington into one of his rare fits of temper. According to Tobias Lear, the news arrived on a Friday evening during Martha's drawing room. He clenched his jaw but held his temper until everyone had left.[5] The ill-fated expedition of 1791 was not only St. Clair's or the militia's fault, however. Both Harmar and St. Clair had been sent on their errands by Knox and Hamilton, men wholly lacking in frontier experience. It is surprising that Washington would forget all he knew about the Ohio wilderness to sanction these impossible undertakings.

Washington concluded that the war "must be prosecuted upon different principles."[6] As long as the British remained in posts on American soil, a new military strategy would be necessary to intimidate the Indians to negotiate. To that end, Washington worked closely with Knox to provide Congress with documents demonstrating that state militias were inadequate for achieving a national objective. Congress regularized the militia and gave the president more control of it in national emergencies. Congress also agreed to increase the size of the regular army temporarily to handle the current crisis. As one congressman noted, to defeat the Indians would "require a powerful army and a Judicious commander."[7]

Other problems, however, were moving matters in the West to a critical juncture. The region south of the Ohio River was filling up and getting angry. Hamilton's excise and fiscal policies seemed either intrusive or remote from the immediate needs of Mississippi navigation and quelling the Indian menace. In late 1791, westerners had the growing impression that the government did not care for their safety or their opinions. For them the St. Clair disaster proved the former and Hamilton's fiscal policies the latter. It confirmed everything they thought was wrong with the national government. Neither a powerful army nor a judicious commander could correct that impression.

By early 1792, Washington's cabinet and informal advisers divided on almost every question that came before them. The pattern of Hamilton and Knox taking one side and Jefferson and Randolph the other was well established by this time. The frequency of meetings contributed to disagreements, though Washington hoped the opposite would occur. He still preferred to mull over written opinions to reach his own conclusions, but he also believed that men who could sit down together could resolve their differences. Because nobody was disposed to be deliberately rude, everyone at least appeared to get along when discussing things in person. They often dined together, sometimes at Washington's house in the morning over breakfast or at informal "family" dinners. They attended Washington's formal Thursday afternoon dinners and visited each other's houses or ran into one another at other people's homes. Sometimes they actually seemed convivial. As winter passed into spring in 1792, though, their differences became more noticeable because they were more serious. Washington consoled himself that they were men of principle and would not let personal animosity cloud their judgment. He liked to believe that, at least.

It became harder to believe when he began receiving anonymous letters warning him of the duplicitous activities of Thomas Jefferson and his "cunning little friend" James Madison.[8] There were three of these letters, all apparently written by the same person, likely a member of the House of Representatives. The anonymous accuser charged Jefferson with naked ambition, most particularly a desire for Washington's retirement so that Jefferson could replace him. Jefferson was godless, a radical, and deceitful in using Madison and Freneau's *Gazette* to turn Washington and the country against Alexander Hamilton. On the heels of these letters an anonymous pamphlet accused Jefferson of sacrificing the nation's interests to his pro-French policies. Eliza Powel sent Washington a copy of the pamphlet, and he thanked her with a note saying that the author should have been a bit more careful with his facts.[9]

It had been a trying congressional session for the president as he watched men he had known and trusted for years reach levels of surprising rancor in the press and in Congress. Thinking the future of the country was at stake made them vicious. By 1792, Madison, Jefferson, and their followers believed their opponents wanted a monarchy or something resembling one. The word "republican" (lowercased) became the label for those claiming to stand against monarchists.[10] It was used to describe Madison's faction, though he would not have liked the term "faction." Nobody believed that Washington wanted a monarchy, let alone that he dreamed of himself as a king. But Madison and Jefferson feared the people around the president and worried that he uncritically trusted them.

Hamilton and his supporters believed that Jefferson and Madison were disloyal to the government, that they supported French interests at the expense of their own country, and that they intended to undo the good that had been done at the Constitutional Convention. Democratic government, no matter how romanticized by Hamilton's foes, meant mob rule to him and his supporters. Falling back on the rhetorical tactics that had succeeded during ratification, they called themselves Federalists to emphasize their allegiance to the federal Constitution and the glory days of 1787 and 1788.

Making political disagreements into questions of potential subversion turned congressional apportionment, coinage, the presidential succession, state debts, and local political races into life-or-death issues. The 1790 federal census for the first time provided figures for state populations, making it necessary to reapportion the House of Representatives. Doing so had ramifications beyond altering the congressional clout of certain states. The adjustment of House delegations would, in turn, determine each state's electoral votes in the next presidential election. The Constitution stipulated a ratio of one congressman per 30,000 people, except for states that did not have 30,000 people, which would have one. Fractions of population complicated the formula. A state with 59,000 people would essentially have almost half of its population unrepresented. To reach the 1:30,000 ratio, the House divided the entire population of the country by 120—the total number of representatives in the House. It worked out that an extra congressman would be allotted to eight states with the largest fractional populations. The problem was that some states, such as Virginia, would lose representatives under the new apportionment formula. Virginians such as Madison, Jefferson, and Randolph understandably thought this arbitrary and unfair, and they had a point. Rather than standardizing the ratio, the House had contrived a way to favor some states and penalize others. The eight states receiving an extra congressman had more than one representative for every 30,000 citizens. Jefferson urged Washington to veto the measure as unconstitutional.

Washington understood the objection and agreed with Jefferson. But he was also worried that because Knox, Hamilton, and many northern congressmen supported the bill, his veto could be interpreted as catering to southern sectionalism and specifically favoring Virginia. Jefferson was near exasperation over this excessive regard for appearance over constitutional common sense. He enlisted Randolph to persuade the president. Jefferson and Hamilton's chronic disagreements had increasingly steered Washington to Edmund Randolph for policy as well as legal advice. Jefferson hoped that this would be one of the times Washington listened to the measured counsel of his attorney general.

Washington had known the Randolph family for as long as he could remember. It seemed like yesterday that the boy who now sat as his attorney general had shown up in Cambridge more than ten years earlier to become an aide-de-camp, all bright-eyed intelligence and dark good looks. Edmund at twenty-three had avoided the stoutness that eventually made most of the men in his family resemble stacks of large and small spheres with legs. He looked more like his father, who had been King's Counsel in Virginia and had returned to England rather than participate in American treason against that king. Edmund's father then became a nasty propagandist for the Crown, penning fictions about Washington to discredit him, but Washington never held that against young Randolph.[11] His uncle Peyton had been a solid patriot, and when Peyton fell dead of a stroke one afternoon and forced Edmund to leave Washington's Boston household prematurely, everyone missed him. Randolph was the rarity of a first-class mind with an amiable personality. He began to look like his uncle—large growing larger—but he took to law the way painters take to paint pots, for Randolph was truly an artist in the tangles of English common law and American jurisprudence. Washington liked his affairs steered by the best of experts, so he routinely had Randolph handle his legal matters. It had kept the two of them in touch. Washington always tried to pay him. Randolph never took a penny.

After his brief time as Washington's aide, Randolph had become Virginia's rising star, an ascent that foreshadowed Madison's rise in the same generation. Randolph became the new state's first attorney general following independence, strangely retracing his tarnished family's footsteps by restoring luster to the Randolph name in the post his Loyalist father had held while serving the hated Crown.

Madison and Randolph sat together in Virginia's delegation to the Congress during the chaotic postwar years and had shared contempt for the body's failings and the system's faults. Beneath official relations, their mutual personal experience encouraged friendly affection. Madison fretted along with his friend over the poor health and difficult pregnancies of Randolph's wife, Betsy. The daughter of prominent Virginia jurist and legislator Robert Carter Nicholas, Betsy had been a spritely child who stunned Edmund Randolph the instant he laid eyes on her when they were childhood playmates. Growing up, Betsy Nicholas became young Randolph's sweetheart as they developed a deep, abiding love. Their friend Jemmy was godfather to their son John, born in October 1785, and he shared their grief when the baby died not long afterward. It had happened just months before the Annapolis Convention. For Madison and Randolph, going to that meeting had been therapeutic.[12]

As governor of Virginia, Randolph led his delegation to Philadelphia to serve in the Constitutional Convention and presented the so-called Virginia Plan, authored by James Madison, to the convention. At the end, however, along with two other delegates, he objected to the Constitution and refused to sign it. Before the Virginia ratification convention, his dear friend James Madison told him his decision was all wrong. Theirs was not a choice between the Constitution and a better one to be wished for, but between the Constitution and the Articles of Confederation. The Antifederalists were dividing the country over a pointless issue, Madison explained, and the defects in the Constitution could be, and would be, repaired later. They talked it out, and after a while Madison could see a fleeting glimmer of doubt passing across his friend's eyes. Randolph always wanted what was best for his neighbors—what was best for his fellow citizens everywhere. Jemmy Madison said he knew that, he had always known that, and he watched Randolph stare into the distance frowning. Anything could happen, but Madison was all but certain that his once-lost friend was now being found.

Governor Edmund Randolph announced on the second day of Virginia's ratification convention that he had reconsidered his refusal to sign the Constitution the previous September. He declared that he now supported ratification as the lesser of the evils confronting the country. The number of people who anticipated this announcement is difficult to say, but it came at some cost. George Mason, a leading opponent of ratification, sat stunned and hollow-eyed as he seemed to sink into himself. "Young Arnold, young Arnold," he muttered, a reference to the arch-traitor of the American Revolution.[13] It was the worst epitaph any American could settle on another, and as it turned out, George Mason would not be the last man to see Edmund Randolph this way.

At the time, however, Washington and Madison were not only aware of Randolph's change of heart, they had been crucial in bringing it about, and they could not have been happier.

Randolph's influence with the president was significant, and it was now to prove crucial in bringing about the first presidential veto. April 5, 1792, was the day before Washington would have to veto, sign, or simply allow the apportionment bill to become law. That morning he went to Jefferson's rooms to discuss the matter. Back home before noon, Washington sent Randolph and Madison instructions to convene with Jefferson to draft a veto message explaining why the bill was unconstitutional. Randolph took their draft to Washington and parsed it at length, with Washington probing Randolph's views. They finally seemed finished, but as Washington walked Randolph to the door, he still seemed uncertain. He again asked if Randolph completely approved of the views in the veto message. Randolph said that upon his honor he did. After Randolph left the house, Washington copied what the three Virginians had provided him. It was the first presidential veto. The victory for Randolph, Jefferson, and Madison was significant, but it was less satisfying than it could have been because Washington had so agonized over the decision, apparently out of fear he would offend Hamilton and the North. Congress repaired the vetoed bill by establishing a standard ratio of 1:33,000, and Washington signed it.[14]

★ ★ ★

The apparently simple task of establishing a mint to coin the country's money became a political issue that embarrassed Washington in an unexpected way. A mint was clearly needed. Too many different kinds of money passed for currency in the United States. Spanish dollars, French louis d'or, and British coins of different denominations were all in various stages of mutilation as a result of making change by cutting them up. The practice of quartering or cutting into eighths Spanish dollars, for example, led to the term for the fragments as "pieces of eight." It was time for the United States to standardize its money.[15]

Jefferson had been working on the question from the moment he became secretary of state. Yet it took an incredible three years for Congress to come to terms with creating the mint, and by that time everything about governance had become a source of suspicion and a cause for dispute. The Senate finally sent a bill to the House with plans to engrave Washington's image on the new coins. The House was aghast at a plan with such obvious parallels to monarchy. The suggestion appalled Washington as much as anyone, but he again kept silent while the question played out in Congress, which meant he received little popular credit for his modesty. Madison led the House in opposing Washington's image on American coins. The House passed the mint bill with the understanding that Lady Liberty would grace the country's coins. Washington signed the amended bill and placed the mint under the State Department, which made no organizational sense. Though Jefferson was the prime mover behind coinage plans, Treasury was the logical place for the mint. Washington was trying to balance the placement of the post office, and politics made organizational logic a secondary consideration.

Meanwhile, headaches over the mint continued to bedevil the government. Filling the position of chief coiner led to one. Jefferson did not recommend someone to Washington before Congress went into recess. When he did name a man, the Senate was not in place to confirm him. Jefferson asked Edmund Randolph if Washington could make a recess appointment, but Randolph said only if Congress had not been in session when the vacancy occurred. Otherwise, the president would create a precedent of waiting until Congress adjourned to avoid Senate consultation.[16] Washington and the country had to wait until Congress returned to have a chief coiner. He was sure to be scrutinized for the potential of partisanship to infect the business of fashioning money.

As 1791 closed and the New Year dawned, Alexander Hamilton had been watching a growing volatility in government securities and bank stocks. Long before most people knew a problem was brewing, Hamilton had become quite nervous.

Americans, whether as colonials or newly independent citizens, had a long history of speculation, usually in land. George Washington speculated in land all his adult life, and the abundant tracts still available in the United States lured many to the promise of riches that always seemed a sure thing. Companies sprouted like weeds and clustered like flies on honey to acquire and sell land in the Northwest and Southwest. Investors flocked to these enterprises. Some of the ventures were honest and bankable; others were riddled with corrupt practices based on flimsy lies. Henry Knox sank small fortunes of his own into efforts to amass vast acreages in the Maine District of Massachusetts in the hope of making a large fortune. He used intermediaries to mask his involvement, not because there was anything illegal about his dealings, but because he sometimes devoted more time to his private affairs than to the War Department. In addition, his finances were often precarious, and he worried about creditors, debtors, and confidence men. The last of these could appear from nowhere.

A speculative land venture in the federal district ruined Robert Morris. Thirty-five lots were sold at the October 1791 auction, raising only $2,000, which was worse than a poor showing. Washington even bought a few lots, too, and a lottery ticket (as a gift for Tobias Lear's infant son), but his efforts to lead by example yielded little good. It was the frustration of having land nobody wanted that ultimately goaded the government to do with this place what it had done elsewhere. It sold to speculators—people who bought in volume in the federal district just as they had in the western surveys. James Greenleaf, Robert Morris, and James Nicholson formed a syndicate to purchase three thousand lots for a bargain price in return for their providing a monthly loan of $2,200 while the public buildings were being erected. They were themselves to build ten houses a year for the coming seven years. Washington agreed to this unlikely arrangement, but it was completely unworkable. For a time, he thought all was going swimmingly and even tried to interest the partners in his holdings on the Ohio and Kanawha. He was unsuccessful, which was just as well because the venture in the district was quite enough to ruin everyone associated with it.

Confidence men, after all, could appear from nowhere. In the case of James Greenleaf, it was from Massachusetts by way of Holland. Greenleaf was young and exuded a confidence that seemed of a good sort when he met Washington. Greenleaf talked convincingly with Boston Brahmin sonority about his considerable assets and his ability to secure foreign backing. His stay in Holland made him seem conversant with the leading banking houses there, some of them the same establishments funding American debts to France and others, and though Washington was inclined to be cautious, his zeal for the district blunted his better judgment. Greenleaf soon added four thousand lots to his original three thousand. In the end, though, Greenleaf was revealed to be a poseur with empty pockets and Nicholson an embezzler. Morris was left holding the bag. Debtor's prison was his fate.[17]

The federal district survived, but another financial escapade nearly destroyed the country. Toward the end of 1791, a group of economic adventurers, including wealthy New York merchant Alexander Macomb, sought to corner the market on government securities and Bank of the United States script, which were certificates held for down payments on bank stock. These men began buying as much paper as they could lay their hands on, driving the price of those securities and Bank of the United States stock sky high. The trick in cornering the market in anything is to dry up its supply. In the case of securities, it required purchasing all that were available, with the key word being "all."

It is not for the fainthearted. The very scale of purchases by a cornering operation forces prices higher and then higher still, and the last few pieces of paper become very, very dear. Everything, in fact, hinges on the scarcity of the commodity with the aim of ultimately setting its price by managing the supply. These men could make a killing only if prices continued as high as they forced them. If something altered the supply to force prices down, the men of the syndicate would be worse than ruined, and they would take many people down with them. In fact, the scheme's scope and its targeting of securities backed by the Treasury had the power to take down the government. That nearly happened when the issuance of new state bank stocks at the end of January 1792 started a gradual decline in prices that quickly turned precipitous. It rapidly became a catastrophic financial crash.

With it came panic over the value of government securities. Petty malfeasance abounded, but the worst pile of exposed rubble was not petty at all, and surveying it turned Alexander Hamilton's blood to ice. He had to stop the panic. Even his opponents knew the health of government securities and the Bank of the United States were inextricably tied to the health of the American economy and by implication the survival of the country. Henry Lee grimly noted that "the destruction of the one will convulse the other."[18]

Hamilton quickly resolved to put out the economic panic the way one would put out a raging fire. One would throw water at a fire, money at a panic. When he moved to stabilize the price of government securities by having the government itself buy as many of them as possible, he was given more room than even his supporters eventually thought wise. Yet Hamilton acted with the sort of resolve that marked the most admirable facet of his character. He sent Treasurer of the United States Samuel Meredith into the market to buy and buy, and then buy yet more. Only after beginning the process did he begin to worry if it was technically legal. Initially, there had been no time, but afterward he consulted both Vice President Adams and Secretary Jefferson. He wanted their approval, just in case there were questions later. Jefferson had not the slightest doubt that Hamilton had exceeded his authority with his profligate spending of public money, and the dizzying pace of the disaster made Adams very nervous. He immediately requested an informal opinion from Chief Justice Jay.[19]

Jay provided a curious endorsement based on financial performance rather than legal precedent or fixed principles. In short, he provided a partisan explanation as a committed Federalist rather than a learned opinion as the country's top jurist. He saw nothing illegal in Hamilton's strategy as long as it did not lose the government's money. As prices for government securities stabilized, and the panic stubbornly continued, Jay's view also made Hamilton a hostage to multiple economic factors. On April 12, 1792, Macomb defaulted on all of his obligations, which gave new life to smoldering apprehension. "This misfortune," Hamilton sighed, "has I fear a long tail to it."[20] He again moved with rapid resolve. His friend William Seton, the director of the Bank of New York, helped him buy up even more securities. The flood of money at last put out the fire, averting the national panic everyone had thought inevitable.

By mid-spring, the worst of the crisis had passed. Jefferson, Madison, and their followers, however, identified a larger and more enduring problem. Stock jobbing (a pejorative for trading in securities) created false prosperity and encouraged unhealthy volatility in security and bank stock markets for a reason. The volatility was how speculators made money. They were supremely indifferent to the possibility it might also destroy America. Jefferson compared it to "nine pins knocking one another down."[21] The gamblers wagered on the knocking down or the standing with no regard to the piles of pins that buried the lives of ordinary people.

In the midst of the panic, the House considered a recommendation made by Hamilton. It was not the best time for another of his proposals, but Hamilton was audacious if nothing else. This time he wanted the federal government to assume all remaining state debts in addition to those tied to the war effort. James Madison wearily stood to argue that creditors were hardly clamoring for the money that would flow unfairly from the federal fount to states careless with their ledgers. Jefferson had lost patience with this relentless perpetuation of the country's debt, whether by the buying of securities or the bailing out of impecunious states. Hamilton and his minions, said Jefferson, believed "that a public debt is a public blessing, so they think a perpetual one is a perpetual blessing, and therefore wish to make it so large that we can never pay it off."[22]

The two braced for the certainty that Hamilton would again have his way.[23] Yet the method Hamilton's supporters had used to get their way finally ran its string. Henry Lee denounced how "they bespatter the character of every individual who dares to utter an opinion hostile to the fiscal measures so that the chance of successful opposition is more and more doubtful."[24] Rattled by the panic and tired of Treasury's bare-knuckle tactics, Congress refused to endorse additional assumption.

The loss was a setback, but it had been a mixed legislative session for

Hamilton in any case. He had failed to obtain the bounties he wanted for industry and to secure further assumption of state debts, but he had indirectly won a higher tariff. And he had narrowly fended off an attempt to change his relationship with Congress that many had mistaken for a minor procedural matter. Madison knew better. He had long objected to Hamilton directly recommending policies to Congress without sending them through the president. Madison argued that the other department heads did not have this direct access to Congress, and that there was no reason why Hamilton should. He proposed that Hamilton communicate with the legislature only when the House or the Senate requested information from him, as was the case with the other department heads.

Whatever its merits, Madison's proposal showed more irritation than consistency. The legislation that created the Treasury, which Madison had helped to write, gave the Treasury secretary closer ties to Congress because his role had originally been envisioned as a chancellor of the exchequer. For his part, Hamilton judged Madison's move as a personal assault, an outrageous attempt to make a policy maker a mere clerk. He marshaled his supporters to defeat Madison by a vote of 31 to 27. Both men remained angry, one defeated and the other again victorious, but Hamilton knew lightning when he saw it. The vote was so close that it challenged his carefully cultivated aura of invincibility.

He brooded. He was now at war with two men too dangerous to underestimate. They certainly saw themselves at war with him for a salient far more important than political dominance in the government. This fight was over the ideological future of the country. At the end of May, Hamilton wrote one of the most important letters of his career. It was to a revenue supervisor in the state of Virginia named Edward Carrington.

A reliable Federalist, Carrington was a surprising correspondent for Hamilton's purpose, which was to portray himself as a wronged patriot thwarted in doing his duty. Carrington was also James Madison's friend. Accordingly, Hamilton claimed to be more hurt than angered by Madison's behavior, and he painted Thomas Jefferson as the evil influence behind Madison's animus. Hamilton called Jefferson "a man of profound ambition and violent passions." Madison and Jefferson had formed a party, he told Carrington, to undermine the government and satisfy Jefferson's ambition and their "womanish attachment to France." The effort to limit his contact with Congress was meant to push him out of the government. Madison and Jefferson knew that he would resign rather than become a clerk.[25]

On he went for page after page, bleeding woe and listing grievances, but he ended triumphantly. He would not leave the administration, he crowed. George Washington needed him in a sea of partisans.

Hamilton was certain that George Washington would hear these sentiments and perhaps even see the actual letter to Revenue Supervisor Edward Carrington, friend of James Madison. Alexander Hamilton, in a sea of partisans, was preparing to chart a more coherent course.

15

"Spirit of Party"

Before Congress left Philadelphia in the spring of 1792, Washington asked James Madison to his house on the morning of May 5. He told Madison that he wanted to retire at the end of his current term. Washington did not ask Madison's advice. He had already told Hamilton, Jefferson, Knox, and Randolph. Washington simply wanted to consult with Madison about the best time to reveal his decision to the American people. The news likely did not surprise Madison. More than anyone he knew how reluctant Washington had been to accept the presidency. Madison told Washington that his plan boded ill for the nation. Washington wearily said his presence was no longer essential. There had always been other people more qualified to understand the law and the Constitution. Washington had, he told Madison, "from the beginning found himself deficient in many of the essential qualifications for the job." It was somebody else's time now.

Washington was also tired, in constant pain, and felt himself "in the decline of life, his health becoming sensibly more infirm, & perhaps his faculties also." He was also worried about the "spirit of party" that hopelessly divided Jefferson and Hamilton, though he did not mention them specifically. Madison could not reassure Washington about his health, but he insisted that only Washington could calm the current political tensions and sustain the country's unity, that his retirement "might have effects that ought not to be hazarded." Moreover, Madison wanted to know who these people were Washington thought his superiors in judging the law and the Constitution. In short, if not Washington, who? Jefferson wanted to retire, but even if he had wanted to stay, the North did not like him. He did not mention it, but Madison believed John Adams and John Jay had become monarchists, and Washington knew his opinion of Hamilton.

They parted with the issue unresolved. Four days later, Congress had adjourned, and Washington intended to leave for Virginia early the next day. Madison returned and told the president that if he was resolved to retire, he should tell the American people before the election. Madison recommended a written address. Washington nodded. Reminiscent of a time before the bad feelings, the rival newspapers, and the forming of factions, he asked Madison to think about what such an address should say and then walked Madison to the door. Washington seemed tired. As they said their good-byes, it was almost like everything had been before.[1]

From Mount Vernon, Washington drafted a pensive letter to Madison. He understood why everyone wanted him to stay, but he was determined to go. He said he would not live much longer and wanted to spend the time he had left on his farm. He now made his request a formal instruction. Madison was to use the congressional recess to write a farewell address. It would state Washington's general reasoning by mentioning the need for rotation in office to prevent service from becoming a sinecure. Yet he also wanted to counsel caution in preserving the government. He never sent this note but was able to deliver it personally. Madison was at Georgetown inspecting the progress on the new capital when Washington arrived on the same errand. Madison sadly promised to begin a draft. In a few weeks, it was ready. He suggested September would be a good time to have it published in newspapers. Madison again implored Washington to reconsider and make "one more sacrifice, severe as it may be, to the desires and interests of your country."[2]

Those who did not know suspected his determination to quit. The mail pouch from Alexandria brought a chorus of persuasive arguments, but the letter from Thomas Jefferson brought him up short. It was dated May 23, 1792, but did not reach Mount Vernon until July, long after Washington had fixed his resolve to retire. Jefferson couched his argument in more compelling terms than any other writer would have or, more important, could have. The letter indicted Alexander Hamilton as a dangerous man. Jefferson had all but said this in February, but for Washington to see it on paper in blunt language was different. Jefferson told Washington that if he retired, political divisions would become so venomous that the country would not likely survive. Jefferson described a government corrupted by Hamilton's financial policies, its citizens developing "habits of vice and idleness instead of industry and morality," and a Congress either blind to or collaborating in the perversion of the American experiment.[3]

This was hard enough to read, but Jefferson spared Washington his deepest fears, alarms he revealed to a few friends. Jefferson believed that too many in the government were "itching for crowns, coronets, and mitr[es]." He was prepared to "cut them off";[4] the gentle philosopher who mumbled and shambled was prepared like Hamilton to chart a more coherent course among a sea of partisans, but he knew that without Washington all would be lost. In July, Jefferson made his case in person at Mount Vernon, but he found Washington somewhat defensive on the subject of Hamilton's financial policies. The president exclaimed to Jefferson that critics of the administration by implication "condemned him, for if they thought there were measures pursued contrary to his sentiment, they must conceive him too careless to attend to them or too stupid to understand them."[5]

Discussions about retirement continued into the fall, with Randolph again entering the mix. In letters and conversations he pleaded with Washington to remain in office for the good of the country, warning that too many people saw the Constitution as a temporary arrangement, and that the nation was "at the eve of a crisis." He continued that "in this threatening posture of our affairs, we must gain time, for the purpose of attracting confidence in the government," and that only one man could "check the assaults."[6] Only Washington could make the government permanent. Washington longed desperately to stay at Mount Vernon and still looked for an honorable way to lay down his burden, but when Washington told Eliza Powel that he was considering stepping down, she, too, weighed in with a recitation of reasons why he should remain for the good of the country. "Resignation wou'd elate the Enemies of good Government," she warned, "and cause lasting regret to the Friends of humanity."[7] That would have mildly shaken him; it summoned the image of tyrants biding their time in the shadows, smiling.

Yet by the time Mrs. Powel wrote her letter, he had likely, if bitterly, decided to stay put anyway. We shall likely never know when he made that final decision, but even before he confided in Eliza Powel, he gradually talked less and less about retirement. The growing partisanship apparently convinced him that he should stay, at least a little while longer. In that regard, Jefferson's May 23, 1792, letter had struck a nerve.

Jefferson's indictment of Hamilton disturbed Washington more than any of the earlier squabbles between the two, and he resolved to test the unifying powers everyone seemed to think he possessed to bring about a reconciliation. First, he wrote to Hamilton that several concerns had come to light regarding his policies. Washington posed twenty-one questions based on Jefferson's objections. Washington did not name Jefferson as their source, but Hamilton surely guessed their origin.[8] He relished this kind of challenge. His response stretched to fourteen thousand words. He answered every question and then some.

Washington then wrote heartfelt appeals to both men, urging them to put aside their differences for the good of the country. The United States had many enemies. Infighting encouraged those enemies while riling the people. Washington hoped "that liberal allowances will be made for the political opinions of one another," for without the effort he could "not see how the Reins of Government are to be managed, or how the Union of the States can be much longer preserved."[9]

Both responded in letters dated September 9, 1792, Jefferson from Monticello and Hamilton from Philadelphia. The other man was responsible for the feud, each claimed. Each perceived himself the injured party with no option other than to defend himself. Yet Hamilton read his chief with a more discerning eye than Jefferson. He expressed concern that Washington continued to worry about such things and promised to "cheerfully embrace" any opportunity to end the feud. Jefferson, on the other hand, would not let the matter go. He was obstinate enough to revisit old controversies and divulge that for him they remained fresh wounds. He said he never would have become involved in the fight over assumption had he not been "duped into [it] by the Secretary of the Treasury." Now, he said, he saw his concession as his greatest mistake, one that "has occasioned me the deepest regret." From stubbornness, he moved to affected indifference. He still planned to retire soon and re-move himself from this disreputable business of government. After his ceaseless reminders to Washington about his duty, Jefferson's mention-ing his imminent escape from public life must have struck the president as unintentionally ironic, but in his next breath Jefferson made matters worse. He revealed resentment and snobbery by announcing he would not have his "retirement . . . clouded by the slanders of a man [Hamil-ton] whose history, from the moment at which history can stoop to no-tice him, is a tissue of machinations against the liberty of the country which has not only received and given him bread, but heaped its honors on his head."[10]

Jefferson gave either a remarkably candid performance or an amaz-ingly tin-eared one, possibly both. Bitterness was not in the president's plan, though. Washington still hoped to bring the two together. He did not care who started the argument or who felt the most victimized by the other's camp; he simply wanted harmony for himself and the na-tion. From Mount Vernon, he continued to call for a truce. He spoke at length with Jefferson when the secretary of state visited on his way back to Philadelphia, but the conversation did not go well. Jefferson's blithe references to his own retirement had stuck in Washington's craw, and he grew heated when Jefferson repeated his plan to retire at the end of the first term. He wanted to retire, too, Washington snapped, especially now that his nephew and farm manager George Augustine Washing-ton was near death. But if duty required him to put aside his personal desires, did not duty require the same of Jefferson?

Washington switched the subject to Jefferson's quarrel with Hamil-ton. Washington admitted their animosity surprised him, hidden as it was until recently, but he insisted their differences were hardly insur-mountable. Yet "insurmountable" was precisely the word for those dif-ferences, because Jefferson was convinced that Hamilton wanted to establish a monarchy. He told Washington that he had heard Hamilton "say that this constitution was a shilly shally thing of mere milk & water, which could not last, & was only good as a step to something better." He had heard stories from others that Hamilton amused dinner compan-ions with praise for crowns and kings. Washington was flabbergasted. Jefferson was misreading his experiences with Hamilton to exaggerate rumors and secondhand talk from parties. He assured Jefferson that he and other vigilant patriots would never allow kings to rise in the United States. Jefferson visibly harbored his doubts. Washington could not understand how the dispute had gotten so out of hand.[11]

Likely Jefferson's visit to an old friend the day before he arrived at Mount Vernon had reinforced his doubts. George Mason of Gunston Hall was one of George Washington's closest neighbors, and for more than three decades he regarded himself as one of Washington's closest friends. Thus, it is strange we have so little understanding of their friendship. Their acquaintance reached back to when young Washington visited Mount Vernon as his brother Lawrence's guest, and it was said that at fourteen Washington was mildly infatuated with pretty Ann Eilbeck, Mason's bride.[12] Theirs was, in other words, the association of a lifetime, and it bears some of the features of friendship, but as Mason's recent biographer observes, it was also "ambiguous."[13]

Mason's Gunston Hall, an elegant brick Georgian house he named for the ancestral seat of his maternal grandfather, was about twelve miles by road from Mount Vernon and even closer via the Potomac. That made him and Washington close neighbors by plantation standards, and they saw each other often, trading gifts of produce and seed and game, hunting and working together, and socializing in the convivial circle of Tidewater planters. They agreed on everything regarding England's mulish policies and cooperated in efforts to oppose them, such as Virginia's boycott of British goods in 1769. In 1774, both signed the Fairfax Resolves, a list of grievances against the British government that saw wide distribution throughout the colonies, and the following year they agreed that active resistance had become the only option. Their unblemished record together in such matters should have mirrored their personal dealings, but that wasn't always the case.

As in many of Washington's friendships, he never completely abandoned a certain aloofness and measured formality with George Mason. It is natural that they would occasionally disagree, sometimes over the kind of local squabbles that make for amusing parables in folk tales, such as a tiff over building Truro Parish's new church nearer to Mount Vernon than Gunston Hall. But at least one of their disagreements was jarring. In 1775, Washington thought Mason was trying to cheat him out of money they had loaned to Fairfax County to establish a local militia. Washington's icy notes and Mason's puzzled responses did not carry the colors of friendship, but this was Washington's fault for jumping to a conclusion and losing his temper.

He seems to have regretted it, later asking Mason to help manage Jack Custis's finances when Washington was away in the war. He prefaced the request with the assurance that he trusted no friend more than Mason, which sounds very much like George Washington was apologizing, in a roundabout way, for something he preferred not to mention, like his suspicions over a militia loan. Washington wrote Mason during the war that "it would afford" him "very singular pleasure to be favored at all times with your sentiments" regarding the struggle. He urged Mason to take an active part in the government, the ideological outcome of the war being every bit as important as military success. By the time they attended the Constitutional Convention together, Mason's ideas on government had been a strong influence on Washington for decades.[14]

Mason was self-taught, but his knowledge of John Locke and the political theories of the Scottish Enlightenment was unsurpassed. Contemporaries were awed by Mason's easy command of difficult ideas that allowed him to state them in plain, understandable language. Jefferson thought he belonged to "the first order of greatness," and Madison praised him as "the ablest man in debate" he had ever seen. Randolph ranked him as among the first men of Virginia, and though he noted that Mason was occasionally sarcastic when conversing with slower wits—Randolph called it "manly" elocution—Mason was never "wantonly" so.[15]

Mason was always sickly. His skin was prone to blisters and violent rashes, age dimmed his vision, and gout frequently tormented his hands, feet, and digestion, robbing him of sleep and doubtless prompting his "manly" sarcasm. Ill health and a nervous temperament made him a homebody. His wife Ann Eilbeck Mason died in 1773, leaving a profoundly grief-stricken husband to raise a brood of children while managing a large estate and trying to mend the hole in his heart. He eventually remarried, but he was never the same and always gave the impression of being "in the shade of retirement."[16] Aside from being a burgess, he had never served in a public office outside of Fairfax County until he was placed on the Virginia delegation to the Constitutional Convention. His trip to Philadelphia in May 1787 was an adventure, for Mason had never been so far from home. Unfortunately, he did not care for it. He found social events in the evenings tedious and the people of the city boorish. Even the work at the convention, which he at first plunged into with boyish enthusiasm, eventually ceased to invigorate. In fact, by the end of the summer, the work had him hopping mad.

Mason's reputation had preceded him as the author of Virginia's "Declaration of Rights," which Mason drafted in 1776 for inclusion in the Virginia state constitution. It was the same year Jefferson wrote the Declaration of Independence, which he partly modeled on Mason's work. The Declaration of Rights was often called the "Bill of Rights" at the time, a comparison to the English document of 1689, but the American version would also take inspiration from Mason later. Like Washington, Mason would always be a farmer, but he was also perfectly comfortable talking about political philosophy, and his colleagues on the delegation as well as nationalists in the convention regarded him a valuable ally.

Nationalists unwisely focused on Mason's occasional denunciation of state governments as unruly nests of corruption and self-interest that undermined liberty and thwarted national progress. Yet Mason harbored an abiding fear of human institutions at any level. Unlike Washington and Madison, Mason had little faith in government. He saw it as apt to be controlled by moneyed interests—men of the merchant class he loathed for trading honor the way they did dry goods. These rich manipulators were likely to use government to bludgeon competitors rather than preserve order, let alone protect liberty. That sort of attitude made George Mason a Jeffersonian before there was such a thing. But unlike Jefferson, Mason did not have much faith in the people, either. He thought that as a mass they were emotional and stupid. Most of all, Mason was vigilant for anything that might erode republicanism, and that was to be much of the problem he would have with the document that the Constitutional Convention produced.

None of this was apparent at first. Mason supported the nationalist agenda and worked heartily to advance it, though there were glimmerings of his dissatisfaction over the elitism of the upper house of the legislature and the powers of the presidency. Then in late July 1787 something snapped, and he simply dug in his heels on significant parts of the proposed constitution and gradually found it a bad idea entirely, a very bad idea indeed.

The broad powers inherent in a constitutional president bothered Mason early, but he was not alone.[17] The debates about establishing the executive branch were usually delicate exchanges because all the delegates knew when talking about the abstract office they were indirectly talking about George Washington. Even so, it was an enormously complicated task since someone other than Washington would eventually be president. Sparing his feelings with ambiguous arrangements that a lesser man could exploit was folly.

In the end, no compromise, no accommodation, no placation could put to rest Mason's reservations. He would not sign the final document. He recited a whopping sixteen reasons the proposed government was unacceptable. The highlights cut to the core of his displeasure: The president was too powerful, the vice president was superfluous, the Senate was too privileged, the commercial measures favored shipping at the expense of agriculture, and the twenty-year moratorium on the foreign slave trade was too long. Mason insisted the only remedy was a bill of rights to protect basic liberties from the elasticity of "necessary" intrusions that could on the whim of a congressional majority be deemed "proper."

When his fellow delegates refused to make any further changes, Mason left the convention in disgust. He went home where he fought—perhaps harder than anyone—against ratification of the Constitution in Virginia. He failed, and the relationship between Washington and Mason would never be the same. Mason publicly announced that he would support the new government, but Washington never forgave him.[18] Mason privately wondered why. When Washington left Virginia to become president, Mason almost timidly offered to take care of anything for Washington in his absence. It was a sad attempt to reprise the reconciliation of fifteen years earlier when a misunderstanding over militia money had been smoothed over by mutual expressions of trust. But this time George Washington had nothing he wanted Mason to take care of.

The broken friendship seemed to bewilder the old man at Gunston Hall. After the Virginia ratification convention, Mason kept his misgivings about the new government to himself and only rarely murmured his opinions to his closest friends. He wrote wistfully to his son to recall "the friendship which has long existed (indeed from our early youth) between General Washington and myself" and that "there are few men in whom he placed greater confidence." He ventured that "it is possible my opposition to the new government . . . may have altered the case."[19] But he knew that this was more than a possibility. It was what had happened.

And possibly the broken friendship did not bewilder Mason after all. Possibly there was more, something that only Washington and Mason knew about and never mentioned. Washington forgave other men for opposing the Constitution, some of them close friends like Mason and others mere casual acquaintances. It suggests that another rift had happened between these two, possibly a private conversation in Philadelphia that went horribly wrong and was therefore unrecorded or an unfortunate letter from Mason that Washington did not want to survive. Had Mason's "manly sarcasm" been on display with the man least likely to indulge it? Had the exasperated neighbor overstepped to say bluntly what was all too true, that he knew more about the philosophy of government and understood better the perils of the one being created? Did George Mason, in short, imply that George Washington was stupid, or at least act in such a way that Washington inferred it?

In early fall 1792, George Mason was dying. His chronic digestive problems were taking their final toll, an illness referred to at the time as "stomach gout." Though Mason remained mentally sharp, he was in great pain and wasting away. Washington had not seen him in years and did not visit during his last illness. Jefferson and Mason, though, had a long talk about the state of the country, and Jefferson listened to his reminiscences of the Constitutional Convention. Mason said the changes made to the Constitution during the last weeks of the convention convinced him he could not sign the document. Jefferson knew this, as he knew the parts Mason found objectionable, but he listened to an old man remember.

Mason denounced Hamilton's financial policies and Hamilton himself "as having done us more injury than Gr. Britain and all her fleets and armies."[20] Jefferson had always admired Mason for his candor and intellect. They had cooperated closely during the Revolution. It was from this sad interview that Jefferson met with Washington the following day. The quiet philosopher had refreshed reasons for his anger at Alexander Hamilton. A week later George Mason was dead. It could not have comforted Thomas Jefferson that one of the vigilant patriots George Washington insisted would protect the republic was a man he had completely cut from his life. In fact, the vigilant patriots were passing.

Newspaper and pamphlet attacks had stepped up over the summer of 1792. Because Hamilton and Jefferson believed the other responsible for starting the public phase of the conflict, each thought the other should stop the assaults first. Hamilton and his supporters saw Philip Freneau's establishment of the *National Gazette* in the fall of 1791 as a declaration of war, but Freneau's columns initially were light on political commentary and heavy on literature and other cultural topics. In November 1791, however, Madison began anonymous contributions that would eventually span across eighteen essays of the *Gazette*. Madison's pen was subtle. He first laid the groundwork and then more pointedly condemned moneyed interests, cronies that Madison charged Hamilton with trying to empower. He explained why state governments were necessary to check national power, why public opinion and a free press were important guardians of liberty, and how political parties were inevitable in a republic. This last was a significant departure for Madison, because it broke with the American tradition of eschewing political parties as inherently corrupt. Madison now distinguished parties from factions, which he had discussed in *Federalist,* no. 10.[21]

In the spring of 1792, Madison's essays became increasingly partisan. Others joined in to fill the *National Gazette* with criticisms of Hamilton's system for causing the recent financial panic. In his March 31, 1792, essay "The Union: Who Are Its Real Friends?" Madison used the crash to attack Hamilton's schemes as leading to speculation, debt, and unconstitutional laws. Madison sprinkled the specter of monarchy and aristocracy throughout. The real friends of the Union wanted power invested in the people. They loved liberty and limited government while opposing hereditary privilege and public debt.[22] More and more Madison used the capitalized word "Republican" to describe those who agreed with him, and thus played the same rhetorical trick on the Federalists that they had pulled during ratification. Madison could paint those who disagreed with him as "Antirepublicans." A measure of this tactic's effectiveness was evidenced when Freneau also began using the term "Republican" to describe those who supported their views.[23]

Hamilton fought back with newspaper essays of his own. Fixating on Jefferson as the real author of Madison's attacks, Hamilton's anonymous essays in John Fenno's *Gazette of the United States* accused the secretary of state of hiring Philip Freneau "to vilify those to whom the voice of the people has committed the administration of our public affairs." A variety of pseudonyms conveyed the same message: Jefferson had never supported the Constitution, Jefferson had placed a man on the government payroll to undermine the government, and Jefferson had always opposed paying the country's debts.[24]

Freneau insisted that Jefferson had nothing to do with establishing his newspaper. The editor played the controversy as high drama by swearing an oath before the mayor of Philadelphia to that effect and publishing it in his *National Gazette* as well as Fenno's *Gazette of the United States*. He contrasted Fenno's generous printing contracts from the Treasury Department to his measly $250 salary in terms of real as opposed to purported patronage.[25] Meanwhile, Jefferson's friends augmented Freneau's efforts with their own strategy to defend the secretary of state. Personal jabs and Hamilton's direct aim at Jefferson brought Madison, James Monroe, and Attorney General Edmund Randolph to the ramparts. Randolph's participation, though secret, provided an additional involvement of the executive branch in the controversy. For their parts, Madison and Monroe wrote essays with excerpts from Jefferson's letters to disprove Hamilton's accusations. Randolph appeared to be righteously indignant over the attacks and replied directly to Fenno's *Gazette of the United States,* calling the person who had written Hamilton's essays "a cowardly assassin."[26]

Jefferson conferred with his defenders but refused to write in his own defense, apparently believing it beneath his dignity to write for a newspaper. He could at least honestly claim never to have done so. Less honestly, he would later tell Washington that he had no idea how the anonymous authors who quoted his letters could have acquired them. Otherwise, Jefferson took a broad and resigned view of the controversy with correspondents. He lamented that "under a government like ours, personal dislikes often assume the garb of public dissension." Airing differences was, however, one of the "evils to be set off against the innumerable blessings of a free press."[27]

The fight in print cemented in the popular mind the differences between competing visions for the American future and their champions. Though Madison wrote many of the newspaper essays and kept his supporters in Congress organized, many people saw Jefferson as the head of the Republicans. Hamilton was the face of Madison's Antirepublicans, a concept that stuck despite the durability of "Federalist" as a label for that faction as it became a party.[28]

Hamilton had managed to avert widespread panic in the spring, but the country's finances continued to be a concern. Revenue was increasing, but had not yet reached the levels hoped for by Washington and Hamilton. Renewed opposition to the whiskey excise did not promise revenue would be increasing soon.[29]

Rumors had circulated since the first of the year that people on the Virginia frontier intended to evade the tax and possibly resist revenue collectors with force. By late summer 1792, most of the signs pointed to problems in western Pennsylvania. Reports reached Philadelphia that collectors there were being threatened and attacked. Angry distillers joined with concerned citizens at a meeting in Pittsburgh. Hamilton initially sent investigators into the area to gauge the extent of disaffection, but he warned Washington that harsh treatment for tax evaders could be necessary to discourage similar movements elsewhere. On the other hand, Chief Justice Jay urged caution. He warned that a threatening proclamation would create the worst impression, especially since Washington had not yet enlisted legislative support. Edmund Randolph agreed. Threatening to prosecute people before they broke the law was simply unacceptable. While Washington was still at Mount Vernon he issued a proclamation stating that the laws would be enforced and pledging to have anyone interfering with them prosecuted. And that seemed to work, for the time being.[30]

Washington's fourth annual message to Congress was again an effort by committee, but this time he did not ask for James Madison's help. Washington reminded Congress that it had not acted yet on Randolph's recommendations for judicial reforms that the Supreme Court justices had requested, and he mentioned the latest bad news regarding the Indian war in the Northwest. He also referred to the difficulties in collecting the whiskey excise. The president would likely have profited from discussing the excise issues with Madison, but the aborted farewell address was to be the Virginia representative's last composition for Washington. Madison again chaired the House committee that drafted the response to Washington's message, and he could not stop his fellow committee members from disparaging tax evaders in western Pennsylvania. Madison did manage to include a section in the response that reminded a government of free people "to be always ready to listen to the representations of its Constituents."[31]

The presidential, vice presidential, and congressional elections came and went that fall in the shadow of these developments. Washington said nothing about serving another term. He did not take James Madison's advice about publishing a farewell address in the newspapers, so most people assumed he had decided to remain in office. The vice presidential and congressional elections merited the most attention. The opposition concentrated on winning as many congressional races as possible and unseating Vice President Adams. Replacing Adams with one of their own seemed all the more pressing given an assumption by Jefferson that Washington might be planning to serve only half of his second term. For a while, Governor Clinton seemed the most likely man to challenge Adams. He had an Antifederalist reputation but was by no means thought of as a firebrand, as his continued friendship with Washington showed. He could carry New York and had a national following. Then events in the spring of 1792 dashed his chances.

John Jay found the chief justice's duties tiring because he had to ride a circuit, and boring because the court heard few cases. He wanted to become governor of New York and challenged Clinton for the post in the spring elections. The campaign was hard fought through proxies who adopted the tactic of the day by making it personal. Matching charges about Clinton's supposedly dubious loyalty to the Constitution, the governor's camp smeared Jay as a radical abolitionist. Clinton barely eked out a victory, but it was tainted by charges of vote tampering and official malfeasance. Authorities tossed out returns from three counties over technicalities, which cost Jay the election. Even Clinton supporters were embarrassed about how he won the election, and New York Republicans began questioning the wisdom of putting him up against Adams. Madison and Monroe squelched a last-minute effort to substitute Senator Aaron Burr, saying it was too late to permit proper organization.

Hamilton monitored all these maneuvers and kept Adams informed. He did not like John Adams, but he was willing to do anything to keep Clinton or Burr out of the vice presidency. In fact, when Hamilton heard that the "antis"—the Federalist label to tar Republicans—were considering replacing Clinton with Burr, he redoubled his efforts. Clinton roused old family rivalries that preceded the Constitution, but Burr's sins against Hamilton's relatives were recent and galling. Burr had become a senator by unseating Philip Schuyler, Hamilton's father-in-law.

No one need have worried. Adams defeated Clinton 77 to 50, and Washington won unanimous reelection. Neither Adams nor Washington seemed to pay much attention to the election. When Washington received congratulations from Henry Lee, he wistfully repeated his wish to retire but also revealed a trace of vanity. He told Lee that he would "have experienced chagreen if my re-election had not been by a pretty respectable vote."[32]

The national contest pleased the Hamiltonians, considering "the unparalleled exertions" against Adams, but congressional elections revealed the "antis" had formidable local organizations.[33] Madison was the architect for Republicans in these congressional elections. When Washington was at Mount Vernon, Randolph informed him about political activity in Philadelphia, telling his boss, "Parties run high here in the choice of electors and representatives."[34] It worried Hamilton. If Madison won major gains in both houses, Hamilton's entire financial plan was in jeopardy. "If the federalists sleep whilst their enemies are awake and vigilant," a friend warned, "some mischief may be done."[35]

It was difficult to tell how much mischief had already been done.

States voted at different times, and returns were slow to come in. Many members arrived for the final session of the Second Congress not knowing if they had been reelected.[36] Though slow, it was gradually sure that Madison's party had made substantial gains in the House. He would have a majority when the Third Congress opened at the end of 1793.

It is possible James Reynolds knew from the beginning that his wife was having an affair with Alexander Hamilton. Some have even concluded that James and Maria were partners in the "badger game," a usually short-term confidence scheme in which the wife lures the mark to her bed to be discovered by the husband, who then sells his silence. There is no evidence to support or disprove this contention, but letters between Hamilton and the Reynolds couple make plain Hamilton's visits to her, the discovery by her husband of the affair, and a subsequent pattern of blackmail that bled Hamilton of more than one thousand dollars over the course of a year. It is also apparent that if this were a badger game, there was nothing short-term about it. Hamilton continued to visit Maria Reynolds after the blackmail commenced, and with the knowledge of James Reynolds. It was a sordid business. As much as he could, Hamilton kept Betsey out of Philadelphia and out of the way during the affair; Reynolds extorted one thousand dollars to start with and then began returning for smaller "loans" now and then; Maria wrote plaintive letters that appealed to Hamilton's vanity and a bizarre sense of chivalry. She also cried often, but not all the time. Hamilton did what he could to make her happy.[37]

The shadowy couple thus had a pretty lucrative run. Selling Maria was, in fact, the most successful venture her husband ever managed. Otherwise he was a penny-ante crook whose greatest accomplishment was marrying a pretty sixteen-year-old Connecticut girl whom Hamilton (and others) later found fetching. As a commissary officer during the Revolution, Reynolds became acquainted with people careless about how they made money. After the war, they involved him in various speculative intrigues, such as defrauding army veterans of their pay vouchers. When Reynolds showed up in Philadelphia to "reconcile" with Maria, he not only squeezed Hamilton for hush money but solicited a job in the Treasury Department on the claim he could snitch on former partners in crime. Hamilton had the scruples to deny Reynolds at least the job, if not the sense to deny himself Reynolds's wife. Everything began to unravel rapidly in December 1792, when authorities arrested Reynolds for his ongoing schemes to cheat veterans. He expected his benefactor in the Treasury to rescue him, but Hamilton finally drew the line, and Reynolds began dropping dark hints to his captors about information that would implicate Hamilton in corrupt Treasury practices. The opposition in Congress was all ears.

Pennsylvania Republican congressman Frederick Muhlenberg visited Reynolds in jail, but he proved an enigma of vague charges and insinuations that he could incriminate Alexander Hamilton. Muhlenberg called in Congressman Abraham Venable and Senator James Monroe to help with the investigation. The trio visited both Reynolds and Maria, but could determine only that Hamilton had for some reason been giving Reynolds money. They concluded what they thought was the worst: that Hamilton had enlisted Reynolds for personal speculations in government securities, arming him with insider information and giving him funds for transactions. They could have gone to Washington, but as gentlemen they chose to confront the culprit in person. On December 15, 1792, the three marched into Hamilton's office.

Hamilton invited Oliver Wolcott, Jr., to sit in on the meeting. Both listened to the allegations, and Hamilton instantly decided to tell them everything. He had engaged in no corruption, he insisted. He had not used Reynolds or anyone else to buy securities. He had not profited in any way from his government position; in fact, his government service had left him in bad financial straits, which was true. He had to borrow from a friend to make the first payment to Reynolds. No, said Hamilton, he was not a speculator trading on insider information. He was an adulterer being blackmailed by a parasitic husband. He told his accusers that he had been paying hush money to Reynolds for months.[38]

Every man in the room sat stunned by Hamilton's confession and marveled over his candor. Hamilton produced letters from Maria and James Reynolds as evidence. The trio looked them over and declared themselves satisfied that there had been no public malfeasance. Furthermore, they promised to keep everything secret. They all considered

Hamilton a political enemy, but this was different from catching a man with his hand in the till.

Their pledge of silence could be interpreted as the winking collusion of worldly men shrugging off a bit of harmless fun with a comely woman who had an inconvenient husband. But that is not why they chose to remain silent. Monroe, Muhlenberg, and Venable were not prudes, and they certainly knew about, if not of, the compulsive urge to risk the wreck of reputation for a passing passionate frisson. Yet Muhlenberg was a Lutheran minister, Monroe was a committed moralist, and Venable was a respected jurist. It is impossible to know precisely how Hamilton's confession struck them on a personal level that December day in the Treasury office. Wolcott's eyes traveled to each of them, Hamilton included, as the Treasury secretary spun out his sordid story. The awkward silence as they passed around the tawdry notes from Maria Reynolds—pathetic in one phrase, seductive in the next, badly spelled throughout—must have made the faint rustle of her and her husband's makeshift stationery deafening. The documents revealed the soiled truth. The passionate excitement had long passed to become an expensive prison whose warden was her oily husband. The truth was that not until ten days after Betsey gave birth to their most recent child, a boy, had Alexander Hamilton finally told Maria Reynolds that he would not be returning to her bed.

Monroe, Muhlenberg, and Venable would not be returning to Hamilton's office. There was and there would be the faint suspicion that he was lying about the affair, using it as a cloak so awful that no one could imagine it might be hiding anything worse, but Monroe took with him the letters that convinced him and his colleagues that Hamilton's sorry tale was true. Monroe and the others gave their word that the matter was closed, but Monroe left the office with the letters. Hamilton seems to have thought he had no choice, but he likely recalled then and certainly would remember later Benjamin Franklin's observation about the sanctity of secrets.

The other players in the drama finished their parts in the wings. James Reynolds ran like a rabbit, a final exit that virtually expunged him from the record. Maria divorced him, helped by her lawyer Aaron Burr, and married her husband's shady associate, a former clerk in

Hamilton's Treasury Department. Betsey knew nothing, and by all evidence neither did George Washington, ignorance preserved by the investigative trio's decision to confront Hamilton rather than unmask him to his chief or certainly his wife. But Franklin's warning about a secret—that two men could keep it, if one of them were dead—waited for its day.

16

"The Look of an Upstart"

Alexander Hamilton soon had other problems in Congress. Suspicion lingered about the abrupt end to the investigation of his alleged corruption, and the mistrust was revived when Hamilton asked Congress for authority to borrow $2 million at 5 percent interest from Dutch bankers. He intended to pay back $2 million the government owed the Bank of the United States at 6 percent to save the government $20,000 in interest. Critics in both houses promptly wanted an accounting of all past loans and what the money had been used for. The Treasury provided the figures, but the report revealed that Hamilton had made previous transactions with neither congressional nor presidential approval as the law required. No evidence of corruption touched on Hamilton's actions, but he had acquired a reputation for careless favoritism that benefited "the Monied and commercial Interest at the expense of the Landed or Agricultural Interest."[1] People with raised hackles over this were prepared to conclude the worst from the slightest irregularities.

Philadelphia was abuzz for weeks with gossip about these events. Adams believed Hamilton would weather the storm. He decried the attempts by "Ambitious Members of a Legislature" to take down "Ministers of State."[2] Jefferson watched congressional proceedings with growing interest, and possibly was hoping to direct them. He had a conversation with Washington at the end of December 1792 to voice worry over the nation's many loans, and after Hamilton submitted his first reports on them, Jefferson met with Washington again. The tentacles of financial dependency ensnared too many in Congress, he said, and caused corruption to run deeply enough to jeopardize the republic. His "wish was to see both houses of Congr. cleansed of all persons interested in the bank or public stocks."³ Jefferson also conferred privately with friends in Congress, including young William Branch Giles of Virginia, a family friend. Giles was earnest and talented but volatile. Jefferson always appreciated earnest and talented men; he had reached a point where he especially appreciated politically volatile ones.

Hamilton's reports made clear that he had gone beyond his instructions, but not that he had intentionally done anything wrong. As for borrowing money without the president's approval, he asked Washington for what amounted to a postdated grant of authority, but Washington was wary. More than the spendthrift Jefferson, Washington had a farmer's concern for tidy bookkeeping. Much of what Hamilton had done seemed honest if risky, but Washington liked things orderly and regular. When Hamilton asked him for retroactive consent, Washington would agree only to a vague statement. From now on, he watched things more closely. Hamilton's critics saw his questionable practices and Washington's tepid support as proof of guilt.

Jefferson had been working on a series of resolutions to spell out his concerns, and it was William Branch Giles who presented them to the House on February 27, 1793. Giles wanted Hamilton censured for violating the Funding Act of 1790 and for financial misconduct. The House of Representatives debated the resolutions, with Madison pressing their case and William Loughton Smith and Fisher Ames defending the secretary of the Treasury. There was no evidence to support the attack, however, and the resolutions went down to a resounding defeat.⁴

The vote tallies revealed the lack of cohesion in the Republican opposition. The resolutions were mainly a regional protest reflecting the frustration of southern agrarians. Parties cannot flower on such narrow ground. Republicans, explaining a defeat made lopsided by defections in their own ranks, interpreted the setback as a clear indication that the rot ran even deeper than they had imagined in the House of Representatives.

The Republican charges reinforced Jefferson's warnings and troubled Washington. He evinced the same old confidence in Hamilton, but he monitored foreign loans more vigilantly. Hamilton felt the subtle change and pressed for a full vindication so vigorously that the House of Representatives in February 1794 commenced a fourteen-month investigation by a fifteen-man committee. It included Giles and other implacable foes of the secretary, and for a time Hamilton seemed very vulnerable.

This episode hastened Jefferson's transition from statesman to active partisan, a change intensified by the brewing disagreements over events in Europe.[5] Jefferson's friends wanted him to remain in the government. He decided to stay at State for a while longer and informed Washington, who expressed relief while repeating his wish that Jefferson and Hamilton try to get along. Jefferson made no promises, other than to say he would do nothing to undermine the administration. It seemed an odd thing to say, even if it were completely true. Jefferson apparently did not consider his first draft of the Giles resolutions a peculiar way to promote administrative harmony.

Washington opened his mind to Jefferson about the growing rancor in the press. Attacks on him were a new development, marking a shift since the election.[6] John Adams wrote to Abigail that "the Hellhounds are now in full cry in the Newspapers against the President, whom they treat as ill—as ever they did me."[7] After the lavish celebration of Washington's birthday in Philadelphia and in cities across the nation, Freneau's *National Gazette* printed an anonymous letter that mocked them as a "monarchical farce."[8] Franklin's grandson Benjamin Franklin Bache criticized the Washingtons' levees in his Philadelphia *General Advertiser* (later the *Aurora*). Another paper sneered that such customs came "from the uniform habits of Royalty."[9] A satire signed by "A Farmer" claimed that someone in Philadelphia mistook Washington's carriage and horses as those of George III's son.

Washington confided briefly in Jefferson, but he turned to Edmund Randolph for advice, marking a shift of his own in response to the drift in his administration. Randolph told him to consider stopping the levees, but Washington would not. He did stop his subscription to the *National Gazette*. Freneau cheekily had extra copies delivered to the president's residence.[10]

The charge that he loved formal ceremony stung Washington. As the Second Congress prepared to adjourn, and the president began thinking how to begin his second term, the wounds were fresh. Did the Constitution even require a second inauguration? Washington asked his "family." All four of his primary advisers thought he should take the oath again on March 4, 1793, but they divided on the form of the ceremony, taking positions that created peculiar points of agreement. Jefferson and Hamilton said it should be as simple as possible, better to occur at the president's house, and best to include only a small number of dignitaries. Hamilton cited "prudential considerations of the moment."[11] Randolph and Knox countered with a recommendation for a public occasion to include Congress.[12] Washington liked the latter suggestion. If the newspapers objected, he could always cancel more subscriptions.

He turned over arranging the entire event to Edmund Randolph, increasingly the man he trusted most in his fractious family. Vice President Adams told Congress to forget adjourning on March 2. Everyone would be expected to remain in town for a one-day special session on March 4. Just before noon on that day, George Washington climbed into his carriage for the short drive to Congress. When he entered the Senate chamber, Adams showed him to the vice presidential chair. He soon delivered the shortest inaugural address in presidential history, a record likely to stand. Justice William Cushing administered the oath, Washington left the building, and that was it. A crowd had gathered outside during the short ceremony. It cheered enthusiastically as Washington appeared and climbed back in his carriage. The occasion's simplicity did not impress George Hammond's secretary. "The French principles are gaining ground fast in this country," he grumbled.[13]

It was indeed a simple ceremony. The Washingtons were in mourning over George Augustine Washington's passing and had refused an invitation to Eliza Powel's lavish fiftieth birthday party a few days earlier. The straightforward public inaugural ceremony had conformed to Washington's mood, but it was also a bow to the duty of office, a bow to the people, and another opportunity to impress upon them the dignity of their sovereignty and the majesty of their republic.

Soaring rhetoric could wait for another day. Washington was sixty-one years old, and his hair was like snow. The carriage rattled back to the house, bruising his sore backside. His dentures hurt his gums. His dead nephew weighed on his mind. His "family" hurt his heart, except for good, mild Randolph, who never complained. Randolph found the balance in any affair, as he had in his plans for the inauguration. Jefferson and Hamilton were at daggers. But Randolph spoke sense softly and was possibly the man to get everyone through the two remaining years Washington planned to serve. The soft cadence of Randolph's voice was comforting. He sounded like home.

The French Revolution that began in 1789 had all the features of idealism informed by the Enlightenment and action guided by the Age of Reason. Most Americans rejoiced. The example of their unlikely revolution against Britain seemed to be inspiring an unlikely revolution in Paris, signaling the end of absolutely empowered kings. The hope was that events in France would spread throughout Europe, possibly throughout the rest of the world. Americans would soon be reminded to be careful what they wished for, in that sometimes wishes come true with unexpected consequences. France's revolution would eventually trigger world events that plagued no less than four American presidential administrations with one diplomatic crisis after another.

Some, including Gouverneur Morris, were concerned early, but it was easy to dismiss their warnings as cynical. As the Federalists developed from Hamilton's faction into a political party, it was easy to dismiss their objections as typical aristocratic resistance to change, reform, and "mobocracy." But events in France took an ominous turn in 1792. The revolutionary assembly declared war on Austria and thereby unleashed muscular military ambitions on the continent and stoked nationalist paranoia at home. Centuries of repression had created a large, angry underclass in France that was neither enlightened nor rational, and it found representatives of increasingly radical stripe. Parties formed rapidly around ideas and for a while took labels from places, as the rising Girondists did from the Gironde department in southwestern France, the home of their leaders. The Girondists seemed quite edgy when they assumed power. They installed ministers who were at one with the revolution and eager to advance it, but the Girondists had rivals in the Jacobins, who started out as a political club that met in the monastery from which they took their name.

After Louis XVI was deposed in the late summer of 1792, Morris asked Jefferson if he was to consider himself the minister to the new government. Jefferson impatiently told Morris that he was to treat any government supported by the people as legitimate. Jefferson believed rumors that Morris had offered advice to the royal family. He knew that Morris had written negative reports about the new government to Washington. Jefferson tried to counter them by assuring the president that events in France were progressing naturally. He instructed his protégé William Short at The Hague to soften his descriptions of violence in France, particularly by the Jacobins. Jefferson proved remarkably blind to the chaos that a general European war all but promised. "Were there but an Adam & an Eve left in every country, & left free," he told Short, "it would be better than as it now is." Jefferson insisted his opinion reflected that of the vast majority of Americans, but Short doubted that anyone who saw what was developing in France would agree with it.[14]

Americans celebrated the September 1792 French victory over the Prussians at Valmy, but they paid little attention to the September Massacres that occurred in Paris at the same time, the expression of underclass rage fueled by famine and anxiety. By early 1793, however, the alarming radicalism of revolutionary factions forced Americans to notice ugly trends. The former king was now "Citizen Louis" to his countrymen, but that was the least of the indignities that quickly became callous and then cruel. In the end, ominous talk about trying him for treason produced a trial for show with a foreordained verdict. Morris reported that the king had been condemned to death, and the news of his January 21 execution quickly followed. Last-minute efforts to save the king included one by Thomas Paine, who tried to persuade the Girondists to exile the royal family to America. In the end, the French government could not risk compassionate gestures that suggested royalist sympathy. Girondists were fighting for their political lives against the rival Jacobins and rightly suspected that should things go wrong, they would be fighting for their literal lives in the end. They bowed to a bloodlust unsatisfied until their ex-king became a dead one, and then remained unsatisfied still. Morris wrote that Louis XVI had "died in a Manner becoming his dignity."[15]

Beheading the king was only the start. His wife, the despised Marie-Antoinette, had become an even greater symbol of royal indifference to common suffering, and her trip to the guillotine was only a matter of time in coming. Federalists had always looked askance at the French Revolution. Now they felt vindicated, and they were repelled by Jeffersonians who claimed to rue the bloodshed but insisted that despotism could not become liberty "in a feather-bed."[16] Federalists wondered if such talk from the supposedly gentle philosopher would long remain just talk in America.

The king's execution and the growing savagery in Paris jarred all but the most committed friends of the French Revolution, and Washington had been wary of it in the first place. Now he questioned whether the United States should continue to recognize the alliance of 1778 or even to recognize the new French government and receive its minister.

Washington had personal reasons for his disenchantment. When the monarchy was dissolved and the royal family imprisoned, the Marquis de Lafayette swam against the radical current and broke with the revolutionary leadership by leading troops to free them. His rescue failed and forced him to flee France or face his own arrest and the likelihood that his head would soon join others "on pikes."[17] Prussians captured him as he crossed the border and turned him over to the Austrians, who promptly threw him in prison. Lafayette spirited out a letter to William Short at The Hague asking for help. Lafayette wanted to be released on the grounds that he was an American citizen, citing an honor bestowed on him by a grateful Congress after the Revolution. But Short's appeal to Gouverneur Morris brought a response that was only marginally encouraging. Lafayette was not an American citizen, said Morris, but he offered to help as best he could. Morris knew he couldn't do much beyond giving money to Lafayette's wife while trying to keep her alive. Washington was in despair as he subordinated his personal feelings to his official duty. The United States did not have diplomatic relations with Austria. Washington told Jefferson to have Morris look into informal options to free Lafayette. Nothing came of their efforts. Lafayette languished in an Austrian jail for the rest of Washington's presidency.

Events moved quickly in France. In addition to Morris's report that the new French republic would soon be replacing Jean-Baptiste Ternant, John Adams's son-in-law William Stephens Smith arrived with fresh news from France. Whispered talk painted Smith as a paid agent of the Girondists, but he was more eager to spear Morris than advance the interests of a French political faction. He told Jefferson and Washington that the current French government despised Morris, especially for his indiscreet support of the king. "At his own table in the presence of company and servants," Jefferson recalled Smith as saying, "he cursed the French ministers as a set of damned rascals."[18]

Smith told them that the new minister to the United States would have the power to negotiate a better commercial treaty with the United States. The conversation seemed a dream come true to Thomas Jefferson, who was ecstatic on both fronts. He had never wanted Morris in Paris. He abhorred the New Yorker's anti-French prejudice and thought Morris's personal relationship with Washington undermined his official relations with the president. The French, per Smith, had discredited Morris's gloomy reports and had satisfied Washington's desire for better trade relations, something Washington had wanted for some time.

Morris's behavior troubled the president, and he sadly told Jefferson that the minister would have to be recalled. Jefferson then suggested what he saw as a diplomatic solution: Simply swap Thomas Pinckney in Great Britain with Morris in France. Washington hesitated because he was certain it would be unsatisfactory for both men. He proposed to Jefferson what he thought would be the ideal solution. Jefferson wanted to retire from the State Department; would he go to France? Jefferson told Washington he wanted to retire, not change jobs, which was precisely the wrong thing to say. Washington barked that Jefferson "had pressed him to a continuance in public service & refused to do the same" himself. Yes, said Jefferson, because Washington was essential to the nation's unity. Any number of people, Jefferson said, could do his job.[19]

This was no help at all, and Washington turned to Edmund Randolph. The charges against Morris had come in an irregular fashion, Randolph remarked, which was a tactful way to suggest Smith was a dubious source. He told Washington to wait for an official request from the French government to remove Morris. To act preemptively would be inappropriate and, worse, it would be unfair to Morris. "Before such a stroke is given to the reputation of any man," Randolph said, "ought he not be heard?"[20] Washington had sent Randolph to an awkward interview with the secretary of state, and during it Randolph had probably revealed that he disagreed with the Morris-Pinckney switch, which was Jefferson's idea. Jefferson could be touchy about his prerogatives, and Washington's consultation with Randolph about State Department business likely irked him.

While Washington was pondering what to do with Gouverneur Morris, Ternant requested the United States pay three million livre of its debt to France. Ternant acted out of compelling necessity. His government was strapped for almost everything, and the United States was technically in arrears on its payments because it had suspended them while Paris was in flux. Ternant wanted these back payments as well as an advance on future ones. The cabinet had considered the request on February 25, 1793, and immediately fell to squabbling. Hamilton opposed the payment, but Knox, Randolph, and Jefferson supported it, creating an odd alignment that broke the usual pattern in the cabinet. Washington ultimately agreed to pay the amount the United States currently owed, but the meeting gave rise to an interesting point when it turned to the question of Ternant's pending replacement. Hamilton wondered aloud if it would be appropriate to receive the new French minister. Jefferson and Randolph were puzzled by the question, and answering it was left for another time.[21]

Washington went home after his second inauguration. He needed to see to his farms, given the recent death of George Augustine Washington, for whom Washington held a delayed funeral attended by a few friends and family. Burying the major took a lot out of him—not only because of the personal loss and disruption in Mount Vernon's management, but because Washington was feeling his age more than at any other time in his life. He did not feel like riding the circuit of his farms, a troubling sign for a man who loved to do nothing more. Content to visit James Craik and David Stuart and stroll the piazza, Washington might have found it a restful prelude to tackling his second term in earnest. He was still at Mount Vernon when he received news he had been dreading. France had declared war on Great Britain.

Americans were aware of the rising tensions that had caused the British to pull their diplomats from certain European cities.[22] Now that war had come, the question for the United States was not if it could stay

The Toll

George Washington's presidency established many precedents, including the relentless physical costs the office imposed. French sculptor Jean-Antoine Houdon fashioned this bust of Washington from a life mask he made at Mount Vernon in 1785 when Washington was fifty-three, and it is the most realistic of all physical representations of Washington. It shows a man still in his prime. *(National Portrait Gallery, Smithsonian Institution)*

Only ten years separate Houdon's bust from Gilbert Stuart's "Vaughan Portrait" of the president, but those years included two terms in office that doubled the decade in Washington's careworn features. *(National Gallery of Art)*

Only another year passed before Stuart began the portrait that he would never finish, the "Anthanaeum Portrait," which reveals what foreign enemies, domestic discord, and constant criticism did to the man Houdon had found content and vigorous eleven years earlier at his farm on the Potomac River. *(Library of Congress)*

Taking Office

The engraving shows Federal Hall in New York City and its surrounding buildings as they looked in the 1790s. Washington took the oath of office for the first time on the second-floor balcony of this building. *(Yale University Art Gallery)*

Washington's inauguration is depicted at the Museum and Education Center at George Washington's Mount Vernon, where computer models have helped produce stunningly life-like wax effigies. Robert Livingston is administering the oath while Washington's hand rests on the Bible brought from Livingston's Masonic Lodge. Diminutive Samuel Otis, secretary of the Senate, stoops to hold it at a comfortable angle for the president-elect. *(Courtesy of the Mount Vernon Ladies' Association. Photograph by Robert Creamer.)*

The First Cabinet

As a member of Washington's staff during the Revolution, Alexander Hamilton was a young man in a hurry, eager to improve and anxious to get ahead. Sometimes his temper was his master, and he left Washington's headquarters near the end of the war angry over a perceived insult to his dignity. Their contact afterward was cordial but slight, and nothing suggested that Hamilton would become the most important man in Washington's administration.
(Library of Congress)

Thomas Jefferson was the last member of the cabinet to take his place, having recently returned from his duties as minister to France. He was the perfect choice for secretary of state and with Hamilton made George Washington's first cabinet the most intellectually gifted in the history of the United States. Jefferson was gentle and soft-spoken by nature, and he lived by the rule that, when angry, one should count to ten before speaking. In a fateful interview with George Washington, Jefferson violated his rule and changed his relationship with the president forever.
(Yale University Art Gallery)

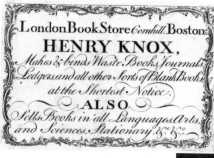

London Book Store *Cornhill* Boston.
HENRY KNOX,
Makes & binds Waste Books, Journals, Ledgers, and all other Sorts of Blank Books, at the Shortest Notice.
ALSO
Sells Books in all Languages, Arts, and Sciences, Stationary, &c. &c.

Before the American Revolution, Henry Knox's London Bookstore on Boston's Cornhill Street offered services customary for such an establishment. More unusual was the reputation of the owner as a radical that put him at risk with British authorities. *(Nathanial Hurd, 1771)*

Henry Knox became Washington's artillery commander during the Revolution and in that post managed one of the most impressive feats of the war, one that earned Washington's unalloyed admiration. Knox's lapses in the cabinet, however, would test Washington's patience.
(National Portrait Gallery, Smithsonian Institution)

Friends and Counselors

Tobias Lear came to Mount Vernon in 1784 to tutor the Washingtons' grandchildren and work as Washington's private secretary. Although a Harvard-educated New Englander, Lear quickly fit in at Mount Vernon, but his relationship with his employer was marred by Lear's occasional tardiness and Washington's habitual chilliness. Lear became punctual, however, and Washington warmed. In time, the secretary grew indispensable at Mount Vernon and continued to be a crucial assistant as the first presidential secretary. *(Courtesy of the Mount Vernon Ladies' Association)*

John Adams combined a first-class mind with an erratic temperament that could impress and exasperate friends and enemies in equal measure. Adams was the first to discover the vice-presidency's frustrations that were compounded by the office's insignificance if the president were to stay alive and remain relatively healthy. Adams, however, tended to make matters worse by fussing over trivial details and openly feeling sorry for himself. *(Yale University Art Gallery)*

Many missed the measure of James Madison by miles, at least at first. Sooner or later, almost everyone was impressed by the towering intellect packed into the diminutive frame with a boyish face. Like his friend Thomas Jefferson, Madison read voraciously but with more focus, amassing an encyclopedic knowledge of governance from both a philosophical and procedural vantage. The combination made him an indispensable advisor for the new president. *(Library of Congress)*

As governor of New York, George Clinton adopted a populist approach that pitted him against the state's elite families, a group that included the Schuylers, who had Alexander Hamilton as an in-law. The connection made Hamilton a bitter enemy of Clinton's, but nothing could diminish the governor's friendship with George Washington, who forgave even Clinton's early opposition to the Constitution. *(Library of Congress)*

Another of Washington's aides from the Revolution, David Humphreys came to live for a time at Mount Vernon after the war and was one of the few people outside Washington's family that he treated with casual friendliness. Humphreys had a poet's heart and a troubadour's mind, which showed when he composed a draft of Washington's first inaugural address that ran more than seventy pages. *(Yale University Art Gallery)*

A descendant of French Huguenots, Gouverneur Morris had the reputation of a rake from stories of sexual liaisons and near misses with jealous husbands. These tales were often imaginary, but Morris had a way of causing people to consider them plausible. He challenged life with caustic quips and a flippant manner that many found to be tedious affectations. It made him an unlikely friend for George Washington, but Gouverneur Morris's visit to Valley Forge in the winter of 1777 cemented an unbreakable bond between the two men. *(Library of Congress)*

The second British minister to the United States, Robert Liston was a refreshing change after the chronic petulance of his predecessor, the very young and inexperienced George Hammond. Liston was wise from age and knowledge-able about the world, and his wife, Henrietta, was likable. He shared with Washington a love of farming. *(National Gallery of Art)*

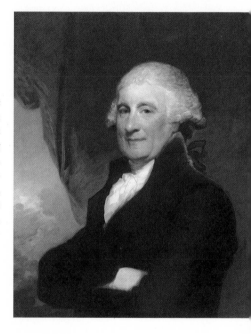

Washington became close friends with John Jay during the Revolution, partly because of Jay's unstinting support in the Continental Congress of the army. After the war, Jay was the Confederation's secretary for foreign affairs and when Washington became president, he offered Jay the similar position of secretary of state. Jay preferred to become chief justice, a decision that he came to regret. In 1794 he went to Great Britain to negotiate a controversial treaty that would bear his name. *(Library of Congress)*

A Certain Species of Property

Edward Savage's *The Washington Family* includes Wash, Nelly, and Martha, but also a slave (see detail, right). William Lee came to Mount Vernon in 1767 and became Washington's manservant and constant companion, accompanying him to Williamsburg for meetings of the House of Burgesses as well as riding with him on fox hunts. He was at his side throughout the Revolutionary War and traveled with Washington to Philadelphia for the Constitutional Convention. Lee suffered crippling injuries while still in his thirties and could not join the presidential residence in New York. Instead, he became a cobbler in Mount Vernon's slave quarters. It was a cruel demotion in status, but in the end, it was revealed that George Washington had not forgotten him. *(Yale University Art Gallery)*

Possessing great dignity and a commanding presence, Hercules was Mount Vernon's talented cook who became the presidential chef in Philadelphia. Nicknamed "Uncle Harkless" by Nelly and Wash, Hercules enjoyed significant freedom of movement and many privileges that made him seem a valued employee rather than a slave. When a series of events reminded him of his real status, he refused to submit to it and vanished from Mount Vernon in early 1797.

Rumors would place him in Europe where he was said to preside over the kitchens of titled aristocracy. Based on Gilbert Stuart's portrait that purports to be Hercules, he had the bearing for it. *(Madrid, Museo Thyssen-Bornemisza)*

In the Company of Women

George Washington was more relaxed in the
company of women. Even with those he counted
as mere acquaintances, he deftly mixed a courtly
bearing with a casual manner. This never happened
with men, and the result was almost universal
female admiration that verged on the starry-eyed.
Philadelphia's social maven Eliza Willing Powel
was unique, however, for her deep friendship
that allowed her to tease Washington one minute
and counsel him the next. He always laughed
at the one and often listened to the other.
(Philadelphia Museum of Fine Art)

Abigail Adams first met Washington when
he came to Massachusetts to take command
of the Continental Army in 1775. Husband
John had told her she would be impressed,
but that did not predict the half of it. After
Washington's courtesy call, Abigail was forever after a steadfast admirer.
(Library of Congress)

Eleanor Parke Custis was
Martha's granddaughter, who came with
her brother, Wash, to live at Mount Vernon after
the death of her father, Jack Custis, Martha's only
surviving child. "Nelly" was a sprightly girl
with a talent for music and a natural charm,
but she also blossomed into a great beauty,
something foreshadowed on the eve of
Washington's presidency in a miniature
of her when she was ten.
(National Gallery of Art)

Poised and pretty, Sally Cary Fairfax as the wife of George Washington's neighbor, friend, and mentor, but he loved her and in a singular instance of impulsiveness and poor judgment, he told her so in writing. He was twenty-six, and she was only two years older, but she had the good sense to rebuff him and the lovely temperament to do so gently. *(Virginia Historical Society)*

A Scot who had lived in the West Indies, Henrietta Liston was in her forties, yet a newlywed, when she came to Philadelphia as the wife of the British minister. The world saw in Henrietta Liston precisely what she was, a mature and perceptive woman with an open manner and a talent for making friends. She closely observed the closing days of Washington's presidency. *(National Gallery of Art)*

Neither maturity nor matrimony dulled
Nelly's loveliness, but as her winsome
expression suggests in this portrait,
after her marriage to Lawrence Lewis,
the idyllic years of her youth in the grand
house on the Potomac gradually became
a remote memory, and life would not
always be kind. *(National Gallery of Art)*

Fannie Bassett was Martha's niece but came to live at
Mount Vernon and was soon like a daughter. Fannie
married Washington's nephew Major George Augustine
Washington and managed Mount Vernon's household
while he ran the estate when the Washingtons left for
New York and the presidency. The major's untimely
death from tuberculosis made her a young, widowed
mother, but she found love again with an old friend.
(Courtesy of the Mount Vernon Ladies' Association)

Martha Washington had lost a husband
and two children by the time she married
George Washington, but this good,
even-tempered woman took life in stride
and made the world her friend. Pictured here
in her later years, Martha is fixed in the
American memory as this portly grandmother,
but George Washington always saw little
Martha Dandridge, the girl who never
pretended to be clever but always tried to be
pleasant. Many thought their marriage loveless
and a mere mixture of opportunism and
convenience, but they could not bear to be
apart. When George Washington died,
Martha grieved herself to death.
(Library of Congress)

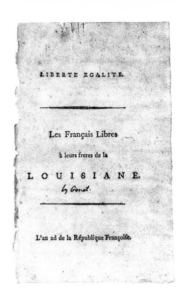

LIBERTE EGALITE.

Les Français Libres

à leurs freres de la

LOUISIANE.

by Genet.

L'an 2d de la République Françoise.

Troubles

Edmond-Charles Genet's arrival from revolutionary France as Paris's minister to the United States raised the expectations of those eager to believe that events in Europe were the logical result of the American quest for freedom and equality. Many Americans were dazzled as well as charmed, but President Washington was not among them. *(Harper's Encyclopaedia of United States History)*

Genet wrote an address from "the free French to the brothers in Louisiana" in 1793 as part of his plan to incite French inhabitants there to rise up against Spanish authorities. Jefferson added "by Genet" to the title page. By then, the secretary of state's high hopes for the Frenchman were waning because of his repeated violations of American neutrality and diplomatic protocol. *(Library of Congress)*

While serving as a Republican senator from Virginia in 1794, James Monroe received the appointment as U.S. Minister to France to replace Washington's friend Gouverneur Morris. He was at first reluctant to accept the post, just as Washington had been reluctant to offer it, but both men were being advised to look beyond past differences and use the event as a way to heal the wounds of faction. In Paris, however, Monroe threatened to undermine Washington's policy of neutrality regarding the Anglo-French war and forced the president to make an awkward decision. *(Yale University Art Gallery)*

Pierre L'Enfant was a French major who had served in the Revolutionary War before he became the original planner of the proposed capital in the federal district. He quickly exasperated everyone by ignoring the district's commissioners and trampling on the property rights of locals. In this 1989 depiction, Bryan Leister captured L'Enfant's confidence tinged with arrogance.
(The Historical Society of Washington, D.C., © Bryan Leister)

L'Enfant had a grand vision for the city of Washington, as indicated by the map he eventually produced. The president's advisors, however, were concerned about burdensome costs and the unseemliness of a republic erecting a sprawling monument to government.
(Library of Congress)

The Second Cabinet

George Washington had known Edmund Randolph as a babe in arms and had watched him grow into a young, eager man full of promise. He often engaged Randolph as his lawyer after the war, and Randolph routinely refused payment for his services. Completely devoted to advancing Washington's best interests, Randolph sought to restrain the political passions of his colleagues that threatened to disrupt the cabinet. His efforts only made them regard him as weak and untrustworthy.
(Library of Congress)

Oliver Wolcott, Jr., was an able assistant to Alexander Hamilton at the Treasury Department, and when Hamilton retired, he secured Wolcott's elevation to head the department. Wolcott was a staunch Federalist suspicious of anyone who did not support Hamilton's program and willing to eliminate all opposition to it in the government. The attitude made him a formidable enemy, as Edmund Randolph was to discover. *(Yale University Art Gallery)*

Despite his tendency to be suspicious of everyone and his habit of scheming, Timothy Pickering's administrative competence made him a palatable addition to Washington's second cabinet, but only just so. Pickering especially excelled at being the second man in almost everything. He was the second postmaster general and the second secretary of war. Pickering become Washington's last secretary of state, finally occupying a post that exceeded his competence. *(Library of Congress)*

An Irish immigrant educated as a physician, James McHenry was an officer during the Revolution and became friends with Alexander Hamilton and the Marquis de Lafayette. Despite these sterling connections, McHenry could not land a place in the administration until 1796. As Washington's last secretary of war, McHenry proved a languid administrator who was fortunate to have a peaceful tenure in the closing days of the Washington presidency. Looming troubles with France during the Adams administration laid bare McHenry's shortcomings. *(Library of Congress)*

Long Shadows

During the Revolution, Washington so admired the daring of Benedict Arnold that he overlooked his flaws. The opportunism, self-promotion, touchy pride, and petty corruptions that marked Arnold's career during the war were warning signs that should have been impossible to ignore, but George Washington managed. When it was finally uncovered, Arnold's treason did more than stun George Washington. It later made this extremely careful man willing to listen to accusations of disloyalty and leap to the worst conclusions.
(Library of Congress)

Few in America, let alone Virginia, could match the farmer-philosopher George Mason's clear understanding of the Scottish Enlightenment and its meaning for limiting government and promoting liberty. Mason was George Washington's neighbor and friend, and he remained his neighbor but ceased to be his friend when he vigorously opposed the ratification of the Constitution because he thought its government too strong, too central, and too intrusive. Yet there was more to their estrangement than that, and the long shadow of it fell on another man long after George Mason had died.
(Virginia Historical Society)

In stark contrast to Benedict Arnold, the Marquis de Lafayette served the American cause in the Revolution selflessly and in deep sympathy with its ideals and purpose. Washington met him when he was only nineteen years old and a newly minted major general, courtesy of the Congress. Lafayette was humble, eager, and soon proved able. That was enough to impress George Washington, but their mutual affection came to resemble that of a father and son.
(National Portrait Gallery, Smithsonian Institution)

Lafayette returned to France after the American victory at Yorktown, but he visited America in 1784. Although he promised to return, it would be the last meeting between him and Washington, something Washington sensed when they parted. Despite all the differences between Benedict Arnold and the Marquis de Lafayette, they were similar in forever shaping Washington's perceptions of how the most trusted men can betray and the most unlikely one enchant. *(Yale University Art Gallery)*

Place

The western aspect of Mount Vernon greeted visitors who approached it from the land and was the result of more than twenty years of renovations. Washington began major improvements before the Revolution, which were continued during the war and completed shortly before he assumed the presidency. *(Collection of the authors)*

Mount Vernon's piazza overlooked the Potomac River and was one of the most popular places on the estate. An expanse of lawn gave way to a steep grade to the river that made Mount Vernon impressive from the water while providing a majestic view from the house. When the piazza enjoyed cooling breezes in summer, people lingered there for hours. *(Library of Congress)*

When Washington died in December 1799, he was buried in the family crypt at Mount Vernon, but it was already in the early stages of deterioration, and Washington had provided in his will for a new tomb. There were plans to place him in a vault at the new Capitol in Washington, D.C., but by the time it was completed, the family would not consent to his removal. The tomb pictured here was completed in 1831, and Washington, Martha, and others were moved to this final resting place on Mount Vernon's grounds, where they remain to this day. *(Yale University Art Gallery)*

above the fray, but should it. Washington informed Hamilton and Jefferson that he was returning to Philadelphia immediately and wanted their counsel about a proper course and a prudent one.[23] He arrived on Thursday, April 18, 1793, and assembled his cabinet the following day. He wanted answers to thirteen questions he had prepared to examine the impact of the European war on American sovereignty and security. The war between Great Britain and France was of immediate concern because of American obligations under the French treaty of 1778. In essence, Washington wanted to know if American neutrality was the best policy.

It was a contentious meeting. Jefferson concluded afterward that most of the discussion had been prearranged and the policy already decided. He thought Washington's questions were really from Hamilton's pen, and he knew from Randolph that Hamilton had previously discussed the cabinet's agenda in detail.[24] Hamilton's intimate involvement in preparations for the meeting convinced Jefferson in hindsight that everything about a proclamation of neutrality had been more or less resolved before April 19. The process of debate seemed a sham. Jefferson believed, without saying so, that Hamilton wanted neutrality because it would favor Britain. Jefferson wanted to delay any policy announcement to give him time to bargain with the British, perhaps to exchange neutrality for eased commercial restrictions. Jefferson expected Knox to be in Hamilton's corner, "like a fool he is."[25] But the main reason Jefferson later thought that he had been trying to influence a foregone conclusion was Randolph's unexpected alignment with Hamilton and Knox. His friend's shift surprised Jefferson to the point of bafflement during the meeting. It was later that he concluded that he had been set up for a fall.

At the meeting, Hamilton did state what were apparently well rehearsed arguments. A proclamation of neutrality was necessary, he said, because the president did not have the power to declare war and needed to maintain peace until Congress could consider the matter. Jefferson disagreed with Hamilton's constitutional interpretation. Since only Congress could declare war, he pointed out, only Congress could proclaim neutrality. Washington chose to issue a proclamation and told Randolph to draft it, and Jefferson had the uneasy feeling he had been wasting his breath.

Yet when it came to recognizing the new French government, receiving France's minister, and reassessing the treaty of 1778 as possibly inoperative, Jefferson would eventually win the day. Hamilton argued that the treaty had been made with Louis XVI, and his removal meant that it was no longer in force. Randolph joined with Jefferson on this point to counter that treaties are made with nations, not specific governments. Washington agreed that the new minister should be received but asked for written opinions on the other points. Randolph was to have the proclamation ready as soon as possible.[26]

The cabinet convened on Monday morning to hash out Randolph's draft. Jefferson won a small victory in having the word "neutrality" omitted, and in its final form the president's proclamation was not technically about neutrality. It sought to prohibit Americans from helping any belligerents and to describe the United States as apart from the conflict, which meant neutrality without saying so and was a small concession to Jefferson. The proclamation was made official that day, April 22, 1793, and was published in the newspapers.[27]

Initial reactions to it were worse than mixed. Almost nobody liked it. James Madison at least kept private his doubt that Washington had the authority to issue such a proclamation. He agreed with Jefferson that only Congress could establish neutrality through statute. "The proclamation," Madison concluded, "was in truth a most unfortunate error." Jefferson made a halfhearted attempt to defend it by pointing out that it never mentioned the word "neutrality," but he conceded that "the instrument was badly drawn, and made the P. go out of his line to declare things which, tho' true, it was not exactly his province to declare."[28]

Jefferson and Madison represented measured criticism. Others were not so sedate. Supporters of France condemned the proclamation as helping Great Britain and staged strident public meetings to say so. Typifying the sentiments, an unsigned letter to Washington expressed disapproval of the proclamation and accused the president of betraying France. The anonymous writer predicted that when France won the war she would "distain her unfeeling Sister."[29]

Meanwhile, the new French minister had arrived in the United States but was not yet officially recognized as his government's emissary. On April 8, 1793, the thirty-six-gun French frigate *Embuscade* landed with Edmond-Charles Genet on board at Charleston, South

Carolina.[30] A rousing welcome by the people was matched by effusive declarations of affection and fidelity from Governor William Moultrie. South Carolinians despised Great Britain as an oppressor and hated Spain for riling southern Indians and choking off American commerce from the Mississippi. They also had great affection for France as the ally who had helped secure independence. In Charleston these sentiments reached a high pitch because of the large number of citizens with French lineage that dated back to the Huguenot (Protestant) exodus from Catholic France. Huguenots had helped shape Charleston's culture, even providing the charming and eccentric way that Charlestonians pronounced certain words.

Genet's decision to begin his American mission in their city flattered Charlestonians to the point of making everyone forget to ask the obvious question: Why was he there? The U.S. capital was Philadelphia, and protocol required accredited diplomats to present their credentials to their host government immediately after arriving in country. Genet used the threat of capture by the Royal Navy as an excuse for his catch-as-catch-can selection of a port of debarkation, but he would have been more convincing if he had behaved more convincingly. As it was, there was a reason for his landing in pro-French Charleston, and it wasn't to escape capture by the British.

Even though he was only thirty years old, Genet already had long served in the French diplomatic corps. His father was chief clerk in the French Bureau of Interpreters and dealt with the U.S. commissioners to France during the American Revolution. Edmond-Charles Genet was only fifteen when he met John Adams and only eighteen when he inherited his deceased father's post. He rose rapidly in the diplomatic service because he was intellectually gifted and a natural polyglot. He possessed a boyish charm that made every man his friend and every woman his mother. As chargé d'affaires to the French Embassy in Russia, Genet had that effect on Catherine the Great. And yet, he also revealed a common failing of prodigies accustomed to admiration: They think praise is always deserved and disdain criticism as misguided. Heedless of where he was or careless about the opinions of his hosts, Genet voiced forthright support for the pending revolution in France when restraint was necessary in the court of a Russian autocrat, no matter how enlightened. The empress Catherine was not amused. She soon ceased to indulge Genet's irritating habits. The most flagrant was his ignoring conventions about the proper way to communicate with her, which was never directly but always supposed to be through her government. He was sent home under a cloud, and that might have been the end of his career had not the revolution resurrected it.[31]

Genet, in fact, became a fervent revolutionary during a time when talent was percolating to the top. He deeply resented the reprimand he had earned at the Russian court and revealed a dangerous inability for introspection and self-appraisal. It was a crippling flaw in a diplomat in the best of times, a lethal one during revolutionary upheavals.[32]

The Girondists sent Genet to America to replace Ternant, the king's last minister. They were not blind to his flaws or unaware of his history, and his superiors warned him about the consequences of brash conduct. While offering this sensible advice, however, they also saddled him with impossible instructions, to which the ambitious Genet likely contributed. Gouverneur Morris had Genet to dinner before he left France and immediately formed the impression that the young Frenchman had "the Look of an Upstart," was in way over his head, and talked too much. Nevertheless, Morris thought that these character flaws might very well work to the United States' advantage.[33]

Genet was expected to enlist the United States in the revolution's challenge of Europe's monarchical regimes. The war France started would continue with different players and only occasional interruptions for the next quarter century. Genet was supposed to secure the United States as a helpmate in the undertaking, though France knew American help would likely be limited. If the United States could lend material support in driving Spaniards from Louisiana and Britons from Canada, all the better.

Thus Genet's instructions took form. First, he was to follow through on Ternant's request to secure a significant portion of the American debt to France, a sum roughly $4.5 million as reckoned by the French. Genet was then to use this money to purchase equipment and provisions for the war effort. Second, he was to negotiate a new commercial treaty whose scope would have surprised even Thomas Jefferson, had he known all of its potential stipulations. Third, the United States was to allow privateers to outfit in American harbors that would also serve as safe havens. And finally, Genet was to launch aggressive military operations against Spanish Louisiana and British Canada. The French expected American acquiescence in this last project because its success would eliminate quarrelsome neighbors to the west and north.

Genet would try to achieve these goals in ways stunningly wrongheaded. He was not stupid, but the key to understanding his behavior is to know that he was fundamentally misinformed. Neither he nor his superiors understood the way the American government worked under the Constitution. They did not realize that the primacy of the legislature had limits and that the executive was something other than an appendage of Congress. Genet's notion of the way things worked in America would leave his hosts aghast, and he did not have an inkling why, until it was too late.

Thus he began his efforts with a ten-day stay in Charleston, where he tried to enlist South Carolina's pro-French leaders in raising forces to march against Spanish territory while he armed privateers to take British prizes in the Atlantic. He carried officers' commissions for Americans willing to fight for the French republic and letters of marque for ships willing to make fortunes under the French flag. Before leaving Charleston he commissioned no less than four ships to prey on the British merchant fleet.

He did not take the *Embuscade* to Philadelphia but traveled overland to the American capital, rallying crowds and meeting important people along the way. The universal adulation shown him was in part a result of sympathy for the French cause and in part a sentimental recollection of Lafayette, another young man from France who had charmed Americans without breaking a sweat. Yet Genet was not Lafayette. The adoration swelled his head and would mislead him about the limits of charm in a hardheaded political world. His trip resembled a royal progress, with his entourage of secretaries and servants, and moved with the deliberation of one. It took him twenty-three days to travel to Philadelphia, where he would finally complete the ritual of presenting his credentials. The landing at Charleston and the long cross-country trip were provocative enough. Commissioning privateers was beyond understanding. Pausing in Virginia to persuade George Rogers Clark to raise an army in Kentucky and attack Spanish territory defied all reason. Yet the lavish receptions, the cheering crowds, and the bowing city dignitaries became a fixture of his journey. Genet was convinced he could do no wrong.

In reality, he had all but undone his embassy before it was officially established. Washington and his cabinet had studied assessments of Genet from Americans in Europe. From Paris, Joel Barlow wrote to Jefferson that Genet "bears a good character."[34] Jefferson certainly hoped so. Yet before President Washington ever laid eyes on "Citizen" Edmond-Charles Genet, he mildly despised him.

17

"Laugh Us into War"

Aware of Genet's fantastic journey, Washington and his advisers had to determine how the government would enforce neutrality. Jefferson exploded when Hamilton suggested that customs officials report violations and enforce Washington's proclamation. Jefferson sputtered that it would turn collectors into "an established corps of spies and informers against their fellow citizens." He was not comforted when Randolph calmly asked him if it was not natural for a government "to gather information from its executive officers."[1]

Randolph proposed a compromise that Washington found agreeable. Customs officials could gather information but would defer to the nearest U.S. attorney to decide if the case warranted prosecution. As happened more often lately, Jefferson was more disgusted with Randolph than angry with Hamilton. Randolph, Jefferson muttered, had "found out a hair to split, which, as always, became the decision." Washington's increasing reliance on Randolph as his primary counselor meant that all decisions hung "on the opinion of a single person, and that the most indecisive one I ever had to do business with. He always contrives to agree in principle with one, but in conclusion with the other." A few days after the proclamation was made public, Jefferson wrote to Madison, "I dare say you will have judged from the pusillanimity of the proclamation, from whose pen it came."[2]

Clearly by the spring of 1793, Jefferson and Randolph's friendship had suffered grave injury. Randolph seems to have been completely unaware of the change. When reports that Virginia was extremely critical of neutrality prompted Washington to dispatch Randolph to gauge public opinion there, Jefferson was again disgusted. Randolph said that opposition in Virginia was the work of John Taylor of Caroline, the state's new rabble-rousing senator who was writing a pamphlet attacking the Bank of the United States. Most people, said Randolph, supported neutrality. Others praised Washington's sensible course. They wanted every effort made "to prevent a breach of Neutrality" and hoped "the vigorous measures of the Government will soon put pointedly in check" those who violated the proclamation.[3]

The initial criticism of the proclamation and Genet's activities had put Washington in a foul mood by the time the French minister arrived in the capital. Jefferson looked forward to meeting with him, especially because Genet was said to have the authority to negotiate new trade agreements. But that was before Genet's primary purpose became clear. Initially Genet charmed Jefferson. It was a common reaction; Genet's first impression was often mesmerizing. He was "a handsome man," said a male admirer, "with a fine open countenance and pleasing and unaffected manners."[4] Genet was neither too tall nor too short. He had auburn hair and blue eyes that women found exciting. A man who was "quite active and seems always in a bustle," he exuded attractive vigor and was exceedingly good humored. A rare skeptic said that Genet's jovial nature was fashioned "to laugh us into war."[5] Jefferson wasn't in the least skeptical. The ebullient Frenchman was all eagerness and earnest confidence. He represented the culmination of four years of revolution in France, a true republican for a true republic in the image of America.

Philadelphia certainly thought so. Town fathers had planned a lavish welcoming ceremony, but Genet arrived unannounced on May 16, 1793. Undaunted, the city staged ceremonies the following day. A reception committee delivered the official welcome, and Genet replied with the enthusiasm that had enlivened his speeches during his trip north. He announced a reassuring intention and repeated it to Jefferson when they met. "France did not expect the United States would take an active part in the war in their favor," or, as Jefferson put it, "he offers every thing and asks nothing."[6] After this cheerful meeting with Jefferson, Genet had his first official audience with President Washington.

At 2 P.M. on May 18, Jefferson, Genet, and Ternant entered Washington's parlor. Months later, Genet described Washington as coldly formal during this first meeting, though at the time he said nothing about being offended by Washington's manner.[7] Given Washington's irritation over Genet's behavior since his landing at Charleston, it was a wonder that the president was not icy. Washington's parlor did, after all, have a bust of Louis XVI conspicuously displayed.

Jefferson's goal of negotiating a more meaningful commercial agreement with France seemed certain with the arrival of the personable, engaging, and presumably compliant French minister. Gone, it seemed, were the cobwebbed and duplicitous ways of the cunning ancien régime. Per his instructions, Genet's government was quite keen to have a more meaningful commercial agreement. Jefferson just had no idea how much more meaningful France intended it to be. The goal was to use commerce to gain American cooperation in separating Louisiana from Spain and Canada from Britain. Jefferson did not know this in the spring of 1793, but Genet hoped to gain access to American ports for armed naval vessels in addition to merchantmen.

Unaware of the broad scope that Genet wanted, Jefferson apprised Washington of what he did know on May 24, 1793. As it happened, this was the very day that Washington responded to a request from Ternant for a letter to the new French government praising his diplomatic mission. The request had put Washington in a muddle, because he wasn't certain why the new revolutionary government had recalled Ternant. Did the diplomat's ties to the Bourbon establishment taint him and therefore would praise from the United States risk offense?

Washington gave Jefferson the job of drafting the letter for Ternant, and his first crack at it left Washington cold. The president objected to Jefferson's reference to the United States as "our republic," because he saw it as insulting American Federalists. In addition, he didn't care for a reference to the French government as a "republic" since the highly volatile nature of the revolution did not assure that a republic was this event's final chapter.

Jefferson made the mistake of seeming to disagree by explaining himself. Washington hotly informed Jefferson that he had no fear that the United States would become a monarchy, but "that there was more danger of anarchy being introduced." Washington was not feeling well and the strain over recent events was weighing on him. He became "sore and warm" as he revealed his preoccupation with critics who accused him of overreaching his authority with the neutrality policy. He said sharply that the last thing he wanted was a monarchy. He was tired of insinuations from people like Freneau that he did. Jefferson hurried away as soon as he could comfortably end the conversation.[8] He made the revisions, and the letter was ready for Washington's signature and dispatch on May 24, the same day Jefferson approached the president with a glowing report on France's eagerness to strengthen commercial ties.[9]

Jefferson could not have been surprised then by Washington's reluctance. His reservations were precisely the same as those over the Ternant letter. Prudence dictated a slow and wary approach to making agreements with people who might soon prove disagreeable. Three days later, Jefferson tried again, supplying translated documents to the president and the cabinet; the group would mull the matter periodically throughout the summer. In all these discussions, only Jefferson supported the initiative, and it came to nothing. Stalling the Frenchman, Jefferson told Genet that everything would have to wait until the Senate reconvened in the fall—a claim that likely seemed plausible to a man with only a dim understanding of executive authority under the Constitution.

Jefferson's promotion of a new commercial agreement seemed irrelevant in the face of a thorny problem caused by Genet's other activities. Jefferson had doubted Genet would abuse privileges, especially by invoking the right to outfit privateers. Yet Genet had done just that, beginning in Charleston. One ship named the *Citoyen Genet* had sallied forth to seize British prizes, including the merchant ship *Grange* in Delaware Bay, which placed the action squarely in American waters. British minister George Hammond had not had anything meaningful to do since arriving in America, but he suddenly had everything to do all at once. He fumed that Genet's privateers made American claims of neutrality preposterous. The ships not only sailed from American ports but were crewed in part by Americans as they merrily seized British ships. It was painful to admit that George Hammond was correct.

The cabinet met on May 15, 1793, to decide how to respond. Division ensued on the customary lines. Hamilton and Knox said the government should restore British property; Jefferson and Randolph said it should not. They pointed out that no one in Charleston could have known about Washington's neutrality proclamation before the ships put to sea, and that technicality provided a way out of the difficulty. Washington privately conferred with Randolph and decided that the French could keep the captured British ship *Little Sarah* as well as any other prizes taken before the proclamation became common knowledge. Randolph told Washington that he had urged Jefferson to talk to Genet to discover his part in the current imbroglio and what the French minister considered to be proper conduct for the future. As it stood following these meetings, the French could no longer outfit privateers in American ports or recruit American citizens into French service. The case of the *Grange,* however, posed a different difficulty. If Hammond's claims were correct about its location when it was seized, the French would have to return the ship to its owners. Advised that the ship had been taken in American waters, Genet agreed to return it.[10] It was to be his only attempt at placating his hosts.

These mounting problems increasingly frayed Washington's temper during that June. Everywhere he turned, duty and protocol constrained him. He felt he had to refuse a private meeting with the Viscount de Noailles, a Royalist refugee and an old friend from the Revolution, because it could offend the new French government. His cabinet squabbled and sniped more than ever, always over Genet and everything French. Hamilton and Jefferson were both considering retirement, and Tobias Lear broached his plan to leave as Washington's indispensable factotum by the end of the summer and start his own business. "The President is not well," Jefferson wrote to Madison. "Little lingering fevers have been hanging about him for a week or ten days, and have affected his looks most remarkeably."[11] George Washington desperately needed to go home, if only for a short time.

On June 22, 1793, as Washington prepared to leave Philadelphia, he and the cabinet received a message from Pennsylvania governor Thomas Mifflin that one of the French prizes docked at Philadelphia, the brig *Little Sarah,* was being refitted as an armed privateer complete with a new name, *La Petite Démocrate.* Genet had begun another exasperating project. Washington quickly gave instructions to Henry Knox. It was significant that he turned the matter over to the War Department. Initial reports were encouraging. Rather than augmenting the armaments on the *Little Sarah,* crews had transferred two of her cannons to the *Citoyen Genet.* Washington had already departed for Mount Vernon, and both Mifflin and the cabinet thought it best to let the sleeping dog lie.

Washington arrived at Mount Vernon and broke his personal rule to avoid local events lest his calendar get clogged and force him to choose one over another. In this case, he accepted an invitation from Alexandria's leaders to attend a July 4 celebration. He wanted to talk to citizens himself and learn their opinions of his proclamation. To his relief, he found people generally positive. With everything temporarily settled at home and comforted by the visit with his neighbors, Washington returned to Philadelphia on July 11, 1793. He went immediately to his desk to find that everything he had hoped to escape was not only waiting for him but had multiplied.

Six days before, new and unsettling information about the former *Little Sarah* had come to light. Genet hoped to dispatch her against Spaniards in New Orleans. The next day, July 6, Governor Mifflin's secretary of state Alexander Dallas learned that she would be ready to sail within twenty-four hours. Mifflin was quite agitated and clearly baffled about how much he should do at the risk of an international incident, possibly one that could provoke war with France. He adopted the halfway measure of preparedness by calling out a squadron of militia without specifying its purpose. At least it would be ready to stop *La Petite Démocrate* if it came to that.

Dallas proposed an alternative by offering to talk some sense into Genet. In a dramatic scene worthy of the theater, Dallas met with Genet just before midnight on July 6, 1793. It did not go well. Genet would not listen to reason and took over the conversation with an excited denunciation of American neutrality as dishonorable on moral grounds and illegitimate under treaty obligations. At this point, he thought he had identified the chief culprits behind the policy as Alexander Hamilton and Hamilton's doddering marionette George Washington. It was from this meeting that a claim arose that would dog Genet for the rest of his life. It was said that he angrily threatened to bypass Washington and his policy by appealing directly to the American people.[12] Genet believed they were more than sympathetic to his cause.

Jefferson met with Genet the following day and was marginally more successful than Dallas; at least, he was prepared to think so. He interpreted the vague concessions of Genet as a "promise" not to send out *La Petite Démocrate* until Washington had returned from Virginia and could review the matter. The cabinet was not reassured, though, and its mood did not improve when Genet abruptly had the brig moved downriver to Chester, Pennsylvania, a point below American batteries on Mud Island, the only thing that could have stopped her progress.

Thomas Jefferson now had a sinking feeling that everything about the Frenchman was poison. He had never shared with the cabinet Genet's plans to oust Spain from Louisiana, which he knew about because the plans involved the botanist André Michaux, who was bound for Kentucky to study western flora—a trip already in the works with Jefferson's enthusiastic support. Genet wanted Michaux to recruit an army in Kentucky, and asked Jefferson to write a letter of introduction to Kentucky leaders to smooth Michaux's way. He wanted the letter to be more of a general character reference rather than the one Jefferson had planned, which described Michaux's botanical credentials. Jefferson obliged, writing that Michaux was trustworthy. The cabinet knew nothing of these plans. Neither did George Washington.

On Washington's desk that July 11 was a packet of papers labeled "instant attention." Jefferson had left them. They outlined everything the cabinet knew about *La Petite Démocrate* and Genet's plans for her. What Washington did not find was Thomas Jefferson. He was at his country house outside of town. The papers Jefferson had provided to Washington told the story of Dallas and Jefferson's separate meetings with Genet and of the cabinet deliberations. Jefferson included a letter from Genet protesting that the United States had violated its obligations under its treaty with France. Washington was furious. He fired off a note to Jefferson. "Is the Minister of the French Republic," he snapped, "to set the Acts of this Government at defiance—with impunity? and then threaten the Executive with an appeal to the People."[13] Jefferson merely said he was sorry he could not appear in person, but he was ill. He promised to pull himself into town for the cabinet meeting the next day. By that time, *La Petite Démocrate* was heading out to sea.

Hamilton and Knox now matched Washington's fury. They demanded that the French government be told to recall Genet. Knox wanted Genet stripped of all diplomatic responsibilities while they waited for the response from Paris. Jefferson tried to salvage the wreck. He suggested that Genet's actions and correspondence be sent to the French government.[14]

Genet finally realized he had gone too far—that he had alienated his hosts just as he had at the Russian court. He rushed to Jefferson, whom Genet still believed was his friend. He told the secretary of state that he wanted to make everything right with Washington by personally visiting the president at his residence that very evening. Jefferson listened to Genet's plan with growing horror. He told Genet that barging in uninvited would be an unforgivable and consequently irreparable mistake. Genet ignored the advice. He found the president enjoying a quiet evening at home with Martha and his close friend Robert Morris. Genet had his interview, a brief encounter with the president who was at first startled but then impassive. Genet vehemently denied that he had ever been disrespectful to Washington or had written anything for the newspapers. Washington's eyes had the look of a sphinx. He said he never read newspapers.[15] Genet finally ran out of words and gracelessly withdrew. Washington had never liked Genet, and his taking such license with proper procedure was the last straw—at least for that evening.

Though Washington's patience with Genet and the controversies he caused was wearing thin, by the next day the president was again showing his famous restraint. Opponents to his proclamation seemed a minority, but they were a vocal one with voices getting louder. "Clubs"—the label reminded Federalists of how the Jacobins started in France—had been forming all over the country to show their support for the French. They called themselves "Democratic Societies" and, in fact, were partly inspired by the Jacobin Club. They were not as numerous as they would become in 1794, but they made up for low numbers with volume, raucously praising Jefferson, Madison, and Genet. Federalists denounced the Democratic Societies as "the most wicked and dangerous attempt ever made in this country to render all government unnecessary."[16] Supporters of neutrality countered with meetings of their own. They passed resolutions, published them in newspapers, and sent copies to the president. Those gestures were only marginally reassuring.

Jefferson knew that Washington was "extremely affected by the attacks made & kept up on him in the public papers." Jefferson believed that the president felt "those things more than any person I ever yet met."[17] The *National Gazette* instructed Washington that "sovereignty still resides with THE PEOPLE."[18] Washington had already hinted to Jefferson that he should fire Freneau from the State Department, but Jefferson ignored the suggestion. He could not ignore Washington's exploding in a cabinet meeting that "that rascal Freneau" refused to cancel his subscription but impudently sent him three copies of each issue of his paper.[19]

Washington's friends were soon giving as good as the president got. Hamilton took the lead in defending neutrality and Washington's wisdom in establishing it. As "Pacificus," he insisted that the president's power to set foreign policy derived from the Constitution.[20] The use of pseudonyms in these newspaper articles was more for form than concealment because the public was familiar with the styles of authors, making them easy to identify. Jefferson was among those who recognized Hamilton as Pacificus. He urged Madison: "For god's sake, my dear Sir, take up your pen."[21] Madison was at home waiting for the Third Congress to convene that fall, but he did as he was told. As "Helvidius" Madison criticized Washington's proclamation as exceeding legitimate presidential power. Madison did not disagree with the neutrality policy; he simply did not believe that it was within the president's power to declare it. Still, it was the first time he publicly disagreed with George Washington directly about anything. There would be no going back.[22]

Jefferson finally gave up hope that Genet could improve relations with France; in fact, he had given up on Genet altogether. He wrote to Madison that "never in my opinion, was so calamitous an appointment made, as that of the present minister."[23] All Jefferson could do was mitigate the damage.

Washington and his cabinet tried to set a standard for handling the French prizes that continued to arrive in American ports, and other violations of American neutrality. Despite Hamilton's bravura as Pacificus, the administration still floundered amid uncertainties about presidential power, the force of an executive proclamation as compared to a congressional statute, and the extent of authority to prosecute neutrality violators. Arriving at a consensus about these issues was almost impossible. The cabinet met almost daily and finally hammered out eight "Rules Governing Belligerents."

The process had been exhausting. At one meeting Knox told a story from Senator Rufus King of New York who had heard a lady say she had heard a man say that the president was a tyrant. It was mischief bordering on malice for Knox to relate this thirdhand gossip, but it would not be the last time he said something apparently designed to make George Washington lose his temper. Knox's collaboration with Alexander Hamilton on questions before the cabinet had become automatic, and this new tactic of abrading already raw nerves was apparently meant to remind Washington that Jefferson and Madison were really the sly authors of all the talk of tyrants and charges of monarchism. Their agents were the subsidized Freneau and the execrable Bache, their minions the seditious assemblies styling themselves Democratic Societies. Washington worked his jaw over the Rufus King story, but he held his temper.

Tempers held in check became scarce for everybody as they wrestled with their proposed rules. When Randolph caught Hamilton in a lie on July 29, 1793, everything almost blew up. Hamilton had circulated his notes of a previous meeting in which a particularly difficult point had proved impossible to resolve. Yet Hamilton's notes said the issue had been settled his way with everyone in agreement. To Jefferson, "it was pretty evident from" Hamilton's "warmth, embarrassment, eagerness, that he wanted to slip in something." Like Knox's mischief bordering on malice, Hamilton's inventive note taking smacked of bad faith.[24]

The cabinet finally set rules defining conduct that violated neutrality. Their list included a foreign belligerent outfitting privateers in the United States, recruiting for combat of any kind against other belligerents, and launching military operations from the United States against other belligerents. By then, word had arrived that Genet's sponsors the Girondists had fallen to the Jacobins, making Genet's days as the French minister almost certainly numbered. The cabinet nevertheless took up the issue of formally requesting his recall. Everyone agreed it should be done but could not come to a consensus on how to accomplish it. Their sessions were lengthy, and they frequently dined at Washington's family table, where they likely suspended angry debates in front of Martha and the children.

It was during one of these meetings that Knox returned to his tactic of baiting the president by reminding him of excesses in the opposition press. Knox produced a recent broadside printed by Freneau. Washington examined it as the cabinet fell silent. Over the title "The Funeral Dirge of George Washington and [Supreme Court justice] James Wilson, King and Judges," Washington was depicted facing a guillotine. This was too much.

Washington became "much inflamed" and "got into one of those passions when he cannot command himself." He ranted about "the personal abuse which had been bestowed on him" and "defied any man on earth to produce one single act of his since he had been in the government which was not done on the purest motives." He continued to rage "that *by god* he had rather be in his grave than in his present situation. That he had rather be on his farm than be made *emperor of the world* and yet that they were charging him with wanting to be king." Everyone, including Knox, sat stunned.[25] For Jefferson, any doubts about malign collusion between Knox and Hamilton vanished during these heated sessions in the hot room on High Street.

Jefferson had always felt these discussions should include Congress, and he continually urged Washington to call the legislature into special session. Washington seemed to agree but faced expected opposition from Hamilton and Knox. One day Knox blurted out that it was fortunate that Congress had not been in session to intrude on their deliberations. Jefferson later noted that "the fool thus let out the secret" and described how Hamilton had tried to cover for him.[26] Worse was when Randolph sided with them. Washington, as usual, agreed with the majority. Yet again, Jefferson was more disgusted with Randolph than angry with Knox. They both had become cyphers doing Hamilton's bidding.

In fact, his disgust over the futility of his efforts became more than Jefferson could take. Madison had earlier reacted to Jefferson's plan to leave the government by writing him that "every consideration private as well as public require a further sacrifice." Jefferson replied with a rare show of temper. Being "committed singly in desperate & eternal contest against a host who are systematically undermining the public liberty & prosperity," was more than he could endure. He was "cut off from my family & friends, my affairs abandoned to chaos & derange-ment, in short giving up every thing I love, in exchange for every thing I hate."[27] He told Washington that his planned retirement could be postponed no longer. He would go home for good at the end of Sep-tember.

Washington was nearing the end of his tether, too. Losing his temper was unlike him. He made a rare personal call to visit Jefferson's home on the Schuylkill River. He insisted Jefferson would be difficult to replace, as would Hamilton, who was threatening to retire as well. Mentioning Hamilton did not help Washington's case, but that he did mention Jefferson's enemy showed how desperately he thought that he needed their help. With a sigh of resignation, Washington listed possi-ble replacements for both. They were mostly Federalists, and Jefferson disliked them all. The prospect of Wolcott as Hamilton's replacement especially bothered him. Jefferson told Washington that Wolcott was "a cunning man."[28]

Washington mentioned Randolph as Jefferson's possible successor at State, and the resentments of weeks instantly rose to the surface. Jef-ferson had just refused to cosign a loan for Randolph, citing his pending retirement as constraining his finances. It was a flimsy excuse to mask the real reason for Jefferson's reluctance to help the attorney general out of a financial bind. Jefferson told Madison that Randolph was "the poorest Chameleon I ever saw having no colour of his own, and reflect-ing that nearest him."[29] He was, in short, a turncoat who betrayed his friends.

Yet Washington's suggestion about placing Randolph to head the State Department gave Jefferson the opportunity to use the criticism he knew would be most effective with Washington. Jefferson acted hesi-tant, played to the pause, and then told the president that Randolph was always in various stages of financial embarrassment. Philadelphia mer-chants were constantly having to dun him, and with that Jefferson—a spendthrift himself—left unsaid but obviously implied that Randolph's money problems could make him too reliant on loans, possibly from unsavory people who could compromise if not direct his actions. He did not say it in so many words, of course, but Jefferson believed the suggestion was sufficient, a seed planted on fertile ground. It was a rotten thing to do.

Washington had not really wanted Jefferson's opinion, however. He simply wanted Jefferson to remain in his post, at least until the end of the year. Jefferson agreed to stay on for the few extra months. Possibly as an incentive, very likely as a reward, Washington had Jefferson draft the request for Genet's recall.[30] Though Jefferson certainly wanted the task rather than let it fall to Hamilton, he had to tread a thin line. His draft letter to Gouverneur Morris set forth the reasons for requesting Genet's recall while making clear that his transgressions—rather than any displeasure with France—prompted the request. Meanwhile, the cabinet debate on whether to make public Genet's impertinent correspondence with the administration continued. Hamilton and Knox wanted to use the incident and the damning documentary trail to discredit the French Republic and its revolution, which is precisely what Jefferson feared. Yet Hamilton's tactics to create a backlash against Genet unintentionally frustrated his goal when Federalists staged rallies that seemed to show overwhelming public support for the administration. Rather than emboldening Washington to publish the documents, it persuaded him that doing so was not necessary.

Jefferson's letter to Morris produced some unexpected results as well. The cabinet quibbled over the document for days, with Hamilton and Knox, and finally Randolph also (to Jefferson's disgust), complaining about its excessive expressions of friendship toward France. The trio perceived gratuitous insults to the European coalition fighting France. They specifically objected to the phrase that described any possible serious disagreement between France and the United States as an unseemly situation that would have "liberty warring on herself," and they succeeded in having it removed.[31]

As Jefferson labored on the letter, John Jay and Rufus King published a joint affidavit asserting that they had heard from a reliable source—Hamilton—that Genet had threatened to appeal to the people over the authority of the president.[32] It prompted Genet, who was in New York, to breach protocol yet again and write directly to Washington denying the allegation. Washington refused to answer the letter. He told Jefferson to answer Genet explaining that he was never again to write directly to the president of the United States. All communications had to come through the secretary of state.[33]

Edmond-Charles Genet's world was falling apart. He was in New York to greet a French fleet carrying refugees from the rebellion in Saint-Domingue, but the crews were near mutiny and many sailors were jumping ship to vanish in the city. He knew that he had made matters worse with his brazen visit to Washington's residence, though it was never apparently clear to him why he had made things worse. Jefferson's curt reply about the proper mode of communication was devastating.

Jefferson sent his letter and supporting documents to Morris shortly after August 20, 1793, by express vessel. He did not advise Genet of the recall request for two weeks for fear the minister would try to have the ship intercepted. Thus, Genet did not know he was already under threat of a recall when the Jay-King affidavit appeared. He was intent on vindicating his behavior against the Jay-King accusations, in the courts if necessary. In the meantime, he forlornly went about his duties as if nothing were wrong.

There was one bright spot for Genet. At a party hosted by Governor Clinton, he saw the most enchanting girl. She was Clinton's daughter Cornelia. Genet could not take his eyes off her. Smart and usually outspoken about politics, Cornelia, upon meeting Genet, for the first time in her life could not put two words together. She was twenty, ten years his junior, and was infatuated the moment she saw him. It would take only a few days, possibly hours, before she was in love with him for the rest of her life. As for Cornelia's father, he at first believed Hamiltonian rumors that Genet had a wife and little Genets back in France, but Cornelia persisted. Genet would rename *La Petite Démocrate* the *Cornelia,* and not too many suitors could do as much. He gradually charmed Governor Clinton the same way Lafayette had captivated Washington.

Eventually Americans would forgive Genet's faults because they were Americans. They would also do something more. When the time came, Americans would save Edmond-Charles Genet's life.[34]

* * *

That summer Polly Lear became seriously ill and rapidly declined. In only days, Toby's young wife and mother of his child died on Sunday afternoon, July 28, 1793. The heat compelled them to bury her in haste, so the next day her funeral was held with Supreme Court associate justices walking solemnly with Secretaries Hamilton, Knox, and Jefferson as Polly's pallbearers. Washington stood with Lear during the ceremony. Polly's death nearly killed Toby and cast a pall over the Washington household. Toby had loved her "from infancy" and now was alone with a two-year-old son.[35] The family had been excited about embarking on a new life with Lear setting up a business and settling them in a place of their own. Then the illness came and she was suddenly gone. George and Martha knew loss, but Polly's death seemed remarkably tragic. Vibrant and kind, the young woman was Martha's companion and kin, but for the bloodline.

Polly's death was more than a tragedy, however. It was a portent of horrible things to come in Philadelphia.[36] Modern scholars are sure what killed Polly Lear, but at the time physicians were at first baffled. They, too, would soon know what killed her, but never what caused it. She was one of the earliest victims of the yellow fever outbreak that terrorized Philadelphia in the summer of 1793. Relatively few deaths marked its early appearance, and doctors were slow to realize what they faced. By the first week of September, they knew.

City leaders did their best to organize medical care and efficient burials. Many people fled, but cities barred fugitives from Philadelphia because of fears of contagion. No one knew what caused yellow fever. In Philadelphia, bad air coming from the harbor's fetid water was blamed. Mosquitos seemed especially thick during the late summer of 1793, but no one would make the connection for more than a century.[37]

All were soon well aware, however, that yellow fever was a horrifying malady that tortured victims before killing them. A low fever, listlessness, and aches signaled its onset. A rising fever soon came on, sometimes to break briefly and rouse hopes of recovery. After a short time, though, the fever would return, raging. A jaundiced complexion gave the disease its name, liver failure being an eventual development, along with internal bleeding, vomiting, and diarrhea. Those who lived alone or were abandoned by frightened relatives died in their own filth.

By mid-September, Philadelphia resembled a ghost town. Stores closed, newspapers stopped printing, and government work ceased. Some of Washington's official family were among the refugees, but Hamilton and Betsey began showing signs of the disease. By September 8, 1793, they were confirmed cases. From his house on the Schuylkill, Jefferson scoffed that Hamilton only had "an autumnal fever." He sneered that Hamilton had wanted to catch something and chuckled that "a man as timid as he is on the water, as timid on horseback, as timid in sickness, would be a phaenomenon if the courage of which he has the reputation in military occasions were genuine."[38] It was becoming more and more apparent that public life brought out the worst in the quiet philosopher.

Hamilton was treated by Dr. Edward Stevens, who hailed from St. Croix and had been a boyhood friend in the West Indies. Stevens was a product of the University of Edinburgh and subscribed to treating yellow fever with cold baths, a therapy that came to be known as the West Indies treatment. This directly opposed Benjamin Rush's advocacy of bleeding and blistering, a technique known as the depletion treatment. Bleeding and blistering was Rush's preferred treatment for everything, and the method often killed rather than cured. Hamilton's recovery boosted the popularity of the West Indies treatment, and he recommended Stevens and his methods to the college of physicians. Yellow fever, like everything else, showed the country's preoccupation with politics. Stevens's West Indies treatment was cited as the Federalist cure and Rush's depletion method as the Republican one.[39]

Jefferson left Philadelphia with his younger daughter, Polly, who had been living with her father for about a year. The trip to Monticello was planned for the fall, but concerns for the child caused him to start out early. Knox and Randolph left as well, though Randolph went only as far as Germantown, where the disease had not reached. The town was nearly bursting at the seams with refugees. People everywhere urged Washington to leave Philadelphia for his "own sake & that of mankind," but he recoiled from the potential charge that, like a cowardly captain, he had jumped a sinking ship. It was Martha's refusal to leave without him that caused him to move up his own fall journey home.

The Washingtons invited Samuel and Eliza Powel to go with them to Mount Vernon, but Samuel refused to leave, and Eliza would not go without him. If she would not cast him aside as a suitor because some ninnies thought him too plain and her too pretty, she was not going to leave him because of a silly epidemic. George and Martha Washington left Philadelphia while the Powels remained.

As the scope of the diseased worsened, Powel persuaded Eliza at least to go her brother's home in the country. In due course, he also retreated to his own country house. The need for "a humane visit" to see about a servant soon brought him back into Philadelphia, which his friends knew was just the kind of thing he would do. Samuel contracted yellow fever. Dr. Rush bled him until he died.[40] Years earlier, young Eliza Powel had born the indescribable grief of losing two small children, but losing Samuel was different. She would never again laugh as heartily, never again wish to preside over a sparkling party without the gentle soul who had courted the improbable girl and lived the exquisitely caring life. Eliza survived the great yellow fever epidemic of 1793. Her heart would have begged to differ.

In the midst of wrenching personal loss, official life went on. As soon as Washington arrived at Mount Vernon, he began worrying about the upcoming meeting of Congress. He asked his advisers how to arrange for Congress to meet someplace other than Philadelphia, and, more important, who had the authority to designate a site. Jefferson visited Mount Vernon on his way home and told Washington that the president did not have the power to name another location. Randolph agreed.

The specter of Congress missing its scheduled opening and setting an exceedingly bad precedent seems to have unnerved Washington. He yearned to have anyone credible tell him that he could name a place other than the plague-ridden capital. Washington even asked Madison's opinion, but he was disappointed that Madison agreed with Randolph and Jefferson that only Congress could change its meeting place. Washington planned to return to Pennsylvania, if not Philadelphia, in the third week of October. He told Randolph to find him a house in Germantown and summoned others in the cabinet to meet him there. He felt it imperative to put some part of the government in operation. Jefferson met Washington early in his journey and traveled most of the way with the president. In Germantown, Jefferson was surprised by the mass of people. He managed to hire a bed in the public room of an inn and was grateful to have it.

The fever was abating but still lingered lethally in Philadelphia. About four to five thousand people had died, which was a devastating blow to the city's population. Into November, Washington met with his cabinet in Germantown, nervously counting the days until Congress was supposed to convene in December. Eventually hearing that no new cases of the fever had occurred for several days, Washington slipped away to Philadelphia on horseback. When he returned, his cabinet was aghast at his recklessness. But Washington was convinced the fever was gone. Hard frosts had ended the nightmare. No one knew why.

Over the next few days, congressmen, senators, and other government officials trickled back into town. Much unfinished business remained from the terrifying summer, not the least of which was what to do about Edmond Genet while they waited for a response from Paris.

Washington could count at least one casualty of the yellow fever with morbid satisfaction. The *National Gazette* had been forced out of business by the fever. That "rascal Freneau" would never again trouble Washington.

18

"Earnest Desire to Do Right"

Citizen Genet never understood that George Washington's proclamation of neutrality proved the oldest maxim of diplomacy: Self-
interest is the foundation for all alliances. In 1778, both France and
America benefited from their association. Fifteen years later the circumstances had changed. Only France could gain from an alliance in
1793, and the United States had much to lose. The proclamation had
not included the word "neutrality," but it had nonetheless unequivocally proclaimed the U.S. government's impartial response to the expanding European war. The proclamation was the country's first rehearsal of
an enduring policy grounded in the belief that altercations across the
Atlantic were none of America's business. The Atlantic Ocean seemed
an effective barrier to bolster an isolationist tradition. The ocean as an
avenue of commerce would, however, become the tradition's primary
weakness, an Achilles' heel for the Washington administration and all
that came after it.

The Neutrality Proclamation deeply troubled pro-French followers
of Jefferson and Madison—mainly because of how it was announced
without consulting Congress, though Congress essentially endorsed the
proclamation with the Neutrality Act of 1794. On the other side, pro-
British followers of Hamilton were encouraged. They were briefly unnerved by the enthusiastic reception given to Genet. But Genet's
eagerness to commission privateers and otherwise invoke the Franco-
American alliance instantly displeased Washington and gradually

eroded Genet's standing with Jefferson. Genet never believed that neutrality reflected the true sentiments of the American people, but he was right only in that neutrality did not reflect the true sentiments of *part* of the American people. The result was an embassy that lasted only a few months following his arrival in Philadelphia.

He was, in some measure, the victim of the impossible instructions he received from his Girondist superiors in Paris, but he also labored under serious misunderstandings about the structure and function of American constitutional government. These two circumstances were compounded by his own personal eccentricities that could charitably be ascribed to his irrepressible ardor, less kindly described as impetuosity and a pugnacious temperament. John Jay and Rufus King's letter accusing Genet of showing disrespect to George Washington unhinged the French minister. By mid-September 1793 he was behaving like "a madman," according to James Madison, who marveled over the injury Genet was doing to the French cause.[1]

Neither Madison nor Jefferson had seen the half of it yet. In November, Genet reopened the controversy with an appeal to Edmund Randolph as attorney general. Genet claimed that he was now eager to pursue the public prosecution of his libelers. That these men were the chief justice of the United States and a senator from New York did not daunt Citizen Genet. He wrote to Jefferson, enclosing a copy of his letter to Randolph, to explain his intention to clear his name in the courts. Randolph did not dismiss Genet out of hand but said he would be willing to meet when Genet returned to Philadelphia. Then the real trouble started.

Genet's public letter incensed John Jay and Rufus King, but the behavior of the administration as represented by Jefferson and Randolph infuriated them. Jay and King felt humiliated by having to prove their statement. They asked Hamilton and Knox to provide signed verification to include in a complete account they planned to publish. Hamilton and Knox obliged, and the Jay-King statement appeared with the imprimatur of the secretaries of Treasury and War. The administration's soiled laundry was well on display.

That fall this apparently simple controversy became dreadfully complicated. At the heart of the Jay-King accusation was Genet's threat to ignore President Washington's authority and appeal directly to the

American people. This was supposed to have been said to Alexander Dallas during their midnight meeting in July. Yet Dallas suddenly wasn't certain he had quoted Genet accurately. Dallas now said the word "appeal" could have been his own rather than Genet's, when Dallas described the interview to Mifflin. That meant the account that had started the entire controversy was hopelessly compromised, even useless, and had deeply wronged Genet.

When Congress reconvened on December 2, 1793, Genet was already the main topic of all political conversations, especially because George Washington had become involved. Jefferson had the president review Genet's complaint against Jay and King. On December 18, Jefferson told Randolph that Washington would make no recommendation other than Randolph should do his duty as he saw fit.

In referring the matter to Randolph in such a seemingly casual way, Washington unintentionally but profoundly offended Jay and King, who thought the president was tacitly impugning their actions. They wrote Washington to denounce Jefferson and Randolph, and came close to instructing Washington to publish Jefferson's account from July, confident that it would vindicate them. Everyone now felt wronged. Jefferson and Randolph took umbrage at Jay and King's attack and more or less insisted that Washington forcefully respond with a defense of them and a justification of himself. Hamilton said Washington should supply Jefferson's account but with a cover letter that obliquely deflected the charge that the president had shown the chief justice and the senator any disrespect. Yet it was Knox who stepped in to prevent what could have been a serious breach among principal figures of the government. He proposed that Jay and King withdraw their offensive letter to Washington and seek an interview with the president to salve the bad feeling it had caused.

Jay and King refused to do this, but Washington did invite Jay for an extended conversation. Washington gave no ground in this interview and, in fact, said that his actions were justified. Jefferson and Randolph had meant no offense, Washington said, and Jay and King had, on the other hand, given considerable offense with the tone of their letter. Jay explained his and King's perspective. As the meeting wore on, the two men softened. Washington finally declared his continued friendship for John Jay and his regard for Rufus King. Seizing that as an opening, Jay proposed a solution. If Washington would supply a copy of Jefferson's account, it would not be used unless Genet brought Jay and King into court. In return, they would give Washington the original draft of their offending letter. In his meeting with King, Washington read the letter he had written iterating a defense of his actions. He then burned all the correspondence. King left with Jefferson's report and the understanding that he would not make it public unless Genet's suit was brought. It never was, and Jefferson's July account remained undisturbed in King's papers for the rest of all their lives. Washington would never completely forgive Rufus King for his haughty tone, though.[2]

When Congress learned of the government's request for Genet's recall and saw all of the relevant correspondence, the administration was shown to have handled the matter so reasonably that even the most committed partisans of the French cause were silenced. Genet looked more the fool than ever.[3] Meanwhile, Jefferson's lengthy explanation, correspondence, and supporting documents reached Gouverneur Morris. In a way the letter and the request were superfluous, made irrelevant by the rapid ascension of the Jacobins in Paris. When Morris presented Jefferson's letter to the new government, it was already primed to recall Genet for his failures. The letter only incensed the Jacobins further as they blamed Genet for deliberately alienating America. The Jacobins vilified Genet and published pamphlets to explain his recall as a prelude not only to bringing him home but killing him when he arrived. Morris suspected they would follow through. He had seen the Reign of Terror unfold and the killing of the queen. He told Washington that Genet's replacement would likely try to send him back in irons to the guillotine.[4]

In the summer of 1793 the British government began restricting foreign trade with France with decrees called Orders in Council, which were issued by the king's council under his royal prerogative. The Order in Council issued in November extended the restrictive policy to the French West Indies. Washington and his government learned of the November order in an unpleasant way at the dawn of 1794 through reports that the British had seized hundreds of American merchant vessels in the Caribbean. In addition, the British had brokered a temporary truce between Portugal and the Barbary pirates, which dealt American commerce with Europe an indirect blow while laying bare the U.S. government's weakness to do anything about it.

The Barbary pirates operated primarily out of Algiers, where the government had grown fat extorting "tribute" from Europeans for as long as anyone could remember. The process was a simple protection racket in which the Algerine bey (the venerable Ottoman title for a provincial chieftain) guaranteed safe passage on the Mediterranean in exchange for annual payments. It was cheaper to pay off the pirates than bear the cost of sending naval squadrons to clean out their nests, but the United States was proud, feisty, and broke. The problem for American merchant mariners was their proud government's scruples were made meaningless by their insolvent government's inability to provide either naval protection or annual payments. Smart American captains did not venture inside the Straits of Gibraltar.

And that was the problem created by the British-sponsored truce. It gave several corsairs the chance to get out of the Mediterranean, which Portuguese patrols usually prevented. The cavorting Algerine pirates soon captured eleven American merchant vessels and brought their crews back to Al Djazair as prisoners. They had company, because American relations with the Algerines had been rancorous for years. When Jefferson and John Adams were in Paris during the 1780s, the two had differed on ways to handle the Barbary pirates. Adams saw the utility in simply paying the tribute as a cost-effective way of doing business in the Mediterranean. Jefferson wanted to bring the thugs in North Africa to reason at gunpoint, which French foreign minister Comte de Vergennes agreed was the only thing beside money that the bey and his fellow brigands respected. Jefferson did not change his opinion when he became secretary of state in 1790, but reality dictated cautious responses to the situation. Thirteen American sailors had been captives in Algiers for almost five years. They petitioned the new constitutional government of the United States for help, and Jefferson prepared three options for Congress to consider in dealing with the pirates.

The first option was to deal with them. The United States could pay the tribute as most European countries did. Or the government could warn American merchants about the perilous Mediterranean. Finally, the United States could build a navy to protect American shipping. Jefferson preferred the navy, but the government could not afford it. Congress appropriated $40,000 to ransom the thirteen Americans and made provisions for $100,000 a year to pay in tribute.

Disaster beset even the effort to make the offers. Jefferson's first choice for an emissary was John Paul Jones, the naval hero from the American Revolution, but Jones died in Europe while planning his trip. Jefferson's second choice died as well, finally leaving David Humphreys, who by then was the U.S. minister to Portugal. Humphreys arrived in Algiers at the end of 1793 shortly after the pirates had added the crews from the additional eleven American ships to the original thirteen captives. All manner of other complications frustrated a resolution, and not until the end of 1795 did 119 Americans finally gain freedom through ransom. The treaty that achieved this was ratified by the Senate in 1796, and by then Federalists were prepared to vote money for bulking up the U.S. Navy. Yet, at that point political divisions were so starkly drawn that Republicans—led by Madison in the House and encouraged by Jefferson in retirement—reflexively opposed the very naval building program Jefferson had earlier advocated.[5]

The seeds of that kind of blind disagreement were planted in 1793 during the developing domestic crisis about how to cope with the European war. The new British policy announced in June defined food as contraband under the "provision order." The seizing of American ships in the West Indies goaded Jefferson to complete a report he had been tinkering with for several years. Gathering information from numerous sources, including Treasury figures supplied by Tench Coxe, Jefferson submitted *Privileges and Restrictions on the Commerce of the United States in Foreign Countries* to Congress on December 16, 1793. Jefferson recommended that the United States enact retaliatory laws against nations that restricted American trade and refused to make commercial treaties. It was his swan song as secretary of state—he would not be dissuaded from resigning at the end of the year—and it caused quite a stir among the Federalists. Jefferson drew compelling conclusions and made provocative recommendations.

Given the offensive behavior of the Royal Navy in the West Indies, his timing could not have been better. His report was more than a reprise of James Madison's restrictive measures that Hamilton had been thwarting for four years. This time Jefferson had the advantage of facts, figures, and events behind him.

By the time the report arrived in Congress, rumors about Jefferson's coming departure were in currency. William Loughton Smith predicted that Randolph would succeed him three weeks before Washington offered the post to the attorney general.[6] Others were not so accurate, as gossip had Hamilton, Knox, and Jefferson all resigning, or that Randolph as well as Jefferson was leaving. Hamilton's college roommate Robert Troup mused about how pleasant it was "to see Jefferson, Randolph & Genet by the ear!"[7] John Adams heard that Jefferson would soon resign and did not think Jefferson would be happy in retirement. "His soul is poisoned with Ambition," Adams told Abigail. In any case, Jefferson's leaving was "good riddance of bad ware." Adams wished for Jefferson the greatest curse he could imagine—that he become the next vice president where he could learn the true meaning of the words "irrelevance" and "futility." "If he could do no good," Adams growled, at least "he could do no harm."[8]

Jefferson submitted his final resignation on December 31, 1793. Near the letter's close Jefferson told Washington, "I carry into my retirement a lively sense of your goodness, & shall continue gratefully to remember it." Washington answered the next day with a fond farewell. "The opinion," he said, "which I had formed, of your integrity and talents . . . has been confirmed by the fullest experience."[9] A few days later, Jefferson left for Monticello.

His tenure as secretary of state and his influence on George Washington are difficult to assess outside the partisan battles that produced the First American Party System. But Jefferson functioned outside of those battles, and he accomplished significant things aside from them. He founded the American diplomatic corps and gave it structure and purpose. Along with Hamilton, Jefferson wrote the most influential reports in the history of American government. His work on standardized weights and measures, the fisheries, and on American foreign trade would establish fixed policies or greatly influence them for generations. He allowed his enthusiasm for the French Revolution to cloud his judgment early with Genet, but he came to his senses and worked with Washington to reach the appropriate solution.

Jefferson was pro-French and Hamilton was pro-British, but their

differences in that regard could be seen as a question of personal preference. Even so, their opinions about America's place in the world were
not rigid or impervious to external events. Jefferson believed in free
trade, but as secretary of state he realized that endorsing free trade as an
immutable principle was foolish when other nations erected tariffs and
closed off their ports. Hamilton believed so thoroughly that the nation's
prosperity was linked to its commercial relationship with Great Britain
that he was prepared to truckle to the most blatant British provocations,
but he had his limits when the British acted as if he would accept anything with a smile.

Jefferson and Hamilton differed in more basic and essential ideas
that represented more than opposing views for the future of America.
They personified the choices that have bedeviled Americans from colonial times to ours. When does liberty become license? When does order
become oppression? How does government have enough power to perform its basic functions without incrementally creeping toward intru-
siveness and then lurching toward tyranny? It sounds too simple to say
that Jefferson loved liberty and Hamilton loved order, but that basically
distills their sentiments and illuminates their differences, for everything
about them stemmed from those core beliefs.

When Thomas Jefferson left Philadelphia, he left George Washington. They had been growing apart for months, but Jefferson's presence
was a counterweight to Hamilton's influence with the president, which
appeared more significant than it really was in the first term but became
more significant than it should have been after Jefferson was gone. As
for Jefferson, everything that proceeded in the government after he left
it would convince him that the basic direction of the country was horribly wrong. Because news came to Jefferson from people who feared
and hated Hamilton, his objectivity suffered as much from his departure as did Washington's. They both lost the balance that had existed, if
uneasily, while they worked together for the same ends—a strong, stable, republican government accountable to a free and happy people.
Americans wanted the country Thomas Jefferson envisioned; they got
the government Alexander Hamilton planned.

★ ★ ★

By the time Jefferson left Washington's "family," Tobias Lear had left it as well. Washington hated losing him, but he understood Lear's wish for change. Lear's departure was different from Jefferson's. For seven years he had lived with the Washingtons and handled many of the most personal details of their lives. He *was* family. But the job as Washington's general factotum was grueling. Lear had spent almost a decade tending to correspondence, accounts, children, servants, and scores of miscellaneous duties that came and went in fatiguing frequency. He had swallowed his repugnance to slavery and had learned how to weather Washington's darker moods and natural reticence, perhaps better than anyone because he saw those moods every day.

Marrying his childhood sweetheart was the beginning of Lear's plan to seek out a wider world. He had always thought of his job as Washington's principal secretary as a temporary arrangement, something to do while he figured out what he really wanted to do. For a while he thought about farming, but business beckoned after his marriage. He and Polly had been planning to move away and move on when she died.

Losing Polly was too typical a turn of events for Toby Lear, for his life was to be stalked by occasional heartbreak and frequent disappointment. Untethered before he showed up at Mount Vernon as a callow youth in need of a reliable watch and a thicker skin, he found it hard to fit in. He wound his watch and grew used to criticism, but most of all he felt an anchor that was reassuring and comforting as Washington relied on him for everything, sent him to New York City as the trusted advance man for his presidency, and visited his mother during the first presidential tour. But the anchor gradually tugged with more weight than comfort, and Lear did not feel so much grounded as aground. He thought to leave Washington's family, not realizing that he had been fated to join it and would never be quite steady away from it. Losing Polly untethered him again. He left his little boy with his mother in New Hampshire, and put himself as far away from the scenes of death and mourning as possible. Business could take him away to Europe. He booked passage out of New York.

Almost at the last minute, as the ship weighed anchor and sailors scurried aloft to unfurl snapping sails, Lear wrote a farewell to the man he saw as a father. He told George Washington that he would "never cease to remember with gratitude & affection your goodness to me & my dear boy." Lear promised "to act in a manner worthy of such recollection."[10] That would prove easier said than done. Lear bounced around Europe for only a few months before returning to the United States in 1794. He wasn't any good at business and was dogged by debt as he caromed from one venture to the next, even mixing himself up in the land speculations of the federal district.

He visited the Washingtons, which is to say he went home. There he found himself in the company of Fanny Washington, George Augustine Washington's young widow and Martha's niece, a girl who as the major's bride had always been a close friend and treated Toby as family. The widower and widow were too young to grieve forever, and they filled the yawning gaps in their lives with each other, making a marriage that was happy for them and reaffirming for Martha and George. Toby was doting, a man made to care, and he took the major's children as his own, creating a safe haven for them along with his own little boy.

But there were no safe havens in Lear's life. When Fanny developed a chronic cough, it became apparent that, like her late husband, she was a consumptive. Everyone held out hope. Everyone who confronted tuberculosis always clung to hope. But Toby watched her slowly die. Amid a series of disappointments, this was another enormous heartbreak. Once again, he made his way back to the Washingtons, the ties too strong to break. They welcomed him with open arms.

During the Genet controversy, Washington took the unusual step of consulting John Adams, which made the vice president as proud as he was touched by Washington's obviously "earnest desire to do right."[11] For two days in two separate meetings they adopted a semblance of closeness that many supporters of the Constitution had thought would be the natural order of things in the new government. Adams was among the first to discover, though, that the vice presidency was a superfluous position only useful when the U.S. Senate couldn't reach a plurality or the president couldn't keep himself alive. Washington and Adams discussed the Genet business privately, and apparently Washington's talks with Adams were not just for show. He emerged from the sessions willing to wait a little longer before suspending Genet as an accredited representative to the U.S. government. The meetings marked a shift, if only slightly, in the two men's relationship as well as in Washington's approach to governing in his second term. Washington began conferring more often with Adams, particularly about foreign affairs, and thus brought Adams into the inner circle of presidential advisers. When William Short was sent to Spain and Washington nominated John Quincy Adams to replace him at The Hague, John Quincy's father had to reassess his sour opinion about Washington. Possibly he really was a Great Man.

Edmund Randolph wasn't aware of any shift, and he tried to maintain balance in the cabinet, though he would find doing so increasingly difficult over the next twenty months. Friends worried that he had "placed himself on a bed of thorns," and the position would "make him the mark at which all who are dissatisfied with public measures will aim their shafts."[12] For different reasons, neither Jefferson nor Hamilton was happy with Washington's choice of Edmund Randolph to head the State Department, and the former attorney general wasn't too thrilled himself. He had hoped to retire soon to resume his legal practice and repair his finances from his four years of government service. As always for Edmund Randolph, duty to Washington trumped everything.

Washington asked him if he would take the job on December 24, 1793, a week before Jefferson's official retirement. The president had come to rely on Randolph as the only politically neutral adviser, and Randolph's acceptance two days later pleased him. As soon as Jefferson officially resigned, Washington sent Randolph's nomination to the Senate, and Randolph took the oath of office from Justice James Wilson on January 2.

Randolph immediately sent a letter to his two colleagues in the cabinet. It was an earnest plea for peace and understanding. If they could work harmoniously, Randolph said with the eagerness of a schoolboy, they could better serve the president. "There are too many opportunities for misconception and misrepresentation," he said, and declared himself bound by a simple rule: If he heard something disagreeable about another department, he would hold his tongue until he talked to the head of it. Randolph said he hoped they would do the same.[13] This sincere gesture by the new secretary of state as his first official act was the admirable effort of a conscientious man, an earnest man, and the very worst kind of man to work amid vulpine politicians. In retrospect, it was worse than poignant. It was pathetic.

His colleagues in the cabinet had never regarded Randolph's attempts to strike a fair balance between the irreconcilable Jefferson and Hamilton as anything other than a continuation of Randolph's legendary indecisiveness. It was just another version of his presenting the plan at the Constitutional Convention, then opposing it, and then still later supporting it. Hamilton and Knox did not interpret Randolph's gesture as sincere but as weak. Pangloss had improbably landed in Philadelphia.

Washington valued Randolph's opinion, though, and that exasperated his colleagues even more. Three weeks after Randolph left the attorney general's post, Washington followed Randolph's recommendation to appoint Pennsylvania Supreme Court judge William Bradford as his replacement.[14] Only thirty-eight years old when named to replace Randolph, Bradford was a confirmed Federalist living in Philadelphia and able to take office immediately. He had served as an officer in the Continental Army under Washington at Trenton and Valley Forge, but Bradford had been young then, and they were never close. His delicate health had forced him from the army, but there was nothing frail about his mind or legal acumen. He had studied law before the war and became Pennsylvania's attorney general when only twenty-five. For eleven years he served as state attorney general and then was named to Pennsylvania's Supreme Court. Bradford worked tirelessly from the bench to reduce the number of offenses in Pennsylvania that carried the death penalty. He had been a close friend of James Madison's from college days, but they had grown apart politically. In fact, Randolph's recommendation was another instance of the Virginian striking a fair balance. Yet Washington from now on would never appoint anyone but a strong Federalist to his official family. The exception was Edmund Randolph.

On January 3, 1794, James Madison introduced resolutions in the House of Representatives to implement Jefferson's recommendations from his commerce report, particularly those that called for commercial discrimination against Great Britain. Federalists attributed Virginians' hatred of the British to the fact that "they owe them money,"[15] but it was impossible to dismiss arguments that Great Britain's new policy was seriously damaging American shipping. Hamilton worried that this time Madison would ride a wave of anti-British resentment to implement the restrictive policy he had always wanted. Hamilton's supporters in the House delayed debate on Madison's resolutions until they could be ready to parry them.

The Republicans had won a majority in the House in the previous election, but they were not well organized. They managed to defeat Hamilton's candidate William Loughton Smith for Speaker to place Pennsylvanian Frederick A. C. Muhlenberg back in the chair (he had been the first Speaker under the Constitution), but after that success, Republicans splintered on using commercial retaliation to bring the British into line. The Federalists hoped to exploit Republican disarray when Smith rose to refute Madison's arguments as impetuous and impractical. With some four-fifths of American imports coming from Great Britain and about one-half of American exports going there, Hamilton calculated that restrictions would devastate U.S. import duties and predicted that retaliation by Great Britain would demolish American exports.[16]

Smith lengthily portrayed the dangers of commercial restriction and argued they could even cause a war with Great Britain. Madison sent Smith's remarks to Jefferson, who saw Hamilton's hand in every word. He recognized exact phrases Hamilton had used in their previous arguments.[17] Jefferson's memory was accurate. Years later, Smith's speech was found in Hamilton's papers in the secretary of the Treasury's handwriting.

The issue was serious because it opened wounds still raw from the Revolution and added the salt of seized ships and confiscated cargoes. Smith received anonymous death threats for his stand against Madison's resolutions,[18] but he continued to advance Hamilton's arguments as the debate continued for the next three months. To Hamilton's chagrin, relations with Great Britain deteriorated. To Madison's delight, those with France seemed to improve.

The arrival of France's new minister helped to repair the damage done by Genet. In the first place, Jean Antoine Joseph Fauchet was all business and punctilio. He appeared in Philadelphia on February 21, 1794, immediately contacted Randolph, and presented unsealed copies of his instructions. Before Randolph formally presented Fauchet to Washington the following day, he provided the president with an agenda listing every step in the complicated diplomatic dance of ministers meeting heads of state. It was the sort of detail Randolph excelled at. He also was mindful that February 22 was Washington's birthday, and the president's calendar would be filled with official visits, the serving of cake and punch throughout the day, and a "splendid ball" presided over by the Washingtons that evening.[19]

Fauchet's first meeting with Washington went well. The two men were alike in resorting to formality in new and uncomfortable situations, and Fauchet was just as parochial as the president, for as Washington did not speak French, Fauchet could not speak English. Randolph served as the interpreter and kept things moving briskly along. John Adams reckoned Fauchet to be "about 33" and "not quite So unreserved as his Predecessor." That night "at the Birthnight Ball, he was placed by the Managers on the right hand of the President, which gave great Offence to the Spanish Commissioners: and it is Said Mr Hammond has left the Theatre, offended or disgusted at some partial popular distinctions there."[20]

Adams also noted that Fauchet seemed to him "to be in great distress."[21] Possibly it was from the fact that by the time Adams was writing to Abigail, Fauchet had realized that his hosts did not intend to grant one of his government's principal requests. The French minister had arrived in Philadelphia with four grim-faced commissioners, and Randolph knew what they were about. Gouverneur Morris suspected that Fauchet's instructions called for the arrest of Genet and his return to France. It was no secret that Genet would likely face execution. Morris had not found this likelihood particularly disturbing. To the contrary, he encouraged the idea. "Such a public act," Morris reminded Washington, "will place in a contemptible light the faction connected with Mr. Genet."[22] Yet when Fauchet requested Genet's arrest, Randolph stalled. Washington did not like Genet, but he would not send him home to die. Fauchet eventually dropped the matter as potentially counterproductive to his primary goal, which was to restore good relations with the United States. His embassy at an end and without a country to return to, Citizen Genet was essentially granted asylum.

Genet's trajectory was spectacular at the start and sorry at the end. Hamilton likened him to a comet.[23] Genet should have done better by all appearances. He was equipped with a fine education, came from a good family, and was extremely civil in his private dealings with friends and strangers alike. In the end, however, he was too earnest to survive the game he should have known how to play. Brashly confident at the outset and a groveling supplicant at the end, he was a victim of circumstance but also a victim of his own impetuosity, ungovernable temperament, and skewed intuitions. Because Washington was kind and Randolph resolute, Genet was able to stay in the United States and marry Cornelia Clinton. After she died, he married the daughter of Samuel Osgood, fathering children and living the rest of his life in a kind of genteel poverty. Genet's career promised greatness. It ended in ruin.

Washington found the reticent Fauchet a breath of fresh air, even if he seemed a cold fish. Fauchet did not need to be ebullient and charismatic. Indeed, he did not need to do anything. The growing animosity between the United States and Great Britain allowed him to sit quietly and watch. The British were doing plenty to drive the United States into a French embrace.[24]

19

"A War Soon with Britain"

Boorish Britain vexed Washington's neutrality policy, but the British had been vexatious ever since the end of the Revolution. Because London wanted to cultivate the profitable fur trade in the Great Lakes region and hoped to create an Indian buffer state to seal off land-hungry Americans, they refused to relinquish the chain of frontier posts on American soil. This alone was an act of brash noncompliance with the terms of the peace treaty of 1783, but British agents also openly sold weapons and whiskey to the Indians. As Indians mounted raids on American settlers, the administration sent two military expeditions into the wilderness with disastrous results.

At sea the British worked to isolate the French West Indies, and toughened Royal Navy captains mounted a savage program that swept up American shipping along with French traders. The British seized some three hundred American merchant ships in the Caribbean, abducted American seamen for service on British warships, and held others captive on filthy prison ships or in dank jails. Adding to American outrage, rumors told of Governor-General of British North America Lord Dorchester encouraging northwestern Indians to make war on the United States.[1]

Washington had chosen one of his bravest combat commanders from the Revolution to command yet another expedition into the Ohio Country, the third in as many years. Anthony Wayne was not a universally popular choice, for he was heavily in debt, had trouble holding a job, and was known to drink. Yet Washington overlooked it all because he had to. Wayne was a political as well as a military choice. Aside from being an effective commander, Wayne was from Pennsylvania, a state that had received relatively few high-ranking federal appointments. Light-Horse Harry Lee complained about the appointment, but Washington explained that "an appointment which may be unpopular in one place, or with one set of men, may not be so in another place or with another set of Men."[2]

Wayne had the rank of major general and the command of what was called the Legion of the United States, a body of temporary regulars, trained extensively by Wayne and his subordinates before their march toward the Miami Indian villages. Although he would have "many and great difficulties in forming an Army & introducing discipline & subordination," he would also face a covert British policy to have the expedition stopped or hobbled.[3] An Indian buffer state could not happen if there were no Indians.

Anthony Wayne's men were not only trained in traditional infantry drill but also in scouting and frontier warfare. He dressed some as Indians and staged mock battles to hone skills of stealth and surprise. When Wayne moved out, he had a trained militia and savvy veterans. They made for the Maumee River with a purpose, a far different army than the two that had preceded it.[4]

It was in this highly charged atmosphere of western expeditions and Canadian misconduct that Congress considered how to respond to the British. Washington never publicly commented on discussions in Congress and did so only rarely in private, but his scrupulous separation of powers in this instance dismayed the Federalists. The British had given Republicans an irresistible momentum that Federalists despaired of stopping. Washington could check it with a single word. While Madison and his supporters pushed for measures to punish the British commercially, Hamilton urged Federalists to kill their opponents with excessive kindness—to give their opponents as much rope as needed to undo them. Federalist anger over British depredations soon eclipsed that of Republicans. They shouted that if the British refused to respect American neutral trade and encouraged the Indians to make war on the American frontier, the nation had no choice but to prepare for war. Rather than half measures to punish the British economically, the United States should build a navy and increase its army to meet foreign aggression. Knox did his part to raise the alarm. He told governors to ready their states for war.[5]

It was all for show, a Federalist pageant of smoke and mirrors to give the Republicans pause, but it was only half-effective. Congress passed and Washington signed a temporary embargo on foreign trade toward the end of March, increasing the feeling that the nation "shall have a war soon with Great Britain."[6] Those who believed that the "fiery spirits" among them were pushing the unprepared nation "to an open rupture" found tactical shenanigans and debating tricks less than amusing.[7] And, in reality, neither Republicans nor Federalists wanted war.

The Republicans wanted to retaliate against violations of American neutral rights with discriminatory duties, hoping that the British would remove their restrictions. The Federalists accused the Republicans of fomenting war with commercial retaliation and introduced measures to build frigates and increase the army rather than impose sanctions. Federalists claimed they hoped it would demonstrate to the British that seizing American merchant ships and stirring up northwestern Indians had serious consequences. They suspected Republican efforts to punish the British were just barely veiled attempts to help the French, and the Republicans suspected the Federalists wanted to expand the military to use it against domestic critics. In short, both claimed to have the same goal of forcing the British to behave, but each suspected the other of nefarious aims.

In point of fact, the prospect of war with Britain terrified the Federalists. Party leaders in Congress met regularly with Hamilton and fashioned a plan to avert the catastrophe. On March 10, 1794, Senator Oliver Ellsworth of Connecticut suggested to Washington that a special envoy to Great Britain could smooth things over while negotiating a resolution of differences. The idea of a special envoy seems to have occurred to a wide variety of people roughly at the same time. Edmund Randolph apparently came up with the idea as well and later claimed that he, not Ellsworth, had first suggested it to Washington.

Whoever was first to mention it, Washington was not keen on the idea. Thomas Pinckney was on the ground in London as the accredited U.S. minister to Great Britain, and Washington was reluctant to supplant him. Ellsworth argued that the very appearance of a special envoy would impress upon the British the American desire for peace. When Ellsworth suggested Alexander Hamilton as an excellent choice for the mission, Washington dismissed the possibility out of hand. He reminded Ellsworth that Hamilton was sufficiently unpopular to make his work at Treasury difficult; the prospect of naming him as the envoy to England brought to mind detonated bombs.

Hamilton had to know his name would come up. He had been working closely with the Senate peace caucus, and as Washington expected, rumors that Hamilton might be sent to London spread alarm throughout the opposition. Republicans feared Hamilton working with the British more than they did an enlarged navy and army, so the House leadership staged a distraction. William Branch Giles proposed and the House passed resolutions requesting Treasury documents relating to Dutch loans secured back in 1790. Madison and his lieutenants were fishing. They wanted to see if Hamilton had received presidential authorization for relatively ancient transactions. As it turned out, Hamilton had apparently violated a legal technicality in moving money from place to place, especially in making unauthorized deposits in the Bank of the United States. It was nothing worthy of prosecution, but it was a violation all the same, and Giles took up the cold scent of Hamilton using his position to benefit the bank and its stockholders. That many of those stockholders were members of Congress suggested dark doings indeed.

Hamilton provided a smattering of documents, but he explained that he had frequently resorted to the legitimate practice of obtaining the president's verbal approval for transactions. The House countered by asking Washington to confirm that he had given this verbal approval where written permissions did not exist. Hamilton had the fresh recollection of Washington's public support but private wariness during the recent congressional investigation. He therefore gently reminded Washington that "he always received his [Washington's] sanction for what was adopted."[8] The president frowned over this development. He wanted to help Hamilton, but he could not with certainty claim that he gave such approval each time. Age and time had fogged his memory. In any event, there was the matter of the law. Presidential permission would not matter if Hamilton had broken the law. In fact, it would implicate the president as well.

Bradford might have been consulted, but Washington again turned to Edmund Randolph, whom he still considered to be his primary legal adviser. Randolph received Washington's urgent note while suffering from a blinding headache that made reading and concentrating difficult, but he scrutinized the documents and weighed Washington's questions. That evening Randolph sent Washington a carefully worded statement for him to use. Yes, it said, he had given his verbal approval on many occasions, but he could not remember each time. Randolph's response had Washington attest "that my sanction was always expressly or tacitly qualified with the condition that whatever was to be done was to be agreeable to the law." Washington answered Hamilton on April 8, 1794, with almost this exact phrasing, which was so cautious as to be hardly a ringing endorsement of Hamilton's probity. Hamilton bitterly viewed the legalese as a rebuke, however mild. Madison chuckled that "the letter from the P is inexpressibly mortifying to his [Hamilton's] friends."[9]

At one point, Washington had actually considered sending Hamilton to Great Britain, but this latest controversy, caused by rumors that he might, all but struck the secretary from the list. It also put Washington in a dark mood and set the table for his angry protection of presidential prerogatives. It could have been Randolph's persuasiveness, but something convinced Washington that a special envoy to England was a good idea. He mulled the question of who was best for the job, speaking privately with Robert Morris about possible choices and revealing that he was considering John Adams, Thomas Jefferson, John Jay, and Alexander Hamilton. Morris preferred Hamilton, and possibly Washington would have, too, but too many problems disqualified the Treasury secretary. And that was when the Republicans, finding Hamilton's chances as a candidate quite dead, decided to kill them again.

Letters from Republican senator James Monroe and congressman John Nicholas all but demanded that Washington not send Hamilton. Monroe said the selection would be "injurious to the public interests" and to the president himself. Washington thought the letters impertinent and offensive. He didn't plan to send Hamilton, but he certainly didn't like upstart senators and congressmen telling him who not to appoint to foreign missions. He curtly wrote Monroe the next day. If the senator had information that would disqualify Hamilton, he should be man enough to relate it, and in writing. Otherwise, Washington said, "I alone am responsible for a proper nomination." The president showed the exchange to Randolph, which was uncomfortable. Monroe was close to Randolph, and Nicholas was his brother-in-law. Randolph assured Washington that the two were acting on their own with no guidance from him. Washington must have reassured Randolph that it had never crossed his mind, for Randolph thanked Washington for "friendly remarks" that only added "to the many obligations" he owed him.[10]

With Hamilton out of the question, Robert Morris told Washington that John Jay was best because Adams and Jefferson would alienate different but important factions. Hamilton apparently wanted the appointment, but he bowed to reality and endorsed Jay as well. Washington promptly invited Jay to a private dinner, and by April 15, 1794, he had made his decision. He would appoint Jay, even though the chief justice showed little enthusiasm for the mission. Jay wrote to his wife, Sarah, that only Washington's appeal to duty had persuaded him to travel to Europe again.[11]

Republicans wished that Jay had not been so duty bound. Next to Alexander Hamilton, they considered John Jay to be the supreme representation of all that was Federalism. His involvement in the recent controversy over Genet shattered for Republicans the notion that the chief justice was aloof from politics. They were convinced that his coldly formal demeanor was a façade to hide another rank partisan. They had no reason to doubt that he would sacrifice American interests to punish the French and genuflect before the British. They were not surprised that Jay remained in his position after accepting the London mission, collecting his $4,000 annual salary as chief justice in addition to remuneration and expenses for his diplomatic chore. Republicans grumbled that it was just the sort of thing a stockjobbing Federalist would do.

★ ★ ★

Washington had known Jay since the Revolution and had developed a strong respect and affection for the New Yorker during that conflict. On the eve of the Revolution, Jay had married Sarah Livingston, a pretty seventeen-year-old daughter of the powerful New York clan. The new responsibilities of marriage made Jay, a cautious man by temperament, a reluctant revolutionary. The prospect of starting out married life by discarding everything that was familiar and safe seemed most uncertain. The likelihood of becoming an outlaw in the process was simply foolhardy.

Jay was never foolhardy. As a boy he learned to look on life as a series of calculated risks. His family's considerable wealth could not save it from the smallpox that laid low a younger brother and an older sister. The illness had nearly killed them but their recovery was profoundly marred. They were blind. Money could not make another brother right in his head. For John Jay, growing up wasn't even a case of paying your money and taking your chances in life's lottery; it was a case of life being frequently a rigged game that rewarded winners with cruel payoffs and losers with hard lessons. It made him somber. George Washington would have understood how that happened.

Cruel payoffs and hard lessons, however, could not make him dour or discouraged. By the time Washington met him, Jay had already made a name for himself in New York's legal circles. With his college chum Robert R. Livingston (from a collateral branch of wife Sarah's family), Jay became prominent in state politics, which is why he landed in the First Continental Congress. He was tall with an angular face and an intense stare that belied his prudent and usually soft-spoken manner. Washington was almost thirteen years older than Jay, but he always appreciated young people with talent and the good sense not to flaunt it. It was also refreshing to meet a man able to balance dignity and deference in his relations with almost everyone, Washington included. The quality made it possible for John Jay to tread a path between the radicals pushing for independence and moderates wanting reconciliation. Seeking the middle way could have been Jay's motto: Always weigh both sides of a question. The habit made him a good lawyer and a respected politician. People, himself included, would in time suspect that the habit made him an uncertain diplomat.

Washington was not one of them. He never questioned Jay's character or abilities, and the renewing of their acquaintance when the president-elect arrived in New York City was one of the pleasant and reassuring events of his inauguration. Washington valued Jay as a counselor precisely because of his caution, yet he also knew that Jay was rather like himself. Though slow to decide, once committed, he was unwavering. That had happened in the Revolution. At first, Jay recoiled from what he saw as a mad rush for independence, but British outrages—their wanton destruction of Norfolk, Virginia, was an example—changed his mind. When Jay embraced independence, he became one of its most resolute proponents. When Jay became president of the Continental Congress in the hard years of 1778 and 1779, he and Washington became close allies. Washington was, by then, disgusted with endless congressional bickering but saw in John Jay a quiet and stalwart champion.

Jay spent most of the 1780s in Europe, beginning with a diplomatic mission to Spain, part of Congress's efforts to enlist additional help against Britain. Sarah was unique in accompanying him on his foreign postings and made sacrifices in doing so. Transatlantic journeys during the Revolutionary War were risky for American patriots. John and Sarah thought it safer to leave their little boy Peter Augustus in the care of his grandparents, with the result that five years of his childhood were spent safely but outside their orbit. Later in life Jay recommended that his son read Plutarch because it would afford him "the experience of others without paying the price which it often cost them."[12] Separation was the price for this prudence, and everyone paid it.

Splitting up the family was prudent, but all the caution in the world could not shield them from loss. Sarah became pregnant while they were in Madrid, but their little girl born in July 1780 lived only briefly. The blow was doubly devastating because it fell so far from home. Sarah would have two more girls while in Europe, both of whom were healthy, but possibly the vulnerability resulting from the loss of his infant amplified Jay's penchant for showing charity to people who didn't deserve it. One of these was Lewis Littlepage, a young Virginian from a good family but with adventurous ways and expensive tastes. He was a guest of the Jays in Madrid, but soon wore out his welcome with his sponging. Jay loaned him money, though, a good deed that encouraged in Littlepage a debtor's resentment.

Jay did good work in Europe, and the Confederation rewarded his service by entrusting him with its foreign office when he returned to the United States in 1785. Unfortunately, Jay had the impossible job of advancing the interests of a bankrupt country that had disbanded its army and could not afford a navy. He did not need the post, or any other for that matter. He was one of the richest men in New York City, which meant the country as a whole.[13]

In the course of his tenure, it became apparent that Jay was unsuited to shape foreign policy. He seriously misjudged the mood of the West and the South by making the ill-fated deal with Spain's Don Diego de Gardoqui y Arriquibar that relinquished Mississippi navigation for a trade agreement. The arrangement was rejected by Congress but not before it made Jay look like a scheming partner of northeastern merchant interests from a southern and western perspective, or an unreliable advocate from a national one. Gardoqui did not help by wrongly assessing Jay's affability as indecision, privately boasting that he had taken advantage of Jay, and describing him as henpecked by Sarah.

Nabby Adams thought Jay "a most pleasing man, plain in his manners, but kind, affectionate, and attentive." She saw that "benevolence is engraved in every feature."[14] Nabby saw Jay in his ideal setting—that of a quiet, pious man surrounded by a loving family. A spirit of public service still animated him, despite his missteps with foreign affairs, and he regularly expressed his political opinions but always in his deliberate, dignified manner. He did not attend the Constitutional Convention in Philadelphia, but he was an important supporter of ratification in New York and a collaborator with Madison and Hamilton on *The Federalist*.[15] From his experience, he knew that a strong central government was the country's only chance to survive in a hostile world.

John Jay was obviously qualified for the envoy position, but prominent Republicans such as Aaron Burr, James Monroe, and John Taylor led the fight against his confirmation. When Jay won easily and began preparing for his voyage, the opposition did not stop. Southerners denounced his antislavery views, and westerners of long memory recalled his lack of concern for them during the Jay-Gardoqui negotiations of 1786. Citizens in Lexington, Kentucky, burned Jay in effigy before he left the country, anticipating behavior that would be widespread upon his return.[16] It would have been a miracle for him to bring home anything acceptable to large parts of America, something Washington surely realized but had ceased to care about. He had given up Hamilton, but he would not be lectured about appointments. His selection of John Jay marked another shift in the president's attitude toward opponents and his assessment of their motives.

With Jay confirmed, Washington and the cabinet worked on his instructions. Hamilton produced a thorough version of what he thought Jay should seek. Secretary of State Randolph was responsible for Jay's final instructions, but Washington approved most of Hamilton's suggestions, requiring Randolph to incorporate them. The arrangement gave rise to mistaken assertions that Randolph was shoved aside and Hamilton exclusively wrote Jay's instructions, but this was not the case. Washington followed his usual practice of consulting with everyone, and everyone freely discussed various proposals. The result was a consensus that Washington approved.

In fact, Jay's final instructions stated goals that Republicans would have found perfectly acceptable. The problem derived from Jay having considerable latitude within supposedly definite guidelines. He was to secure the evacuation of the northwestern forts, preferably within a year; he was not to agree to any commercial arrangements that violated the treaty with France; he was to secure compensation for recent ship seizures; he was to secure reimbursement for slaves the British had taken from the country at the end of the Revolutionary War; he was to settle the issue of American debts to British creditors; and finally he was to negotiate a commercial treaty. Jay knew he would not be negotiating from strength, which meant he knew that the British were not likely to give him as much as he wanted on any of these points. He did not know, however, that the British would know that they didn't have to.

Jay departed for Great Britain with his son Peter and the artist John Trumbull as his secretaries and was pleasantly surprised that Great

Britain had already lifted some of the worst restrictions on American trade with France by the time he arrived in London. The British government's courtesy and attention encouraged him, and social events hosted by the British aristocracy and Foreign Secretary Lord Grenville flattered him. The king and queen received him. In fact, the only person unhappy about Jay's gadding about was the current U.S. minister to Great Britain, Thomas Pinckney. He understandably felt insulted by Jay's appointment, and he was not immune to Republican prejudices about the character of the special envoy. Diplomatic lore always harkened back to Don Diego de Gardoqui's acid description of Jay as willing to curry favor with concessions while trying to please the imperious Sarah Livingston's whims. Pinckney noticed and Republicans back home heard that during the audience with the queen, Jay had bowed and kissed her hand. Republicans slapped their hands to their foreheads.

So did the administration after a while, except for Hamilton. Months passed with nothing from Jay about tangible progress as stories about his social life continued to provide fodder for the opposition press. Jay regularly reported to Randolph, but his letters became a tedious litany about tedious negotiations that started nowhere and stalled over minutiae. Meanwhile, Jay saved the real details for his private letters to Hamilton. When Washington and his advisers learned that Sweden and Denmark wanted the United States to join its League of Armed Neutrality—a coalition to enforce the rights of neutral shippers in European waters—Hamilton and Knox were opposed, but Randolph thought it a good way to pressure Great Britain. Marking another stride in his shift toward the Federalists, Washington agreed with Hamilton and Knox, which was just as well. Hamilton had already told George Hammond that the United States would not join the league. Hammond immediately sent the information to London. Jay could not have threatened this or any other potential action by the United States even if he had wanted to without Lord Grenville knowing exactly what was bluff and what was real. Jay was not negotiating a treaty. He was formalizing an arrangement that would please Britain, infuriate France, and move the Republican opposition to defiance.

★ ★ ★

Despite their differences, Madison and Washington continued an informal relationship with friendly correspondence about agricultural matters. Washington and Jefferson were lately limited to that subject as well. Not allowing politics to intrude in their letters meant that Washington could still close with such phrases as "Affectionately Yours," words he reserved for friends. At least once after the disagreeable times had set in, Washington had Madison to a "family" dinner, and Madison once mentioned in a letter to Jefferson that he had a private conversation with the president.[17] Such events recalled better days, if dimly. Madison at forty-two had decided to marry, and stories tell of how the Washingtons abetted his courtship. Possibly the stories are true.

The sprightly young widow Dolley Payne Todd had lost her husband in the yellow fever epidemic only months before, but Madison felt time was running out on matrimonial chances, and he wasted no time enlisting Aaron Burr to serve as a go-between and set up a meeting. It's likely he and the bubbly extrovert Dolley already knew each other, but it was also obvious that Madison's intentions of late were more affectionate than friendly. Sure enough, shortly after their interview, Madison told Dolley he loved her, which was hardly a surprise. Who, asked their mutual friends, would not find fetching the soft-eyed girl with the infectious laugh? People wondered, however, why Dolley would have him. Madison seems to have conducted his courtship by proxy. Dolley so consumed his thoughts, she was told, that "he has Lost his Tongue, at Night he Dreames of you & Starts in his Sleep a Calling on you to relieve his Flame for he Burns to such an excess that he will be shortly consumed & he hopes that your Heart will be calous to every other swain but himself."[18] If Madison were not struck dumb and in flames, he was worried about rivals.

According to family lore, Martha Washington told the young widow to marry "the great little Madison," and so she did, but they were an odd pair. His ardor was real, but things she said, and didn't say, suggest that she wanted a father for her orphaned little boy more than a husband for herself. Nevertheless, in September 1794, Dolley married Jemmy at Harewood, the western Virginia home of Washington's nephew George Steptoe Washington, the place where George Steptoe had eloped with Dolley's younger sister the year before. On the night of her wedding, Dolley seemed to wake from a dream verging on nightmare. She scrawled in a forlorn letter to a friend, "Dolley Madison! Alas!"[19] He would grow on her.

Perhaps the Washingtons were never involved in Madison's love life, but the president continued to rely on Madison for his peerless knowledge of the Constitution. The controversy that arose over Gouverneur Morris was a case in point. As they were trying to stop Jay's confirmation, Senate Republicans had spent weeks clamoring to see Morris's letters to the administration. They were confident that the correspondence would disclose such transparent support for the French monarchy that it would force Washington to recall him. Washington's first instinct was to refuse, but Randolph persuaded him to reconsider. He had Randolph meet with Madison and Justice James Wilson, one man the expert on the Constitution and the other the architect of the presidency in the Constitutional Convention. Madison and Wilson agreed that the president could withhold information he deemed sensitive, but otherwise the letters should be turned over to Congress. Washington released all but one letter. Republicans read them with disappointment. They contained "little of what is exceptionable."[20]

Though Gouverneur Morris had not written about everything he said or did to alienate the French government, he had repeatedly offended that government, and the Jacobins formally requested his recall. Washington had to find a replacement. Initially, he thought a simple solution would be to have Jay remain in Great Britain as the permanent minister and move Pinckney to France. Washington broached the idea with Jay before his departure and was disappointed that Jay refused to stay beyond his special mission.

The cabinet was full of suggestions. Some had a political cast. Hamilton suggested Randolph, presumably as a way to remove him from the country as well as the cabinet. Randolph had not wanted to stay in Philadelphia as secretary of state, and he was certainly not going to uproot his family to move to Paris. Washington had Randolph approach James Madison, but Madison immediately declined, citing his delicate health. More likely his pursuit of Dolley was more a factor; he did not want to leave a clear field for rivals. Madison urged the selection of Aaron Burr, but Washington detested Aaron Burr. Nobody knows exactly why, but something about Burr raised Washington's hackles. Washington would not be alone in this as the years went by.

Washington's offer to Madison suggests that he still held him in high regard, or maybe the president was simply trying to balance the Federalist Jay with a bona fide Republican. His offer to Madison lost some of its luster when the president finally settled on Senator James Monroe, the lecturing legislator who had audaciously defined who was appropriate for Jay's job. That made Monroe one of Washington's least favorite people, but he would at least please the Republicans. Monroe hesitated, though, and only after Madison and colleagues implored him to accept did he agree. In all, the entire affair was distasteful for Washington. He sent a sorrowful letter to Gouverneur Morris assuring him that "my confidence in, and friendship & regard for you remains undiminished."[21] It seemed a lifetime ago that General Washington had greeted the carriages carrying Continental congressmen as they rattled into the encampment at Valley Forge. Gouverneur Morris, instead of flashing his customary smile and saying something witty, had looked at the wraiths in rags through falling snow and almost wept. Washington liked him enormously.

Monroe's time in France would be tumultuous. His exclusive motive for accepting the appointment was his desire to improve relations with France, for he believed that Morris had been an American Genet, a man thoroughly unsuited to his task and incompatible with his hosts. Morris's aristocratic air and simpering over the royal family had done as much as Genet's silly enthusiasms and insulting tactics to fray the bonds connecting their nations. Monroe sailed believing this as much as he believed anything, but he was young and not without silly enthusiasms of his own. Upon his arrival in Paris, he heard the French government was fearfully behind in fulfilling diplomatic protocols, and he joined other foreign emissaries in a long wait to have his credentials accepted while the government began killing its own officials and everyone else it could lay hands on. Maximilien Robespierre, who had sent countless people to their deaths on mere revolutionary whims, had himself been sent to the guillotine just before Monroe arrived.

Morris was typically gracious regarding his change of status, and he presented Monroe to what passed for the French Foreign Office. Morris was jaded by months of incredible events whose horrific nature defied description. Nobody who had not seen the long queues of trundles filled with the forlorn waiting for their appointment with the National Razor could have believed it. Nobody who had not smelled it could have imagined the way lengthy Parisian streets had become like charnel houses, the stench of baking blood so horrendous that residents would finally demand that the guillotines be moved elsewhere. William Short had seen the portents of this, and Jefferson had told him to shut up about it. Gouverneur Morris wrote freely to his government and spoke his mind a bit more than was wise at dinner parties, and he was having to give way to an earnest pup for the trouble. Morris likely mused over the reach of revolutionary whims.

Even after Morris had arranged a semblance of diplomatic ritual to have Monroe present his credentials, it soon became apparent that the ceremony was meaningless. As weeks promised to pass without his recognition becoming formal, Monroe grew impatient and then impetuous. On the advice of a low-level bureaucrat, he requested a meeting with the entire National Convention, an enormous body of seven hundred men. The convention was so stunned by the irregularity that it agreed to it. James Monroe entered the hall on August 14, 1794, and addressed the seven hundred delegates as well as a sizable audience of spectators. His speech was sentimental and flowery, with soaring phrases about the undying friendship that should always exist between the two republics.[22] After the new American minister finished, the president of the convention recited his own soaring phrases about the bonds of brotherhood between France and the United States. He warmly embraced Monroe and kissed his cheeks in the French style. The convention resolved to place the flag of the United States next to their own in the great hall. Monroe counted his exploit a great success.

Other Americans, however, did not. Reports of this curious event soon reached Philadelphia. One came from John Jay, who had read about it in the London newspapers and was livid. He could not begin to measure the damaging impression Monroe's exhibition had made on the British government. Randolph and Washington thumbed through the correspondence and worried that they had made a mistake. Randolph wrote to Monroe to tone down his rhetoric and not to get too chummy with his hosts. Monroe "was hurt at the criticism & equally surprised" by the mild admonishment, especially since it came from his close friend.[23]

Randolph and Washington were right. They had made a mistake.

20

"Do Not Turn Your Back"

The summer of 1794 saw a new round of newspaper attacks of Jay's mission. His appointment revived a slumbering Republican press, and it exploded the number of Democratic Societies. By midsummer, their number throughout the nation had increased into the forties. Hamilton's Federalists smelled subversion and the emulation of France's Jacobin Club with the ultimate goal of overthrowing the government. The societies saw themselves as keepers of America's revolutionary flame, lights of liberty that embraced simple republican principles in the spirit of '76.

Federalists formed their own clubs to counter the Democratic Societies, but they were never as numerous or as vocal as the Republican groups because they operated from an entirely different disposition. Federalists didn't embrace citizen participation the way Republicans did. In that regard, Federalist clubs by the very act of their proposed activism were a contradiction. Republicans believed that Americans should not just follow political events but should express views to their elected representatives. Federalists believed in a passive citizenry, one that performed its civic duty by voting but left governing to those they elected. If the people disapproved of elected officials, the people could vote them out of office in the next election. Otherwise, boisterous dissent at meetings and in newspapers seemed nothing short of seditious.

The Democratic Societies said things at their meetings, in the press, and even in letters addressed to the president that Washington found rude and impertinent. His was not a new attitude but one old and venerable, a tradition of Virginia politics that was grounded in deference to the propertied planters whose seats in the burgesses were virtually hereditary and whose decisions were beyond question. Hamilton felt that way by temperament rather than experience. He regarded the people as a great beast that was best kept passive lest it become violent.

As Washington read accounts of Democratic Society meetings and newspaper attacks on him, his experience melded with his temperament to cloud his better judgment. Despite Edmund Randolph's determination to strike a balance and promote harmony, Washington's official family became tinted with increasingly Federalist hues that dismissed balance as weakness, saw debate as distracting, and played to win. Washington came to agree with the sentiments, which was a change stemming from his experience as well as his temperament. For a time, Washington remained wary of Federalist methods about winning at any cost, but that, too, would change.

That was the president's frame of mind when reports arrived on July 25, 1794, that a large armed group had burned the house of a western Pennsylvania excise officer. It could not have happened at a worse time, for Washington did not feel well. He had recently wrenched his back when his horse slipped crossing the falls of the Potomac on a short trip home. A mildly confrontational letter from the Pennsylvania Democratic Society's Washington County chapter did not improve his mood. Then he heard about the house of the excise officer, a man named John Neville. The attack was only the most recent in a series of violent outbreaks over the collection of the whiskey tax.

Disturbances related to Hamilton's excise had periodically occurred in the western parts of states, and they were usually written off as instances of frontier exuberance, the way ornery pioneers expressed themselves. Some of these incidents were serious, as in 1792 when frontier exuberance turned mean and rough in western Pennsylvania. Hamilton urged using force, but Washington preferred words. He issued a proclamation with the hope that the protesters would settle down, and they had. They almost always did. The current problem, however, featured more than tar, feathers, and a few potshots at some "revenuers." Washington was prepared to see the rebellion as the inevitable result of Republican efforts to undermine the government. Even Randolph was pretty well fed up with the rhetoric of the Democratic Societies. Arson by a mob directed at a government agent was serious enough to cause the entire cabinet to agree that a military response should at least be prepared.

The administration began putting its constabulary ducks in a row, which presented another series of irritating complications. Washington needed a federal judge to certify that a rebellion was occurring before he could nationalize state militias under the Militia Act of 1792. To that end, he met with Associate Justice James Wilson, but if Wilson refused to issue the certification (he seemed exceedingly deliberate in studying the issue) and the violence continued, Washington would have to rely on the Pennsylvania governor to supply his militia. To cover that possibility, the next step was to meet with Governor Thomas Mifflin and his secretary of state Alexander Dallas. Mifflin and Dallas were Republicans.

At their meeting on August 2, 1794, Washington laid out the evidence that there was indeed an insurrection taking place in the western portions of Mifflin's state. Randolph accordingly asked for the use of the Pennsylvania militia. Mifflin and Dallas paused. It would not be prudent to use militia in this instance, they said, because it could provoke more violence. When they proposed that the courts could best manage the situation, Hamilton lost his temper. He exclaimed that if the rebels continued to flout the law with impunity, the survival of the national government was at risk. In the end, everyone calmed down and reached a temporary compromise: If Mifflin would help begin mobilization, they would make one more attempt at a peaceful solution.

Mifflin's hesitation concerned Washington. If the militia did not respond to his call, the government would look weaker than if it did nothing. Hamilton and Knox continued to urge force, Hamilton arguing it would hammer some respect for the national government into the great beast. Randolph calmly observed that only the people's affection could make the government strong. It was the start of a persuasive argument to send a peace commission to meet with the rebels. By then Wilson had delivered his certification, so Washington had several options, but he listened to Randolph. The president would appoint Attorney General William Bradford, Pennsylvania Supreme Court justice Jasper Yeates, and Federalist senator James Ross to open talks with the rebels. Because all three were Pennsylvanians, they would not likely invite trouble by seeming to be meddlesome outsiders. Ross was also a western Pennsylvania resident—a neighbor, so to speak—and already on-site because Congress was not in session. The commission had the power to grant amnesty and to waive back taxes.

It was difficult by that time to judge how far out of control the situation in western Pennsylvania had spun. A meeting of several thousand insurgents near Pittsburgh suggested widespread discontent and a troubling level of organization. Yeates and Bradford made their way to join Ross in the rebellious counties, and Washington issued another proclamation telling the insurgents to disperse and go home. He warned them he would call up neighboring state militias to stop the unrest if it continued.

The commission was discouraged before it began. Bradford and Yeates met Collector Neville along the way, a man understandably bitter about losing his house to a mob. He gave them little hope that the rebels would lay down their weapons. When Ross joined them, he was also gloomy. Cooler heads were ready to accept terms, which included swearing an oath of loyalty to the United States at their local polling places, but hardliners were having none of it and were threatening the men who wanted to back down. Bradford wrote to Washington that he believed many of the rebels were stalling in the hope that winter weather would prevent a military expedition that year.

By August 23, 1794, Washington had decided that force was necessary, especially when new rumors had insurgents planning to break western Pennsylvania away from the Union and join with the British. Much to Washington's displeasure, Knox had gone home on personal business at the very moment the War Department had something to do for a change: Anthony Wayne was undertaking his campaign against Little Turtle, and the western Pennsylvania rebellion was going to require the application of military force. At the cabinet meeting on the twenty-third, Knox was conspicuous in his absence, and it would be months before Washington felt kindly toward his old friend again. In the meantime, Hamilton and Randolph handled the details of summoning twelve thousand militia troops from Pennsylvania, New Jersey, Maryland, and Virginia.[1]

It was surprising that the two worked well together, but they were in complete agreement that this dire step had to be taken. It was simply unfortunate, however, that it was being taken the way it was. Knox's absence was a bad piece of luck, because Hamilton's stepping in as the acting secretary of war made the affair look more political than necessary. It was inevitable that it would appear an effort to stifle dissent rather than preserve order. For his part, Randolph had come to the conclusion that the Democratic Societies were a threat to the stability of the government and perhaps to the survival of the Union.[2] But his alliance with Federalists on this issue won him no points with them and further estranged him from Republican leaders.

In the early morning of September 30, 1794, Washington's carriage rattled away from his door carrying him, Hamilton in his capacity as acting secretary of war, and Washington's secretary, Martha's young nephew Bartholomew Dandridge, who had stepped up in the staff hierarchy with Lear's departure. They traveled about twenty-five miles the first day and that night received the heartening news of Anthony Wayne's campaign in the Ohio Country. At Fallen Timbers, his legion had at last defeated the Indians in such a signal victory that it would force them to negotiate with Americans rather than act as clients of the British.[3] It was one less thing to worry about and put Washington's companions in a better mood.

Outside of Carlisle at one of the militia rendezvous points on October 4, they received another boost by the appearance of mustering militia. The carriage stopped to allow Washington to mount Prescott and review the troops. Governor Henry Lee of Virginia arrived, and Washington felt better than he had in weeks. He could leave the campaign to Light-Horse Harry and return to Philadelphia. He should have taken Hamilton with him. Hamilton's plan to stay compounded the political blunder of his role so far, convincing many that he had inflated the crisis to make inappropriate military force an acceptable option.

Before Washington left Carlisle, David Reddick, a community leader in western Pennsylvania, and Pennsylvania congressman William Findley brought a message from the "Whiskey Boys" that if they were given enough time, they would meet the government's demands. Washington was at first encouraged enough to meet with Reddick and Findley several times, but he could never get them to provide proof that the rebellion was over. The season was growing late, and Washington had to recall the warnings from his commissioners that stalling until winter was a rebel strategy. Washington did not stop the large militia force from proceeding to the west and decided against immediately returning to Philadelphia. Rather, he moved forward to the final rendezvous point at Fort Cumberland and then to Bedford for a final review of the troops, by this time an impressive force of some thirteen thousand. As he approached the fort, a troop of horse rode out commanded by George Washington Lewis, his sister Betty's boy.[4] Washington was in his company for a few days, and young George commanded the cavalry escort part of the way toward Bedford when his uncle headed back to the capital. "George," he said in farewell, "you are the oldest of five nephews that I have in this Army; let your conduct be an example to them, and do not turn your back until you are ordered."[5]

Washington was back in Philadelphia on October 28, 1794. Harry Lee led the troops toward the scenes of rebellion and encountered no disorder, let alone violent unrest on the march. As soldiers entered localities, insurgents scattered. The Whiskey Rebellion was over. It had been small—fewer than five Whiskey Boys were killed—but its very smallness meant that the repercussions of suppressing it were significant. Enhancing the power of the federal government to enforce the law gave rise to grumbling about the exaggerated display of force and Hamilton's eagerness to use it. Militia commanders had names of rebels and knew the houses they belonged to, and troops all dressed up with no one to shoot began to rough up citizens. Hamilton conducted menacing interrogations, and about twenty men were arrested and paraded back to Philadelphia. Some were forced to wear hand-lettered signs labeling them as traitors. Findley and Reddick had asked Washington to accompany the expedition to prevent this sort of thing, but the president had assured them that officers would not allow it. Yet it had happened.

The roughhousing was perhaps understandable, but Hamilton's interrogations were cringe worthy. The crude branding of prisoners as traitors without trial was regrettably memorable. Two of the detainees were eventually convicted and sentenced to death, which courted the creation of martyrs.

Washington quickly pardoned them.[6]

While Washington was away, Randolph had kept him informed of events in Philadelphia while managing the day-to-day operations of the government. He also regularly visited Martha to make sure that she was not lonely or needed anything. He reported to Washington about her health and moods. When Washington returned, Randolph helped him prepare the annual message, which must have become a troubling exercise, as the president revealed a level of sustained anger in succeeding drafts that was unlike him.

Congress was blissfully unaware of that as it gathered. On November 18, 1794, Senator Aaron Burr arrived in town "as fat as a Duck," giving the Senate a quorum and allowing the Third Congress to open its second session.[7] Most members were happy. Anthony Wayne had not just avoided the fate of his predecessors but had given the country a victory. Washington had put down the Whiskey Rebellion with so little fuss that even Madison was content for the time being, especially as he settled into James Monroe's vacant house with Dolley. Yet everyone would soon find out what Randolph knew—that George Washington was angrier than he had ever been since taking office. He was convinced that babbling Democratic Societies had caused the western insurrection, and that Republican babbling encouraged the groups while nasty newspaper attacks on the administration abetted them.

As a consequence, the message that Congress heard at the end of 1794 included an indignant denunciation of Democratic Societies for threatening the very existence of the nation. He disdainfully referred to them as "self-created societies," which he meant as a pejorative, making the phrase as offensive as it was puzzling. The Continental Congress had been a self-created society. And was a gathering of American citizens made sinister because it was their idea, rather than, say, one promoted by Alexander Hamilton? Quite simply, the fifth annual message surprised Congress as it revealed Washington's belief that the way citizens expressed their views was as important as the views themselves. Courtesy and deference bespoke order and stability, but organized groups whose sole purpose was to complain about their duly elected officials were unseemly at best, subversive at worst. Congressional reaction divided along well-formed party lines, but the cheerfulness melted away on both sides in an instant.

The Federalist-dominated Senate endorsed Washington's views and marched to the residence to present their response, but they smugly treated Washington's words as vindicating them and condemning their opponents, and they clinched hands for a fight more than they applauded the president for finally saying what they believed. The House fell into a heated argument over endorsing or ignoring that part of the president's address. Criticizing it did not occur to anyone, because Washington had stunned Republicans with a blatantly political statement wrapped in obvious anger. The House decided to ignore it, as though it had been an aberration. Yet, behind the scenes, they were shaken. Republicans had sincerely disapproved of the Whiskey Rebellion, but they worried that Federalists intended to use it as a political weapon, tarring Republicans with the brush of sedition to equate dissent with disloyalty. Federalists compared members of Democratic Societies to Jacobins, but it had been the Federalists themselves who paraded citizens into Philadelphia with placards proclaiming them as traitors.

As 1794 came to a close, even the most optimistic American had to think that these were perilous times. Western discontent continued as the question of Mississippi navigation remained unresolved, and the apparent government impotence to solve it was beginning to diminish Washington's popularity in that region. The federal system was unable to quell domestic disaffection with effective foreign policy, and the government appeared to devolve into petty politics and partisan squabbles. These had been occurring behind the scenes since the beginning, but the angry newspaper columns, the arguments in Congress, and now the president's pronouncement put them on public display. The spectacle was enlightening, but not in a good way.

And here was the real cause behind the rise of the Democratic Societies, which was something Washington, Hamilton, and apparently Edmund Randolph could not see. The chief complaint of these associations was that representative government was not working, and in that they resembled the old revolutionary Committees of Correspondence that had spread information and established ties between discontented colonists, except this version in the mid-1790s was committed to scrutinizing government and speaking commonsense ideas about the common good. In a sharp departure from the politics of deference, they insisted that people should participate in government more consistently and directly. That participation, according to the societies, was the only way to find meaningful solutions to unexpected problems. Having the president of the United States describe this as sinister was baffling, at least at first. It would not be long before thoughtful men wondered who had put such ideas in the president's head. It would not be long before they spoke what they thought.

Republicans in Congress winced at Washington's condemnation of "self-created societies," but the Democratic Societies themselves seethed at talk that tied them to the Whiskey Rebellion. Though they had repeatedly disavowed the rebels, they still had to defend against what they rightly regarded as baseless charges. Madison and Jefferson had never been members of any of these societies, and they, too, found Washington's remarks as well as Federalist attempts to tie the groups to the rebellion disturbing.

Moreover, Madison worried that disagreeing with administration policy would soon be characterized as disloyalty to the government. Jefferson shared the concern. He wrote to Giles in December that "the attempt which is being made to restrain the liberty of our citizens meeting together, interchanging sentiments on what subjects they please, and stating the sentiments in the public papers, has come upon us, a full century earlier than I expected." Jefferson told Madison of his disappointment "that the President should have permitted himself to be the organ of such an attack." From that perspective, the move against the Whiskey Boys was inevitably deemed as something more ominous than enforcing the law. It seemed the start of a program to suppress political opposition with force. How else to explain the massive response to what turned out to be a minor disturbance caused by some backwoods moonshiners? Jefferson concluded as much and more by March 1795. The militia campaign in western Pennsylvania had "answered the favorite purposes of strengthening government and increasing public debt; and therefore an insurrection was announced and proclaimed and armed against, and marched against, but never could be found."[8]

Even so, something more troubling was amiss than Jefferson and Madison thought. The societies were a symptom of a larger phenomenon, not its cause. Political alienation was spreading, with discontent arising from something other than a coherent political movement. It bubbled up from the bottom rather than down from orderly gatherings of prominent citizens, which the Democratic Societies often were. The men who tarred and feathered "revenuers" in western Pennsylvania did not need anyone to tell them they were getting a raw deal. Western separatists flirting with Spain wanted a Mississippi doorway to the world and had little time for dignified gatherings drafting resolutions and publishing protests. Separatists could plot secession without formal ado. Dissatisfaction defined the polity, or the lack of it, and violence was not out of the question for a generation that had defined itself with violent resistance to overbearing authority on the one hand and ineffectual government on the other. Giving life to the axiom that when elections do not lead to change, people will find other ways to effect it, some were ready to discard stable procedures and resort to more direct ways to secure their safety and preserve their liberty. George Washington saw that and did not like it, but he saw only the symptoms and did not understand their cause. In short, he had a point, but he was losing his ability to see the other fellow's point, too.

Washington's attitude nevertheless meant a serious problem for the opposition that had formed behind Jefferson and Madison. Their movement's viability required avoiding any hint of disloyalty. They could not risk association with the societies, no matter how much they agreed with their complaints, especially when Washington's narrowing perspective branded them as seditious. Harnessing discontent without seeming to encourage it would be a Republican problem for the rest of the decade. Eventually the Federalists would overreach. In a way, Washington's fifth annual message foreshadowed that.

Yet Jefferson and Madison eschewed the societies for other than strategic reasons. What the societies portended bothered them. The Democratic Societies rejected deferential politics and menaced the system that Madison had so painstakingly constructed to promote the general welfare. He opposed Hamilton's centralizing policies, but he could not accept intense localism. His conflict was freighted with ironies. Southerners, especially influential Virginians, had been unacquainted with the raucous and sometimes unruly democracy of town meetings. They framed the Constitution from an idealized reverence for representative government. In their world, government was made orderly by educated elites who wielded authority wisely and were appreciated by their inferiors. The effort to install idealized, deferential democracy on the nation exasperated New Englanders who were well acquainted with the temper and tone of the town meeting. New Englanders accordingly opposed high levels of such "democracy" in representative government, and they became high Federalists for reasons other than an affinity with Alexander Hamilton's economic programs. The people were indeed a great beast, they said, and when newspapers became virulent and popular opposition violent, even some southerners in some measure gradually agreed. One Virginian, the one who counted the most, was by early 1795 convinced that the high Federalists were more right than wrong about this, which was why he endorsed their position in his annual message, even if inelegantly. Washington was by degrees being isolated from more than his former neighbors. He was distancing himself from their ideas as well.

Washington knew that anger in the West was real and growing, and not just over a tax on whiskey. Efforts to reach an agreement with Spain for American use of the Mississippi had not so much stalled as had never gotten under way. In the spring of 1794, a prominent Kentuckian responded to Washington's insistence that Spain was a peaceful neighbor with sarcasm. It was clearly better, said John Breckinridge, to petition Congress than actually to navigate the Mississippi; after all, the central government in one form or another had been working on the issue since 1783 with grand results. Westerners, proclaimed Breckenridge, should "send forth petitions to Congress . . . and I assure them, the Congress will most certainly, on their petitions being presented, order them to be—read."[9] Nobody in Philadelphia was laughing, because Breckinridge touched on a truth and hit a nerve. The government had been trying for more than a decade to solve the problem, which gave the appearance that the government's exertions were inept or half-hearted.

They were a bit of both, though not in Philadelphia but in Madrid.

The administration had tried to animate William Carmichael, but the State Department was lucky to hear from him, counting the arrival of something from Spain in the diplomatic pouch as cause for celebration in itself, regardless of what it said. When William Short was sent to help Carmichael, Short discovered at least part of the reason correspondence was rare. Carmichael had developed such a severe tremor in his hands that he could not even sign his name. For a time, Short had to forge Carmichael's signature on official documents.[10] Short was a reliable correspondent—and a voluble one; his letters could take the better part of a day to read—but he fared no better with the Spanish court. Short still nursed disappointment over President Washington not considering him to replace Jefferson in Paris, and he was prone to blame Washington for his failure in Madrid. Frustration in Madrid had a way of making men angry with somebody, and George Washington was an easy target.

News of John Jay's arrival in London as special envoy infuriated France, but it also troubled Spain. The possibility that an Anglo-American alliance would result from Jay's negotiations caused Madrid to reassess relations with the United States. A land-hungry neighbor of Spanish Louisiana indignant about the Mississippi and the closure of New Orleans teaming up with the most powerful naval presence in the world seemed a most disagreeable combination. Suddenly the Spanish government was willing to talk about the Mississippi River, and for the American government the prospect of either the young William Short or the ineffectual William Carmichael taking up these negotiations would not do. Washington needed a diplomat with the appropriate gravitas to seize this opportunity and make the most of it. He had Randolph broach the idea with Jefferson, but the former secretary of state quickly said no. Randolph then offered the mission to Patrick Henry, whose support for the constitutional government had grown warmer, at least according to Henry Lee. Yet Henry also said no. Out of the necessity for a speedy response to what could have been a passing whim in Madrid, Washington and Randolph hit upon the idea of making Thomas Pinckney a special envoy to Spain.

It was a rare stroke of good fortune offsetting bad circumstances. Not only had Jay's mission insulted Thomas Pinckney, he had been struck by tragedy when his wife Betsey died suddenly in August 1794.

He coped with grief while trying to comfort their five children. More-over, he leaped at the chance to leave London. On November 21, 1794, Washington submitted Pinckney's name to the Senate to serve as envoy extraordinary to Spain, and he was quickly confirmed. Randolph im-mediately sent instructions, and Pinckney was soon bound for Spain armed with another stroke of luck. Two days before Pinckney's nomi-nation was confirmed in the Senate, John Jay finally signed a treaty with the British government. Its existence would be known in Madrid, but not its terms. His Most Catholic Majesty's ministers were inclined to expect the worst, making them even more pliable to American de-mands. In addition, there would be no American diplomat in Madrid to look upon Pinckney's arrival with irritation. William Carmichael died on February 9, 1795.

The South Carolinian arrived in Madrid to a solicitous greeting and apparently sincere smiles. It was a stark change from his time in Britain. "Lord Grenville presents his compliments to Mr. Pinckney," had been a common communication, and Grenville having "the honor of inform-ing him that the conference of today will not take place" too frequently followed it.[11] Madrid was like the difference between night and day. Pinckney returned the smiles. He had a feeling that American boats would soon be riding a Spanish river, a prelude to American stars run-ning their courses in a formerly Spanish sky.

21

"That Man Is a Traitor"

As he began the third year of his second term, George Washington could not recall a time when fatigue and despondency had been such constant companions. Sleep did not refresh, and anger simmered just below the surface. His memory began to fail like his hearing, and his sense of dignity was never more easily wounded. The newspapers, having long ago shed the taboo of criticizing Washington, treated him as if he were evil or vapid, and sometimes both. He had once revealed to Thomas Jefferson a touchiness about this, "that in condemning the administration of the government they condemned him, for if they thought there were measures pursued contrary to his sentiment, they must conceive him too careless to attend to them or too stupid to understand them."[1] Now he needed only to peruse the public prints for evidence of his growing carelessness and evident stupidity. Jefferson remembered Washington "in every sense of the words, [as] a wise, a good, & a great man," and though he "had obtained a firm and habitual ascendancy over" his temper, if it ever "broke its bonds, he was most tremendous in his wrath."[2] He was most tremendous a lot lately.

"No man," he admitted, "was ever more tired of public life, or more devoutly wished for retirement, than I do."[3] It was something he often said and sometimes meant, but he now meant it to his marrow. John Adams noticed this. "The Man the most to be pitied is the President," he said, reflecting his new appreciation for Washington now that the president had begun to rely on him. "Exertions, Anxieties Responsibilities for twenty Years without fee or reward" were bad enough, but "to be the Butt of the Insolence of Genets and Clubbs is a Tryal too great for human Nature to be exposed."

Adams had grown pensive about other things, too. He began recording the passing of former warriors and Founders, as would an ancient Egyptian chronicler filling in a Book of the Dead. Friedrich von Steuben was gone, as were Roger Sherman and Richard Henry Lee, men worth arguing with and remembering as towering and brave and difficult and admirable—irreplaceable men. Others were leaving Congress, disappearing into private life and local concerns, to sit by home fires and watch their children grow or, as was more likely for the Revolutionary generation, dote on their children's children. Rumors abounded that Knox and Hamilton would soon leave the administration. Adams fretted "that good Men will be worn out and wearied too often into Resignations" and that "the Government will fall for Want of Men to hold it up."[4] He was not alone with these fears.[5]

The rumors about Knox and Hamilton were true. Knox had planned to resign early in 1794. His finances were in their usual precarious state, but the war scare with Great Britain and the unsettled frontier had caused him to stay. Even so, Washington could have wondered what good it did to have Knox remain in the War Department if Knox was seldom physically at the War Department. Financial problems pulled him from Philadelphia when he was most needed, as in August when his absence during the Whiskey Rebellion put a considerable strain on his friendship with the president. Washington would forgive him eventually when the memory returned of the shouting lad with Fort Ticonderoga's cannons on the Cambridge Road.

Henry and Lucy Knox were never truly happy during his time in the government. She entertained well, and laughter always rang through the halls of the home when guests needed a drink and a cheerful word, but she knew what people whispered to one another about her weight. Their five years in New York City and Philadelphia had been shadowed by chronic financial worries, and in 1792 they lost their nine-year-old son to a sudden illness. Laughter did not ring so constantly in their home after that. And while she could chuckle to play the jovial fat girl, a habit she had cultivated in youth, he, too, became heavy and lumbering, and more than a few people thought that reflected a heavy and lumbering mind.

There was always the nagging feeling, which Knox secretly shared, that he was in just a bit over his head in his job and a bit dull in the company of Thomas Jefferson with his faraway stare and Alexander Hamilton with his crackling tongue. Knox confided in John Adams shortly before leaving the administration, telling Adams of his plans to retire in the Maine District and squeeze as much profit as he could from his vast acreage to assure Lucy a comfortable old age. Knox thought his days numbered, and if he died "tomorrow his Wife & Children would not have enough to live on two Years."[6] Adams listened quietly for a change. It made him sad.

Hamilton wanted to quit, too, and for the same financial reasons as Knox. His enemies had never really understood him. They thought him a big-time crook speculating in bank stock and securities, trading on margins with insider information, and selling influence to jobbers for profit and pleasure. But Hamilton had never personally made a penny on his financial policies. It wasn't that he was especially scrupulous. He tampered with elections to punish personal enemies, smeared opponents with lies when the truth would serve better, and betrayed his wife with a pretty trollop while paying her pimp.

But something stayed his hand at Treasury—something his enemies never understood. For Hamilton, theft was vulgar, even when elegantly contrived by aristocratic rogues. Alexander Hamilton might be the bastard child of a West Indies slattern and a Scottish peddler, but he wasn't a thief. The House committee had burned scores of candles scrutinizing the Treasury's books, ledgers, accounts, reports, letters, and loans for month after month after month, looking for Hamilton's indiscretions. When it finally filed its findings in the spring of 1795, Republicans closed their eyes and cursed. Their majority immediately tabled the report into oblivion, and for good reason. Nobody could find the slightest impropriety at Treasury on Hamilton's watch, and the hunt for his hide had become a political embarrassment

Hamilton's growing family and his refusal to use his post for money meant he needed to return to his legal practice in New York and repair his bank account. He could survey a good run at Treasury despite a few missteps, such as trusting aristocratic rogues and initially misjudging the panic in 1792 that nearly brought down the country, but, then, Hamilton lived by the motto of fortune favoring the man who dares. Against impossible odds he had put the government on a sound financial footing, had groomed a provincial backwater to realize its limitless potential for prosperity, and had persuaded the powerful at home and the British abroad that the United States of America was pure profit waiting to happen. He wanted to leave, but he promised Washington that he would stay until the end of January. Hamilton had one last piece of business as the secretary of the Treasury.

In mid-January 1795, Hamilton informed the House that he had prepared a report on retiring the debt. He did not include the report with his letter. The omission mocked House Republicans for their insistence that Hamilton not provide unsolicited reports to Congress, but it also teased them with an irresistible prospect. The debt had been a source of friction since the beginning of Washington's presidency, and budget-conscious Republicans could not refuse to review Hamilton's recommendations. This report was like all previous ones: massive, comprehensive, and daunting. He outlined a long-term plan for retiring the public debt with three separate interwoven sections that reviewed the finances of the country on his watch, discussed at length the meaning and method of public finance, and put forward ten proposals with commentary explaining how to sustain public credit. To round out the matter, he included the obligatory tables and statistical overviews.

In summary, it was far more than just a set of recommendations on retiring the debt. It was an extensive treatise explaining Hamilton's "complete views ... of ... the actual state of our debt and finances."[7] The House of Representatives received it on January 19, 1795, and gave it mixed reviews along partisan lines. Madison joined others in the main objection that Hamilton's plan would span three decades to pay down the debt in the absence of new taxes. Yet the Federalists were charmed, if not by the substance of Hamilton's work (like all of his productions, its length alone was unappealing) but by the march it stole on the Republicans. After all, they had been complaining for years about the debt and were now confronted with a plan to do something about it; when Republicans complained about this latest report, men such as Hamilton's friend Fisher Ames were pleased at the exposure of their hypocrisy. After considerable debate, both House and Senate passed a bill so closely resembling Hamilton's plan that it was in sum if not particulars a Federalist triumph. Republican opponents could only grumble and point out privately how Hamilton's tentacles had grappled away the legislature's principles. But Fisher Ames was right when he crowed that it was "the finale, the crown of federal measures."[8]

The audacity on display in this last effort enchanted Federalists, enraged Republicans, and impressed George Washington. The president politely said farewell to Knox, but he accepted Hamilton's resignation with a rare expression of sincere affection. His distress over losing a man he deemed indispensable was more than evident. "In every relation, which you have borne to me," Washington wrote, "I have found that my confidence in your talents, exertions and integrity, has been well placed."[9] For the remaining two years of Washington's presidency, he never stopped relying on Hamilton for advice. He would not hesitate to dispatch a letter to New York when important questions loomed.

The dependency intrigued Hamilton. Despite their long association, he never developed affection for Washington. Problems of personality always lurked on the edges of their relations. The sharp exchange during the Revolution that partially estranged them was an example, and Washington's reluctance to provide unqualified approval for Hamilton's financial sleight of hand was another. Hamilton was as proud as Washington, just as touchy, and equally alert to suspicions about probity. When Washington watched him more closely after the congressional investigations, Hamilton said nothing, but it rankled as if he were a footman suspected of filching from the pantry. Hamilton had perfected the appearance of affection as part of his arsenal of charm and persuasiveness, whether it was toward his wife, her relations, old chums such as Robert Troup, or George Washington. Without doubt, he loved his children, but that was different from the resonant bonds of selfless friendship that mark the relations of a man with at least some of his associates. The only person who merited that level of unqualified affection from Alexander Hamilton had been John Laurens, dead and buried for many years in a South Carolina grave. Everybody else was someone to use for pleasure (Maria Reynolds) or for advancement (President Washington), to fight (Jefferson and Madison), or to disdain (Randolph).

Washington's continued dependency also gave Hamilton the opening to pursue his program from behind the scenes. Hamilton claimed he was leaving public life forever, but nobody really believed it. He would not, could not disappear completely from the public scene. James McHenry, Hamilton's old friend from the war whom Hamilton had dubbed "Mac," had learned, he said, to appreciate the simple things in life—his wife, his children, gardening—but that sort of talk seemed preposterous to the crackling bundle of energy always on a climb.

When Knox quit, Washington had already decided on Postmaster General Timothy Pickering to become secretary of war. Pickering had served in the war, ending it as quartermaster general, a post that usually consumed careers because most failed at it. Yet Pickering had often done as well as could be expected and sometimes had even exceeded expectations. He had the personality of a clerk, if a grand one, and managed the Post Office Department with a characteristic attention to detail that brought no shame and occasionally merited some accolades.

Born in Salem, Massachusetts, Pickering emulated his father to become a self-righteous meddler, a man who minded other people's business but found it hard to find his own way. He seldom smiled, and near penury increased his stony nature. His early efforts to join the Washington administration stemmed from his need for money, and he settled for what he could get like a scrambler for crumbs. He was socially inept. When his budget made reciprocating invitations difficult, he left his wife at home and attended dinners alone, candidly admitting to his hosts that as a public figure he could not seclude himself from the world and people who might prove "*useful,* as well as agreeable."[10]

Washington never liked the petulant Pickering, and Pickering never cared for Washington, which made his joining the president's official family a peculiar act of necessity mixed with ambition. He was good with Indians, so everyone thought, and the War Department had its hands full with Indians. Nothing more vividly illuminates the diminished talent of Washington's second cabinet than this fact—that he had to choose people because they were available. Though disagreeable, Pickering was near at hand. It had come to that.

Replacing the irreplaceable Hamilton posed an entirely different set of difficulties, for Washington knew that Hamilton's successor in comparison would never be more than a pale placeholder. Energy, brilliance, and creativity were in short supply, so as with his choice of Pickering, Washington settled for competence and convenience, comforted by the fact that the choice had Hamilton's approval. He appointed Hamilton's trusted subordinate Oliver Wolcott, Jr. Like Pickering, Wolcott was also from New England, but from Connecticut and a prominent family. Oliver Wolcott, Sr., had been a general during the war and friends with General Washington, and young Oliver was a contemporary of other Connecticut men such as Joel Barlow and Noah Webster, known collectively as the Hartford Wits. Oliver had even tried his hand at poetry, but it was praised mainly for its brevity in contrast to Barlow's long-winded epics. Webster remembered Wolcott from college as "eccentric." They were all high Federalists; Wolcott's father called the Democratic Societies "demoniacal" and "nurseries of sedition."[11]

Wolcott had been with Hamilton in the Treasury since the beginning and was loyal to his old boss to a fault. That and other problems waited to complicate Washington's life. The fact that both Pickering and Wolcott were from New England marked another shift in Washington's method of governance. He was less concerned about geographical balance in his second term, and he had by design or chance surrounded himself with northeastern reactionaries who thought the Democratic Societies were subversive and their senior colleague Edmund Randolph was too influential. They were not untalented for ordinary times, but they were plopped into place during extraordinary events. They were also much less sophisticated than Jefferson and Hamilton. Unlike those two, for example, Wolcott could not read French and Pickering could make out only a little, which was worse, as it turned out. It would, in fact, have seismic consequences.

Washington knew that John Jay and Lord Grenville had reached an understanding in London, because Jay had immediately written to Randolph (and Hamilton) about signing a treaty on November 19, 1794.[12] Then nothing came for weeks on end. Jay prepared no less than three copies of the treaty for dispatch on three different ships. The hope was to increase the chances of evading French patrols or privateers. Inept messengers, however, undid the plan by placing two copies on the same ship, which was waylaid by the French. The British crew tossed the copies overboard. Another ship with the third copy sailed later, but icy storms and rough seas delayed her arrival in Norfolk until late February. Because Washington knew from Randolph and Hamilton knew directly from Jay about the treaty, everyone with ears knew about it, too, and the long wait gave rumormongers a clear field for rampant speculation.

Without seeing the treaty, Federalists lauded its presumed terms and congratulated one another on Jay's successful negotiations. Republicans were just as ignorant of the treaty's contents but preemptively criticized Jay for granting the British too many concessions. For his part, Jay knew that many people would be unhappy with his work, but he believed it was the best he could do. Randolph was anxious. Jay's letters during negotiations had indicated he was getting nowhere on such issues as reimbursement for confiscated slaves and financial claims for seized American shipping. Randolph had sent Jay fresh instructions, but news of a treaty caused Randolph to fear that they had not arrived in time.

He and Washington could only wait for a treaty that might be completely unacceptable. They at least hoped that it would arrive before Congress adjourned on March 3, 1795, but when it did not, Randolph informed every senator that the president would convene a special session for June 8. Four days after Congress adjourned, the treaty arrived in Philadelphia. Jay had not yet returned from England, and Washington wanted to confer with him before submitting the treaty to the Senate. His first reading of the document left him dispirited. He very much wanted to confer with Jay.

It was officially the Treaty of Amity, Commerce, and Navigation, Between His Britannic Majesty and The United States of America, but almost from the start and enduringly afterward it was called Jay's Treaty. Because the U.S. special envoy had entered negotiations with a weak hand—cards made weaker by Hamilton's revealing what they were—Jay had won few concessions.

The British did promise to evacuate the posts in the American

Northwest, but they had made that promise in Paris in 1783, and to John Jay at that. In any case, under the terms that Jay agreed to this time, the British would not have to leave the Northwest until the following summer. The British opened the British West Indies to limited American trade, but only to small vessels under seventy tons. Americans were also barred from the carrying trade between the Caribbean and Europe. Britain agreed to pay damages for the latest seizures of American ships, but they said nothing about altering their maritime policy, ceasing impressment, or stopping the supply of arms to Indians. Rather, they made Jay bind the United States to pay prerevolutionary debts owed to British merchants while they avoided any mention of reimbursements for slaves taken at the end of the Revolution. Commissions would be convened to determine American debts, set spoliations for American ships seized during the current war, and resolve the disputed boundary between Canada and the United States. Otherwise, the treaty granted each country "most favored nation" status with regard to tariffs, which sounded better than it was. In reality, it meant that Congress could not pass retaliatory commercial measures against the British. About the best that could be said for Jay's work was that it preserved the peace, and Washington hoped that preserving the peace would be enough to see it through. As usual, Edmund Randolph had encouraging words for the president and his emissary. Randolph wrote to Jay that he believed the treaty should be ratified, but he and the president wanted clarification on certain matters.[13]

What they wanted, they did not get. Jay was done with his job and, in fact, was done with the federal experiment. He arrived home in New York at the end of May to find that without his knowledge he had been elected governor in absentia, an election procedure his opponents found irregular, but considering the irregularities of the previous governor's race, their protests had little weight. Jay promptly resigned as chief justice, a post he had never liked and had grown to detest for the burden of travel it entailed, both on the circuit and to Philadelphia once a year to hear cases brought before the Supreme Court.

Despite his disdain for it, Jay's time as chief justice was important and like everything else, controversial. Under his leadership, for example, the court established jurisdiction over state laws, a questionable extension of authority as far as the Republicans were concerned but not the last time they would cavil over judicial supremacy. The president had to find a new chief justice. He quickly offered the post to John Rutledge of South Carolina, who had earlier served as an associate justice on the court. Rutledge accepted, but nobody could have foreseen the problems that Jay's Treaty would cause, including with the appointment of the next chief justice.

Interestingly, Washington did not initially include Wolcott and Pickering in the sensitive discussions about Jay's handiwork. It was with Randolph that he decided to submit the flawed document to the Senate to seek its advice as well as consent, as the Constitution directed. The decision was sensible, but the way Washington and Randolph implemented it was not. Because the document was sure to be controversial, they had kept its terms secret, which was a surprising accomplishment and not without merit. Yet when the Senate convened, Washington and Randolph requested that it, too, keep the terms secret. Senate Republicans wanted the treaty published but did not have the votes to force the issue, and from that failure and the administration's seeming covertness, a regrettable perception eventually formed in the public mind. The Senate debate held behind closed doors contributed to the notion that all the secrecy was meant to hide something sinister. In reality, the debates were mainly "temperate, grave, decent, and wise."[14] It would have been better politics for the people to see that.

Despite the mature nature of debate, treaty supporters realized that they had an uphill climb in the Senate. Article XII that opened the British West Indies to American trade was quite unpopular, not just because of its restrictions on ship size but for its listing of coffee, molasses, cotton, sugar, and cocoa as prohibited for export. One could ponder what else the West Indies had that was worth exporting, which meant that Article XII was enough to prevent Senate ratification. Treaty proponents found the solution in simply removing it, and with Article XII duly deleted, the final vote was 20 to 10 in favor, the very minimum needed for ratification.

Garnering just enough votes was hardly a ringing endorsement, but the Senate's solution to produce those votes created another problem for the administration. Washington did not know how to address the Senate's removal of Article XII. The action was certainly beyond the constitutional prescription of advice and consent. Washington asked Randolph for his options in what turned out to be an enormously complicated issue. For example, if the executive substituted different wording for Article XII, would it require a separate Senate approval? If so, the Senate would have to stay in session while a draft article was produced and submitted. Randolph thought the actual problem was a less obvious one: If the administration resubmitted draft articles for a ratified treaty, the very act implied that the president was setting a condition that, if met, would assure his signing the treaty. Randolph knew that Washington had not yet made that decision. This reasoning effectively removed the Senate from any additional participation in the process, and the administration did nothing to stop its adjournment on June 26, 1795. After that day, George Washington had the fate of Jay's Treaty exclusively in his hands.

That was when the real trouble started. After Senate ratification, Washington thought secrecy was no longer necessary and told Randolph to publish the treaty, but one thing and then another delayed its release. Meanwhile, Senator Stevens Thomson Mason, George Mason's nephew, was among those Republicans chafed by the administration's request for confidentiality, which had been interpreted as an order, and by the Senate's self-imposed silence. Mason did not feel bound by any such arrangement and gave the treaty to Benjamin Franklin Bache, who published a synopsis in the *Aurora* and the entire document as a pamphlet. Because these publications happened to precede the administration's release, they seemed to force Washington and Randolph to make a decision to publish the treaty—one they had actually already made. The damage to public perceptions of administration transparency contributed to the rising anger over the treaty's terms being kept under wraps and the way it was secretly ratified. The country was up in arms before Washington had even begun weighing if he should sign Jay's Treaty.

That decision was hardly certain. It was the first issue of substance that Washington brought before his new cabinet as a group, specifically whether to draft an alternative to Article XII or leave it out altogether. Should he sign the treaty? And if he signed a treaty with a new Article XII, should it be resubmitted to the Senate? Washington wanted written opinions, and he solicited Alexander Hamilton's views for good measure. (Hamilton thought it was a bad treaty but the best the United States could expect.)

Meanwhile, opposition to the treaty gave new life to Democratic Societies previously discredited by Federalist efforts to tie them to the Whiskey Rebellion. They held meetings and passed resolutions with renewed fervor. At a Fourth of July rally in New York, protesters heaped abuse on their new governor John Jay, mirroring behavior that was occurring everywhere in the country. When dissidents began scheduling their meetings after sundown so his burning effigy would be more visible, Jay was said to have quipped that nighttime travelers could use him to illuminate their journeys throughout the United States. But most of his critics were not joking. One hoped Jay's lips would be "blistered to the bone" for having kissed the queen's hand,[15] and an especially loquacious graffiti artist in New York City painted on a wall "Damn John Jay! Damn everyone who won't damn John Jay. Damn everyone who won't put lights in the windows and sit up all night damning John Jay!"[16]

Some feared the bad treaty would have grim consequences. A New Englander noted the strong opposition to the treaty in the South that could mean "an ultimate separation between us & them."[17] It was true that many southerners saw the treaty as a pathetic capitulation to Britain that betrayed their section. Planters would have to pay prerevolutionary debts, but Federalist merchants would collect damages for British assaults on shipping. But anger was not a sectional preserve. Hamilton tried to explain to a rally of protestors in New York City the treaty's good points. The crowd shouted him down, threw rocks, and then marched to Jay's home to burn the treaty at his front door. Hamilton gave up on public meetings. As "Camillus," he published essays that were so persuasive that Jefferson, who viewed the treaty as a "monument to folly or venality," again urged Madison to take up his pen to counter Hamilton.[18]

The controversy over the treaty began to compromise George Washington's heretofore inviolable popularity with the general public and, worse, it breached the dignity he thought more precious than acclaim, as when disrespectful citizens directly told him not to sign the treaty. Whether these communications came from fractious individuals or official groups such as the Boston Board of Selectmen, his response was uniform: It was his decision to make, and he always decided things for the good of the country as he saw it. Before long, President Washington saw all protests, letters, and petitions against the treaty as completely inappropriate, and that impression likely persuaded him to sign it as much as any measured opinions from the cabinet or advisers such as Hamilton. Randolph agreed that it should be signed, at least until the British recommended enforcing their provision order by seizing American ships carrying food to France. Washington was equally nonplussed. What was the point of a treaty if the British were intent on provoking a war? He huddled with Randolph, and both concluded he could not sign the treaty unless British policy was immediately changed. Randolph promptly called on George Hammond to lodge the president's objections.

Their meeting was worse than awful. Hammond had never liked Randolph, because he believed he was part of the Jefferson-Madison pro-French cabal, but when the secretary of state appeared on this occasion, the British minister was more supercilious than usual. He flippantly told Randolph that his government could rescind the provision order to allow Washington the political leeway to sign the treaty. But Hammond went on to say that afterward London would simply reinstate it following the exchange of ratifications. Randolph could not believe his ears. He returned to the president in a near daze. Randolph described the meeting. Washington was tremendous in his wrath.[19]

It was likely fortunate that personal business at just that moment required him to leave Philadelphia for home. In a trembling rage, he essentially told Randolph to forget the ignorant puppy traveling under the name of George Hammond and prepare a direct message to Lord Grenville. The treaty was in such jeopardy at this point that no one, including Randolph, knew what Washington would do, but the secretary of state was steadfast to his chief in insisting that Washington's decision would be the right one. He wrote to William Short of his certainty that Washington at the helm would "by his fortitude and wisdom steer us into safe port."[20] While Washington was in Virginia, Randolph thus worked to stay the course with his own even keel. He commenced a routine of sending the president regular reports, conferring with his colleagues in the cabinet, and coping with diplomatic reverberations from Jay's Treaty, particularly with the French. None of these tasks was pleasant, but dealing with the French was exasperating. Jean Antoine Joseph Fauchet was exceptionally angry.

From the start the French minister had been nervous about Jay's mission and spent months peppering the State Department with questions about its purpose. The French government had done the same with Monroe in Paris and became suspicious when Monroe seemed evasive. The Jacobins suspected that Monroe was withholding information, but the truth was he had no information to withhold. Monroe all but begged Jay for reports on the negotiations, but Jay would have been vague even if he had not been angry with Monroe over the way the Virginian had opened his embassy in Paris. As it was, Jay was downright uncommunicative in repeating to Monroe the standard line that nothing was being done to violate understandings between the United States and France. After signing the treaty, Jay remained mum. At most, he offered to send his secretary to brief Monroe on the treaty's terms, but only if Monroe promised to keep them secret. Monroe refused to agree to the condition.[21]

Fauchet had earned early praise for not being Genet, which was to say he had remained aloof from America's domestic political squabbles. Yet it was inevitable that he would gravitate toward the Republicans, and he seems to have thought he had a friend in Edmund Randolph by way of the secretary of state's seeming association with Jefferson and Madison. In his first year, Fauchet often talked over issues with Randolph well into the night, grateful for a man fluent in French and seemingly sympathetic to the plight of France in a hostile Europe. When Jay's Treaty appeared, Randolph labored to reassure Fauchet that it did not at all imperil Franco-American relations, but he also obeyed Washington's wishes for secrecy. Unable to divulge its contents, Randolph watched Fauchet cool and then turn petulant. It mattered less to Fauchet than he let on. For months he had quietly believed that the Jacobin interlude in his country's revolution was fated to be brief. When the Reign of Terror finally ended in exhaustion, its sponsors had worn out their welcome. Fauchet soon received news that his replacement was on the way. Pierre Adet arrived in June 1795, and Fauchet gladly turned everything over to him and prepared to go home. He was glad to be shed of Americans, because he judged them as ungrateful for the help France had given in the break with Britain. He would not miss Edmund Randolph. Fauchet had thought of Randolph as his friend. Friends did not keep secrets from each other.

Randolph drafted the message to Lord Grenville objecting to the provision order and offered to take it to Mount Vernon to hasten Washington's final review and approval. Washington told him not to take the trouble because he had decided to come back earlier than planned. Randolph, Pickering, and Wolcott all agreed that Washington's early return could be interpreted as signaling his uneasiness about Jay's Treaty. Randolph related their concerns in a letter of July 29, 1795. Shortly after the mail pouch left for Alexandria, Pickering and Wolcott appeared in Randolph's office to announce they had changed their minds. Perhaps it would be best for Washington to return to Philadelphia sooner after all, they said, especially in light of recent reports that George Hammond was soon leaving for Britain. He could personally carry Washington's message to Lord Grenville. Randolph thought this sensible and accordingly wrote a new letter to Washington on July 31. The vagaries of eighteenth-century mail delivery brought Randolph's two letters—one saying to stay, and the other to come back—to Mount Vernon on the same day, August 5. Another letter arrived that day from Timothy Pickering, also written on July 31. The dates of Randolph's letters made relatively clear that the most recent one asking for Washington's return contained the most current information. Pickering's letter must have been puzzling, however, particularly because of a cryptic remark and a mildly alarming instruction.

Pickering urged more than Washington's early return to Philadelphia; he wanted the president back as soon as possible. He told Washington that Randolph's letter had been written at his and Wolcott's urging, and even referred to William Bradford joining in from his sickbed, which rather inaccurately described the calm discussion that had prompted Randolph to write his letter of July 31. But Pickering then became mysterious. "On the subject of the treaty I confess that I feel extreme solicitude," he confided, "and for a special reason, which can be communicated to you only in person." He closed by telling Washington that the "letter is for your eye alone."[22]

Washington hurriedly left for Philadelphia the next day and arrived in the capital on August 11, 1795. He invited Randolph to an informal afternoon dinner and sent word to Pickering to come that afternoon as well to elaborate on his curious letter. Washington and Randolph were chatting over dinner when Pickering arrived. It is likely that Pickering's instruction to keep his note confidential caused Washington to meet him in private rather than include the secretary of state. Washington rose from dinner and took Pickering to another room. Washington asked Pickering what he had meant in his letter. Pickering dramatically raised an arm to point toward the dining room where the door was closed and Randolph remained, calmly continuing his meal. Pickering sputtered, "That man is a traitor!"

22

"To You I Shall Return"

Washington first met Benedict Arnold when he appeared at army headquarters outside Boston in 1775 with an audacious proposal. Arnold was thirty-four, short, and stocky, but striking in appearance. He had a dark complexion and brown hair; his gray eyes appeared to glow, and he impressed Washington. He had already notched some memorable achievements in a war that had not being going well for the Americans.

Washington was receptive to Arnold's proposal. He wanted to lead a small force through the Maine wilderness to cooperate with the main American attack on Quebec. The Maine country, then a part of Massachusetts, was a mysterious place never adequately mapped and likely to have unimagined obstacles, but Arnold was confident. This first conversation with Washington thereby set a pattern of sorts. A tincture of self-interest colored Arnold's desire to advance the patriot cause in this instance and, looking back, many would see more than tinctures of self-interest in everything Benedict Arnold did.[1]

The Quebec campaign was the first large undertaking that Washington planned as commander in chief, and it was a terrible mistake. Arnold's contingent reached the outskirts of Quebec, but only after an arduous trek that cost him more than half his command with the rest reduced to eating their dogs and gnawing their boots to stay alive. The American siege that followed ended during a blizzard when a disastrous American attack left Arnold wounded. Washington counted himself oddly indebted to Arnold. Perhaps Washington's own unfortunate history during the French and Indian War shaped his thinking. There were similarities in Arnold's quixotic participation in the Quebec campaign and Washington's efforts twenty years earlier to protect the enormous Virginia frontier from hostile Indians. In addition, Arnold's daring against long odds was admirable. As the ill-fated Canadian campaign concluded with a general American retreat before superior British forces, Arnold managed to extricate the army and even mount a defense of Lake Champlain in October 1776. Though it was another defeat, Washington correctly judged it to have delayed British operations in the region for months. From then on he trusted Arnold without question, up to the day he discovered that Arnold had betrayed him.[2]

It was the first meaningful treachery George Washington ever encountered and unfortunately, in his mind, it would not be the last. Benedict Arnold came from a prominent Rhode Island family that had fallen on hard times because of his father's alcoholism. The family's plummeting finances forced young Arnold to work as an apprentice in his cousins' apothecary learning the medicine-mixing trade, but the cousins were kind and staked him to his own establishment. He moved to New Haven, Connecticut, where he drove himself as he would for the rest of his life, always chased by the shameful specter of his drunken father. He grew a drugstore and bookshop into a merchant house, a small empire with its own ships that allowed Arnold to become a seafaring captain, work the rich Caribbean and Canadian trade, have adventures, and make a name for himself as a shrewd bargainer and a bad enemy. Wealth won him a wife from a prominent family, and they were happy as three boys came in quick succession, but the marriage was soon clouded by Arnold's incessant travel and rumors that he was consorting with low women in the West Indies.[3] Ugly rumors would be a constant in Benedict Arnold's life.

Trouble with Britain was made to order for his love of action and adventure. He responded to Lexington and Concord by helping to capture lightly defended Fort Ticonderoga on Lake Champlain, which was the reason Henry Knox could bring its cannons to Boston. The exploit won Arnold applause and recognition, but it also revealed a fundamental flaw in the man he had become. He saw praise of others as detracting from his reputation and diminishing the value of his exploits. A quarrel over command at Fort Ticonderoga ended with his resigning his state commission before his conduct in the failed Quebec assault won him promotion to brigadier general. Even so, the Congress placed other officers in command of the army Arnold had saved. Washington knew from experience how such treatment could provoke a wronged man.

Others, however, saw something troubling in Benedict Arnold's character. Here was a potentially great man who easily committed petty and sometimes pointless transgressions. He solicited small graft for puny profits, actions that made him enemies and jarred his admirers. Careful men who had to work with and for him found him a disconcerting bundle of contradictions. Americans angry over his treachery later portrayed him as a coward and invented stories about his youth that recalled his killing baby birds and strewing paths with broken glass to cut the bare feet of schoolmates. But Benedict Arnold was much more complex than an operatic villain. He was courageous when the challenge was most daunting, and his exploits made him easy to admire, even if his ugly temper, constant complaints, and little corruptions made him hard to like.

The Congress passed Arnold over for major general in early 1777, and Washington was barely able to talk him out of resigning by appealing to his vanity as much as his loyalty. When Arnold finally received his promotion but immediately complained that he was junior to officers unfairly promoted before him, Washington persisted in overlooking his unattractive insecurities and egocentrism.[4] In fact, Arnold's anger over almost everything and his turbulent associations with brother officers became one of the hallmarks of his service, yet Washington only weighed Arnold's battlefield exploits, which were evidently impressive enough to eclipse accusations that he routinely used his position to line his pockets. And thus Benedict Arnold became a great and courageous soldier, peerless in the crucial hours of the American Revolution, while at his core he harbored a despicable combination of opportunism and avarice that ironically would also make him peerless in the crucial hours of the American Revolution.

George Washington never saw the trouble coming. Instead, he continued to sympathize with Arnold and ignore his flaws. He sent Arnold back to New York to help oppose John Burgoyne's invasion in 1777, and Arnold quickly exhibited both his worst and best sides. He argued with his commanding officer beyond the point of insubordination and was relieved of command. Then he ignored the dismissal and led the decisive charge that sealed Burgoyne's fate at Saratoga, an American victory that forever crippled the British war effort, but also forever crippled Benedict Arnold. He was badly wounded again. His shattered left leg was badly set, making it a couple inches shorter than the other and giving him a halting limp for the rest of his life.

Washington thought the military governor's post at Philadelphia would be a placid assignment for a semi-invalid. He appointed Arnold to it, but it was a mistake. At first, Arnold seemed only to trifle in small schemes while lavishing money on ladies. A court-martial reprimanded him in 1779, but Washington took great pains to soften the reproach. Meanwhile, Arnold was also involved in more serious transgressions. He made secret investments in British firms and used his authority to boost their profits. He lived ostentatiously, socialized with Loyalists, and married the daughter of a Tory family—his second marriage, but the first for his bride Margaret (Peggy) Shippen, who was half his age. For many years Peggy Arnold was pitied as another of her husband's victims, but her family had connections to British headquarters in New York City, and Peggy was complicit in everything Arnold planned. They married on April 8, 1779, with Arnold barely able to stand at the altar because of his bad leg. The happy couple was already well into a scheme that was hardly trifling. It was meant to betray George Washington and destroy the American cause. And it was all for money.

From the start of the war, foreigners sought commissions in the American army, and George Washington found almost all of them bothersome. That was his first impression of the Marquis de Lafayette in August 1777 when they met at a Philadelphia dinner party. Washington was mildly dismayed to be introduced to what seemed a mere child with a preposterous rank. Lafayette was slim with a self-consciousness to his posture that caused him to stand very erect, possibly to make him seem taller than his five feet nine inches. He had sandy reddish hair, blue eyes, and a prominent slope to his forehead that made his hairline seem to be receding, even though he was only nineteen. Despite Lafayette's youth, the Congress had made him a major general because of "zeal, illustrious family and connexions."[5] Washington could see only a major headache in the move, another instance of politicians placating potentially influential foreigners rather than giving him competent officers. He could only imagine the reaction of his staff and of line officers such as General Nathanael Greene, who had clawed his way up from the lowly rank of private in a Rhode Island militia company.

Yet before the evening was through, Washington was no longer dismayed but profoundly confused. He had never met anyone like this young man. Lafayette had a charming modesty, a sort of clumsy eagerness, and a disarming desire to learn. When they parted that August evening after only a few hours, George Washington knew he had been in the company of a boy born into noble rank and high privilege and from a world alien to everything the Virginia farmer had ever known. But something had happened. If Lafayette as a toddler had padded along the halls of Mount Vernon, or had come bolting out of one of its stables spurring a young colt, or had pondered great questions while gazing from the piazza across the Potomac, or had grown to his current age in years spent under Virginia rather than French skies, it would have been just like this. To Washington, Lafayette was not a foreigner, his world was not alien, his horrible English was not strange.

Washington invited him to visit headquarters the next day. He would introduce him around and take him on an inspection tour of Philadelphia's batteries. Lafayette appeared early. He was wearing a uniform of his own purchase, a resplendent and colorful collation of braid and shiny buttons, which contrasted sharply with the shabby ordinariness of Washington's aides and the tattered condition of the army's officers, not to mention its rank and file, many of whom wore dirty linen hunting shirts. Washington awkwardly commented that it must not seem much of an army to one accustomed to the pomp and precision of Europe's military. Lafayette replied simply, "I've not come to teach but to learn." Perfect.

His name was Marie-Joseph-Paul-Yves-Roch-Gilbert du Motier, but Americans would always know him as the Marquis de Lafayette. The sole son of a soldier descended from a long line of soldiers, Lafayette was only two when his father was killed in the Battle of Minden in 1759. His mother died after a brief illness eleven years later. The boy was the inheritor of not just a title but of considerable estates and capital that gave him an annual income of 120,000 livres without his ever needing to touch the principal. Except for his money, however, nothing about him was particularly remarkable. He was enrolled as a military cadet and received the sort of education typical for martial nobility in France, which is to say, not very much in quality or quantity. Though still a child, he was shoved into an arranged marriage with a pleasant girl, also a child, so it is understandable that his home life was not marked by more than cordial affection. He remained awkward and clumsy, so stilted at formal balls that Marie-Antoinette and her ladies-in-waiting made him a figure of fun. He was bashful and often at a loss for words until an idea seized him. Then he would erupt in torrents of exclamations that gushed with exaggerated and flowery phrases, the sort of fellow who knocks over everyone's wineglass when gesticulating during a story. He had no military experience and owed his position as a garrison captain to his wife's influential family.

Lafayette had to overcome many obstacles to help America. King Louis XVI tried to stop Lafayette from traveling to America (possibly for show—it was before the French alliance), and the marquis used his own money for a down payment on a ship to transport him and several dozen adventurers to America. By the time he arrived in Philadelphia, foreigners armed with commissions and spouting braggadocio far beyond their talents had disgusted both the Congress and George Washington. Congressional leaders treated Lafayette so dismissively—his interview was conducted at curbside outside Independence Hall—that a less determined man would have gone home. Yet Lafayette persisted, and within three days the Congress had made him a major general in the Continental Army. Something the nineteen-year-old said had struck a chord. He had asked of America only two indulgences: to be allowed to serve in her army and not to be paid for it. The Congress sat stunned.

The tongue-tied boy often at a loss for words had found just the right ones.

The commission he received was merely honorary, and the Congress took him at his word about no compensation. Yet, Washington soon worried that Lafayette did not understand the terms of his commission. The young man outfitted himself with horses and uniforms and haunted headquarters, always quiet and modest but all ears and eyes. In due course, Washington wondered what the lad wanted and, more important, what he expected. What exactly had the Congress done? Washington asked, and Benjamin Harrison told him that the Congress had done nothing more than provide the young man with an honorific rank that did not have anything to do with a field command. Yet Lafayette had begun to offer his services, indicating that a command of any size would do.[6]

In the space of three months, Lafayette's earnestness and sincerity earned Washington's affection with a meaningful command soon to follow. At the encampment the day after their first meeting, Lafayette's humble statement about learning rather than teaching matched his humble message to the Congress, and from there it only got better. As the British moved on Philadelphia, Lafayette was at Washington's side helping to rally stragglers at the Battle of Brandywine when a bullet hit Lafayette's leg. Washington told the surgeons to take care of the young man is if he were his own son.

From then on, Lafayette moved above the jealousies and suspicions that older officers trained on one another, always managing himself without incurring their wrath or their displeasure. When the French alliance was announced in the spring of 1778, he became an official brother in arms for his American compatriots. He adopted American customs, including using his knife as a spoon, not using a napkin, and drinking from the same goblet as it was passed around.[7]

Benedict Arnold negotiated with British commander Sir Henry Clinton for sixteen months during 1779 and 1780 to hammer out a bargain grand enough to suit Arnold's pride and pocketbook. His initial tactics included small betrayals of Americans to show the British his "good faith" by providing bits of marginally useful information that were not significant enough to attract attention and could never be traced back to him. For his larger scheme, Arnold proposed to turn over the Hudson River citadel of West Point, the gateway to upstate New York because the river's sharp turn below it exposed vessels to devastating fire. Arnold's price for West Point was £20,000, an enormous sum but one the British would have found reasonable for the prize. If Clinton had West Point, he could isolate New England, open up interior lines of supply, and divide the rebellion to conquer it. To accomplish it, Arnold needed to place himself in a position to deliver West Point. It seemed strange to Washington that Arnold was insisting on a command at the remote post, but Arnold invoked his pathetic leg, and Washington relented.

Once in command on the Hudson, Arnold wasted no time in putting his betrayal in motion. He stripped West Point's defenses and scattered its garrison to make surrender a fait accompli. Everything in his plan nearly happened just as he wanted, but the arrest of his British contact and an unexpected inspection visit by Washington and his staff disrupted everything at the eleventh hour. Arnold escaped just before Washington arrived. Once the plot was uncovered, Washington sent Hamilton racing to arrest Arnold but it was too late. Arnold left Peggy and their infant son behind when he fled, but she would be fine. As Washington and his companions approached West Point the morning of the barely foiled treason, Lafayette had been eager to proceed to Arnold's residence, because he said breakfast was likely waiting. "Ah, Marquis," Washington had bantered, "you young men are all in love with Mrs. Arnold."[8] While Washington and his aides sorted out the particulars of the treason later that day, Peggy Arnold feigned madness so convincingly that Washington sent her home to her family without question. Not only the young men were susceptible to the lovely Mrs. Arnold.

Benedict Arnold did not deliver West Point, but the British rewarded him with some £6,000 pounds and reimbursements for his losses, and made his family pensioners. The British also commissioned him a brigadier general and sent him to Virginia with 1,600 soldiers where he commenced destructive raids that further confirmed his infamy for

Americans. Lafayette headed the force that pursued Arnold with orders to execute him immediately upon his capture. But the traitor was able to extricate himself and return to New York City unscathed and unrepentant.

Though George Washington maintained an even strain when he discovered Benedict Arnold's treachery, it had to jolt him more than any other event of the Revolution. In their obviously contrasting impact on Washington, Benedict Arnold and the Marquis de Lafayette shaped his thoughts in the future. One was the homegrown patriot he unwisely trusted, and the other was the earnest foreigner he grew to love. The stark difference between them became etched in Washington's consciousness and cast a shadow over the rest of his life. He must have pondered his incredible lapse of judgment about the man who should have cared but did not. He must have ruminated over his dismissive first impression of the man who had no reason to care but did.

Arnold was not just highly placed with delicate responsibilities in the American military cause; he was a hero to many. His devotion to the cause of independence proven with personal sacrifice on battlefields outside Quebec and in upstate New York, Arnold wore his loyalty to the Revolution in his crippling limp and his crutches. His treason cut to the core of everything the Revolution was about, touching as it did on civic virtue. Everybody, including George Washington, was shaken, even if he did not show it. Its significance larger than the man, Arnold's act left the troubling sense that civic virtue would never provide enough protection against opportunism and avarice. After the events of late 1780, men began to consider the need for a strong central government because, as James Madison would put it, men were not angels.

The ethereal concept of virtue was imperative, and George Washington supplied that in abundance for American patriots wary of power and suspicious of ambition.[9] A coin minted during the early years of the Republic conveyed the message. It featured George Washington in profile with the motto *"Non vi virtute vici."*[10] "I prevailed by virtue, not might." It had a resounding ring to it, and it could have been applied to Lafayette also as he stood with Washington while British pomp and arrogance at last lay humbled and bowed.

Lafayette was civic virtue personified. Like Lafayette, American soldiers had little or no experience as they leveled guns and stood their ground, but they had something better. They had the purity of good motives and the unyielding courage that comes with them. Armed with that, American victory was certified as a triumph of will and virtue, a miracle against all odds, a gift from the hand of Providence to a deserving people.

Lafayette returned to France in the 1780s to become an important reformer in the causes of abolition and religious toleration, a celebrated figure before the French Revolution began to tear at the flesh of celebrated men. In the halcyon days of victory and vindication, however, he visited Washington at Mount Vernon. That was in 1784, and for several glorious days they basked in each other's glow as father and son, home together again from long and separate journeys.

It was nonetheless a bittersweet visit, for Washington counted his years and measured the ocean as barriers to another meeting. When they parted, he said as much. "No, my dear general, our late parting was by no means a last interview," Lafayette wrote to him from the ship that was weighing anchor to take him back to France. Lafayette knew that Washington would never travel to France, "but to you I shall return."[11] He surely meant to, but he would not. Lafayette would never again stroll Mount Vernon's piazza with Washington. Yet neither would Lafayette ever leave his heart.

And neither would Benedict Arnold leave his memory. Among Americans who fought for independence, Arnold profited the most, and that was by trying to sell it out. There were other traitors, but Arnold's betrayal was unfathomable to Americans. Nathanael Greene muttered that "never since the fall of Lucifer has a fall equaled this," and Benjamin Franklin marked the traitor as "too base to be forgot." Yet it was Lafayette who found the best epitaph. When the British had placed Arnold on general staff in command of a brigade, Lafayette casually observed, "There is no accounting for taste."[12]

Washington would carry a scar for the rest of his days from Arnold's incident, although it would be for many years all but invisible. Eventually and most sadly, the wound would open again in due course, and Washington would see its cause to be another man he trusted. Another, better man would pay for Benedict Arnold's treachery, the man who had seemed rather like Lafayette but was abruptly revealed to be a prisoner of money, the man who was passively sitting at George Washington's dining table on the other side of the door as Timothy Pickering pointed and accused.

"To you," Lafayette had promised, "I shall return." He had never left. Neither had Arnold. Both of them were sitting at the dining table on the other side of that door.

The events that rapidly unfolded in the wake of Timothy Pickering's accusation did little credit to anyone. Randolph's shifting positions during the Constitutional Convention and ratification debates had earned him the reputation of a political chameleon willing to take the complexion of whatever company he found current. His reputation may have been fairly earned, but it unfairly dogged him as he tried to strike a balance between Hamilton and Jefferson's antagonism in Washington's first cabinet. Jefferson's anger about Edmund Randolph's supposed inconsistency was actually resentment over Randolph's perceived inconstancy to Jefferson's ideas. Jefferson had bitterly said unkind things about Randolph, always behind his back. While Randolph counted Jefferson a friend, Jefferson viewed him as something worse than a turncoat: a weakling. Jefferson told Washington that Randolph was a chronic debtor, implying that financial embarrassment could make Randolph prone to blackmail or bribery.

Oliver Wolcott shared Hamilton's disdain for Randolph, and for the same reason as Jefferson. Wolcott believed that Randolph's fairness was really weakness, that his careful consideration of each issue was not to discover what was best, but what was expedient. Pickering brought a unique smallness to the cabinet with his bitterness about having to pinch pennies. His childhood habit of childishly meddling in a spirit of self-righteous rectitude endured. He resented the soft-voiced mediocrity at the head of the State Department, a closet Republican whom Washington unwisely trusted. And George Washington, standing in his Philadelphia residence weary from his trip, listening to the stony-faced Pickering speak of treason, had to have flash through his memory

Alexander Hamilton clutching the papers that proved Benedict Arnold a traitor.

Pickering broke into an excited ramble to tell Washington a convoluted story. One of the letters from France's new minister Joseph Fauchet to his government had been captured when the British stopped the vessel and thwarted the customary method of tossing papers overboard by fishing them out of the water. The letter was sent to Lord Grenville, who forwarded it to George Hammond. On July 26, 1795, Hammond summoned Oliver Wolcott to his home and briefly summarized the letter's contents, a helpful précis for his guest who could not read French. Hammond was kind enough to give the letter to the Treasury secretary.[13] Fauchet had designated it as Dispatch no. 10.

Wolcott relied on Hammond's summary, which was provocative enough for him to rush to Pickering with the letter he could not read. They pooled their linguistic ignorance as Pickering quickly procured either a French dictionary or a French grammar book (accounts would differ) and set about translating the letter. He made a hash of it. His English version distorted French idioms and ignored Fauchet's nuance to produce convincing proof in Dispatch no. 10 that Edmund Randolph had sold Fauchet confidential government information. They also concluded that Randolph's odious relationship with Fauchet had caused Randolph to persuade Washington not to sign Jay's Treaty.

Wolcott and Pickering had to ignore compelling contrary evidence to reach these conclusions. Dispatch no. 10 said nothing about Jay's Treaty, having been written before the treaty was finalized, and Randolph had approved of Washington's intention to sign the treaty until the British revived the provision order. But the two sleuths congratulated themselves for uncovering Randolph's nefarious plot, and hatched a plan to unmask him. The first phase played out when Wolcott and Pickering went to Randolph on July 31, 1795, to have him write to Washington urging the president's return. Pickering had emphasized the necessity with his Delphic letter. The second phase was informing Washington, which Pickering did with barely veiled relish.

Washington listened in silence. He suggested that Pickering accompany him to the dining room. Randolph and Washington finished their meal. Randolph left with Pickering, and Wolcott timed his visit to miss them. In due course, he called on the president to present the original

Dispatch no. 10 with Pickering's translation. For hours, Washington studied the documents, but he, too, could not read French and had to trust the Pickering version, in which Washington found many troubling things. For instance, Pickering had interpreted Fauchet's reference to Randolph's *précieuses confessions* as meaning "precious confessions," which was logical for a schoolboy licking his pencil and thumbing through a foreign dictionary. But the phrase actually meant "valuable disclosures" and referred to information about British activities rather than anything confidential about the U.S. government. In another part of the dispatch, Fauchet told his superiors that Randolph believed Hamilton had maneuvered Washington into the rash suppression of the Whiskey Rebellion to increase the federal government's power.

Washington was to pass a fitful night pondering Dispatch no. 10. Parts of it seemed garbled beyond the bad translation. For example, Fauchet said that Randolph had enormous influence over Washington, but that seemed to contradict the notion of Hamilton as the master puppeteer in the administration. Just as strangely, it made little sense for Randolph to claim that Hamilton was responsible for excessive force in putting down the Whiskey Rebellion when Randolph himself had agreed to its suppression, had helped to arrange the militia response, and had never criticized the government's policy afterward. Finally, Fauchet's mention of money was quite vague and cited earlier dispatches (nos. 3 and 6) as providing a fuller explanation as to his meaning. If George Hammond had Dispatches no. 3 and no. 6, he did not show them to Wolcott.[14]

The next morning, Washington called a meeting of the entire cabinet. When it convened, Washington asked each man for an opinion about immediately signing Jay's Treaty. Pickering and Wolcott did not hesitate before saying yes, by all means, but Randolph was clearly puzzled. He repeated what he thought had been settled policy, that the president should wait until the British rescinded the obnoxious provision order. Washington seemed to mull the conflicting advice but suddenly announced that he would sign the treaty. He told Randolph to prepare the documents—work that would take several days. The secretary of state was surprised but did not protest. He left to begin the task.

In the days that followed, Washington and Randolph conferred on routine business with no hint of the president's suspicion intruding. On August 14, 1795, Washington visited Randolph's home to review the message they were sending with Hammond. Washington planned to inform Grenville that he was signing the treaty without Article XII and that he was unhappy about the provision order. Randolph followed these instructions, and Washington had Randolph attend a formal dinner that afternoon at the presidential residence. The event occurred without a trace of any change in George Washington's attitude toward Edmund Randolph. Finally, the secretary of state had everything ready for the formal signing of the treaty on August 18. After Washington had placed his name on the document, he invited Randolph to a convivial dinner that afternoon.

The next morning, Randolph rose early to prepare for a 9 A.M. appointment with Washington. In town at his office in plenty of time, he was about to leave for the presidential residence when Washington's steward appeared. The president wanted Randolph to wait until 10:30. Randolph worked at his office and arrived at Washington's door right on time. A servant took him to Washington's office, telling him that Wolcott and Pickering were already with the president. Randolph was surprised. He did not know there was to be a cabinet meeting. He entered and exchanged pleasantries with everyone. Their responses were cool. With a grim face, Washington handed Randolph papers. "Mr. Randolph," he said, "here is a letter which I desire you to read, and make such explanations as you choose."[15]

Edmund Randolph was the only man in the room who could read French. His head was bowed over Fauchet's dispatch for a few minutes before he looked up, puzzled. He seemed to think that the need was for a translation of a document nobody but he could decipher. He explained the section that vaguely referred to money by reminding Washington how a year earlier they had heard about British plans to exploit discontent over the excise by luring western Pennsylvania from the Union. Randolph admitted that he could not be completely certain that Fauchet had meant that incident without seeing the other two dispatches mentioned in no. 10. He offered to go through the letter line by line and provide a written explanation of what he believed was meant in each instance.

Washington asked Wolcott and Pickering if they had any questions for Randolph. Wolcott certainly did. He curtly asked what Fauchet meant when he said that the British wanted to "destroy" certain people. By then, Randolph did not like the tone of the proceedings. He said that Fauchet obviously meant that the British wanted to damage certain people's ability to shape opinion. As Randolph was speaking, a servant appeared at the door, a normal occurrence when something required the president's attention. Washington stepped out of the room. Randolph broke the silence to ask Wolcott where the letter came from. Wolcott curtly said that Washington would tell him. Washington returned after a few minutes. He asked Randolph to wait in another room.

Randolph did not know that George Washington had meant the meeting to be an investigation but had clumsily allowed it to become an inquisition. The president had submitted a list of questions to Wolcott and Pickering to plan the best way to approach Randolph about the letter, but those very questions indicated he believed Randolph was guilty of something. It is likely that Washington was angered by Fauchet's insinuation that he was Hamilton's dupe, and possibly Randolph's as well. For their part, Pickering and Wolcott were early convinced Randolph was guilty of much more than boasting about his influence over the president. It is possible that after his lengthy study of Pickering's version of Dispatch no. 10, Washington was convinced that Randolph had betrayed him and the country. He asked Pickering and Wolcott the best way to remove Randolph from office if they found him guilty of selling information and influence, how the public should be informed, and how they could protect State Department files from a former secretary of dubious loyalty and vengeful intent.[16] These were questions posed by someone who had already come to a conclusion.

The result was a shameful episode, possibly the worst incident to mar an almost unblemished life. George Washington, in league with Oliver Wolcott and Timothy Pickering, became Randolph's inquisitor, proceeding from Pickering's flawed interpretation of a document that related an incomplete story even if it had been translated correctly. Randolph's understanding of French and his knowledge of what had actually passed between him and Fauchet made him so calm during the questions that he actually disappointed two of his accusers and might have relieved the one who counted. Before Randolph had arrived that morning, they had agreed to scrutinize his reaction as he read the letter, watching for the slightest sign of panic. With Randolph out of the room, they had to admit that he had not acted frightened or guilty. Yet waiting in a room by himself with time to brood over his treatment, Edmund Randolph gradually realized what everyone had been driving at. He of the soft voice and balanced temperament became so enraged he could barely talk. He did not just return to the room of his recent inquisition, he burst into it, glaring at the three men, two of whom he had tried to treat as colleagues and one he had always admired and revered more than anyone in the world. Washington asked Randolph when he could complete a written explanation. Randolph snapped that it would not take long, but without nos. 3 and 6, knowing Fauchet's mind was impossible. He would supply the explanation all right, he said, but not as secretary of state. Randolph fairly shouted he would not remain in the post "one second after such treatment."[17] He stormed out of the house and marched straight to his office, where he had a clerk lock it down so that he could not be accused of taking any papers. Edmund Randolph went home and heatedly penned his resignation. He had it delivered to President Washington the next day.

Randolph asked in his resignation that Washington keep the matter quiet, giving Randolph time to conduct an investigation to clear his name. This much Washington agreed to do.[18] Randolph set out for Newport, Rhode Island, where Fauchet was awaiting passage to France aboard the *Méduse*.

Nothing nefarious had happened between Edmund Randolph and Joseph Fauchet. The secretary of state had done nothing wrong except engage in some harmless gossip with the French minister. Except for George Washington, trading gossip with foreign diplomats was a common diversion for everyone in the government. As Randolph raced to Newport, he must have regretted greatly his participation in the seemingly innocuous pastime.

At Newport, the British had unwittingly done Randolph a favor.

HMS *Africa* lay off Newport ready to seize the *Méduse,* and the result was a delay that gave Randolph time to catch Fauchet, but just barely. Fauchet was not happy to see him, yet Randolph's unexpected fall from grace stirred Fauchet's pity, and the accusations Fauchet knew to be false offended his sense of justice. He agreed to write an exculpatory statement and have it ready for Randolph the following day. Randolph came to Fauchet's lodgings the next morning, but the Frenchman was not there. The captain of the *Méduse* had grabbed a chance to escape when a storm forced the *Africa* to put to sea. The French had sailed with Fauchet aboard. Randolph was near panic when the captain of the pilot boat that had escorted the *Méduse* to sea brought back a message. Fauchet's signed statement exonerating Randolph had been sent to the new French minister Pierre Adet. Randolph rushed back to Philadelphia and called on Adet. Sure enough, he supplied Randolph with not only Fauchet's statement but also true copies of the pertinent sections of Dispatches no. 3 and no. 6.[19]

Randolph was now able to piece together what Fauchet meant about money in Dispatch no. 10. It was just as he deduced. It pertained to his discussion with Fauchet about British attempts to split western Pennsylvania from the Union. Fauchet had told Randolph about British agents stifling pro-French sentiment in New York by threatening to call in debts owed London merchants. This was the money! Randolph had suggested that Fauchet arrange early payments to French supporters for flour he planned to purchase for his government. They could then pay off their British debts and be free to act as they wished. It was plainly clear that Randolph had never solicited money for himself.

Swirling rumors about the cause for his resignation prompted Randolph to publish all this information to clear his name. His *Vindication* of his conduct was to appear in a pamphlet, but with a lawyer's caution, Randolph wanted more information, particularly about the infamous Dispatch no. 10's chain of custody. He wrote Washington to ask when Grenville had obtained Dispatch no. 10, when Grenville had sent it to Hammond, when Wolcott had received it from Hammond, when Washington had first learned of it, and if he or anyone else had ever seen Dispatches no. 3 and no. 6. Washington's reply was in the main

formal and brief: He first saw Dispatch no. 10 on August 11; he had
never seen nos. 3 and 6; he knew nothing about Grenville's or Hammond's roles. And then George Washington dropped the formal reserve for just an instant as he closed. "No man would rejoice more than
I should," he told Randolph, "to find that the suspicions which have
resulted from the intercepted letter, were unequivocally, and honorably
removed."[20] There was no going back, though. These were the last letters with any semblance of cordiality between George Washington and
Edmund Randolph.

Randolph's anger had become his relentless master. His *Vindication*
was published that December, and its commentary was almost unhinged. Washington saw the pamphlet and was never more tremendous in his wrath. The documents Randolph included proved that he
had done nothing illegal, but his accompanying remarks attacked
Washington personally for taking part in his disgrace. That was most
regrettable. It would have been better for Randolph to publish the
documents with a slight exegesis rather than ventilate his personal
bitterness over Washington's actions. Randolph accused the president
of hypocrisy and duplicity for waiting an entire week after learning
of Dispatch no. 10 before confronting him, and even Washington's
most admiring biographers admit that the president's behavior was
uncharacteristically unfair and his attitude toward Randolph strangely
deceitful. Nevertheless, Edmund Randolph was to learn, as others
had and would, that there was no future in attacking George Washington.

The president's defenders descended in droves to pummel Randolph
in the press. They accused him of corruption, dishonesty, and for protesting too much, a sure sign of his misconduct. Hamilton wrote to
Washington that the *Vindication* was nothing more than an admission
of guilt.[21] Others cited Randolph's chronic money problems as "proof"
of his guilt. His friends grew distant, even if, like Jefferson, they believed his story. Jefferson refused to have his name linked to someone
who had publicly attacked George Washington.

Randolph survived the ordeal and would resume his successful legal
career, but for the rest of his life someone somewhere would always
remember, often imperfectly, that Randolph had left George Washing-

ton's administration under a cloud and that he had said unthinkable things about the idol. The mild odor of corruption hung about him as gossip endured that the need for money had soiled his soul. He could have noted the irony. Randolph had performed countless hours of personal legal work for the man who had cast him off but had never drawn up a bill and had never taken a penny.

Why did George Washington never concede that two second-rate political partisans had wrongly accused his most trusted and loyal adviser and most devoted friend? It would seem that at first Washington's anger also became his relentless master. Randolph's publishing private letters enraged Washington, but the *Vindication* made it impossible for the president to forgive, even if he no longer believed Randolph was a traitor. A fair reading of the documents properly translated showed that Randolph had never taken money from Fauchet. Yet there was also something else in Dispatch no. 10 that could have done worse than anger George Washington.

Randolph had gossiped to the French minister, but it was not, according to Fauchet, commonplace gossip. Fauchet said Randolph had talked about Washington in a demeaning way and had dismissed him as dull-witted, the dupe of Hamilton, or the pawn of Edmund Randolph. Nobody throughout the entire controversy seems to have examined Joseph Fauchet's possible motives for writing such things in Dispatch no. 10. Yet he very likely distorted Randolph's words for his own reasons: His sponsors the Jacobins had fallen from power that summer and the new government was questioning his performance; Fauchet's dispatches began exaggerating his influence with the American government in part by depicting Randolph as a confidant. Pickering's flawed translation that Washington first saw did not materially differ from the correct one in Randolph's *Vindication* in this regard, and Washington had to notice that.

Washington could never forgive attitudes that implied personal disregard, especially if they stemmed from a belief that he was wrong about something because he was too dense to understand it. He had revealed to Thomas Jefferson a concern that people would "conceive him too careless . . . or too stupid" to understand Hamilton's policies.[22] Washington could be quite touchy about this, and though his anger, like violent storms, would pass, the hurt of disregard always lingered. He never forgave Randolph. And thus, in the end, Edmund Randolph neither lived up to being Lafayette nor stooped to being Arnold. He had become an arrogant scholar talking out of school to a sniggering Frenchman. He had become George Mason.

23

"A Magic in His Name"

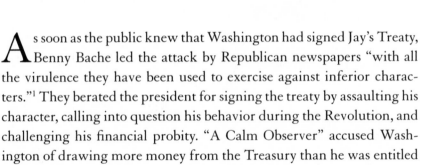

As soon as the public knew that Washington had signed Jay's Treaty, Benny Bache led the attack by Republican newspapers "with all the virulence they have been used to exercise against inferior characters."[1] They berated the president for signing the treaty by assaulting his character, calling into question his behavior during the Revolution, and challenging his financial probity. "A Calm Observer" accused Washington of drawing more money from the Treasury than he was entitled to, implying that Washington led a lavish lifestyle at the taxpayer's expense. Wolcott and Hamilton published refutations to show that presidential draws on the Treasury never exceeded his $25,000 annual salary. Wolcott suspected Randolph was "A Calm Observer," but the accuser was House clerk John Beckley, who had access to financial records.[2] The enemies had multiplied.

Washington had an abundance of defenders, but suddenly he was all alone in Philadelphia. He could ask Hamilton for advice, but Hamilton was in New York. Everyone else was gone, too. Lear was making a new life for himself in the federal district. Jefferson had seemed to leave even before departing for his mountaintop; Madison led the opposition; Randolph had been the last of his original coadjutors. Attorney General William Bradford had died during the Randolph controversy a month shy of his fortieth birthday, and though Washington was never particularly close to Bradford, the ordeal of replacing him became emblematic of an official family that was official but hardly familial. Future chief justice John Marshall refused to become attorney general, and Washington finally resorted to Light-Horse Harry's younger brother Charles Lee to fill the post.[3]

Replacing Randolph at the State Department proved almost impossible. Five people, including Patrick Henry, turned down the position. In the end, Washington turned to the acting secretary, Timothy Pickering, who behaved like a churl when he received the offer. Pickering felt himself badly used. He was irked that he had performed the duties at both State and War while Washington scoured the countryside looking for someone—anyone but Pickering, in fact—to head the State Department. He initially turned down the position, and Washington was forced to have Wolcott salve Pickering's wounded feelings. The president was finally able to talk the sour little man into taking the position. It must have been galling.

Pickering moving to State meant that Washington needed a new secretary of war. Everyone, again including Patrick Henry, refused him. Ultimately Washington asked his former aide James McHenry to take the post. He had been soliciting federal employment from Washington for years, but no one had ever considered McHenry as especially qualified for anything. "Mac" was born and raised in Ireland, came to America in 1771, and eventually studied medicine under Benjamin Rush. He served in the war, which Washington always noticed, but that was about all there was to notice. On General Washington's staff he was a pleasant but undistinguished colleague. At the end of the war, he was on Lafayette's staff, and Lafayette liked him immensely, but that confirmed only Mac's affability rather than talent; Lafayette liked everybody who was in the least likable. McHenry represented Maryland at the Constitutional Convention and supported ratification, and his friendship with Alexander Hamilton chugged along in the adequate way that bespoke all things McHenry. In fact, McHenry's nonabrasive temperament was his most sterling quality. Being pleasant and available had become the most important qualifications for service in Washington's cabinet.

This new (and final) official family was a collection of competence tempered by traces of mediocrity. Wolcott was the best of them, which speaks volumes. James Madison surveyed the executive branch with acute melancholy, because nobody but highly partisan Federalists now had the president's ear. He and Washington were still cordial, trading letters about nothing of importance and dining together at formal events, where Jemmy appeared with bubbly Dolley on his arm, a favorite of Martha's. But Madison told friends that talking to Washington about policy had become impossible. Washington told Pickering that he would never again make the mistake of appointing anyone who opposed his positions.[4] Madison did not know of the remark, but it would not have surprised him.

Despite his difficulties, Washington was determined to make his seventh annual message positive by emphasizing all that was right in America. All that was right did not necessarily include his new cabinet, though, for he did not ask Pickering and Wolcott for help with his address but turned to Hamilton. Washington told Congress on December 8, 1795, that the nation was prosperous, and was at peace with foreign neighbors as well as previously hostile Indians. He had unofficial word about Thomas Pinckney's successful negotiations with Spain for one claim, and Anthony Wayne's victory and subsequent treaty with the Miami and associated tribes for the other. The House and Senate commended the president for his superb performance in office, but many Republicans noted that Washington's picture of relations with Great Britain, a subject barely mentioned in the address, was too cheerful. The British were still interfering with American commerce, which Virginia senator Henry Tazewell believed should have been addressed before proclaiming the nation's "situation is prosperous."[5] Old heads criticized more in sadness than anger. When William Branch Giles grumbled that Jay's Treaty was nothing more than a bundle of errors, Jefferson told the young congressman that Washington "errs as other men do, but errs with integrity."[6]

Virginians were angry, though, and in December 1795 their General Assembly proposed constitutional amendments that sought to close the door after Jay's Treaty had escaped from the barn. One would have given the House of Representatives right of review for treaties that involved trade. Others proposed to halve Senate terms to three years and specifically ban federal judges from holding additional government positions, a slap at Jay as special envoy while remaining chief justice. Other states were not receptive to the proposals, but Virginia Republicans meant them as a warning that House Republicans intended to discuss the validity of the treaty itself when Washington finally placed it before them to ask for the money to implement it.[7]

Meanwhile, the treaty itself complicated Washington's appointment of John Rutledge to replace Jay as chief justice, which took place during the growing popular reaction to Jay's Treaty. Rutledge denounced Jay's Treaty in the strongest possible terms in a public address that some reported as including insults aimed at Washington. This last would have seemed unlikely to anyone who knew Rutledge, and Washington could hardly believe it. The two had long been friends. They had served in the Constitutional Convention together, and Washington had named Rutledge one of the original associate justices of the high court. Yet credible witnesses said Rutledge had been behaving oddly ever since his wife died in 1792.

By the fall of 1795, lurid stories about Rutledge's irrational behavior had created a strange coalition of senators worried about the dignity of the court and Federalists eager to punish an opponent of Jay's Treaty. Thus, for different reasons, a majority of the Senate was on course to block Rutledge's confirmation. Those senators possibly had Washington's tacit approval after he read Rutledge's offending speech. The Senate rejected him that December because some believed him "insane" but most "because he was unfriendly to the Treaty with England."[8]

Washington eventually turned to Federalist senator Oliver Ellsworth for the chief justiceship. As one of Connecticut's first senators, he was a reliable administration supporter and the architect of the Judiciary Act of 1789, which established the federal court system. Ellsworth was thoroughly qualified for the high court, yet John Adams lamented his departure from the Senate. It meant the "the firmest pillar of his [Washington's] whole administration" would be absent at a crucial time.[9]

Adams saw trouble coming. The administration would need a staunch Senate to balance the increasingly volatile House of Representatives. Although the House had been more than usually agreeable in its response to Washington's seventh annual message, Republicans had a large majority and were better organized than in years past. They could barely wait to get their hands on Jay's Treaty when it returned from the exchange of ratifications in London. Washington and his advisers were not at all sure what their opponents would do and how far they would go. A partial answer to those questions was disclosed when a House resolution to extend best wishes to the president on his sixty-fourth birthday was defeated 52 to 38. The House had behaved similarly the previous year, but the enormous margin in 1796 was a shock. As the country staged the usual birthday celebrations and Philadelphia "celebrated with unexampled splendor," the stark fact that fifty-two congressmen did not want to wish the president returns of the day had to cast a cloud.[10]

The treaty arrived from Great Britain ratified and with no mention of Article XII. While House Republicans wanted to begin the debates opposing the treaty right away, they could do nothing until Washington declared it in effect and laid it before them. Their urgency was not unfounded. The previous fall, publications criticizing the treaty and Washington were "read by the People with an astonishing avidity."[11] But at the time of Washington's annual message the treaty was being credited for growing prosperity. Republicans told themselves that waning criticism of the treaty was the result of "the astonishing exertions and artifices employed" by the Federalists, but that did not change the fact that waning criticism of the treaty indicated the Republicans were losing the public opinion battle.[12]

Fortune smiled on the Federalists. Before Washington proclaimed Jay's Treaty to be in force, Thomas Pinckney's Treaty of San Lorenzo and the treaty with Algiers arrived in Philadelphia. Both would be exceedingly popular. San Lorenzo was quickly dubbed Pinckney's Treaty and hailed as a triumph in all quarters. It established a permanent southern boundary between the United States and Spain at the thirty-first parallel, granted the United States navigation of the Mississippi, and established the right of deposit at New Orleans. In short, it resolved every western grievance with the federal government. The treaty with Algiers arranged for the United States to pay annual "tribute" in naval stores—protection payments that were exasperating but at least provided American merchants some safety from pirates in the Mediterranean.

Washington announced these two treaties a few days before he proclaimed Jay's Treaty in force on February 29, 1796. The House received it on March 1 and the following day at last revealed how far the Republican majority was prepared to go. New York congressman Edward Livingston called for Washington to turn over all documents related to the negotiations in London, including letters between Jay and the administration. Livingston was the much younger brother of the man who had administered the oath to George Washington at the first inaugural, and like his brother had become a Republican. Livingston held no brief for the conservative and respectful tactics of Madison and other old hands in the House, and while they were likely aware of the intent, if not the scope, of his confrontational resolution, it seems most veteran Republicans were not quite ready for it. Nevertheless, the debate was on.

Federalists pointed out that the treaty had been ratified by the Senate and signed by both the president and the king. The House had no constitutional role in this process in the first or last place, unless Republicans intended to impeach the president. Livingston responded with a shocking observation. Only the documents themselves, he said, could determine the necessity for impeachment proceedings. Federalists and Republicans alike sat stunned. After regaining their composure, older Republicans scurried to reign in the firebrand. Livingston finally agreed to temper his resolution to exclude documents that could impinge on current negotiations, and in that form it passed on March 25, 1796, by a vote of 62 to 37. It was a better margin for the Republicans—worse for Washington—than the birthday rebuke a month earlier.

Washington initially considered giving the House what it wanted, but after consulting with Pickering and his new attorney general Charles Lee, he paused. He also wanted Hamilton's opinion and soon received a detailed explanation of why executive compliance with this untoward demand from the legislature was out of the question. Hamilton prepared his critique expecting it to be used as Washington's response, but its late arrival forced the president to send the House only Pickering's remarks with Lee's minor editorial changes. Because it was an emphatic "no," the Republicans assumed it had come from Hamilton's pen. Madison had privately disapproved of Livingston's tactics, but Washington's response was "as unexpected, as the tone & tenor of the message, are improper & indelicate."[13] The development was interesting in the way that peculiar misunderstandings can be. Pickering and Lee's creation was not different from Hamilton's in substance, but the arguments were framed less delicately, as Madison noticed. Pinning the blame on Hamilton, however, resurrected a convenient bugbear that could, like the ritualized scapegoat, deflect the direct responsibility for improper and indelicate remarks from George Washington.

Washington agreed with those remarks, though, and obviously found their force appropriate. It was the first instance of invoking executive privilege, something considered when Congress had wanted documents relating to the disastrous St. Clair expedition, but Washington had supplied information at the time. Madison had, in fact, tried to have Livingston shape his request for documents to conform with that earlier instance by allowing Washington to select the material he would provide, but the House refused to approve the alteration. Madison's moderation eroded his influence as a Republican leader and forced him to fall in line with the more radical arm of the party or risk being shoved completely to the sidelines.

In his response, Washington instructed the House that because it had no constitutional role in treaty making, he was under no obligation to supply them with any documents related to any treaty's negotiations and consequently would not relinquish papers about Jay's Treaty.[14] Executive privilege is a necessary constitutional safeguard, and the Washington administration was on firm constitutional ground when it protected communications between the president and any correspondent. Subjecting such documents to congressional review would subordinate the executive to the legislature, tilting the constitutional balance of coequal branches of government. Yet, executive privilege is an awkward political device, because its invocation invites speculation about why the president does not want Congress to see documents, speculation that almost always tends to bolt past the generality of a constitutional safeguard to dwell on the specifics of a particular controversy.

Republicans saw the negotiation and ratification of Jay's Treaty as having produced something more than a disagreeable agreement with Great Britain. Rather, it was a process "viewed as a means of strengthening the Executive department of the Government." Republicans were concerned that "the disposition to accumulate power in the hands of that Department [the presidency] is formidable, and [has] now become very serious." If allowed to proceed unchecked, where would it stop, and what would be the consequences? "If from the doubtfulness of the extent of their power, danger is reasonably to be apprehended of its swallowing up the powers of the other departments . . . it is high time to amend & explain the Constitution in this particular." Jay's Treaty was more than it appeared to be: "That such danger does exist, the British Treaty affords the most striking evidence."[15]

People with these fears either did not see or did not care that Washington's refusal to comply with the House request was constitutionally acceptable and perhaps even necessary. They were interested in stopping the treaty as a means to curb executive power, and to that end Republicans continued the debate. They intended to insert themselves in the process by refusing to fund those parts that required appropriations, such as the commissions that were to resolve issues not covered in the treaty.

Madison had little choice in tagging along with the more radical Republicans in the House lest he be left behind, but Federalists bellowed that he had crossed a line in doing so. And so he had, even if not altogether willingly. Federalists insisted that Madison had to know that blocking the treaty in the House proceeded from no constitutional authority.[16] Though events pulled at Madison, his enemies—including Hamilton—insisted he was directing them. He was the architect of a campaign whose success meant "the Constitution would at once vanish!"[17] By early April 1796, the Federalist perception, once false, was at last accurate. Madison had decided to block the treaty.

The day after Washington invoked executive privilege, the House voted to debate the president's message. It was essentially an announcement that they had the right to consider the treaty itself. Republicans had the votes to defund the treaty, and Federalists scrambled to thwart them. They pondered the bundling of all three treaties—British, Spanish, and Barbary—in the hope that the popular Spanish and Algerine agreements would quash objections to Jay's. Federalists consulted with Hamilton about the strategy, and he adamantly opposed it because it accepted the principle that the House had a right to pass judgment on treaties. Hamilton knew what this was all about at its base, and he must have winced that Federalists were prepared to surrender a principle for a policy. Political battles could be won that way, but never philosophical wars. Protecting principle was key; policy would follow, in due course.

Left with little else, the Federalists stalled by keeping the House debate alive for weeks while they used their newspapers and pamphleteers to flood the country with glowing predictions of prosperity if the treaty were funded and equally dire projections of ruin if it were not. War with Great Britain was inevitable if the treaty failed, they said. To galvanize business discontent, they pressured insurance companies not to underwrite voyages and banks not to extend credit to merchants who traded overseas. When petitions from merchant groups began to mount in the House—some from people who had originally opposed the treaty—Republicans wavered.[18]

And then came April 28, 1796, a day in the House of Representatives that would be remembered by Federalists as long as they had banquets for heroes and gave trophies to champions. Virginia congressman Francis Preston had just finished criticizing the treaty, and Fisher Ames rose to rebut not just Preston but every word uttered against Jay's Treaty.

Some claimed that the Massachusetts Federalist was the most brilliant orator of his generation, which could be dismissed as an exaggeration except for the fact that he was likely the most brilliant orator in the House of Representatives until it saw the likes of Henry Clay almost two decades later. During the early part of the debate on Jay's Treaty, only illness could silence the Federalists' ablest advocate. As the frail figure stood and tried to catch his breath, members of the Senate began filling the House galleries and were soon joined by the Supreme Court. Associate Justice James Iredell settled in next to Vice President Adams. When Ames began, his weak, raspy voice gradually took on resonance and power.

Then he hit his stride. Biting wit speared what he portrayed as the Republican hypocrisy of claiming to be guardians of the Constitution while unconstitutionally meddling in the nation's diplomacy. As the speech arced and ebbed, he finally took it to its emotionally logical conclusion by raising the specter of war, describing frightened mothers rocking cradles, their nights long and tense, the war cry of Indians their greatest terror—Indians loosed by Britons stubbornly ensconced in America's frontier posts, their pledges in Jay's Treaty to leave made meaningless for the want of a few dollars. Ames concluded and fell into his chair. In the brief silence before the raucous applause, a gasping voice blurted out, "My God! How great he is!"[19] It was Iredell talking to Adams, but it was the cue to bring the house down in a House of Representatives that had seen something rare and irresistible.

The Committee of the Whole voted the next day with ten of Madison's most reliable men changing their minds to vote with the Federalists. The result was a 49 to 49 tie. Speaker of the House Frederick Muhlenberg broke it in favor of the treaty. His motives stemmed from principle rather than policy. Muhlenberg feared a constitutional crisis and explained himself privately that the House could still defund the treaty if it chose.[20] The final vote occurred the next day with 51 to 48 in favor of the treaty, which was followed by a vote to fund it. Petitions from wounded parties, threats by banks and insurance companies, and oratorical lightning in the well of the House had combined to give the Federalists a victory against overwhelming odds. The treaty would stand.

The body count after the battle was sobering. One casualty was Muhlenberg, who never recovered his political status and was forsaken by Republican supporters in Pennsylvania who refused to renominate him for his House seat. It was an epic fall for a Speaker of the House, but even that was not the greatest humiliation. Muhlenberg's brother-in-law attacked him with a knife, over his tie-breaking vote it was said.[21] Muhlenberg survived the stab wound, as did the stories of its political motivation, even though it's likely his assailant was insane and spurred by "private motives."[22]

Fisher Ames, on the other hand, would be lionized. Washington saw the House vote on the treaty as a referendum on his foreign policy, and the conclusion of the episode was more than gratifying. After Congress adjourned, Ames planned a trip to the federal district, and knowing that Washington's calendar would keep him in the capital, Ames wondered if he could tour Mount Vernon in his absence. Washington immediately wrote to his farm manager with instructions to give Fisher Ames anything he wanted, including the most lavish hospitality of the house. It was the closest George Washington came to giving a trophy to a champion, the least he could do for the man who had done so much for him.[23]

★ ★ ★

Lafayette's son bore his father's looks and the name of his father's best friend. When Henry Knox and George Cabot wrote the president separate letters telling him that sixteen-year-old Georges Washington Motier de Lafayette had arrived in Boston with his tutor Felix Frextel, Washington's first impulse was to have the boy and Frextel come to Philadelphia to live with him. But they were exiles, and since he had refused to meet with other French refugees, Washington struggled with the conflict between duty and conscience. With young Lafayette he remained wary about violating neutrality by extending hospitality to anyone fleeing the French Revolution. He had asked Hamilton for advice when the House passed a generous resolution calling for financial aid for the boy, and Washington's mind was eased a bit. Before extending the invitation, he asked Madison for advice as well. At last, Washington invited the boy, and he settled into the presidential household. The sight of him became a daily reminder of his father's plight, and soon Washington was quietly trying to open channels of communication with Emperor Francis II of Austria to secure the release of the marquis.[24]

The president's household was happy that summer in 1796. Young Lafayette and his tutor became part of the family, the controversy over Jay's Treaty was finally at an end, and everyone looked forward to a long sabbatical at Mount Vernon. There was even a breath of fresh air from an unexpected quarter. The new British minister Robert Liston and his charming wife, Henrietta, arrived in New York and soon came to Philadelphia to take up his duties. They were Scots by heritage, she the heiress of a West Indies merchant, and newlyweds. Liston was almost fifty-four and a confirmed bachelor when he met Henrietta, who was a bit younger but hardly a child, being in her forties when he courted her. Liston was a veteran of the British diplomatic service with postings from Munich to Madrid to Stockholm to Constantinople, but he had finally grown lonely in faraway places with no one to share them with, and in Henrietta he had found a bonnie lass after his own heart. The Atlantic voyage had been a dreadful affair with storms and towering waves. Henrietta found it bracing.

They made a jolly couple, a good antidote to the grating, scheming George Hammond, and the Washingtons thought them delightful. The president and Liston both loved to farm and never tired of talking about the latest innovations. Henrietta was soon enchanting Philadelphia society, rather like Dolley with a lilting burr. She thought Washington was fascinating, but "gaiety was not natural to him." Nevertheless, "there is a Magic in his name more powerful in this Country than the Abilities of any other man can ever acquire." Washington invited them to Mount Vernon.[25]

The Listons' affability marked a thaw following the treaty in official British attitudes that began appearing in private ones as well. Thomas Twining, a British colonial official who had recently served under Lord Cornwallis in India, called at the presidential residence on May 13, 1796, but Washington was busy. Martha, however, sat Twining down to hear details about his recent visit to the federal district, especially about his meeting Martha's granddaughter Elizabeth Parke Custis Law. In the middle of their conversation, Washington walked into the room. Martha announced, "The president," as they both stood. Only a couple of years before George Hammond's secretary had penned snide descriptions of George Washington as vain, pompous, and ordinary. Twining saw the polar opposite in "the impressive dignity of his person" but also "the benevolence of his countenance and the kindness of his address." Twining marveled at how "so completely did he look the great and good man he really was." Washington asked about Lord Cornwallis and inquired about conditions in India, giving Twining the better part of an hour for pleasant conversation on that mid-May morning that would forever remain among the "most memorable days" of Twining's life. It was a remarkable interlude in many ways. Twining did not realize that the thaw was evident in George Washington, too. When Washington was first introduced to him, Twining saw "the tall, upright, venerable figure of this great man advancing toward me to take me by the hand."[26] George Washington never shook hands.

24

"Friends and Fellow Citizens"

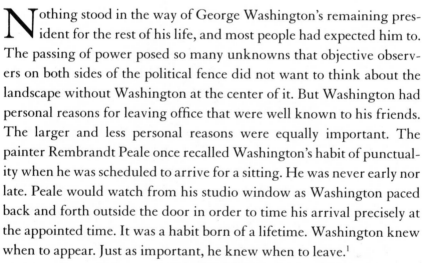

Nothing stood in the way of George Washington's remaining president for the rest of his life, and most people had expected him to. The passing of power posed so many unknowns that objective observers on both sides of the political fence did not want to think about the landscape without Washington at the center of it. But Washington had personal reasons for leaving office that were well known to his friends. The larger and less personal reasons were equally important. The painter Rembrandt Peale once recalled Washington's habit of punctuality when he was scheduled to arrive for a sitting. He was never early nor late. Peale would watch from his studio window as Washington paced back and forth outside the door in order to time his arrival precisely at the appointed time. It was a habit born of a lifetime. Washington knew when to appear. Just as important, he knew when to leave.[1]

As early as February 1796, Washington had told Hamilton he planned to retire rather than stand for reelection. He intended to issue a statement as he had planned when considering retirement in 1792. It was to be a valedictory address assessing his presidency and giving advice for the future. Washington liked much of what Madison had prepared for him four years earlier, and he wanted Hamilton to help him update that document. He also told John Adams in confidence over a private dinner about his plan to retire. The number of people Washington was telling about his decision called into question the level of its secrecy. Gouverneur Morris was still in Europe but noted rumors about the matter in his diary that February. Martha Washington giddily spoke about her impending return to private life at social events throughout the spring.[2]

On May 8, 1796, Washington wrote two letters, one to John Jay explaining the resolve to retire and the other to Hamilton repeating the request for help. A week later he sent Hamilton a draft he had been working on that included the text of Madison's 1792 version. Washington carefully placed Madison's parts in quotation marks with attribution. He again told Hamilton he liked the Madison draft and wanted it included in the final document. Hamilton was to apply his editorial skills to produce a complete address.

That June, Hamilton traveled to Philadelphia and discussed with the president what he had written so far. During this visit, Kentucky senator John Brown asked Hamilton about rumors that Washington planned to resign, and Hamilton told him that the stories were not true. He should have let the matter drop at that. Instead, he said that Washington planned to refuse reelection and would be issuing an address to announce that before the election. Brown told House clerk John Beckley who immediately wrote to James Madison.[3] Secrecy has always been a rare commodity in politics.

That was proven with a vengeance during Washington's stay at Mount Vernon that summer. In Philadelphia someone gave Benny Bache the list of questions Washington had submitted in writing to each member of the cabinet in the spring of 1793. At the time, the cabinet was discussing how best to preserve American neutrality at the start of the war between France and Great Britain, which meant the matter was old but not outdated. With the war still very much on, France was smarting over the implications of Jay's Treaty, and when Bache published the questions in the *Aurora* it revived an old controversy to amplify a new one. Worse, the questions revealed how the Washington administration considered and discarded contingencies. Thomas Jefferson at Monticello read the exposé in the *Aurora* with a mounting sense of dread. He assumed Washington would suspect him of being Bache's source.

He immediately wrote the president denying any part in the messy business. Washington replied noncommittally. Others had mentioned that Jefferson was saying "derogatory" things about him, Washington said, but he assured Jefferson that his "answer invariably has been, that I had never discovered any thing in the conduct of Mr. Jefferson to raise suspicions, in my mind, of his insincerity." Washington insisted that he still considered political parties a bane and that he wished he could "reconcile them." It was the last meaningful written communication between George Washington and Thomas Jefferson. The letter ended with the president abruptly changing the subject to agricultural pursuits.[4]

Washington was less sanguine about this incident than he let on. He wrote David Humphreys that "these attacks, unjust and unpleasant as they are, will occasion no change in my conduct" except to increase his determination to retire.[5] Humphreys could only surmise how bad it had gotten. Timothy Pickering had stopped Randolph's practice of sending diplomats newspapers representing all political views, with the result that embassies and consulates only received the Federalist press.[6] Yet it was true that the relentless attacks had begun to wear Washington down, giving him "a slight air of moroseness." When he was at Mount Vernon that summer, the arrival of every new dispatch or bundle of newspapers opened wounds, making him regret that he "did not publish my valedictory address the day after the Adjournment of Congress."[7] The attacks had to start changing the sentiments of citizens. "Drops of Water," sighed Washington, "will Impress (in time) the hardest Marble."[8]

As much as it could under these circumstances, the prospect of permanently returning to Mount Vernon buoyed his spirits. Tobias Lear came to the house that summer after Fanny died, a man now shrouded in chronic sorrow but, like Washington, drawing strength from the place he, too, more or less called home. Washington treated young Lafayette "more as his child than as a guest."[9] Happy family scenes unfolded one upon another that July. British architect Benjamin Latrobe arrived one day with a letter of introduction from Washington's nephew Bushrod. The architect lately lived in Richmond, but he felt like he was really at home as soon as he knocked on Mount Vernon's door.

Washington at first showed his customary reticence and was aloof but cordial as they talked about agriculture, canals, and weather. Latrobe thought his host had "an air of reserve in his manner," and the "extreme correctness of his language . . . almost seemed studied." Then the transformation resembled an opening flower. As the hours passed, Latrobe was folded into the family. He saw in Washington "something uncommonly majestic and commanding in his walk, his address, his figure, and his countenance." When Latrobe met Nelly Custis, he lost his heart. She was seventeen and, to his eyes, flawless. "More perfection of form, of expression, of color, of softness, and of firmness of mind," he hymned, "than I have ever seen before or conceived consistent with mortality."[10]

At dinner Washington exchanged "a few jokes" with young Lafayette, something that never happened at formal dinners in Philadelphia. "He seemed to enjoy a humorous observation," recalled Latrobe, "and made several himself." Washington even "laughed heartily several times in a very good-humored manner." Washington insisted Latrobe stay the night, and when the architect left Mount Vernon, the president treated him "as if I had lived for years in his house, with ease and attention."[11] Benjamin Latrobe in the summer of Washington's satisfaction saw something few people outside a small circle ever witnessed. Drops of water could erode marble the way the newspapers could scar a president. But at Mount Vernon, George Washington was neither stone nor statesman. He was a man.

In response to Jay's Treaty, French privateers began preying on American merchant ships. One American vessel, ironically named *Mount Vernon,* was taken just off the coast of Delaware. Reports of this plundering coincided with Pickering's estimation of James Monroe as increasingly ineffective in his relations with the French government. Yet the treaty had placed Monroe in an awkward position. From the start of Jay's mission, Monroe had assured the French that any agreement with London would not harm their interests. When the treaty's terms were revealed, the clause that granted Great Britain most-favored-nation status alone made Monroe look like either a liar or a fool. Monroe persevered in trying to persuade the French that Jay's Treaty was harmless, but it was no use.

Pickering despised Monroe—the people Pickering despised would have made a long list—and he seems to have let his prejudice color his communications with Washington about their minister to France.

Washington had his own reasons to find fault with Monroe, including France's increasingly hostile reaction to Jay's Treaty, but he was also aware that Pickering was trying to bias his views.[12] And Pickering had a point; Monroe was not completely blameless in his conduct toward his own government. He had allowed the publication of a letter in which he was openly critical of the treaty. Worse, he wrote directly to Washington to chastise him for writing a personal letter to Gouverneur Morris that the French government had intercepted. Only Monroe's skewed compass could match his impertinence: Rather than criticize a man for writing a private letter, he should have condemned the French for reading it. By July, Washington had seen enough of this sort of thing, but even if Monroe's behavior had been flawless, it is doubtful he would have survived after Washington consulted with Hamilton and Jay. The president told Pickering to recall him.[13]

Washington first offered the position to John Marshall, who refused, a circumstance lately so common that Washington enclosed a proffer to Charles Cotesworth Pinckney with instructions for Marshall to forward it to South Carolina in case he refused the post.[14] Pinckney accepted. As his brother, Thomas, made plans to return from Europe, Charles Cotesworth sailed for Philadelphia with his wife and youngest daughter to receive his instructions. They were friends of the Washington family, and the attachment suggested a return to the old days of geographical, personal, and political balance that had been missing from many appointments in the second term. It was a shame that the Pinckneys were headed to Paris.

They soon had reason to think so, too. After Charles Cotesworth received his instructions from Pickering and the president, the Pinckney family commenced a voyage to France that could have been seen as an ominous omen of things to come. Violent storms were the least of their troubles. The ship's captain became so erratic that Pinckney had to foment a mutiny led by the first mate to save the vessel. When they finally arrived at Bordeaux, they found their carriage in disrepair. Its overhaul gave them time to tour the city and soak up some of the culture. At the theater, they encountered more culture than they bargained for. Mary figured out that she was sitting next to "two ladies of pleasure."

The Pinckneys finally arrived in Paris on December 5, 1796, and found Monroe angry over the treatment by his government but cordial to fellow Americans, a philosophical approach that perhaps recalled the sanguine attitude of Gouverneur Morris when he faced the same situation. In any case, as Morris had done for him, Monroe escorted Pinckney to his first meeting with the French government. He then took his family to Holland, where they would wait for spring weather to arrive before returning to the United States.[15]

Pinckney was on his own, and things that were bad at his first meeting with the French soon turned worse. They initially refused to receive him. Several weeks later they told him they never would. Shortly after these inhospitable gestures, Pinckney was menacingly told to leave the country. He did not have to be told twice. The Pinckneys thus followed the Monroes to Holland to await instructions from home. In Philadelphia, relations with Pierre Adet had also collapsed in retaliation for Jay's Treaty, a disorder provoked by neither Monroe nor Pinckney. The French issued a decree to treat all neutral trade as Britain did, which was to define only allies as "neutral." Aimed primarily at the United States, the decree authorized the French navy and privateers to seize American cargoes meant for British ports. Adet was to announce the new French policy, express extreme displeasure over Jay's Treaty, and suspend diplomatic relations with the American government.

Adet thought French anger could influence the upcoming presidential election, and he timed his announcements and their mode of delivery accordingly. He sent his letter not only to Pickering at the State Department but to Bache at the *Aurora*. These developments had the look of a crisis, prompting Washington to leave his family at Mount Vernon and return to Philadelphia. Adet's communication to the State Department was troubling, but his publication of it in a newspaper was a major embarrassment. Washington immediately wrote Hamilton for advice, but for once Hamilton did not promptly respond. Time being of the essence, Pickering was allowed to publish his caustic response to Adet. Soon these exchanges appeared in newspapers throughout the country.[16]

Hamilton saw what the blinkered advisers in the cabinet could not. Adet's primary purpose in publishing his announcement in the *Aurora* was to influence the selection of presidential electors in Pennsylvania. It was Pickering who had turned it into a national spectacle. Washington generally disapproved of using the press in this manner, but he had been pressed for time. When Hamilton did write in the wake of Pickering's publication, he expressed reservations about publishing official correspondence. In this instance, he thought Pickering's letter was remarkably ham-fisted, but that damage was already done. As Hamilton suspected, however, more was on the way.

Adet's response revealed more diplomatic shambles. He informed Americans that he would no longer correspond with their government because he was no longer the French minister. Hamilton quickly advised Washington not to allow anyone to respond to Adet ever again. Instead, the president should write a measured letter to Pinckney in Europe explaining the American position and provide a copy to Congress. That was how seasoned professionals made government statements available to the public. Washington told Pickering to draft the letter, but he heavily edited it before sending it to Hamilton for his review. Only then did Washington dispatch it to Pinckney and Congress. The president needed a seasoned professional more than ever. In the space of months he had had enough domestic and diplomatic dislocations to last a lifetime.[17]

Before the storm over Adet, Washington had put the finishing touches on his Farewell Address and had Lear deliver it to the newspaper he had chosen for its appearance, *Claypoole's American Daily Advertiser*. With Hamilton he had decided that the best time for publication was approximately two months before presidential electors were chosen across the country. Hamilton hoped to the last minute that the delay would give Washington time to change his mind. It had not mattered.

How much of this creation that generations of schoolchildren would memorize was from the mind of George Washington or Alexander Hamilton or James Madison or even John Jay? Part of the question is easy to answer. The sentiments belonged to George Washington. Even ideas framed by Madison in 1792 were Washington's in the beginning and at the end. Madison had fashioned them into polished prose, and that was what Hamilton did in 1796. Four more years of experience had rounded out Washington's attitudes, particularly about foreign affairs, which had dominated the second term and left him embittered toward

France and estranged from parts of America. Hamilton seasoned the draft with his pepper, but the dish was Washington's. He meant every word of the advice (hold fast to the Union; understand and revere the Constitution; preserve "religion and morality"); of the warnings (there are people, foreign and domestic, who will try to break the nation apart, political parties being perhaps the biggest danger); of his greatest unease (that foreign interference and "the spirit of party" would subvert all that they had worked so hard to build).

Washington never used the words "entangling alliances" as something to avoid; those were Jefferson's a half decade later in his first inaugural address. Washington instead warned about "permanent alliances" that would tie the nation to foreigners long after their interests and aims had diverged from America's. It was plainly advice stemming from his exasperating experience with France, but he meant something broader in application and more enduring as a principle. Washington had found himself comfortable with Jefferson and Hamilton because, like him, they had always understood the difference between principle and policy, even when violently disagreeing about the latter from a profound understanding of the former. The enduring principle should always be reflected in the ever-adjustable policy. The country's own interests rather than ad hoc policies born of expedience—or, worse, of sentimentality—should always guide the United States.[18]

The ideas were his, but as with almost everything in Washington's life, the Farewell Address was a collaborative effort, and not only with the authors of various drafts. It was the product of the people and their words and their ideas that had influenced him from youth onward. His father's industry and risk, his mother's flinty and unpleasant resolve, his older half brother's heedlessness and its consequences, Sally's affection, Martha's love, Lafayette's devotion—on and on, and more unnamed but remembered, down through the seasons of youth, hope, ascent, achievement, disappointment, loss, and finally farewell. They all had a part in this, but as with all important tasks Washington moved at his own pace and toward his own destination. When he had received Hamilton's final draft, he sat down and painstakingly wrote it out in his own hand to make numerous stylistic and substantive changes. When he finished, he had thirty-two pages of quarto letter paper "with many

Alterations," expunged paragraphs, and interlined notations, all in his hand.

Lear summoned the publisher David Claypoole, who found Washington sitting in his drawing room. They discussed the schedule for publication, and Lear soon delivered the manuscript to Claypoole's office. The printer knew the subject of the manuscript from his and Washington's discussion, but as he set the type he realized that he was reading something worth remembering. He returned to Washington several times with galleys to proofread before readying the final printing and taking the original manuscript back to the president. Claypoole said he hated to part with the pages because he had grown so attached to them. Washington casually told him to keep the manuscript. It is now lost.[19]

On September 19, 1796, Washington rose early as always. Not too much later that morning, he stepped into his carriage and rode out of town toward Virginia and Mount Vernon, where he would rest for a couple of weeks. As Washington's carriage rattled southward, Philadelphia opened its copies of *Claypoole's American Daily Advertiser.* On the second page there was a small headline: "To the PEOPLE of the United States." Below that was the opening line of a long column, "Friends and fellow Citizens."[20] Even with all the rumors, most people were surprised as they read, but even those certain of Washington's plans had cause to sit down if standing, to look up and away for a moment after they realized what they were reading. There had always been the chance that he had not meant it, or that he would reconsider, as he had in 1792. Seeing his decision in type made it seem final and irreversible.

From this distance and given the subsequent sanctity of Washington's Farewell Address, it is surprising that Republicans so quickly attacked it in both their private letters and their newspapers. It was, they said, a partisan document meant to influence the upcoming election for the Federalists. Though that was not Washington's primary purpose, the Republicans were partly correct. Washington always agreed with the Federalist desire for a strong central government and a neutral foreign policy, but he had also come to believe that Republican dissent from the government and criticism of him were signs of disloyalty. His attack on the corrosive spirit of party in the Farewell Address was a swipe at those activities that was buried amid eternal principles meant to steer the government along a correct path. The address then was both a political document for the present and a guiding doctrine for the future.

At least one Republican overlooked the one as the expression of a proud and angry man grown old in the service of his country; he valued the other as a shining moment. Thomas Jefferson knew immediately as he read and pondered Washington's words that he was holding something remarkable. Like the ringing phrases in the Declaration of Independence that Jefferson had penned twenty years before, the Farewell Address soared when it was supposed to, a remembrance of when they had all been proud and angry men.[21]

Perceptions of politics in the Farewell Address whipped the election campaign of 1796 into full tilt. John Beckley complained that Washington had waited until September to announce his retirement to help John Adams as the presumptive Federalist candidate for the presidency. Beckley was wrong, of course, but he had known enough about Washington's plans to organize Jefferson's supporters in Pennsylvania, just as Republican operatives were doing in every state where he stood a chance. If anything, Washington had done them a favor by allowing them to pursue the prize far more openly after it was clear he would not be available for reelection.

Washington seldom mentioned the election. The one exception to this otherwise inviolable aloofness was his obvious disgust over the meddling of Pierre Adet, but he was not alone in that.[22] Madison and other Republicans also disapproved of Adet's unseemly attempts to interfere with the election, partly from the fear that his pro-Republican statements would drive citizens to vote for Federalists.

While Washington seemed to ignore the election, those around him talked of little else. Hamilton led the Federalist wing that was secretly opposed to Adams because of uncertainty about his commitment to Federalist principles. Since spring they had been casting around for alternatives, even considering Patrick Henry, but could persuade none to stand for election. They were forced to settle on Adams, with Thomas Pinckney as his second. Attempts to manipulate the Electoral College— by Hamilton, it was presumed—into elevating Pinckney over Adams were blocked by Adams men who discovered the trickery and refused to cast a vote for Pinckney. The result surprised everybody, especially Hamilton.

Republicans had no such chicanery to deal with because they had no doubts about their candidate. They wanted Thomas Jefferson despite his insistence that his retirement was final. To pull votes from all-important New York and neighboring northern states, they selected Senator Aaron Burr to stand as Jefferson's second. James Madison did not give Jefferson a chance to refuse recruitment. Madison simply did not talk to him about the election until after it was over.

Madison and Beckley managed the campaign, though not in a modern sense. John Beckley most closely resembled a campaign operative of today. His work in Pennsylvania, the only place he could regularly reach, probably gave that state to Jefferson. Using Philadelphia printers, Beckley had handbills printed by the thousands listing the Republican electors.[23] Otherwise, candidates issued no statements and made no speeches; they simply made themselves available and awaited the results. Newspapers were partisan organs to tout their candidate's virtues and attack their opponent's vices. If virtues or vices were not evident, they would be invented to suit the occasion, though sometimes that wasn't necessary. Hamilton published anonymous attacks aimed at Jefferson's character, but Jefferson's friends recognized Hamilton's style and published anonymous rejoinders that cryptically mentioned skeletons and closets. The shadow of Maria Reynolds loomed, and Hamilton stopped.

The absence of George Washington meant the absence of certainty in the election of 1796. The most sagacious could only discern that the contest would be close. "Appearances at this moment are in favor of Mr. Jefferson," said some reports, but others insisted the tally would end with a tie.[24] When Jefferson heard the word "tie," he immediately authorized Madison "fully to solicit on my behalf that Mr. Adams may be preferred." Madison was not happy to read this, but Jefferson was sincere in stating his reasons about giving way to Adams. "He has always been my senior from the commencement of our public life," said Jefferson, "and the expression of that public will being equal, this circumstance ought to give him the preference."

Madison hoped it would not come to that, but two weeks later he had another letter from Jefferson that made him even unhappier. It included a letter to Adams that Madison was free to read, said Jefferson, and deliver or not, depending on his judgment. The letter was an earnest attempt at reconciliation that would have moved Adams and pleased Washington. Jefferson preemptively congratulated Adams on his victory, and though he cautioned that Hamilton could still find a way to foil him, he said such kind things about Adams and the future of the country that Madison tucked the letter away.[25] Adams would never see it.

Madison was possibly wise in quashing Jefferson's sentimental gesture. Shortly after he received the letter from Jefferson, the election results were not quite official but otherwise certain. Adams won the presidency with 71 electoral votes, but his Federalist second Thomas Pinckney did not come in second. The Republican Thomas Jefferson did with 68 electoral votes. Ironically, Jefferson was the beneficiary of Federalist efforts to supplant Adams with Pinckney, though Jefferson would have argued about the benefits of the result. Becoming vice president required him to come out of retirement, beginning with a trip to Philadelphia to be sworn in. He would see George Washington, for the last time.

Adams had returned to Philadelphia from a visit home before the results of the election were known. He dined privately with Washington the evening after his arrival. The president showed him a pamphlet published by Bache. It was an open letter to Washington from Thomas Paine, who berated Washington for abandoning him to prison in France. Paine scorned the president for becoming a puppet of the British, and for good measure accused him of wanting to become an American king.[26] Washington was now accustomed to personal attacks, though he never quite became immune to the hurt.

Washington had been working on his eighth annual message since late October. Hamilton and Jay, rather than his cabinet, had by now become his principal advisers. Hamilton's contributions chiefly concerned foreign affairs, particularly because they had unraveled regarding the French. For the last time on December 7, 1796, Washington staged the grand parade of cabinet and court with accompanying escorts for the short trip to Congress. He entered the House chamber to the largest audience ever in its gallery and certainly the largest ever to attend one of his addresses.

It was a broad message and slightly disappointing, despite its talk of good Indian relations, the progress of treaties with Great Britain, Spain, and Algiers, and the need to encourage manufacturing and agricultural advances. Washington called for a national university and a military academy, but it was his desire to expand the navy to protect American trade that caught most ears. A brief reference to deteriorating relations with France provided little detail but promised more information in a special message soon to come. Washington closed by congratulating everyone on eight years of successful government and expressed his hope that "the Supreme Ruler of the Universe" would continue to extend "His providential care."[27] Jefferson was not yet in Philadelphia, but he read the address at Monticello and saw storms at its margins. "The President is fortunate to get off as the bubble is bursting," he wryly noted, "leaving others to hold the bag."[28]

As promised, Washington's special message came a month later. In it he called for a peaceful resolution to the French problem but included a copy of Timothy Pickering's instructions to Pinckney insisting he take a hard line with the French government. Pinckney had already been kicked out of France, but nobody in Philadelphia knew that yet. Washington would not hear that news until he was safely out of office and back at Mount Vernon. By then, the storms were moving out of the margins.

Washington did not slow his work schedule during his last two months in office, but he appeared increasingly relaxed as his day of liberation neared. Bache and others were printing stories celebrating Washington's impending exit, but friends noticed that for him the jabs mattered little and hurt less. He, too, was celebrating. Henrietta Liston was puzzled by his retirement, and he compared his situation to the *Adventures of Gil Blas,* a popular novel of the time and apparently one of the few works of fiction Washington ever read. In a particular scene, the archbishop of Grenada employed the hero Gil Blas on the pledge that Gil Blas would tell him when he began slipping because of age. When Gil Blas did so, the archbishop fired him. Washington said he never wanted to need someone to tell him he was slipping. Mrs. Liston thought him lighthearted and told him she could see it in his face.

Washington insisted his face never revealed his emotions. It "was the only weak or vain thing I ever heard Washington utter," she said.[29]

The days passed. Plans for the biggest birthday celebration of his presidency included pageants and balls from Boston to Savannah, with the most impressive to be in Philadelphia, and Republicans commenced their grumbling about monarchical trappings, but nothing could blunt the enthusiasm. In Philadelphia, parades streamed down every main thoroughfare during the day, and that night a special show at John Ricketts's circus building preceded a supper and a ball for more than a thousand people. Eliza Powel made a rare appearance because she, like every other friend and acquaintance, wanted to bask in George and Martha Washington's happiness. Washington's face was impressive with his emotions.[30]

They wrote dear friends to say good-bye and, in Washington's case, sometimes to say more than farewell. He told John Adams that he should not worry over keeping his son John Quincy in office, because "Mr. Adams is the most valuable public character we have abroad." He wrote to Henry Knox one of the most sympathetic letters of condolence he ever framed. Henry and Lucy had buried three more children, and Washington said his feelings came "from the friendship I have always borne you."[31]

The entire household was bubbly about the big move as if it were to an exotic locale rather than the hill above the Potomac. Washington was not so bubbly as to abandon thrift. He had incurred considerable expenses furnishing and equipping the houses on Broadway in New York City and High Street in Philadelphia, and he no longer needed many of the things he had purchased. He offered John Adams furniture at bargain prices. He sold horses to Eliza Powel for her nephew and made gifts of odds and ends or arranged for their sale at public auction. Servants packed eight years of belongings from the private quarters.[32]

Adams was staying at the Francis Hotel until the Washingtons vacated the High Street house, and he soon had a caller. Jefferson had arrived in Philadelphia on March 2, 1797, and briefly stayed with the Madisons before moving into the Francis Hotel also. Jefferson and Adams talked about foreign affairs and old times.

The poisons of the past seemed to recede under the constitutional prescription for new starts with peaceful transfers of power. No revolution or barracks rebellion was required to dislodge George Washington from the presidency. He was simply going home. Adams sat with Jefferson on the eve of their elevation to the first and second places in the executive branch not as the beneficiaries of a conspiracy but as Americans elected to public office. Anything seemed possible that March in 1797. Adams told Jefferson that he was thinking of sending a special mission to France—an idea proposed by Fisher Ames, who had gotten it from Hamilton. Adams asked Jefferson to invite Madison to join the mission. Jefferson correctly doubted Madison would accept, but anything seemed possible that March day in America.[33]

On the last afternoon of his presidency, Washington held a formal dinner for foreign dignitaries and department heads. Henrietta Liston sat next to him and later remembered that "vanity in him was a very limited passion, & prudence his striking trait." After the last course, Washington filled and raised his glass. "Ladies and gentlemen," he said, "this is the last time I shall drink your health as a public man. I do it with sincerity, and wishing you all possible happiness!" Henrietta Liston wept.[34]

The following morning, March 4, 1797, Washington breakfasted with his family. As the clock neared eleven thirty, he left the house for Congress Hall. No grand processional of ministers and judges and postilions and servants trailed behind his progress. George Washington was on foot. He walked to leave the stately parades to his successor.

Washington was the first of the official party to enter the House chamber. Members of Congress rose to applaud and continued as Thomas Jefferson entered. Finally John Adams walked into the House chamber and took his place. The president-elect was "a dumpy little man" as he stood next to the physical giants, but the tableau the three presented was unimportant in that respect.[35]

The brief ceremony of the oath preceded an inaugural address full of praise for George Washington, and then it was time to leave. Adams noticed the "serene" expression on Washington's face. He later told Abigail that he could almost hear the former president saying, "I am fairly out and you fairly in! See which of Us will be happiest." Congressmen and senators began a smattering of applause again that soon reached full volume as the three began to exit. The U.S. Congress was in tears.[36] Jefferson paused in deference to Washington and motioned for him to follow Adams. Washington would not. He insisted that the vice president depart next. George Washington was consequently the last one of them to step out of the building into the Philadelphia sunshine.

The crowd that had assembled to watch them arrive had lingered. An eerie silence descended as the throng soundlessly followed Washington as he walked to the Francis Hotel to call on the new president as a ritual courtesy. Washington entered the building, but only for an instant. As though he had forgotten another form of courtesy, he reappeared and bowed. Everyone watched the gesture in silence, and Washington, having paid his first respects to the real sovereign of the republic, vanished through the hotel's lobby door to visit the sovereign's servant, at that moment President John Adams.[37]

With such majestic respect for the majesty of the people, "the machine . . . worked without a creak."[38] Yet it was as hard to let go as it was to accept the change. That evening Philadelphia dignitaries staged an elaborate dinner for George Washington rather than John Adams. It took place at Ricketts's, where an enormous transparency showed Washington being crowned with a laurel wreath, a creation of Charles Willson Peale, the first man to capture Washington on canvas a quarter century before. The rousing strains of "Washington's March" filled the air as guests went to their tables.

At High Street, the packing by servants continued with even more urgency as Washington hosted a final dinner as a courtesy for Adams and Jefferson on the sixth. Three days later, Nelly, young Lafayette and his tutor, the servants, and finally Martha and the general pulled away from the house in carriages as Tobias Lear and Bartholomew Dandridge waved good-bye. They were staying behind to gather stray odds and ends and supervise the cleaning of the house for President Adams and his Lady. On the trip south to Mount Vernon, Nelly and Martha suddenly remembered something they had left behind. Two members of the family were missing. Washington wearily wrote to Lear that, "on one side I am called on to remember the Parrot, and on the other to remember the dog. For my own part I should not pine too much if both were forgot."[39]

After stopping in the federal district to visit with Martha's grand-daughters and their husbands, the group commenced the last leg of the journey. Outside of Alexandria, Virginia, a troop of militia rode out and escorted the family to Mount Vernon. After a six-day trek, George Washington was at last home, and with Martha could count the days to a blossoming spring as a blessing.

25

"Already Turned Farmer Again"

George Washington's first concern upon returning home was cor-
recting the disrepair of his house and farms. He spent months supervising artisans restoring neglected structures. He ordered furnishings
and bric-a-brac from Philadelphia and was like a kid at Christmas
when they arrived. In fact, everyone noticed that he and Martha were
having the time of their lives. She wrote Lucy Knox that "the General
and I feel like children just released from school or from a hard task-
master, and we believe that nothing can tempt us to leave the sacred
roof-tree again."[1] Nelly had never seen her grandfather so thoroughly
in his element. He had "already turned Farmer again," she laughingly
reported.[2]

And so he had. Washington drew up elaborate plans for every field
on every farm. He discussed with neighbors and corresponded with distant acquaintances about what to plant and when. He experimented
with new types of crops, always searching for what thrived in Virginia's
climate and Mount Vernon's marginal soil. His manager James Anderson did not much care for Washington's ubiquity in the daily operations, and the two had to work out an arrangement to keep him on. The
overseers at the five farms had no such leverage, though, and they grew
accustomed to the appearance of the tall rider wearing a black slouch
hat and making sure the wheels were in motion, his saddle tricked out
with an umbrella and a lunch pail.

Visitors flocked to see the great man and tour his estate, making

Mount Vernon resemble a well-resorted tavern as in the days before his presidency. Washington probably enjoyed more privacy in Philadelphia. Except for the levees and Thursday dinners, the family usually dined alone at High Street and spent evenings in quiet conversation, reading aloud, or listening to Nelly play. In Washington's final retirement, people came in large numbers every day of the week, every day of the year. The only time the Washingtons were not personally extending the hospitality of their home was when they were visiting nearby family or friends. Even so, strangers with letters of introduction or strangers with merely open hands and empty stomachs continued to appear and were never turned away. When in residence, Washington followed his routine of rising early, writing letters, eating a quick breakfast, and riding his farms. He returned an hour before dinner, still held at three o'clock, sharp.

In October 1797 everyone joyfully greeted the news that the Marquis de Lafayette had been released from the Austrian prison and would be returning to France. Yet, it meant that Georges Washington Lafayette would be returning home to meet a father he had not seen in years, while leaving the man who had been acting like one. They parted as Washington had parted with the boy's father almost fifteen years earlier, likely with the promise of meeting again sooner or later, both knowing it was never to be.

Almost all partings were final, in fact. Shortly after his return home, Washington received word from Fredericksburg that his sister Betty Lewis had died after a short illness. He wanted to do something to help her family and soon came up with a way: Washington wrote to his nephew Lawrence Lewis, Betty's thirty-year-old son whose first wife had died seven years before, asking him to live at Mount Vernon and help entertain evening guests. Providing overnight visitors with entertaining conversation burdened Martha and bothered him. Lawrence could restore their usual bedtime of 9 P.M., but Washington was careful to tell him that the position carried no salary, only room and board.

Lawrence quickly became part of the household, a pleasant young man, if a bit shy and self-effacing. Everyone liked him for that, though, and when Wash was between schools—withdrawn or kicked out and waiting for another to enroll him—Lawrence was like an older brother. But it was Nelly who surprised everyone, including Lawrence and likely herself as well. Within a year of Lawrence's arrival, the young woman everyone described as the most beautiful person they had ever met had fallen in love with Washington's shy nephew. They married on Washington's birthday in 1799 in a candlelight ceremony at Mount Vernon. Ten months later, the Washingtons had a great-granddaughter, Frances Parke Lewis.[3] Her family would call the girl "Parke." It would be her preferred name for the rest of her life.

Washington's retirement made the charges of monarchy seem more foolish than ever, and critics could never afterward use alleged pretensions to kingship to criticize him. To the contrary, Washington's presidency had been a great success, and his reputation was fated to grow in stature with every passing year. Bache and his successor William Duane continued to carp, never really learning the maxim Thomas Jefferson had tried to instill in the opposition, that denouncing George Washington was a losing tactic for petty losers. Accusing him of incompetence was just as ineffective as charging him with malfeasance, for doing either only made Americans angry. The people trusted Washington to do what was right rather than what was smart. It mattered not at all that he was not brilliant, for the world was full of brilliant but bad people. Americans preferred his wisdom born of experience, the certainty of self that feared no other man's greater intelligence, and the moral compass that always pointed the way to promises kept. In a world where everything is trying to kill you, promises have to mean something.

George Washington had left Mount Vernon in April 1789 fearful that his return to public life would place his reputation in peril. He worried that the job was beyond his abilities, but the deliberation that could exasperate quicker men was just right for the task he shouldered. He was a bit deaf and growing deafer, but that made him seem impervious to chattering arguments. He paused and hesitated when he spoke, but that made him seem thoughtfully averse to hair-triggered opinions. Saddled with ordinary flaws, Washington forged them into armor that protected him, burnished his reputation, and increased people's admiration. He left office with storms Jefferson saw clearly gathering on the horizon—the French problem was becoming unmanageable—but he left the country more prosperous, more stable, and just as free as he had found it. It would be strong enough to handle the crises to come. Americans credited Washington with these achievements, because few doubted his "purity of motive," and they were confident that because of George Washington a bright future was coming to life for them "in the womb of time."[4]

Washington had retired, but he sometimes found it impossible to avoid the tribulations of public life. In May 1797, Federalist newspapers printed a private letter Thomas Jefferson had written the previous year during the controversy over Jay's Treaty. It was to an Italian friend named Philip Mazzei. Jefferson never intended for the letter to be made public, and he doubtless thought its dispatch to someone an ocean away would preserve its confidentiality. But neither the ocean nor the recipient's judgment saved Jefferson. Mazzei foolishly extracted the sections about American politics and published them in an Italian newspaper. These excerpts were translated into French and published in Paris. They found their way back across the ocean to be translated back into English and were published in the United States that first spring of Washington's retirement. They were exceedingly embarrassing.

In the original letter Jefferson had written Mazzei that "an Anglican, monarchical and aristocratical party has sprung up" and that "it would give you a fever were I to name to you the apostates who have gone over to these heresies, men who were Samsons in the field and Solomons in the council, but who have had their heads shorn by the harlot England."[5] Federalists understandably assumed Jefferson's reference to Samson and Solomon was about Washington. The multiple translations had actually garbled much of what Jefferson had said, but the essence of his sentiments remained. Because he could not truthfully forsake the letter, he decided to ignore the controversy.[6] Nevertheless, he had broken his own rule by criticizing George Washington. Washington did not stoop to notice the matter. He and Jefferson had not corresponded in months. They never would again.[7]

Jefferson tried to keep his young friend James Monroe from a similar mistake. When Monroe returned from France in the summer of 1797, he was a bundle of angry resentment over his treatment by Washington and Pickering. He was determined to defend himself by publishing an account of his diplomacy in Paris. It was to be a pamphlet in the style of Edmund Randolph's *Vindication*. Jefferson strongly advised against it, noting that the tactic had done Randolph no good, but Monroe ignored the advice, published his own vindication, and almost irredeemably shattered his own reputation. Washington publicly ignored Monroe, too, but he read the pamphlet thoroughly and filled a copy with marginalia refuting Monroe's version of events.[8]

President Adams tried to prevent a final break with France by sending a special commission to Paris, but the gesture only made matters worse when the French demanded bribes and a large loan to open talks. Under pressure from Republicans, who suspected Adams of provoking the French, he released the dispatches that described this sorry course of events. Republicans were flabbergasted, but Americans were furious and demanded war to avenge the country's honor. Adams did not want war, but he understood the political and practical reasons for expanding the nation's military under the circumstances. As Congress set about that task, the question became who would command the provisional army. By summer 1798, Federalists were insisting that Washington be called from retirement to lead it.

It took considerable coaxing, but Washington agreed. He did have specific conditions. First, the War Department and his subordinates would handle recruiting and the organizing of the new force. Second, he insisted on the right to name the three major generals authorized by Congress and to set their order of seniority. In any case, Washington said he would assume command of the army only if France invaded the United States. John Adams issued Washington's commission on July 4, 1798, and Secretary of War James McHenry personally delivered it at Mount Vernon.

Washington named the men to serve under him, including the inspector general, who would essentially be his second-in-command, but his choices and their seniority sparked a heated controversy while wounding an old friend's feelings. He designated Alexander Hamilton as inspector general. For the next senior officer, he named Charles Cotesworth Pinckney, recently returned as one of Adams's commissioners to the French. Only then did Washington select Henry Knox as the third officer under Hamilton and Pinckney. It was an astonishing humiliation. Hamilton had never moved higher than the rank of colonel in the Continental Army and was always junior to both Pinckney and Knox. Knox had been senior to both Hamilton and Pinckney and could not help but see his place in the provisional army as a mortifying demotion. Washington's preferences had skewed his better judgment, for he knew that Hamilton would not accept a commission except with special preferment, and he very much wanted Hamilton as his second-in-command. If Henry Knox was too insulted to accept Washington's offer, then so be it.

As it happened, Knox was not only too insulted to accept Washington's offer, he made no effort to hide his bitterness over the slight. Washington finally came to his senses and gave Knox a way to soothe his pride by letting him act as if personal matters kept him from accepting.[9] If Pinckney had any qualms, he hid them, telling Washington that he would do anything to be of service during the crisis. President Adams, however, was quite troubled by Hamilton's high rank. Adams had an inkling by then of Hamilton's actions in the election of 1796 and was irritated by his ongoing sense of privilege in freely advising him as well as the cabinet. Adams had kept Pickering and Wolcott to assure everyone of administrative continuity, and they repaid him by acting as Hamilton's minions. Adams only reluctantly agreed to Hamilton when he was told that Washington would not serve without him.

These early tiffs set the tone for the episodes that followed—events that were either tragicomic or objectionable. Washington remained at Mount Vernon examining papers and plans sent to him by Hamilton, McHenry, and others as the army slowly expanded. He busied himself with strange preoccupations and took uncharacteristic liberties with the public trust.[10] For example, he approved the design of a new, elaborate uniform for himself and his officers, and he secured a cornet's commission (the equivalent of today's second lieutenant) for an excited seventeen-year-old Wash. For a time he peppered the War Department with suggestions about recruiting and occasionally hectored McHenry about his listless administrative methods, but after a while he grew bored with the business. He had little to do with the army he officially commanded. Only once did he take an active part in anything remotely connected to it, and that involved a trip to Philadelphia in late 1798 to meet with President Adams and others involved in planning. Congress had authorized and budgeted a secretary for him. In an act of forgiveness and loyalty, he immediately appointed Tobias Lear, despite his discovery earlier in the year that Lear had used rent money he was collecting from Washington's tenants to pay his own bills. Washington sternly reproached him, but Lear was too close to his heart to cast off. He gave Lear the rank of colonel and brought him to Philadelphia.[11]

Military matters took up so little time during his visit that he enjoyed many pleasant reunions with friends in Congress—most poignantly with Robert Morris, for several years by then a resident of the Prune Street Prison, the debtors' wing of the Walnut Street Prison. Morris had a small apartment in the jail where friends supplied him with meager comforts. On December 7, 1798, Washington dined there with Robert and Mary Morris in a makeshift room of the little apartment. Doubtless all had penetrating memories of sumptuous dinners enjoyed on High Street, but it's likely no one mentioned them.

Washington also called on Eliza Powel at least twice, and she helped him pick out gifts for the ladies back at Mount Vernon. Her note of farewell revealed a deep sadness over his leaving, a persistent mood since Samuel's death but heightened by the likelihood that she and General Washington would never see each other again. Eliza Powel wished "that God may take you into his holy keeping and preserve you safe both in Traveling and under all Circumstances, and that you may be happy here and hereafter is the ardent Prayer of Your affectionate afflicted Friend."[12] The once wealthy Morris languished in jail and was reduced to relishing modest victuals supplied by the charity of friends. Sparkling Mrs. Powel had become a virtual shut-in who succumbed to brown studies. Washington was glad to go home.

Not everyone in the country had war fever, and Federalists reacted to growing criticism of the government's military plans with some of the most improbable legislation in the history of Congress. The series of laws passed in 1798 became known as the Alien and Sedition Acts, and they were at best a medley of understandable apprehension and inexcusable odium. The first two were aimed generally at foreigners in the United States but really sought to discourage French agents. The Alien Act increased a five-year residency requirement to fourteen years to become eligible for American citizenship; the Enemy Alien Act gave the president power to deport aliens he deemed a threat to American security.[13] These measures were coherent responses to an impending war.

Yet the third law was simply foul. The Sedition Act made criticism of the government a prosecutable offense if a court found it "false, scandalous, and malicious."[14] The stipulation was broad enough to reveal the purpose, which was to silence dissent with dungeons, a clear violation of the First Amendment. Even some high Federalists—Alexander Hamilton and John Marshall among them—saw the act as a political disaster less likely to silence Republicans as it was to stir them to ferocious efforts.[15] Sadly, George Washington refused to condemn the Sedition Act. He had been the victim of too many "malicious" attacks, to be sure, but his belief that Republican newspapers should be subjected to government intimidation was an appalling instance of a petty pique impinging on a more important principle.[16]

Fate saved Washington from additional folly by keeping the war from happening. The U.S. Navy and American merchant ships clashed with the French on the high seas in what became known as the Quasi-War, but there would be no land battles, no chance for Hamilton to win martial glory, and no occasion for Washington to don his comic opera uniform. In 1799, President Adams again turned to diplomacy to secure a peaceful understanding with France, and both Federalists and Republicans calmed down.

In that, Eliza Powel's prayer became more than a heartfelt expression to an old friend. It was answered: Her friend had been kept safe in traveling and in all circumstances, including protection from his own pride.

Those who saw George Washington during the summer of 1799 thought he had never seemed happier. The Listons visited, and though not of long acquaintance, Henrietta was an astute observer. She commented that "he now converses with more ease & less guardedly than when in public life."[17] Most noticeably Washington at long last had cast off a lifelong habit of hesitation when speaking.

Whether a premonition or simple responsibility guided him, Washington drew up a new will that summer. In it he left a life estate in Mount Vernon to "his dearly beloved wife" Martha, in addition to outright title to other property and most of the mansion's contents. The exceptions were keepsakes specifically meant for certain people. Otherwise, the bequests were of material rather than sentimental value. He handed down property to nephews, nieces, and step-grandchildren and arranged a rent-free life tenancy on a farm for Tobias Lear. He also made several charitable bequests, primarily to educational institutions, and drew up the provisions for emancipation. After drawing up the document, he tucked it away in his desk.

Washington had reasons to think about the vagaries of life that year. Like others, this one was full of fear, loss, and hope. Martha became seriously ill, which brought Dr. Craik and other physicians to dose her with the usual medicines. She survived, but as she recovered, it was apparent that each bout of illness was becoming more difficult to fight off, and each recuperation was less of a rebound. Then Charles, his last surviving sibling, died in western Virginia, making George, who "was the first," in the end "the last of my fathers Children by the second marriage."[18] Somber reflections were soon put away when Lawrence and Nelly's baby came healthy and fat, allowing Martha to dote and the house to hear again the cry and gurgle of a newborn. That December, Nelly's new baby made the mansion cheerful. Washington's nephew Howell Lewis came to visit with his young wife but didn't stay, and when the proud new father Lawrence left with Wash after breakfast to attend to some business in New Kent County, the house was pleasantly empty for at least a couple of days. Nelly slept, Parke gurgled, and Martha fussed over both, the best medicine in the world for her. By the eleventh, Mount Vernon was again full of visitors. Many stayed for dinner.

Washington rode out to inspect the farms the next morning. As usual, neither guests nor unsettled weather could disrupt his routine. As he made his way, rain became snow, and it hailed. He was late returning to the mansion and would not delay dinner by changing into dry clothes. The Washingtons awoke the next morning to three inches of snow on the ground. It was very cold, and because he had a sore throat—a sign of a cold, he thought—Washington stayed in for most of the day. Around four o'clock, he went out to tag some trees he wanted taken down. His throat still bothered him, but the Washingtons and Tobias Lear sat in the parlor that evening as usual with Washington reading to them from that day's delivery of newspapers. Martha retired early, first looking in on Nelly and Parke before padding off to bed.

Washington and Lear chatted a while longer until Lear went to bed, leaving Washington in his study writing in his diary, though not for long. He was in bed near nine o'clock, as usual.

All was as usual, in fact, as the comforting rhythms of the household thrummed along in the cold December hours. Yet in Mount Vernon's stables, the horses impatiently hoofed at the straw in their stalls as the sun rose on the fourteenth when the hostler brought no saddles and the tall rider did not appear. The morning wasted away as the familiar circuit of the five farms went uninspected. They could snort, flare nostrils, flick tails, and put back their ears, but he would not come.

The night before had gone from bad, as his every swallow became like flame, to worse, as his throat began to close. He woke Martha. It was past midnight, and he was having trouble breathing. He insisted that she not stir, and they were still abed when a maid came to build a fire just before dawn. Martha told her to bring Mr. Lear. After seeing Washington, Lear immediately sent a message to Dr. Craik in Alexandria: Come at once. Lear also sent for Dr. Gustavus Brown.

Washington insisted that his manservant Christopher Sheels dress him. Craik found Washington in the bedroom sitting in a chair. Washington already had pressed an overseer into service to bleed him. He suggested that Craik bleed him again. He was helped back to bed, and Craik performed the procedure. Thus began the medieval medical rituals that never cured and sometimes killed. Washington was bled at least four times during the day of December 14, 1799.

Dr. Brown answered Lear's call, and Craik sent for Dr. Elisha Cullen Dick as well. This team did what they knew best, which was to open veins, administer purgatives, and ultimately heat tumblers to blister Washington's feet and legs, a procedure thought effective in drawing out toxins.[19] They were fairly certain he had quinsy, their name for a throat abscess on or near the tonsils. They were likely wrong; Washington probably had epiglottitis, a severe infection of the flap that covers the windpipe when one swallows. The malady causes the epiglottis to swell and gradually cut off respiration.[20] It qualifies as a surgical emergency that can test modern skills. Washington in the year 1799 could not survive what was wrong with him.

As the hours passed and his breathing became more labored, he asked to be helped to a sitting position, which eased his wheezing. After a time he became too weak to sit up. Despite his struggle for every breath, he tried to talk. In the afternoon he noticed Christopher Sheels still standing as he had been since dawn and insisted that he sit down. He sent Martha for two documents in his desk, examined them, and directed that one be thrown in the fire. It was the older will superseded by the one he had written just that summer. He rasped to Craik, "I die hard; but I'm not afraid to go." As the afternoon grew dim with twilight, he bore up under the torture passing for medical treatment but finally whispered to the physicians, "I feel myself going. I thank you for your attention. You had better not take any more trouble about me; but let me go off quietly; I cannot last long."

They allowed him to rest. Craik sat by the fire while his colleagues conferred outside the room. About 10 P.M., Washington motioned for Lear to lean in close. He had been thinking; being buried or entombed alive was a great fear before the invention of embalming. Washington told his secretary, "I am just going. Have me decently buried, and do not let my body be put into the vault in less than two days after I am dead." Lear could not make his voice work. Washington rasped with urgency, "Do you understand me?" Lear finally could say that he did. Washington calmly whispered, "'Tis well." They were his last words.

The room seemed calmer then with the light low and the fire crackling. Dr. Craik returned to the chair by the fire. Martha sat silently at the foot of the bed. Lear held Washington's hand. As the clock neared eleven o'clock, Washington drew his hand away from Lear's and felt for his own pulse. They all watched this strange gesture. His hand fell away from his wrist. His shallow breathing stopped. Lear was frozen, and after a few minutes Craik reached over him to close Washington's eyes.

Martha quietly asked, "Is he gone?"

Lear could not speak.

George Washington's beloved wife simply said, "'Tis well. All is now over. I have no more trials to pass through. I shall soon follow him."[21]

On the following day, friends and family gathered. Lear went to Alexandria to order a lead-lined mahogany coffin and came back to the house to arrange the funeral to be held at the house in two days, per Washington's instructions. He also wrote letters to inform the government, especially President Adams, of the death. Martha's granddaughters, their husbands, and their children came, as well as neighbors and friends. The amateur architect William Thornton arrived with Thomas and Elizabeth Custis Law from the federal district. Thornton had won the contest for the design of the U.S. Capitol, a plan that required significant rescaling to conform to a reasonable budget, but Thornton was neither offended nor difficult, which Washington had always appreciated. Nothing was beyond Thornton's notice, and he had included in his studies strange remedies for death. Hearing that Washington was in cold storage awaiting burial, Thornton proposed that they try to reanimate him by thawing the corpse and using lamb's blood as a restorative. There must have been a long and clumsy pause. The matter was dropped.[22]

By custom, most widows did not attend their husbands' funerals, and Martha was no exception. She was absent from the simple ceremony and did not join the more elaborate military, Masonic, and religious services that followed. After brief obsequies, the procession began shortly after three o'clock. A ship in the Potomac fired minute guns (a report every sixty seconds, hence the name), and a military band played a dirge for the infantry and dragoons who led the way. Washington's riderless stallion followed, and pallbearers bore the mahogany coffin, followed by Masons and local citizens. A few of Washington's nephews, Eleanor Calvert Custis Stuart, and her children stood at the tomb where musket and artillery salutes were fired. Masonic funeral rites and then prayers followed before the coffin was placed in the family crypt.[23]

As the news spread across the country, the grief was almost convulsive. Some three hundred eulogies were delivered throughout the nation over the coming months. Gouverneur Morris spoke in New York City and sent a copy of his remarks to Martha, but only after waiting several months to let her grief abate. Morris knew her well enough to know it would abate only a bit, no matter the length of time.[24] Congress adjourned immediately after the news arrived and with President Adams commemorated the sad occasion with a state funeral in Philadelphia on the day after Christmas. Light-Horse Harry Lee delivered the eulogy that summarized Washington's contributions, praised his virtues, and enjoined Americans to celebrate his legacy by fulfilling their destiny. Lee's eulogy provided the most enduring phrase of these many sad remembrances when he proclaimed that Washington had been "first in war, first in peace, and first in the hearts of his countrymen."

Wearing full formal military dress, Alexander Hamilton led the procession honoring Washington in New York City. He had written to Charles Cotesworth Pinckney soon after hearing the news of Washington's passing. "Perhaps no friend of his has more cause to lament, on personal account, than my self," he mused. To Martha, Hamilton wrote "there can be few, who equally with me participate in the loss you deplore."[25] Hamilton was always most stilted when most moved.

James Madison had retired from Congress in 1797 and had just been elected to the Virginia House of Delegates when Washington died. To that assembly, Madison expressed his belief that "death has robbed our country of its most distinguished ornament, and the world of one of its greatest benefactors."[26] Thomas Jefferson said little, but weeks after the death he answered a correspondent who had sent him a pamphlet extolling Washington's virtues. Jefferson spent a lifetime decrying the corruption of power as the ruin of foolish men, and in the end he viewed Washington's greatest contribution as having avoided that snare. "The example which has been set by the great man who was the subject of it [the pamphlet]," he said, "will be of immense value to mankind if the Buonapartes of this world, & those whose object is fame & glory, will but contemplate & truly calculate the difference between that of a Washington & of a Cromwell."[27]

But that was not Thomas Jefferson's last word on the subject. Almost fifteen years would pass before he came to terms with having walked with a giant. "His mind was great and powerful," said Jefferson, even if not "of the very first order." Yet George Washington's almost supernatural ability to pluck the best solution from an abundance of advice had made him "in every sense of the words, a wise, a good, and a great man." Jefferson's memory was possibly performing the trick of erasing unpleasantness and burnishing the past with a brush of regret. Yet by 1814 he was prepared to say, "I felt on his death, with my countrymen, that verily a great man hath fallen in Israel."[28]

★ ★ ★

Her husband's death immediately changed Martha Washington and gradually transformed her as well. After midnight on December 15, 1799, when servants carried Washington's body downstairs to Mount Vernon's parlor, Martha had them move her belongings to the house's third floor, where she settled into a room. It was little more than an attic. She had their bedroom closed as well as the general's study below it. Possibly Lear had access to the study for a few months as he organized Washington's papers. By all accounts, Martha never entered either room again.

She spent most of her time in the third-floor room with her Bible and her needles and threads. Visitors continued to stream to the mansion to see the great Washington's house. She occasionally came down to greet them and often served refreshments. She answered a few condolence letters, but left most of those chores to Lear. She could barely write more than a few lines to her closest friends.

President Adams wrote her that the government had plans to place Washington's body in an elaborate tomb being prepared under the new Capitol's rotunda. The thought of his leaving Mount Vernon broke her heart, but she consented for the sake of the country.[29] After many years' delay, the tomb was completed. It still waits for Washington's remains; by the time the government finished the project the owner of Mount Vernon, Washington's great-nephew John Augustine Washington, refused permission. The family had already moved Washington's remains from the old crypt to a more substantial tomb on Mount Vernon's grounds. That was done in 1831, and George Washington is in that place today.

On January 1, 1801, Martha signed a document freeing the 123 slaves her husband had intended for freedom after she died. Her views on slavery hadn't changed substantially; she still saw slavery as the natural order of the world. It has been inferred that she freed those slaves because her life was the only thing standing between them and their liberty.[30] Some remained at Mount Vernon because of ties to the plantation's dower slaves whom she could not free; many left to make a life somewhere else.

Martha continued her household routines with the help of the housekeeper Eleanor Forbes, whom Washington had hired a few years before. She still had Nelly and Lawrence with her. Washington had left them considerable property nearby where they were building a house, but they meant to stay with Martha as long as she lived. The little family and the visitors broke the monotony of the days. The Listons came to say good-bye before leaving the country and were shocked at how Martha had aged since their last visit. Henrietta had always thought the Washingtons' marriage was at most companionate, but the sight of Martha in mourning opened her eyes. "This excellent Woman," she noted, was "grieving incessantly."[31]

During visits with friends, Martha did something that she had almost never done during her husband's lifetime and revealed a trait few knew she possessed. One story circulated that at the High Street house one day, she had pointed out a greasy spot and muttered that it had likely been left by a Republican, but the instances of her expressing any opinion about such things were so rare as to be remarkable. After Washington died, she talked freely about politics and was especially bitter about Republican successes. When Thomas Jefferson and Aaron Burr were tied in the presidential election of 1800 and the contest was being decided in the House of Representatives, Federalists sneered that Jefferson's visit to Mount Vernon was pure political show. It was certainly a social mistake. He paid his respects to Washington at the tomb and then went to the mansion to see Martha. Their meeting must have been worse than awkward. Martha later said "that, next to the loss of her husband, it was the most painful occurrence of her life."[32]

She made her will from a draft prepared by Attorney General Charles Lee. She had said the night Washington died that she would soon follow him, and her health soon gave proof to the prediction. Fragile before December 1799, she began unraveling as the months passed afterward. Her tumbling stomach had troubled her for years, but increasing respiratory problems gradually made the climb to her garret apartment a slow, halting ordeal. In May 1802 an illness was serious enough to put her in bed and worry Nelly, who summoned Dr. Craik. He remained nearby for the three weeks it took her to die. Her grandchildren were around her on May 22, 1802, when she simply slipped away.

The family gathered again in the New Room to hear the Anglican service. Eleanor Calvert Custis Stuart, the girl who had made Jacky happy and had given them lovely Nelly and lovable Wash, was the chief mourner. She followed the coffin to the crypt, where Martha Dandridge Custis Washington was placed beside her husband. The house seemed hopelessly empty, the world seemed gray and dull, the boys less witty and the girls less charming, now that all were deprived of the woman who was always more interested than interesting. They returned to the mansion for a while, to remember.

Epilogue

Closing the Circle

John Adams

John Adams had a tumultuous four years as president marred by Alexander Hamilton's meddling and the contempt of Washington's second cabinet. Adams kept Wolcott, Pickering, and McHenry in place to ensure administrative continuity, but it was a mistake that he waited too long to correct by firing Pickering and McHenry while castigating Hamilton. Adams had already alienated many Federalists with his peace diplomacy that ended the Quasi-War, and his open break with Hamilton completed the disastrous political odyssey. Defeated in the election of 1800, Adams went home embittered but spent his remaining years working his Massachusetts farm as long as he was able, filling books with vehement marginalia, and corresponding with anyone who would trade an argument or share a laugh. Family tragedies intruded with painful regularity. His son Charles died an alcoholic, and his dear Nabby contracted breast cancer and underwent a gruesome mastectomy but died two years later. Abigail's death in 1818 completed a cycle of devastating loss for the entire family and deprived Adams of the only person in the world he had habitually called "friend." He took solace in his books and watching the successful rise of his son John Quincy Adams, who became president in 1825. His many correspondents by 1812 included Thomas Jefferson, their reconciliation mending a mutual alienation that preceded the bitter campaign of 1800, which had seemingly finalized it. As old men, they exchanged letters for the rest of their lives to discuss everything from American manufacturing to politics. The approach of the fiftieth anniversary of their greatest collaboration on the Declaration of Independence saw both in failing health and sep-arated by five hundred miles, but they sank as though tethered, as in fact they had become. In one of the great coincidences of history, these two remarkable statesmen died within hours of each other on July 4, 1826. The last words of John Adams were, "Jefferson lives."

George Washington Parke Custis ("Wash")

George Washington Parke Custis lived most of a long life at Arlington House, the palatial mansion he built on land inherited from his father's estate. He began building it shortly after Martha Washington died. The house overlooked the Potomac and the new federal city. Custis married Mary Lee Fitzhugh in 1804, and they had one child who survived to adulthood, Mary Anna Randolph Custis. Custis fancied himself a play-wright, but his life's work was preserving Washington artifacts and re-cording his memories of the first president with imaginative accounts that were sometimes so embellished as to be unreliable. In 1831, his daughter married Robert E. Lee, a professional army officer who was the son of George Washington's friend Light-Horse Harry Lee and later commanded the Confederate Army of Northern Virginia. The Lees had seven children who spent much of their childhood at Arling-ton listening to their grandfather spin stories about George and Martha Washington. When Custis died in 1857, Robert E. Lee served as execu-tor of the estate, with Arlington slated to be inherited by the Lees' oldest son, George Washington Custis Lee, upon his mother's death. During the Civil War, the federal government confiscated Arlington and estab-lished a national cemetery there. A court battle following the war re-turned Arlington to George Washington Custis Lee, but he subsequently sold it back to the government.

Alexander Hamilton

Before George Washington died, the Maria Reynolds scandal was made public. John Beckley supplied the information to the scandalmongering journalist James Callender, who printed the details with the claim that they proved Hamilton's corruption at the Treasury Department. Against much advice, Hamilton published a lengthy pamphlet denying the corruption but also explaining with lurid explicitness how the affair started and how James Reynolds blackmailed him. Hamilton's enemies condemned his immorality. His supporters praised his candor and condemned James Monroe, who was suspected of disclosing the information to Callender. Washington never commented on the affair, at least in writing. Hamilton remained active in the political life of New York and the nation while running his lucrative law practice. In the presidential contest of 1800, he returned to his old trick of manipulating electors to elect Federalist vice presidential candidate Charles Cotesworth Pinckney to the presidency over John Adams. When Jefferson tied the Republican vice presidential candidate Aaron Burr, Jefferson prevailed in the final House vote partly because Hamilton urged Federalists to vote for Jefferson over fellow New Yorker Burr, a man Hamilton believed to be thoroughly unprincipled. Hamilton subsequently undermined Burr's political career in New York, but it was the report that he had impugned Burr's honor at a dinner party that led the sitting vice president to challenge Hamilton to a duel. On July 11, 1804, Burr mortally wounded Hamilton at Weehawken, New Jersey. It destroyed Burr's political career and made Hamilton a martyr to the Federalist Party. His widow Betsey became a mourner in the truest Victorian fashion, always dressing in black and laboring tirelessly to burnish her husband's image. She died on her birthday in 1854 at age ninety-seven.

John Jay

When Washington died, John Jay was still governor of New York. He counted as one of his greatest achievements his successful advocacy of gradual emancipation by statute of all slaves in the state. His administration was notable for such visionary goals as well as strict probity. Jay refused his party's nomination for another term as governor, as well as President Adams's offer to appoint him chief justice of the United States Supreme Court when Oliver Ellsworth resigned. (Adams finally nominated John Marshall.) Jay was resolved to retire to his farm and the house he was building in Westchester County, but all the pleasure of those plans was shattered when Sarah died in 1802. They had looked forward with excitement to a tranquil life in the country, and he was never quite the same after her death. Deeply religious before, he became more so afterward, dividing his time between his church and his grandchildren. In May 1829, Jay suffered a stroke and died a few days later at his home surrounded by his family. He was eighty-three.

Thomas Jefferson

Mostly at Monticello during his four years as vice president, he came to Philadelphia to preside over the Senate and drew up rules that guided procedures there for decades. As vice president, he was in the odd position of leading the Republican opposition to his own administration, and in 1800 was the presidential candidate for his party against incumbent John Adams. When he tied with his running mate Aaron Burr in the Electoral College in their victory over Adams, the House eventually chose Jefferson, partly at the urging of Alexander Hamilton. President Thomas Jefferson scored his greatest triumph by purchasing Louisiana from France in 1803, a deed that Federalists charged contravened his previously strict view of executive authority. He was less successful in resolving growing differences with Britain over neutral trade and impressment. It was all part of the reality that leading the nation in a troubled world was a complicated matter and that economic sanctions did not always work against an implacable foe. Jefferson left the presidency in the midst of the crisis with Great Britain, and his successor, James Madison, had to cope with the war that finally resulted. Jefferson retired to Monticello where he indulged his love of agriculture, played with his grandchildren, and founded the University of Virginia, which he considered his greatest accomplishment. He also spent money he did not have and struggled to pay off debts he had inherited or unwisely vouched for. At the end, he was living at Monticello on the charity of his creditors. He died there on July 4, 1826, just hours before John Adams passed away in Quincy, Massachusetts.

Henry Knox

His relationship with George Washington had already suffered because of his absence during the Whiskey Rebellion, but his leaving the cabinet softened the edges of their discontent until the 1798 dispute regarding rank and seniority in the provisional army. When Washington allowed

Knox to refuse the niggardly commission with excuses about time and personal concerns, things were smoothed over yet again. Knox never surrendered the hope that he would make a fortune with his land speculation and other business ventures, but he invariably moved from one financial mishap to another. He built a mansion he named Montpelier on part of his acreage in the District of Maine and lived there with Lucy as contented as a man could be who was always a half step away from financial ruin. The sobering family losses that had dimmed their years in Philadelphia continued until all but one of their thirteen children died young. In 1806, Knox choked on a chicken bone. It apparently perforated his throat, and the ensuing infection killed him a few days later. He was fifty-six.

Tobias Lear

For two years Lear lived on the farm for which Washington had left him life tenancy. In addition to helping Martha with the estate, Lear organized Washington's papers, leading to speculation that he destroyed some of them and deleted portions of Washington's diary. There is no proof. More clearly, Lear became bitter over the Washington family's treatment of him. In 1802, he married Martha Washington's niece, Frances Dandridge Henley, but by then Martha's death had broken the last tie to the family, and his drift into the Republican camp and especially toward Thomas Jefferson meant complete estrangement from the surviving members of the family. Some wondered if Lear had removed items damaging to Jefferson from Washington's files and thus warranted special favors. Again, there is no proof that Jefferson brought Lear into his administration for any other reason beyond his personal fondness for him and their mutual agreement on politics. During the summer of 1801, Jefferson appointed him consul to Saint Domingue and in 1803 made him consul general to Algiers with authority to negotiate a treaty. In Algiers he secured the release of American prisoners and negotiated a trade treaty that ended the First Barbary War. Yet he exceeded his instructions with secret arrangements about other hostages that put him out of favor. He never received another diplomatic appointment, though Madison did place him in a low-level War Department post. Lear's business problems had continued over the years as he kited loans and delayed payments to his business partner. At one point, he was at such low ebb that he was thinking of killing himself. Yet by the time he accepted the job in the War Department, his investments began to pay off, and he and Fanny were comfortable. Still, he suffered from painful headaches and was sensitive about Federalist attacks on him as a turncoat for his work with Republicans. Profoundly depressed, he committed suicide in 1816. His widow Fanny survived him by forty years. His only child was his son with Polly, Benjamin Lincoln Lear, who was born at the High Street residence in Philadelphia. He died in the cholera outbreak of 1832.

Eleanor Parke Custis Lewis ("Nelly")

Nelly and Lawrence Lewis lived at Mount Vernon until Martha's death in 1802 and then at Woodlawn on the property left them by George Washington. Lafayette, with his son Georges Washington Lafayette, visited Woodlawn during his 1825 tour of the country. Such festive events were rare in a life strangely shadowed by unhappiness. Nelly's mother and stepfather—Washington's friend David Stuart—died within a few years of each other, though she was only fifty-three at the time of her death in 1811. Nelly and Lawrence had eight children, but only four lived past early childhood. After they acquired Audley, a plantation in western Virginia, Lawrence began spending more time there as he and Nelly grew apart. In the 1830s, she visited their daughter Angela and her husband in Louisiana. These "visits" were actually extended spans of residence. Shortly after Nelly left Louisiana in 1839, Angela suddenly died. Lawrence also died that year, at age seventy-two, and Nelly buried him at Mount Vernon in the new tomb. For the rest of her life she lived at Audley, at first with her son and his wife, Esther, and after his death in 1847 with his widow. Nelly traveled occasionally. President Zachary Taylor invited her to the White House during a visit to Washington, D.C. She died at Audley following a stroke on July 15, 1852. She was taken back to Mount Vernon, the place where she had turned heads, struck men speechless with a smile, and finally fell in love with the bashful fellow who married her and then drifted away. They placed her in the family tomb next to him. The only one of Nelly's children to outlive her was Parke, the girl born at Mount Vernon just weeks before Washington's death.

James Madison

James Madison went briefly into retirement the year before Washington died, but he soon left Montpelier for Richmond as a member of the House of Delegates, where he was serving when news came of Washington's death. He remained active beyond Virginia politics, corresponding with Republicans, drafting the Virginia Resolution of 1798 against the Alien and Sedition Acts, and serving as Jefferson's unofficial campaign manager for the election of 1800. With Jefferson's victory in the House vote in early 1801, James and Dolley Madison moved to the new federal capital where Madison became Jefferson's secretary of state. Dolley was Jefferson's unofficial hostess throughout his presidency. Secretary of State Madison was involved with the Louisiana Purchase, the Barbary crisis, and growing tensions with Great Britain and France. When he succeeded Jefferson to the presidency in 1809, British relations were at a nadir and only worsened in the next three years. In June 1812, Madison asked Congress for a declaration of war and commenced a conflict hampered by America's military unpreparedness and Federalist dissent that bordered on disloyalty. Although the army would improve, and competent commanders would score victories, Madison had to abandon the capital in August 1814 when a British raid occupied the town and burned public buildings, including the Capitol and the executive mansion. As she had left the presidential residence, Dolley cut one of Gilbert Stuart's replicas of the "Lansdowne" portrait of George Washington from its frame, rolled it up, and took it with her. The war revealed for Madison and other Republicans the wisdom in some of Hamilton's financial policies, particularly a national bank's utility in funding unexpected government emergencies. With Madison's encouragement, Republicans repented of allowing Hamilton's creation to expire in 1811 and created the Second Bank of the United States in 1816. Madison left office the following year. He and Dolley retired at Montpelier. The little man who had always been sick was remarkably resilient. He lived for almost two more decades, finally dying in June 1836.

Dolley survived him by thirteen years, but she had to sell Montpelier to pay debts and spent her final year in Washington. She paid her way at the end by selling her husband's papers to Congress.

Gouverneur Morris

Because Gouverneur Morris left the country on business as George Washington was becoming president and was drafted into diplomatic service abroad during the 1790s, he never saw Washington again after the Constitutional Convention. He returned to the United States at the end of 1798 and always intended to visit Mount Vernon but postponed the trip until it was too late. After a brief stint in the U.S. Senate, Morris lived in genteel retirement. He corresponded with political friends around the country but largely stayed out of the fray. In 1809, the fifty-seven-year-old bachelor surprised everyone by marrying his housekeeper Anne ("Nancy") Cary Randolph. Nancy was the sister of Thomas Jefferson's son-in-law Thomas Mann Randolph. She had come to New York to work as a domestic after a scandal in Virginia made her life unbearable. While a teenager, Nancy had an illegitimate child. The alleged father was either her brother-in-law Richard Randolph or his younger brother Theodorick, who died before the baby's birth. When the infant was found dead under mysterious circumstances, Nancy and Richard were suspected of killing the child. The inquest cleared them—Patrick Henry and John Marshall represented Nancy—and no formal charges followed, but the odor of impropriety clung to her. Morris was a friend of Nancy's father, had met her when she was a child, and could not have cared less about whiffs of scandal and impropriety. Their marriage, in fact, was scandalously happy. In 1813, Nancy gave birth to Gouverneur Morris, Jr. The elder Morris died in 1816 after trying to relieve a urinary blockage with a self-administered catheter. The infection that resulted killed him.

Robert Morris

Robert Morris remained in the Prune Street Prison for almost two years after Washington died but was finally released when Congress passed the nation's first bankruptcy law in 1800, partly inspired by his situation. Morris was physically broken, though. A group of friends that included Gouverneur Morris arranged for a modest stipend to be paid to Mary Morris to support her husband, and he lived in relative comfort until his death in May 1806. His brother-in-law Bishop William White, who had said obsequies at Washington's Philadelphia funeral in 1799, set aside space in his family's crypt for Morris's resting place. Mary lived for another twenty-one years, a revered matron of Philadelphia society.

Marie-Joseph-Paul-Yves-Roch-Gilbert du Motier, Marquis de Lafayette

Lafayette's release from the Austrian prison in 1797 did not end his troubles. He, his wife, and daughters remained in exile in northern Europe because the French government feared he would try to take power. Georges Washington Lafayette soon joined them from America. Not until the end of 1799 were Lafayette and his family allowed to return to their rural estate in France. They hoped to live there in obscurity. Napoleon Bonaparte's rise to power made that unlikely as he worried about Lafayette's popularity. Although Lafayette did not openly work against Napoleon's regime, he remained in France to serve as a symbol against the empire. Responding to the invitation of the U.S. government, Lafayette traveled to America with Georges Washington Lafayette in 1824. His tour took him to every state, but he made a special point to visit old friends, including Adams, Jefferson, and President James Monroe. Lafayette contracted pneumonia in 1834 and died in Paris that May. Georges sprinkled soil from Bunker Hill on his grave. It was a battle that had taken place before Lafayette arrived in America, but symbolism and reality were blurred by then for a generation passing into shadow. When Lafayette visited America in 1824, the veterans turned out paunchy or frail, and he had seemed fragile as well as he made his way along a tiring journey. Yet nothing could keep him from Mount Vernon, which he visited twice during the tour. He stood at the tomb of George Washington and for a few moments was again the brash boy who had said he would fight for America because he believed in her cause, a bundle of sparkling enthusiasm, broad gestures, and limitless energy. He bowed his head and wept before the grave of the finest person he had ever known.

Elizabeth Willing Powel

Eliza Powel lived quietly in Philadelphia for the remainder of her long life. In contrast to her days as a social maven, she seemed reclusive, but in reality she quietly visited friends and exchanged letters with distant ones. Following Washington's death, she wrote a tender letter of condolence to Martha. She was confident that because Washington was a Christian, he was in a better place. Eliza remained close to Nelly, who visited whenever she came to Philadelphia. In 1823, Eliza sent Nelly a beautiful silver inkstand, inscribed, "A testimony of cherished affection from E[lizabe]th Powel to her favorite Eleanor P. Lewis."[1] The death of her infant sons had prompted Eliza to shower maternal affection on all the children of friends and relatives, but her attachment to her sister's son John Hare was extraordinary. When he reached his majority, she persuaded him to change his name to John Hare Powel and made him her principal beneficiary. Eliza remained a staunch Federalist, but she strongly endorsed American efforts in the War of 1812. She was one of the people Lafayette singled out for a special visit in 1824, and they doubtless reminisced about the Washingtons. When Eliza died at eighty-seven in 1830, she left the bulk of her enormous estate to her nephew John, but she also made numerous bequests of money and personal items to friends, family, and servants. She was always amusing but always kind, loved by quiet Samuel Powel and esteemed by George Washington, a lady with money, and manners.

Edmund Randolph

His voice sounded like home, and he had been George Washington's devoted friend until he wasn't, something he could never understand nor forgive. After the break, Edmund Randolph remained an important attorney in Virginia, but he never completely dug out from his chronic financial problems. He also never completely shook off the accusation, kept current by Federalists, that he had taken money from the French. Those who knew him never doubted his integrity, and the trust of friends sustained him. He became something of a celebrity for taking up unpopular causes, as when he served as one of Aaron Burr's defense attorneys in Burr's treason trial in 1807. Randolph's beloved Betsy died in 1810 after a long illness, and her medical bills placed Randolph into even greater debt. He suffered an apparent stroke not long after and was partially paralyzed, which meant more medical bills and mounting debt. For years he had been writing a history of Virginia, and paralysis did not distract him from it. It was published in 1811. By then, he had long lost both the strength and the desire to practice law. He rented out his Richmond home and spent most of his time with his children. He was visiting a friend in September 1813 when he became ill, worsened as the days passed, and died on September 12, 1813. His short obituary in newspapers throughout the country closed with the observation "His history is blended with that of his country.—In private life he displayed all the domestic charities which distinguish the man of sensibility."[2] His real friends never doubted it for a minute.

Acknowledgments

G enerous archivists across the country made our labors productive and often pleasant. Efficiency and good cheer define the people who manage the Manuscript Reading Room of the Library of Congress, and our many visits over the years have made them friends as well as fellow scholars. Charleston, South Carolina, has charms on its own, but the South Carolina Historical Society's setting and staff always add to the treat. The Charleston Library Society's Janice Knight, D. Carol James, Anne W. Cleveland, and Robert C. Salvo can make research seem festive, delighting in their patrons' discoveries while guiding them to new ones. Kind people at the Library of Virginia in Richmond, the Albert and Shirley Small Special Collections Library at the University of Virginia, and the Manuscript Department at the Earl Gregg Swem Library at the College of William and Mary are equally peerless, and describing the archivists at the New York Public Library and the New York Historical Society as helpful does not do them justice. The society's Edward O'Reilly and Tammy Kiter are exemplars of professionalism and consideration.

Graphic arts managers made possible the collection of images that enliven as well as illustrate our story. Dawn Bonner at George Washington's Mount Vernon was generous with her time and steadfastly cheerful in the face of frequent and what surely were mildly exasperating queries. Deborah Sisum at the National Portrait Gallery, Smithsonian Institution, and Laura Barry at the Historical Society of Washington,

D.C., were as prompt as they were friendly when answering questions and supplying images. Bryan Leister is a talented artist with a disposition that Gilbert Stuart would have found congenial. The good people at the Virginia Historical Society simplified complications, as did Cristina Seghi in Florence, Italy, as we wrestled with the obstacles of distance and currency conversion.

Acting as our agent, Geri Thoma has read every draft of this book, but it has been as a friend that she heartened us at every step, and we could not have done it without her. We will be forever grateful. At Random House, our editor Jonathan Jao and his assistant Molly Turpin have vastly improved the book with their blue pencils and cogent recommendations. Jonathan saw languishing in our first draft a slightly different book than we had written, and his insistence that we find it has made for a better result. Will Murphy has been crucial in bringing everything to a happy conclusion. Michelle Daniel's copyediting of the manuscript has saved us from countless embarrassments while providing suggestions that in every instance resulted in improvements.

Many colleagues have been generous with time and counsel. We must make special mention of Mary V. Thompson at George Washington's Mount Vernon for allowing us to intrude on a busy schedule to discuss Washington's personal life. Her unrivaled knowledge of George Washington's religion gave us invaluable insights about his spiritual evolution, and her observations regarding slavery at Mount Vernon provided a vivid portrait of life on Washington's farms as well as his relations with individual slaves. Not only Washington scholars but the world is indebted to Mary for her research and writings. If we have erred in our interpretation of these matters, it is because we misheard or misread this remarkable historian. The inestimable Mary Thompson does not make mistakes.

Professor Kathryn E. Holland Braund read parts of the manuscript, and as she has done before with other projects, she offered for this one a unique blend of encouragement to bolster our spirits and suggestions to improve everything in significant ways. A remarkable combination of brains and beauty would set Kathryn apart in any case, but her humor and thoughtfulness are the stuff of legend among students and scholars alike.

We cannot adequately thank our family, whose encouragement was indispensable in chasing away weary moods. Sarah Twiggs and brothers Jack and Dub Heidler and Mike Twiggs inspire us with their love.

Finally, dear friends Steve and Leslie Bentley have been with us since the beginning of all our adventures, and this was simply to be the latest. To commemorate its start Steve gave us a bust of General Washington, which we proudly display in our dining room. Their amazing children—John, Richard (our godson), and Richard's lovely wife, Alexis—make us smile the way Nelly and Wash did the Washingtons. Steve's passing made this the last adventure for us and him, depriving us of a friend, but Leslie's incredible courage has humbled the saints and made the angels smile. To these remarkable people we have dedicated this book.

Notes

Abbreviations Used

AFC	*The Adams Papers: Adams Family Correspondence*
AHP	*The Papers of Alexander Hamilton*
FHS	Filson Historical Society
GWP, LOC	George Washington Papers, Library of Congress
JMP	*Papers of James Madison*
LOC	Library of Congress
LOV	Library of Virginia
CLS	Library Society of Charleston
MHS	Massachusetts Historical Society
NYHS	New York Historical Society
NYPL	New York Public Library
SCHS	South Carolina Historical Society
TJP	*The Papers of Thomas Jefferson*
UVA	Albert and Shirley Small Special Collections Library, University of Virginia
WD	*The Diaries of George Washington*
WM	Earl Gregg Swem Library, College of William and Mary
WOW	*The Writings of George Washington*
WPCOLS	*The Papers of George Washington,* Colonial Series
WPCS	*The Papers of George Washington,* Confederation Series
WPPS	*The Papers of George Washington,* Presidential Series
WPRS	*The Papers of George Washington,* Retirement Series
WPRWS	*The Papers of George Washington,* Revolutionary War Series
WTJ	*The Works of Thomas Jefferson*

Introduction

1. Wood, *Radicalism of the American Revolution,* 206.
2. The problem only got worse. See Washington to Greenwood, January 25, 1797, GWP, LOC.
3. Howard, *Painter's Chair,* 372.
4. Niemcewicz, *Travels,* 84, 85.
5. Louis-Guillaume Otto to Comte de Montmorin Saint-Hérem, June 13, 1790, in O'Dwyer, "French Diplomat's View," 434.
6. Serle, *Journal,* 309; Niemcewicz, *Travels,* 5.
7. Mail Contracts, July 24, 1791, *TJP,* 20:666.

1: "A Citizen of So Much Consequence"

1. Washington to Lafayette, April 28, 1788, *WOW,* 29:479.
2. Hamilton to Washington, September 1788, *WPPS,* 1:23–24.
3. Ibid., 1:24.
4. An excellent discussion of Washington and Morris's relationship can be found in Kline, "Gouverneur Morris and George Washington," in McDonald, *Sons of the Father,* 169–88.
5. Adams, *Morris,* 14.
6. Jay to Morris, September 16, 1780, Papers of John Jay, Columbia University.
7. Morris to Washington, November 12, 1788, *WPPS,* 1:103.
8. Morris to Washington, December 6, 1788, *WPPS,* 1:165–66.
9. Washington to Richard Conway, March 4, 1789, March 6, 1789, Washington to George Clinton, March 25, 1789, Washington to Madison, March 30, 1789, Washington to James McHenry, April 1, 1789, *WPPS,* 1:361–62, 368, 443–44, 464, 2:3; Freeman, *Washington,* 6:159; Robert Morris to John Jay, April 20, 1789, Papers of John Jay, Columbia University. For a sample of the many letters to Washington and his replies, see Washington to William Pierce, January 1, 1789, Samuel Meredith to Washington, February 23, 1789, Benjamin Harrison to Washington, February 26, 1789, Washington to Gustavus Scott, March 21, 1789, *WPPS,* 1:227–28, 336–37, 345, 420.
10. Washington to Knox, April 1, 1789, *WPPS,* 2:2.
11. *American State Papers, Miscellaneous,* 1:5.
12. Journal of Samuel Powel, in Lee, *Experiencing Mount Vernon,* 52
13. Knox to Washington, April 2, 1789, GWP, LOC.
14. Address by Charles Thomson, April 14, 1789, GWP, LOC. Ray Brighton's biography of Tobias Lear says that in addition to Thomson and Washington, Martha Washington was present with Lear, David Humphreys, and two men from Alexandria that he does not name. Most accounts, however, have Lear departing earlier to arrange for Washington's arrival in New York City. Washington's close friend James Craik was in the New Room as well, according to Brighton. See Brighton, *Lear,* 57–58.
15. Washington to Thomson, April 14, 1789, GWP, LOC.
16. *WPPS,* 2:152.
17. Arthur S. Lefkowitz put it more bluntly (and unfairly) by describing Humphreys as "a pompous windbag." See Lefkowitz, *George Washington's Indispensable Men,* 271.
18. Washington to Humphreys, October 10, 1787, *WOW,* 29:287.
19. Beall, "Military and Private Secretaries of George Washington," 111–12.

20. Brighton, *Lear,* 44.

21. Lear to George Long, ca. 1788, quoted in Decatur, *Private Affairs,* 315.

22. Bourne, *First Family,* 102–3.

23. The Lewises' house near Fredericksburg is usually referred to as "Kenmore," but it was never called that during their lifetimes. A subsequent owner named it Kenmore in 1819 after his ancestral home in Scotland.

24. Bourne, *First Family,* 86; Freeman, *Washington,* 5:252.

25. Washington to Mary Ball Washington, February 15, 1787, GWP, LOC.

26. George Augustine Washington is sometimes described as serving as one of Washington's aides during the war, but he was never officially designated as one.

27. Washington to Bassett, May 23, 1785, GWP, LOC.

28. Washington to George Augustine Washington, 1785, *WPPS,* 4:307–9.

29. Freeman, *Washington,* 6:63; Washington to George Augustine Washington, October 25, 1786, *WPCS,* 4:307–10.

30. Morgan, "Washington: The Aloof American," 412–13.

31. His detailed instructions on the eve of his departure for New York City were a prelude for what was to come. See Washington to George Augustine Washington, March 31, 1789, *WPPS,* 1:472–75; Washington to George Augustine Washington, June 10, 1787, *WOW,* 29:231; Ellis, *His Excellency,* 192; Lee, "Mount Vernon Plantation," in Schwarz, *Slavery at the Home of George Washington,* 24.

32. Articles of Agreement, May 20, 1790, *WPPS,* 5:332n–333n.

33. Washington to Henry Knox, September 3, 1792, Washington to George Augustine Washington, January 27, 1793, *WPPS,* 11:67; 12:53; Martha Washington to Fanny Bassett Washington, December 3, 1792, February 10, 1793, Washington, *"Worthy Partner,"* 241, 243.

2: "The Most Insignificant Office"

1. John Caldwell to James McHenry, April 8, 1789, Jensen, *Documentary History of First Federal Elections,* 4:228.

2. Rogers, *William Loughton Smith,* 171.

3. Jefferson to Madison, July 29, 1789, James Madison Papers, LOC.

4. Adams to Taylor, April 15, 1814, Adams, *Works of John Adams,* 6:642.

5. Maclay, *Journal,* 201, 242.

6. Ibid., 2–3.

7. Adams to Abigail Adams, December 19, 1793, John Adams Papers, MHS, Digital Collection.

8. Waldstreicher, *In the Midst of Perpetual Fetes,* 49; Freeman, *Washington,* 6:171–76.

9. Freeman, *Washington,* 6:179–82.

10. Decatur, *Private Affairs,* 100.

11. Kaminski, *George Clinton,* 57.

12. Ibid., 19.

13. Ibid., 165.

14. Chernow, *Washington,* 544.

15. Kaminski, *George Clinton,* 35; "HG" Letter VI, February 26, 1789, *AHP,* 5:273–74.

16. Rorabaugh, *Alcoholic Republic,* 48.

17. Kaminski, *George Clinton,* 5, 18, 51–52, 188, 191; Spaulding, *George Clinton,* 155, 194–95, 253–54; Maier, *Ratification,* 320–21.

18. Kaminski, *George Clinton,* 109–11; Stahr, *John Jay,* 235.

19. Berg, *Grand Avenues,* 60.

20. Remini, *House of Representatives,* 37–38.

21. Smith, *New York in the Year of Washington's Inauguration,* 7–9, 63.

22. Maclay, *Journal,* 4.

23. Kite, *L'Enfant and Washington, 1791–1792.* He was also "Major Longfont" in *The Georgetown Weekly Ledger.* See March 1791.

24. Dangerfield, *Robert R. Livingston,* 242.

25. Jensen, *Documentary History of First Federal Elections,* 4:269; McNamara, *Days of Jubilee,* 25.

26. Washington's First Inaugural Address, April 30, 1789, *WPPS,* 2:174–76.

27. Ames to George Richard Minot, May 3, 1789, Ames, *Works,* 1:34.

28. Stahr, *Jay,* 269–70.

29. *George Washington's Rules of Civility & Decent Behaviour in Company and Conversation* has been produced by the Colonial Williamsburg Foundation in pamphlet and online form, the latter at http://www.history.org/almanack/life/manners/rules2.cfm.

30. Lillback, *Sacred Fire,* 287.

31. Thompson, *Religion in the Life of George Washington,* 77–80, 185.

32. The various interpretations of Washington's views on religion and its place in government are summarized well in Lillback, *Sacred Fire;* Muñoz, "Washington on Religious Liberty"; Muñoz, *God and the Founders;* Curry, *First Freedoms;* Lambert, *Place of Religion;* Grizzard, *Religion & George Washington;* and Noll, *America's God.* As mentioned, Mary Thompson's *Religion in the Life of George Washington* is authoritative.

33. Lillback, *Sacred Fire;* Thanksgiving Proclamation, October 3, 1789, *WPPS,* 4:131.

34. His one exception was to receive the Speaker of the House should he call on Sunday afternoon. See Lillback, *Sacred Fire,* 264–65.

35. Washington to Hebrew Congregation of Newport, Rhode Island, August 17, 1790, GWP, LOC.

3: "Not the Tincture of Ha'ture About Her"

1. Washington to Alton, April 1, 1759, *WOW,* 2:318–19.

2. *WD,* 1:211. Ford notes that Washington must have had the measles as a child because Martha did not give them to him. Ford, *True George Washington,* 48.

3. Bryan, *Martha Washington,* 29.

4. Ibid., 72.

5. All of this is conjectural, of course, but it does amount to the consensus among most Washington biographers. Freeman, *Washington,* 2:401–4; Bryan, *Martha Washington,* 88.

6. Washington also had a troubling health history. In addition to being struck by "agues and feaver" in 1748 and contracting smallpox in Barbados when traveling with his brother Lawrence in 1751, he had an attack of pleurisy in 1752, high fevers and dysentery during his militia service in the 1750s, an attack of "river fever" (a mild form of malaria) in 1761 that recurred in 1786, and chronic rheumatism from 1787 on. Surprisingly, the healthiest period of his life was during the American Revolution.

7. Bryan, *Martha Washington,* 113–14, finds it highly unlikely based on her assessment of Washington's character in all other instances.

8. Washington to Mrs. George William Fairfax, September 12, 1758, *WOW,* 2:287–88.

9. Washington to Mrs. George William Fairfax, September 25, 1758, *WOW,* 2:292, 293.

10. Flexner, *Washington,* 4:355.

11. Cary, *Sally Cary,* 49.

12. Henriques, *Realistic Visionary,* 84, effectively pleads Sally Fairfax's case.

13. Wilstach, *Mount Vernon,* 102.

14. Washington to Bassett, June 20, 1773, *WOW,* 3:138.

15. Bourne, *First Family,* 89. Eltham burned in the late nineteenth century. Its bricks were used in the Rockefeller restoration of Williamsburg.

16. Eleanor Parke Custis to Elizabeth Bordley, October 13, 19, 1795, Brady, *Washington's Beautiful Nelly,* 20, 21.

17. Washington to Gordon, November 3, 1784, March 8, 1785, Washington to Custis, January 7, 1798, GWP, LOC; Chernow, *Washington,* 616.

18. Chernow, *Washington,* 615.

19. Hamlin, *Latrobe,* 77; Niemcewicz, *Travels,* 96; "Lady Henrietta Liston's Journal," 520.

20. Fleming, *Intimate Lives,* 24; Decatur, *Private Affairs,* 66.

21. Chernow, *Hamilton,* 126.

22. Bryan, *Martha Washington,* 242.

23. Pope, *Eloisa to Abelard,* 8.

24. Rice, *Early American Taverns,* 187–88.

25. Adams to Mary Smith Cranch, June 28, 1789, *AFC,* 8: 379.

26. Washington to Martha Washington, June 18, 23, *WD,* 3:336–38.

27. Ibid. Also see Samuel Johnston to James Iredell, March 4, 1790, McRee, *Life and Correspondence of Iredell,* 284–85; Thomas Lee Shippen to Dr. William Shippen, September 16, 1790, Ethel Armes Collection of Lee Family Papers, LOC.

28. Sarah Jay to John Jay, April 23, 1790, Papers of John Jay, Columbia University.

29. Flexner, *Washington,* 3:360.

30. Freeman, *Washington,* 6:248.

4: "His Person Is Little and Ordinary"

1. Irving Brant believed that Madison suffered from "epileptoid hysteria," a malady that mimics epilepsy but is psychosomatic and related to circumstantial stress. Ralph Ketcham does not dismiss the conclusion but points out that Madison's chronic bouts throughout his life do not match the age-related nature of epileptoid hysteria, which is associated with puberty. See Ketcham, *Madison,* 51; Cheney, *Madison,* 4.

2. Zacks, *Pirate Coast,* 315.

3. *Resolutions of Virginia and Kentucky,* 70.

4. Madison's attempt in August to remove exclusive responsibility for appropriations from the popularly elected House and allow the elite (nationalist) Senate to share in the task indicates that he was not interested in promoting the interest of large states but of subsuming all the states equally.

5. Leibiger, *Founding Friendship,* 2–3.

6. Randolph to Madison, November 10, 1788, *JMP,* 11:339.

7. Madison to Randolph, November 23, 1788, *JMP,* 11:363.

8. Carrington to Madison, November 18, 1788, *JMP,* 11:352.

9. Monroe to Jefferson, July 12, 1788, quoted in Maier, *Ratification,* 318.

10. Madison to Washington, January 14, 1789, *WPPS,* 1: 244; Banning, *James Madison,* 273.

11. Maier, *Ratification,* 357.

12. Rutland, *Ordeal of the Constitution*, 297.
13. William Loughton Smith to Edward Rutledge, August 9, 1789, William Loughton Smith Papers, SCHS.
14. Ames to George Minot, May 3, 1789, May 18, 1789, Ames, *Works*, 1:35, 42.
15. Cahn, "Firstness of the First Amendment," 465–67.
16. Lee to Patrick Henry, September 14, 1789, Henry, *Patrick Henry*, 3:399.
17. Ames to George Minot, May 3, 1789, Ames, *Works*, 1:35–36.
18. Smith to Rutledge, June 21, 1789, William Loughton Smith Papers, SCHS. Washington corrected the oversight. See Washington to the Senate, June 15, 1789, *WPPS*, 2:498.
19. Washington to Bushrod Washington, July 27, 1789, *WPPS*, 3:334.
20. Decatur, *Private Affairs*, 58–60; Chernow, *Washington*, 591; Washington to Senate, August 6, 1789, *WPPS*, 3:391–92.
21. Phelps, *Washington and Constitutionalism*, 148; Currie, *Constitution in Congress*, 23.
22. Maclay, *Journal*, 128; McDonald, *Presidency*, 27–28.
23. McDonald, *Presidency*, 36–37.
24. Jefferson to Jay, February 14, 1790, *TJP*, 16:181.
25. Smith to Rutledge, July 5, 1789, William Loughton Smith Papers, SCHS.
26. Maclay, *Journal*, 109.

5: "Republican Court"

1. Madison to Samuel Johnson, June 21, 1789, *JMP*, 12:249.
2. William Loughton Smith to Edward Rutledge, June 21, 1789, William Loughton Smith Papers, SCHS.
3. Langstaff, *Doctor Bard*, 170.
4. Ibid., 171.
5. Madison to Edmund Randolph, June 24, *JMP*, 12:258.
6. Chernow, *Washington*, 577.
7. Washington to Stuart, June 15, 1790, *WPPS*, 5:527.
8. Martha Washington to Fanny Bassett Washington, June 8, 1789, Washington, *"Worthy Partner,"* 215.
9. Smith, *New York in the Year of Washington's Inauguration*, 91.
10. Decatur, *Private Affairs*, 116.
11. Quoted in Charles, "Hamilton and Washington," 253.
12. Maclay, *Journal*, 135, 201.
13. Thompson, *Rum Punch*, 192.
14. Decatur, *Private Affairs*, 97–98; Brookhiser, *Founding Father*, 151–53.
15. Abigail Adams to Mary Smith Cranch, August 9, 1789, *AFC*, 8:399.
16. Cooke, *Tench Coxe*, 131.
17. Rush to Marshall, September 15, 1789, *Letters of Rush*, 2:807.
18. *Gazette of the United States*, April 22, 1789.
19. *WD*, 5:447.
20. Maclay, *Journal*, 15.
21. Christopher Gore to Rufus King, Rufus King Papers, NYHS.
22. *Gazette of the United States*, May 30, 1789.
23. Jones, *King of the Alley*, 89n4.
24. James Warren to Gerry, August 23, 1789, Gardiner, *Warren-Gerry Correspondence*, 235.
25. Decatur, *Private Affairs*, 276.

26. Freeman, *Affairs of Honor,* 43–44.

27. Maxey, "Portrait of Elizabeth Willing Powel," 19.

28. Maclay, *Journal,* 341.

29. Adams to Smith, December 26, 1790, Adams to Cotton Tufts, February 6, 1791, *AFC,* 9:167, 185.

30. O'Dwyer, "French Diplomat's View," 434.

6: "A Stranger in This Country"

1. Betty Lewis to Washington, July 24, 1789, *WPPS,* 3:301.

2. Henriques, "Grim King," 76.

3. Washington to Lewis, September 13, 1789, *WPPS,* 4:32–33.

4. Hamilton to Stevens, November 11, 1769, *AHP,* 1:4.

5. Hamilton to Laurens, January 8, 1780, *AHP,* 2:255.

6. Hamilton to Gordon, September 5, 1779, *AHP,* 153.

7. Hamilton to Greene, October 12, 1782, *AHP,* 3:184.

8. Fleming, *Perils of Peace,* 271.

9. See Kohn, "Inside History," 187–220; Rappleye, *Morris,* 301, 332–33.

10. Nelson, "Gates at Newburgh," 143–58; Skeen, "Newburgh Reconsidered," 273–98.

11. Freeman, *Washington,* 5:160n122.

12. "Conjectures about the New Constitution," ca. September 17–30, 1787, *AHP,* 4:276; T. Lowther to James Iredell, May 9, 1789, McRee, *Life and Correspondence of Iredell,* 259.

13. Hamilton to Henry Lee, December 1, 1789, *AHP,* 6:1.

14. For Washington's views on political philosophy, government, and dissent, see: Phelps, *Washington and Constitutionalism,* 131; Jones, "Washington and Politics of the Presidency," 29; Bradley, "Political Thinking of Washington," 470–79; Lienesch, "Constitutional Tradition," 6; Chambers, *Political Parties,* 5; Wood, *Empire of Liberty,* 97, 104; Winik, *Great Upheaval,* 153; Phelps, "Founding of the Presidency," 347–61.

15. Mary Smith Cranch to Abigail Adams, November 1, 1789, *AFC,* 8:433; Moats, *Celebrating the Republic,* 51. For a defense of Hancock, see Proctor, "John Hancock," 670–75.

16. John Trumbull to Oliver Wolcott, December 9, 1789, Gibbs, *Wolcott,* 33.

17. Benjamin Hawkins to John Jay, October 6, 1789, Papers of John Jay, Columbia University.

18. For good discussions of this evolution of ceremonies surrounding Washington, see Newman, "Washington and Political Culture," and *Politics of the Street.*

19. O'Dwyer, "French Diplomat's View," 412.

20. Washington's First Annual Message, January 8, 1790, *WPPS,* 4:543–46.

21. For explanations of Hamilton's plan, see Perkins, *American Public Finance,* 213–17, and Ferguson, *Power of the Purse.*

22. For Hamilton's plans regarding a sinking fund, see Swanson and Trout, "Hamilton's Hidden Sinking Fund."

23. Henry Lee to Madison, March 4, 1790, Henry Lee Papers, LOV.

24. Ferguson, *Power of the Purse,* 252, 254, 298.

25. Quoted in Rappleye, *Robert Morris,* 315.

26. Schwarz, "Hamilton, Madison," 407.

27. *The Federalist* no. 51, 266.

7: "A Certain Species of Property"

1. For several interesting discussions of early petitioning, see Bowling, *House and Senate,* 31–47, 107.
2. For Franklin on slavery, see Isaacson, *Benjamin Franklin,* 463–66.
3. Smith to Rutledge, February 13, 1790, William Loughton Smith Papers, SCHS.
4. Wolcott, Sr., to Wolcott, Jr., April 23, 1790, Gibbs, *Wolcott,* 1:45.
5. Kaminski, *Great Virginia Triumvirate,* 166–71; Brant, *Madison,* 3:380.
6. Bailyn, *To Begin the World Anew,* 48–49.
7. Finkelman, "Jefferson and Antislavery," 201.
8. Jefferson, *Notes,* 272.
9. For discussions of the debates on the petitions, see Elkins and McKitrick, *Age of Federalism,* 142–43, 151–52; Meleney, *Burke,* 187–90; Rogers, *William Loughton Smith,* 196–97; Bowling, *House and Senate,* 36, 66; Ellis, *Founding Brothers,* 113–15.
10. Washington to Stuart, March 28, 1790, *WPPS,* 5:288.
11. Certificate to John Dandridge to sell Anderson, May 28, 1795, *WOW,* 34:208.
12. Kaminksi, *Great Virginia Triumvirate,* 38; Stetson, *Washington and His Neighbors,* 115; Thompson, "Private Lives," 80–81; Jean Butenhoff Lee, "Model for the Republic," in Schwarz, *Slavery at the Home of George Washington,* 28.
13. Niemcewicz, *Travels,* 88; Parkinson, *Tour in America,* 2:420.
14. Johnson, *Taxation No Tyranny,* 89.
15. Casper, *Sarah Johnson's Mount Vernon,* 7–9.
16. Hirschfeld, *Washington and Slavery,* 85.
17. Carretta, *Phillis Wheatley,* 22.
18. Some have suggested that the poem is not a tribute to Washington but an entreaty for him to address the problem of patriots in Boston living under the British. Carretta, *Phillis Wheatley,* 156.
19. Washington to Wheatley, February 28, 1776, GWP, LOC. Wheatley's recent biographer thinks that if this meeting occurred, it was probably in Providence, Rhode Island. See Carretta, *Wheatley,* 157.
20. Carretta, *Wheatley,* 157.
21. McLeod, *Dining with the Washingtons,* 75.
22. Wiencek, *Imperfect God,* 272.
23. Morgan, "Problem of Slavery," 299.
24. Washington to Biddle, July 28, 1784, GWP, LOC.
25. *WD,* 4:125.
26. Ibid., 5:73.
27. Entry of June 24, 1788, *WD,* 5:349.
28. McLeod, *Dining with the Washingtons,* 25.
29. Lear to Washington, April 5, 24, 1791, Washington to Lear, April 12, 1791, *WPPS,* 8:67, 130, 85; Decatur, *Private Affairs,* 223–26.
30. Martha Washington to Fanny Bassett, June 5, 1791, Washington, *"Worthy Partner,"* 231.
31. Lear to Washington, June 5, 1791, *WPPS,* 8:232; Chernow, *Washington,* 639.
32. Mary V. Thompson's important discovery about the place whence Hercules fled resulted from her careful study of Mount Vernon's farm records and other documentary evidence. She also has posed to us the possibility that the type of work that raised Hercules's objections was not punishment but in character with Washington's dictum that there be no idle hands at Mount Vernon. In any case, the fate of Hercules remains

a mystery. Some speculate that he went from Mount Vernon to Philadelphia and from there to Europe, where he worked in fashionable households as a chef. A portrait in the style of Gilbert Stuart shows a black man wearing a chef's toque and fine linens and is thought to be Hercules.

33. Washington to Mercer, September 9, 1786, *WOW,* 29:5.

34. Washington to John Fowler, February 2, 1788, *WOW,* 29:388; also see Parkinson, *Tour in America,* 2:248–31. Dr. James Craik confided to a visitor that slaves were a financial bane, their labor marginal, and their cost considerable. See Niemcewicz, *Travels,* 104.

35. Washington to Young, December 12, 1793, GWP, LOC.

36. Washington was careful not to mention liberating his slaves to Young, but he made clear that this object was one of the reasons for his plan. See Washington to Lear, GWP, LOC.

37. Hirschfeld, *Washington and Slavery,* 233.

38. The 1786 inventory is found in *WD,* 4:277–83; 1799 is in *WPRS,* 4:528–40.

39. *Philadelphia Gazette,* May 24, 1796.

40. Schwarz, *Slavery at the Home of George Washington,* 97.

41. Decatur, *Private Affairs,* 226; Chernow, *Washington,* 637–39.

42. "Washington's Runaway Slave," interview with Oney Judge, *The Liberator,* August 22, 1845.

43. *Philadelphia Gazette,* May 24, 1796.

44. *The Liberator,* August 22, 1845. See Finkelman, *Slavery and the Founders,* 80, for the origins of the Fugitive Slave Act of 1793.

45. Whipple to Wolcott, October 14, 1796, Whipple to Washington, December 22, 1796, GWP, LOC.

46. Washington to Whipple, November 28, 1796, *WOW,* 35:297.

47. *WD,* 4:278; Wiencek, *Imperfect God,* 383n13. In Decatur's edited record of Lear, he states that Washington did not try to recapture Oney, which is not true given his many attempts to do so that failed. See *Private Affairs,* 314.

48. The 1867 Currier and Ives illustration changed Savage's seating arrangement and eliminated Lee. See Howard, *Painter's Chair,* for the slavery metaphor.

49. Washington was careful to mention Lee's meritorious service in connection with his manumission. This possibly harkened back to the old process that required an explanation for the act of freeing a slave. Washington could have been protecting Lee's status from future interpretations of emancipation that might nullify it.

8: "This May End Disagreeably"

1. Jefferson to Martha Jefferson, May 5, 1787, *Works of Jefferson,* 5:281.

2. Abigail Adams to Elizabeth Shaw Smith, September 27, 1789, *AFC,* 8:411.

3. Kaminski, *Great Virginia Triumvirate,* 113.

4. Jefferson to Washington, December 15, 1789, *TJP,* 16:34.

5. Jefferson to Madame de Tesse, March 11, 1790, *TJP,* 16:228.

6. Washington to Jefferson, January 21, 1790, Washington to Madison, February 20, 1790, *WPPS,* 5:29–30, 164.

7. Jefferson to Washington, December 15, 1789, *TJP,* 16:34.

8. Randolph to Madison, October 10, 1789, *JMP,* 12:435.

9. Jefferson to Mason, June 13, 1790, *Papers of George Mason,* 3:1201.

10. Madison to Washington, January 4, 1790, *WPPS,* 4:536–37.

11. Bailyn, *To Begin the World Anew,* 58.
12. Rahe, "Jefferson's Machiavellian Political Science," 472.
13. Jefferson to Madison, February 14, 1790, Jefferson to Washington, February 14, 1790, *TJP,* 16:182, 184.
14. Reuter, "George Beckwith," 483. For the best exegesis on the importance of the Beckwith-Hamilton relationship, see Boyd, *Number 7.*
15. See, for instance, Morris to Carmichael, February 25, 1789, quoted in Ferguson, *Power of the Purse,* 251.
16. Morris, *Diary and Letters,* 1:137.
17. William Nelson, Jr., to William Short, December 17, 1789, William Short Papers, WM.
18. Morris, *Diary and Letters,* 1:137.
19. Morris to Washington, July 31, 1789, *WPPS,* 3:360–61.
20. *WD,* 6:51.
21. For Washington's consultative style, see White, *Federalists,* 32–40; Phelps, *Washington and Constitutionalism,* 162–63; Wood, *Empire of Liberty,* 86; McDonald, *Presidency of George Washington,* 40–41.
22. Washington to Lafayette, June 3, 1790, *WPPS,* 5:468.
23. For different views on the relationship between Thomas Jefferson and James Madison, see Rakove, *James Madison and the Creation of the American Republic,* 14; Bailyn, *To Begin the World Anew,* 47; Burstein and Isenberg, *Madison and Jefferson;* Fleming, *Intimate Lives,* 364; and Staloff, *Hamilton, Adams, Jefferson,* 300.
24. Maclay, *Journal,* 265, 302.
25. Madison to Randolph, May 6, 1790, *JMP,* 13:189.
26. Jefferson to Randolph, June 6, 1790, *TJP,* 16:475.
27. Peterson, *Jefferson,* 269–70, 388.
28. Jefferson to Madison, June 9, 1793, *TJP,* 15:27.
29. Jefferson to Samuel Osgood, October 5, 1785, Samuel Osgood Papers, NYHS.

9: "A Spirit of Accommodation"

1. Washington to Adams, May 12, 1790, *AFC,* 9:55.
2. Flexner, *Doctors on Horseback,* 167; Shultz, *Body Snatching,* 80.
3. Lamb and Harrison, *History of the City of New York,* 2:305.
4. Maclay, *Journal,* 258.
5. Martha Washington to Mercy Otis Warren, June 12, 1790, Washington, *"Worthy Partner,"* 226.
6. Bickford and Bowling, *First Congress,* 83.
7. Butler to Rutledge, May 15, 1790, Butler, *Letters,* 42.
8. Stuart to Lee, May 23, 1790, Custis-Lee Family Papers, LOC.
9. Smith to Rutledge, May 24, 1790, William Loughton Smith Papers, SCHS.
10. Wolcott, Sr., to Wolcott, Jr., December 23, 1789, Gibbs, *Wolcott,* 1:33.
11. Richard Bland Lee to Theodorick Lee, March 14, 1790, Custis-Lee Family Papers, LOC.
12. William Page to Nicholas Gilman, April 1, 1790, Nicholas Gilman Correspondence, LOC.
13. Maclay, *Journal,* 229–30.
14. Rose, "David Stuart," 9–10. Eleanor Calvert Custis had seven pregnancies while she was married to Martha's son John Parke Custis, though only four of those children

lived. With Stuart she had at least thirteen more children and perhaps sixteen pregnancies.

15. Rose, "David Stuart," 11.
16. Stuart to Washington, March 15, 1790, *WPPS,* 5:235–7.
17. Stuart to Washington, June 2, 1790, *WPPS,* 5:460–61.
18. Washington to Stuart, June 15, 1790, *WPPS,* 5:524–25.
19. Tench Coxe to James Madison, May 4, 1790 *JMP,* 13:188.
20. Cooke, *Tench Coxe,* 161.
21. William Loughton Smith to Edward Rutledge, May 24, 1790, June 14, 1790, William Loughton Smith Papers, SCHS.
22. Rappleye, *Morris,* 476–77.
23. "The Assumption," February 1793, *WTJ,* 7:224–25.
24. Katz, "Jefferson's Liberal Anticapitalism," 8.
25. Jefferson to Mason, June 13, 1790, *TJP,* 16:493.
26. Risjord, "Compromise of 1790: New Evidence," 309–10.
27. "The Assumption," February 1793, *WTJ,* 7:226–27.
28. Bickford and Bowling, *First Congress,* 195.
29. Maclay, *Journal,* 304, 319.
30. Richard Bland Lee to Theodorick Lee, June 26, 1790, Custis-Lee Family Papers, LOC.
31. Madison to James Monroe, July 24, 1790, *JMP,* 13:282.
32. Memorandum from Thomas Jefferson, August 29, 1790, Memorandum from James Madison, August 29, 1790, *WPPS,* 6:368–70.
33. Dumbauld, "Jefferson and the City of Washington," 69–74.
34. Morales-Vazquez, "President's House," 40–41; Berg, *Grand Avenues,* 186; Reps, *Monumental Washington,* 22.
35. Washington to Commissioners of the Federal District, December 1, 1791, *TJP,* 22:367–68.
36. Washington to Jefferson, January 18, 1792, *WPPS,* 9:469.
37. Berg, *Grand Avenues,* 193.
38. Kite, *L'Enfant and Washington, 1791–1792,* 159n111.

10: "The Sensation of a Philosophic Mind"

1. Puls, *Henry Knox,* 9.
2. Ibid., 30.
3. Abigail Adams Smith to Abigail Adams, June 17, 1788, *AFC,* 8:273.
4. Knox to Washington, July 7, 1789, *WPPS,* 3:134. For difficulties in the Southeast, see William Loughton Smith to Edward Rutledge, June 21, 1789, William Loughton Smith Papers, SCHS; Warley to Andrew Pickens, July 27, 1788, George Handley to Andrew Pickens, August 31, 1788, Andrew Pickens to Richard Winn, May 16, 1789, Andrew Pickens Papers, CLS; John Cleves Symmes to Richard C. Anderson, June 15, 1789, Anderson-Latham Collection, LOV.
5. Anthony Wayne to James Madison, June 15, 1789, Anthony Wayne Papers, LOC.
6. Braund, *Deerskins and Duffels,* 171.
7. McGillivray to Panton, May 8, 1790, Caughey, *McGillivray,* 260.
8. Charles Pinckney to Andrew Pickens, July 4, 1790, Andrew Pickens Papers, CLS.
9. Anderson, *Crucible of War,* 55.
10. Ellis, *His Excellency: George Washington,* 213.

11. Knox could not completely isolate McGillivray, though, and Beckwith likely visited him at least once.

12. Adams to Mary Smith Cranch, August 8, 1790, *AFC,* 9:85.

13. Hamilton to Washington, July 8, 1790, *WPPS,* 6:24; *WD,* 6:87–89, 93; Reuter, *Washington's Foreign Policy,* 83.

14. Jefferson's Opinion, July 12, 1790, *WPPS,* 6:59; Jefferson to James Monroe, July 11, 1790, Jefferson to Randolph, July 11, 1790, *TJP,* 17:25.

15. Boyd, *Number 7,* 41; Harper, *American Machiavelli,* 79; Adams, *Gouverneur Morris,* 219; DeConde, *Entangling Alliance,* 72; "Conversations with Beckwith," July 15, 1790, August 7, 1790, *AHP,* 6:497, 547; Jefferson to Morris, August 12, 1790, *TJP,* 17:128.

16. Miller, *Hamilton,* 368.

17. Stahr, *Jay,* 124, 136–37.

18. Jefferson to Luis Pinto de Souza, August 11, 1790, Jefferson to Humphreys, August 11, 1790, *TJP,* 17:118–19, 125–26; Reuter, *Washington's Foreign Policy,* 128; Stahr, *Jay,* 124; Boyd, *Number 7,* 73, 75–76.

19. Jay to Washington, August 28, 1790, Jefferson to Washington, August 28, 1790, Adams to Washington, August 29, 1790, Knox to Washington, August 29, 1790, Hamilton to Washington, September 15, 1790, *WPPS,* 6:353, 356–66, 440–47.

20. Campbell to Steele, March 2, 1792, Papers of Arthur Campbell, FHS; Symmes to Richard C. Anderson, June 15, 1789, Anderson-Latham Collection, LOV; John Brown to Harry Innes, April 27, 1790, Innes Papers, LOC.

21. Henry Knox to Isaac Shelby, July 20, 1790, Isaac Shelby Papers, FHS.

11: "A Particular Measure Proceeding from a Particular Officer"

1. Abigail Adams to Abigail Rogers, September 5, 1790, *AFC,* 9:98.

2. Quoted in Sword, *Washington's Indian War,* 121.

3. Niemcewicz, *Travels,* 37.

4. Wenger, "Jefferson, Tenant," 249–50, 253.

5. Madison to Jefferson, March 31, 1791, *TJP,* 19:107.

6. Wansey, *American Journal,* 73.

7. Niemcewicz, *Travels,* 54.

8. Adams to Smith, January 8, 1791, *AFC,* 9:177.

9. Niemcewicz, *Travels,* 55.

10. Thompson, *Rum Punch,* 191–92, 197–98; Eberlein and Hubbard, "American 'Vauxhall,'" 163–65.

11. George Thatcher to wife, December 9, 1790, George Thatcher Papers, LOC.

12. Freeman, *Washington,* 6:303; Hamilton to Washington, December 22, 1790, *AHP,* 7:378.

13. Madison remarks, December 27, 1790, *JMP,* 13:336.

14. Perkins, *American Public Finance,* 233–34.

15. Robert Troup to Hamilton, January 19, 1791, *AHP,* 7:445.

16. McCraw, *Founders and Finance,* 62–64, 111.

17. *Report on Proposed Bank, AHP,* 7:305–42; Perkins, *American Public Finance,* 235–44; Flexner, *Washington,* 3:279; McDonald, *Presidency,* 61.

18. John Beckley to William Anderson, January 1, 1791, John J. Beckley Family Papers, LOC.

19. Madison's remarks, February 2 and February 8, 1791, *JMP,* 13:373–85; Hammond, *Banks,* 104, 116.

20. Ames to George Richards Minot, February 17, 1791, Ames, *Works,* 1:95.

21. Randolph to Washington, February 12, 1791, *WPPS,* 7:330–37.

22. Malone, *Jefferson,* 2:341–44.

23. Madison to Washington, February 21, 1791, *WPPS,* 7:395.

24. Madison, et al., *The Federalist,* 148.

25. Washington to Humphreys, March 16, 1791, *WPPS,* 7:583; also see Malone, *Jefferson,* 2:344–48.

26. Klubes, "First Federal Congress," 22; Banning, "Triumph of the Constitution," 181; Maclay, *Journal,* February 23, 1791, 387.

27. Hamilton to Jay, November 13, 1790, Lincoln to Hamilton, *AHP,* 7:149–50, 197.

28. Siemers, "Electoral Dynamics," in Bowling, *House and Senate,* 255–56.

29. Rakove, *Madison and the Creation of the Republic,* 95–96; Sheehan, "Madison v. Hamilton," 408–21; Ben-Atar, *Jeffersonian Commercial Policy,* 101; McCoy, "Madison and Commercial Discrimination," 642.

30. James Madison to Ambrose Madison, March 2, 1791, *JMP,* 13:402.

12: "Positively Unable to Articulate a Word"

1. Gore to Lear, December 28, 1791, Tobias Lear Papers, LOC; Jefferson to Hancock, February 2, 1791, *TJP,* 19:237.

2. Editorial Note, *TJP,* 16:237, 245, 247.

3. Jefferson to Freneau, February 28, 1791, *TJP,* 19:351.

4. Axelrad, *Philip Freneau,* 198–221; Brant, *Madison,* 3:334–36; Pasley, *Newspaper Politics,* 64.

5. Rogers, *William Loughton Smith,* 210–13; Smith, *Journal,* 35–37.

6. Washington to Hamilton, Jefferson, and Knox, April 4, 1791, *WPPS,* 8:59–60.

7. *WD,* 6:107.

8. Anna Jean Simpson to Mrs. Christian Fleming, April 25, 1791, Henderson, *Southern Tour,* 115.

9. Harriott Pinckney Horry Diaries, Pinckney-Lowndes Papers, SCHS.

10. Henderson, *Southern Tour,* 139–40.

11. Liscomb, *South Carolina in 1791,* 21.

12. Robert Mills Account of Washington's Visit, SCHS; *Virginia Herald,* May 26, 1791, in Kaminski and McCaughan, *Eyes of His Contemporaries,* 191.

13. *WD,* 6:131.

14. Liscomb, *South Carolina in 1791,* 64.

15. Caldwell, *Autobiography,* 91–92.

16. Washington to Hamilton, June 13, 1791, *AHP,* 8:470–71.

17. Liscomb, *South Carolina in 1791,* 81–83.

18. Henderson, *Southern Tour,* 80–83.

19. Brant, *Madison,* 3:339; Burstein and Isenberg, *Madison and Jefferson,* 229.

20. Reynolds Pamphlet, 1797, *AHP,* 21:250–51.

13: "Political Heresies"

1. Coxe to Jefferson, April 16, 1791, *TJP,* 20:232–33.

2. Jefferson to Madison, July 27, 1791, Madison to Jefferson, July 31, 1791, *TJP,* 20:682, 708.

3. Charles Francis Adams made this observation in the 1851 edition of the work. See *Works of John Adams,* 4:274.

4. Jefferson to Smith, April 26, 1791, *TJP,* 20:290.

5. Jefferson to Washington, May 8, 1791, *WPPS,* 8:163.

6. Jefferson to Madison, May 9, 1791, *TJP,* 20:293.

7. Lear to Washington, May 8, 1791, *WPPS,* 8:166.

8. Jefferson to Adams, August 30, 1791, *TJP,* 20:311.

9. Washington to Jefferson, June 26, 1791, *WPPS,* 8:300.

10. Beckwith to Grenville, March 11, 1791, quoted in Boyd, *Number 7,* 83.

11. Thornton to James Bland Burges, April 2, 1792, June 11, 1792, Jackman, "Thornton to Burges," 104, 110.

12. Hamilton to Knox, October 3, 1791, *AHP,* 9:270.

13. Memorandum of Conversation between Philemon Dickinson and George Hammond, March 26, 1792, *TJP,* 23:344.

14. Thornton to Burges, February 2, 1792, December 5, 1792, Jackman, "Thornton to Burges," 96–97.

15. Hammond to Jefferson, November 30, 1791, *TJP,* 22:356–57.

16. Record of conversation between Hamilton and Hammond, January 18, 1792, March 31, 1792, July 1–2, 1792, *AHP,* 10:494, 11:212–13, 12:1; Editorial Note, *TJP,* 22:411.

17. Draft of a message to the U.S. Senate, ca. January 3–4, 1792, *WPPS,* 9:381.

18. Hawkins's notes on the debate in the Senate, ca. January 3, 1792, *WPPS,* 9:376–80.

19. Sherman speech on Morris appointment, January 1792, Rufus King Papers, NYHS.

20. Morris to Hamilton, March 21, 1792, *AHP,* 11:162.

21. Jefferson to Morris, January 23, 1792, *TJP,* 23:55–57.

22. Washington to Morris, January 28, 1792, *WPPS,* 9:515–17.

23. For more on the United States' role in the Saint-Domingue rebellion, see Brown, *Toussaint's Clause;* Matthewson, "Washington's Policy Toward the Haitian Revolution" and "Jefferson and Haiti"; Jones, *America and French Culture;* Hickey, "Slave Revolt in Haiti"; DeConde, *Entangling Alliance,* 271–74; Scherr, *Jefferson's Haitian Policy.*

24. Jefferson to Lafayette, June 16, 1792, *TJP,* 24:85.

14: "Sweets of Office"

1. Hamilton to Nicholas Low, July 22, 1792, May 13, 1793, Ebenezer Stevens Papers, NYHS.

2. Hamilton to Madison, November 24, 1791, *AHP,* 9:528.

3. Madison to Henry Lee, January 1, 1792, *JMP,* 14:180.

4. Memoranda of Conversation with the President, March 1, 1792, *TJP,* 23:184–87.

5. Editorial note, *WPPS,* 9:275.

6. Robert Smith to Wilson Cary Nicholas, January 10, 1792, Wilson Cary Nicholas Papers, 1789–1827, LOC.

7. John Steele to Arthur Campbell, January 29, 1792, Papers of Arthur Campbell, FHS; see also Clarfield, "Defense Policy and the Tariff," 448; Egbert Benson to Nicholas Low, December 26, 1790, Philip Schuyler, Nicholas Low Papers, NYHS.

8. Anonymous to Washington, January 3, 1792, *WPPS,* 9:370.

9. Anonymous to Washington, ca. January 20, 1792, March 1792, Powel to Washington, April 21, 1792, Washington to Powel, April 23, 1792, *WPPS,* 9:481–82, 10:174, 305, 313.
10. Gutzman, *Madison,* 262.
11. Ford, *Spurious Letters.*
12. Reardon, *Randolph,* 65, 75, 78.
13. Broadwater, *Mason,* 229.
14. Memoranda of Consultations with the President, April 9, 1792, *TJP,* 23:264; Freeman, *Washington,* 6:346–47.
15. Taxay, *United States Mint and Coinage,* 15.
16. Lear to Jefferson, June 30, 1792, Randolph's opinion, July 7, 1792, *TJP,* 24:165–67; Reardon, *Randolph,* 205.
17. Reps, *Monumental Washington,* 26.
18. Lee to Madison, August 14, 1791, Henry Lee Papers, LOV.
19. Hamilton to Adams, March 20, 1792, Hamilton to Jefferson, March 20, 1792, Adams to Jay, March 21, 1792, *AHP,* 11:158, 159.
20. Hamilton to Seton, April 12, 1792, *AHP,* 11:273.
21. Jefferson to Randolph, April 19, 1792, *TJP,* 23:436.
22. Jefferson to Nicholas Lewis, April 12, 1792, *TJP,* 23:408.
23. Richard Bland Lee to unknown, February 7, 1792, Custis-Lee Family Papers, LOC.
24. Lee to Madison, January 8, 1792, Henry Lee Papers, LOV.
25. Hamilton to Carrington, May 26, 1792, *AHP,* 11:426–45.

15: "Spirit of Party"

1. Madison's Notes on Conversations with Washington, May 5, 9, 1792, *JMP,* 14:299–303.
2. Washington to Madison, May 20, 1792, Madison to Washington, June 20, 1792, Draft Address, ca. June 20, 1792, *WPPS,* 10:399–401, 478–83; Brant, *Madison,* 3:356.
3. Notes on Conversation with Washington, July 10, 1792, *TJP,* 23:535–40.
4. Jefferson to Jean Antoine Gautier, June 8, 1792, *TJP,* 24:42.
5. Notes on Conversation with Washington, July 10, 1792, *TJP,* 23:535–40, 24:210–11.
6. Randolph to Washington, August 5, 1792, *WPPS,* 10:629–30.
7. Powel to Washington, November 17, 1792, *WPPS,* 11:395.
8. Washington to Hamilton, July 29, 1792, *WPPS,* 10:588–91.
9. Washington to Hamilton, August 26, 1792, *WPPS,* 11:39.
10. Hamilton to Washington, September 9, 1792, Jefferson to Washington, September 9, 1792, *WPPS,* 11:91, 97–98.
11. Jefferson's Conversation with Washington, October 1, 1792, *WPPS,* 11:82–84; Steele, *Jefferson and American Nationhood,* 204–5.
12. Broadwater, *Mason,* 4.
13. Ibid., 57.
14. Ibid., 57–58; Henriques, "George Washington and George Mason," 185; Washington to Mason, May 10, 1776, March 27, 1779, GWP, LOC; Moore, "Mason, Statesman," 13.
15. Broadwater, *Mason,* 55; Rowland, *Mason,* 1:178.
16. Rowland, *Mason,* 1:178.
17. Edmund Randolph called the single executive a "foetus of monarchy," and John Blair also voted against the single executive. U.S. Constitutional Convention, *Debates,* 38.
18. Mason to Public, July 8, 1788, *Papers of George Mason,* 3:1122.
19. George Mason to John Mason, March 13, 1789, *Papers of George Mason,* 3:1142.

20. Jefferson's Notes of a Conversation with George Mason, September 30, 1792, *TJP,* 24:428–29.
21. Madison's Essays, December 3, 1791, December 19, 1791, December 31, 1791, January 23, 1792, February 4, 1792, *JMP,* 14:137–39, 170, 178–79, 197, 217; Siemers, *Ratifying the Republic,* 116.
22. Madison's Essay, March 31, 1792, *JMP,* 14:274.
23. Pasley, *Newspaper Politics,* 67–68.
24. Hamilton's Essays, July 25, 1792, July 28, 1792, August 4, 1792, August 11, 1792, *AHP,* 12:107, 123–24, 157–64, 188–94.
25. *Gazette of the United States,* August 8, 1792.
26. Quoted in Clifford, "Politics of Edmund Randolph," 291.
27. Jefferson to Morris, October 4, 1792, *TJP,* 24:440.
28. Butler to Gunn, September 12, 1792, Butler, *Letters,* 185.
29. Rorabaugh, *Alcoholic Republic,* 53.
30. Edward Carrington to Zachariah Johnston, January 19, 1792, Zachariah Johnston Papers, LOV; Hamilton to Washington, September 1, 1792, Hamilton to Jay, September 3, 1792, Jay to Hamilton, September 8, 1792, Randolph to Hamilton, September 8, 1792, *AHP,* 12:311–12, 316–17, 334–35, 336–40; Proclamation, September 15, 1792, *WPPS,* 11:122–23.
31. Supreme Court Justices to Washington, August 9, 1792, Randolph to Washington, October 28, 1792, 4th Annual Message, November 6, 1792, *WPPS,* 10:643, 11:272, 345; Jefferson suggestions, October 15, 1792, Washington to Jefferson, November 11, 1792, *TJP,* 24:486, 567–68; House Response, November 9, 1792, *JMP,* 14: 403; Brant, *Madison,* 3:366.
32. Washington to Lee, January 20, 1793, *WPPS,* 12:30.
33. Smith to Rutledge, January 3, 1793, William Loughton Smith Papers, SCHS.
34. Randolph to Washington, August 5, 1792, *WPPS,* 10:627.
35. Elisha Boudinot to Hamilton, September 13, 1792, *AHP,* 12:370.
36. Christopher Greenup to Richard C. Anderson, August 15, 1792, Anderson-Latham Collection, LOV; Fisher Ames to John Lowell, December 6, 1792, Fisher Ames Correspondence, LOC.
37. Reynolds to Hamilton, December 15, 1791, December 17, 1791, December 19, 1791, December 22, 1791, January 3, 1792, January 17, 1792, April 3, 1792, April 10, 1792, April 17, 1792, April 23, 1792, May 2, 1792, *AHP,* 10:376–77, 387–88, 396, 401, 503, 519–20, 11:222, 254–55, 297, 330, 354. Cerniglia, "An Indelicate Amor," is one of the more recent treatments of this improbable episode and how it affected Hamilton's career.
38. Hamilton to Monroe, Muhlenberg, and Venable, December 17, 1792, Monroe to Hamilton, December 20, 1792, 13:330, 344; Cogan, "Reynolds Affair," 394.

16: "The Look of an Upstart"

1. Butler to John Hunter, February 6, 1793, Butler, *Letters,* 238.
2. Adams to Abigail Adams, January 24, 1793, February 27, 1793, *AFC,* 9:381, 413.
3. Conversation with Washington, February 7, 1793, *TJP,* 25:154–55.
4. Editorial Note, Madison Remarks, March 1, 1793, *JMP,* 14:455–68; Anderson, *Giles,* 22–23; Rogers, *William Loughton Smith,* 240–41; Sheridan, "Jefferson and Giles Resolutions," 593–98.

5. Editorial Note, *TJP*, 25:280–92.
6. Notes on Conversation with Washington, February 7, 1793, *WPPS*, 12:105.
7. Adams to Abigail Adams, January 24, 1793, *AFC*, 9:381.
8. *National Gazette,* March 2, 1793.
9. *The Carlisle* (PA) *Gazette,* March 6, 1793.
10. Tagg, "Bache's Attack on George Washington," 200; Newman, "Washington and Political Culture," 487; Randolph to Washington, February 18, 1793, *WPPS*, 12:176; Decatur, *Private Affairs,* 301–2.
11. Cabinet Meeting, March 1, 1793, *AHP*, 14:176.
12. Cabinet Opinion on Administration of Presidential Oath, February 28, 1793, *WPPS*, 12:231.
13. Thornton to Burges, March 5, 1793, Jackman, "Thornton to Burges," 120.
14. Jefferson to Short, January 3, 1793, *TJP*, 25:14.
15. Morris to Jefferson, January 25, 1793, *TJP*, 25:95.
16. Jefferson to Lafayette, April 2, 1790, *TJP*, 16:293.
17. Smith to Rutledge, ca. 1792, William Loughton Smith Papers, SCHS.
18. Notes on Conversation with Smith and Washington, February 20, 1793, *TJP*, 25:244.
19. Notes on Conversation with Washington, February 20, 1793, *WPPS*, 12:193.
20. Randolph to Washington, February 22, 1793, *WPPS*, 12:199.
21. Jefferson's Notes, March 30, 1793, *WPPS*, 12:392–93; Staloff, *Hamilton, Adams, Jefferson,* 105; Sheridan, "Jefferson and Giles Resolutions," 599–600.
22. Humphreys to Lear, November 28, 1792, Tobias Lear Papers, LOC.
23. Washington to Hamilton, Washington to Jefferson, April 12, 1793, *WPPS*, 12:447–48.
24. Jefferson's Notes, May 6, 1793, *WPPS*, 12:529.
25. Ibid., 530.
26. Minutes on Cabinet Meeting, April 19, 1793, *WPPS*, 12:459.
27. Neutrality Proclamation, April 22, 1793, *WPPS*, 12:472–73.
28. Madison to Jefferson, June 13, 1793, Jefferson to Monroe, July 14, 1793, Jefferson to Madison, August 11, 1793, *TJP*, 26:273, 501, 677–78; Madison to Jefferson, June 19, 1793, *JMP*, 15:33.
29. Anonymous to Washington, May 3, 1793, *WPPS*, 12:506–7.
30. The *Embuscade*'s ordnance is described in James, *Naval History of Great Britain, from the Declaration of War by France in 1793, to the Accession of George IV,* 1:110.
31. Minnigerode, *Genet,* 34–35, 65, 117; Ammon, *Genet Mission,* 5–9; Bowman, *Struggle for Neutrality,* 45.
32. Minnigerode, *Genet,* 121; Ammon, *Genet Mission,* 2–3, 7.
33. Morris to Washington, January 6, 1793, *WPPS*, 11:593.
34. Barlow to Jefferson, March 8, 1793, *TJP*, 25:336.

17: "Laugh Us into War"

1. Jefferson to Randolph, May 8, 1793, Randolph to Jefferson, May 9, 1793, *TJP*, 25:691, 700.
2. Jefferson to Madison, May 13, 1793, Jefferson to Madison, May 19, 1793 *TJP*, 26:26, 61.
3. Christopher Gore to Tobias Lear, June 2, 1793, Tobias Lear Papers, LOC; John Leeds Bozman to William Vans Murray, May 27, 1793, John Leeds Bozman Family Papers, LOC; W. S. Smith to William Constable, July 19, 1793, Constable-Pierrepont Papers, NYPL.

4. Ammon, *Genet Mission,* 53.
5. John Steele to Hamilton, April 30, 1793, *AHP,* 14:359.
6. Alexander Macomb to William Constable, May 25, 1793, Constable-Pierrepont Papers; Jefferson to Madison, May 19, 1793, *TJP,* 26:62.
7. Ammon, *Genet Mission,* 59.
8. Ternant to Washington, May 17, 1793, Washington to Ternant, May 17, 1793, *WPPS,* 12:605–6; Notes of a Conversation with George Washington, May 23, 1793, *TJP,* 26:101–2.
9. Washington to the Provisional Executive Council of France, May 24, 1793, *TJP,* 26:111.
10. Memorandum from Hamilton, May 15, 1793, Memorandum from Knox, May 16, 1793, Cabinet Opinion on French Privateers, *WPPS,* 12:577, 595, 13:1; Reardon, *Randolph,* 228–31; Ammon, *Genet Mission,* 54.
11. Jefferson to Madison, June 9, 1793, *JMP,* 15:27.
12. Young, "Connecting the President and the People," 454; Freeman, *Washington,* 7:101.
13. Washington to Jefferson, July 11, 1793, *TJP,* 26:481.
14. Cabinet Notes, July 12, 1793, *WPPS,* 13:214.
15. Minnigerode, *Genet,* 269–71.
16. A Gentleman in the Country to Rufus King, December 17, 1793, Rufus King Papers, NYHS.
17. Jefferson to Madison, June 9, 1793, *JMP,* 15:27.
18. Daniel, *Scandal and Civility,* 103.
19. Axelrad, *Philip Freneau,* 257.
20. Pacificus no. 1, June 29, 1793, Hamilton and Madison, *Pacificus-Helvidius Debates,* 8.
21. Jefferson to Madison, July 7, 1793, *TJP,* 26:444.
22. Helvidius no. 1, August 24, 1793, Hamilton and Madison, *Pacificus-Helvidius Debates,* 55–64.
23. Jefferson to Madison, July 7, 1793, *TJP,* 26:444.
24. Notes on Cabinet Meeting, July 29, 1793, *TJP,* 26:579–80.
25. Notes on Cabinet Meeting on Edmond Charles Genet, August 2, 1793, *TJP,* 26:601–3.
26. Notes on Cabinet Meeting, August 3, 1793, *TJP,* 26:608.
27. Madison to Jefferson, May 27, 1793, Jefferson to Madison, June 9, 1793, *JMP,* 15:22, 26–27.
28. Notes on conversation with Washington, August 6, 1793, *TJP,* 26:629
29. Jefferson to Madison, August 11, 1793, *TJP,* 26:652.
30. Ammon, *Genet Mission,* 104; Harper, *American Machiavelli,* 125.
31. Hamilton's Outline for a Letter of Recall, ca. August 2, 1793; Proposed Addition, ca. August 15, 1793; Jefferson's Analysis of Letter of Recall, ca. August 15–20, 1793, Jefferson to Gouverneur Morris, August 16, 1793, *TJP,* 26:693–95, 697–711.
32. *The Albany Gazette,* August 19, 1793; Jay and King Affidavit, August 12, 1793, Rufus King Papers, NYHS.
33. Genet to Washington, August 13, 1793, *WPPS,* 13:436–37; Jefferson to Genet, August 16, 1793, *TJP,* 26:684.
34. Jefferson to Madison, November 2, 1793, *TJP,* 27:298; George Clinton to Cornelia Clinton, March 19, 1793, Genet Family Papers, NYPL; Wansey, *American Journal,* 76; Ann Cobham to Cornelia Clinton Genet, November 21, 1794, George Clinton Papers, NYPL.
35. James Iredell to Mrs. Tredwell, July 30, 1793, McRee, *Life and Correspondence of Iredell,* 397.
36. Freeman, "Slander, Poison Whispers," 35–36; Notes on Conversations with Lear and Beckley, April 7, 1793, Lear on Public Debt, May 15, 1793, *TJP,* 25:517, 26:17.

37. Powell, *Yellow Fever,* 24.
38. Jefferson to Madison, September 8, 1793, *TJP,* 27:62.
39. Washington to Hamilton September 6, 1793, *AHP,* 15:324–25; Rush to Julia Rush, October 3, 1793, Rush, *Letters of Rush,* 2:701.
40. Oliver Wolcott, Jr., to Washington, October 20, 1793, *WPPS,* 14:239.

18: "Earnest Desire to Do Right"

1. Madison to Monroe, September 15, 1793, *JMP,* 15:111.
2. Ammon, *Genet Mission,* 152; "Genet, etc, etc," Rufus King Papers, NYHS; King to Jay, December 15, 1793, Papers of John Jay, Columbia University.
3. Smith to Rutledge, December 6, 1793, William Loughton Smith Papers, SCHS; Jay to King, December 12, 1793, Rufus King Papers, NYHS; James Morris to Lewis Morris, January 5, 1794, Morris Family Papers, NYHS; Francis Preston to William Preston, January 1, 1794, Preston Family Papers, FHS; Ralph Izard to Herman LeRoy, January 22, 1794, Ralph Izard Letter, SCHS.
4. Editorial note, *TJP,* 26:xiii; Morris to Washington, October 18, 1793, October 19, 1793, *WPPS,* 14:229–30, 233.
5. Jefferson to Humphreys, March 21, 1793, *TJP,* 25:420–21; Alexander Macomb to William Constable, December 17, 1793, Constable-Pierrepont Papers, NYPL; Kitzen, "Tripolitan War," 603–4; Allison, *Crescent Obscured,* 17–22; James Simpson to Jefferson, January 12, 1793, James Simpson Letterbook, LOC.
6. Smith to Rutledge, December 6, 1793, William Loughton Smith Papers, SCHS.
7. Troup to King, January 1, 1794, Rufus King Papers, NYHS.
8. Adams to Abigail Adams, December 26, 1793, January 6, 1794, *AFC,* 9:485, 10:30.
9. Jefferson to Washington, December 31, 1793, Washington to Jefferson, January 1, 1794, *TJP,* 27:656, 28:3.
10. Lear to Washington, October 10, 1793, *WPPS,* 14:193.
11. Adams to Abigail Adams, January 9, 1794, *AFC,* 10:36.
12. George Nicholas to Madison, February 9, 1794, *JMP,* 15:256.
13. Randolph to Hamilton, January 2, 1794, *AHP,* 15:604.
14. Randolph to Washington, January 22, 1794, *WPPS,* 15:105.
15. Wolcott, Jr. to Wolcott, Sr., January 18, 1794, Gibbs, *Wolcott, 157.*
16. Burk, *Great Britain and America,* 200.
17. Jefferson to Madison, April 3, 1794, *JMP,* 15:301.
18. "15 Republicans" to Smith, 1794, William Loughton Smith Papers, LOC.
19. Mary Smith Otis to Abigail Adams, April 23, 1794, *AFC,* 10:89.
20. Adams to Abigail Adams, March 2, 1794, *AFC,* 10:95; also Madison to Jefferson, March 2, 1794, *JMP,* 15:250.
21. Adams to Abigail Adams, March 2, 1794, *AFC,* 10:95.
22. Minnigerode, *Genet,* 288.
23. "Relations with France," ca. 1795, *AHP,* 19:96, 526.
24. Ammon, *Genet's Mission,* 159–60; DeConde, *Entangling Alliance,* 305; Madison to Jefferson, March 2, 1794, *TJP,* 28:27.

19: "A War Soon with Britain"

1. New York *Columbian Gazetteer,* March 27, 1794.
2. Lee to Washington, June 15, 1792, Washington to Lee, June 30, 1792, *WPPS,* 10:455, 508.
3. Wayne to William R. Atlee, December 12, 1792, Anthony Wayne Papers, LOC.
4. John Preston to William Preston, June 1, 1792, December 7, 1792, Preston Family Papers, FHS. For detailed accounts of Washington's Indian wars in the Northwest Territory see Sword, *Washington's Indian War;* Gaff, *Bayonets in the Wilderness;* Nelson, *Anthony Wayne;* and Downes, *Council Fires on the Upper Ohio.*
5. Samuel Adams to Knox, April 4, 1794, Samuel Adams Papers, LOC; Paine Wingate to Josiah Bartlett, April 2, 1794, Paine Wingate Correspondence, LOC.
6. Christopher Greenup to Nathaniel Pendleton, March 26, 1794, Nathaniel Pendleton Papers, NYHS.
7. Paine Wingate to Josiah Bartlett, March 22, 1794, Paine Wingate Correspondence, LOC.
8. Hamilton to Washington, March 24, 1794, *WPPS,* 15:444.
9. Hamilton to Washington, March 24, 1794, Randolph to Washington, April 1, 1794, Washington to Hamilton, April 8, 1794, Hamilton to Washington, April 8, 1794, *WPPS,* 15:443, 486–87, 541–42; Madison to Jefferson, April 14, 1794, *TJP,* 28:52.
10. Monroe to Washington, April 8, 1794, Washington to Monroe, April 9, 1794, Randolph to Washington, April 19, 1794, *WPPS,* 15:548, 551, 621.
11. Jay to Sarah Jay, April 15, 1794, Jay, *Correspondence,* 4:3–4.
12. Stahr, *John Jay,* 282–83.
13. Ibid., 224.
14. Ibid., 225.
15. Washington to Jay, August 13, 1788, *WOW,* 30:34.
16. Bowling, *House and Senate,* 168, 170.
17. Washington to Madison, February 8, 1794, Madison to Jefferson, March 23, 1795, Bartholomew Dandridge to Madison, March 31, 1795, *JMP,* 15:253, 493, 505.
18. Coles to Todd, June 1, 1794, *JMP,* 15:342.
19. Brant, *Madison,* 3:406–10; Fleming, *Intimate Lives,* 368.
20. Randolph to Washington, January 26, 1794, *WPPS,* 15:130.
21. Washington to Morris, June 19, 1794, *WPPS,* 16:248.
22. Monroe to Madison, September 2, 1794, *JMP,* 15:355.
23. Monroe to Madison, February 18, 1795, Hamilton, *Writings of Monroe,* 2:209.

20: "Do Not Turn Your Back"

1. Washington to Hamilton, August 12, 1794, *AHP,* 17:88–89.
2. Randolph to Short, August 18, 1794, Daniel Family Papers, LOV.
3. The treaty the following year at Greenville arranged the removal of virtually all Indians from what would become the state of Ohio.
4. *WD,* 6:192.
5. Freeman, *Washington,* 7:209–10. The other nephews with the Virginia militia were Lawrence Lewis, who would later marry Nelly Custis; Howell Lewis; Samuel Washington (Charles's son); and Lawrence Washington (Samuel's son).
6. For full coverage of the Whiskey Rebellion see Hogeland, *Whiskey Rebellion;* Slaughter, *Whiskey Rebellion;* Rich, "Washington and Whiskey Insurrection"; Kohn, "Deci-

sion to Crush the Whiskey Rebellion"; Brackenridge, *Western Insurrection;* and Findley, *Insurrection in the Four Western Counties.*

7. Adams to Abigail Adams, November 18, 1794, *AFC,* 10:262.
8. Jefferson to Giles, December 17, 1794, Jefferson to Madison, December 28, 1794, Jefferson to Monroe, May 26, 1795, *TJP,* 28:219, 228, 359.
9. Winship, "Western Ways," in Bowling, *House and Senate,* 164.
10. Short to Jefferson, November 13, 1793, *TJP,* 27:358.
11. See, for example, Grenville to Thomas Pinckney, January 1, and October 2, 1794, Pinckney Family Papers, SCHS.

21: "That Man Is a Traitor"

1. Jefferson to Washington, May 23, 1792, Notes on Conversation with Washington, July 10, 1792, *TJP,* 23:535–40, 24:210–11.
2. Jefferson to Walter Jones, January 2, 1814, Thomas Jefferson Papers, LOC.
3. Washington to Pendleton, January 22, 1795, *WOW,* 34:98.
4. Adams to Abigail Adams, December 7, 1794, December 30, 1794, January 20, 1795, *AFC,* 10:290–91, 329, 355.
5. John E. Van Alen to Peter Van Schaack, February 4, 1795, Peter Van Schaak Papers, LOC.
6. Adams to Abigail Adams, December 30, 1794, *AFC,* 10:328.
7. Robert Goodloe Harper to Arnoldus Vanderhorst, February 20, 1795, Vanderhorst Papers, SCHS.
8. Ames to Christopher Gore, February 24, 1795, Ames, *Works,* 1:167.
9. Washington to Hamilton, February 2, 1795, *WOW,* 34:109.
10. Pickering to Bingham, December 17, 1795, Pickering, *Pickering,* 3:171, emphasis in original.
11. Wolcott, Sr., to Wolcott, Jr., March 26, 1795, Gibbs, *Wolcott,* 216.
12. Jay to Hamilton, November 19, 1794, *AHP,* 17:390; Jay to King, November 19, 1794, Jay, *Correspondence,* 4:136; Peter Jay to Sarah Jay, February 8, 1795, Jay Family Papers, NYPL.
13. Randolph to Jay, May 30, 1795, Conway, *Randolph,* 234–35.
14. John Adams to Abigail Adams, June 14, 1795, *AFC,* 10:449.
15. Miller, *Federalist Era,* 168.
16. Estes, *Jay Treaty Debate,* 104.
17. Webster to Wolcott, July 30, 1795, Noah Webster Papers, NYPL.
18. Jefferson to Thomas Mann Randolph, August 11, 1795, *TJP,* 28:435.
19. Clifford, "Politics of Edmund Randolph," 305.
20. Randolph to Short, July 25, 1795, Daniel Family Papers, LOV.
21. Monroe to Madison, June 13, 1795, *JMP,* 16:16–17; Bowman, *Struggle for Neutrality,* 187.
22. Pickering to Washington, July 31, 1795, Pickering, *Pickering,* 3:188–89.

22: "To You I Shall Return"

1. Hatch, *Thrust for Canada,* 62–64.
2. Washington, 4:225.

3. Ibid., 49–50, 52.
4. Wallace, *Traitorous Hero,* 7.
5. Ford, *Journals of the Continental Congress,* 8:593.
6. Freeman, *Washington,* 4:458.
7. Kramer, *Lafayette in Two Worlds,* 22.
8. Arnold, *Life of Benedict Arnold; His Patriotism and His Treason,* 295.
9. Royster, *Revolutionary People at War,* 191–93.
10. Schwartz, *American Symbol,* 149. This is also cited in Neely, "Myth of Braddock's Defeat," 45.
11. Lafayette to Washington, December 21, 1784, Butler, *Memoirs of the Marquis de La Fayette,* 2:103.
12. Martin, *Benedict Arnold, Revolutionary Hero,* 6–7; *Complete Works of Benjamin Franklin,* 7:240–41; Lafayette to Mme. de Lafayette, February 2, 1781, Butler, *Memoirs of the Marquis de La Fayette,* 1:386.
13. Clifford, "Politics of Edmund Randolph," 307.
14. Randolph, *Vindication,* passim.
15. Randolph, *Vindication,* 6.
16. Washington's Queries, Gibbs, *Wolcott,* 291.
17. Reardon, *Randolph,* 312.
18. Washington to Randolph, August 20, 1795, *WOW,* 34:277.
19. Tachau, "Washington and Randolph," 31.
20. Randolph to Washington, September 21, 1795, Randolph, *Vindication,* 19–20; Washington to Randolph, September 27, 1795, *WOW,* 34:316–17.
21. Hamilton to Washington, December 24, 1795, *AHP,* 19:514.
22. Notes on Conversation with Washington, July 10, 1792, *TJP,* 23:535–40, 24:210–11.

23: "A Magic in His Name"

1. Christopher Gore to Tobias Lear, October 10, 1795, Tobias Lear Papers, LOC.
2. Philadelphia *Aurora General Advertiser,* October 24, 1795; Concord *Courier of New Hampshire,* December 12, 1795; Cunningham, "John Beckley," 46.
3. Charles Lee to Richard Lee, December 17, 1795, Custis-Lee Family Papers, LOC.
4. Washington to Pickering, September 27, 1795, *WOW,* 34:315.
5. Henry Tazewell to Sylvanus Bourne, January 6, 1796, Sylvanus Bourne Papers, LOC.
6. Jefferson to Giles, December 31, 1795, *TJP,* 28:565.
7. Farnham, "Virginia Amendments of 1795," 82–85; Arnoldus Vanderhorst to South Carolina House of Representatives, December 1, 1796, Vanderhorst Papers, SCHS.
8. Henry Tazewell to John Ambler, January 22, 1796, Henry Tazewell Papers, LOC.
9. Toth, *Ellsworth,* 20–22; Brown, *Oliver Ellsworth,* 231.
10. Madison to Jefferson, February 29, 1796, *TJP,* 28:624.
11. Stevens Thomason Mason to Henry Tazewell, October 6, 1795, Tazewell Family Papers, LOV.
12. Giles to Jefferson, December 20, 1795, *TJP,* 28:558–59.
13. Madison to Jefferson, April 4, 1796, *JMP,* 16:286.
14. Washington to House of Representatives, March 30, 1796, *WOW,* 35:2–3.
15. Henry Tazewell to John Ambler, January 22, 1796, Henry Tazewell Papers, LOC.
16. George Cabot to John Lowell, March 26, 1796, George Cabot Correspondence, LOC.
17. Hamilton to William Loughton Smith, William Loughton Smith Papers, LOC.

18. Madison to Jefferson, April 23, 1796, *JMP,* 16:335; Banner, *To the Hartford Convention,* 20; Daniel Morgan to William Loughton Smith, April 21, 1796, William Loughton Smith Papers, LOC.
19. Freeman, *Washington,* 7:372.
20. Seidensticker, "Frederick Augustus Conrad Muhlenberg," 204.
21. Wilson, *Peter Porcupine,* 22.
22. Charles Lee to John Marshall, May 5, 1796, Marshall, *Papers of John Marshall,* 3:26.
23. Gilbert, *To the Farewell Address,* 120; Bernard, *Fisher Ames,* 277.
24. Washington to Hamilton, November 23, 1795, *WOW,* 34:374–76; Washington to Madison, January 22, 1796, March 6, 1796, *JMP,* 16: 200–201, 252; Washington to Hamilton, February 13, 1796, April 9, 1796, May 8, 1796, *AHP,* 20:55, 109, 166.
25. "Lady Henrietta Liston's Journal," 511, 515; Liston to her uncle, October 6, 1796, Perkins, "Letters of Henrietta Liston," 596, 604.
26. Twining, *Travels in America,* 114, 128–32.

24: "Friends and Fellow Citizens"

1. Howard, *Painter's Chair,* 214.
2. Morris, *Diaries of Gouverneur Morris,* February 22, 1796, 247; Charles Lee to Marshall, May 5, 1796, Marshall, *Papers of John Marshall,* 3:27; Washington to Madison, May 12, 1796, *JMP,* 16:355.
3. Beckley to Madison, June 26, 1796, *JMP,* 16:371.
4. Washington to Jefferson, July 6, 1796, *WOW,* 35:118–19.
5. Washington to Humphreys, June 12, 1796, *WOW,* 35:91–92; Tagg, "Bache's Attack on George Washington," 217.
6. Pickering to Webster, February 18, 1796, Noah Webster Papers, NYPL.
7. Washington to Hamilton, June 26, 1796, *AHP,* 20:239; Latrobe, *Journal,* 63.
8. Washington to Wolcott, July 6, 1796, *WOW,* 35:126.
9. Latrobe, *Journal,* 58.
10. Ibid., 57–58, 62.
11. Ibid., 58, 62–63.
12. Washington to Pickering, July 27, 1796, *WOW,* 35:156–57.
13. Pickering to King, August 29, 1796, King, *Life and Correspondence of Rufus King,* 2:84.
14. Washington to Pickering, July 8, 1796, *WOW,* 35:127.
15. Zahniser, *Charles Cotesworth Pinckney,* 136–43.
16. See Boston *Polar-Star,* November 11, 1796; *New Hampshire Journal,* November 15, 1796; and Charleston *Columbian Herald,* November 22, 1796.
17. Clarfield, *Timothy Pickering and American Republic,* 174–77; Bowman, *Struggle for Neutrality,* 269–70; Coleman, "'Second Bounaparty?'" 191.
18. Farewell Address, September 19, 1796, *WOW,* 35:214–38.
19. Statement of David Claypoole, February 26, 1826, in Graff, *Genealogy of the Claypoole Family,* 86–87; Flexner, *Washington,* 4:303.
20. Spalding and Garrity, *Farewell Address,* 45.
21. For different views on the purpose and perceptions of the document, see Kaufman, *Washington's Farewell Address;* Morrison, *Political Philosophy of Washington;* Markowitz, "Washington's Farewell"; Spalding, *Farewell Address;* Pessen, "Washington's Farewell"; and Gilbert, *To the Farewell Address.*
22. Perkins, "Letters of Henrietta Liston," 605.

23. Cunningham, "John Beckley," 47–51.

24. Dabney Carr to Richard Terrell, December 30, 1796, Papers of the Carr and Terrell Families, UVA.

25. Jefferson to Madison, December 17, 1796, January 1, 1797, Madison to Jefferson, January 15, 1797, Madison to James Maury, January 18, 1797, *JMP,* 16:431–32, 440–41, 455, 462.

26. Philadelphia *Aurora General Advertiser,* December 19, 1796; Baltimore *Federal Gazette,* January 4, 1797; Nelson, *Thomas Paine,* 292.

27. Eighth Annual Message, December 7, 1796, *WOW,* 35:310–20.

28. Jefferson to Madison, January 8, 1797, *JMP,* 16:448.

29. "Lady Henrietta Liston's Journal," 515–16.

30. Chernow, *Washington,* 766; Newman, "Washington and Political Culture," 494; Freeman, *Washington,* 7:432.

31. Washington to Adams, February 20, 1797, Washington to Knox, March 2, 1797, *WOW,* 35:394, 408.

32. Eberlein, "190, High Street," 173–74; Flexner, *Washington,* 4:337–38.

33. Brant, *Madison,* 3:449–50.

34. "Lady Henrietta Liston's Journal," 514; Freeman, *Washington,* 7:436.

35. Niemcewicz, *Travels,* 29.

36. Adams to Abigail Adams, March 5, 1797, Adams Family Papers, MHS, Digital Collection.

37. Freeman, *Washington,* 7:436–38.

38. Quoted in Rogers, *William Loughton Smith,* 296.

39. Washington to Lear, March 9, 1797, *WPRS,* 1:25.

25: "Already Turned Farmer Again"

1. Washington to Knox, May 1797, Washington, *"Worthy Partner,"* 303.

2. Eleanor Parke Custis to Elizabeth Bordley, March 18, 1797, Brady, *Washington's Beautiful Nelly,* 32.

3. Martha Washington's first husband's maternal grandfather had stipulated in his will that any of his descendants who expected to inherit any of the Parke estate would have to have the name "Parke" inserted somewhere, no matter how awkwardly, in their name.

4. Henry Tazewell to John Ambler, December 18, 1796, Henry Tazewell Papers, LOC.

5. Jefferson to Mazzei, April 19, 1796, *TJP,* 29:82.

6. For an analysis of the different versions see Marraro, "Four Versions of Jefferson's Letter to Mazzei."

7. An especially insightful student of Washington attributes their permanent estrangement to the Mazzei letter. See Henriques, *Realistic Visionary,* 117.

8. Freeman, *Washington,* 7:491–92; Kaplan, *Jefferson and France,* 71.

9. Knox to Washington, July 29, 1798, Washington to Knox, August 9, 1798, Knox to Washington, August 26, 1798, *WPRS,* 2:469–72, 502–6, 562–63.

10. Flexner noted how Washington was scrupulous about not using his influence when president but had no such qualms in retirement when he never hesitated to use his name to gain special privileges in business dealings or land sales. Flexner, *Washington,* 4:372.

11. Nutting, "Lear," 720.

12. Powel to Washington, December 3, 1798, Washington to Powel, December 4, 1798, Powel to Washington, December 7, 1798, *WPRS,* 3:242, 243, 246.

13. Because the United States never declared war on France, the terms of the Enemy Alien Act were never invoked.

14. *Statutes at Large,* 1:596.

15. Coleman, "'A Second Bounaparty?,'" 210.

16. See Smelser, "Washington and the Alien and Sedition Acts."

17. "Lady Henrietta Liston's Journal," 516.

18. Washington to Burgess Ball, September 22, 1799, *WPRS,* 4:318.

19. Henriques, "George Washington and the Grim King," 81.

20. Ibid., 79.

21. Freeman, *Washington,* 7:24–25; Lear, *Letters and Recollections,* 132–35.

22. Brown, *Incidental Architect,* 25.

23. New York *Weekly Museum,* December 28, 1799.

24. Kahler, *Long Farewell,* 28–33; Morris to Washington, April 7, 1800, Washington, *"Worthy Partner,"* 373–74; *The New-York Gazette,* December 30, 1799.

25. Hamilton to Pinckney, December 22, 1799, Hamilton to Martha Washington, January 12, 1800, *AHP,* 24:116, 184.

26. Madison's remarks on the "Death of George Washington," *JMP,* 17:295.

27. Jefferson to Uzal Ogden, February 12, 1800, *TJP,* 31:369.

28. Jefferson to Walter Jones, January 2, 1814, Jefferson Papers, LOC. Jefferson was paraphrasing 2 Samuel 3:38 in the King James version of the Holy Bible. The precise quotation is "And the king said unto his servants, 'Know ye not that that there is a prince and a great man fallen this day in Israel?'"

29. Thornton, "Mrs. Thornton's Diary," 90.

30. Casper, *Sarah Johnson's Mount Vernon,* 5.

31. "Lady Henrietta Liston's Journal," 519.

32. Smith, *Correspondence,* 224–25.

Epilogue: Closing the Circle

1. Lewis to Elizabeth Bordley Gibson, October 25, 1823, Brady, *Washington's Beautiful Nelly,* 137.

2. Washington, D.C. *Daily National Intelligencer,* September 22, 1813.

Bibliography

Primary Sources

Manuscript Collections

American Philosophical Society, Philadelphia, Pennsylvania
  Papers of Benjamin Franklin, Digital Edition

Rare Book and Manuscript Library, Butler Library, Columbia University, New York, New York
  Papers of John Jay

Charleston Library Society, Charleston, South Carolina
  Andrew Pickens Papers
  Charles Cotesworth Pinckney Papers
  Thomas Pinckney Papers
  John Rutledge Letters

Filson Historical Society, Louisville, Kentucky
  John Brown Papers
  Papers of Arthur Campbell
  Preston Family Papers
  Isaac Shelby Papers
  Richard Sprigg, Jr., Papers

Library of Congress, Washington, D.C.
  Samuel Adams Papers
  Theodosia Burr Alston Papers
  Fisher Ames Correspondence
  Ethel Armes Collection of Lee Family Papers, 1671–1936
  John J. Beckley Family Papers, 1789–1918
  William Bingham Papers, 1776–1801

Sylvanus Bourne Papers, 1775–1859
John Leeds Bozman Family Papers, 1688–1883
George Cabot Correspondence
Carroll Family Papers
Joshua Coit Correspondence, 1792–98
Custis-Lee Family Papers
William Duer Papers, 1776–89
Gabriel Duvall Papers, 1780–1920
Alexander Gillon Correspondence, 1793
Nathaniel Gilman Papers, 1776–1824
Nicholas Gilman Correspondence, 1790–1808
Henry Glen Correspondence
David McMurtrie Gregg Papers, 1716–1916
Robert Goodloe Harper Papers, 1796–1823
John Henry Correspondence, 1780–93
Harry Innes Papers, 1754–1900
Thomas Jefferson Papers
Rufus King Papers, 1784–1822
John Langdon Correspondence, 1776–1809
Tobias Lear Papers
James Madison Papers
Wilson Cary Nicholas Papers, 1789–1827
Roger Sherman Papers
James Simpson Letterbook
William Loughton Smith Papers
Caleb Strong Papers
Henry Tazewell Papers
George Thatcher Papers
John Trumbull Papers
Peter Van Schaack Papers
George Washington Papers
Anthony Wayne Papers
Paine Wingate Correspondence

Library of Virginia, Richmond, Virginia

Anderson-Latham Collection, 1777–1881
Daniel Family Papers, 1794–1898
Patrick Henry Letters, 1778–99
Zachariah Johnston Papers, 1742–1856
Henry Lee Papers, 1768–1816
Lewis Family Papers, 1779–1841
John Peter Gabriel Muhlenberg Letter

Edmund Pendleton Letters, 1773–1800
Tazewell Family Papers, 1623–1930
Virginia Miscellany Papers, 1657–1931

Massachusetts Historical Society, Boston, Massachusetts

Adams Family Papers, Electronic Archive
John Adams Papers, Digital Collection

New York Historical Society, New York, New York

Richard Harrison Letterbooks
John Jay Papers, Gilder Lehrman Collection
Rufus King Papers, 1783–1826
Morris Family Papers
Samuel Osgood Papers
Nathaniel Pendleton Papers
Philip Schuyler, Nicholas Low Papers
Ebenezer Stevens Papers

New York Public Library, New York, New York

George Clinton Papers
Constable-Pierrepont Papers, 1762–1911
Genet Family Papers
Gerry-Townsend Papers
Jay Family Papers
Livingston Family Papers
Robert Morris Papers
Noah Webster Papers

Albert and Shirley Small Special Collections Library, University of Virginia, Charlottesville, Virginia

Papers of the Carr and Terrell Families
Carr-Cary Papers
Papers of James McDowell
Thomas J. Randolph Reminiscences
Stuart-Baldwin Family Papers

South Carolina Historical Society, Charleston, South Carolina

DeSaussure Family Papers
Grimke Family Papers
Journal of the Charleston Chamber of Commerce
Henry Laurens Papers
Manigault Family Papers

Pinckney-Lowndes Papers

Pringle Family Papers

Ralph Izard Letter

Harriott Horry Ravenel Papers

Read Family Correspondence

Robert Mills's Account of George Washington's Visit to Charleston, S.C., May 2, 1791

William Loughton Smith Papers

Arnoldus Vanderhorst Family Papers

Earl Gregg Swem Library, College of William and Mary, Williamsburg, Virginia

Powell Family Papers, Hepburn Addition

Short Papers, 1675–1789

William Short Papers

Published Primary Sources

Adams, Charles Francis, ed. *The Works of John Adams, Second President of the United States: With a Life of the Author, Notes and Illustrations, by His Grandson Charles Francis Adams.* 10 vols. Boston: Little, Brown, 1850.

Adams, Samuel. *The Writings of Samuel Adams.* 4 vols. Edited by Harry Alonzo Cushing. New York: G. P. Putnam's Sons, 1904.

American State Papers, Miscellaneous. 2 vols. Washington, DC: Gales and Seaton, 1834.

Ames, Fisher. *Works of Fisher Ames.* Edited by Seth Ames. 2 vols. Boston: Little, Brown, 1854.

Annals of Congress. 42 vols. Washington, DC: Gales and Seaton, 1834.

Bailyn, Bernard, ed. *The Debate on the Constitution.* 2 vols. New York: Library of America, 1993.

Bard, Samuel. *An Enquiry into the Nature, Cause and Cure, of the Angina Suffocativa, or, Sore Throat Distemper, As It Is Commonly Called by the Inhabitants of This City and Colony.* New York: S. Inslee and A. Car, 1771.

Bear, James Adam. *Jefferson at Monticello.* Charlottesville: University Press of Virginia, 1967.

Beckley, John James. *Justifying Jefferson: The Political Writings of John James Beckley.* Edited by Gerard W. Gawalt. Washington: Library of Congress, 1995.

Brackenridge, H. M. *History of the Western Insurrection in Western Pennsylvania.* New York: Arno Press, 1969.

Bradford, William, ed. *Life and Correspondence of Joseph Reed: Military Secretary of Washington, at Cambridge, Adjutant-general of the Continental Army, Member of the Congress of the United States, and President of the Executive Council of the State of Pennsylvania.* 2 vols. Philadelphia: Lindsay and Blakiston, 1847.

Breck, Samuel. *Recollections of Samuel Breck.* Philadelphia: Porter and Coates, 1877.

Brewster, Charles Warren, William Henry Young Hackett, and Lawerence Shorey. *Rambles About Portsmouth: Sketches of Persons, Localities, and Incidents of Two Centuries: Principally from Tradition and Unpublished Documents.* Portsmouth, NH: C. W. Brewster and Son, 1859.

Brock, R.A., ed. *The Official Records of Robert Dinwiddie, Lieutenant-Governor of the Colony of Virginia, 1751–1758, Collections of the Virginia Historical Society.* Richmond, VA: The Society, 1884.

Burnett, Edmund Cody, ed. *Letters of Members of the Continental Congress.* 8 vols. Washington, DC: Carnegie Institution of Washington, 1921.

Butler, Frederick. *Memoirs of the Marquis de La Fayette: Major General in the Revolutionary Army of the United States of America, Together with His Tour Through the U.S.* Wethersfield, CT: Deming and Francis, 1825.

Butler, Pierce. *The Letters of Pierce Butler, 1790–1794: National Building and Enterprise in the New American Republic.* Edited by Terry W. Lipscomb. Columbia: University of South Carolina Press, 2007.

Butterfield, L. H. et al., eds. *The Adams Papers: Adams Family Correspondence.* 11 vols. Cambridge: Belknap Press of Harvard University Press, 1963.

Caldwell, Charles. *Autobiography of Charles Caldwell, M.D.* Philadelphia: Lippincott, Grambo, 1855.

———. *Memoirs of the Life and Campaigns of the Hon. Nathaniel Greene, Major General in the Army of the United States, and Commander of the Southern Department, in the War of the Revolution.* Philadelphia: Published by Robert Desilver and Thomas Desilver, 1819.

Carroll, B. R., ed. *Historical Collections of South Carolina.* 2 vols. New York: Harper, 1836.

Caughey, John Walton. *McGillivray of the Creeks.* Norman: University of Oklahoma Press, 1938.

Cobbett, William, and David A. Wilson. *Peter Porcupine in America: Pamphlets on Republicanism and Revolution.* Ithaca, NY: Cornell University Press, 1994.

Conway, Moncure Daniel. *Omitted Chapters of History Disclosed in the Life and Papers of Edmund Randolph—Governor of Virginia—First Attorney-General United States—Secretary of State.* New York: Putnam's, 1888.

Custis, George Washington Parke, Mary Randolph Custis Lee, and Benson John Lossing. *Recollections and Private Memoirs of Washington, by His Adopted Son, George Washington Parke Curtis, with a Memoir of the Author, by His Daughter; and Illustrative and Explanatory Notes, by Benson J. Lossing.* New York: Derby and Jackson, 1860.

Cutler, William Parker, and Julia Perkins, eds. *Life, Journals, and Correspondence of Rev. Manasseh Cutler, LL.D.* 2 vols. Cincinnati: Robert Clarke, 1888.

Decatur, Stephen Jr., ed. *Private Affairs of George Washington, from the Records and Accounts of Tobias Lear, Esquire, His Secretary.* New York: Da Capo, 1969.

DePauw, Linda Grant, and Charlene Bangs Bickford, eds. *Documentary History of the First Federal Congress of the United States.* 20 vols. Baltimore: Johns Hopkins University Press, 1972.

Devins, Richard Mille. *The National Memorial Volume: Being a Popular Descriptive Portraiture of the Great Events of Our Past Century.* Springfield, MA: C. A. Nichols, 1879.

Findley, William. *History of the Insurrection in the Four Western Counties of Pennsylvania.* Philadelphia: S. H. Smith, 1796.

Fithian, Philip Vickers. *Journal and Letters 1767–1774, Student at Princeton, 1770–1772, Tutor at Nomini Hall in Virginia.* Carlisle, MA: Applewood Books, 2007.

Foner, Philip S., ed. *The Democratic-Republican Societies, 1790–1800; A Documentary Sourcebook of Constitutions, Declarations, Addresses, Resolutions, and Toasts.* Westport, CT: Greenwood Press, 1976.

Ford, Worthington Chauncey, ed. *Journals of the Continental Congress, 1774–1789.* 33 vols. Washington, DC: Government Printing Office, 1904.

Franklin, Benjamin. *The Autobiography of Benjamin Franklin.* Boston: Houghton, Mifflin, 1888.

———. *The Complete Works of Benjamin Franklin.* 10 vols. Edited by John Bigelow. New York: G. P. Putnam's Sons, 1887.

Gallatin, Albert. *The Writings of Albert Gallatin.* Edited by and Henry Adams. Philadelphia: J. B. Lippincott, 1879.

Gardiner, C. Harvey, ed. *A Study in Dissent: The Warren-Gerry Correspondence, 1776–1792.* Carbondale: Southern Illinois University Press, 1968.

Gibbs, George, ed. *Memoirs of the Administrations of Washington and John Adams, Edited from the Papers of Oliver Wolcott, Secretary of the Treasury.* 2 vols. New York: W. Van Norden, 1846.

Gist, Christopher. *Christopher Gist's Journals: With Historical, Geographical, and Ethnological Notes and Biographies of His Contemporaries by William M. Darlington.* Pittsburgh: J. R. Weldin, 1893.

Hamilton, Alexander. *The Papers of Alexander Hamilton.* 27 vols. Edited by Harold C. Syrett and Jacob E. Cooke. New York: Columbia University Press, 1961.

Hamilton, Alexander, and James Madison. *The Pacificus-Helvidius Debates of 1793–1794.* Edited by J. Morton Frisch. Indianapolis: Liberty Fund Inc., 2007.

Hamilton, Alexander, James Madison, and John Jay. *The Federalist.* London: Phoenix, 1992.

Hamilton, John C. *History of the Republic of the United States of America, as Traced in the Writings of Alexander Hamilton and of His Contemporaries.* 7 vols. New York: D. Appleton, 1857.

Hamilton, Stanislaus Murray, ed. *The Writings of James Monroe: Including a Collection of His Public and Private Papers and Correspondence Now for the First Time Printed.* 7 vols. New York: G. P. Putnam's Sons, 1899.

Hazen, Charles D. *Contemporary American Opinion of the French Revolution.* New York: Kessinger, 2007.

Henry, William Wirt, ed. *Patrick Henry: Life, Correspondence, and Speeches.* 3 vols. New York: Charles Scribner's Sons, 1891.

Hirschfeld, Fritz. *George Washington and Slavery: A Documentary Portrayal.* Columbia: University of Missouri, 1997.

Jackman, S. W., ed. "A Young Englishman Reports on the New Nation: Edward Thornton to James Bland Burges, 1791–1793." *William and Mary Quarterly* 18 (January 1961): 85–121.

James, Alfred Procter, ed. *Writings of General John Forbes Relating to His Service in North America.* Menasha, WI: Collegiate, 1938.

Jay, John, and Henry P. Johnston, eds. *Correspondence and Public Papers of John Jay.* 4 vols. New York: Putnam's, 1890.

Jefferson, Thomas. *Cod and Whale Fisheries: Report of Hon. Thomas Jefferson, Secretary of State, on the Subject of Cod and Whale Fisheries, Made to the House of Representatives, February 1, 1791. Also, Report of Lorenzo Sabine, Esq., on the Principal Fisheries of the American Seas, Being Part of House Executive Document No. 23, of the Second Session, Thirty-Second Congress.* Edited by Lorenzo Sabine. Washington, DC: U.S. State Department, 1872.

———. *Notes on the State of Virginia.* London: Stockdale, 1787.

———. *The Papers of Thomas Jefferson.* Edited by Julian P. Boyd et al. 39 vols. Princeton, NJ: Princeton University Press, 1950.

———. *The Works of Thomas Jefferson.* Edited by Leicester Ford. 12 vols. New York: G. P. Putnam's Sons, 1904.

———. *The Writings of Thomas Jefferson.* Edited by Andrew A. Lipscomb and Albert Ellery Bergh. 20 vols. Washington, DC: Thomas Jefferson Memorial Foundation, 1903.

Jensen, Merrill, and Robert A. Becker, eds. *The Documentary History of the First Federal Elections.* 4 vols. Madison: University of Wisconsin Press, 1976.

Johnson, Monroe. "Washington Period Politics." *William and Mary Quarterly* 12 (July 1932): 159–66.

Johnston, Elizabeth Bryant. *George Washington: Day by Day.* New York: Kessinger, 2008.

Jones, Hugh. *The Present State of Virginia.* London: J. Clarke, 1724.

King, Rufus. *The Life and Correspondence of Rufus King.* 6 vols. New York: Putnam's, 1894.

Lafayette, Marie-Joseph-Paul-Yves-Roch-Gilbert du Motier, Marquis de. *Memoirs, Correspondence, and Manuscripts of General Lafayette.* 3 vols. New York: Saunders and Otley, 1837.

Latrobe, Benjamin Henry. *The Journal of Latrobe; Being the Notes and Sketches of an Architect, Naturalist and Traveler in the United States from 1796 to 1820.* New York: D. Appleton, 1905.

Laurens, Henry. *The Papers of Henry Laurens.* Edited by Philip M. Hamer. 16 vols. Columbia: University of South Carolina Press, 1968.

Lear, Tobias. *Letters and Recollections of George Washington.* New York: Doubleday, Page, 1906.

Lee, Charles. *The Life and Memoirs of the Late Major General Lee.* Carlisle, MA: Applewood Books, 2009.

Lee, Jean B., ed. *Experiencing Mount Vernon: Eyewitness Accounts, 1784–1865.* Charlottesville: University of Virginia Press, 2006.

Lee, Richard Henry. *The Letters of Richard Henry Lee.* Edited by James Curtis Ballagh. 2 vols. New York: Macmillan, 1911.

Liston, Henrietta. "Lady Henrietta Liston's Journal of Washington's 'Resignation', Retirement, and Death." Edited by James C. Nicholls. *Pennsylvania Magazine of History and Biography* 95 (October 1971): 511–20.

Livingston, William. *The Papers of William Livingston.* Edited by Carl E. Prince. 5 vols. New Brunswick, NJ: Rutgers University Press, 1979.

Maclay, William. *Journal of William Maclay, United States Senator from Pennsylvania, 1789–1791.* New York: Albert and Charles Boni, 1927.

Madison, James. *Papers of James Madison.* Edited by William T. Hutchinson et al. 17 vols. Chicago: University of Chicago Press, 1962.

———. *The Writings of James Madison.* Edited by Gaillard Hunt. 9 vols. New York: Putnam's, 1900.

Madison, James, Thomas Jefferson, and Virginia General Assembly, House of Delegates. *Resolutions of Virginia and Kentucky.* Richmond, VA: R. I. Smith, 1826.

Marcus, Maeva, and James R. Perry, eds. *The Documentary History of the Supreme Court of the United States, 1789–1800.* 8 vols. New York: Columbia University Press, 1985.

Marshall, John. *The Papers of John Marshall.* Edited by Charles T. Cullen and Herbert A. Johnson. 12 vols. Chapel Hill: University of North Carolina Press, 1974.

Mason, George. *The Papers of George Mason, 1725–1792.* Edited by Robert A. Rutland. 3 vols. Chapel Hill: University of North Carolina Press, 1970.

McRee, Griffith John. *Life and Correspondence of James Iredell.* 2 vols. New York: D. Appleton, 1857.

Mill, John Stuart. *On Liberty.* Boston: Ticknor and Fields, 1863.

Morris, Gouverneur. *The Diaries of Gouverneur Morris: European Travels, 1794–1798.* Edited by Melanie Randolph Miller. Charlottesville: University Press of Virginia, 2011.

———. *The Diary and Letters of Gouverneur Morris, Minister of the United States to France.* 2 vols. New York: Charles Scribner's Sons, 1888.

Morris, Robert. *The Confidential Correspondence of Robert Morris, the Great Financier of the Revolution and Signer of the Declaration of Independence.* Philadelphia: S. V. Henkels, 1917.

Niemcewicz, Julian Ursyn. *Under Their Vine and Fig Tree: Travels Through America, 1797–1799, 1805 with Some Further Account of Life in New Jersey.* Translated and edited by Metchie J. E. Budka. Elizabeth, NJ: Grassman, 1965.

O'Dwyer, Margaret M., ed. "A French Diplomat's View of Congress, 1790." *William and Mary Quarterly* 21 (July 1964): 408–44.

Parkinson, Richard. *The Experienced Farmer's Tour in America: Exhibiting, in a Copious and Familiar View, the American System of Agriculture and Breeding of Cattle, with Its Recent Improvements.* 2 vols. London: John Stockdale, 1805.

Perkins, Bradford, ed. "A Diplomat's Wife in Philadelphia: Letters of Henrietta Liston, 1796–1800." *William and Mary Quarterly* 11 (October 1954): 592–632.

Pope, Alexander. *Eloisa to Abelard.* Glasgow: R. and A. Foulis, 1751.

The Public Statutes at Large of the United States of America. 16 vols. Boston: Little, Brown, 1845.

Randolph, Edmund. *A Vindication of Mr. Randolph's Resignation.* Philadelphia: Samuel H. Smith, 1795.

Randolph, Sarah N. *The Domestic Life of Thomas Jefferson. Compiled from Family Letters and Reminiscences*. New York: Harper and Brothers, 1871.

Rush, Benjamin. *The Letters of Benjamin Rush*. Edited by Lyman Henry Butterfield. 2 vols. Princeton, NJ: Princeton University Press, 1951.

Serle, Ambrose. *The American Journal of Ambrose Serle, Secretary to Lord Howe, 1776–1778*. Edited by Edward Howland Tatum. San Marino, CA: Huntington Library, 1940.

Smith, John Cotton. *The Correspondence and Miscellanies of the Hon. John Cotton Smith, LLD, Formerly Governor of Connecticut*. New York: Harper and Brothers, 1847.

Smith, Margaret Bayard. *The First Forty Years of Washington Society: Portrayed by the Family Letters of Mrs. Samuel Harrison Smith (Margaret Bayard) from the Collection of Her Grandson, J. Henley Smith*. New York: Charles Scribner's Sons, 1906.

Smith, William Loughton. *Journal of William Loughton Smith, 1790–1791*. Cambridge, MA: Harvard University Press, 1917.

———. *The Politicks and Views of a Certain Party, Displayed*. Philadelphia: T. Dwight, 1792.

Steiner, Bernard Christian, ed. *The Life and Correspondence of James McHenry: Secretary of War Under Washington and Adams*. Cleveland: Burrows Brothers, 1907.

Thornton, Anna Maria. "Diary of Mrs. William Thornton, 1800–1863." Edited by Worthington Chauncey Ford. Records of the Columbia Historical Society, Washington, D.C. Vol. 10. Washington, DC: The Society, 1907.

Trumbull, John. *Autobiography, Reminiscences, and Letters of John Trumbull*. New York: Wiley and Putnam, 1841.

Twining, Thomas. *Travels in America 100 Years Ago: Being Notes and Reminiscences*. Carlisle, MA: Applewood Books, 2007.

United States Constitutional Convention. *The Debates in the Federal Convention of 1787 Which Framed the Constitution of the United States of America, Reported by James Madison, a Delegate from the State of Virginia*. Edited by Gaillard Hunt and James Brown Scott. New York: Oxford University Press, 1920.

Wansey, Henry. *Henry Wansey and His American Journal: 1794*. Edited by David John Jeremy. Philadelphia: American Philosophical Society, 1970.

Washington, George. *The Diaries of George Washington*. 6 vols. Edited by Donald Jackson and Dorothy Twohig. Charlottesville: University of Virginia Press, 1976.

———. *The Papers of George Washington*. Colonial Series. 10 vols. Charlottesville: University of Virginia Press, 1983.

———. *The Papers of George Washington*. Confederation Series. 6 vols. Charlottesville: University of Virginia Press, 1992.

———. *The Papers of George Washington*. Presidential Series. Edited by Dorothy Twohig et al. 17 vols. Charlottesville: University of Virginia Press, 1987.

———. *The Papers of George Washington*. Retirement Series. Edited by Dorothy Twohig et al. 4 vols. Charlottesville: University of Virginia Press, 1998.

———. *The Papers of George Washington*. Revolutionary War Series. Edited by David R. Hoth. 22 vols. Charlottesville: University of Virginia Press, 1985.

———. *Rules of Civility & Decent Behaviour in Company and Conversation: A Book of Etiquette*. Williamsburg, VA: Beaver Press, 1971.

_____. *The Writings of George Washington*. Edited by John Clement Fitzpatrick and David Maydole Matteson. 39 vols. Washington, DC: Government Printing Office, 1931.

Washington, George, and Tobias Lear. *Letters from George Washington to Tobias Lear: With an Appendix Containing Miscellaneous Washington Letters and Documents*. Edited by William Keeney Bixby and William Holland Samson. Rochester, NY: Genesee Press, 1905.

Washington, Martha. *"Worthy Partner": The Papers of Martha Washington*. Edited by Joseph E. Fields. Westport, CT: Greenwood Press, 1994.

Weld, Isaac. *Travels Through the States of North America, and the Provinces of Upper and Lower Canada, During the Years, 1795, 1796, and 1797*. 2 vols. London: John Stockdale, 1807.

Newspapers and Magazines

The Albany Gazette
Baltimore *Federal Gazette*
Boston *Polar-Star*
The Carlisle (PA) *Gazette*
Charleston *Columbian Herald*
Claypoole's American Daily Advertiser
Concord *Courier of New Hampshire*
Gazette of the United States
The Georgetown Weekly Ledger
Harper's
Maryland Gazette
National Gazette
New Hampshire Journal
New York *Columbian Gazetteer*
New York *Weekly Museum*
New-York Gazette
Philadelphia *Aurora General Advertiser*
Philadelphia *Gazette*
Philadelphia *General Advertiser*
St. Louis *Daily Globe-Democrat*
The Liberator
The Washington Post
Washington, DC, *Daily National Intelligencer*

Secondary Sources

Books

Abernethy, Thomas Perkins. *The Burr Conspiracy*. New York: Oxford University Press, 1954.

_____. *The Origin of the Franklin-Lee Imbroglio*. Raleigh: North Carolina Historical Commission, 1938.

Achenbach, Joel. *The Grand Idea: George Washington's Potomac and the Race to the West.* New York: Simon and Schuster, 2004.

Adams, Henry. *The Life of Albert Gallatin.* Philadelphia: J. B. Lippincott, 1879.

Adams, William Howard. *Gouverneur Morris: An Independent Life.* New Haven, CT: Yale University Press, 2003.

Alden, John R. *Robert Dinwiddie: Servant of the Crown.* Williamsburg, VA: Colonial Williamsburg, 1973.

Alden, John Richard. *General Charles Lee: Traitor or Patriot?* Baton Rouge: Louisiana State University Press, 1951.

Alexander, John K. *Samuel Adams: America's Revolutionary Politician.* Lanham, MD: Rowman and Littlefield, 2002.

Allgor, Catherine. *Parlor Politics: In Which the Ladies of Washington Help Build a City and a Government.* Charlottesville: University Press of Virginia, 2000.

_____. *A Perfect Union: Dolley Madison and the Creation of the American Nation.* New York: Henry Holt, 2006.

Allison, Robert. *The Crescent Obscured: The United States and the Muslim World, 1776–1815.* Chicago: University of Chicago Press, 2000.

Amar, Akhil Reed. *The Bill of Rights: Creation and Reconstruction.* New Haven, CT: Yale University Press, 2000.

Ambler, Charles H. *George Washington and the West.* Chapel Hill: University of North Carolina Press, 1936.

Ammon, Harry. *The Genet Mission.* New York: W. W. Norton, 1973.

Anderson, Dice Robins. *William Branch Giles: A Study in the Politics of Virginia and the Nation from 1790–1830.* Gloucester, MA: Peter Smith, 1965.

Anderson, Fred. *The Crucible of War: The Seven Years' War and the Fate of Empire in British North America, 1754–1766.* New York: Vintage, 2001.

Appleby, Joyce. *Capitalism and a New Social Order: The Republican Vision of the 1790s.* New York: New York University Press, 1984.

_____. *Inheriting the Revolution: The First Generation of Americans.* Cambridge, MA: Belknap Press of Harvard University Press, 2001.

_____. *Liberalism and Republicanism in the Historical Imagination.* Cambridge, MA: Harvard University Press, 1992.

Arnebeck, Bob. *Through a Fiery Trial: Building Washington, 1790–1800.* Lanham, MD: Madison Books, 1991.

Arnold, Isaac N. *The Life of Benedict Arnold: His Patriotism and His Treason.* Chicago: Jansen, McClurg, 1890.

Axelrad, Jacob. *Philip Freneau: Champion of Democracy.* Austin: University of Texas Press, 1967.

Bailyn, Bernard. *The Origins of American Politics.* New York: Vintage, 1970.

_____. *To Begin the World Anew: The Genius and Ambiguities of the American Founders.* New York: Vintage, 2004.

_____. *Voyagers to the West: A Passage in the Peopling of America on the Eve of the Revolution.* New York: Vintage, 1988.

Baker, William Spohn. *Washington After the Revolution: 1784–1799*. Philadelphia: J. B. Lippincott, 1897.

Baldwin, Leland D. *Whiskey Rebels: The Story of a Frontier Uprising*. Pittsburgh: University of Pittsburgh Press, 1939.

Bancroft, George. *Joseph Reed: A Historical Essay*. New York: W. J. Widdleton, 1867.

Banner, James. *To the Hartford Convention: The Federalists and the Origins of Party Politics in Massachusetts*. New York: Knopf, 1970.

Banning, Lance. *The Jeffersonian Persuasion: Evolution of a Party Ideology*. Ithaca, NY: Cornell University Press, 1978.

————. *The Sacred Fire of Liberty: James Madison and the Founding of the Federal Republic*. Ithaca, NY: Cornell University Press, 1995.

Barnard, Ella Kent. *Dorothy Payne, Quakeress: A Side-light Upon the Career of "Dolley" Madison*. Philadelphia: Ferris and Leach, 1909.

Barratt, Carrie Rebora, Gilbert Stuart, and Ellen Gross Miles. *Gilbert Stuart*. New York: Metropolitan Museum of Art, 2004.

Baseler, Marilyn C. *Asylum for Mankind: America, 1607–1800*. Ithaca, NY: Cornell University Press, 1998.

Bass, Robert D. *Gamecock: The Life and Campaigns of General Thomas Sumter*. New York: Holt, Rinehart, and Winston, 1961.

Beeman, Richard R. *The Old Dominion and the New Nation, 1788–1801*. Lexington: University Press of Kentucky, 1972.

Bell, Malcolm, Jr. *Major Butler's Legacy; Five Generations of a Slaveholding Family*. Athens: University of Georgia Press, 1987.

Bell, Rudolph M. *Party and Faction in American Politics: The House of Representatives, 1789–1801*. Westport, CT: Greenwood Press, 1973.

Bemis, Samuel Flagg. *Jay's Treaty: A Study in Commerce and Diplomacy*. New Haven, CT: Yale University, 1962.

————. *Pinckney's Treaty: America's Advantage from Europe's Distress, 1783–1800*. New Haven, CT: Yale University Press, 1965.

Ben-Atar, Doron S. *The Origins of Jeffersonian Commercial Policy and Diplomacy*. New York: Palgrave Macmillan, 1993.

Ben-Atar, Doron S., and Liz B. MacMillan. *Federalists Reconsidered*. Charlottesville: University of Virginia Press, 1998.

Berg, Scott W. *Grand Avenues: The Story of Pierre Charles L'Enfant, the French Visionary Who Designed Washington, D.C.* New York: Vintage, 2008.

Berkeley, Edmund, and Dorothy Smith Berkeley. *John Beckley: Zealous Partisan in a Nation Divided*. Philadelphia: American Philosophical Society, 1973.

Berlin, Ira. *Many Thousands Gone: The First Two Centuries of Slavery in North America*. Cambridge, MA: Belknap Press of Harvard University Press, 2000.

Bernard, Winfred E. A. *Fisher Ames: Federalist and Statesman, 1758–1808*. Chapel Hill: University of North Carolina Press, 1965.

Bernier, Olivier. *Lafayette: Hero of Two Worlds*. New York: E. P. Dutton, 1983.

Beveridge, Albert J. *The Life of John Marshall*. 4 vols. Boston: Houghton Mifflin, 1919.

Bickford, Charlene Bangs, and Kenneth R. Bowling. *Birth of the Nation: The First Federal Congress, 1789–1791*. Lanham, MD: Rowman and Littlefield, 1989.

Billias, George Athan. *Elbridge Gerry, Founding Father and Republican Statesman*. New York: McGraw-Hill, 1976.

Binger, Carl. *Revolutionary Doctor: Benjamin Rush, 1746–1813*. New York: W. W. Norton, 1966.

Blanning, Tim. *The Pursuit of Glory: Europe 1648–1815*. New York: Viking, 2007.

Bockstruck, Lloyd DeWitt. *Virginia's Colonial Soldiers*. Baltimore: Genealogical, 1998.

Bodenhorn, Howard. *State Banking in Early America: A New Economic History*. New York: Oxford University Press, 2002.

Bourne, Miriam Anne. *First Family: George Washington and His Intimate Relations*. New York: W. W. Norton, 1982.

Bowling, Kenneth R. *The Creation of Washington, D.C.: The Idea and Location of the American Capital*. Fairfax, VA: George Washington University Press, 1991.

Bowling, Kenneth R., and Donald R. Kennon. *The House and Senate in the 1790s: Petitioning, Lobbying, and Institutional Development*. Athens: Ohio University Press, 2002.

Bowman, Albert Hall. *The Struggle for Neutrality: Franco-American Diplomacy During the Federalist Era*. Knoxville: University of Tennessee Press, 1974.

Boyd, Julian. *Number 7, Alexander Hamilton's Secret Attempts to Control American Foreign Policy, with Supporting Documents*. Princeton NJ: Princeton University Press, 1964.

Boylan, Brian Richard. *Benedict Arnold: The Dark Eagle*. New York: W. W. Norton, 1973.

Brady, Patricia, ed. *George Washington's Beautiful Nelly: The Letters of Eleanor Parke Custis Lewis to Elizabeth Bordley Gibson, 1794–1851*. Columbia: University of South Carolina Press, 1991.

———. *Martha Washington: An American Life*. New York: Penguin, 2006.

Brant, Irving. *The Bill of Rights: Its Origins and Meaning*. Indianapolis: Bobbs-Merrill, 1965.

———. *James Madison*. 6 vols. Indianapolis: Bobbs-Merrill, 1941.

Braund, Kathryn E. Holland. *Deerskins and Duffels: Creek Indian Trade with Anglo-America, 1685–1815*. Lincoln: University of Nebraska Press, 1993.

Brighton, Ray. *The Checkered Career of Tobias Lear*. Portsmouth, NH: Portsmouth Marine Society, 1984.

Brinkley, M. Kent, and Gordon W. Chappell. *The Gardens of Colonial Williamsburg*. Williamsburg, VA: Colonial Williamsburg, 1996.

Broadwater, Jeff. *George Mason, Forgotten Founder*. Chapel Hill: University of North Carolina Press, 2006.

———. *James Madison: A Son of Virginia and a Founder of the Nation*. Chapel Hill: University of North Carolina Press, 2012.

Brookhiser, Richard. *Founding Father: Rediscovering George Washington*. New York: Free Press, 1997.

———. *The Rules of Civility*. Charlottesville: University of Virginia Press, 2003.

Brown, Gordon S. *Incidental Architect: William Thornton and the Cultural Life of Early Washington, D.C., 1794–1828*. Athens: Ohio University Press, 2009.

———. *Toussaint's Clause: The Founding Fathers and the Haitian Revolution*. Jackson: University Press of Mississippi, 2005.

Brown, William Garott. *The Life of Oliver Ellsworth*. New York: Macmillan, 1905.

Brumwell, Stephen. *George Washington: Gentleman Warrior*. London: Quercus, 2012.

Bryan, Helen. *Martha Washington: First Lady of Liberty*. New York: Wiley, 2002.

Bryan, Wilhelmus Bogart. *A History of the National Capital from Its Foundation Through the Period of the Adoption of the Organic Act*. New York: Macmillan, 1914.

Buel, Richard. *Securing the Revolution: Ideology in American Politics, 1789–1815*. Ithaca, NY: Cornell University Press, 2000.

Bullock, Steven C. *Revolutionary Brotherhood: Freemasonry and the Transformation of the American Social Order, 1730–1840*. Chapel Hill: University of North Carolina Press, 1998.

Burk, Kathleen. *Old World, New World: Great Britain and America from the Beginning*. New York: Atlantic Monthly Press, 2007.

Burrage, Henry Sweetser, and Albert Roscoe Stubbs. *Genealogical and Family History of the State of Maine*. New York: Lewis Historical, 1909.

Burstein, Andrew, and Nancy Isenberg. *Madison and Jefferson*. New York: Random House, 2010.

Callahan, North. *George Washington Soldier and Man*. New York: William Morrow, 1972.

Carbone, Gerald M. *Nathanael Greene: A Biography of the American Revolution*. New York: Palgrave Macmillan, 2010.

Caroli, Betty Boyd. *First Ladies*. New York: Oxford University Press, 1987.

Carp, E. Wayne. *To Starve the Army at Pleasure: Continental Army Administration and American Political Culture, 1775–1783*. Chapel Hill: University of North Carolina Press, 1984.

Carretta, Vincent. *Phillis Wheatley: Biography of a Genius in Bondage*. Athens: University of Georgia Press, 2011.

Cartmell, Thomas Kemp. *An Historic Sketch of the Two Fairfax Families in Virginia*. New York: Knickerbocker Press, 1913.

Cary, Wilson Miles. *Sally Cary: A Long Hidden Romance of Washington's Life*. London: Ulan Press, 2011.

Casper, Scott E. *Sarah Johnson's Mount Vernon: The Forgotten History of an American Shrine*. New York: Hill and Wang, 2008.

Casto, William R. *The Supreme Court in the Early Republic: The Chief Justiceships of John Jay and Oliver Ellsworth*. Columbia: University of South Carolina Press, 1995.

Cerami, Charles A. *Dinner at Mr. Jefferson's: Three Men, Five Great Wines, and the Evening That Changed America*. New York: Wiley, 2009.

Cerniglia, Keith Andrew. "'An Indelicate Amor': Alexander Hamilton and the First American Sex Scandal." MA thesis, Florida State University, 2002.

Chambers, William Nisbet. *Political Parties in a New Nation: The American Experience, 1776–1809*. New York: Oxford University Press, 1963.

Cheney, Lynne. *James Madison: A Life Reconsidered*. New York: Penguin, 2014.

Chernow, Barbara Ann. *Robert Morris, Land Speculator, 1790–1801*. New York: Arno, 1978.

Chernow, Ron. *Alexander Hamilton*. New York: Penguin, 2005.

———. *Washington: A Life*. New York: Penguin, 2010.

Clarfield, Gerard H. *Timothy Pickering and American Diplomacy, 1795–1800*. Columbia: University of Missouri Press, 1969.

———. *Timothy Pickering and the American Republic*. Pittsburgh: University of Pittsburgh Press, 1980.

Clark, Christopher. *Social Change in America: From the Revolution to the Civil War*. Chicago: Ivan R. Dee, 2007.

Clary, David A. *Adopted Son: Washington, Lafayette, and the Friendship That Saved the Revolution*. New York: Bantam Books, 2007.

Cogliano, Francis D. *Thomas Jefferson: Reputation and Legacy*. Charlottesville: University of Virginia Press, 2006.

Combs, Jerald. *The Jay Treaty: Political Battleground of the Founding Fathers*. Berkeley: University of California Press, 1970.

Conley, Patrick T. *The Bill of Rights and the States: The Colonial and Revolutionary Origins of American Liberties*. Madison, WI: Madison House, 1992.

Conway, Moncure Daniel, ed. *George Washington and Mount Vernon*. New York: Long Island Historical Society, 1889.

Cooke, Jacob E. *Tench Coxe and the Early Republic*. Chapel Hill: University of North Carolina Press, 1978.

Cox, Joseph W. *Champion of Southern Federalism;: Robert Goodloe Harper of South Carolina*. Port Washington, NY: Kennikat, 1972.

Cress, Lawrence Delbert. *Citizens in Arms: Army and Militia in American Society to the War of 1812*. Chapel Hill: University of North Carolina Press, 1982.

Cunningham, Noble E., Jr. *The Jeffersonian Republicans: The Formation of Party Organization, 1789–1801*. Chapel Hill: University of North Carolina Press, 1957.

Currie, David P. *The Constitution in Congress: The Federalist Period, 1789–1801*. Chicago: University of Chicago Press, 1997.

Curry, Thomas J. *The First Freedoms: Church and State in America to the Passage of the First Amendment*. New York: Oxford University Press, 1987.

Cushman, Paul. *Richard Varick: A Forgotten Founding Father—Revolutionary War Soldier, Federalist Politician, and Mayor of New York*. Amherst, MA: State University of New York Press, 2010.

Dalzell, Robert F., Jr., and Lee Baldwin Dalzell. *George Washington's Mount Vernon: At Home in Revolutionary America*. New York: Oxford University Press, 2000.

Dangerfield, George. *Chancellor Robert R. Livingston of New York, 1746–1813*. New York: Harcourt, Brace, 1960.

Daniel, Marcus. *Scandal and Civility: Journalism and the Birth of American Democracy*. New York: Oxford University Press, 2009.

Davis, David Brion. *The Problem of Slavery in Western Culture*. New York: Oxford University Press, 1988.

DeConde, Alexander. *Entangling Alliance: Politics and Diplomacy Under George Washington*. Durham: Duke University Press, 1958.

DePauw, Linda Grant. *The Eleventh Pillar: New York State and the Federal Constitution*. Ithaca, NY: Cornell University Press, 1966.

Deppisch, Ludwig M. *The White House Physician: A History from Washington to George W. Bush*. Jefferson, NC: McFarland, 2007.

Dill, Alonzo Thomas. *George Wythe, Teacher of Liberty*. Richmond: Virginia Independence Bicentennial Commission, 1979.

Downes, Randolph C. *Council Fires on the Upper Ohio: A Narrative of Indian Affairs in the Upper Ohio Valley Until 1795*. Pittsburgh: University of Pittsburgh Press, 1989.

Drake, Francis S. *Life and Correspondence of Henry Knox: Major-General in the American Revolutionary Army*. Boston: Samuel G. Drake, 1873.

Dunlap, William. *History of the Rise and Progress of the Arts of Design in the United States*. Boston: George P. Scott, 1834.

DuPriest, James E. *William Grayson: A Political Biography of Virginia's First United States Senator*. Prince William, VA: Prince William County Historical Commission, 1977.

Durey, Michael. *Transatlantic Radicals and the Early American Republic*. Lawrence: University Press of Kansas, 1997.

Edling, Max M. *A Revolution in Favor of Government: Origins of the U.S. Constitution and the Making of the American State*. New York: Oxford University Press, 2008.

Elkins, Stanley, and Eric McKitrick. *The Age of Federalism: The Early American Republic, 1788–1800*. New York: Oxford University Press, 1995.

Ellis, Joseph J. *After the Revolution: Profiles of Early American Culture*. New York: W. W. Norton, 2002.

_____. *First Family: Abigail and John*. New York: Alfred A. Knopf, 2010.

_____. *Founding Brothers: The Revolutionary Generation*. New York: Alfred A. Knopf, 2000.

_____. *His Excellency: George Washington*. New York: Alfred A. Knopf, 2004.

Estes, Todd. *The Jay Treaty Debate: Public Opinion, and the Evolution of Early American Political Culture*. Boston: University of Massachusetts Press, 2006.

Faler, Paul G. *Mechanics and Manufacturers in the Early Industrial Revolution: Lynn, Massachusetts, 1780–1860*. Albany: State University of New York Press, 1981.

Fennessy, R. R. *Burke, Paine and the Rights of Man: A Difference of Political Opinion*. The Hague: M. Nijhoff, 1963.

Fenstermaker, Joseph Van. *The Development of American Commercial Banking: 1782–1837*. Kent, OH: Kent State University Press, 1965.

Ferguson, E. James. *The Power of the Purse: A History of American Public Finance*. Chapel Hill: University of North Carolina Press, 1961.

Ferling, John. *The Ascent of George Washington: The Hidden Political Genius of an American Icon*. New York: Bloomsbury, 2009.

Finkelman, Paul. *Slavery and the Founders: Race and Liberty in the Age of Jefferson*. Armonk, NY: M. E. Sharpe, 1996.

Fischer, David Hackett. *The Revolution of American Conservatism: The Federalist Party in the Era of Jeffersonian Democracy*. New York: Harper and Row, 1965.

Fleming, Thomas. *The Intimate Lives of the Founding Fathers*. Washington, DC: Smithsonian, 2009.

_____. *The Man Who Dared the Lightning: A New Look at Benjamin Franklin*. New York: William Morrow, 1971.

_____. *The Perils of Peace: America's Struggle for Survival After Yorktown*. New York: HarperCollins, 2009.

Flexner, James Thomas. *Doctors on Horseback: Pioneers of American Medicine*. New York: Fordham University Press, 1993.

_____. *George Washington*. 4 vols. Boston: Little Brown, 1965.

_____. *On Desperate Seas: A Biography of Gilbert Stuart*. New York: Fordham University Press, 1955.

Ford, Henry Jones. *Washington and His Colleagues: A Chronicle of the Rise and Fall of Federalism*. New Haven, CT: Yale University Press, 1918.

Ford, Paul Leicester. *The True George Washington*. Philadelphia: J. B. Lippincott, 1896.

Ford, Worthington Chauncey. *Inventory of the Contents of Mount Vernon, 1810*. Cambridge, MA: Harvard University Press, 1909.

Ford, Worthington Chauncey, John Randolph, John Vardill, and John Carey. *The Spurious Letters Attributed to Washington*. Brooklyn, NY: Privately Printed, 1889.

Formisano, Ronald P. *The Transformation of Political Culture: Massachusetts Parties, 1790s–1840s*. Oxford: Oxford University Press, 1984.

Fowler, William M. *The Baron of Beacon Hill: A Biography of John Hancock*. Boston: Houghton Mifflin, 1980.

Frank, Andrew K. *Creeks and Southerners: Biculturalism on the Early American Frontier*. Lincoln: University of Nebraska Press, 2005.

Freeman, Douglas Southall, John Alexander Carroll, and Mary Wells Ashworth. *George Washington: A Biography*. 7 vols. New York: Scribner, 1948.

Freeman, Joanne B. *Affairs of Honor: National Politics in the New Republic*. New Haven, CT: Yale University Press, 2001.

Furstenberg, Francois. *In the Name of the Father: Washington's Legacy, Slavery, and the Making of a Nation*. New York: Penguin, 2006.

Gaff, Alan D. *Bayonets in the Wilderness: Anthony Wayne's Legion in the Old Northwest*. Norman: University of Oklahoma Press, 2004.

Gaines, James R. *For Liberty and Glory: Washington, Lafayette, and Their Revolutions*. New York: W. W. Norton, 2007.

Gaustad, Edwin S. *Faith of Our Fathers: Religion and the New Nation*. New York: Harper and Row, 1987.

_____. *Neither King Nor Prelate: Religion and the New Nation 1776–1826*. Grand Rapids, MI: Eerdmans, 1993.

_____. *Proclaim Liberty Throughout All the Land: A History of Church and State in America*. New York: Oxford University Press, 2003.

Gelles, Edith. *Abigail and John: Portrait of a Marriage*. New York: William Morrow, 2009.

Genovese, Eugene D. *Roll Jordan Roll: The World the Slaves Made.* New York: Vintage, 1976.

Gerlach, Don R. *Philip Schuyler and the American Revolution in New York, 1733–1777.* Lincoln: University of Nebraska Press, 1964.

Gilbert, Felix. *To the Farewell Address.* Princeton, NJ: Princeton University Press, 1970.

Gilje, Paul A. *The Road to Mobocracy: Popular Disorder in New York City, 1763–1834.* Chapel Hill: University of North Carolina Press, 1987.

Gillespie, Michael Allen. *Ratifying the Constitution.* Lawrence: University Press of Kansas, 1989.

Gipson, Lawrence Henry. *The British Empire Before the American Revolution: The Great War for the Empire: The Victorious Years, 1758–1760.* New York: Knopf, 1949.

Glenn, Thomas Allen. *Some Colonial Mansions and Those Who Lived in Them.* 2 vols. Philadelphia: Henry T. Coates, 1897.

Goldwin, Robert A. *From Parchment to Power: How James Madison Used the Bill of Rights to Save the Constitution.* Washington, DC: AEI, 1997.

Golway, Terry. *Washington's General: Nathanael Greene and the Triumph of the American Revolution.* New York: Macmillan, 2007.

Goodman, Paul. *The Democratic Republicans of Massachusetts: Politics in a Young Republic.* Cambridge, MA: Harvard University Press, 1964.

Gottschalk, Louis Reichenthal. *Lafayette.* 6 vols. Chicago: University of Chicago Press, 1935.

Graff, Rebecca Irwin Vanuxen Trimble. *Genealogy of the Claypoole Family of Philadelphia, 1588–1893.* Philadelphia: J. B. Lippincott, 1893.

Greene, George. *The Life of Nathanael Greene.* Carlisle, MA: Applewood Books, 2009.

Greene, Jack P. *The Intellectual Construction of America: Exceptionalism and Identity From 1492 to 1800.* Chapel Hill: University of North Carolina Press, 1997.

Grizzard, Frank E., Jr. *The Ways of Providence: Religion and George Washington.* Buena Vista, VA: Mariner, 2005.

Gutzman, Kevin R. *James Madison and the Making of America.* New York: St. Martin's, 2012.

Haines, Charles Grove. *The American Doctrine of Judicial Supremacy.* Berkeley: University of California Press, 1932.

Hall, Edward Hagaman. *Philipse Manor Hall at Yonkers, N.Y.* New York: American Scenic and Historic Preservation Society, 1912.

Hall, Kermit L. *The Oxford Companion to the Supreme Court of the United States.* New York: Oxford University Press, 2005.

Hamlin, Talbot. *Benjamin Henry Latrobe.* New York: Oxford University Press, 1955.

Hammond, Bray. *Banks and Politics in America from the Revolution to the Civil War.* Princeton, NJ: Princeton University Press, 1991.

Hansen, Marcus Lee. *The Atlantic Migration, 1607–1860: A History of the Continuing Settlement of the United States.* Cambridge, MA: Harvard University Press, 1945.

Harland, Marion. *The Story of Mary Washington.* Boston: Houghton, Mifflin, 1892.

Harley, Lewis Reifsneider, and Charles Thomson. *The Life of Charles Thomson: Secretary of the Continental Congress and Translator of the Bible from the Greek*. Philadelphia: George W. Jacobs, 1900.

Harper, John Lamberton. *American Machiavelli: Alexander Hamilton and the Origins of U.S. Foreign Policy*. New York: Cambridge University Press, 2007.

Harris, Neil. *The Artist in American Society: The Formative Years*. Chicago: University of Chicago Press, 1982.

Hart, Charles Henry, and Edward Biddle. *Memoirs of the Life and Works of Jean Antoine Houdon: The Sculptor of Voltaire and of Washington*. New York: Kessinger, 2006.

Hart, James. *The American Presidency in Action, 1789*. New York: Macmillan, 1948.

Hatch, Robert McConnell. *Thrust for Canada: The American Attempt on Quebec in 1775–1776*. Boston: Houghton Mifflin, 1979.

Haw, James. *John and Edward Rutledge of South Carolina*. Athens: University of Georgia Press, 1997.

Haworth, Paul Leland. *George Washington: Farmer*. Indianapolis: Bobbs-Merrill, 1915.

Hayes, Kevin J. *The Road to Monticello: The Life and Mind of Thomas Jefferson*. New York: Oxford University Press, 2008.

Henderson, Archibald. *Washington's Southern Tour 1791*. Boston: Houghton Mifflin, 1923.

Hendricks, James Edwin. *Charles Thomson and the Making of a New Nation, 1729–1824*. Rutherford, NJ: Fairleigh Dickinson University Press, 1979.

Hendrickson, Robert A. *The Rise and Fall of Alexander Hamilton*. New York: Van Nostrand Reinhold, 1981.

Henriques, Peter R. *Realistic Visionary: A Portrait of George Washington*. Charlottesville: University of Virginia Press, 2006.

Henry, Florette. *The Southern Indians and Benjamin Hawkins, 1796–1816*. Norman: University of Oklahoma Press, 1986.

Higginbotham, Don. *George Washington Reconsidered*. Charlottesville: University Press of Virginia, 2001.

Hill, George Canning. *Benedict Arnold: A Biography*. London: Ulan Press, 2012.

Hoadley, John F. *Origins of American Political Parties, 1789–1803*. Lexington: University Press of Kentucky, 1986.

Hoffman, Ronald, and Peter J. Albert, eds. *Diplomacy and Revolution: The Franco-American Alliance of 1778*. Charlottesville: University of Virginia Press, 1981.

———, eds. *Launching the "Extended Republic": The Federalist Era*. Charlottesville: University of Virginia Press, 1996.

Hofstadter, Richard. *Anti-intellectualism in American Life*. New York: Alfred A. Knopf, 1963.

———. *The Idea of a Party System: The Rise of Legitimate Opposition in the United States, 1780–1840*. Berkeley: University of California Press, 1970.

Hogeland, William. *The Whiskey Rebellion: George Washington, Alexander Hamilton, and the Frontier Rebels Who Challenged America's Newfound Sovereignty*. New York: Scribner, 2006.

Holton, Woody. *Abigail Adams*. New York: Free Press, 2009.

Howard, Hugh. *The Painter's Chair: George Washington and the Making of American Art*. New York: Bloomsbury Press, 2009.

Huston, James L. *Securing the Fruits of Labor: The American Concept of Wealth Distribution, 1765–1900*. Baton Rouge: Louisiana State University Press, 1998.

Hutson, James H. *Religion and the Founding of the American Republic*. Washington, DC: Library of Congress, 1998.

Innes, Stephen, ed. *Work and Labor in Early America*. Chapel Hill: University of North Carolina Press, 1988.

Isaacson, Walter. *Benjamin Franklin: An American Life*. New York: Simon and Schuster, 2003.

Isenberg, Nancy. *Fallen Founder: The Life of Aaron Burr*. New York: Viking, 2007.

James, William. *The Naval History of Great Britain, from the Declaration of War by France in 1793, to the Accession of George IV: A New Ed., with Additions and Notes, Bringing the Work Down to 1827*. 6 vols. London: R. Bentley, 1878.

Johansen, Bruce Elliott, and Barbara Alice Mann. *Encyclopedia of the Haudenosaunee (Iroquois Confederacy)*. Westport, CT: Greenwood Publishing, 2000.

John, Richard R. *Spreading the News: The American Postal System from Franklin to Morse*. Cambridge, MA: Harvard University Press, 1998.

Johnson, Samuel. *Taxation No Tyranny: An Answer to the Resolutions and Address of the American Congress*. London: T. Cadell, 1775.

Jones, Howard Mumford. *America and French Culture, 1750–1848*. Chapel Hill: University of North Carolina Press, 1927.

Jones, Robert. *The King of the Alley: William Duer, Politician, Entrepreneur, and Speculator, 1768–1799*. Philadelphia: American Philosophical Society, 1992.

Kahler, Gerald E. *The Long Farewell: Americans Mourn the Death of George Washington*. Charlottesville: University of Virginia Press, 2008.

Kaminski, John P. *George Clinton: Yeoman Politician of the New Republic*. Lanham, MD: Rowman and Littlefield Publishers, 1993.

————. *The Great Virginia Triumvirate: George Washington, Thomas Jefferson, and James Madison in the Eyes of Their Contemporaries*. Charlottesville: University of Virginia Press, 2010.

Kaminski, John P., and Jill Adair McCaughan, eds. *A Great and Good Man: George Washington in the Eyes of His Contemporaries*. Lanham, MD: Rowman and Littlefield, 2007.

Kammen, Michael. *People of Paradox: An Inquiry Concerning the Origins of American Civilization*. New York: Vintage Books, 1972.

Kaplan, Lawrence S. *Jefferson and France*. New Haven, CT: Yale University Press, 1967.

Kasson, John F. *Civilizing the Machine: Technology and Republican Values in America, 1776–1900*. New York: Grossman, 1976.

Kaufman, Burton Ira. *Washington's Farewell Address: The View from the 20th Century*. Chicago: Quadrangle Books, 1969.

Kenyon, Cecelia M., ed. *The Antifederalists*. Indianapolis: Bobbs-Merrill, 1966.

Ketcham, Ralph. *James Madison: A Biography*. Charlottesville: University of Virginia Press, 1990.

———. *Presidents Above Party: The First American Presidency, 1789–1829*. Chapel Hill: University of North Carolina Press, 1984.

Ketchum, Richard M. *The World of George Washington*. Rockville, MD: American Heritage, 1974.

Kidd, Thomas S. *Patrick Henry: First Among Patriots*. New York: Basic Books, 2011.

Kirschke, James J. *Gouverneur Morris: Author, Statesman, and Man of the World*. New York: Thomas Dunne Books, 2005.

Kite, Elizabeth. *L'Enfant and Washington, 1791–1792*. Baltimore: Johns Hopkins Press, 1929.

Knudson, Jerry W. *Jefferson and the Press: Crucible of Liberty*. Columbia: University of South Carolina Press, 2006.

Koch, Adrienne. *Jefferson and Madison: The Great Collaboration*. Old Saybrook, CT: Konecky and Konecky, 2004.

Kohn, Richard H. *Eagle and Sword: The Federalists and the Creation of the Military Establishment in America, 1783–1802*. New York: Free Press, 1975.

Kramer, Lloyd. *Lafayette in Two Worlds: Public Cultures and Personal Identities in an Age of Revolutions*. Chapel Hill: University of North Carolina Press, 1996.

Kranish, Michael. *Flight from Monticello: Thomas Jefferson at War*. New York: Oxford University Press, 2010.

Labunski, Richard. *James Madison and the Struggle for the Bill of Rights*. New York: Oxford University Press, 2006.

LaCroix, Alison L. *The Ideological Origins of American Federalism*. Cambridge, MA: Harvard University Press, 2010.

Lamb, Martha Joanna, and Mrs. Burton Harrison. *History of the City of New York: Its Origin, Rise, and Progress*. New York: A. S. Barnes, 1896.

Lambert, Frank. *The Founding Fathers and the Place of Religion in America*. Princeton, NJ: Princeton University Press, 2003.

Langstaff, John Brett. *Doctor Bard of Hyde Park: The Famous Physician of Revolutionary Times, the Man Who Saved Washington's Life*. New York: E. P. Dutton, 1942.

Lefkowitz, Arthur S. *George Washington's Indispensable Men: The Thirty-Two Aides-De-Camp Who Helped Win American Independence*. Mechanicsburg, PA: Stackpole Books, 2002.

Leibiger, Stuart Eric. *Founding Friendship: George Washington, James Madison, and the Creation of the American Republic*. Charlottesville: University of Virginia Press, 1999.

Lengel, Edward G. *General George Washington: A Military Life*. New York: Random House, 2005.

Levy, Leonard Williams. *Jefferson and Civil Liberties: The Darker Side*. Cambridge, MA: Belknap Press of Harvard University Press, 1963.

———. *Origins of the Bill of Rights*. New Haven, CT: Yale University Press, 2001.

Levy, Philip. *Where the Cherry Tree Grew: The Story of Ferry Farm, George Washington's Boyhood Home*. New York: St. Martin's, 2013.

Lewis, James E., Jr. *The American Union and the Problem of Neighborhood: The United States and the Collapse of the Spanish Empire, 1783–1829*. Chapel Hill: University of North Carolina Press, 1998.

Lewis, William Terrell. *Genealogy of the Lewis Family in America: From the Middle of the Seventeenth Century Down to the Present Time*. Louisville, KY: Courier-Journal Job Printing Company, 1893.

Lillback, Peter A. *George Washington's Sacred Fire*. King of Prussia, PA: Providence Forum, 2006.

Link, E. P. *Democratic Republican Societies 1790–1800*. New York: Octagon Books, 1990.

Liscomb, Terry W. *South Carolina in 1791: George Washington's Southern Tour*. Columbia: South Carolina Department of Archives and History, 1993.

Lossing, Benson John. *The Home of Washington; or, Mount Vernon and Its Associations, Historical, Biographical, and Pictorial*. Hartford, CT: A. S. Hale, 1871.

Loveland, Anne C. *Emblem of Liberty: The Image of Lafayette in the American Mind*. Baton Rouge: Louisiana State University Press, 1971.

Mackie, John Milton. *The Administration of President Washington*. Edited by Frank E. Grizzard, Jr. Buena Vista, VA: Mariner, 2006.

Maier, Pauline. *Ratification: The People Debate the Constitution, 1787–1788*. New York: Simon and Schuster, 2010.

Main, Jackson Turner. *The Antifederalists: Critics of the Constitution, 1781–1788*. Chapel Hill: University of North Carolina Press, 1961.

Malone, Dumas. *Jefferson and His Time*. 6 vols. Boston: Little, Brown, 1948.

Mann, Barbara Alice. *George Washington's War on Native America*. Westport, CT: Praeger, 2005.

Mapp, Alf J., Jr. *Thomas Jefferson: America's Paradoxical Patriot*. Lanham, MD: Rowman and Littlefield, 2007.

Marcus, Maeva. *Origins of the Federal Judiciary: Essays on the Judiciary Act of 1789*. New York: Oxford University Press, 1992.

Martin, James K. *Benedict Arnold, Revolutionary Hero: An American Warrior Reconsidered*. New York: New York University Press, 2000.

Matthews, Richard K. *The Radical Politics of Thomas Jefferson: A Revisionist View*. Lawrence: University Press of Kansas, 1984.

May, Henry F. *The Enlightenment in America*. New York: Oxford University Press, 1978.

Mayer, Henry. *A Son of Thunder: Patrick Henry and the American Republic*. New York: Grove, 2001.

McCraw, Thomas K. *The Founders and Finance: How Hamilton, Gallatin, and Other Immigrants Forged a New Economy*. Cambridge, MA: Harvard University Press, 2012.

McCullough, David. *John Adams*. New York: Simon and Schuster, 2001.

McDonald, Forrest. *Alexander Hamilton: A Biography*. New York: W. W. Norton, 1982.

_____. *The Presidency of George Washington*. Lawrence: University Press of Kansas, 1974.

McDonald, Robert M. S., ed. *Sons of the Father: George Washington and His Protégés*. Charlottesville: University of Virginia Press, 2013.

McGaughy, J. Kent. *Richard Henry Lee of Virginia: A Portrait of an American Revolutionary*. Lanham, MD: Rowman and Littlefield, 2004.

McInnis, Maurie D., and Louis P. Nelson, eds. *Shaping the Body Politic: Art and Political Formation in Early America*. Charlottesville: University of Virginia Press, 2011.

McLeod, Stephen A., ed. *Dining with the Washingtons*. Chapel Hill: University of North Carolina Press, 2011.

McNamara, Brooks. *Days of Jubilee: The Great Age of Public Celebrations in New York, 1788–1909*. New Brunswick, NJ: Rutgers University Press, 1997.

Meacham, Jon. *Thomas Jefferson: The Art of Power*. New York: Random House, 2012.

Meleney, John C. *The Public Life of Aedanus Burke: Revolutionary Republican in Post-Revolutionary South Carolina*. Columbia: University of South Carolina Press, 1989.

Middlekauff, Robert. *The Glorious Cause: The American Revolution, 1763–1789*. New York: Oxford University Press, 1982.

Miller, Helen Hill. *George Mason: Gentleman Revolutionary*. Chapel Hill: University of North Carolina Press, 1975.

Miller, John C. *Alexander Hamilton*. New York: Barnes and Noble Books, 2003.

———. *The Federalist Era 1789–1801*. New York: Harper and Row, 1960.

Miller, Melanie Randolph. *An Incautious Man: The Life of Gouverneur Morris*. Wilmington, DE: ISI Books, 2008.

Minnigerode, Meade. *Jefferson, Friend of France, 1793: The Career of Edmond Charles Genet, Minister Plenipotentiary from the French Republic to the United States, as Revealed by His Private Papers, 1763–1834*. New York: G. P. Putnam's Sons, 1928.

Moats, Sandra. *Celebrating the Republic: Presidential Ceremony and Popular Sovereignty, from Washington to Monroe*. DeKalb: Northern Illinois University Press, 2010.

Moore, George Henry. *"Mr. Lee's Plan—March 29, 1777": The Treason of Charles Lee, Major General, Second in Command in the American Army of the Revolution*. New York: C. Scribner, 1860.

Morgan, Edmund S. *American Slavery, American Freedom*. New York: W. W. Norton, 2003.

———. *Inventing the People: The Rise of Popular Sovereignty in England and America*. New York: W. W. Norton, 1989.

Morison, Samuel Eliot. *Harrison Gray Otis, 1765–1848: The Urbane Federalist*. Boston: Houghton Mifflin, 1969.

Morrison, Jeffry H. *The Political Philosophy of George Washington*. Baltimore: Johns Hopkins University Press, 2009.

Morton, Joseph C. *Shapers of the Great Debate at the Constitutional Convention of 1787: A Biographical Dictionary*. Westport, CT: Greenwood, 2005.

Muñoz, Vincent Phillip. *God and the Founders: Madison, Washington, and Jefferson*. New York: Cambridge University Press, 2009.

Nagel, Paul C. *The Adams Women: Abigail and Louisa Adams, Their Sisters and Daughters*. New York: Oxford University Press, 1987.

Nathans, Heather S. *Early American Theatre from the Revolution to Thomas Jefferson: Into the Hands of the People*. New York: Cambridge University Press, 2007.

Neil, J. Meredith. *Toward a National Taste: America's Quest for Aesthetic Independence*. Honolulu: University Press of Hawaii, 1975.

Neill, Edward D. *The Fairfaxes of England and America in the Seventeenth and Eighteenth Centuries*. Albany, NY: Joel Munsell, 1868.

Nelson, Craig. *Thomas Paine: Enlightenment, Revolution, and the Birth of Modern Nations*. New York: Viking, 2006.

Nelson, Paul David. *Anthony Wayne: Soldier of the Early Republic*. Bloomington: Indiana University Press, 1985.

Newman, Simon P. *Parades and the Politics of the Street: Festive Culture in the Early American Republic*. Philadelphia: University of Pennsylvania Press, 1997.

Noll, Mark A. *America's God: From Jonathan Edwards to Abraham Lincoln*. New York: Oxford University Press, 2002.

Nordham, George W. *Age of Washington: George Washington's Presidency, 1789–1797*. Chicago: Adams, 1989.

North, Douglass C. *The Economic Growth of the United States: 1790–1860*. Englewood Cliffs, NJ: Prentice-Hall, 1961.

O'Brien, Conor Cruise. *The Long Affair: Thomas Jefferson and the French Revolution*. Chicago: University of Chicago Press, 1996.

O'Brien, Michael Joseph. *A Hidden Phase of American History: Ireland's Part in America's Struggle for Liberty*. New York: Dodd, Mead, 1919.

Papenfuse, Eric Robert. *Evils of Necessity: Robert Goodloe Harper and the Moral Dilemma of Slavery*. Philadelphia: American Philosophical Society, 1997.

Pasley, Jeffrey L. *The First Presidential Contest: 1796 and the Founding of American Democracy*. Lawrence: University Press of Kansas, 2013.

————. *The Tyranny of Printers: Newspaper Politics in the Early American Republic*. Charlottesville: University of Virginia Press, 2001.

Patterson, Caleb Perry. *The Constitutional Principles of Thomas Jefferson*. Gloucester, MA: Peter Smith, 1967.

Perkins, Bradford. *The First Rapprochement: England and the United States, 1795–1805*. Philadelphia: University of Pennsylvania Press, 1955.

Perkins, Edwin J. *American Public Finance and Financial Services, 1700–1815*. Columbus: Ohio State University Press, 1994.

Peterson, Merrill D. *The Jefferson Image in the American Mind*. Charlottesville: University of Virginia Press, 1998.

————. *Thomas Jefferson and the New Nation: A Biography*. New York: Oxford University Press, 1975.

Phelps, Glenn A. *George Washington and American Constitutionalism*. Lawrence: University Press of Kansas, 1993.

Pickering, Octavius. *The Life of Timothy Pickering*. 4 vols. Boston: Little, Brown, 1867.

Pogue, Dennis J. *Founding Spirits: George Washington and the Beginnings of the American Whiskey Industry*. Buena Vista, VA: Harbour Books, 2011.

Pomerantz, Sidney I. *New York, an American City, 1783–1803: A Study in Urban Life*. Port Washington, NY: I. J. Friedman, 1965.

Posey, John Thornton. *General Thomas Posey: Son of the American Revolution*. East Lansing: Michigan State University Press, 1992.

Poulet, Anne L. *Jean-Antoine Houdon: Sculptor of the Enlightenment*. Chicago: University of Chicago Press, 2005.

Pound, Merritt B. *Benjamin Hawkins: Indian Agent*. Athens: University of Georgia Press, 1951.

Powell, J. H. *Bring Out Your Dead: The Great Plague of Yellow Fever in Philadelphia in 1793*. New York: Time, 1965.

Prince, Carl E. *The Federalists and the Origins of the U.S. Civil Service*. New York: New York University Press, 1977.

Pryor, Sara Agnes Rice. *The Mother of Washington and Her Times*. New York: Macmillan, 1903.

Puls, Mark. *Henry Knox: Visionary General of the American Revolution*. New York: Palgrave Macmillan, 2010.

Rahe, Paul Anthony. *Montesquieu and the Logic of Liberty: War, Religion, Commerce, Climate, Terrain, Technology, Uneasiness of Mind, the Spirit of Political Vigilance, and the Foundations of the Modern Republic*. New Haven, CT: Yale University Press, 2009.

_____. *Soft Despotism, Democracy's Drift: Montesquieu, Rousseau, Tocqueville, and the Modern Prospect*. New Haven, CT: Yale University Press, 2009.

Rakove, Jack. *James Madison and the Creation of the American Republic*. New York: Longman, 2006.

_____. *Revolutionaries: A New History of the Invention of America*. Boston: Houghton Mifflin Harcourt, 2010.

Randall, Henry Stephens. *The Life of Thomas Jefferson*. 3 vols. New York: Derby and Jackson, 1858.

Randall, Willard Sterne. *George Washington: A Life*. New York: Macmillan, 1998.

Raphael, Ray. *Mr. President: How and Why the Founders Created a Chief Executive*. New York: Alfred A. Knopf, 2012.

Rappleye, Charles. *Robert Morris: Financier of the American Revolution*. New York: Simon and Schuster, 2010.

Reardon, John J. *Edmund Randolph: A Biography*. New York: Macmillan, 1975.

Remini, Robert V., and Library of Congress. *The House: The History of the House of Representatives*. New York: Harper, 2007.

Reps, John. *Monumental Washington: The Planning and Development of the Capital Center*. Princeton, NJ: Princeton University Press, 1967.

Reuter, Frank. *Trials and Triumphs: George Washington's Foreign Policy*. Fort Worth: Texas Christian University Press, 1983.

Rice, Kym S. *Early American Taverns: For the Entertainment of Friends and Strangers*. New York: Fraunces Tavern Museum, 1983.

Rigal, Laura. *The American Manufactory: Art, Labor, and the World of Things in the Early Republic*. Princeton, NJ: Princeton University Press, 2001.

Risch, Erna. *Supplying Washington's Army*. Washington, DC: Center of Military History, United States Army, 1981.

Risjord, Norman K. *Chesapeake Politics, 1781–1800*. New York: Columbia University Press, 1978.

Roger, Philippe, and Sharon Bowman. *The American Enemy: The History of French Anti-Americanism*. Chicago: University of Chicago Press, 2006.

Rogers, George C. *Charleston in the Age of the Pinckneys*. Columbia: University of South Carolina Press, 1980.

_____. *Evolution of a Federalist: William Loughton Smith of Charleston 1758–1812*. Columbia: University of South Carolina Press, 1967.

Rorabaugh, W. J. *The Alcoholic Republic: An American Tradition*. New York: Oxford University Press, 1979.

Rosenfeld, Richard N. *American Aurora: A Democratic Republican Returns*. New York: St. Martin's, 1997.

Rossie, Jonathan Gregory. *The Politics of Command in the American Revolution*. Syracuse, NY: Syracuse University Press, 1975.

Rossman, Kenneth R. *Thomas Mifflin and the Politics of the American Revolution*. Chapel Hill: University of North Carolina Press, 1952.

Rowland, Kate Mason. *The Life of George Mason, 1725–1792*. New York: G. P. Putnam's Sons, 1892.

Royster, Charles. *A Revolutionary People at War: The Continental Army and American Character, 1775–1783*. New York: W. W. Norton, 1979.

Rutland, Robert Allen. *George Mason: Reluctant Statesman*. Baton Rouge: Louisiana State University Press, 1980.

_____. *The Ordeal of the Constitution: The Antifederalists and the Ratification Struggle of 1787–1788*. Norman: University of Oklahoma Press, 1966.

Scherr, Arthur. *Thomas Jefferson's Haitian Policy: Myths and Realities*. Lanham, MD: Lexington Books, 2011.

Schlenther, Boyd Stanley. *Charles Thomson: A Patriot's Pursuit*. Newark: University of Delaware Press, 1990.

Schwartz, Barry. *George Washington: The Making of an American Symbol*. New York: Free Press, 1987.

Schwarz, Philip J., ed. *Slavery at the Home of George Washington*. Mount Vernon, VA: Mount Vernon Ladies' Association, 2002.

Sears, Lorenzo. *John Hancock: The Picturesque Patriot*. Boston: Little, Brown, 1912.

Sellers, Charles Coleman. *The Artist of the Revolution: The Early Life of Charles Willson Peale*. Philadelphia: Feather and Good, 1939.

Setser, Vernon G. *The Commercial Reciprocity Policy of the United States 1774–1829*. Philadelphia: University of Pennsylvania Press, 1937.

Sharp, James Roger. *American Politics in the Early Republic: The New Nation in Crisis*. New Haven, CT: Yale University Press, 1993.

Sheehan, Bernard W. *Seeds of Extinction: Jeffersonian Philanthropy and the American Indian*. Chapel Hill: University of North Carolina Press, 1973.

Shields, David S. *Civil Tongues and Polite Letters in British America*. Chapel Hill: University of North Carolina Press, 1997.

Shultz, Suzanne M. *Body Snatching: The Robbing of Graves for the Education of Physicians in Early Nineteenth Century America*. Jefferson, NC: McFarland, 2005.

Shy, John W. *A People Numerous and Armed: Reflections on the Military Struggle for American Independence*. New York: Oxford University Press, 1976.

Siemers, David J. *Ratifying the Republic: Antifederalists and Federalists in Constitutional Time*. Stanford: Stanford University Press, 2002.

Silbey, Joel. *The Congress of the United States, 1789–1989*. Brooklyn, NY: Carlson Publishing, 1991.

Simpson, Henry. *The Lives of Eminent Philadelphians, Now Deceased*. Philadelphia: W. Brotherhead, 1859.

Slaughter, Thomas P. *The Whiskey Rebellion: Frontier Epilogue to the American Revolution*. New York: Oxford University Press, 1988.

Sloan, Herbert E. *Principle and Interest: Thomas Jefferson and the Problem of Debt*. New York: Oxford University Press, 1995.

Smith, Daniel B. *Inside the Great House: Planter Family Life in Eighteenth-Century Chesapeake Society*. Ithaca, NY: Cornell University Press, 1986.

Smith, Page. *James Wilson: Founding Father, 1742–1798*. Chapel Hill: University of North Carolina Press, 1956.

———. *John Adams*. Garden City, NY: Doubleday, 1962.

Smith, Richard Norton. *Patriarch: George Washington and the New American Nation*. New York: Houghton Mifflin, 1993.

Smith, Thomas E. V. *The City of New York in the Year of Washington's Inauguration*. New York: A. D. F. Randolph, 1889.

Spalding, Matthew, and Patrick J. Garrity. *A Sacred Union of Citizens: George Washington's Farewell Address and the American Character*. Lanham, MD: Rowman and Littlefield, 1996.

Sparks, Jared. *The Life and Treason of Benedict Arnold*. London: Ulan, 2012.

Sparks, Jared, and Henry Reed. *Lives of Charles Lee and Joseph Reed*. Boston: Little, Brown, 1846.

Spaulding, E. Wilder. *His Excellency George Clinton: Critic of the Constitution*. Port Washington, NY: Ira J. Friedman, 1964.

Spruill, Marjorie Julian, Joan Marie Johnson, and Valinda W. Littlefield. *South Carolina Women: Their Lives and Times*. Athens: University of Georgia Press, 2009.

Stahr, Walter. *John Jay: Founding Father*. New York: Bloomsbury, 2006.

Staloff, Darren. *Hamilton, Adams, Jefferson: The Politics of Enlightenment and the American Founding*. New York: Hill and Wang, 2007.

Steele, Brian. *Thomas Jefferson and American Nationhood*. New York: Cambridge University Press, 2012.

Stegeman, John F., and Janet A. Stegeman. *Caty*. Athens: University of Georgia Press, 1977.

Stetson, Charles W. *Washington and His Neighbors*. Richmond, VA: Garrett and Massie, 1956.

Stourzh, Gerald. *Alexander Hamilton and the Idea of Republican Government*. Stanford: Stanford University Press, 1970.

Sword, Wiley. *President Washington's Indian War: The Struggle for the Old Northwest, 1790–1795*. Norman: University of Oklahoma Press, 1985.

Sydnor, Charles S. *American Revolutionaries in the Making*. New York: Free Press, 1965.

Taft, Lorado. *The History of American Sculpture*. New York: Macmillan, 1903.

Tagg, James D. *Benjamin Franklin Bache and the Philadelphia "Aurora."* Philadelphia: University of Pennsylvania Press, 1991.

Taxay, Don. *The United States Mint and Coinage: An Illustrated History from 1776 to the Present*. New York: Arco, 1966.

Thacher, James. *American Medical Biography: Or, Memoirs of Eminent Physicians Who Have Flourished in America. To Which Is Prefixed a Succinct History of Medical Science in the United States, from the First Settlement of the Country*. Boston: Richardson and Lord, 1828.

Thayer, Theodore. *The Making of a Scapegoat: Washington and Lee at Monmouth*. Port Washington, NY: Kennikat Press, 1976.

Thompson, Mary V. *"In the Hands of a Good Providence": Religion in the Life of George Washington*. Charlottesville: University of Virginia Press, 2008.

Thompson, Peter. *Rum Punch and Revolution: Tavern Going and Public Life in Eighteenth-Century Philadelphia*. Philadelphia: University of Pennsylvania Press, 1999.

Todd, Charles Burr. *The Real Benedict Arnold*. Charleston, SC: Nabu, 2012.

Toth, Michael C. *Founding Federalist: The Life of Oliver Ellsworth*. Wilmington, DE: Intercollegiate Studies Institute, 2011.

Unger, Harlow G. *John Hancock: Merchant King and American Patriot*. Edison, NJ: Castle Books, 2005.

Van Doren, Carl. *The Great Rehearsal: The Story of the Making and Ratifying of the Constitution of the United States*. New York: Viking, 1948.

————. *Secret History of the American Revolution: An Account of the Conspiracies of Benedict Arnold and Numerous Others Drawn from the Secret Service Papers of the British Headquarters in North America, Now for the First Time Examined and Made Public*. New York: Viking, 1941.

Varg, Paul A. *Foreign Policies of the Founding Fathers*. East Lansing: Michigan State University Press, 1963.

Vipperman, Carl J. *The Rise of Rawlins Lowndes, 1721–1800*. Columbia: University of South Carolina Press, 1978.

Waldstreicher, David. *In the Midst of Perpetual Fetes: The Making of American Nationalism, 1776–1820*. Chapel Hill: University of North Carolina Press, 1997.

Wallace, Willard M. *Traitorous Hero: Benedict Arnold*. New York: Harper, 1954.

Walters, Raymond. *Albert Gallatin: Jeffersonian Financier and Diplomat*. New York: Macmillan, 1957.

Waring, Alice Noble. *The Fighting Elder: Andrew Pickens, 1739–1817*. Columbia: University of South Carolina Press, 1962.

Weems, Mason Locke. *The Life of George Washington*. Philadelphia: J. B. Lippincott, 1858.

Wertenbaker, Thomas J. *The Planters of Colonial Virginia*. Baltimore: Genealogical, 2009.

White, Leonard D. *The Federalists: A Study in Administrative History, 1789–1801*. New York: Free Press, 1948.

Whitley, William T. *Gilbert Stuart*. Cambridge: Harvard University Press, 1932.

Wick, Wendy C., and Lillian B. Miller. *George Washington, an American Icon: The Eighteenth-Century Graphic Portraits*. Washington, DC: Smithsonian Institution Traveling Service, 1982.

Wiencek, Henry. *An Imperfect God: George Washington, His Slaves, and the Creation of America*. New York: Farrar, Straus and Giroux, 2004.

Wilentz, Sean. *Chants Democratic: New York City and the Rise of the American Working Class, 1788–1850*. New York: Oxford University Press, 1986.

Williams, Frances Leigh. *A Founding Family: The Pinckneys of South Carolina*. New York: Harcourt Brace Jovanovich, 1978.

Wills, Garry. *Cincinnatus: George Washington and the Enlightenment*. Garden City, NY: Doubleday, 1984.

Wilstach, Paul. *Mount Vernon: Washington's Home and the Nation's Shrine*. New York: Doubleday, Page, 1916.

Winik, Jay. *The Great Upheaval: America and the Birth of the Modern World, 1788–1800*. New York: Harper Perennial, 2008.

Winterer, Caroline. *The Culture of Classicism: Ancient Greece and Rome in American Intellectual Life, 1780–1910*. Baltimore: Johns Hopkins University Press, 2004.

Wood, Gordon S. *Empire of Liberty: A History of the Early Republic, 1789–1815*. New York: Oxford University Press, 2009.

———. *The Radicalism of the American Revolution*. New York: Vintage, 1993.

———. *Revolutionary Characters: What Made the Founders Different*. New York: Penguin, 2007.

Woodward, W. E. *Lafayette*. New York: Farrar and Rinehart, 1938.

Wright, J. Leitch, Jr. *Creeks and Seminoles: The Destruction and Regeneration of the Muscogulge People*. Lincoln: University of Nebraska Press, 1986.

Wyatt-Brown, Bertram. *The Shaping of Southern Culture: Honor, Grace, and War, 1760s–1880s*. Chapel Hill: University of North Carolina Press, 2001.

Young, Alfred F. *Beyond the American Revolution: Explorations in the History of American Radicalism*. DeKalb: Northern Illinois University Press, 1993.

Zacks, Richard. *The Pirate Coast: Thomas Jefferson, the First Marines, and the Secret Mission of 1805*. New York: Hyperion, 2005.

Zagarri, Rosemarie. *Revolutionary Backlash: Women and Politics in the Early American Republic*. Philadelphia: University of Pennsylvania Press, 2008.

Zahniser, Marvin R. *Charles Cotesworth Pinckney, Founding Father*. Chapel Hill: University of North Carolina Press, 1967.

Zuckert, Michael P. *The Natural Rights Republic: Studies in the Foundation of the American Political Tradition*. Notre Dame, IN: University of Notre Dame Press, 1999.

Articles

Alexander, Sally Kennedy. "A Sketch of the Life of Major Andrew Ellicott." *Records of the Columbia Historical Society, Washington, D.C.* 2 (1899): 158–202.

Ammon, Harry. "Agricola Versus Aristides: James Monroe, John Marshall, and the Genet Affair in Virginia." *Virginia Magazine of History and Biography* 74 (July 1966): 312–20.

Bailey, Worth. "General Washington's New Room." *Journal of the Society of Architectural Historians* 10 (May 1951): 16–18.

Banning, Lance. "Jeffersonian Ideology Revisited: Liberal and Classical Ideas in the New American Republic." *William and Mary Quarterly* 43 (January 1986): 3–19.

———. "Republican Ideology and the Triumph of the Constitution." *William and Mary Quarterly* 31 (April 1974): 167–88.

Barksdale, Kevin T. "Our Rebellious Neighbors: Virginia's Border Counties During Pennsylvania's Whiskey Rebellion." *Virginia Magazine of History and Biography* 111 (2003): 5–32.

Beall, Mary S. "The Military and Private Secretaries of George Washington." *Records of the Columbia Historical Society, Washington, D.C.* 1 (1897): 89–118.

Bedini, Silvio A. "Benjamin Banneker and the Survey of the District of Columbia, 1791." *Records of the Columbia Historical Society, Washington, D.C.* 69/70 (1969–70): 7–30.

———. "The Survey of the Federal Territory: Andrew Ellicott and Benjamin Banneker." *Washington History* 3, no. 1 (Spring/Summer 1991): 76–95.

Bemis, Samuel Flagg. "John Quincy Adams and George Washington." *Proceedings of the Massachusetts Historical Society* 67 (October 1941): 365–84.

Bogin, Ruth. "'Measures So Glaringly Unjust': A Response to Hamilton's Funding Plan by William Manning." *William and Mary Quarterly* 46 (April 1989): 315–31.

Boller, Paul F., Jr. "George Washington and Religious Liberty." *William and Mary Quarterly* 17 (October 1960): 486–506.

———. "Washington, the Quakers, and Slavery." *Journal of Negro History* 46 (April 1961): 83–88.

Bowling, Kenneth R. "Dinner at Jefferson's: A Note on Jacob E. Cooke's 'The Compromise of 1790.'" *William and Mary Quarterly* 28 (October 1971): 629–48.

———. "Good-by 'Charle': The Lee-Adams Interest and the Political Demise of Charles Thomson." *Pennsylvania Magazine of History and Biography* 100, no. 3 (July 1976): 314–35.

———. "'A Tub to the Whale': The Founding Fathers and Adoption of the Federal Bill of Rights." *Journal of the Early Republic* 8 (Autumn 1988): 223–51.

Boyd, Steven R. "Antifederalists and the Acceptance of the Constitution: Pennsylvania, 1787–1792." *Publius* 9 (Spring 1979): 123–37.

Boyett, Gene W. "Developing the Concept of the Republican Presidency, 1787–1788." *Presidential Studies Quarterly* 7 (Fall 1977): 199–208.

Bradley, Harold W. "The Political Thinking of George Washington." *Journal of Southern History* 11 (November 1945): 469–86.

Brant, Irving. "Edmund Randolph: Not Guilty!" *William and Mary Quarterly* 7 (April 1950): 179–98.

Brooks, Robin. "Alexander Hamilton, Melancton Smith, and the Ratification of the Constitution in New York." *William and Mary Quarterly* 24 (July 1967): 339–58.

Brown, Stuart Gerry. "The Mind of Thomas Jefferson." *Ethics* 73 (January 1963): 79–99.

Caemmerer, H. Paul. "The Life of Pierre Charles L'Enfant." *Records of the Columbia Historical Society, Washington, D.C.* 50 (1948–50): 323–40.

———. "The Sesquicentennial of the Laying of the Cornerstone of the United States Capitol by George Washington." *Records of the Columbia Historical Society, Washington, D.C.* 44/45 (1942–43): 161–89.

Cahn, Edmond. "The Firstness of the First Amendment." *Yale Law Journal* 65 (February 1956): 464–81.

Campbell, Karlyn Kohrs, and Kathleen Hall Jamieson. "Inaugurating the Presidency." *Presidential Studies Quarterly* 15 (Spring 1985): 394–411.

Cayton, Andrew R. L. "'Separate Interests' and the Nation-State: The Washington Administration and the Origins of Regionalism in the Trans-Appalachian West." *Journal of the Early Republic* 79 (June 1992): 39–67.

Charles, Joseph. "Hamilton and Washington: The Origins of the American Party System." *William and Mary Quarterly* 12 (April 1955): 217–67.

Clarfield, Gerard. "Protecting the Frontiers: Defense Policy and the Tariff Question in the First Washington Administration." *William and Mary Quarterly* 32 (July 1975): 443–64.

Clark, Allen C. "Doctor and Mrs. William Thornton." *Records of the Columbia Historical Society, Washington, D.C.* 18 (1915): 144–208.

Clifford, John Garry. "A Muddy Middle of the Road: The Politics of Edmund Randolph, 1790–1795." *Virginia Magazine of History and Biography* 80 (July 1972): 286–311.

Cogan, Jacob K. "The Reynolds Affair and the Politics of Character." *Journal of the Early Republic* 16 (Fall 1996): 389–417.

Coleman, Aaron N. "'A Second Bounaparty?' A Reexamination of Alexander Hamilton During the Franco-American Crisis, 1796–1801." *Journal of the Early Republic* 28 (Summer 2008): 183–214.

Conlin, Michael F. "The American Mission of Citizen Pierre-Auguste Adet: Revolutionary Chemistry and Diplomacy in the Early Republic." *Pennsylvania Magazine of History and Biography* 74 (October 2000): 489–520.

Conway, Moncure D. "Footprints in Washingtonland." *Harper's* (April 1889): 738–44.

Cooke, Jacob E. "Alexander Hamilton's Authorship of the 'Caesar' Letters." *William and Mary Quarterly* 17 (January 1960): 78–85.

———. "The Compromise of 1790." *William and Mary Quarterly* 27 (October 1970): 523–45.

Crabb, A. L. "George Washington and the Chickasaw Nation, 1795." *Mississippi Valley Historical Review* 19 (December 1932): 404–8.

Cunningham, Noble E. "John Beckley: An Early American Party Manager." *William and Mary Quarterly* 13 (January 1956): 40–52.

Daniel, Frederick S. "A Visit to a Colonial Estate." *Harper's* (March 1888): 517–23.

DeConde, Alexander. "Washington's Farewell, the French Alliance, and the Election of 1796." *Mississippi Valley Historical Review* 43 (March 1957): 641–58.

Dulany, Daniel. "Military and Political Affairs in the Middle Colonies in 1755." *Pennsylvania Magazine of History and Biography* 3 (1879): 11–31.

Dumbauld, Edward. "Thomas Jefferson and the City of Washington." *Records of the Columbia Historical Society, Washington, D.C.* 50 (1980): 67–80.

Eberlein, Harold Donaldson. "190, High Street (Market Street Below Sixth) the House of Washington and Adams, 1790–1800." *Transactions of the American Philosophical Society* 43 (1953): 161–78.

Eberlein, Harold Donaldson, and Cortlandt Van Dyke Hubbard. "The American 'Vauxhall' of the Federal Period." *Pennsylvania Magazine of History and Biography* 68 (April 1944): 150–74.

Edling, Max M. "'So Immense a Power in the Affairs of War': Alexander Hamilton and the Restoration of Public Credit." *William and Mary Quarterly* 64 (April 2007): 287–326.

Einhorn, Robin L. "Patrick Henry's Case Against the Constitution: The Structural Problem with Slavery." *Journal of the Early Republic* 22 (Winter 2002): 549–73.

Estes, Todd. "The Art of Presidential Leadership: George Washington and the Jay Treaty." *Virginia Magazine of History and Biography* 109 (2001): 127–58.

Farnham, Thomas J. "The Virginia Amendments of 1795: An Episode in the Opposition to Jay's Treaty." *Virginia Magazine of History and Biography* 75 (January 1967): 75–88.

Finkelman, Paul. "Thomas Jefferson and Antislavery: The Myth Goes On." *Virginia Magazine of History and Biography* 102 (April 1994): 193–228.

Fishback, Frederick L. "Washington City, Its Founding and Development." *Records of the Columbia Historical Society, Washington, D.C.* 20 (1917): 194–224.

Fisher, George Harrison. "Brigadier-General Henry Bouquet." *Pennsylvania Magazine of History and Biography* 3 (1879): 121–43.

Fitzpatrick, John C. "The Aides-de-Camp of General George Washington." *Daughters of the American Revolution Magazine* 57 (January 1923): 1–16.

Ford, Paul Leicester. "The George Washington Scandals." *Scribner's Magazine* 81 (April 1927): 393–94.

Freeman, Joanne B. "Slander, Poison, Whispers, and Fame: Jefferson's 'Anas' and Political Gossip in the Early Republic." *Journal of the Early Republic* 15 (Spring 1995): 25–57.

Ganter, Herbert Lawrence. "The Machiavellianism of George Mason." *William and Mary Quarterly* 17 (April 1937): 239–64.

Giacomantonio, William C. di. "All the President's Men: George Washington's Federal City Commissioners." *Washington History* 3 (Spring/Summer 1991): 52–75.

Goldfarb, Stephen J. "An Inquiry into the Politics of the Prohibition of the International Slave Trade." *Agricultural History* 68 (Spring 1994): 20–34.

Grant, C. L. "Senator Benjamin Hawkins: Federalist or Republican." *Journal of the Early Republic* 1 (Autumn 1981): 233–47.

Grant, U. S., III. "The L'Enfant Plan and Its Evolution." *Records of the Columbia Historical Society, Washington, D.C.* 33/34 (1932): 1–23.

Gray, Arthur P. "Washington's Burgess Route." *Virginia Magazine of History and Biography* 46 (October 1938): 299–315.

——. "The White House—Washington's Marriage Place." *Virginia Magazine of History and Biography* 42 (July 1934): 229–40.

Greenfield, Edward W. "New Aspects of the Life of Daniel Parke." *Virginia Magazine of History and Biography* 54 (October 1946): 306–15.

Harris, C. M. "Washington's 'Federal City.' Jefferson's 'Federal Town.'" *Washington History* 12 (Spring/Summer 2000): 49–53.

——. "Washington's Gamble, L'Enfant's Dream: Politics, Design, and the Founding of the National Capital." *William and Mary Quarterly* 56 (July 1999): 527–64.

Harris, Marc L. "'Cement to the Union': The Society of the Cincinnati and the Limits of Fraternal Sociability." *Proceedings of the Massachusetts Historical Society* 107 (1995): 115–40.

Harrison, Joseph H., Jr. "'Sict Et Non': Thomas Jefferson and Internal Improvement." *Journal of the Early Republic* 7 (Winter 1987): 335–49.

Henriques, Peter R. "The Final Struggle Between George Washington and the Grim King: Washington's Attitude Toward Death and an Afterlife." *Virginia Magazine of History and Biography* 107 (Winter 1999): 73–97.

——. "Major Lawrence Washington Versus the Reverend Charles Green: A Case Study of the Squire and the Parson." *Virginia Magazine of History and Biography* 100 (April 1992): 233–64.

——. "An Uneven Friendship: The Relationship Between George Washington and George Mason." *Virginia Magazine of History and Biography* 97 (April 1989): 185–204.

Hickey, Donald R. "America's Response to the Slave Revolt in Haiti, 1791–1806." *Journal of the Early Republic* 2 (Winter 1982): 361–79.

Higginbotham, Don. "Virginia's Trinity of Immortals: Washington, Jefferson, and Henry, and the Story of Their Fractured Relationships." *Journal of the Early Republic* 23 (Winter 2003): 521–43.

Holcombe, Arthur N. "The Role of Washington in the Framing of the Constitution." *Huntington Library Quarterly* 19 (August 1956): 317–34.

Hornor, Marian Sadtler. "A Washington Affair of Honor, 1779." *Pennsylvania Magazine of History and Biography* 65 (July 1941): 362–70.

Horsman, Reginald. "The Dimensions of an 'Empire of Liberty': Expansion and Republicanism, 1775–1825." *Journal of the Early Republic* 9 (Spring 1989): 1–20.

Hoxie, R. Gordon. "The Presidency in the Constitutional Convention." *Presidential Studies Quarterly* 15 (Winter 1985): 25–32.

Hutson, James H. "John Adams' Title Campaign." *New England Quarterly* 41 (March 1968): 30–39.

Jones, Robert F. "George Washington and the Politics of the Presidency." *Presidential Studies Quarterly* 10 (Winter 1980): 28–35.

Katz, Claudio. "Thomas Jefferson's Liberal Anticapitalism." *Journal of Political Science* 47 (January 2003): 1–17.

Kitzen, Michael. "Money Bags or Cannon Balls: The Origins of the Tripolitan War, 1795–1801." *Journal of the Early Republic* 16 (Winter 1996): 601–24.

Klubes, Benjamin B. "The First Federal Congress and the First National Bank: A Case Study in Constitutional Interpretation." *Journal of the Early Republic* 10 (Spring 1990): 19–41.

Knupfer, Peter B. "The Rhetoric of Conciliation: American Civic Culture and the Federalist Defense of Compromise." *Journal of the Early Republic* 11 (Autumn 1991): 315–37.

Kohn, Richard H. "The Inside History of the Newburgh Conspiracy: America and the Coup d'Etat." *William and Mary Quarterly* 27 (April 1970): 188–220.

———. "The Washington Administration's Decision to Crush the Whiskey Rebellion." *Journal of American History* 59 (1972): 567–84.

Koontz, Louis Knott. "Washington on the Frontier." *Virginia Magazine of History and Biography* 36 (October 1928): 305–27.

Lee, Jean Butenhoff. "The Problem of Slave Community in the 18th Century Chesapeake." *William and Mary Quarterly* 43 (July 1986): 133–61.

Leibiger, Stuart. "James Madison and Amendments to the Constitution, 1787–1789: 'Parchment Barriers.'" *Journal of Southern History* 59 (August 1993): 441–68.

———. "'To Judge of Washington's Conduct': Illuminating George Washington's Appearance on the World Stage." *Virginia Magazine of History and Biography* 107 (Winter 1999): 37–44.

Levy, Philip. "'Crystallized into Solid Reality': How Mason Locke 'Parson' Weems Shaped George Washington's Boyhood Home." *Virginia Magazine of History and Biography* 121 (Spring 2013): 106–45.

Lienesch, Michael. "The Constitutional Tradition: History, Political Action, and Progress in American Political Thought, 1787–1793." *Journal of Politics* 42 (February 1980): 2–30.

Lindgren, James M. "'Pater Patriae': George Washington as Symbol and Artifact." *American Quarterly* 41 (December 1989): 705–13.

Loss, Richard. "Alexander Hamilton and the Modern Presidency: Continuity or Discontinuity?" *Presidential Studies Quarterly* 12 (Winter 1982): 6–25.

Maier, Pauline. "Coming to Terms with Samuel Adams." *American Historical Review* 81 (February 1976): 12–37.

Marcus, Maeva, et. al. "'It Is My Wish as Well as My Duty to Attend the Court': The Hardships of Supreme Court Service, 1790–1800." *Yearbook of the Supreme Court Historical Society* (1984): 118–26.

Markowitz, Arthur A. "Washington's Farewell and the Historians: A Critical Review." *Pennsylvania Magazine of History and Biography* 94 (April 1970): 173–91.

Marraro, Howard R. "The Four Versions of Jefferson's Letter to Mazzei." *William and Mary Quarterly* 22 (January 1942): 18–29.

Marsh, Philip. "Jefferson and Journalism." *Huntington Library Quarterly* 9 (February 1946): 209–12.

_____. "John Beckley—Mystery Man of the Early Jeffersonians." *Pennsylvania Magazine of History and Biography* 72 (1948): 54–69.

_____. "The Griswold Story of Freneau and Jefferson." *American Historical Review* 51 (October 1945): 68–73.

Matthewson, Timothy M. "George Washington's Policy Toward the Haitian Revolution." *Diplomatic History* 3 (July 1979): 321–36.

_____. "Jefferson and Haiti." *Journal of Southern History* 61 (May 1995): 209–48.

Maxey, David W. "A Portrait of Elizabeth Willing Powel (1743–1830)." *Transactions of the American Philosophical Society* 96 (2006): i–91.

McCarthy, Daniel J. "James Wilson and the Creation of the Presidency." *Presidential Studies Quarterly* 17 (Fall 1987): 689–96.

McCormick, Richard P. "New Jersey's First Congressional Election, 1789: A Case Study in Political Skulduggery." *William and Mary Quarterly* 6 (April 1949): 237–50.

McCoy, Drew R. "Republicanism and American Foreign Policy: James Madison and the Political Economy of Commercial Discrimination, 1789 to 1794." *William and Mary Quarterly* 31 (October 1974): 633–46.

McPherson, Elizabeth G. "The Southern States and the Reporting of Senate Debates, 1789–1802." *Journal of Southern History* 12 (May 1946): 223–46.

Miller, William. "The Democratic Societies and the Whiskey Insurrection." *Pennsylvania Magazine of History and Biography* 62 (July 1938): 324–49.

Mitchell, Broadus. "Alexander Hamilton, Executive Power and the New Nation." *Presidential Studies Quarterly* 17 (Spring 1987): 329–43.

Moore, R. Walton. "George Mason, the Statesman." *William and Mary Quarterly* 13 (January 1933): 10–17.

Morales-Vazquez, Rubil. "George Washington, the President's House, and the Projection of Executive Power." *Washington History* 16 (Spring/Summer 2004): 36–53.

Morgan, Edmund S. "George Washington: The Aloof American." *Virginia Quarterly Review* 52 (July 1976): 410–36.

Morgan, Kenneth. "George Washington and the Problem of Slavery." *Journal of American Studies* 34 (August 2000): 279–301.

Morison, Samuel Eliot. "Elbridge Gerry, Gentlemen-Democrat." *New England Quarterly* 2 (January 1929): 6–33.

Morris, Richard. "The Origins of the Presidency." *Presidential Studies Quarterly* 17 (Fall 1987): 673–87.

Muñoz, Vincent Phillip. "George Washington on Religious Liberty." *Review of Politics* 65 (Winter 2003): 11–33.

Neely, Sylvia. "Weems's Life of Washington and the Myth of Braddock's Defeat." *Virginia Magazine of History and Biography* 107 (Winter 1999): 45–72.

Nelson, Paul David. "Horatio Gates at Newburgh, 1783: A Misunderstood Roll." *William and Mary Quarterly* 29 (January 1972): 143–58.

Bibliography

Nelson, William E. "Reason and Compromise in the Establishment of the Federal Constitution, 1787–1801." *William and Mary Quarterly* 44 (July 1987): 458–84.

Nettels, Curtis P. "Alexander Hamilton and the Presidency." *Presidential Studies Quarterly* 4 (Summer/Fall–Winter 1974–75): 23–25.

Newman, Simon P. "Principles or Men? George Washington and the Political Culture of National Leadership, 1776–1801." *Journal of the Early Republic* 12 (Winter 1992): 477–507.

Nutting, P. Bradley. "'Tobias Lear, S.P.U.S.': First Secretary to the President." *Presidential Studies Quarterly* 24 (Fall 1994): 713–24.

Palmer, R. R. "The Dubious Democrat: Thomas Jefferson in Bourbon France." *Political Science Quarterly* 72 (September 1957): 388–404.

————. "Notes on the Use of the Word 'Democracy,' 1789–1799." *Political Science Quarterly* 68 (June 1953): 203–26.

Pasley, Jeffrey L. "'A Journeyman, Either in Law or Politics': John Beckley and the Social Origins of Political Campaigning." *Journal of the Early Republic* 16 (Winter 1996): 531–69.

————. "The Two National 'Gazettes': Newspapers and the Embodiment of American Political Parties." *Early American Literature* 36 (2000): 51–86.

Perry, James R. "Supreme Court Appointments, 1789–1801: Criteria, Presidential Style, and the Press of Events." *Journal of the Early Republic* 6 (Winter 1986): 371–410.

Pessen, Edward. "George Washington's Farewell Address, the Cold War, and the Timeless National Interest." *Journal of the Early Republic* 7 (Spring 1987): 1–25.

Peterson, Merrill D. "Thomas Jefferson and Commercial Policy, 1783–1793." *William and Mary Quarterly* 22 (October 1965): 584–610.

Phelps, Glenn A. "George Washington and the Founding of the Presidency." *Presidential Studies Quarterly* 17 (June 1987): 345–63.

————. "George Washington and the Paradox of Party." *Presidential Studies Quarterly* 19 (December 1989): 733–45.

Phillips, Ulrich B. "The South Carolina Federalists, II." *American Historical Review* 14 (July 1909): 731–43.

Pomerantz, Sidney I. "George Washington and the Inception of Aeronautics in the Young Republic." *Proceedings of the American Philosophical Society* 98 (April 1954): 131–38.

Posey, John Thornton. "Governor Thomas Posey: The Son of George Washington?" *Indiana Magazine of History* 86 (March 1990): 28–49.

Proctor, Donald J. "John Hancock: New Soundings on an Old Barrel." *Journal of American History* 64 (December 1977): 652–77.

Rahe, Paul A. "Thomas Jefferson's Machiavellian Political Science." *The Review of Politics* 57 (Summer 1995): 449–81.

"Rebecca Dinwiddie, Wife of Gov. Dinwiddie." *William and Mary Quarterly* 1 (July 1921): 214.

Reuter, Frank T. "'Petty Spy' or Effective Diplomat: The Role of George Beckwith." *Journal of the Early Republic* 10 (Winter 1990): 471–92.

Rhodehamel, John H. "The Growth of Mount Vernon." Mount Vernon Ladies' Association of the Union, *Annual Report,* 1982, 18–24.

Rich, Bennett M. "Washington and the Whiskey Insurrection." *Pennsylvania Magazine of History and Biography* 65 (July 1941): 334–52.

Richard, Carl J. "A Dialogue with the Ancients: Thomas Jefferson and Classical Philosophy and History." *Journal of the Early Republic* 9 (Winter 1989): 431–55.

Richardson, Edgar P. "A Penetrating Characterization of Washington." *Winterthur Portfolio* 3 (1967): 1–23.

Riggs, John Beverly. "Certain Early Maryland Landowners in the Vicinity of Washington." *Records of the Columbia Historical Society, Washington, D.C.* 48/49 (1946–47): 249–63.

Risjord, Norman K. "The Compromise of 1790: New Evidence on the Dinner Table Bargain." *William and Mary Quarterly* 33 (April 1976): 309–14.

Robinson, Donald L. "The Inventors of the Presidency." *Presidential Studies Quarterly* 13 (Winter 1983): 8–25.

Rolater, Fred S. "Charles Thomson: 'Prime Minister' of the United States." *Pennsylvania Magazine of History and Biography* 101 (July 1977): 322–48.

Rose, Ruth P. "Dr. David Stuart: Friend and Confidant of George Washington." *Northern Virginia Heritage* 10 (February 1988): 9–14.

Sayen, William Guthrie. "George Washington's 'Unmannerly' Behavior: The Clash Between Civility and Honor." *Virginia Magazine of Biography and History* 107 (Winter 1999): 5–36.

Schoenbachler, Matthew. "Republicanism in the Age of Democratic Revolution: The Democratic-Republican Societies of the 1790s." *Journal of the Early Republic* 18 (Summer 1998): 237–61.

Schwartz, Barry. "George Washington and the Whig Conception of Heroic Leadership." *American Sociological Review* 48 (February 1983): 18–33.

Schwarz, Michael. "The Great Divergence Reconsidered: Hamilton, Madison, and U.S. British Relations, 1783–1789." *Journal of the Early Republic* 27 (Fall 2007): 407–36.

Scott, Pamela. "Stephen Hallet's Designs for the United States Capitol." *Winterthur Portfolio* 27 (Autumn 1992): 145–70.

Seidensticker, Oswald. "Frederick Augustus Conrad Muhlenberg, Speaker of the House of Representatives, in the First Congress, 1789." *Pennsylvania Magazine of History and Biography* 13 (July 1889): 184–206.

Sheehan, Colleen. "Madison v. Hamilton: The Battle Over Republicanism and the Role of Public Opinion." *American Political Science Review* 98 (August 2004): 405–24.

Sheridan, Eugene R. "Thomas Jefferson and the Giles Resolutions." *William and Mary Quarterly* 49 (October 1992): 589–608.

Skeen, Edward C. "The Newburgh Conspiracy Reconsidered." *William and Mary Quarterly* 31 (April 1974): 273–98.

Slaughter, Thomas P. "The Tax Man Cometh: Ideological Opposition to Internal Taxes, 1760–1790." *William and Mary Quarterly* 41 (October 1984): 566–91.

Smelser, Marshall. "The Federalist Period as an Age of Passion." *American Quarterly* 10 (Winter 1958): 391–419.

————. "George Washington and the Alien and Sedition Acts." *American Historical Quarterly* 59 (February 1954): 322–34.

————. "The Jacobin Phrenzy: The Menace of Monarchy, Plutocracy, and Anglophilia, 1789–1798." *Review of Politics* 21 (January 1959): 239–58.

Swanson, Donald F., and Andrew P. Trout. "Alexander Hamilton's Hidden Sinking Fund." *William and Mary Quarterly* 49 (January 1992): 108–16.

————. "Thomas Jefferson on Establishing Public Credit: The Debt Plans of a Would-Be Secretary of the Treasury?" *Presidential Studies Quarterly* 23 (Summer 1993): 499–508.

Tachau, Mary K. Bonsteel. "George Washington and the Reputation of Edmund Randolph." *Journal of American History* 73 (June 1986): 15–34.

Tagg, James D. "Benjamin Franklin Bache's Attack on George Washington." *Pennsylvania Magazine of History and Biography* 100 (April 1976): 191–230.

Tarter, Brent. "George Mason and the Conservation of Liberty." *Virginia Magazine of History and Biography* 99 (July 1991): 279–304.

Thompson, Harry C. "The Second Place in Rome: John Adams as Vice President." *Presidential Studies Quarterly* 10 (Spring 1980): 171–78.

Thompson, Mary V. "The Private Life of George Washington's Slaves." *Virginia Cavalcade* 48 (Autumn 1999): 178–90.

Tinling, Marion. "Cawsons, Virginia, in 1795–1796." *William and Mary Quarterly* 3 (April 1946): 281–91.

"Virginia Gleanings in England." *Virginia Magazine of History and Biography* 20 (October 1912): 372–81.

Wallenstein, Peter. "Flawed Keepers of the Flame: The Interpreters of George Mason." *Virginia Magazine of History and Biography* 102 (April 1994): 229–60.

Webking, Robert H. "Melancton Smith and the Letters from the Federal Farmer." *William and Mary Quarterly* 44 (July 1987): 510–28.

Wenger, Mark R. "Thomas Jefferson, Tenant." *Winterthur Portfolio* 26 (Winter 1991): 249–65.

Wood, Gordon S. "The Authorship of the Letters from the Federal Farmer." *William and Mary Quarterly* 31 (April 1974): 299–308.

Wright, Esmond. "'Mr. President' . . . George Washington's New Clothes." *History Today* 39 (April 1989): 22–28.

Young, Christopher J. "Connecting the President and the People: Washington's Neutrality, Genet's Challenge, and Hamilton's Fight for Public Support." *Journal of the Early Republic* 31 (Fall 2011): 435–66.

Zahniser, Marvin R. "Edward Rutledge to His Son, August 2, 1796." *South Carolina Historical Magazine* 64 (April 1963): 65–72.

Ziesche, Philipp. "Exporting American Revolutions: Gouverneur Morris, Thomas Jefferson, and the National Struggle for Universal Rights in Revolutionary France." *Journal of the Early Republic* 26 (Fall 2006): 419–47.

Zimmerman, John J. "Charles Thomson, 'The Sam Adams of Philadelphia.'" *Mississippi Valley Historical Review* 45 (December 1958): 464–80.

Zuppan, Jo. "John Custis of Williamsburg, 1678–1749." *Virginia Magazine of History and Biography* 90 (April 1982): 177–97.

Index

About the Authors

DAVID S. HEIDLER and JEANNE T. HEIDLER have written numerous scholarly books and articles dealing with the history of the early American republic, the Antebellum period, and the Civil War. They are the authors of the acclaimed biography *Henry Clay: The Essential American.* David S. Heidler taught history for many years at the university level, and Jeanne T. Heidler is professor of history at the United States Air Force Academy, where she is the senior civilian member of her department.

About the Type

This book was set in Granjon, a modern recutting of a typeface produced under the direction of George W. Jones (1860–1942), who based Granjon's design upon the letterforms of Claude Garamond (1480–1561). The name was given to the typeface as a tribute to the typographic designer Robert Granjon (1513–89).